101 975 630 6

The Criminal Pro

D1435141

BLACKSTONE'S GUIDE TO

The Criminal Procedure Rules

SECOND EDITION

By

Duncan Atkinson
Barrister, 6 King's Bench Walk

Tim Moloney QC
Barrister, Tooks Chambers

OXFORD
UNIVERSITY PRESS

OXFORD

UNIVERSITY PRESS

Great Clarendon Street, Oxford OX2 6DP

Oxford University Press is a department of the University of Oxford.
It furthers the University's objective of excellence in research, scholarship,
and education by publishing worldwide in

Oxford New York

Auckland Cape Town Dar es Salaam Hong Kong Karachi
Kuala Lumpur Madrid Melbourne Mexico City Nairobi
New Delhi Shanghai Taipei Toronto

With offices in

Argentina Austria Brazil Chile Czech Republic France Greece
Guatemala Hungary Italy Japan Poland Portugal Singapore
South Korea Switzerland Thailand Turkey Ukraine Vietnam

Oxford is a registered trade mark of Oxford University Press
in the UK and in certain other countries

Published in the United States
by Oxford University Press Inc., New York

© Duncan Atkinson and Tim Moloney 2011

British Library Cataloguing in Publication Data
Data available

Library of Congress Cataloging-in-Publication Data
2010941968

Typeset by Glyph International Private Ltd, Bangalore, India
Printed in Great Britain
on acid-free paper by
CPI Antony Rowe, Chippenham, Wiltshire

ISBN 978-0-19-958870-1

1 3 5 7 9 10 8 6 4 2

Foreword

The introduction of the Criminal Procedural Rules in 2005 was one of the most controversial developments in the law governing English criminal procedure in decades if. At first it appeared, perhaps predictably, that their introduction had generated substantial mistrust in many members of the legal profession. There was anxiety about the detail within individual Rules, and a more general concern about even matters as fundamental as the overriding objectives being expressed in 'Rules' (discussed in Ch. 2). There was an open hostility from many who, it seems, regarded the Rules as introducing to the criminal trial in both the Crown Court and the Magistrates' Court an unnecessary and undesirable managerialism. The truth is that the courts were already well on their way to imposing greater procedural regulation on the trial process via the common law: see cases such as *R v Jisl* [2004] EWCA Crim 696; *R v Chabban* [2003] EWCA Crim 1012 (discussed in see Ch 3) and the foundation laid in Auld LJ's *Review of the Criminal Courts of England and Wales* (2001).

Since the introduction of the Rules in 2005, the appellate courts have used them to press ahead, emboldened in their desire to reduce delay and maximize efficiency in the process. This has on occasions led to an over exuberance, with attempts to use the Rules for purposes far beyond that for which they were intended. Examples include *R v FB* [2010] EWCA Crim 1857 (in which attempts were made to use the Rules as a basis for a judge to quash indictments on the basis that he did not believe that a prosecution was worthwhile or in the public interest when compared with the needs of other cases); *R v Rochford* [2010] EWCA Crim (where it was sought to use the Rules to compel service of a defence case statement); and *Hubner v District Court of Prostejov Czech Republic* [2009] EWHC 2929 (Admin) where it was sought to use the Rules to create a new exception to the Extradition Act 2003.

Even ignoring these cases in which the courts have strayed too far, there can be no doubt that the Rules have frequently been used to develop the law in significant ways. For example, in *Ensor* [2009] EWCA Crim 2519 the judge excluded defence expert evidence because it had not been served in time; in *R v C* [2009] EWCA Crim 2614 the rules were used to read strict limits onto the statutory powers of prosecution appeals under the Criminal Justice Act 2003; in *Musone* [2007] EWCA Crim 1237 the Rules were held to confer a power for a court to exclude bad character evidence as between a co-accused where there had been a breach of the prescribed requirements); and in *R v Penner* [2010] EWCA Crim 1155 Thomas LJ commented in frustration: 'The Criminal Procedure Rules have been in force in this country for some time. They have abolished what is known as "trial by ambush". Sometimes it appears that people do not appreciate that...'

On some occasions, judicial attempts to use the Rules to change trial procedures, although rejected by the appellate courts as being unjustified, have served as a catalyst for legislative development. For example, in *R. (Kelly) v Warley JJ* [2007] EWHC 1836 (Admin) the Divisional Court had ruled that the courts' general powers of case management do not extend to requiring the defence to identify their witnesses. This has now been superseded by s 6C of the Criminal Procedure and Investigations Act 1996, and the Criminal Justice Act 2003 (Commencement No. 24 and Transitional Provisions) Order 2010 (SI 2010/1183) (see the discussion in Ch 3 at para 3.16).

Aside from these more notorious examples at the developing boundaries of the law on criminal trial procedure, the Crim PR havehad an impact on more mundane and routine matters that arise in all criminal trials. Many practitioners who were initially resistant have therefore already come to accept that there is no point in maintaining a stubborn hostility (coupled in more extreme cases with an indignant purported ignorance of their contents). Many have realized that it is now fruitless to deny that the Crim PR are here to stay. The Crim PR form an integral part of the criminal trial and will be likely to have ever greater impact in the future, particularly as efforts to render the process more efficient take on a keener financial significance. Practitioners could go beyond merely accepting the existence of the Crim PR by beginning to *use* them more effectively. In some instances the Rules might be used positively to support a particular trial tactic, in others, knowledge of the Rules may be crucial in seeking to resist an opponent's procedural stance. In either situation, it is clear that a well-prepared practitioner now requires a sound working knowledge of the Rules and the growing jurisprudence developing around them. This book will provide the information necessary to acquire that knowledge. It offers a comprehensive lucid and up-to-date account accompanied throughout by high quality commentary from the authors.

The subject matter is, of course, an intensely practical one. It is vital that the reader can rely with confidence on the content of the book as being relevant to, and reflecting, what actually happens in practice. There is no doubt on that score. Both authors are extremely highly regarded experts in this area with significant practical experience in defending and prosecuting. Their incisive analysis of the Rules is set within a logical framework following the order of the Crim PR and dealing with all aspects of pre-trial, trial, sentencing, confiscation, appeals, and costs. The authors also provide welcome assistance with practical checklists of time limits and key tasks to be performed (eg paras 6.64 and 10.40)

This new edition is a timely one. Since the 2005 there have been numerous updates to the Rules. The updates have included some very significant additions (eg those governing witness anonymity discussed at para 10.55 et seq) as well the constant refinement of the details within the Rules. In 2010 the first consolidation of the many amendments took place, and this volume provides comprehensive coverage of the new consolidated 2010 version of the Rules and the Consolidated Criminal Practice Direction. They are appended in full.

It is a privilege to have been asked to write the foreword for such a helpful guide. Rules, especially those on procedure, can be boring even for lawyers, but this volume renders the subject clear and accessible. I am confident it will prove indispensible for criminal practitioners.

David Ormerod

Acknowledgements

Both authors were lured into their work on the Criminal Procedure Rules through membership of the Criminal Bar Association Rules Group, which was set up to provide the perspective of the Criminal Bar to the work of the Criminal Procedure Rules Committee. This book owes a great deal to the analysis and ideas of the Rules Group and especially to its chairman, David Fisher QC.

The authors would like to acknowledge the patient assistance in the production of this work of Ben Lloyd, Tim Devlin, Duncan Campbell, and Tanya Burgess, and the efficiency, support, and enthusiasm of all those at Oxford University Press and of Faye Judges in particular.

Contents

Table of Cases

Table of Primary Legislation

Table of Secondary Legislation

Table of Abbreviations

The following abbreviations have been used in the text that follows:

BA 1976	Bail Act 1976
CAJA 2009	Coroners and Justice Act 2009
CDA 1998	Crime and Disorder Act 1998
CJA 1987	Criminal Justice Act 1987
CJA 1988	Criminal Justice Act 1988
CJA 1991	Criminal Justice Act 1991
CJA 2003	Criminal Justice Act 2003
CPIA 1996	Criminal Procedure and Investigations Act 1996
CYPA 1933	Children and Young Persons Act 1933
DPP	Director of Public Prosecutions
DTA 1994	Drug Trafficking Act 1994
DVCVA 2004	Domestic Violence Crime and Victims Act 2004
DX	Document Exchange
EA 1989	Extradition Act 1989
MCA 1980	Magistrates' Court Act 1980
PACE 1984	Police and Criminal Evidence Act 1984
PCC(S)A 2000	Powers of Criminal Courts (Sentencing) Act 2000
PCMH	plea and case management hearing
POCA 2002	Proceeds of Crime Act 2002
RTOA 1988	Road Traffic Offenders Act 1988
The 1965 Act	Backing of Warrants (Republic of Ireland) Act 1965
The Practice Direction	The Consolidated Criminal Practice Direction
The Rules	The Criminal Procedure Rules
YJCEA 1999	Youth Justice and Criminal Evidence Act 1999

NOTE: Throughout this book words connoting the masculine include the feminine.

1

THE OVERRIDING OBJECTIVE AND UNDERSTANDING AND APPLYING THE RULES

A. INTRODUCTION

On 4 April 2005 Statutory Instrument 2005 No 384 (L 4) brought into effect the Criminal Procedure Rules (the Rules), the first consolidation of the panoply of procedural rules governing the criminal justice system of England and Wales.   1.01

The conceptual framework for the rules had its origins in Lord Justice Auld's *Review of the Criminal Courts of England and Wales*. It was recommended in Chapter 10 paragraph 274 that: 1.02

> What is needed is not a consolidation of all relevant provisions but a concise and simply expressed statement of the current statutory and common law procedural rules and the product of the present overlay of practice directions, codes of guidance and the like. It should be in a single instrument and laid out in such a form that it, the Code, can be readily amended without constant recourse to primary legislation. . .
>
> That instrument should begin with a clear statement of purpose and general rules of application and interpretation, as successfully pioneered in the civil justice rules flowing from Lord Woolf's reforms of the civil law. It should combine the various sources into a concise summary of rules, reducing them so far as possible into a discipline common to all levels of jurisdiction, using the same language and prescribing the same forms. It should make separate provision only insofar as necessary to allow for procedural differences at each level flowing from the court's composition and nature and volume of its work. It should be capable of ready and orderly amendment, by secondary legislation along the lines of that enabling the Lord Chancellor to amend the Civil Procedure Rules.

Those recommendations found acceptance by the Government and reiteration in the White Paper '*Justice for All*' and their essential features were embodied in sections 69 to 73 of the Courts Act 2003.   1.03

1.04   As a result, for the first time in this jurisdiction, criminal procedure was at once consolidated in one document and also subject to an explicit philosophy governing its operation embodied in an overriding objective.

1.05   Since then, the Rules have been subjected to three significant sets of amendments which have culminated in the version of the Rules now operative since 4 October 2010. In most cases the amendments have led to a simplification of procedures to be followed and a consistency of approach throughout the Rules.

B. PART 1—THE OVERRIDING OBJECTIVE

1.06   Part 1 of the Rules sets out the overriding objective and the duties of the participants and the court in respect of that overriding objective. It underpins the aspirations for the criminal justice system of the architects of the Rules, as foreshadowed in Lord Justice Auld's *Review of the Criminal Courts of England and Wales* when he stated:

> A criminal trial is not a game under which a guilty defendant should be provided with a sporting chance. It is a search for truth in accordance with the twin principles that the prosecution must prove its case and that a defendant is not obliged to inculpate himself, the object being to convict the guilty and acquit the innocent.

1.07   The Rules have, in a relatively short time, become important to the daily operation of the criminal justice system. Rule 1.1 sets out the overriding objective and factors important to its achievement. Rule 1.2 stipulates the duties of the participants in relation to the overriding objective. Rule 1.3 sets out the corresponding duties of the court.

1. The overriding objective

1.08   At rule 1.1(1) the overriding objective is explicitly, and very concisely, stated to be that criminal cases be dealt with justly. Rule 1.1(2) then sets out some factors which dealing with a case justly include. Amongst the more noteworthy of those, at (a) of that part is acquitting the innocent and convicting the guilty; a clear expression of the sentiment contained in the passage from the *Review* by Lord Justice Auld cited in the preceding paragraph. In addition, the prosecution and defence should be dealt with fairly (1.1(2)(b)) and the interests of witnesses, victims, and jurors should be respected, with them being kept informed of the progress of the case (1.1(2)(d)).

1.09   Rule 1.1(2)(c) stipulates that the rights of a defendant, including those under Article 6 of the European Convention on Human Rights, should be recognized if a case is to be dealt with justly.

1.10   Rule 1.1(2)(e) incorporates into the concept of justly dealing with a criminal case that it is dealt with efficiently and expeditiously. That sentiment reflects the Case Management aspect of the Rules found in Part 3 which are set out and discussed in the next chapter. It was emphasized in *R (Robinson) v Sutton Coldfield Magistrates' Court*[1] the objective that all cases be dealt with efficiently and expeditiously depends upon adherence to the timetables set out in the Rules. The court thus emphasized the balance between the rights and duties of participants in the criminal justice process and highlighted the

---

[1] [2006] EWHC 307.

importance of active case management in ensuring that the overall objective is achieved. However, that such timetables do not constrain the court from doing justice was emphasized in *R (Robinson) v Sutton Coldfield Magistrates' Court*. The Rules allow for the extension of a time limit by the court even after it has expired, and the balance of the interests of justice in that case permitted the later service of applications by the Crown.

Rule 1.1(2)(g) then allows for a degree of proportionality in the way that cases are   1.11 approached taking into account the gravity of the offence alleged, the complexity of what is in issue, the severity of the consequences for the defendant and others affected and the needs of other cases.

The other factor stipulated as being of core importance to dealing with a case justly is   1.12 ensuring that appropriate information is available to the court when bail and sentence are considered (rule 1.1(2)(f)).

C. THE DUTY OF THE PARTICIPANTS IN A CRIMINAL CASE

Rule 1.2 sets out the duties of the participants in relation to the overriding objective.   1.13 A participant is defined within the Rules at rule 1.2(2) as anyone involved in any way with a criminal case. As a category it is wider than a 'party' which is defined in the glossary as 'a person or organisation directly involved in a criminal case, either as prosecutor or defendant'. Thus participants must include court staff, probation officers, organizations tasked with bringing prisoners to court and arguably even jurors.

The duties imposed upon participants by rule 1.2 include a requirement to inform the   1.14 court of any significant failure to take any step required by the Rules, any practice direction or any direction of the court. A significant failure is defined as one which might hinder the court in furthering the overriding objective. If a participant fails to inform the court of a significant failure by another, then that participant is also potentially vulnerable to sanction from the court (see rule 3.5(2)(i) at 2.15). The importance of the parties adhering to their duties as spelled out under this Part of the Rules was emphasized by Clarke J in *Philips*[2] when he stated 'not only must judges be robust in all their case management decisions. . .but the parties who are ordered to take steps must take them'.

D. THE APPLICATION BY THE COURT OF THE OVERRIDING OBJECTIVE

Rule 1.3 sets out the duties of the court in relation to the overriding objective. Baldly,   1.15 the court must further the overriding objective and in particular when exercising any legislative power or applying any practice direction or interpreting any rule or practice direction. Thus the duties imposed on participants are shared by the court which is itself required to work towards the overriding objective. Such an approach is ensured by the case management duties of the court set out in Part 3 of the Rules and dealt with in the next chapter.

---

[2] [2007] EWCA Crim 1042.

E. PART 2—UNDERSTANDING AND APPLYING THE RULES

1.16　Part 2 of the Rules is explanatory of their scope and meaning. Rule 2.1 dictates that the Rules apply to all criminal cases in all relevant courts (including the Court of Appeal Criminal Division) unless an individual rule stipulates that it applies only to a specific court or courts. In addition, the Rules do not affect any direction made by a court prior to the implementation of the Rules, that is to say any direction made before 4 April 2005.

1.17　　Rule 2.2 defines certain terms used within the Rules. A 'court' is a tribunal with jurisdiction over criminal cases. A 'court officer' means the appropriate member of staff of the court and 'Practice Direction' means the Lord Chief Justice's Consolidated Practice Direction which is reproduced at Appendix 2 to this publication.

1.18　　Rule 2.4 introduces the glossary to the Rules.

2

CASE MANAGEMENT

A. INTRODUCTION

Part 3 of the Rules is the practical cornerstone upon which the remainder of the Rules   2.01
are built. Its requirements complement Part 1, the recommended model practice set out
in the Adult Criminal Case Management Framework and the Consolidated Criminal
Practice Direction (the Practice Direction). In cases of serious fraud, the 'Serious Fraud
Protocol' must also be taken into account and in terrorism cases, the 'Terrorism Protocol'
requires similar consideration. There is also a short protocol concerned with sexual
offences in the youth court to which regard should be had in appropriate cases.

The rules contained within this part apply to the management of cases from the first   2.02
appearance in a magistrates' court through to the conclusion of proceedings in either the
magistrates' court or Crown Court (rule 3.1) (the procedural rules relevant to proceedings in the Court of Appeal Criminal Division are contained within Parts 65 to 73).
These rules impose explicit duties on the court (rule 3.2) and the parties (rule 3.3). They
also require each party to appoint a case progression officer and that case progression
officer has duties imposed by these rules (rule 3.4).

Powers exercisable by the court in carrying out its case management function, including   2.03
the power to make orders as to costs, are also set out in this Part (rule 3.5). In addition, provision is made for the parties to vary any direction made by the court (rules 3.6 and 3.7).

The parties are expected to ensure readiness for trial and the court may require the   2.04
parties to certify their readiness (rule 3.9). The court may also be proactive in setting
down a timetable for trial proceedings (rule 3.10).

Finally, this Part of the Rules introduced case management forms which are now used   2.05
as a matter of course at plea and case management hearings (rule 3.11).

2.06   The Court of Appeal Criminal Division has repeatedly and consistently encouraged this type of case management. The most notable early examples were *R v Chaaban*[1] and *R v Jisl (and others)*.[2] In the latter case Lord Justice Judge (as he then was) foreshadowed the importance in the Rules of case management by saying:

> 116. The principle therefore, is not in doubt. This appeal enables us to re-emphasise that its practical application depends on the determination of trial judges and the co-operation of the legal profession. Active, hands on, case management, both pre-trial and throughout the trial itself, is now regarded as an essential part of the judge's duty. The profession must understand that this has become and will remain part of the normal trial process, and that cases must be prepared and conducted accordingly.
>
> . . .
>
> 118. Once the issue has been identified, in a case of any substance at all. . .the judge should consider whether to direct a timetable to cover pre-trial steps, and eventually the conduct of the trial itself, not rigid, nor immutable, and fully recognising that during the trial at any rate the unexpected must be treated as normal, and making due allowance for it in the interests of justice. To enable the trial judge to manage the case in a way which is fair to every participant, pre-trial, the potential problems as well as the possible areas for time saving should be canvassed. In short, a sensible informed discussion about the future management of the case and the most convenient way to present the evidence, whether disputed or not, and where appropriate, with admissions by one or both sides, should enable the judge to make a fully informed analysis of the future timetable and the proper conduct of the trial. The objective is not haste and rush, but greater efficiency and better use of limited resources by closer identification of and focus on critical rather than peripheral issues. When trial judges act in accordance with these principles, the directions they give, and where appropriate, the timetables they prescribe in the exercise of their case management responsibilities, will be supported in this Court. Criticism is more likely to be addressed to those who ignore them.

2.07   The support promised in *Jisl* for those who pursue active case management has since materialized on a number of occasions in the Court of Appeal. For example, in *Bryant*,[3] the Court of Appeal re-emphasized that it will continue to support efforts on the part of a trial judge to keep a case moving forward at a reasonable speed. Moreover, in *Heppenstall*,[4] the Court of Appeal stated that a judge was entitled to seek a time estimate from counsel for the length of cross-examination and see that they kept to it as active case management required that cases were presented in a focussed manner. Consequently, a culture of active case management is now much more readily apparent in any magistrates' or Crown Court than it was when the Criminal Procedure Rules first saw the light of day in 2005.

B. RULES 3.2 AND 3.3—THE DUTIES OF THE COURT AND THE PARTIES

2.08   Under rule 3.2, a positive duty is placed on the court to actively manage proceedings in pursuit of the overriding objective. Many aspects of the exhortation to active case

---

[1] [2003] EWCA Crim 1012.
[2] [2004] EWCA Crim 696.
[3] [2005] EWCA Crim 2079.
[4] [2007] EWCA Crim 2485.

management found within the dictum of Lord Justice Judge are contained within this rule. The court is required to manage cases in ways which include the following means:

(a) Identifying the real issues in the case at an early stage (rule 3.2(2)(a)). In *R(DPP) v Chorley Justices*,[5] Thomas LJ emphasized the importance of requirement, stating:

> If a defendant refuses to identify what the issues are, one thing is clear: he can derive no advantage from that or seek, as appears to have happened in this case, to attempt an ambush at trial. The days of ambushing and taking last-minute technical points are gone. They are not consistent with the over-riding objective of deciding cases justly, acquitting the innocent and convicting the guilty.

Those sentiments were echoed in *Writtle v DPP*.[6] In pursuance of the aim of the early identification of the real issues, the requirement in the Criminal Justice Act 2003 (CJA 2003) of detailed particulars to be provided in any defence statement has undoubtedly been much more rigidly enforced in recent years.

(b) Identifying the needs of witnesses at an early stage (rule 3.2(2)(b)).

(c) Securing certainty as to what needs to be done by each participant and by what date through, in particular, setting a timetable for the progress of the proceedings at an early stage (rule 3.2(2)(c)).

(d) Monitoring the progress of the case and ensuring that directions are complied with (rule 3.2(2)(d)). (See rule 3.4(2) at 2.11, which requires the court, where appropriate, to nominate a court officer to be responsible for progressing a case.)

(e) Making sure that evidence is presented in the clearest and most concise manner (rule 3.2(2)(e)).

(f) Discouraging delay, dealing during the course of one hearing with as many issues as possible and avoiding unnecessary hearings (rule 3.2(2)(f)). (Rule 3.5, at 2.13, which permits the court to receive applications for directions in writing and subsequently make any necessary directions without recourse to a hearing, undoubtedly has helped to facilitate the avoidance of many unnecessary hearings in the more lengthy cases.)

(g) Encouraging the participants to cooperate in the progression of the case (rule 3.2(2)(g)).

(h) Employing technology (rule 3.2(2)(h)).

Rule 3.2(3) requires the court to make any direction necessary to achieve the desired case management. 2.09

Rule 3.3 requires the parties to assist the court in its case management duties outlined above. 2.10

C. RULE 3.4—CASE PROGRESSION OFFICERS AND THEIR DUTIES

The Rules require that, unless the court directs otherwise, each party to a case appoints a case progression officer at the commencement of the proceedings and informs the other parties and the court of who that person is and how they can be contacted (rule 3.4(1)). 2.11

---

5 [2006] EWHC 1795 (Admin).
6 [2009] RTR 28.

Likewise, where appropriate, the court, in order to fulfil its duty to further the overriding objective must also nominate a case progression officer and make that person and his contact details known to the parties (rule 3.4(2)).

2.12   The case progression officer is an important element of the framework and is required to supervise the compliance by participants with directions from the court and inform the court of anything that might affect the progress of the case. In reality, it is the case progression officer that, in accordance with rule 1.2(c), will most often be required to inform the court of any significant failings to carry out a task. The case progression officer is also obliged to make himself available to be contacted during ordinary business hours and, if contacted about the case, he must reply promptly and reasonably. If he is to be unavailable, then he must appoint a replacement and inform the other case progression officers (rule 3.4(4)).

D. RULES 3.5 TO 3.7—THE CASE MANAGEMENT POWERS OF THE COURT AND DIRECTIONS

2.13   Rule 3.5 gives the court a wide-ranging power to make any direction or take any step designed to achieve the overriding objective, provided it is not inconsistent with any legislation, including the Rules. This rule establishes the basis for proactive case management by the courts in that it provides for the court to appoint a person (a judge, magistrate, justices' clerk or assistant to a justices' clerk) to manage a case (rule 3.5(2)(a)) and make directions of its own initiative or on application (rule 3.5(2)(b)) with or without a hearing (rule 3.5(2)(e)).

2.14   In addition, rule 3.5 lays the ground for more expeditious and less time-consuming methods of progressing a case by allowing for the receipt of representations in relation to a direction by letter, telephone or any other means of electronic communication. A court may also hold a directions hearing by way of any of those means (rule 3.5(2)(d)). The court may also ask or allow a party to propose a direction (rule 3.5(2)(c)), fix, vary, and cancel the date for a hearing (rule 3.5(2)(f)), and vary a deadline imposed by a direction (even after that deadline has expired) (rule 3.5(2)(g)).

2.15   The court may also require that the issues in the case should be determined separately and stipulate the order in which they will be determined (rule 3.5(2)(h)). Finally, the court may specify the consequences of failing to comply with a direction. The potential scope of that provision, at rule 3.5(2)(i), has been significantly added to since it was originally implemented. If a party fails to comply with a direction, rule 3.5(6) allows the court, first, to fix, postpone, bring forward, extend, cancel, or adjourn a hearing. But the court may also make an order as to costs and impose such other sanction as it deems appropriate. Rule 3.5(3) and (4) respectively allow for the magistrates' court to give a direction that will apply in the Crown Court if the case is to continue there and vice versa. Any power to give such a direction includes the power to vary or revoke that direction (rule 3.5(5)). In *R (Kelly) v Warley Magistrates' Court*,[7] it was recognized that, in the absence of express statutory provision to the contrary, the case management powers within the Rules do not override legal professional privilege or litigation privilege.

---

[7] [2008] 1 Cr App R 14.

(So far as the facts of the *Warley Magistrates' Court* case are concerned, it should be noted that section 34 of the CJA 2003 came into force in May 2010, creating section 6C of the Criminal Procedure and Investigations Act 1996 (CPIA 1996) and requiring the defence to notify details of witnesses it proposes to call.)

Rules 3.6 and 3.7 provide for the variation of a direction made by the court. Rule 3.6 allows a party to apply to vary a direction if it was made without a hearing (rule 3.6(1)(a)) or without that party being present (rule 3.6(1)(b)). In addition, greater leeway for the making of such an application is allowed under rule 3.6(1)(c) where a party may apply to vary a direction if 'circumstances have changed'. If a party is to apply to vary a direction, then it must do so as soon as practicable after becoming aware of the grounds for making the application and must give the other parties as much notice as possible (rule 3.6(2)). 2.16

Rule 3.7 allows the parties to vary a direction by agreement provided that the court has not prohibited such an agreement and the agreement would not put any hearing date in jeopardy or significantly affect the progress of the case. The court's case progression officer must be promptly informed of any such agreement (rule 3.7(1)(c)) and if he is not satisfied that the agreement will not jeopardize a hearing date or significantly affect the progress of the case, he must refer the agreement to the court (rule 3.7(2)). 2.17

E. RULES 3.8 TO 3.10—CASE PREPARATION, READINESS FOR TRIAL, AND THE CONDUCT OF A TRIAL OR APPEAL

Rules 3.8 to 3.10 impose further case management duties on the court and the parties to ensure efficient case progression. If a case is not to be concluded at a particular hearing, rule 3.8(1) requires the court to give directions designed to ensure that it can be concluded as soon as possible. If the defendant is absent the court must decide whether to proceed nonetheless (rule 3.8(2)(a)). It is nowadays routine at any plea and case management hearing (PCMH) that the defendant is warned that if he fails to attend for his trial it may proceed in his absence. It is not at all uncommon that a trial proceeds in the defendant's absence. If the plea of the defendant is not entered at a hearing then, at every hearing, the court should enquire as to the likely plea in the future (rule 3.8(2)(b)). 2.18

The court should also set, follow, or revise a timetable for the progression of the case, which may include a timetable for any hearing including the trial or appeal in the Crown Court (rule 3.8(2)(c)). This rule also requires the court to ensure when it is making directions that, whenever appropriate and practicable, there is continuity of representation and court in the proceedings (rule 3.8(2)(d)). This requirement is echoed in the Practice Direction (paragraph IV.41.8), in the context of plea and case management hearings, when it states: 2.19

Resident Judges in setting the listing policy should ensure that list officers fix cases as far as possible to enable the trial advocate to conduct the PCMH and the trial.

If a direction has not been complied with, the court is required to find out why not and who is responsible for the failure to comply with the direction. The court must then take any appropriate action (rule 3.8(2)(d)). This provision has to be viewed in the light of the powers of the court identified in rule 3.5(6). In the Crown Court, a plea and case management hearing must be held in order to prepare for the trial unless the circumstances 2.20

make it unnecessary (rule 3.8(3)). The increasing recognition of the importance of properly taking into account the needs of witnesses is reflected in rule 3.8(4). It did not form part of the original rules and provides that, in order to prepare for trial, the court must take every reasonable step to encourage and facilitate the attendance of witnesses when they are needed.

2.21   Duties in respect of case preparation are imposed on the parties by rule 3.9. The parties must comply with the directions of the court (rule 3.9(2)(a)) and must promptly inform the court of anything that may jeopardize the date for a hearing or significantly affect the progress of the case (rule 3.9(2)(d)). In addition the parties must make the necessary and appropriate arrangements for the presentation of any written or other material in the case (rule 3.9(2)(c)) and take every reasonable step to ensure that their witnesses attend when they are supposed to (rule 3.9(2)(b)). The court may also require the parties to certify that they are ready for trial (rule 3.9(3)).

2.22   The court is also able to require the parties to stipulate a number of features of the presentation of its case with the aim of managing the case properly. The court may require a party to identify:

(a) which witnesses he intends to give evidence;
(b) the order in which he intends that those witnesses will give their evidence;
(c) whether he needs an order compelling the attendance of a witness;
(d) any arrangements he proposes to facilitate a witness giving evidence;
(e) any arrangement he proposes to facilitate the participation of any other person including the defendant;
(f) any written evidence he intends to adduce;
(g) what other material he intends to use in the presentation of his case;
(h) any points of law he intends to raise that could affect the conduct of the trial or appeal; and
(i) what timetable he proposes and expects to follow.

F. RULE 3.11—CASE MANAGEMENT FORMS AND RECORDS

2.23   Rule 3.11 requires the court and the parties to use the case management forms stipulated in the Practice Direction wherever they are available. If no form is available then the participants do not have to adopt any particular formality. The court is required to make available to the parties a record of the directions given. This rule also lists other rules and legislation which might affect case management.

2.24   The use of forms is discussed below in relation to Part 5 of the rules, which is dedicated to the issue, in chapter 3 (at 3.12), and in relation to the case progression forms utilized when a case is transferred to the Crown Court, and at PCMHs, in chapter 5.

3

SERVICE, FORMS, AND RECORDS

A. INTRODUCTION

Parts 1 and 3 of the Rules demonstrate that the intention of the Rules is to enhance the   3.01
efficiency and expedition of the criminal justice system by increasing communication
between the parties, monitoring of the activities of the parties, and ensuring certainty as
to what has been done and what needs to be done in managing criminal cases. Parts 4 to
5 provide the mechanics for achieving these improvements in three important areas:

(a) how documents are to be served;
(b) the forms that need to be completed; and
(c) the records that are to be kept of decisions and orders.

In the last edition of this Guide, criticism was levelled at the decision to replicate in the   3.02
2005 Rules the old Magistrates' Court Rules 1981 in relation to the service of documents. As a result various opportunities to inject technology into the process by, for
example, allowing the service of various documents and notices by email, had been lost.
Fortunately, that criticism was recognized by the Rules Committee and the Rules were
amended by the Criminal Procedure (Amendment) Rules 2007[1] to increase significantly
the option of electronic service, communication, and storage.

B. SERVICE OF DOCUMENTS

The two key issues in this context are: 3.03

(a) how to serve a document; and
(b) how to prove that it has been served.

---

[1] SI 2007/699.

3.04 In the first edition of the 2005 Rules, Part 4 was divided into service in the magistrates' court and the Crown Court. This preserved the differences of service between the two courts that had previously resulted from rules 67 and 99 of the Magistrates' Court Rules 1981[2] and rule 28 of the Crown Court Rules 1982.[3] The 2010 Rules now apply equally to both. In the same way, whereas the 2005 Rules maintained different pre-existing rules for the service of particular documents, such as witness summonses, the 2010 Rules apply to the service of 'any document in a case', unless there is specific identified exception (rule 4.1).

1. Methods of service

3.05 The Rules identify four methods of service of general application by which any document may be served (rule 4.2), subject to certain limitations identified in rule 4.7.[4] The methods are:

(a) service by handing over the document (rule 4.3);
(b) service by leaving the document at a service address or posting it to that address (rule 4.4);
(c) use of Document Exchange (DX) (rule 4.5), fax, email, or other electronic means (rule 4.6);
(d) another method that has been approved by the court (rule 4.9).

It should also be noted that there is specific provision for how someone who is in custody can serve a document (rule 4.8). In addition, it should be noted that just as the court may specify a method of service (pursuant to rule 4.9), it may also specify the time and date on which it is to be served (rule 4.12(1)).

3.06 Service by handing over the document, for the purposes of rule 4.3, involves placing it into the hand directly of an individual (or an appropriate adult if the individual is under 17), a senior office holder or the legal representative of a corporation, the prosecution's representative or an officer with requisite authority at the relevant court office or Criminal Appeal Office (rule 4.3). The date of service by this method is the date on which it has handed over (rule 4.10(1)).

3.07 Service by leaving the document at a service address or posting it to that address by first-class post, for the purposes of rule 4.4, is limited to service within the United Kingdom. There are specific provisions for the service of documents elsewhere, such as under section 1139 of the Companies Act 2006, but these rules are not concerned with those specific instances. The rules define, at rule 4.4(2), what will be accepted as a service address. In summary:

(a) in the case of an individual it is an address 'where it is reasonably believed that he or she will receive it'. The wording no longer includes specific reference to the individual's last known address as an option, but it is clear that a last known address would amount to one at which the document would be expected to reach him;

---

[2] SI 1981/552.
[3] SI 1982/1109.
[4] See 3.9 below.

(b) where a document is to be served on a corporation by delivery or post the appropriate address is either its principal offices or to the place in the United Kingdom from which it carries out its business (rule 4.4(2)(b)). As an alternative, the document may be served on the corporation's legal representative (rule 4.4(2)(c));

(c) where the document is to be served on the prosecution or the court, it may be delivered or posted to the prosecutor, Court of Appeals office as appropriate (rule 4.4(2)(d)–(f)).

The date of service for a document left at an address is taken to be the next business day (rule 4.10(2)(a)). The date of service where a document has been posted is the second business day after it has been placed in the first-class post (rule 4.10(2)(c)). 3.08

It should be noted that pursuant to rule 4.7, delivery by hand, by leaving at the service address or by post (in accordance with rule 4.3 to 4.4) are the only means that may be used for service on an individual or a corporation, subject to rule 4.9, for the categories of documents identified in rule 4.7(2). These documents can be categorized as the important means by which proceedings are initiated and culminated, and records of court orders and directions. On the same basis, an application to punish an individual or corporation for contempt of court[5] must be delivered by hand (rule 4.7(3)). 3.09

Limitations are also inevitable where the sender is a person in custody. Such a person serves a document by handing it to a custodian, who then forwards it to the addressee (rule 4.9). The time of service is that time at which the prisoner hands the document to the custodian, and it is this time and date that is recorded (rule 4.9(2)). 3.10

Service by DX, fax, email, or other electronic means is only permitted where the person (or presumably corporate body) to be served includes a DX number and/or fax number or email address on their writing paper and has not indicated that they will not accept service by those means (rule 4.5 to 4.6). In a rare concession to the environment, the rules permit a party to serve a document electronically which is not also served on paper (rule 4.6(2)). The date of service will be taken as two business days after a document has been sent by DX (rule 4.10(2)(c)) or one day after it has been faxed or sent electronically (rule 4.10(2)(d)). 3.11

2. Proof of service

The reason why limitations are put on the methods by which important court documents can be served is so that there can be certainty that they have arrived. Proof of service was a focus of the Rules when they first came into force in 2005. However, those provisions have been removed, save for the following limited rules: 3.12

(a) service of any process or document can be proved by a certificate from the person who served it (rule 4.11);

(b) any process or document produced by a court computer on a given day will be taken to have been sent on the next day (rule 4.10(4));

(c) where the recipient of a document responds to it, this is taken to have been the date of its receipt if it is earlier than any of the dates specified in rule 4.10 (rule 4.10(2)(e)), and the court will treat it has having been served in accordance with the Rules even

---

[5] Pursuant to r 62.3, see Chapter 17.

if this has not been the case (rules 4.12(2)). It follows that technical objections to service will avail a recipient nothing if he has, in fact, received the document in question.

C. FORMS

3.13   No aspect of the introduction of the Rules in 2005 received as much public attention, or was subject to as much comment and complaint from the judiciary, the legal profession, and beyond, as the new forms that were introduced in conjunction with the Rules by the Consolidated Criminal Practice Direction. Because the forms were actually issued pursuant to the Practice Direction, the Rules themselves said very little about them, and that little was to be found in the 2005 version of Part 5 of the Rules. The 2010 Rules have reduced the status of the forms section yet further by amalgamating it with the section of court records, which had appeared in Part 6 of the 2005 Rules.

3.14   The Practice Direction seeks to supplement the rules in various areas, including in relation to the forms. The obvious merit of this approach is that the forms can be amended and replaced by direction of the Lord Chief Justice rather than by amendment to the Rules, which are, of course, a statutory instrument. This, therefore, explains the bald statement to be found in rule 5.1, that the forms set out in the Practice Direction shall be 'used as appropriate in connection with the rules to which they apply'.

3.15   This is amplified by paragraphs I.14.1 to I.14.3 of the Practice Direction and, most especially by Annex D to the Practice Direction. This Annex sets out the forms to be used in the criminal courts by reference to the rule to which they apply. The information in Annex D is in columns that relate to the rule in question, the form reference number and the rules that have been replaced in the particular context in issue.

3.16   Throughout the Rules there are references to the need to provide a notice or other document 'in the form set out in the Practice Direction', for example at rule 13.2(1) in relation to the notice of an application to dismiss, rule 16.1, in relation to the application for reporting restrictions, and rule 34.2, which relates to the notice for adducing hearsay evidence. In each case, these references alert the reader to the need to refer to Annex D to identify which form is required for compliance with that rule.

3.17   Part 5 also addresses two specific issues in relation to the documentation necessary to dealing with the Rules. These are:

(a) use of Welsh language forms (rule 5.2); and
(b) signatures on forms (rule 5.3).

1. Use of the Welsh language

3.18   Paragraph III.23.1 of the Practice Direction seeks to 'reflect the principle of the Welsh Language Act 1993 that in the administration of justice in Wales the English and Welsh languages should be treated on a basis of equality'.

3.19   The remainder of that paragraph addresses the use of the Welsh language in court, and especially at trial. With the same principle in mind, rule 5.2 addresses the use of the Welsh language in forms. These may be used in connection with magistrates' court proceedings in Wales either exclusively (rule 5.2(1)) or in conjunction with English language forms (rule 5.2(2)). Moreover, the forms should make clear that they are available in Welsh, in the terms set out in rule 5.2(3), and should be provided in that form by the justices' clerk on request (rule 5.2(4)).

Although paragraph III.23 of the Practice Direction speaks of equality of the two languages, this equality is subject to the further qualification, in rule 5.2(6), that where there is any discrepancy between the English and Welsh language versions of the forms, the former prevails over the latter. 3.20

2. Signatures

Rule 5.3 seeks to increase the efficiency of the processing of magistrates' court paperwork by allowing the clerk to the justices to sign forms that would otherwise have to be signed by a justice of the peace. There is a list of exceptions to this relaxation in rule 5.3(2), in relation to various forms that are the product of judicial decisions, such as informations and warrants, although it is of note that the purely administrative warrants of commitment can be signed by the clerk. As a further time saving, electronic signatures can be used on forms, save for warrants (rule 5.3(3)). 3.21

D. COURT RECORDS

Whilst section 2 of Part 5 of the rules continues to deal with the same theme of court paperwork as those addressed above, the focus in this section is neither on the forms that need to be completed nor on the service of those forms, but on the records that need to be made thereafter by the court. It replaces that which appeared in Part 6 of the 2005 Rules, but retains the wording of that earlier version. 3.22

The importance of this section of the Rules is twofold. First, it provides certainty as to what has been decided and what the outcome of a hearing, argument, or case has been, and, secondly, it allows for a record that can be proved in evidence of what decisions have been, for example the proving of a memorandum of conviction. 3.23

The main focus of the rules is the magistrates' court register, which is the place in which a minute or memorandum is made of all adjudications and proceedings of which a record is required (rule 5.4(1)). This register can be an electronic record, which includes data under the headings set out in rule 5.4(2) held on the court computer system and should be open to inspection during reasonable hours by any justice of the peace or authorized person (r.5.4(15)). 3.24

Rule 5.4 lists various specific types of hearing that should result in an entry in the register. In summary these are as follows: 3.25

Rule	Hearing
5.4(4)	Consent of the defendant to the hearing and determination of an application for his remand on the adjournment of his case happening in his absence, pursuant to section 128(3A) of the Magistrates' Court Act 1980 (MCA 1980)
5.4(5)	Withdrawal of consent of the defendant to the hearing and determination of an application for his remand on the adjournment of his case happening in his absence, pursuant to section 128(3A) of the MCA 1980

(continued)

Rule	Hearing
5.4(6)	Plea of defendant in summary proceedings
5.4(7)	Consent of defendant to be tried summarily at the mode of trial stage
5.4(8)	Whether or not the defendant was present for the decision as to the mode of trial of triable either way offences, and the reasons for his absence if applicable
5.4(9)	Decision as to the value involved in an offence (criminal damage/aggravated vehicle taking) where this is determinative of where it should be tried, pursuant to section 22 of the MCA 1980
5.4(10)	Consent of the defendant to make the order, pursuant to section 53(3) of the MCA 1980, for which a civil complaint is made to the court under section 51 of the MCA 1980
5.4(11)–(12)	Conviction of the defendant or the dismissal of the charge against him, setting out the dates of the offence and of the order, and the nature of the offence
5.4(13)	Reasons, required under section 130(3) of the Powers of Criminal Courts (Sentencing) Act 2000 (PCC(S)A 2000), for not making an order as to compensation for personal loss, damage, or injury resulting from the offence or to make payment towards funeral expenses or bereavement in respect of a death resulting from the offence, under section 130(1)
5.4(14)	Confirmation that a pre-sentence report has been obtained and considered, in accordance with section 81 of the PCC(S)A 2000, where a custodial sentence is then passed

3.26   The rule also recognizes that separate records will be kept in certain areas, which nevertheless form a part of the complete register. This refers to the following:

Rule	Hearing/Decision	Separate Book
5.4(3)	Remand decisions, reasons for bail decisions, certificates of fully argued bail applications (pursuant to section 5(6A) of the Bail Act 1976)	Bail register
5.4(17)	Register of youth court proceedings	Youth court register
5.5	Particulars of an endorsement on a driving licence where a fixed penalty has been imposed without a hearing (pursuant to section 57 of the Road Traffic Offenders Act 1988 (RTOA 1988))	Endorsement book
5.6	Particulars of fine in default of a fixed penalty (pursuant to section 70 of the RTOA 1988)	Endorsement book

3.27   In terms of the evidential use to be made of this register, rule 5.4(16) states that extracts from the register can be used as a record of summary conviction or of an order made on a complaint where this is required for an appeal or for another legal purpose. Rule 5.7 adds to this, by stating that the register, or a certified extract from it, shall be admissible in any legal proceedings as evidence of these proceedings.

3.28   The uses of this register would include proving a conviction as part of an appeal against it or in relation to an offence consequent upon it, or for that matter as part of the adducing of the bad character of a defendant or another.[6]

---

[6] Under Chapter 1 of Part 11 of the CJA 2003, see Chapter 12 in this book.

4

PRELIMINARY PROCEEDINGS IN THE MAGISTRATES' COURT

A. INTRODUCTION

It is recognized in the Rules that for the overriding objective to have its proper effect, it must be addressed in proceedings in the magistrates' courts because it is there that all criminal cases start. With that end in mind, the Rules seek to enhance the efficiency of the whole criminal process by taking steps to enhance the case management function that is now firmly made part of the magistrates' court's role.   4.01

The Rules, in seeking to do this, do not seek to replace the existing structure of the Magistrates' Court Act 1980 (MCA 1980). Rather, they seek to address proceedings in the magistrates' courts in a number of areas, which have hitherto been covered by a combination of statutory instruments and rules made pursuant to statute. Each of the areas addressed is covered by a part of the rules.   4.02

It is of note that the Rules Committee were clearly primarily concerned to address the case management of Crown Court cases. This can be seen from the fact that most of the rules primarily relate to the Crown Court, and from the fact that the rules for pre-trial hearings in the magistrates' court,[1] which were not included in the 2005 Rules have still not been drafted, whilst the Crown Court position is extensively dealt with by those parts of the Rules that deal with preliminary proceedings.   4.03

Some of these rules are of general application, such as: 4.04

(a) the process by which Proceedings are commenced in the magistrates' court—Part 7;

(b) the procedure for objecting to discontinuance of such proceedings—Part 8;

(c) the procedures for pre-trial hearings—Part 9.

These are addressed in this chapter.

---

[1] Part 9 of the Rules.

4.05   The parts of Rules most important to the attempt to create a more efficient case management role for the magistrates' courts are contained in those parts that deal with the different means by which cases are transferred, committed, or sent to the Crown Court. These Rules[2] are addressed in the next chapter.

4.06   The Rules then seek to deal with the preliminary stages of proceedings once they have reached the Crown Court,[3] which are concerned with the rules relating to the preferring of indictments and the preparatory hearing regime. These are also dealt with in the next chapter.

4.07   Finally, the Rules address two specific areas, the rules restricting reporting of and public access to proceedings,[4] and self contained jurisdiction of the magistrates' courts in relation to extradition.[5] These discrete areas are addressed in Chapter 6, below.

B. COMMENCING PROCEEDINGS

4.08   Part 7 of the Rules deals with some of the different ways in which it is possible to commence proceedings in the magistrates' court, giving effect to relevant provisions of the MCA 1980 and the Criminal Justice Act 2003 (CJA 2003).

4.09   Under section 1 of the MCA 1980,[6] the magistrates' court will issue a summons requiring someone to attend court, or issue a warrant for that person's arrest (if the offence is one triable in the Crown Court that is punishable with imprisonment and the person's address cannot be established to allow for the service of a summons), on receipt of a formal information. Part 7 deals addresses this process (rule 7.1).

4.10   Since the 2005 Rules, sections 29 and 30 of the CJA 2003 have come into force. Under section 29, a public prosecutor (as defined in section 29(5) of the Act as including all public prosecuting authorities, including the Crown Prosecution Service) can initiate proceedings, through the issuing of a written charge, alleging that someone has committed an offence and of a requisition, requiring that person to attend court to answer it.[7] Part 7 of the 2010 Rules addresses this process (rule 7.1).

4.11   In the last edition of this Guide, it was observed that whilst section 30(4) of the CJA 2003 makes clear that the court will retain its role in relation to the issuing of warrants,[8] pursuant to section 29 proceedings will be initiated in most cases by communication from the prosecution to the defendant, rather than from the court. The aim of the rules in relation to this procedure is to ensure that the magistrates' court is nevertheless involved in the process, rather than being taken unaware when the defendant makes his first appearance at court.

4.12   There is, of course, a third route by which a defendant can make his first appearance at the magistrates' court. The 2005 Rules in no way impinged on the rights of the police to initiate proceedings by arresting a suspect in one of the ways enunciated in the Police and

---

[2] Contained in Parts 10–12.
[3] Parts 13–15 of the Rules.
[4] Part 16.
[5] Part 17.
[6] As amended by s 43 of the Courts Act 2003.
[7] The section 29 procedure is dealt with at *Blackstone's Criminal Practice 2011*, para. D5.2.
[8] Warrants are discussed in Chapter 7 below.

Criminal Evidence Act 1984 (PACE 1984), and to then bring those that they have arrested before the magistrates' court.

The process remains that once an arrest has been made, compliant with PACE 1984,[9]   4.13
and once there is sufficient evidence, a suspect should be brought before the custody sergeant to be charged.[10] They then appear before the magistrates' court and the procedures of that court come into effect. Rule 7.1(1)(c) makes clear that Part 7 of the Rules now applies where a person in custody has been charged with an offence, and it is clear that this is a reference to a person charged pursuant to section 37 of PACE 1984. Part 7 of the 2010 Rules does address the production at court of a person charged with an arrestable offence by the police (rule 7.1).

The 2005 Rules had also dealt with notices/declarations under the Road Traffic   4.14
Offenders Act 1988. This is no longer the case.

1. Laying an information

The rules in relation to the laying of an information originate from rules 4, 12, and 100   4.15
of the Magistrates' Court Rules 1981[11] as they stood at 3 April 2005.

The Rules have now been slimmed down and simplified into one unified procedure.   4.16
In relation to the section 1, MCA 1980, procedure, they can be summarized as follows:

(a) Where a prosecutor requires the magistrates' court to issue a summons, an information should be provided to the court officer. This should either be served in writing (rule 7.2(1)(a)) or, where permissible for the offence in question, presented orally providing that the allegations are set out in writing (rule 7.2(1)(b)).

(b) Where a prosecutor requires the issue of a warrant, the same procedure applies, namely that a written information and written charges are provided to the court (rule 7.2(2)(a)) or these documents are presented orally to the court (rule 7.2(2)(b)).

(c) The information should be served within six months of the offence, where that offence may only be tried in the magistrates' court, unless other legislation proscribes otherwise (rule 7.2(5)). Where the offence may be tried in the Crown Court, the time limit depends on the offence in question (rule 7.2(6)). The case management powers of the court (under Part 3 of the Rules) will also have application.

The Rules do not alter the previous law in relation to the meaning of prosecutor. It has   4.17
been made clear, for example in *Rubin v DPP*,[12] that an unincorporated association, such as a police authority, could not commence proceedings and there is therefore still a need for an individual to act as the informant, even if that individual is acting on behalf of a prosecuting authority or the local police authority.[13] The Rules do not affect the position for prosecutions by persons other than the Crown Prosecution Service.[14] The Note to rule 7.2 makes clear that the officer responsible for applying to the court for

---

[9] See para D1.21 of *Blackstone's Criminal Practice 2011*.
[10] Pursuant to s 37 of PACE 1984. See para D1.32 of *Blackstone's Criminal Practice* 2011.
[11] SI 1981/552.
[12] [1990] 2 QB 80.
[13] See para D3.37 of *Blackstone's Criminal Practice 2011*.
[14] As set out in s 6(1) of the Prosecution of Offences Act 1985, for the details of which, see para D3.45 of *Blackstone's Criminal Practice 2011*.

breach, revocation, or amendment of a community order,[15] is a prosecutor for these purposes and is therefore obliged to follow this procedure.

4.18   The Rules also do not seek to alter the considerations to which the magistrates' court should have regard when deciding whether or not to issue a summons. This remains a judicial rather than an administrative function.[16] The Rules do, however, address the contents of the information. The information needs to describe the offence with necessary particulars in ordinary language, together with a reference to any relevant statute/ statutory instrument/rule which creates the offence in question (rule 7.3(1)(a)). The degree of detail that is required as to the offence is more general than the old rule 4(3) which required the summons to particularize 'an exception, exemption, proviso, excuse or qualification' to liability. The information should also provide such particulars of the conduct constituting the commission of the offences as to make clear that which is alleged against the defendant (rule 7.3(1)(b)).

4.19   Under the 2005 Rules (and the Magistrates' Court Rules 1981 which they replaced), it was stated that an information could only charge one offence, although a number of informations each charging different offences could be laid at the same time. Under the 2010 Rules, it remains the case that more than one information and more than one charge may be included in the same document (rule 7.2(4)). In addition, however, if more than one incident of an offence is alleged to have occurred in the context of a course of conduct, these incidents may all be included in the same allegation (rule 7.3(2)). The document including the information, or series of informations, may also include the summons (rule 7.4(4)).

4.20   Again, under the 2005 Rules, if it became apparent to the court that more than one offence was alleged in an information, the court was empowered to put the prosecutor to his election, with the sanction that the information could be dismissed if the prosecutor failed to elect. That power is not reproduced in the 2010 Rules, and the combined effect of this and the rules described in the last paragraph is that the document provided to the court by the prosecutor may allege more than one offence, with no immediate route of objection to that course on behalf of the court or defendant.

2. Issuing a written charge

4.21   In relation to the section 29, CJA 2003, procedure, the rules may be summarized as follows:

(a) Where a public prosecutor has issued a written charge to a defendant, pursuant to section 29, the magistrates' court officer must be notified immediately (rule 7.2(3)).

(b) The written charge should be issued within six months of the alleged offence where that offence may be tried only in the magistrates' court (rule 7.2(5)(b)), save where legislation imposed a different time limit. Where the offence may be tried in the Crown Court, as with the procedure for the laying of an information, the time limit is offence specific (rule 7.2(6)(b)).

---

[15] See Part 44 of the Rules.
[16] This was held in *Gateshead Justices, ex p Tesco Stores Ltd* [1981] QB 470. The considerations relevant to the execution of this judicial function are addressed at para D5.5 of *Blackstone's Criminal Practice 2011*.

(c) The charge should describe the offence in ordinary language, together with a reference to any relevant statute/statutory instrument/rule which creates the offence in question (rule 7.3(1)(a)), and should provide such particulars of the conduct constituting the commission of the offences as to make clear that which is alleged against the defendant (rule 7.3(1)(b)).

(d) Section 29 permits the public prosecutor to issue a requisition, requiring the defendant served with a written charge to attend the magistrates' court, the content of such a requisition is the same as that of a summons, which is described below. The requisition may be included in the same document as the written charge (rule 7.4(5)), and one requisition may be issued for a number of offences (rule 7.4(2)).

3. Summonses, warrants, and requisitions

Once the court has received an application for a summons or warrant, it may issue the document in question without the necessity of a hearing, or otherwise entertaining representations from the parties (rule 7.4(1)). One summons or warrant may be issued for more than one offence (rule 7.4(2)).[17]   4.22

The content of a summons, and in the same terms of a requisition, are identified in rules 7.4(3). It should tell the defendant where and when he should attend which court, which offence or offences the document relates to, and identify the person who issued it. When a summons is issued, it should be served on the defendant by either the prosecutor or the court, there being communication between the prosecutor and the court in this regard (rule 7.4(6)). It is always the responsibility of the prosecutor to serve the requisition on the defendant, together with a copy of the charge. A copy of each document should be provided to the court (rule 7.4(7)).   4.23

Under section 34A of the Children and Young Persons Act 1933, a summons issued for the attendance of the parent/guardian of a child/young person under section 34A takes the same form set out above. This is a summons issued where a youth is charged with an offence and the court wish his parent or guardian to accompany him at any stage of the proceedings, and where it is not unreasonable to request such attendance. The summons or requisition to the parent/guardian may be included in the same document as that addressed to the child, but may also appear in a separate document (rule 7.4(9)).   4.24

The service of such summonses and requisitions is governed by rule 4.1,[18] which deals with the service of summonses, which had previously been dealt with by rule 99 of the 1981 Rules. A replacement summons or requisition may be issued, subject to any specific legislative provision to the contrary, without the necessity for the prosecutor to serve new information or the public prosecutor to serve a new written charge. The only pre-condition to the issue of a replacement document is that the original was served by being left at, or posted to an address at which it can be show to have arrived (rule 7.4(8)).   4.25

---

[17] Warrants are addressed in more detail in Part 18 of the Rules, and at Chapter 7 below.
[18] This rule is dealt with in Chapter 3 above.

C. OBJECTING TO THE DISCONTINUANCE OF PROCEEDINGS

4.26 Previously, the Magistrates Courts (Discontinuance of Proceedings) Rules 1986[19] provided the framework for raising objection to a decision by the prosecuting authority to discontinue proceedings. The power to discontinue proceedings, to which the 1986 Rules formerly gave effect, and which are not contained in Part 8 of the Rules, is contained in section 23(3) of the Prosecution of Offences Act 1985. This states:

> Where, at any time during the preliminary stages of the proceedings, the Director gives notice under this section to the justices' chief executive for the court that he does not want the proceedings to continue, they shall be discontinued with effect from the giving of that notice but may be revived by notice given by the accused under subsection (7) below.

4.27 Part 8 of the Rules, which have not been amended between their 2005 and 2010 incarnations, replace the Magistrates Courts (Discontinuance of Proceedings) Rules 1986. The scenario envisaged by the Rules is that the Director of Public Prosecutors may discontinue proceedings, pursuant to section 23(3) of the 1985 Act:

(a) before the start of a summary trial;
(b) before an indictment is preferred in a case that has been sent pursuant to section 51 of the Crime and Disorder Act 1998 (CDA 1998); or
(c) before the defendant is committed (which provision, section 23(1)(b)(i), will become obsolete when committals are abolished on the introduction of Schedule 3 to the Criminal Justice Act 2003).

4.28 The right of a defendant served with such notice is contained in section 23(7) of the 1985 Act, which states:

> Where the Director [of Public Prosecutions] has given notice under subsection (3) above, the accused shall, if he wants the proceedings to continue, give notice to that effect to the justices' chief executive for the court within the prescribed period; and where notice is so given the proceedings shall continue as if no notice had been given by the Director under subsection (3) above.

4.29 The timeline for this procedure is as follows:

Action	Rule
Notice by the accused under s. 23(7) that he wishes to challenge the decision to discontinue must be given within 35 days of that decision.	8.1
Notice to be written and to identify the offence in question.	8.2
The DPP shall make the accused aware that a notice has been served.	8.3
The court shall make any surety of the defendant, or other person responsible for the defendant's compliance with bail, aware of the situation	8.4

---

[19] SI 1986/367.

The Rules do not seek to address the requirement enunciated in section 23(5) of the 4.30
1985 Act, to the effect that where the Director of Public Prosecutions (DPP) gives notice
of discontinuance he should also gives reasons for that decision.

D. PRE-TRIAL HEARINGS IN THE MAGISTRATES' COURTS

There is a gap in the Rules between those parts which deal with the initiation of proceed- 4.31
ings, discussed above, and those which deal with the sending or committal of cases to the
Crown Court, discussed below. The proceedings that occur in between these stages of
the progression of a case are pre-trial hearings in the magistrates' courts. At present, there
are no provisions in the Rules for these hearings, although Part 9 of the Rules is set aside
for this purpose.

The bald statement that there are no provisions in the Rules for pre-trial hearings is 4.32
subject to the qualification that the Rules do address applications for the issuing and
execution of warrants and for decisions in relation to bail, which are both common
components of such pre-trial hearings, and the service of advance information.[20]

The key procedure that are not covered by the Rules at all at present are: 4.33

(a) rules relating to a defendant's first appearance in the magistrates' court; and
(b) the determination of mode of trial.

The Rules similarly do not address the often vexed determination of mode of trial in 4.34
youth court cases.

1. First appearances

Guidance as to the conduct of first appearances is provided in the Criminal Case 4.35
Management Framework ('the Framework'), issued by the Lord Chief Justice in July
2004 to provide guidance to those engaged in criminal cases, and especially cases before
the Rules came into force. The Framework addresses first appearances in two categories,
those where a plea of guilty is entered (Part 5) and those where there is a plea or indication
of a plea of not guilty (Part 15).

In guilty plea cases (Part 5) the objectives of the first appearance, as expressed in the 4.36
Framework, are:

(a) to ascertain the plea and enter it where appropriate. It is clearly envisaged that an
    unrepresented defendant will be assisted to secure representation at court that same
    day to allow this to happen (see paragraph 5.3(d));
(b) to ensure that the case proceeds to an effective sentencing hearing in relation to
    summary and triable either way offences. It is clearly envisaged that this should
    occur at the first appearance where possible;
(c) to prepare indictable-only cases for sending directly to the Crown Court;
(d) to keep the victims and witnesses informed of progress.

---

[20] Warrants are addressed by Part 18 of the Rules, rules for bail applications are set down in Part 19, and
advance information appears in Part 21.

4.37 The procedure will be that, in relation to summary matters, the defendant will be asked to enter his plea, and if it is a guilty plea the case will proceed to sentence (paragraph 5.3(b)). In triable either way cases, the court will expect both parties to proceed to plea before venue (paragraph 5.3(c)), and in indictable-only cases an indication as to plea will be expected before the case is then sent to the Crown Court under section 51 of the CDA 1998 (paragraph 5.3(g)). A decision will be made as to whether a pre-sentence report is required only after the prosecution has opened its case (paragraph 5.4(b)).

4.38 In not guilty plea cases (Part 15) the objectives of the first appearance, as expressed in the Framework, are:

(a) to ascertain the defendant's plea and deal with mode of trial whether this is appropriate;
(b) to prepare to send the case to the Crown Court under section 51 where this applies;
(c) to ensure that the parties prepare for the case properly and are ready for trial when it is listed;
(d) to keep the victims and witnesses informed of progress.

4.39 Where the case is to be tried summarily, at this first hearing the court will either fix a date or require certificates of readiness from the parties by a specified date to allow for the fixing of the trial date (paragraph 15.6(a)). The court may also make directions 'timetabling the future progression of the case' (paragraph 15.6(c)), and fix a 'progression hearing' where necessary (paragraph 15.6(d)).

4.40 Part 17 of the Framework also provides further guidance as to the measures that should be adopted to ensure that trials proceed when listed, maximizing court time and not delaying witnesses. Paragraph V.56.2 of the Practice Direction also addresses efficient progress towards effective summary trials by requiring that the form at Annex E be used to provide a case progression timetable in such cases.

4.41 In other cases, it is envisaged that such further steps as the determination of mode of trial and, where jurisdiction is declined, the transfer of the case to the Crown Court, will happen at this first appearance wherever possible.

4.42 If the court decides to commit the defendant to the Crown Court for sentence,[21] it should provide the Crown Court with the case notes. These should include the reasons given by the magistrates' to commit the defendant for sentence (Practice Direction, paragraph V.52.2).

2. Mode of trial

4.43 Determination of the venue in which an offence either-way should be tried is governed by sections 17A to 21 of the Magistrates' Court Act 1980.[22] It must be remembered that the mode of trial procedure has been subject to significant change as a result of the introduction of Schedule 3 to the Criminal Justice Act 2003 by virtue of section 41 of that Act.

---

[21] Under the Powers of Criminal Courts (Sentencing) Act 2000, ss 3–4, as amended by Sch 3, para 22, to the CJA 2003.
[22] Set out from para D6.4 of *Blackstone's Criminal Practice 2011*.

At paragraph V.51 of the Practice Direction, guidelines are provided 'to help magistrates decide whether or not to commit defendants charged with "either way offences" for trial in the Crown Court. Their object is to provide guidance not direction. They are not intended to impinge on a magistrate's duty to consider each case individually and on its own particular facts'. 4.44

The Practice Direction goes on to identify the mode of trial considerations that should apply in all cases, such as the nature of the case and the court's sentencing powers (paragraph V.51.2 to V.51.3), before addressing factors relevant to particular offences, namely: 4.45

(a) burglary (paragraphs V.51.5 to V.51.6);
(b) theft and fraud (paragraph V.51.7);
(c) handling (paragraph V.51.8);
(d) social security fraud (paragraph V.51.9);
(e) violence (paragraph V.51.10);
(f) public order offences (paragraph V.51.11);
(g) violence to and neglect of children (paragraph V.51.12);
(h) indecent assault (paragraph V.51.13);
(i) unlawful sexual intercourse (paragraph V.51.14);
(j) drug offences (paragraphs V.51.15 to V.51.16);
(k) dangerous driving and aggravated vehicle taking (paragraph V.51.17);
(l) criminal damage (paragraph V.51.18).

5

TRANSFERS TO THE CROWN COURT AND PRELIMINARY CROWN COURT PROCEDURE

A. INTRODUCTION

Under the Magistrates' Courts Act 1980 (MCA 1980), as originally drafted, there were two methods by which a case which had started its life in the magistrates' court could be transferred to the Crown Court: the committal at which the evidence is considered (section 6(1)) and the 'paper' committal without consideration of the evidence (section 6(2)). 5.01

The transfer of cases to the Crown Court has evolved considerably since then. Initially, the focus was on expediting the transfer of certain types of case, such as serious fraud cases (pursuant to sections 4 to 5 of the Criminal Justice Act 1987 (CJA 1987)), and cases involving children as witnesses (pursuant to section 53 of the Criminal Justice Act 1991 (CJA 1991)). 5.02

More recently, legislative efforts have been directed towards reducing to the barest minimum the period of time that a case that is due to end up in the Crown Court has to wait before getting there. Under the Criminal Procedure and Investigations Act 1996 (CPIA 1996) fundamental modifications were made to committals at which the evidence is considered (section 6(1) of the MCA 1980). More importantly, section 51 of the 5.03

Crime and Disorder Act 1998 (CDA 1998) ended the role of committal proceedings in cases where indictable-only offences had been charged, replacing them with early transfer of the case to the Crown Court.

5.04   The Criminal Justice Act 2003 (CJA 2003) has further, and no less fundamentally, altered the procedure. When Schedule 3 to the Act comes into force, the procedure for sending indictable-only cases under section 51 will be extended to all triable either-way offences (paragraph 18). This will mean that all cases being transferred to the Crown Court will thereafter be sent under section 51 and committal proceedings under section 6 will cease. Schedule 3 also brings notice of transfer provisions for serious fraud (section 4 of the CJA 1987) and child witness cases (section 53 of the CJA 1991) under the CDA 1998.

5.05   The Rules seek to regulate this new landscape, and, because the Rules came into force on 4 April 2005 and thus before the new landscape has been brought into effect by Schedule 3, to address the interim position for committals. The Rules therefore deal with three different ways in which cases can be transferred from the magistrates' court to the Crown Court: committal for trial (Part 10), transfer for trial of serious fraud or cases involving children (Part 11), and sending for trial (Part 12).

5.06   An area where the Rules are now radically different from their 2005 predecessors is in relation to indictments. Part 14 of the 2005 Rules dealt with limited procedural requirements, without any real impact on the validity or content of an indictment. The 2010 version (which was in fact first introduced in 2007) has a significant impact in both areas.

B. SECTION 6 COMMITTALS

5.07   Part 10 of the Rules deal with committal proceedings pursuant to section 6 of the MCA 1980. Given that section 6 committals will cease to occur when Schedule 3 to the CJA 2003 comes into force, the 2010 Rules replicate the majority of the 2005 Rules relating to committals unchanged. When the Schedule does come into force, Part 10 of the Rules will become redundant. The Rules are dealt with here according to the topics they address.

1. Reporting restrictions

5.08   Section 8 of the MCA 1980[1] prohibits, subject to certain exceptions, the reporting of committal proceedings beyond certain specified information. The court should explain the restrictions to the defendant before proceeding to committal and inform him of his right to have them lifted (rule 10.1(1)). Further, the court should record a decision to lift the restrictions[2] in the register (rule 10.1(2)), and should restate the order at the beginning of any further hearing (rule 10.1(3)).

---

[1] Set out at *Blackstone's Criminal Practice 2011*, para D10.44.
[2] Pursuant to s 8(2) of the MCA 1980.

2. Rule 10.2—paper committals

Rule 10.2 replaces rule 6 of the Magistrates' Courts Rules 1981.[3] It is of note that **5.09** the new rule 10.2(1) does not accord entirely with its predecessor as to the preconditions to a paper committal. Under the 1981 Rules it was not necessary for the defendant's solicitor to be present in court, as long as he had been instructed. This qualification no longer appears in the rule, and therefore the solicitor must now be present before a section 6(2) committal can occur.

Rule 10.2 otherwise mirrors the 1981 rule, and therefore: **5.10**

(a) the charge should be written down, if this has not already been done (rule 10.2(2));
(b) the court should ask whether the defendant wishes to submit that there is insufficient evidence to put him on trial, and thereby change the committal to a section 6(1) committal where this submission of insufficient evidence will be considered (rule 10.2(2));
(c) if there is no submission of insufficient evidence, the court shall receive the written evidence,[4] and then determine whether or not to commit the defendant without considering that evidence (rule 10.2(3));
(d) if the court decides to commit without considering the evidence, it proceeds to do so. Otherwise, the procedure for a section 6(1) committal is followed.

3. Section 6(1) committals

The rules for committals where the evidence is considered (rule 10.3) replace without **5.11** alterations the previous rules under rule 7 of the Magistrates' Courts Rules 1981. In cases, therefore, where the defendant is unrepresented or his legal representative indicates that it is to be submitted that there is insufficient evidence to put the defendant on trial, the stages, therefore, are as follows:

(a) the prosecutor makes an opening address, if he wishes;
(b) the evidence[5] is tendered by being read aloud (except as the court directs), or an oral account is given of it;
(c) the court shall view the exhibits;
(d) the court shall then hear any submissions and the prosecution's response to them;
(e) the court then decides whether or not to commit, the test being whether there is sufficient evidence to put the accused on trial;[6]
(f) if the court decides to commit, the charge should be written down and read out. If the defendant is not being represented, the charge should be explained to him.

---

[3] Set out at *Blackstone's Criminal Practice 2011* Supplement 1, para R=74.

[4] Written evidence for the purposes of r 10.2 means: (i) written statements and documents/exhibits referred to in those statements (s 5B); (ii) depositions and documents/exhibits referred to in those statements (s 5C); and (iii) written statements that it is believed will be admissible pursuant to ss 23 or 24 of the CJA 1988 (s 5D) (since replaced by ss 116 and 117 of the CJA 2003).

[5] Evidence for these purposes is as listed in s 5A(2) of the MCA 1980.

[6] As set out in *Blackstone's Criminal Practice 2011*, para D10.38.

5.12   Rule 10.4 is the only section of Part 10 of the 2010 Rules in Part 10 that differs from its 2005 predecessor. Under the 2005 Rules, the court was required to remind the defendant who had just been committed that he has fourteen days to indicate which witnesses he requires to attend to give live evidence at his trial. The new rule 10.4 is designed to give effect to Schedule 2 to the CPIA 1996, pursuant to which a statement admitted in evidence at committal may be read at trial without the necessity of the witness in question giving live evidence, unless any party objects within the timeframe laid down by the rules. The deadline for such objection is now fourteen days from the date of committal (rule 10.4(2)). Given the potential significance of this deadline to the defence, they are warned of it twice in committal proceedings, once by the prosecution at the time that the statements are served and once by the court when the case is committed (rule 10.4(4)). In any event, the Crown Court has the power to extend the deadline for giving notice of any objection even after the period has expired (rule 10.4(5)).

5.13   Rule 10.5 lists the documentation that is to be sent to the Crown Court, within four days of committal (unless that period is extended by rule 10.5(2)). This is the list originally laid down by rule 11 of the Magistrates' Court Rules, which can now be found in rule 10.5(1). Under paragraph IV.41.6 of the Practice Direction, it is envisaged that a plea and case management hearing (PCMH) will be held in all cases committed to the Crown Court under section 6 within seven weeks of that committal.[7]

C. TRANSFERS FOR TRIAL IN CASES OF SERIOUS FRAUD OR INVOLVING CHILD WITNESSES

5.14   As a more efficient alternative to the multi-staged process of committal of cases to the Crown Court for trial, the CJA 1987 introduced the notice of transfer procedure for serious fraud cases. Under this process,[8] specified prosecuting authorities remove the jurisdiction of the magistrates' court for all but ancillary matters by the giving of a notice of transfer which empowers the authority in question to prefer a bill of indictment immediately. This notice of transfer procedure was extended to cases involving children as witnesses by section 53 of the CJA 1991.[9]

5.15   Like section 6 committals, the notice of transfer scheme is due to be subsumed into the process under the CDA 1998 when Schedule 3 to the CJA 2003 comes into effect. Thereafter, serious fraud cases will be transferred pursuant to section 51B and child witness cases will be transferred under section 51C of the CDA 1998.

5.16   As with the rules relating to section 6 committals in Part 10, the rules relating to the notice of transfer scheme in Part 11 seek to cover the interim position with the rules necessary to the operation of the notice of transfer procedure, which had previously been found in the Magistrates' Courts (Notice of Transfer) Rules 1988 and the Magistrates' Courts (Notice of Transfer) (Children's Evidence) Rules 1991. As with Part 10, the rules in Part 11 of the 2010 Rules replicate those that had operated under the 2005 Rules.

---

[7] The automatic directions to be made by the magistrates' court in preparation for that hearing are set out below.

[8] Pursuant to ss 4–5 of the CJA 1987.

[9] The notice of transfer regime is discussed at paras D10.45 of *Blackstone's Criminal Practice 2011*.

1. The giving of notice

Under section 4(1)(a) and (b) of the CJA 1987, where it is the opinion of a 'designated   5.17
authority' (as defined by section 4(2)) that there is sufficient evidence for a defendant to
stand trial for an offence or offences of fraud of 'such seriousness or complexity that it is
appropriate that the management of the case should without delay be taken over by the
Crown Court' it should issue a notice to that effect to the magistrates' court which would
otherwise be seized of the defendant's case. The content of the notice, which may be
served electronically (rule 11.1(2)), is defined by section 5(1) and (2) of the 1987 Act.

In very similar provisions, section 53(1) of the CJA 1991 empowers the DPP to issue   5.18
a notice to the relevant magistrates' court in any case where there is sufficient evidence
for the defendant to stand trial for specified offences of violence or of a sexual nature,
where the victim or a witness to the commission of the offence is a child, and the case
should be transferred to the Crown Court without further delay to prevent prejudice to
that child. Again, this notice may be served electronically (rule 11.1(2)).

2. The role of the magistrates' court

Having surrendered its general jurisdiction on receipt of the relevant notice of transfer,   5.19
the residual issue for the magistrates' court to consider is bail. The focus is on three particular administrative matters:

(a) Where a magistrates' court has granted bail to a defendant in relation to whom a
    notice of transfer is subsequently received[10] or who appears before the court on
    receipt of a notice that he is to be transferred and is then granted bail,[11] the court
    should notify the governor of the prison to which the defendant would otherwise
    have been sent. Also, where the defendant transferred under the 1987 Act is a
    corporation, appropriate notice of that fact should be sent to the prison governor
    (rule 11.2).
(b) Similar notice is required to be given to the governor of the prison to which the defen-
    dant would otherwise have been sent and the manager of the hospital in which he is
    in fact detained, where a defendant has been transferred to hospital[12] (rule 11.3).
(c) Where either a defendant or the prosecution wishes to vary the conditions of the
    defendant's bail,[13] the applicant is required to give the court and the other party
    notice of that fact (rule 11.4(1)). If the court then accedes to the application and
    varies bail, it shall send a copy of the record of the variation to the Crown Court
    (rule 11.4(2)).

In a provision very similar to rule 10.5, which relates to committal proceedings, rule   5.20
11.5 lists the documentation that is to be sent to the Crown Court, as soon as practicable
after the notice of transfer has been received and the court has discharged its functions
thereunder. This is the list originally laid down by rule 11 of the Magistrates' Court
Rules. Under paragraph IV.41.7 of the Practice Direction, it is envisaged that a PCMH

---

[10] Section 5(7) of the CJA 1987 or para 2(1) of Sch 6 to the CJA 1991.
[11] Section 5(3) of the CJA 1987 or para 2(7) of Sch 6 to the CJA 1991.
[12] Hospital transfer under either of ss 47 or 48 of the Mental Health Act 1983.
[13] Pursuant to s 3(8) of the Bail Act 1976.

will be held in all cases transferred to the Crown Court by way of a notice of transfer within seven weeks of that committal.[14]

D. SENDING FOR TRIAL

5.21 As will be clear from the sections dealing with committals[15] and the notice of transfer provisions,[16] the sending of cases to the Crown Court will become the only method by which cases will be transferred there from the implementation of Schedule 3 to the 2003 Act.

5.22   Under the amended version of section 51,[17] the magistrates' court is obliged to send a defendant forthwith to the Crown Court, pursuant to section 51(1), where:

(a) he is charged with an offence triable only on indictment (section 51(2)(a));

(b) he is charged with an either-way offence and the court is required to send him to the Crown Court (section 51(2)(b));

(c) notice has been given either:

  (i) by a designated authority under section 51B, that there is sufficient evidence for the defendant to stand trial for an allegation of fraud of 'such seriousness or complexity that it is appropriate that the management of the case should without delay be taken over by the Crown Court';[18] or

  (ii) by the DPP under section 51C, that there is sufficient evidence for the defendant to stand trial for specified offences of violence or of a sexual nature (section 51C(3)), where the victim or a witness to the commission of the offence is a child under the age of 17, and the case should be transferred to the Crown Court without further delay to prevent prejudice to that child.

5.23 The rules, in Part 12, address administrative aspects of the new regime. The 2010 Rules are an exact repetition of Part 12 of the 2005 Rules.

5.24   Rule 12.1, which replaces rule 11A of the Magistrates' Court Rules, is in very similar terms to rule 10.5 in the context of committal proceedings. It lists the documentation that is to be sent to the Crown Court, within four days of committal (unless that period is extended by rule 12.1(2)). This list is now found in rule 12.1(1), which can be summarized generically as including:

(a) the information;

(b) records relating to the grant/refusal of bail, sureties, and any prosecution appeals in relation to bail;

(c) the details of any interpreter engaged for the defendant, together with details of the relevant language or dialect;

(d) a statement, where appropriate, confirming the imposition of restrictions under section 39 of the Children and Young Persons Act 1933; and

(e) documentation relevant to representation orders.

---

[14] The automatic directions to be made by the magistrates' court in preparation for that hearing are set out below.

[15] Part 10.

[16] Part 11.

[17] This is more fully addressed at para D10.33 of *Blackstone's Criminal Practice 2011*.

[18] Section 51B is the replacement for the old notice of transfer regime in s 4 of the 1987 Act.

Under the original version of section 51, section 51(7) required the magistrates' court to   5.25
provide the defendant and the court with a notice which set out the charges on which he
had been sent for trial. In the amended section 51, this subsection no longer exists.
Rather, the new section 51(7) deals with the power of the court to send a youth to the
Crown Court where he is jointly charged with an indictable offence together with an
adult. This change to section 51 does not appear to have been noticed by those who
drafted the new Rules.

This has two consequences: 5.26

(a) rule 12.1 includes in the list of documentation to be provided to the Crown Court,
    at sub-paragraph (b), the 'notice required by section 51(7)'. When Schedule 3 to the
    2003 Act comes into effect there will, of course, be no such notice; and
(b) rule 12.2 requires the Crown Court officer who receives the section 51(7) notice to
    list the defendant's case for its first Crown Court appearance in accordance with the
    directions given by the magistrates' court. Again, Schedule 3 will do away with the
    notice on the basis of which this listing can occur.

If the rules are to have any meaning, and especially rule 12.2 which deals directly with   5.27
the progression of a case through the system, this problem will require rectification.

The significance of rule 12.2 does not end there, however. Under the old rule 27(2)(h)   5.28
of the Crown Court Rules 1982, the Crown Court was obliged to list a defendant's case
for a preliminary hearing within eight days of his being sent to the Crown Court in
custody, or within twenty-eight days of his being sent on bail. These fixed time limits no
longer apply.

The reason for this can be found in paragraph IV.41.2 of the Practice Direction,   5.29
which states:

A preliminary hearing ('PH') is not required in every case sent for trial under section 51 of the
Crime and Disorder Act 1998: see rule 12.2 (which altered the Crown Court rule from which it
derived). A PH should be ordered only where the court considers such a hearing necessary for
some compelling reason.

Paragraph V.56.4 of the Practice Direction further makes clear that the decision as to   5.30
whether or not there should be a preliminary hearing is a decision that may be taken by
either the Crown Court or the magistrates. The latter should, if they deem it appropriate
for there to be such a hearing, order that it should take place within fourteen days.

Save in those cases where it is deemed necessary to have a preliminary hearing, the   5.31
directions necessary for the preparation of the case by the parties so that the matters set
out have been addressed before the PCMH at the Crown Court will be made automatically on the sending of the case by the magistrates' court.[19]

The Practice Direction itself is silent as to the circumstances in which a preliminary   5.32
hearing will be appropriate. However, the guidance notes state that a preliminary hearing should be held in the following circumstances:

    (i) there are case management issues which call for such a hearing;
    (ii) the case is likely to last more than 4 weeks;
    (iii) it would be desirable to set an early trial date;

---

[19] See para 5.36 below.

    (iv) the defendant is a child or young person;

    (v) there is likely to be a guilty plea and the defendant could be sentenced at a preliminary hearing; or

    (vi) it seems to the court it is a case suitable for a preparatory hearing in the Crown Court . . .

5.33   In further guidance provided by the Senior Presiding Judge on 22 April 2005, this list of circumstances was repeated. Resident Judges considering the need for preliminary hearings are exhorted to consider the cost of such hearings, and whether issues such as the fixing of trial dates can be done administratively rather than at a court hearing. The Police and Justice Act 2006, section 45, inserts new sections 57A to 57E into the CDA 1998, permitting an accused who is in police or prison custody to appear at any preliminary hearing via a live link. He is thereby deemed to be present at the hearing. The provisions came into fuller effect for the majority of London and Kent on 14 November 2008.[20]

5.34   Accordingly, rather than having a hearing after eight days in the Crown Court, under paragraph IV.56.5 of the Practice Direction the next hearing of the case will normally be the PCMH which should be held fourteen weeks after sending where the defendant is in custody or after seventeen weeks if he is on bail.

5.35   These time limits are considered in further guidance provided by the Senior Presiding Judge on 22 April 2005. It is made clear that the time limits were set in consultation with the Crown Prosecution Service and other agencies. The guidance goes on to state:

It is, of course, important to ensure that all parties will be ready to deal with all the issues raised at the PCMH in order to reduce the need for any further case management hearings. However, if a Resident Judge is content that the agencies and professions locally can be ready to conduct PCMHs earlier, it is within the judge's discretion to ask that PCMHs be listed earlier, provided that such PCMHs are effective. The word 'within' was inserted in to the time limits in order to ensure that Resident Judges have this discretion.

E. AUTOMATIC DIRECTIONS

5.36   As a major component of the process by which the Criminal Procedure Rules and Practice Direction are seeking to increase the efficiency of the criminal court process, the Practice Direction requires the making of standard sets of directions in the magistrates' court.

5.37   The direction are to be made automatically as part of the process of transferring the case and are set out in the case progression form set out in Annex E of the Direction. There are different versions of this form, the content of which depends on the methods by which the case is transferred to the Crown Court.

5.38   In further guidance provided by the Senior Presiding Judge on 22 April 2005, it was made clear that the magistrates' court must make the directions specified using the prescribed form. The guidance states:

The standard directions are set out in the Magistrates' Court case progression forms for cases sent and committed to the Crown Court and **must** be made in every case: this is not discretionary. However, the Magistrates' Court may decide that additional or alternative directions are required in a particular case.

---

[20] SI 2008/2785.

When they were first introduced in conjunction with the 2005 Rules, the purpose of the 5.39
automatic directions was to govern the preparation of the case by the parties and to
ensure that the matters set out had been addressed before the date of the PCMH at
the Crown Court. All of the directions contained in the relevant form 'apply in every
case unless the court otherwise orders' (paragraph V.56.6). However, it is arguable that
the 2010 Rules have deprived the automatic directions of that purpose.

Under paragraph V.56.3, when a case is sent under section 51 the court is invited to 5.40
make the series of automatic directions, which are drawn from a variety of statutory
provisions concerning certain applications, relating particularly to notice of applications
relating to special measures, hearsay, and bad character.

Originally all timings were derived from the date on which the prosecution serves its 5.41
case and completes primary disclosure. This date would either have been at committal,
where appropriate, or the period of forty-two days from the date of the preliminary hearing, which itself was to occur within eight days (in custody) or twenty-eight days (on
bail) of the case being sent from the magistrates' court.[21]

Because the time limits imposed by the various statutory provisions that informed the 5.42
deadlines included in relevant sections of the Rules had often been decided in isolation,
their combined effect led to a succession of inconsistent time limits. For example, the
defence were required to provide a defence statement within fourteen days of receipt of
primary disclosure,[22] but the prosecution was not required to serve the indictment until
twenty-eight days after the service of its case.[23]

The 2010 Rules has overhauled the position. Most of the starting point for many time 5.43
limits now, for example for the service of a bad character notice[24] or an application for
special measures,[25] is the date on which the defendant enters a not guilty plea. As a
matter of common sense this is understandable. It will only be if a defendant is contest-
ing the charges at trial that it will be necessary to make arrangements for witnesses to be
called, or for applications to adduce bad character or hearsay evidence to be necessary.

It follows, however, that whereas under the 2005 Rules it was expected that many of 5.44
the matters governed by automatic directions would have been addressed before the
PCMH, now that hearing and the defendant's arraignment at it, will be the catalyst for
that activity.

F. DISMISSAL OF CHARGES SENT TO THE CROWN COURT

As a replacement for the right of the defendant to challenge whether the prosecution had 5.45
sufficient evidence to bring him to trial by a section 6(1) ('old style') committal, the

---

[21] With the removal of the need for preliminary hearings, the periods for the service of the case have now
become 50 days when the defendant is in custody (8 days + 42 days) and 70 days when the defendant is on
bail (28 days + 42 days).

[22] In compliance with the terms of the Criminal Procedure and Investigations Act 1996 (Defence Disclosure
Time Limits) Regulations 1997, SI 1997/2680.

[23] In compliance with r 5 of the Indictment (Procedure) Rules 1971, SI 1971/2084.

[24] Pursuant to r 34.2 of the Criminal Procedure Rules 2010.

[25] Pursuant to r 29.3 of the Criminal Procedure Rules 2010.

CDA 1998 introduced a new procedure whereby, before the defendant had been arraigned, he could apply to dismiss all or some of the charges he faced.

5.46   With the extension of the procedure for the sending of cases to the Crown Court under section 51 of the CDA 1998, the procedure for making an application to dismiss will similarly be extended to all cases that find themselves in the Crown Court.

5.47   The ability to apply to dismiss the charges against a defendant had previously been included in relation to the Notice of Transfer provisions under the CJA 1987 and CJA 1999. When these methods of transfer are subsumed into the section 51 regime, the rules governing section 51 applications to dismiss will similarly apply to these types of cases. In the meantime, the Rules seek to address all relevant transfer schemes in this Part of the Rules.

5.48   In 2005, Part 13 of the Rules replaced the previous rules[26] and the 2010 Rules largely follow the 2005 version of Part 13. The Rules seek to achieve two things:

(a)   to set out the timetable for the stages of processing of an application to dismiss, calculated from the time either that the notice of transfer was given or the case was sent; and

(b)   to set out what is required at each stage of the timetable.

5.49   The timetable is as follows:

Time	Action	Rule
14 days from 1991 notice or section 51 sending	Written notice of an intention to apply to dismiss the charges or a specified charge to be served on the court and the prosecutor. Written application to dismiss similarly to be served.	13.2(2)(b) and (c) 13.3(4)(b) and (c)
28 days from 1987 notice	Written notice of an intention to apply to dismiss the charges or a specified charge to be served on the court and the prosecutor. Written application to dismiss similarly to be served.	13.2(2)(a) 13.3(4)(a)
7 days from receipt of notice—21 days from 1991 notice or section 51 sending, 35 days from 1987 notice	Prosecution application to adduce oral evidence at the application to dismiss hearing.	13.4.(1)
7 days from receipt of notice—21 days from 1991 notice or section 51 sending, 35 days from 1987 notice	Prosecution to apply for an oral hearing of the application.	13.4(2)
14 days from receipt of notice/written application to dismiss—28 days from 1991 notice or section 51 sending, 42 days from 1987 notice	Prosecution to serve written reply to application to dismiss, or further evidence/video material relied on in response to such an application.	13.4(5)

---

[26] The Criminal Justice Act 1987 (Dismissal of Transferred Charges) Rules 1998, the Criminal Justice Act 1991 (Dismissal of Transferred Charges) Rules 1992 and the Crime and Disorder Act 1998 (Dismissal of Charges Sent) Rules 1998.

To further explain some of the stages of this timetable: 5.50

1. Notice

- There is a power to apply to the Crown Court to extend the period for the service of the notice (rule 13.2(3)), by an application to be served on the prosecution and any other defendant (rule 13.2(4)). The application for an extension is then decided on the papers by the judge, whose decision is then communicated to all parties (rule 13.2(5)).
- Notice is normally to be given in writing of an intention to apply to dismiss the charges, identifying the charge the dismissal of which is sought, whether there is an application to adduce oral evidence in support, and if so which witnesses are required for this purpose (rule 13.2(6)).
- An application to adduce oral evidence is also required to be in writing. Again, the judge will make a decision on this application on the papers and then all parties are notified of his decision (rule 13.2(7)). The court may allow such an application even if the procedural requirements have not been complied with (rule 13.5(1)). The application itself can be made orally, rather than on paper. In that situation the court is required to list the matter for hearing (rule 13.2(8)).

2. Written application

- In addition to the need for a notice of an application, rule 13.3 requires a written application to be sent to the court with any supporting documentation (rule 13.3(1) and (2)). This written application is to be provided to the other parties as well as the court (rule 13.3(3)).
- Again, there is provision for applying to extend the time limit, in accordance with the matters set out above (rule 13.3.(4)).

3. Prosecution response

- The prosecution are given time limits to respond to three questions (rule 13.4):
  (a) Do they need to call oral evidence?
  (b) Do they want an oral hearing of the application?
  (c) Do they need to serve a response to the application, or to serve further evidence/material/video evidence to counter the application?
- As with the defence, the prosecution, if seeking to adduce oral evidence, need to identify what witnesses they propose to call, and need to serve all their applications in writing (rule 13.4(3)–(4)). The court may allow such an application even if the procedural requirements have not been complied with (rule 13.5(1)).
- All these applications are to be served on the court and the defendants (rule 13.4(4)). Likewise, any further material served by the prosecution needs to be served on all parties (rule 13.4(5)). The time limits imposed on the prosecution are open to application to extend (rule 13.4(6)). Such application is to be made in writing (rule 13.4(7)), with copies served on the parties.

5.51 Under rule 13.5, the court's ruling on a non-oral application to dismiss will be communicated to the parties as soon as is practicable.

5.52   In the 2005 version of the Rules, rule 13.6 dealt with the service of documents. Unfortunately, because rule 13.6 mirrored the pre-2005 provisions, it did not allow for electronic service. Part 13 now includes no specific provisions for the service of documents, and it follows that the rules that apply are those in Part 4 of the Rules, which do include provision for electronic service.

G. INDICTMENTS

5.53 Once a case has been sent, and assuming the charges have survived any application to dismiss, the next stage is for the indictment to be preferred. Logically, therefore, the next area that is addressed by the Rules is the topic of the indictment, and more especially the rules for the preferment of an indictment that were previously primarily contained in the Indictment (Procedure) Rules 1971.

5.54   Originally, the Criminal Procedure Rules did not seek to address large parts of the 1971 Rules. It remains the case that the 1971 Rules still apply in relation to such matters as Voluntary Bills of Indictment (rules 6 to 10), but the Criminal Procedure (Amendment) Rules 2007[27] made significant changes to the Rules. In part, the aim of these amendments has been to simplify the rules from their 1971 complexity, which had resulted in considerable litigation as to the consequences of the new regime for the trial of specimen counts, pursuant to sections 17-21 of the Domestic Violence Crime and Victims Act 2004 (DVCVA 2004). The 2010 replicates this revised version, which has already had a striking impact.

5.55   The Rules are supplemented by the Consolidated Practice Direction. At paragraph IV.34, direction is given as to the settling of indictments, which can be summarized as follows:

(a) There should only be one indictment extant in any case, even though there is no rule that prevents there being multiple indictments. To avoid such duplication, where further defendants are committed after an original indictment has been signed they may still be joined to that indictment if it is otherwise proper to do so (paragraph IV.34.2).

(b) It is 'undesirable that a large number of counts should be contained in one indictment'. To prevent this, the prosecution should be made to proceed on a limited number of counts, leaving a decision to be taken as to what happens to any remaining counts later. Equally, where a conspiracy count appears on the same indictment as substantive counts, the prosecution should be put to their election. An indictment can be split into two to avoid difficulties of the type outlined here (paragraph IV.34.3).

5.56 As to voluntary bills of indictment,[28] directions are given at paragraph IV.35 of the Practice Direction which deal with the documents which must accompany such an application (paragraph IV.35.2), the circumstances in which such an application should

---

[27] SI 2007/699.
[28] The preferment of a voluntary bill is permitted under s 2(2)(b) of the Administration of Justice (Miscellaneous Provisions) Act 1933.

be made (paragraph IV.35.3), and the fact that the defence need neither be notified of the application nor invited to attend any hearing to make submissions (paragraph IV.35.4). It is within the judge's discretion whether or not to have such an oral hearing before granting or refusing the application (paragraph IV.35.6).

1. The timetable

Rule 14.1 deals with the methods by which a valid indictment may be served, and the timetable for such service. The terminology employed in the 1971 Rules has been replaced. In keeping with the ethos of the rules and that of their civil progenitors, the reason for this has been to update and simplify the language. Whereas before an unsigned indictment was called a 'bill of indictment' it is now called a 'draft indictment' and the lodging of that draft is no longer called its 'preferment' but its 'service'. The presumably inadvertent consequence of this is that the terminology in the Rules now differs from that employed by the legislation to which they are designed to give effect. 5.57

Rule 14.1(1) imposes a timetable for the service of the indictment, as below: 5.58

Time	Action	Rule
28 days from service of the prosecution case (50 or 70 days after the case has been sent)	Draft indictment served in cases where the defendant was sent for trial under s 51 of the CDA 1998.	14.1(1)(a)
28 days from permission	Draft indictment served where a High Court Judge has permitted a voluntary bill of indictment (this use of 'bill of indictment' appears to have survived).	14.1(1)(b)
28 days from order for a retrial	Draft indictment served, following order of the Court of Appeal.	14.1(1)(c)
28 days from committal	Draft indictment served in cases where the defendant has been committed for trial under s 6.	14.1(1)(d)

The time limits can be extended on application by a judge (rule 14.1(2)), even after it has expired. In fact, this largely accords with the position under the 1971 Rules, for example: 5.59

(a) in *Sheerin*,[29] the appellant complained of the decision of the trial judge who had given leave for preferment of a bill of indictment preferred twenty-one days out of time finding that S had not suffered any prejudice by reason of the delay. On appeal, Lawton LJ held:
   (i) first, that the judge had had jurisdiction to grant the extension of time even though the application was not made until after the twenty-eight days had elapsed (this is now expressly confirmed by rule 14.1);
   (ii) secondly, as to the status of the rule, his lordship said (at page 70): 'It is to be noted that the very title of the rules is "Procedure Rules"—that is rules for the

---

[29] (1976) 64 Cr App R 68.

guidance of courts in the administration of justice. They are not rules setting boundaries beyond which the courts cannot go';

(b) in *Soffe*,[30] the argument on appeal was that authorization for an extension of time for preferment had been given by the chief clerk of the Crown Court concerned, not by a judge. Donaldson LJ, giving the Court of Appeal's judgment, said (at 136):

> There must be some doubt in this case whether the chief clerk in fact purported to extend the time limited by rule 5 or whether the bill was preferred out of time. So far as this application is concerned, it matters not which occurred. A breach of [the rules] does not constitute a material irregularity in the course of the trial or in any way invalidate the proceedings, and the applicant accordingly has no valid grounds of appeal.

5.60   The impression that rule 14.1(2) provides no sanction for breach of the time limit is strengthened by section 116(1)(c) of the Coroners and Justice Act 2009 (CAJA 2009), which addresses the consequences of procedural failures in relation to indictments by inserting new subsections (6ZA) to (6ZC) into section 2 of the Administration of Justice (Miscellaneous Provisions) Act 1933. The effect is that, where a draft indictment is served in accordance with section 2(1) and (2), no objection may be taken to it after the commencement of the trial (ie after a jury is sworn or an accused pleads guilty) by reason of any failure to observe the rules relating to indictments.

5.61   Rule 14.1(2) should not, however, be treated by prosecutors as a licence to take as long as they like to draft the indictment. In *Sheerin*,[31] Lawton LJ gave this warning:

> If there is inordinate delay in preferring a bill of indictment, which clearly has caused, or clearly is likely to cause prejudice to accused persons, then the judge may very well not exercise his discretion and leave the prosecution to take such course as they think fit. Prosecutors should not assume that they will always be granted leave to prefer a voluntary bill of indictment.

Similarly, in *Soffe*,[32] Donaldson LJ, 'first and foremost', emphasized 'that it is the duty of all concerned to take all reasonable steps to ensure that bills of indictment are preferred within the 28-day period'.

2. Service

5.62   The service of a draft indictment (the process formerly called the preferment of a bill of indictment) is regulated by the combination of section 2(1) of the Administration of Justice (Miscellaneous Provisions) Act 1933 and rule 14.1(3). Section 2(1) was amended by the CAJA 2009, section 116, which came into force on 12 November 2009, so that it now reads:

> (1) Subject to the provisions of this section, a bill of indictment charging any person with an indictable offence may be preferred by any person before the [Crown Court] and it shall thereupon become an indictment and be proceeded upon accordingly.

The effect of this amendment is to remove the statutory prerequisite that an indictment came into being only once it was signed by a proper officer of the Crown Court.

---

[30]   (1982) 75 Cr App R 133.
[31]   Ibid, at 71.
[32]   Ibid, at 136–7.

Under the Rules there is still a requirement that a draft indictment should be served on   5.63
the court and signed by a court officer; when the draft indictment is signed, the date of
receipt should be added (rule 14.1(3)(a)). Although not explicitly stated, it would appear
that the officer ought to be satisfied that the requirements of section 2(2) of the 1933
Act have been complied with, as these requirements are reflected in rule 14.1(1).

Before the 2010 version of the Rules was introduced, there had been considerable   5.64
litigation as to the consequences of proceedings occurring pursuant to an unsigned
indictment. For example, the Court of Appeal had emphasized in *Morais*[33] and the
House of Lords then reiterated in *Clarke*,[34] that the proper officer's signature is not 'a
comparatively meaningless formality' but a 'necessary condition precedent to the existence of a proper indictment'. The conclusion in *Clarke* was that failure to follow the
correct procedure as to how the indictment should be signed, as opposed to whether it
is signed at all, will not necessarily invalidate subsequent proceedings.

The impact of *Clarke* has been reduced, if not removed entirely, by the combination   5.65
of section 116(1)(c) of the CAJA 2009 and rule 14.1(3). Section 116 inserts new subsections (6ZA) to (6ZC) into section 2 of the 1933 Act. The effect is that, where a draft
indictment is served in accordance with section 2(1) and (2), no objection may be taken
to it after the commencement of the trial (ie after a jury is sworn or an accused pleads
guilty) by reason of any failure to observe the rules relating to indictments. Rule 14.1(3)
permits the court to dispense with the need for the indictment to be signed at all. It
follows that technical objections based on the signing of the indictment may become less
common, as any such procedural irregularity in this regard can now be overcome by the
use of rule 14.1(3).

3. Form and content of indictment

The 1971 Indictment Rules contained a series of provisions which governed the form   5.66
and content of an indictment. These rules have been replaced, in much shorter order, by
rule 14.2. The starting point remains section 3 of the Indictments Act 1915, which
states:

(1) Every indictment shall contain, and shall be sufficient if it contains, a statement of the
specific offence or offences with which the accused person is charged, together with such
particulars as may be necessary for giving reasonable information as to the nature of the
charge.

(2) Notwithstanding any rule of law or practice, an indictment shall, subject to the provisions
of this Act, not be open to objection in respect of its form or contents if it is framed in
accordance with the rules under this Act.

Against that background, the basic requirements as to the layout of an indictment are as   5.67
follows:

(a) Each offence charged should be set out in a separate paragraph or count (rule
14.2(1)). If there is more than one count, then these should be consecutively
numbered (rule 14.2(4)).

---

[33] [1988] 3 All ER 161.
[34] [2008] 1 WLR 338.

(b) Each count should be divided into a statement of offence and particulars of offence (rule 14.2(1)(a) and (b)).

(c) The statement of offence describes the offence shortly in ordinary language, and, if the offence is statutory, should specify by section and subsection the provision contravened (Indictments Act 1915, section 3(1) and rule 14.2(1)(a)).

(d) The particulars of offence should give 'such particulars as may be necessary for giving reasonable information as to the nature of the charge' (Indictments Act 1915, section 3(1)). This is supplemented by rule 14.2(1)(b) which states that there should be included 'such particulars of the conduct constituting the commission of the offence as to make clear what the prosecutor alleges against the defendant'.

5.68 In large part, these provisions mirror those that they replaced. This is also the case in relation to rule 14.2(3), which identifies the circumstances in which the prosecution may lawfully join two or more counts against one accused in a single indictment. Rule 14.2(3) replaces the test formally contained in rule 9 of the 1971 Rules without any significant alteration to its content. The rule has two limbs:

(a) *charges founded on the same facts*: this limb is satisfied if the offences alleged in counts joined in one indictment arise out of a single incident or an uninterrupted course of conduct,[35] and extends to situations where later offences would not have been committed but for the prior commission of an earlier offence;[36]

(b) *series of offences of the same or a similar character*: the circumstances in which two or more offences may be said to amount to a series of offences of the same or similar character within the meaning of the second limb of rule 14.2(3) were considered by the House of Lords in *Ludlow v Metropolitan Police Commissioner*.[37] Lord Pearson delivered the leading opinion. The main points emerging from this opinion are as follows:

(i) two offences are capable of constituting a 'series' for the purposes of rule 9;[38]

(ii) the court should take into account both their legal and their factual characteristics;[39]

(iii) to show the existence of a series of offences, the prosecution must be able to point to some nexus between them. This means 'a feature of similarity which in all the circumstances of the case enables the offences to be described as a series'.[40]

5.69 An indictment containing counts which are not linked in either of the ways mentioned in rule 14.2(3) is invalid (although not a nullity), and any convictions returned on such an indictment are liable to be quashed on appeal (on the basis of *Newland*).[41]

5.70 Rule 14.2(5) reflects the Administration of Justice (Miscellaneous Provisions) Act 1933, section 2(2)(a), which allows a bill of indictment charging an offence to be

---

[35] eg *Mansfield* [1977] 1 WLR 1102, where it was held proper to join counts for arson and murder relating to the same fire.

[36] eg *Barrell* (1979) 69 Cr App R 250.

[37] [1971] AC 29.

[38] *Ludlow*, at 38E–G.

[39] Ibid, at 39B.

[40] *Ludlow*, at 39D.

[41] [1988] QB 402.

preferred if the person charged has been committed for trial or sent for trial, pursuant to the CDA 1998, section 51 and Schedule 3, in each case in conjunction with proviso (i) to the subsection. The proviso is:

. . . where the person charged has been committed [or sent] for trial, the bill of indictment against him may include, either in substitution for or in addition to counts charging the offence for which he was committed [or sent], any counts founded on facts or evidence [either disclosed at committal or contained in the papers served in pursuance to the sending provisions], being counts which may lawfully be joined in the same indictment.

4. Rule 14.2(2)

In contrast to these areas of continuity between the new rules and the 1971 Rules, rule 14.2(2) marks a significant change from the previous position. Before this form of words was incorporated into the Rules in April 2007, it had been argued that it was only possible to allege one incident per count, save where a general deficiency count was drafted, or it was asserted that one continuous offence had been committed.[42] It was suggested that to allege more than one incident in a count fell foul of the rule against duplicity.[43]   5.71

Under rule 14.2(2), a series of incidents amounting to a course of conduct may be included in one count. Circumstances in which it is suggested to be appropriate to use rule 14.2(2) to charge a 'multiple offending count' are identified in the Consolidated Criminal Practice Direction, at paragraph IV.34.10:   5.72

Rule 14.2(2) of the Criminal Procedure Rules allows a single count to allege more than one incident of the commission of an offence in certain circumstances. Each incident must be of the same offence. The circumstances in which such a count may be appropriate include, but are not limited to, the following:

(a) the victim on each occasion was the same, or there was no identifiable individual victim as, for example, in a case of the unlawful importation of controlled drugs or of money laundering;
(b) the alleged incidents involved a marked degree of repetition in the method employed or in their location, or both;
(c) the alleged incidents took place over a clearly defined period, typically (but not necessarily) no more than about a year;
(d) in any event, the defence is such as to apply to every alleged incident without differentiation. Where what is in issue differs between different incidents, a single 'multiple incidents' count will not be appropriate, though it may be appropriate to use two or more such counts according to the circumstances and to the issues raised by the defence.

Counts which allege more than one incident can give rise to certain difficulties amongst these. One[44] is that the accused should be sentenced only for offences on which he has been indicted and of which he has been convicted.   5.73

---

42 See *Blackstone's Criminal Practice 2011*, para D11.29 for a detailed discussion.
43 See *Blackstone's Criminal Practice 2011*, para D11.44.
44 Identified in *Kidd* [1998] 1 WLR 604.

H. PREPARATORY HEARINGS IN SERIOUS FRAUD AND COMPLEX/LENGTHY CASES

1. The statutory framework for preparatory hearings

5.74   Preparatory hearings are a part of the criminal process in complex cases, the aims of which are very much in keeping with the ethos of the rules as a whole, namely the early identification of the issues, and the tailoring of the trial process to those issues.

5.75   Initially, preparatory hearings were introduced in relation to cases of serious fraud by the CJA 1987.[45] The test for having such a hearing is that the evidence on the indictment 'reveals a case of fraud of such seriousness or complexity that substantial benefits are likely to accrue from a [preparatory] hearing'.[46] The availability of preparatory hearings was extended from fraud to other lengthy and complex cases by the CPIA 1996.[47] The test for and purpose of such a hearing is the same as under the 1987 Act.

5.76   Such hearings are likely to be less common in the future as a result of the decision of the Court of Appeal in *I, P, O, I & G*.[48] Although actually addressing the question of whether the same judge was required to preside over both the preparatory hearing and the trial, Hughes LJ said:[49]

It is emphatically not the case that most heavy fraud or similar cases will nowadays call for a preparatory hearing. Virtually the only reason for directing such a hearing nowadays is if the judge is going to have to give a ruling which ought to be the subject of an interlocutory appeal. Such rulings are few and far between and do not extend to most rulings of law. An interlocutory appeal can be a most beneficial process in a few, very limited, circumstances. If a discrete point of law arises, its resolution in this court can if necessary be accomplished within a very short timeframe and this can avoid the risk of many weeks of wasted trial time. On the other hand, many points of law decided in the Crown Court turn out to be fact sensitive and to appear differently, or for that matter to go away, by the time the evidence has been heard. Making a decision on one part of a case only and on necessarily hypothetical facts is normally very undesirable; whereas a ruling in the Crown Court can be varied from time to time if the case proceeds differently from what was expected, a ruling of this court cannot normally be treated similarly. An interlocutory appeal is apt to cause serious disruption to a carefully planned trial timetable, which may involve multiple defendants and their lawyers and large numbers of witnesses. If the timetable of one case is disrupted, it very often has a knockon effect on the timetables of others. Moreover, if the tendency of an interlocutory appeal to have this consequence is to be minimised, it is essential for this court to give it priority over other waiting appeals. This is not only potentially unfair to those who are in custody following conviction; it is also impossible unless interlocutory appeals are very exceptional.

5.77   The Rules do not seek to create preparatory hearings in new areas but to pull together the rules in existing types of cases.[50]

---

[45] The relevant provisions are ss 7–11 of the CJA 1987.
[46] Section 7(1) of the CJA 1987.
[47] Sections 29–43 of the CPIA 1996.
[48] [2009] EWCA Crim 1793.
[49] Ibid, at para 21.
[50] Preparatory hearings are addressed in para D14.46 of *Blackstone's Criminal Practice 2011*.

2. The Rules

The Rules deal with the mechanics of such hearings in the following areas: 5.78

(a) the method by which such a hearing can be brought about, that is the rules for making an application to hold a preparatory hearing (rules 15.1 to 15.4); and
(b) the process by which the cases of the parties should be disclosed and identified (rule 15.5).

One of the parties in a case may make an application for a preparatory hearing under 5.79
section 7(2) of the 1987 Act in fraud cases and under section 29(4) of the 1996 Act in other complex cases. The rules in relation to such applications are as follows:

(a) an application is to be made on the form specified in the Practice Direction (rule 15.1(1)(a)), including a statement of the grounds for the application (rule 15.1(1)(b)), and this application should be served on the Crown Court officer and on the other parties (rule 15.1(1)(c));
(b) the application is to be made within twenty-eight days of committal, consent to the preferment of the bill of indictment or within twenty-eight days of the service of the prosecution's case where the defendant has been sent for trial (rule 15.2(1));
(c) the time limits can be extended, either before or after its expiration (rule 15.2(3));
(d) on receipt of an application by one of the other parties of a case requesting a preparatory hearing, the other parties shall serve such representations as they wish to make on the Crown Court officer and the other parties within seven days (rule 15.3(1));
(e) an application for a preparatory hearing, will be determined by a judge. That decision will normally be on paper (rule 15.4(1)). That it is anticipated that the decision is to be made without an oral hearing in all but an exceptional case is underlined by the fact that the provisions for the holding of such an oral hearing that appeared at rule 15.4(1) of the 2005 Rules have been removed. Once the decision has been made, the Crown Court officer will communicate the judge's decision to the parties (rule 15.4(2)).

Preparatory hearings need not be generated by an application by one of the parties. The 5.80
judge can order one of his own motion (section 7 of the 1987 Act and section 29(4)(c) of the 1996 Act). If he does so, the court officer will communicate his decision to the parties (rule 15.4(2)(b)).

In certain circumstances, a preparatory hearing is required by statute. Those circum- 5.81
stances are where the prosecution is seeking a trial by judge alone,[51] or where a judge-only trial is sought.[52]

An application for a preparatory hearing in such circumstances should be made as 5.82
soon as is reasonably practicable. Ideally this should be within the twenty-eight-day period envisaged for applications for preparatory hearings in other circumstances, but it is recognized that the need for a judge-only trial may not arise within that twenty-eight-day period, and later application is permitted (rule 15.2(2)). Even if there is already to be a preparatory hearing at the behest of the defence, the prosecution is obliged to apply

---

[51] Pursuant to s 43 or 44 of the CJA 2003.
[52] Pursuant to s 17 of the DVCVA 2004.

for a preparatory hearing to allow an application for a judge-only trial to be made (rule 15.1(2)). Almost certainly, the reason for this is that the judge has a discretion whether or not to accede to an application in ordinary circumstances, but must hold such a hearing where a judge-only trial is sought (rule 15.4(1)).

5.83   As part of the process of identifying the issues in a case, the judge can order the service of documents by the parties:

(a) in relation to the prosecution,[53] the judge can order the prosecution to serve:
     (i)   a written case statement setting out the principal facts of the prosecution case, the witnesses who speak to them and exhibits that relate to them, and the relevant propositions of law;
     (ii) documentation to assist the comprehension of the case by the jury, including admissions;
(b) rule 15.5 makes clear that any order made in relation to such prosecution disclosure should specify what documents are to be served and on whom they are to be served, and directs that the court officer should ensure that all parties are on notice of such an order;
(c) in relation to the defence,[54] the judge can direct the service of:
     (i)   a written statement setting out the general nature of the defence and the principal issues with the prosecution. Rule 15.5(2) makes clear that this statement does not require disclosure of what witnesses are to be called for the defence, save for alibi and expert evidence;
     (ii) objections to the prosecution case statement;
     (iii) written notice of any points of law and the authorities relied on in support of these points of law; and
     (iv) the extent to which the defence agree with the documents served by the prosecution or the reasons for disagreeing with them.

5.84   Rule 15.5(3) directs that the court officer should ensure that all parties are on notice of an order for disclosure either by the prosecution or the defence.

5.85   Within the 2005 version of Part 15 there were rules which dealt with the methods by which documents can be served. There is no such specific provision in Part 15 of the 2010 Rules. This is because the service of documents is now covered for all purposes by Part 4. It follows that, in a change from the 2005 Rules, applications and responses to applications in relation to preparatory hearings can be served electronically.

3. The Protocol

5.86   On 22 March 2005, the Lord Chief Justice issued a Protocol for the control and management of heavy fraud and other complex criminal cases. The document, which is referred to where relevant elsewhere in this book, is premised on a general acceptance that trials of fraud and of other complex cases take too long, and need to be controlled. Lord Woolf states 'whatever view is taken, it is essential that the current length of trials is brought back to acceptable and proper duration'.

---

[53] Pursuant to s 9(4) of the CJA 1987 or s 31(4) of the CPIA 1996.
[54] Pursuant to s 9(5) of the 1987 Act or s 31(6)–(7) of the 1996 Act.

The Protocol seeks to achieve this, in conjunction with the Rules, by encouraging   5.87
continuous case management by judges presiding over trials which last more than eight
weeks. This is not the appropriate place for a paragraph-by-paragraph analysis of this
document, which is set out in Appendix 3. However, it does address the following
areas:

(a) the investigation of such offences, seeking to keep the amount of material obtained
within 'manageable limits' (paragraph 1(i)), to avoid interviews which are 'too long
and too unstructured' (paragraph 1(ii)), and to impose on leading counsel for prosecution and defence a responsibility 'to take all necessary decisions in the presentation and general conduct of the . . . case' (paragraph 1(iii));
(b) consideration of the length of trial, requiring the prosecution team to justify the
length of trial where it will exceed eight weeks (paragraph 1(iv)) and to notify
the court and others where the case is likely to exceed that length (paragraph 1(v)).
The trial judge is also expected to 'consider what steps should be taken to reduce the
length of the trial, whilst still ensuring that the prosecution has the opportunity of
placing the full criminality before the court' (paragraph 3(vi)(b));
(c) early appointment of a trial judge where the case will last more than four weeks, who
will then 'manage the case from cradle to grave' (paragraph 2). The judge will require
a more detailed knowledge of the case than would normally be the position (paragraph 3(i)(b));
(d) case management, detailing the matters that should be addressed at directions
hearings (paragraph 3(iii)), with a short preliminary hearing followed by a full case
management hearing attended by trial counsel, before which both prosecution
and defence will have identified their cases and at which there should be 'a real dialogue between the judge and all advocates for the purpose of identifying the focus
of the prosecution case, the common ground and the real issues in the case' (paragraph 3(iv)(b));
(e) disclosure, seeking to set a timetable for structured disclosure and preventing defence
solicitors from spending 'a disproportionate amount of time and incur[ring] disproportionate costs trawling through a morass of documents' (paragraph 4(iii));
(f) trial management, through 'judicial mastery of the case' (paragraph 6(ii)), the ordering of evidence (paragraph 6(iii)), the controlling of 'prolix' cross-examination
(paragraph 6(v)), electronic presentation of evidence (paragraph 6(vi)) and better
management of the timing of the court sitting and jury management (paragraphs
6(viii)–(ix)).

The aspirations behind this Protocol will need to be borne in mind at all stages of such   5.88
serious cases, and especially at any preparatory hearing at which major decisions affecting the trial will be made.

I. PLEA AND CASE MANAGEMENT HEARINGS

The Rules are silent as to the content and conduct of PCMHs. These are, however, hear-   5.89
ings of considerable significance which are to be held in all cases committed, transferred,
or sent for trial to the Crown Court.

5.90   Their purpose is to ensure that all steps necessary for the proper preparation of a case for trial have been taken, or are properly timetabled for future attention. In the Practice Direction,[55] the rationale for such hearings is expressed as follows:

> Active case management at the PCMH should reduce the number of ineffective and cracked trials and delays during the trial to resolve legal issues. The effectiveness of a PCMH hearing in a contested case depends in large measure upon preparation by all concerned and upon the presence of the trial advocate or advocate who is able to make decisions and give the court the assistance which the trial advocate could be expected to give. Resident Judges in setting the listing policy should ensure that list officers fix cases as far as possible to enable the trial advocate to conduct the PCMH and the trial.

5.91   The form to be used at PCMHs is that which appears in Annex E of the Practice Direction. At paragraph IV.41.10 it is indicated that those forms are to be used 'in accordance with the guidance notes' only at specified pilot court centres. At other courts, under paragraph IV.41.11, the manner in which the form is used is a matter within the discretion of the resident judge in consultation with the local criminal justice agencies and practitioners. Where agreement cannot be reached between them as to the manner of use of the form, the Presiding Judge will be the ultimate arbiter.

5.92   In further guidance provided by the Senior Presiding Judge on 22 April 2005, it is made clear that the new PCMH form is the only form that may be used at such hearings. The purpose of this is to ensure uniformity of forms across the country. The guidance goes on to say that the 'discretionary element in respect of the PCMH form is the manner in which the form is used' and stresses the importance of there being a written record of all orders made at the PCMH which is made available to all concerned.

---

[55] At para IV.41.8.

6

REPORTING RESTRICTIONS AND EXTRADITION

A. INTRODUCTION

These two areas, contained in Parts 16 and 17 of the Rules, are put together in this   6.01
chapter not because they have anything in common but because they are discrete areas
of magistrates' court practice that do not conveniently fit anywhere else.

As with other Parts of the Rules, these Parts do no attempt to regulate all aspects of   6.02
these areas, but to replace various specific rules. In the case of reporting restrictions, the
rules are those previously found in the Magistrates' Court (Reports relating to adult witnesses) Rules 2004, the Crown Court (Reports relating to adult witnesses) Rules 2004
and the Crown Court Rules 1982. In the case of extradition, the rules are those previously found in the Magistrates' Courts (Extradition) Rules 1989 and the Magistrates'
Courts (Backing of Warrants) Rules 1965.

In each case, the 2010 Rules reproduce those of 2005 without amendment.   6.03

B. REPORTING RESTRICTIONS AND PUBLIC ACCESS

Part 16 of the Rules addresses two issues which in general terms relate to the protection   6.04
of witnesses:

(a) the enforcement of section 46 of the Youth Justice and Criminal Evidence Act 1999
     (YJCEA 1999), which empowers the courts to restrict reporting of cases in order to
     protect vulnerable adult witnesses;
(b) the holding of crown court proceedings in camera or in private for various reasons,
     including the protection of the identity of a witness.

1. Section 46 of the YJCEA 1999

6.05 Section 46 is intended to provide the Crown Court and magistrates' courts with the power to make reporting restrictions to protect vulnerable witnesses. In summary, its provisions work as follows:

(a) The order is made under section 46(6) 'a direction that no matter relating to the witness shall during the witness's lifetime be included in any publication if it is likely to lead members of the public to identify him as being a witness in the proceedings'. The direction prevents the reporting of the various pieces of information about the witness that are listed at section 46(7).

(b) It is made (pursuant to section 46(2)) where:
  (i) the witness, who is over 18, is eligible for protection on the basis that the court is satisfied (under section 46(3)) that the quality of the witness' evidence and his level of cooperation are likely to be diminished by the witness' fear or distress at being identified by the public as a witness, and the court has considered the factors in section 46(4) and the views of the witness (section 46(5));
  (ii) the reporting restrictions will improve the quality of the evidence of the witness and his level of cooperation with the party calling him;
  (iii) it is in the interests of justice to do so, which outweighs the public interest in press freedom (section 46(8)).

(c) It may be varied, pursuant to section 46(9), where it is in the interests of justice to do so or the order is imposing a 'substantial and unreasonable restriction on the reporting of the proceedings' and it is in the public interest to remove or relax it. It may be revoked by a further court order under section 46(10).

(d) It is made on application by a party to the proceedings (section 46(1)), but not of the court's own motion.

6.06 The rules are as follows:

(a) an application for reporting restrictions may be made orally (rule 16.3) but is normally to be made in writing using the appropriate form issued under the Practice Direction, in which case it must be provided to the court officer and to the other parties (rule 16.1);

(b) if the application is opposed, the opposing party must, within five days of receipt of the application, notify the court officer in writing of that opposition and the reasons for it, spelling out whether there is challenge to the eligibility of the witness or to the likelihood that protection will improve the quality of the evidence or cooperation of the witness (rule 16.2);

(c) application can be made to extend this five-day period, before it has expired, under rule 16.6(1). The application for an extension needs to be in writing, provided to the court officer and the other parties, and explaining why additional time is needed (rule 16.6(2)–(3));

(d) the period may also be reduced in cases of urgency where an application for an earlier decision is made and there are exceptional circumstances requiring it (rule 16.3). Such an application does not need to be preceded by a normal application under rule 16.1 (rule 16.3(2)), and may be made orally, in which case the court should hear and take into account the representations of interested parties, or in writing.

The application, in either form, needs to specify the exceptional circumstances that require such expedition (rule 16.3);

(e) section 46(9) of the YJCEA 1999 allows the court to direct, by what is called an 'excepting direction', that the restrictions may be dispensed with. Under rule 16.4, such an excepting direction may be made on the application of any party to the proceedings or anyone 'directly affected by a reporting direction', the procedure being as follows:

(i) the application, when made in writing, should state the reasons why the order is placing a substantial and unreasonable restriction on the reporting of the proceedings, and why it is in the public interest to 'remove or relax' the order, and should be served on the court officer and the parties (rule 16.4(2) and (4));

(ii) once proceedings have started, the application may be made orally (rule 16.4(3));

(iii) a party receiving an application for an excepting direction can oppose the making of such an order, by submitting a written response to it, setting out the reasons for opposition. That notice is to be given in writing within five days of receipt of the application (rule 16.4(5)), unless application is made within the five-day period for an extension (rules 16.4(6) and 16.6);

(f) section 46(10) allows the court to revoke reporting restrictions, and section 46(11)(b) allows it to vary or revoke an excepting direction. In each case, application for such an order can be made under rule 16.5 by any party to the proceedings or anyone 'directly affected' by them. The application is to be made in writing, setting out the reasons for it (rule 6.5(4)), and sent to the court officer and the parties (rule 16.5(3)). Any recipient party may object to the application, by a written response supported by reasons served within five days of receipt (rule 16.5(5)), unless an extension of time has been granted (rule 16.5(6));

(g) the court may determine an application for reporting restrictions (rule 16.1), urgent application (rule 16.3), excepting direction (rule 16.4) or order varying or revoking any of the other orders (rule 16.5) on the papers, in which case it should notify the parties of its decision, or it can direct an oral hearing, the time and place of which will be notified to the parties (rule 16.7);

(h) the court may hear and take into account the views of anyone with a legitimate interest in the outcome when determining any of these applications (rule 16.7(4)). Where the order is made in the magistrates' court, and the case is then transferred to the Crown Court, a copy of the order should be amongst the papers sent with the case (rule 16.8).

2. Other reporting restrictions

At paragraph I.3, the Practice Direction addresses restrictions that may be placed on the reporting of a case by section 4(2) of the Contempt of Court Act 1981. Section 4(2) permits the court to postpone the publication of any report of proceedings where this is necessary to avoid a substantial risk of prejudice to the administration of justice. In making such an order, the court is encouraged to hear representations from any member of the press (paragraph I.3.2). 6.07

6.08   Any order that is made under section 4(2) must be retained by the court. It must also be expressed in the clearest terms at the judge's direction, so that its precise scope, duration, and purpose are all clear. The court has a responsibility to publicize the terms of the order, and answer any questions that the press may have about them. That said, the primary responsibility for making the press aware of such orders rests on the press (paragraph I.3.3).

3. Restrictions on public access

6.09   As the editors of *Blackstone's Criminal Practice* 2011 observe,[1] the hearing of a trial in camera, with the public excluded, is 'the gravest interference with open justice'. Save for certain statutory provisions that deal with the exclusion of the public in the interests of national security,[2] the principles that govern the decision to hold proceedings in camera are to be found in common law. Other than the needs of national security, the main reason for applying to hear a case in camera is to protect the identity of a witness who is unwilling to give evidence in public.

6.10   Rule 16.10 replaces rule 24A of the Crown Court Rules 1982 as the means by which an application can be made for such an in camera hearing. The procedure now is, however, unchanged. The steps are as follows:

(a) the prosecutor or defendant serves a written notice of his intention to apply for a hearing in camera not less than seven days before the hearing on the court officer and the other parties (rule 16.10(1));

(b) the notice should be displayed prominently in the precincts of the court (rule 16.10(2));

(c) the application itself is then made in camera, unless the court directs otherwise, after arraignment but before the empanelment of the jury (rule 16.10(3));

(d) if the order is granted, the case should be adjourned until either twenty-four hours has passed without an application being made to appeal against the order or the determination of the application for leave or if the appeal of leave is granted.

6.11   The procedure for appealing against such a ruling is to be found in rule 67.2. Appeals are dealt with generally in Chapter 18 below.

6.12   Rule 16.11 deals with a list of other situations in which the court will sit in chambers to deal with specified hearings. In the main, it repeats rule 27 of the Crown Court Rules. The situations are:

(a) applications for bail;

(b) applications to issue summonses and warrants, and applications incidental to early stages of criminal proceedings, such as applications relating to legal aid;

(c) applications under the Rules for:
   (i) the first appearance in the Crown Court of a case that has been sent (rule 12.2);
   (ii) application for a witness summons (rule 28.3);

---

[1] *Blackstone's Criminal Practice 2011*, para D3.78.
[2] Pursuant to the Official Secrets Acts of 1911 and 1920.

    (iii) applications to the Crown Court in relation to extending the time for service of appeal against the decision of the magistrates' court (rule 63.2(5)) and to state a case to the High Court (rule 64.7);

(d) applications under the Rules in relation to:

    (i) evidence of the previous sexual history of the complainant (rule 36);

    (ii) applications to extend custody time limits, and appeals against such extensions (rule 20);

    (iii) appeals against the grant of bail by the magistrates' court or the conditions imposed by that court (rule 19).

6.13 One form of hearing that is directed by the Rules to be heard in chambers, but which is not set out in rule 16.11 is a hearing for an application in restraint or receivership proceedings under the Proceeds of Crime Act 2002. Rule 61.4 directs that such hearings should be held in chambers, and such hearings can therefore be added to the rule 16.11 list.

C. EXTRADITION

6.14 Extradition is the process by which one sovereign state, or the judicial authority of one state, enlists the assistance of another sovereign state, or its judicial authority, to have a person brought back to its territory either to be tried by its courts for a criminal offence or offences, or, having been convicted and/or sentenced for an offence to serve that sentence. It is an area in which the magistrates' courts have a distinct judicial role.

6.15 From 1 January 2004, the extradition procedure has been governed by the Extradition Act 2003. Section 218 of that Act specifically repeals the previous statutory arrangements under the Extradition Act 1989 and the Backing of Warrants (Republic of Ireland) Act 1965.

6.16 In the previous edition of this Guide, criticism was made of the fact that, despite this, the Criminal Procedure Rules 2005 incorporated the old 1989 and 1965 Rules, rather than to introduce any rules under the new 2003 Act. It seemed odd in 2005 that the Rules should have been looking back at the old law, and a very small minority of cases, whilst leaving the vast majority of cases and the new law entirely untouched and unregulated. Five years on, the fact that the Part 17 of the Rules remains unchanged is odder still.

6.17 The result is that rules in Part 17 of the 2005 version of the Rules only relate to requests for extradition received before 31 December 2003. Even though extraditions can be protracted, it seems extremely unlikely that there will now be any cases passing through the magistrates' courts to which the rules under the Extradition Act 1989 apply and even more unlikely that the expedited procedure under the Backing of Warrants (Republic of Ireland) Act will be engaged at all. It follows that Part 17 of the 2010 Rules is almost certain to be without value or relevance.

1. The Extradition Act 1989

6.18 In order to understand the Rules, it is necessary to have an understanding of the procedure in extradition cases as it existed before the Extradition Act 2003 came into force. This is not the appropriate place for a detailed explanation of the extradition process, as it stood before 1 January 2004, especially as there was more than one regime in operation. In summary, however:

(a) a request is made by a foreign state for the return of an individual to the Secretary of State. The Secretary of State then considers the matter and if it is deemed appropriate to do so, issues the necessary authority or order to proceed, pursuant to section 7(1) of the Extradition Act 1989 (EA 1989). This provides the magistrates' court with the jurisdiction needed to deal with an extradition case;

(b) thereafter, the magistrates' court issues a warrant for the arrest of the person whose extradition has been requested ('the defendant') and the defendant is then arrested. The defendant may also have been arrested on a 'provisional' warrant, which is then followed up by a formal request;

(c) the magistrates' court, before which the defendant is then brought, then acts as the court of committal. The court's main purpose in Part III and Convention cases (pursuant to section 9(8) of the EA 1989), but not Schedule 1 cases, is to decide whether or not the offence or offences to which the authority or order relates are extradition crimes and there is a sufficient description of the conduct alleged;

(d) in Schedule 1 and Part III cases, the court must also ask whether the evidence would be sufficient for the defendant to be prosecuted in this country, or, if unlawfully at large after conviction of the offence has been duly convicted;

(e) if the answer to each of these is affirmative, to commit the defendant on bail or in custody to await the Secretary of State's decision as to his return and, if the decision is in favour of return, to await his return;

(f) if the magistrates' court refuses to commit a defendant, the requesting state may question the proceedings on the basis that they were wrong in law by applying to state a case for the opinion of the Administrative Court (pursuant to section 10 of the EA 1989);

(g) where this occurs, the magistrates' court must decide whether to order the detention of the defendant pending the decision of the Administrative Court, or to order his release on bail.

6.19   As the rules in Part 17 only have an extremely limited shelf life, they can be dealt with briefly.

6.20   Rule 17.1 regulates the procedure for a challenge by way of case stated by the requesting state of the refusal of the magistrate's court to commit, pursuant to section 10(1) of the Act. Save for cosmetic amendments of names from 'Crown Office' to 'Administrative Court Office' and from 'clerk' to 'court officer', this replicates exactly rule 4 of the 1989 Rules.

6.21   Section 14 of the EA 1989 creates a 'simplified procedure', under which a defendant may waive his rights under section 11 of the Act to make an application for habeas corpus, which would thereby secure his release from detention, or to consent to his immediate return to the requesting state without having to go through all the formal stages set out in the Act. Each of these measures which a defendant may take to expedite his extradition is governed by the Rules, accompanied by the necessary forms under the Practice Direction:

(a) rule 17.2 governs notice of waiver of the right to habeas corpus. Such a notice must be in writing, using form 1;

(b) rule 17.3 governs notice of consent to an order for committal under section 14, using form 2, and

(c) rule 17.4 governs notice of consent to an order for committal under section 14A, using form 3.

2. The Backing of Warrants (Republic of Ireland) Act 1965

The remaining rules in Part 17 address the process of extradition to the Republic of Ireland which was governed, until 31 December 2003, by the Backing of Warrants (Republic of Ireland) Act 1965 ('the 1965 Act') and the rules thereunder, which it seeks to replicate. As has already been indicated, as this procedure was designed to be speedier than that for extradition to other parts of the world, there is only the most remote chance of that Act, and therefore these rules, having any application at all now.   6.22

The brief summary of the procedure for such cases is as follows: 6.23

(a) a warrant issued by the Judicial Authorities in the Republic for the arrest of a person accused/convicted of an offence is endorsed by the justices in the prescribed form (section 1), and the person is arrested under that warrant. The warrant must first be verified in accordance with rule 17.8;

(b) the person is then brought before the magistrates' court, which shall order him to be delivered to the Irish authorities, and remand him to allow this to happen, unless certain conditions, set out in section 2(2) are met;

(c) if the court refuses to make the order delivering the person to the Irish authorities, the Republic may challenge that decision by way of case stated (section 2A);

d) if the court makes the order, it shall not be carried out for fifteen days unless that period is waived (section 3(1)(a)). Rule 17.5 governs the waiver procedure;

(e) the remand, pending removal to the Republic, can be either in custody or on bail, in the latter case directing the person to surrender himself to a specified police office, if necessary imposing sureties/securities to that effect (section 5);

(f) where a defendant is remanded on bail pending return or pending a challenge by way of case stated, rules 17.6 and 17.7 regulate the provision of necessary paperwork by the court officer;

(g) where the court has refused to make the order sought, the representative of the requesting government has twenty-one days to make a written application to challenge that refusal by way of case stated, identifying the point of law in issue (rule 17.9). The court should then prepare a draft of the case to be stated, and send it to the parties. The parties then have twenty-one days to respond, and the court, a further twenty-one days to perfect, sign, and serve the case (rule 17.10).

7

WARRANTS, CUSTODY, AND BAIL

A. INTRODUCTION

Parts 18 to 20 of the Rules deal with the procedural issues that arise in relation to   7.01
the detention of defendants in custody: the issuing and execution of the warrants that
place a defendant in custody, the applications for bail that seek to extricate him from
custody, and the time limits that determine how long he may legitimately be kept in
custody.

Part 18 is concerned with warrants of arrest and warrants of detention or imprison-   7.02
ment. Part 19, which is one of the longest parts of the Rules, addresses the procedural
aspects of bail in the magistrates' courts and the Crown Court, together with appeals
from the former to the latter, and replaces both the 1981 Rules and the Crown Court
Rules 1982 in this regard. Part 20 is limited to custody time limits in the Crown Court,
thereby replacing rule 27A of the 1982 Rules.

B. WARRANTS OF ARREST, DETENTION, OR IMPRISONMENT

This section of the Rules has been much simplified by the new Part 18, in force from   7.03
4 October 2010. In contrast to the original Rules, Part 18 now governs the issue of
warrants in the senior courts as well as magistrates' courts. Two types of warrant are dealt
with in Part 18, namely:

(a) warrants of arrest, on the basis of which a defendant is arrested and brought before
    the court (rule 18.2);
(b) warrants of detention or imprisonment, on the basis of which a defendant is lawfully
    conveyed from the court to a prison or other place of detention (rule 18.3).

A 'defendant' means anyone against whom a warrant is issued (rule 18.1).

1. Warrants of arrest

7.04 The principal statutory provisions under which a warrant for arrest may be issued are section 4 of the Criminal Procedure (Attendance of Witnesses) Act 1965, section 7 of the Bail Act 1976, sections 1 and 97 of the MCA 1980 and sections 79, 80, and 81(4), (5) of the Senior Courts Act 1981. By virtue of rule 18.2, a warrant for arrest must require the person to whom it is directed to arrest the defendant and bring the defendant to a court specified in the warrant or one required or allowed by law. Alternatively, if the warrant is backed for bail, the defendant should be released on bail (with conditions or without) to attend court at a date, time, and place either specified in the warrant or to be notified by the court.

2. Warrants for detention or imprisonment

7.05 A warrant for detention or imprisonment must require the person to whom it is directed to arrest the defendant, take him to any place specified in the warrant, and deliver him to the custodian of that place. The warrant must also require the custodian to keep the defendant in custody until the defendant is lawfully delivered to the appropriate court or place or released (rule 18.3(1)). If a magistrates' court remands a defendant to police detention under section 128(7) or section 136 of the MCA 1980, or to customs detention under section 152 of the CJA 1988 then the warrant it issues must be directed to a constable or an officer of HMRC. It must require the constable or officer to keep the defendant in custody for a specified period which does not exceed the maximum lawful period or until the defendant is lawfully conveyed to the appropriate court or place (rule 18.3(3)). A defendant can lawfully be taken to and detained in a prison, young offenders' institution, remand centre, or can be detained by the police for up to three days to allow for making further enquiries under section 128(7) of the MCA 1980. Under section 136 of the MCA 1980 a defendant who has been arrested for non-payment of a fine may be ordered to be detained in a police station until 8 am the following day. Under section 152 of the CJA 1988 a customs officer may detain a defendant for up to 192 hours if he has been arrested for drug trafficking under the CJA 1988.

3. Information to be included in a warrant

7.06 All warrants must identify the person to whom it is directed, the defendant against whom it is issued, the reason for its issue, the court that issued it (unless that is otherwise recorded by the court officer) and the court office of the court that issued it (rule 18.4(1)). If the warrant is one for detention or imprisonment it must also include any record of a decision by the court under section 23 of the CYPA 1969 (remand to local authority detention), section 80 of the MCA 1980 (application of money found on defaulter to satisfy a sum adjudged to be owed) or section 82(1) or (4) of the MCA 1980 (conditions for the issue of a warrant) (rule 18.4(2)). If a warrant contains an error, it is not invalid provided it was issued in respect of a lawful decision by a court and it contains enough information for that decision to be identified (rule 18.4(3)).

4. Execution of a warrant

7.07 A warrant may be executed by any person to whom it is directed. If it was issued by a magistrates' court, it may also be executed by anyone authorized to do so under section 125 (warrants), 125A (civilian enforcement officers), or 125B (an approved enforcement agency) of the MCA 1980 (rule 18.5(1)). A person executing the warrant must explain to the defendant what the warrant requires and why. That must be done in terms the defendant can understand. If the person executing the warrant has the warrant with him, he must show the warrant to the defendant. If he does not have the warrant and the defendant asks to see it, he must make arrangements for that to happen. If the defendant asks to see any written statement of the authority a person has to execute the warrant under section 125A or 125B of the MCA 1980 then that must be shown (rule 18.5(2)). Rule 18.5(3) governs the procedure when a person is to be released on bail after arrest. The person executing the warrant must make a record of the defendant's name, the reasons for arrest, his release on bail, and the time and place where the warrant requires the defendant to attend court. That record must then be served on the defendant and the court officer. Rule 18.5(4) governs the procedure when a warrant is executed for detention or imprisonment. The person executing that warrant must take the defendant to any place specified in the warrant. If that is not immediately practicable he may take him to any place where he can lawfully be detained. The warrant then has effect as if it specified that place. On taking him to the place of detention, he must obtain a receipt from the custodian and notify the court officer that the defendant has been taken to the place of detention.

5. Warrants that cease to have effect on payment

Rule 18.6 applies to warrants issued under sections 76, 83, 86, and 136 of the MCA 1980. Those statutory provisions concern the enforcement of sums adjudged to be paid, the process for securing the attendance of an offender, the power of a magistrates' court to fix the date of attendance of a defendant for a means inquiry and the committal for overnight detention for non-payment of an adjudged sum respectively. Such warrants cease to have effect when either the sum is paid to the person executing the warrant, or the sum is offered by the defendant but refused or the defendant shows a receipt for the sum given by the court officer or relevant authority. 7.08

6. Warrants issued when the court office is closed

Where the justice issues a warrant outside normal court hours, the applicant for the warrant has seventy-two hours to serve on the court officer a copy of the warrant and the written information on the strength of which the warrant was issued (rule 18.7). 7.09

C. BAIL

1. Overview

Part 19 of the Rules deals with the procedures that relate to bail at the various stages of the criminal process, that is as first granted by the police following arrest and/or charge, by the magistrates' court after the police have refused bail, or by the Crown Court after it has been refused by the court below. The Rules deal not only with the granting of bail, but with varying its terms, seeking its withdrawal, and other issues raised by its administration. 7.10

7.11   To follow the Rules, which in general terms seek to follow chronologically the stages of the criminal process at which issues of bail arise, this chapter traces that process and incorporates the rules where they become relevant.

2. Police bail

7.12   Where a person is arrested and released without charge he may be bailed with or without conditions under section 37 of PACE. Where a person is arrested and charged by the police, the custody officer is required by section 38 of PACE to decide whether to keep the defendant in custody until he is brought before the magistrates' court, or to release him to attend the magistrates' court on a specified day either unconditionally or on conditional bail (section 47(3A), PACE).

7.13   Section 47(1E) of PACE 1984 and section 43B of the MCA 1980 allow the defendant to apply to vary the conditions that the custody officer has placed on his bail before charge and after charge respectively. Rule 19.1 requires:

(a) such an application is to be made in writing, stating the grounds for the application, the offence charged if any, the reasons that had been given by the custody officer for the conditions, the details of any surety, and the address at which the applicant would reside if the court was to impose a condition of residence (rule 19.1(1));

(b) the application to be sent either to the magistrates' court specified by the custody officer or if no such court has been appointed to a magistrates' court acting for the local justice area in which the police station at which he was granted bail or his conditions of bail were varied, as the case may be, is situated (rule 19.1(2));

(c) the court to arrange a hearing for the application to take place within seventy-two hours of receipt (rule 19.1(4)). Written notice of the place, date, and time of the hearing shall then within twenty-four hours of receipt of the application be communicated to the applicant, prosecution (or if the applicant has not yet been charged to the chief officer of police or other investigator), and sureties (rule 19.1(3));

(d) notice of any application by a party to the magistrates' court to vary or impose conditions of bail under section 3(8) of the Bail Act 1976 to be given to the court officer and the other party at least twenty-four hours before the hearing at which the application is to be made. The notice must specify the variation or conditions proposed and the reasons (rule 19.1(5));

(e) if at the hearing the court agrees to vary the conditions, the surety be notified by the court if the amount is reduced or the condition of surety removed (rule 19.1(6);

(f) the court may vary or waive any time limit in this rule. Whilst there is a form included in the practice direction for the making of such an application, the court may allow notice to be given in a different form or even orally (rule 19.1(7)).

7.14   Section 5B(1) of the Bail Act 1976 allows the prosecution to apply for bail that has been granted by a police officer (section 5B(A1)(b)) to be revoked or varied as to the imposition of conditions or the nature of the conditions, provided that the defendant is charged with offences triable on indictment or either way and they are in possession of information that was not available to the officer who granted bail.

7.15   The requirements as to the content of the application (rule 19.2(2)), and the processing of the application by the court (rule 19.2(3)–(4)), are the same as those that apply to the defendant's application to vary in rule 19.1, save that the notice of the hearing also has to contain notice of the powers available to the court under section 5B and has to be provided to the person affected (rule 19.2(5)). However, it is of note that the matters to be included in the application, as set out in rule 19.2(2), do not include a need to state what material is available to the court which was not available to the bailing officer, even though this is required by the statute (section 5B(3)).

The difference from rule 19.1 occurs at the hearing stage. Under rule 19.2(5), the   7.16
court is required to consider any written or oral representations by the person affected, and, if that person has not provided such representations and does not attend to make them, the court can only proceed to decide on the application if it is proved that the affected party was put on notice of the application (rule 19.2(5)). This is done either on oath or by a solemn declaration before the court, its clerk, or one of the others named in rule 4.1(1).

If the court has been so satisfied, and makes an order in the absence of the person   7.17
affected, the person should be notified by the court of the variation to his bail (rule 19.2(6)(a)), and an order to surrender to custody signed by the clerk to the court if his bail has been withdrawn (rule 19.2(6)(b)).

When a person is released on bail, the custody officer should direct him to attend a   7.18
specified court at a specified time. This time can subsequently be varied by the magistrates' court, which is obliged to notify the defendant, and his sureties, of the change (rule 19.3).

3. Magistrates' court bail

Rules 19.10 and 19.11 echo the earlier provisions of rule 6.1(3) as to the records to be   7.19
kept by the magistrates' courts. The court is obliged to make a note of the arguments deployed during a fully argued bail application (rule 19.10). This is clearly to assist in giving effect to Part IIA of Schedule 1 of the Bail Act 1976, in relation to the number of applications with full argument the court needs to entertain. Section 5 of the Act requires the court to make a note of the reasons for granting bail (section 5(2A) and (2B)) or for refusing it (section 5(3) and (4)) and to issue a certificate that it has heard a fully argued bail application (section 5(6A)). These notes and certificates should be added to the court register (rule 19.11).

The conditions to be imposed on the grant of bail are those necessary to meet the   7.20
concerns set out in section 3(6) of the Bail Act 1976, as it now stands amended by section 13 of the CJA 2003. The Rules seek to address several consequences of this, as follows:

(a) rule 19.4 requires the court to give directions as to the manner in which and the persons before whom requirements are to be complied with. This can be presumed to refer to:
   (i) the taking of a security (section 3(5));
   (ii) making himself available to assist with further inquiries or a report (section 3(6)(d));
   (iii) an interview with an authorized advocate or litigator (section 3(6)(e));
(b) where the court imposes any conditions which need to be complied with before the defendant is released on bail, it shall issue a certificate showing the conditions in question, or the amount and details of a surety if there is one, and the person required

to ensure that the conditions are met or the surety taken cannot act until this certificate has been provided (rule 19.5(2)). The court shall also provide this certificate to the governor or keeper of the prison or place of detention in which the defendant is being detained, and, where there is to be a surety, it should also be provided to them (rule 19.6);

(c) rules 19.5 to 19.8 focus primarily on sureties and securities, and ordain the following:

(i) a surety can be taken by the governor or keeper of the prison or place of detention, and those defined by section 8(4)(a) of the Bail Act 1976 who are also listed in rule 19.5(1)(b), or by a civilian enforcement officer if it is that officer who executed the warrant for the defendant's arrest (rule 19.5(1));

(ii) the certificate referred to above should, under rule 19.5(2), include details of the surety, and therefore needs to be in the possession of that person taking the surety before he does so, and the certificate needs to be communicated to the prison or place of detention;

(iii) if the surety has been taken at court, a certificate confirming that the surety is acceptable should be provided to the prison or place of detention (rule 19.5(3)). If it is taken by someone else, the court needs to be notified of the fact (rule 19.5(4)).

7.21 Once the pre-release conditions have been complied with, the defendant should be released (rule 19.7).

7.22 On granting bail, the court will indicate the date that the defendant is bailed to, that is when he has to return to court. If the court changes that date, it shall notify the defendant and his sureties of the new date (rule 19.3(b)). It should send out a similar notice if it extends a surety from the magistrates' court to the Crown Court, pursuant to section 129(4) of the MCA 1980, when it commits or sends a defendant there, or where it extends the period of remand for a youth pending the obtaining of further information about him under section 48(3) of the Children and Young Persons Act 1933 (rule 19.9).

7.23 Comparable provision is made by rule 19.13 for the alteration of the court for those in custody and in rules 19.14 and 19.15 for those detained under the Mental Health Act 1983. In summary:

(a) section 130(1) of the MCA 1980 allows the magistrates' court to which the defendant is remanded to remand him instead to an alternate court. If it does so, the court must, within two working days, provide the documentation for the case (listed at rule 19.13(1)) to the new court, and alter the order under which the defendant waived his right (section 126(3A) of the MCA 1980) to be produced at the original court every eight days for remand to the new court (rule 19.13(2)). If the case is later returned to the original court, the process mirrors the above (rule 19.13(3));

(b) section 47 of the Mental Health Act 1983 allows the Secretary of State to authorize the removal of a person serving a sentence of imprisonment (which includes a person remanded in custody in criminal proceedings by virtue of section 47(5)(a)) where the necessary conditions are met. During the currency of this transfer, rule 19.14 requires the court to notify the relevant hospital of further remands made under section 128 of the MCA 1980 during the course of the proceedings;

(c) where application is successfully made to the magistrates' court under section 52(5) of the Mental Health Act 1983 to bring such a transfer direction to an end, notice of that decision is to be communicated to the hospital and to the appropriate prison or place of detention (rule 19.15).

4. Breach of bail

The Consolidated Practice Direction addresses the question of breaches of bail at paragraph I.13.2 in the following terms: 7.24

The failure of the defendants to comply with the terms of their bail by not surrendering can undermine the administration of justice. It can disrupt proceedings. The resulting delays impact on victims, witnesses and other court users and also waste costs. A defendant's failure to surrender affects not only the case with which he is concerned, but also the court's ability to administer justice more generally by damaging the confidence of victims, witnesses and the public in the effectiveness of the court system and the judiciary. It is, therefore most important that defendants who are granted bail appreciate the significance of the obligation to surrender to custody in accordance with the terms of their bail and that courts take appropriate action if they fail to do so.

It is, in fact, to the Practice Direction, rather than to the Rules, that one should look in   7.25
relation to breaches of bail (see also paragraph 7.26 below). Where a defendant who has been released on bail fails to comply with the conditions of his bail, whether by failing to attend as required or otherwise, the Practice Direction, at paragraph I.13.3, identifies three courses of action open to the court, namely:

(a) the imposition of penalties for failing to surrender (dealt with at paragraphs I.13.4–13);
(b) revoking the defendant's bail or imposing more stringent conditions (dealt with at paragraphs I.13.14–16);
(c) conducting the proceedings, and especially a trial, in the absconding defendant's absence (dealt with at paragraphs I.13.17–19).

The only involvement that the Rules have in this area is to be found in paragraph 19.12.   7.26
This is concerned with the application of section 7 of the Bail Act 1976. In summary:

(a) if a person fails to surrender to his bail, the court may issue a warrant for his arrest (section 7(1));
(b) if a person fails to surrender to his bail or breaks the conditions, he may be arrested without a warrant (section 7(3));
(c) within twenty-four hours of being thus arrested, the person should be brought before the magistrates' court which will decide whether or not to readmit the defendant to bail. In this context, it should be remembered that section 13(4) of the CJA 2003 has amended Schedule 1 to the Bail Act 1976 to make such a breach of bail an exception to the right to bail.

Rule 19.12 requires the court to make a record of its decision which is to be sent to the   7.27
court in which the defendant's case is otherwise being heard.

5. Appeals to the Crown Court against magistrates' court bail decisions

The Rules address the procedural aspects of two forms of challenge to a decision by the   7.28
magistrates' court as to bail, namely an appeal by the prosecution against a grant of bail (rules 19.16 to 19.17] and a Crown Court bail application (rule 19.18).

7.29   Section 1 of the Bail (Amendment) Act 1993 permits the prosecution to appeal to the Crown Court where a defendant is granted bail, despite the objections of the prosecution. Originally this was only possible in connection with an offence punishable with five or more years' imprisonment or an offence connected with taking a motor vehicle. However, since 4 April 2005, section 18 of the CJA 2003 has extended this to allow appeals in connection with all imprisonable offences.

7.30   The rules for the making of such an application are as follows:

(a) Section 1(4) and rule 19.16(1) require the prosecutor to give oral notice of the appeal to the court and defendant before the defendant is released. The justices' clerk should then announce in open court the time that notice was given (rule 19.16(2)) and enter the decision to appeal and the time of oral notice in the register (rule 19.16(3)). Once such notice has been given, the defendant should be remanded in custody by a warrant of commitment (section 1(6), rule 19.16(4)).

(b) Section 1(5) requires the prosecutor to follow the oral notice with a written notice of application which must be served within two hours of the hearing. This notice should 'be in the form set out in the Practice Direction' (rule 19.17(2)), although in Annex D thereof there is in fact no form identified. It should be served on the court and the defendant (rule 19.17(2)).

(c) Where the notice is not received in time, this failure should be entered in the register (rule 19.16(9)) and the court shall send a notice to the persons in whose custody the defendant is detained, directing his release on bail with such conditions as are deemed appropriate (rule 19.16(7)).

(d) Equally, if the prosecution abandon their appeal, by giving written notice of that fact in a form yet to be specified in the Practice Direction (rule 19.17(6)) to the defendant, and the magistrates' court and Crown Court officers (rule 19.17(7)), this should be entered in the register (rule 19.16(8)) and the court shall send a notice to the persons in whose custody the defendant is detained, directing his release on bail with such conditions as are deemed appropriate (rule 19.16(8)). The prosecution notice may be served by fax (rule 19.17(11)).

(e) Where written notice is received by the court in time, it shall make an entry in the register of that fact, and of the time of receipt (rule 19.16(6)). The notice should then be provided to the Crown Court officer as soon as is practicable, together with the notes of the argument (which it was required to make under rule 19.10) and a note of when the defendant is next due to appear at court (rule 19.16(10)). The Crown Court is required, by section 1(8), to list the case within forty-eight hours from the date of oral notice, and, having listed it, the court is required to inform the prosecution, defence, and magistrates' court (rule 19.17(3)). Such notice can be made by fax, email, or other electronic communication or by telephone (rule 19.17(11)).

(f) Section 1(9) makes clear that the appeal shall be by way of re-hearing of the bail application, and the judge hearing the appeal may remand the defendant in custody, or grant bail with or without conditions, and the necessary particulars of its decision shall be endorsed on the file (rule 19.17(8)). Since 4 October 2010, the defendant is entitled to be present at the hearing (rule 19.17(4)). It should be noted that by virtue of sections 57A and 57B of the Crime and Disorder Act 1998, a person is to be treated as present in court when he attends the hearing via a live link. If the defendant is unrepresented, he may apply to the court for representation by the Official Solicitor (rule 19.17(5)).

(g) The Crown Court officer is required to give notice of the decision, and a statement of either the conditions of bail if any or the reasons for refusing bail if relevant (as set out in rule 19.17(8)), to the defendant, prosecutor, police, magistrates' court, and prison governor, as soon as is practicable after it has been made (rule 19.17(9)). To expedite this process, it may be carried out by fax email, or other electronic communication (rule 19.17(11)).

Under section 3(8) of the Bail Act 1976, the prosecution may apply to the Crown Court to vary or add to the conditions of bail that has been granted by the magistrates' court. In so doing, it follows the same procedure as a defendant applying to the Crown Court for bail, which is set out below (rule 19.18(2)). **7.31**

Since section 17 of the CJA 2003 ended the right of defendants to apply to the High Court for bail, following its refusal in the magistrates' court, the usual route for an appeal against such a refusal of bail is by application to the Crown Court. The Crown Court's jurisdiction to hear appeals in this regard derives from section 81 of the Senior Courts Act 1981. **7.32**

Under rule 19.18, which applies to Crown Court bail applications that do not take place during Crown Court proceedings, the procedure is as follows: **7.33**

(a) Ordinarily, written notice must be given of such an application at least twenty-four hours before it is made, and served on the prosecution or, where it is a section 3(8) application by the prosecution (see paragraph 7.31 above), on the defendant (rule 19.18(2)). The notice should be in the form as yet not identified in the Practice Direction and a copy is to be provided to the court officer (rule 19.18(4)). Paragraph V.53.2 of the Practice Direction requires the application to be accompanied by a certificate confirming that a fully argued application has already been made to the magistrates' court, and issued under section 5(6A) of the Bail Act 1976.

(b) Where a defendant who wishes to make an application relating to bail does not have a solicitor, he may give written notice to the court of these facts and request that the Official Solicitor act for him. If the court considers this appropriate, it may appoint the Official Solicitor to act for the defendant (rule 19.18(6)). In this situation, the court may dispense with the notice requirements above (contained in rule 19.18(2)), and deal with the application in a summary fashion (rule 19.18(7)).

(c) On receiving an application under rule 19.18(2), the other party must indicate whether the party wishes to be represented, whether they oppose the application, and if so on what grounds. The grounds should be set out in a written statement that is to be served on both the court and the applicant (rule 19.18(3)). It should be noted, in relation to this last requirement, that it is one that was found in rule 19 of the Crown Court Rules, even if it was more followed in the breach than the observance. It should also be noted that there is no time limit on when this response is to be made.

(d) Only where the application is made by the prosecution under section 3(8) is there a right for the applicant to be present at the hearing of the application (rule 19.18(5)). Paragraph V.53.3 of the Consolidated Practice Direction indicates that the case will be heard in chambers at the Crown Court Centre to which the defendant has been/ is to be sent (although it erroneously refers to committal in the text) or to the nearest centre that carries out class 4 work if the defendant's case is to be tried summarily.

(e) By virtue of rule 19.18(9), the requirements of section 5 of the Bail Act 1976 apply to these applications. The court is required to make a note of the reasons for granting bail (section 5(2A) and (2B)) or for refusing it (section 5(3) and (4)) and to issue a certificate that it has heard a fully argued bail application (section 5(6A)). These notes and certificates should make clear, where appropriate, the effect of the court's decision, a statement of any conditions imposed or varied, as well as the reasons for refusal.

7.34 Rule 19.18(9) requires the applicant to declare in his application any previous application to the High Court or the Crown Court in the same proceedings. This wording is lifted without alteration from rule 20(1) of the Crown Court Rules 1982. As has already been noted (at paragraph 7.32 above), section 17 of the CJA 2003 has brought to an end 'applications to the High Court'. As this amendment came into effect on 5 April 2004, this wording is unlikely to be intended to cover cases that are still proceeding through the system where a High Court bail application was made before 5 April 2004 and a Crown Court application made after the Rules came into force a year later.

7.35 In the same vein, paragraph V.53.1 of the Consolidated Practice Direction states that rules 19 and 20 of the Crown Court Rules apply to these applications. This is an odd claim for a document that is designed to supplement the Criminal Procedure Rules that supersede those 1982 Rules. In each case, it is therefore much more likely to be an oversight when the old texts were copied.

6. Bail in the Crown Court

7.36 Rules 19.19 to 19.24, relate to the administration of bail in the Crown Court.

7.37 Rules 19.19 to 19.21 relate to the records that must be provided to the place where a defendant has been detained when his case is transferred for trial. They are as follows:

(a) Where an accused is committed for trial, pursuant to section 6 of the MCA 1980 (until that form of transfer ceases to apply on the coming into force of the relevant part of Schedule 3 to the CJA 2003), or is sent for trial, pursuant to section 51 of the CDA 1998, the prison or place of detention to which he would have been sent if in custody should be informed of the fact (rule 19.19(1)). This is the case even where the defendant is a corporation (r 19.19(2)). Where a defendant is transferred to the Crown Court by virtue of the notice of transfer provisions, the same requirement applies by virtue of rule 11.2.

(b) Rule 19.14 imposes an obligation for the court to notify the relevant hospital of further remands where the Secretary of State has authorized the removal of a person remanded in custody in criminal proceedings to a hospital under section 47 of the Mental Health Act 1983. Rule 19.20 imposes the same obligation where the defendant's case has been committed or sent for trial. The same obligation is imposed in notice of transfer cases by rule 11.3.

(c) Where bail conditions are varied by the magistrates' court between the date of committal or sending (rule 19.21) or notice of transfer (rule 11.4), the magistrates' court should send a notice to the Crown Court officer of the notice made under section 5 of the Bail Act 1976.

The remaining rules deal with conditions attached to the grant of bail and to the proce- 7.38
dure to be followed where there is a failure to comply with those conditions. They
mirror in most respects the comparable provisions for the administration of bail in the
magistrates' courts which are now rules 19.5 to 19.6. It should be noted that there is no
rule 19.22(3), for reasons that may owe more to the selective copying of rule 20 of the
1982 Rules than anything else.

In summary they state: 7.39

(a) a surety can be taken by the governor or keeper of the prison or place of detention,
    and those defined by section 8(4)(a) of the Bail Act 1976 (who are also listed at
    paragraph 7.20(c)(i) above) (r 19.22(1)). Where a person proposes to enter into a
    recognizance or give security for bail, he must give the prosecution twenty-four
    hours' notice before he does so, unless the court directs otherwise (rule 19.22(4)).
(b) Where the court imposes any conditions which need to be complied with before the
    defendant is released on bail, it may direct how the condition is to be complied with,
    and before whom (rule 19.22(2)). Once the condition has been complied with, or a
    recognizance has been entered into, a statement to that effect needs to be provided
    to the Crown Court officer, and sent to the relevant governor of the prison or keeper
    of the place of detention unless he participated in the event which the statement
    records (rule 19.22(5)).
(c) Where subsequently either the defendant answers to his bail or the court decides not
    to order the forfeiture of the surety, the court officer shall notify the person before
    whom the surety was taken of this (rule 19.22(6)).

These rules are supplemented by paragraphs III.25.2 to III.25.5 of the Consolidated 7.40
Practice Direction which deal with the administration of bail during a trial in the Crown
Court. In summary, where a defendant appears for trial on bail, his future bail is a matter
within the judge's discretion (paragraph III.25.2). That said, he should retain that bail
overnight, unless there are positive reasons to the contrary, such as an increased fear that
he might abscond or interfere with witnesses (paragraph III.25.3), and should retain it
during the short adjournment unless it is not possible to segregate him from the jury and
witnesses save by a remand into custody (paragraph III.25.2). This remains true during
the summing up (paragraph III.25.4), but, if a defendant is then convicted, further
renewal of bail will depend on the gravity of the offence and the likely sentence (paragraph III.25.5).

In relation to breaches of bail, the relevant rules are to be found in rules 19.23 and 7.41
19.24. These state as follows:

(a) Where it appears to the Crown Court that there has been a default by the defendant
    or his surety in performing the conditions of a recognizance which falls short of a
    failure to surrender, the court 'may order the recognizance to be estreated'. Estreated
    means forfeited, as the Glossary to the Rules makes clear. It was made clear in *R v
    Crown Court at Warwick, ex parte Smalley*[1] that 'default' here means a failure, and

---

[1] [1987] 1 WLR 237.

that there is no need to establish fault on the part of the defendant or surety, providing that there has been a failure.

(b) In either this situation, or where the defendant fails to appear at court in accordance with the terms of the surety and the court declares the surety forfeit as a result (rule 19.24(1)), the procedure is the same. The court should issue a summons to the person by whom the recognizance was entered requiring them to attend court, at a specified time and place, and show cause why the surety should not be forfeited (rule 19.24(2)). If the court is satisfied that the summons has been served (for which see rule 4.3), it may proceed even if the person by whom the recognizance was entered fails to answer this summons (rule 19.24(3)).

(c) Where the defendant fails to answer to his bail but the court decides not to forfeit his surety, however, the court officer shall notify the person before whom the surety was taken of this (r 19.22(6)).

7.42   The Practice Direction provides additional guidance as to the approach to be adopted by the Crown Court after the defendant has failed to surrender in answer to his bail. In so doing without a reasonable cause, the defendant commits an offence under section 6 of the Bail Act 1976. Paragraph I.13.5 requires the court to deal with such an offence 'as soon as is practicable' rather than adjourning the matter to the end of the proceedings, unless there is good reason to postpone. The penalty for such a failure should normally be custodial and consecutive to any other custodial sentence passed.

7.43   Where the bail that has been breached was granted by the court, the person should be brought back before that court after he has been arrested save that, where he has committed further offences on bail, all matters should be dealt with at the court seized of the new offences (paragraph I.13.8). Proceedings for an offence under section 6 will be initiated by the court, but thereafter conducted by the prosecution (paragraphs I.13.9–10). Proceedings will be carried out either under section 6 or as a contempt of court. If necessary, evidence will need to be called, the burden being on the defendant to prove that he had reasonable cause for his failure to surrender (paragraphs I.13.10–22).

7.44   Where, following this procedure, the defendant is convicted of a bail offence, his remand status should be reviewed. Such a failure to surrender will be a 'significant factor weighing against the re-grant of bail' and the court may, as a result, remand the defendant in custody (paragraphs I.13.14–16).

7.45   The Practice Direction then goes on to deal with another consequence of the defendant failing to surrender, namely proceeding to try the defendant in his absence. That is dealt with in paragraphs I.13.17 to I.13.19 of the Practice Direction reproduced at Appendix 2.

7. Specific conditions

7.46   By virtue of rule 25.25, the defendant must notify of any address he would reside at, if granted bail with a condition of residence, as soon as practicable after proceedings are instituted against him and as soon as practicable after any change of address.

7.47   The increasing use of electronic monitoring as a condition of bail is addressed by the Rules at rule 25.26. If a person is granted bail subject to a condition of electronic monitoring, the court officer must inform the monitor of the defendant's name and telephone number, the offences with which he is charged, the details of the address at which he is to be monitored, the times during which he must be monitored and (if fixed) the date on which he must surrender to custody. If, subsequently, there is any variation of the terms of the monitoring requirement or the date of surrender to custody, the court officer must inform the monitor.

Rule 25.27 governs the procedure when a person is released on bail subject to accom- 7.48
modation or support requirements. If a defendant is released on bail with a condition that he reside in accommodation provided for that purpose by, or on behalf of, a public authority or receive bail support provided by, or on behalf of, a public authority, the court officer must inform the person responsible for the provision of such accommodation or support of the defendant's name, and telephone number (if available), the offence or offences with which the defendant is charged, details of the requirement, any other bail condition, and (if fixed) the date on which the defendant must surrender to custody; The court officer must also inform the defendant or (if the defendant is under 16) an appropriate adult of the name of the service provider, how they may be contacted, and the address at which the defendant must reside. Moreover, the court officer must notify the service provider of any variation or termination of the requirement or any other condition of bail and the fixing or variation of any date on which the defendant must surrender to custody.

D. CUSTODY TIME LIMITS

The aim of the Criminal Procedure Rules is to collect the disparate rules that impinge 7.49
upon matters of criminal procedure in one place. In this aim, however, it singularly fails in the context of custody time limits, which dictate how long a defendant may remain in custody awaiting trial.

Before 4 April 2005, this area was governed by the combination of section 22 of the 7.50
Prosecution of Offences Act 1985 and the Prosecution of Offences (Custody Time Limits) Regulations 1987, which were made thereunder. After 4 April, the position remains exactly the same because these Regulations, unusually and inexplicably, have not been incorporated into the Rules.[2]

The only contribution that the Rules make to this important safeguard of the liberty 7.51
of the individual is to be found in Part 20 of the Rules and focusses on appeals against a decision of the magistrates' court when asked to extend the custody time limit of seventy days between first appearance and committal in cases triable on indictment or either way and fifty-six days for summary trial (regulation 4(2)–(4) of the 1987 Regulations).

Under section 22(7) of the 1985 Act, a defendant may appeal to the Crown Court 7.52
where a magistrates' court has either extended the custody time limit in his case or has ruled (pursuant to section 22(6A)) that a period during which he was unlawfully at large, or such other period as the court deems appropriate, may be disregarded for the purposes of calculating custody time limits. Under section 22(8) the prosecution has a reciprocal right of appeal.

---

[2] For these see *Blackstone's Criminal Practice 2011*, paras D11.4–14.

7.53   In either case, the appeal is commenced by the giving of written notice to the court officers of the magistrates' court and Crown Court and to the other parties in the case (rule 20.1(2)) which states the date when the time limit is due to expire, and would have expired but for an extension (where such has been granted) (rule 20.1(3)). On receipt of the notice, the Crown Court officer shall notify the parties and the magistrates' court of when the case will be heard (rule 20.1(4)). Provision is also made for the appellant to abandon their challenge to the custody time limit decision within three days of the date fixed for the hearing (rule 20.1(5)).

8

DISCLOSURE

A. INTRODUCTION

When the first Rules were published, they contained detailed and complex provision for **8.01** the supply of 'advance information' by the prosecution. The 2010 Rules greatly simplify the procedure, providing for the disclosure of initial details of the prosecution case.

The provisions governing disclosure by the prosecution and defence have also been **8.02** greatly simplified. Detailed coverage of the law and practice in respect of disclosure can be found at Chapter D9 of *Blackstone's Criminal Practice 2011*.

B. INITIAL DETAILS OF THE PROSECUTION CASE

By virtue of rules 21.1 and 21.2, in any matter that is triable either way or triable sum- **8.03** marily only, the prosecutor must serve initial details of the prosecution case on the court officer, and make them available to the defence, at or before the beginning of the day of the first hearing. The provision of initial details in respect of matters which are triable on indictment only are dealt with in Part 12 of the Rules (see 5.21)

The initial details of the prosecution case must include a summary of the evidence on **8.04** which the prosecution case is based, whether that be by a summary, statement or extract or some other document, or some combination of material of those types. The defendant's previous convictions must also be disclosed.

C. DISCLOSURE BY THE PROSECUTION AND THE DEFENCE

Part 22 of the Rules governs disclosure in both the magistrates' court and Crown Courts **8.05** where Parts I and II of the CPIA 1996 apply to proceedings (rule 22(1)). It is notewor- thy that the CPIA 1996 was amended in May 2010 with the introduction of section 6C of that Act requiring the defence to notify the details of witnesses to be called for the defence.

8.06   When a prosecutor discloses material to the defence in accordance with section 3 of the CPIA 1996, or informs the defence that there is no such material to disclose, he must also notify the court officer of the same (rule 22(2)).

1. Prosecutor's application for public interest ruling

8.07   If, without a court order, a prosecutor would ordinarily have to disclose material under section 3 but wishes the court to rule on whether it would be in the public interest to disclose it, he must make a written application to the court. That application must be served on the court officer, any person who the prosecutor thinks would be directly affected by disclosure of the material, and the defendant. However, the requirement that the application be served on the defendant is operative only to the extent that serving it on him would not disclose what the prosecutor thinks ought not be disclosed (rule 22.3(1) and (2)). The application must describe the material which the prosecution seeks a ruling on. It must also explain why the prosecutor thinks that it is material that the prosecution would have to disclose and it would not be in the public interest to disclose that material. Moreover, it must set out why no measure such as the prosecutor's admission of any fact, or a form of disclosure by summary adequately would protect both the public interest and the defendant's right to a fair trial. The prosecutor is also required to omit from any part of the application that is served on the defendant anything that would disclose what the prosecutor thinks ought not be disclosed. If no part of the application is served on the defendant, the prosecutor must explain why that is the case (rule 22.3(3)).

8.08   If the issue is of the type that requires the prosecutor to serve only part of the application on the defendant, he must mark the other part, to show that it is only for the court. In that other part, the prosecutor must explain why he has withheld it from the defendant (rule 22.3(4)). If it has not already occurred, the court may direct the prosecutor to serve an application on the defendant and/or any other person who the court considers would be directly affected by the disclosure of the material.

8.09   The subsequent hearing to determine the application at a hearing will be in private, unless the court otherwise directs. Moreover, the court may direct that the hearing take place, wholly or in part, in the absence of the defendant (rule 22.3(6)). If the defendant is present at the hearing, the general rule as regards the order of representations will be as follows. First the prosecutor and any other person served with the application will make representations. Then the defendant may make representations in the presence of all parties. Finally, further representations may be made by the prosecutor and any such other person in the defendant's absence. However, the court has a discretion to direct any other arrangements for the hearing (rule 22.3(7)).

8.10   Upon hearing the application, the court may only determine it if it is satisfied that it has been able to take adequate account of the rights of confidentiality as apply to the material and the defendant's right to a fair trial (rule 22.3(8)). Unless the court otherwise directs, the court officer must not give notice to anyone other than the prosecutor of the hearing of an application under this rule, unless the prosecutor served the application on that person. In addition, no notice should be given of the court's decision on the application. The court officer may keep a written application or representations himself, or arrange for another appropriate person to keep the whole or any part subject to any conditions that the court may impose (rule 22.3(9)).

2. Service of defence statement

By virtue of rule 22.4, any defence statement pursuant to section 5 of the CPIA 1996 **8.11** must be served on both the court officer and the prosecution. The Practice Direction contains a form for the defence statement. In bold type, it warns the defendant only that the court (without mentioning the jury for some reason) may draw inferences about the failure to serve a defence statement. The time for service of a defence statement is prescribed by section 12 of the CPIA 1996 and by the Criminal Procedure and Investigations Act 1996 (Defence Disclosure Time Limits) Regulations 1997. In a magistrates' court, it is not more than fourteen days after the prosecutor discloses material under section 3 of the CPIA 1996, or serves notice that there is no such material to disclose. In the Crown Court, it is not more than fourteen days after either service of copies of the documents containing the evidence, in a case in which the defendant is sent for trial, or service of the draft indictment, in any other case, or fourteen days after the prosecutor discloses material under section 3 of the CPIA 1996, or serves notice that there is no such material to disclose. The fourteen days flows from whichever of those three events happens last. It is of note that there is no corresponding timetable for compliance by the prosecution with the requirements of secondary disclosure.

A defence statement is not obligatory in respect of proceedings in the magistrates' court. **8.12**

3. Defence application for disclosure

Following the service of a defence statement under section 5 of the CPIA 1996, a defen- **8.13** dant may make a request for disclosure under section 8 of the same Act. Rule 22.5 governs the procedure for the making of such an application.

In order to pursue such an application, the defendant must first serve it on the court **8.14** officer and the prosecutor. The application must describe the material that the defendant wants the prosecutor to disclose. Moreover, it must explain why the defendant thinks there is reasonable cause to believe that the prosecutor has that material, and it is material that the CPIA 1996 requires the prosecutor to disclose. If the defendant wants one, the application should also ask for a hearing and explain why it is needed (rule 22.5(2) and (3)).

The court may determine an application under this rule with or without a hearing, in **8.15** public or in private but the court must not require the prosecutor to disclose material unless the prosecutor is present or has had at least fourteen days in which to make representations (rule 22.5(3) and (4)).

A form for use in connection with such an application is set out in the Practice **8.16** Direction.

4. Defence review of public interest ruling

If a public interest ruling in accordance with rule 22.3 has led to the withholding of **8.17** material, the defence may apply for a review of that ruling, or the Crown Court may order such a review of its own initiative, under rule 22.6. The court's power of review is provided by sections 14 and 15 of the CPIA 1996.

Where the defendant wants the court to review that decision, the defendant is required **8.18** to serve an application on the court officer and the prosecutor. The application must describe the material that the defendant wants the prosecutor to disclose, and explain why the defendant thinks it is no longer in the public interest for the prosecutor not to disclose it (rule 22.6(2)). That application must be served by the prosecutor on any person who the prosecutor thinks would be directly affected if that material were disclosed (rule 22.6(3)). Any representations from the prosecutor, and any such person directly affected must be served on the court officer and the defendant (unless to do so would in effect reveal something that either the prosecutor or person affected thinks ought not be disclosed) (rule 22.6(4)). The court may direct the prosecutor to serve any application by the defence on any person who the court considers would be directly affected if that material were disclosed. Moreover, the court may direct the prosecutor and any person directly affected to serve any representations on the defendant (rule 22.6(5)).

8.19   The court must review a decision to which this rule applies at a hearing. Unless the court otherwise directs, that hearing will be in private. In addition the hearing may take place wholly or partly in the defendant's absence if the court directs. If a defendant is present at a hearing the general rule is that the court will receive representations in the following order. The first representations will be by the defendant, followed by the prosecutor and any other person served with the application. The defendant's representations will be in the presence of all parties. There will then be further representations by the prosecutor and any affected person in the defendant's absence. However, the court has a discretion to direct other arrangements for the hearing. The court may only conclude a review under this part if it is satisfied that it has been able to take adequate account both of such rights of confidentiality as apply to the material and the defendant's right to a fair trial.

5. The use of disclosed material

8.20   Section 17 of the CPIA 1996 provides for the court to allow a defence application to use material disclosed by the prosecution otherwise than in connection with the case in which it was disclosed or beyond the extent to which it was displayed or communicated publicly at a hearing.

8.21   Any such application must be served on the court officer and the prosecutor. It must specify what the defendant wants to use or disclose and must explain why he wants to use it. The court may decide the application by way of a hearing (whether that be in public or in private) or without a hearing. The use of such material must not be permitted by the court unless the prosecutor has had at least twenty-eight days in which to make representations. Moreover, the court must be satisfied that it has been able to take adequate account of any rights of confidentiality that may apply to the material (rule 22.7).

8.22   If disclosed material is used in breach of section 17, the court may punish the person responsible for contempt of court (see paragraph 17.01 of this work). Rule 22.8 sets out the procedure to govern such action by the court.

8.23   In such circumstances, the court may punish a person for contempt of court on an application by the prosecutor, or any person directly affected by the disclosure of the material. In addition the court may punish a person on its own initiative. Should the prosecutor or any other person directly affected by the alleged contempt want the court to punish the contemnor he must comply with the rules in Part 62 (Contempt of court) (rule 22.8(2) and (3)). By virtue of rule 22.8(4) the court must not exercise its power to forfeit material used in contempt of court unless the prosecutor, and any other person directly affected by the disclosure of the material, is present, or has had at least fourteen days in which to make representations.

Under rule 22.9 the court may shorten or extend a time limit under this Part even 8.24 after it has expired. The court may also allow a defence statement to be in a different written form to one set out in the Practice Direction, provided it contains what the CPIA 1996 requires. Any application under this Part may also be allowed by the court to be in a different form to one set out in the Practice Direction, or even to be made orally. The court may also specify the period within which any application under this Part must be made, or any material must be disclosed, following a defence application for disclosure pursuant to section 8 of the CPIA 1996 and rule 22.5.

9

WITNESSES AND RESTRICTIONS ON CROSS-EXAMINATION OF AN UNREPRESENTED DEFENDANT

A. INTRODUCTION

Parts 27 to 36 of the Rules are collected together under the heading of 'Evidence'. This title is, in fact, slightly misleading because on the whole they deal not with rules that govern the admissibility of evidence but with various aspects of the procedures that relate to the calling and questioning of witnesses.   9.01

There are several obvious exceptions to this general concept, which are the new rules which deal with the admissibility of hearsay evidence, evidence of bad character, evidence of previous sexual conduct, and the regulation of expert evidence in the wake of the changes brought about by the Criminal Justice Act 2003. These are dealt with below.[1] The remainder are addressed in this chapter.   9.02

These rules must be read as a part of the new framework for the calling of witnesses. The Consolidated Practice Direction devotes much of Part IV, 'Further Directions Applying to the Crown Court', to witness issues and the Protocol for Case Management in Frauds and Complex Cases also has an impact.   9.03

With the exception of Parts 27 and 28, the aims of which are largely mechanistic, the aim of these Parts of the Rules is to ensure that witnesses are able to give their best evidence.   9.04

---

[1] Chapters 11 and 12.

This aspiration was summed up by Paul Boateng, then Minister of State for the Home Office:[2]

> ...the Government recognise that in the past the criminal law and the criminal justice system have not always got it right. All too often, witnesses have not been able to give of their best in court, for a variety of reasons. The measure is designed to protect the public interest and thus the interests of justice, striking a proper balance between the interests and rights of the defendant and those of the victim. That demands that the best evidence possible be laid before the jury. Fear, intimidation and the vulnerability of age or incapacity can militate against witnesses giving their best evidence. The proposal will ensure that the best evidence comes before the jury...

9.05   The areas covered in this chapter are:

(a)   witness statements;
(b)   witness summonses;
(c)   special measures applications;
(d)   use of live links;
(e)   restrictions on cross-examination by the defendant in person.

9.06   There have been a number of important developments under the heading of 'special measures' which call for particular attention. These are the extension of the availability of those measures to a defendant, in particular pursuant to sections 33A to 33C imported to the Youth Justice and Criminal Evidence Act 1999 (YJCEA 1999), and the procedure for witness anonymity orders, pursuant to sections 89 to 90 of the Coroners and Justice Act 2009 (CAJA 2009).

B. WITNESS STATEMENTS

9.07   Although the rules relating to witness statements derive from two related statutory provisions, section 9 of the Criminal Justice Act 1967 (CJA 1967) and section 5A of the Magistrates' Courts Act 1980 (MCA 1980), rule 27.1 limits their application only to statements introduced under section 9.

1. Layout of a witness statement

9.08   Section 9 of the CJA 1967 renders admissible 'to like extent as oral evidence to like effect by that person' a written statement which complies with the conditions set out in subsections 9(2) to (3). Section 5B of the MCA 1980 renders admissible a statement tendered before examining justices which complies with the conditions set out in subsections 5A(2) to (3). In each case the pre-conditions are in very similar terms. The requirements are as follows:

(a)   the statement is signed by its maker, who has given his age if under 18, and is signed by the person who has read the statement to the maker for him to check, if he cannot otherwise read it (rule 27.2);

---

[2] Addressing the House of Commons Standing Committee E on 17 June 1999 in relation to the Youth Justice and Criminal Evidence Act 1999.

(b) the maker has signed a declaration as to the truth of the content of the statement;
(c) where the statement refers to a document or object as an exhibit, that item must be clearly identified and labelled in accordance with the statement (rule 27.3).

The Note to rule 27.2 indicates that the statement should be set out in accordance with the form prescribed by the Practice Direction. **9.09**

2. Editing witness statements

Rule 27.1(4) to (5) of the 2005 Rules addressed the question of editing of a witness statement to remove inadmissible material. Those rules have been reduced in the 2010 Rules to a basic requirement that a party introducing a statement should mark the served copy to make clear what is relied on, where the statement is relied on only in part (rule 27.4(2)). **9.10**

The obligation to edit a witness statement is also addressed at paragraph III.24 of the Practice Direction. This section of the Direction addresses the editing of witness statements with the aim of efficiency and convenience of presentation as well as the requirement to remove that which is inadmissible, for example editing statements where 'a witness has made more than one statement whose contents should conveniently be reduced into a single, comprehensive statement' (paragraph III.24.1). **9.11**

The rules set out in the Practice Direction are as follows: **9.12**

(a) editing should be done by the Crown Prosecution Service or other legal representative rather than by the police (paragraph III.24.1);
(b) a composite statement, reducing into one a number of witness statements by the same maker, should be drawn up in compliance with section 5A of the MCA 1980 or section 9 of the CJA 1967 as appropriate, and should be signed by the maker (paragraph III.24.2). Where such a fresh statement is taken the original should be disclosed, unless there are grounds to withhold it from disclosure (paragraph III.24.7);
(c) single statements should be edited either by:
    (i) the offending passages being lightly struck out or bracketed on a copy of the statement (and not the original that is submitted to the court) and the words 'the prosecution does not propose to adduce evidence of those passages of the attached copy statements which have been struck out and/or bracketed (nor will it seek to do so at the trial unless a notice of further evidence is served)' (paragraph III.24.3(a));
    (ii) the statement being retaken from the witness, with the offending passages omitted, in which case it must be drawn up in compliance with section 5A or section 9 as appropriate, and should be signed by the maker (paragraph III.24.3(b)). This method is preferable where the original deals with the interviews of more suspects than those who are charged (paragraph III.24.4(a)), where the suspect was asked about more offences than those with which he was then charged (paragraph III.24.4(b)), where the part relied on is but a small part of the original (paragraph III.24.4(c)) or where the prosecution is entitled not to disclose the excised passage (paragraph III.24.4(d));
    (iii) where such a fresh statement is taken the original should be disclosed, unless there are grounds to withhold it from disclosure (paragraph III.24.7);

(d) where a section 9 statement which contains inadmissible material, is tendered in summary proceedings, a new statement should be prepared rather than copy edited by striking out or bracketing passages (paragraph III.24.5);

(e) these editing principles do not apply to a document exhibited to a statement or to oral statements made by a defendant recorded in a witness statement. These should remain in the statement in the form that is sent to the Crown Court at Committal (paragraph III.24.6). It is presumed that this requirement will cease to apply when Schedule 3 to the CJA 2003 abolishes committals.

3. The timetable for service and response

9.13   Rule 27.4 regulates the process by which a witness statement is introduced in evidence. A party introducing a witness statement in evidence should serve it on the court and other parties in advance of the hearing (rule 27.4(a)), unless that other party has waived the right to be served with it, by giving notice to that effect on other parties and the court (rule 27.4(5)).

9.14   At the same time that the statement itself is served, the party on whom it is served should also be provided with a notice of his right to object to its being read (rule 27.4(3)). Under section 9 of the CJA 1967 the party on whom a statement is served is given seven days from the date of service to indicate objections to the tendering in evidence of the statement. This explains why a time limit for the provision of witness requirements of seven days is included in the automatic directions given by the magistrates' court in cases that are sent under section 51 (see Chapter 5). That deadline is reflected in rule 27.4(3)(a).

9.15   Even where no objection of the statement is communicated, the court retains the power, in its discretion, to require the witness to attend to give evidence (rule 27.4(3)(b)), either of its own initiative or on application by a party (rule 27.4(4)).

9.16   The remaining provisions of Part 27 of the 2005 Rules had been lifted from the Magistrates Rules, which had been drafted when most defendants were transferred to the Crown Court by committal under section 6 of the MCA 1980. Schedule 3 to the CJA 2003, when it comes into force, will abolish committals, and this may be why these further rules are not replicated in the 2010 Rules.

C. WITNESS SUMMONSES

9.17   In their 2005 form, the rules in Part 28 dealt separately with two forms of witness summonses, namely those issued in the magistrates' court to allow for evidence to be given, a deposition to be taken or for a person to produce a document or thing, and those issued in the Crown Court to secure the attendance of the witness or the production of a document.[3] Like so many other areas of the 2005 Rules, this was a consequence of the unamended replication of the Magistrates Court Rules 1981 and the Crown Court Rules 1982. Part 28 was completely re-written by the Criminal Procedure

---

[3] This is dealt with more fully at para D20.21 of *Blackstone's Criminal Practice 2011*.

(Amendment) Rules 2007[4] to integrate the two systems into one set of rules, and it is this amended version that is to be found in the 2010 Rules.

1. Issuing a summons or order

Rule 28.1 makes clear that the Rules apply to any application for a witness summons, warrant, or order under the following legislation: 9.18

(a) under section 97 of the MCA 1980: a magistrates' court may issue a summons to a person unwilling to attend court voluntarily where that person can give material evidence in summary proceedings or can produce a document or thing that is likely to be material evidence in those proceedings. If, having heard evidence on oath, the court considers that a summons will be insufficient to secure the person's attendance, an arrest warrant can be issued instead;

(b) under sections 2 and 2A of the Criminal Procedure (Attendance of Witnesses) Act 1965: the Crown Court may issue a summons to a person unwilling to attend court voluntarily where that person can give material evidence or can produce a document or thing that is likely to be material evidence in those proceedings;

(c) under section 7 of the Bankers' Book Evidence Act 1879, which permits either the magistrates' court or Crown Court to order the production of a copy of an entry in a banker's book without the attendance of an officer of the bank;

(d) under section 2D of the Criminal Procedure (Attendance of Witnesses) Act 1965: the Crown Court may issue a witness summons on its own initiative.

In any of these instances the court may either issue or withdraw a summons, warrant, or order without a hearing (rule 28.2(1)). If there is a hearing, it will ordinarily be in private (rule 28.2(2)). 9.19

The application, which should be made as soon as is practicable after its necessity has become apparent, may be made orally or in writing. The appropriate method will depend, subject to the overriding view of the court (rule 28.3(3)(b)), on what is sought. If the summons sought is for the production of documents the application must be in writing (rules 28.3(3)(a) and 28.5(2)), unless the court permits otherwise.[5] If not, it may be oral. 9.20

In either event, the application must: 9.21

(a) identify the witness (rule 28.3(2)(a)) (that is the person to whom the summons, warrant, or order is directed, rule 28.1(2));

(b) include a brief description of the evidence or document sought, together with the reasons why it is likely to be material, and why it is in the interests of justice to make the application. It is of note that unlike the 2005 version of the Rules, there is no specific requirement to spell out why the witness will not attend voluntarily, though that may be a factor in the assessment of the interests of justice.

If the application is made in writing, it should be in the form identified in the Practice Direction (rule 28.4(1)), and should be served on the court officer in all cases and, where 9.22

---

[4] SI 2007/699.
[5] Application to make an oral application where it should otherwise be in writing is made pursuant to r 28.8.

it is an application for the production of documents, additionally, subject to the court's direction, on the proposed witness, a person to whom the evidence relates and any other party identified by the court (rules 28.4(2) and 28.5(3)). The application should also contain the same declaration of truth as appears on a witness statement (rule 28.4(1)).

9.23   If there is an application to make orally an application that should otherwise be in writing (rule 28.8(1)), the application should identify the reasons for this, and provide as much notice as is possible to other parties (rule 28.8(2)).

9.24   As was the case before the 2007 amendment, there are additional rules where the application is for a summons requiring the production of a document or other thing.[6] The requirement that the application should be in writing[7] and the special rules as to service[8] have been dealt with. In addition:

(a) if the application is for the person to produce something, those on whom the summons is to be served, as identified by the court, have the right to make representations. The person to be summonsed has fourteen days from receipt of the application to inform the court if he wishes to make representations, including representations as to whether there should be a hearing to resolve the application (rule 28.5(4)(a)). The court may shorten or extend this fourteen-day period, even after it has expired (rule 28.8(1));

(b) in adjudicating upon such an application, the court is required to have regard to the duties and rights of the person on whom the summons is served and any person to whom the evidence relates, including their duty of confidentiality (rule 28.4(b)). This addition clearly has in mind such bodies as local authority social service departments which owe duties of care and confidentiality to children whose files may be the subject of a witness summons in criminal proceedings;

(c) where a party objects to the issuing of a summons on the basis that the item sought is not likely to be material evidence, or the rights and duties of the proposed witness or the person to whom the evidence relates outweighs the reasons for the issuing of the summons (rule 28.6(1)), the court may require the proposed witness to make the item available for the court's inspection (rule 28.6(2)) and invite either the proposed witness or the person to whom the item relates to assist the court in that assessment (rule 28.6(3)). What this addresses is the possibility of the court reviewing the documents sought, with oral or written representations from those objecting, before deciding whether to issue the summons for those documents.

9.25   It should be noted that whilst on one level an application under the Bankers' Books Evidence Act 1879 is an application for the production of documents, such applications are specifically excluded from the additional requirements of rule 28.5 (rule 28.5(5)).

9.26   The remainder of Part 28 deals with the three ways in which a witness summons may be set aside, namely at the applicant's request, at the request of the party to whom the

---

[6] Pursuant to s 2A of the Criminal Procedure (Attendance of Witnesses) Act 1965.
[7] Rule 28.5(2).
[8] Rule 28.5(3).

summons is directed or at the third party's request.[9] The applicable circumstances are as follows:

(a) section 2B of the Criminal Procedure (Attendance of Witnesses) Act 1965 was added by the CDA 1998. It permits the person who has applied to the Crown Court for a summons for third party disclosure to apply again for it to be set aside when he concludes that it is no longer needed. This is reflected in rule 28.7(1)(a);

(b) section 2C of the Criminal Procedure (Attendance of Witnesses) Act 1965 allows the person served with a witness summons to apply to the court for it to be set aside. Under rule 28.7(1), such an application can be made by the person to whom the summons is directed (rule 28.7(1)(b)) or to whom the evidence relates (rule 28.7(1)(c)) because he was not served with notice of the application for the summons, he cannot give or produce material evidence, or the rights and duties of the proposed witness or the person to whom the evidence relates outweighs the reasons for the issuing of the summons.

This application shall be made in writing,[10] setting out why the summons should be withdrawn (rule 28.7(2)(a)), as soon as is practicable after those reasons have become apparent. It shall be served on the court and other relevant parties (rule 28.7(2)(b)).   9.27

D. SPECIAL MEASURES

1. The special measures provisions

Part II, Chapter I of the YJCEA 1999 sought to encourage the attendance of vulnerable witnesses and improve the quality of evidence given by such witnesses at court by introducing a series of special measures.[11] The measures that are regulated by Part 29 of the Rules are identified in rule 29.1. In summary, however, the measures addressed here are: 9.28

(a) screening the witness from the defendant (under section 23);

(b) the use of live links for evidence (under section 24), or allowing the evidence to be given in private (under section 26);

(c) taking steps to make the courtroom less intimidating, such as the removal of wigs (under section 25), and through communication aids for the young or incapacitated (under section 30);

(d) adducing examination-in-chief (section 27) or cross-examination and re-examination (section 28) by video recording, or through the use of an intermediary (section 29).

Those for whom such measures are available are those who are young or incapable (section 16) or those the quality of whose evidence 'is likely to be diminished by reason of fear or distress' in giving evidence (section 17). Within the rules, the term 'witness' is applied to anyone for whose benefit any special measure has been sought (rule 29.2).   9.29

---

[9] It should be noted that the court retains the power, in addition, to withdraw a summons of its own motion pursuant to s 2D of the Criminal Procedure (Attendance of Witnesses) Act 1965.

[10] Unless the court permits the application to be made orally pursuant to r 28.8.

[11] These are set out in more detail at para D14.97 of *Blackstone's Criminal Practice 2011*.

In relation to both young witnesses and others, application has to be made for the appropriate special measure in accordance with section 19. It is in this context that the Rules step in to replace the old procedural regulations[12] with the new Part 29, which is centred on the completion of a new form.

9.30 Part 29 of the Rules also deals with special measures for a defendant, and witness anonymity orders. As these are significant recent extensions to the range of special measures available, they are dealt with separately below.

2. The procedure

9.31 The timetable for the making and resolution of special measures applications has been simplified in the 2010 Rules. The stages are dealt with in Part 29 of the Rules both in Section 2, the 'general rules' section, and Section 3, 'Special Measures Directions'.

(a) *The application*

9.32 The starting point is the application for special measures, using the form set out in the Practice Direction and complying with rule 29.10. The form includes a number of parts, relating to different measures—part B for live link, part C for intermediary, and part D for use of video recording (rule 29.10). In order to qualify for special measures, the witness must fall within a category prescribed by the YJCEA 1999, and the content of the application varies, depending on the category. Witnesses may be eligible for the measures on grounds of youth or incapacity (section 16), or because of the fear or distress they are likely to suffer when giving evidence (section 17).

9.33 In relation to young witnesses (defined as those under 17 until the age is changed to 18 by section 98 of the CAJA 2009), section 21 of the YJCEA 1999 determines the appropriate measures which may be adopted. The 'primary rule' is that the evidence in chief of such witnesses will take the form of a video recorded interview, and that their further evidence will occur via a live link.

9.34 In *R (D) v Camberwell Green Youth Court*[13] it was emphasized that the special measures regime in relation to those requiring special protection would only rarely be disapplied and the court should proceed on the presumption that special measures would be used. This is reflected at rule 29.9, which makes clear that those measures will be given either when requested or of the court's own initiative (rule 29.9(1)). Rule 29.9(2) indicates that the party seeking to rely on the witness should notify the court that the witness is eligible (ie under the appropriate age) and serve the video interview of the witness on the court and other parties.

9.35 The CAJA 2009, sections 98 and 100, make substantial amendments to section 21 but these are not yet in force. Section 100 of the CAJA 2009 widens the availability of special measures for child witnesses in the following ways:

(a) section 21(1)(b) and (5) to (7) are omitted, which has the effect of making special measures available in respect of all child witnesses, whatever the offence in question;

---

[12] The Magistrates' Courts (Special Measures Directions) Rules 2002 and the Crown Court (Special Measures Directions and Directions Prohibiting Cross-examination) Rules 2002.

[13] [2003] 2 Cr App R 257.

(b) new subsections (4)(ba) and (4A) to (4C) are added which enable a child witness to opt out of special measures where 'the court is satisfied that not complying with the rule would not diminish the quality of the witness's evidence' and specify the factors which the court must take into account in such circumstances. In those circumstances, the application for other measures on his behalf should address this issue (rule 29.10(e)).

In relation to other witnesses, to whom section 17 of the YJCEA 1999 applies, the application submitted under rule 29.10 should identify how section 17 is of application, in that it should set out: 9.36

(a) how the witness is eligible;
(b) what measures are sought;
(c) why the quality of the evidence of the witness will be improved by the grant of those measures; and
(d) the views of the witness.

Additional matters that are required for certain specific measures are addressed below.

In relation to the detail to be included in the application, in *Brown*,[14] the Court of Appeal made clear that, although section 17(2) required the court to consider the list of factors in section 17(2)(a) to (d) in deciding whether a witness was eligible for assistance, it was entitled to reach that conclusion solely having regard to the nature and circumstances of the offence (the factor specified in section 17(2)(a)), regardless of the age of the witness or whether he was particularly vulnerable.   9.37

Further, when section 99 of the CAJA 2009 comes into force, section 17 of the YJCEA 1999 will be amended so as to provide for automatic eligibility for special measures for witnesses in proceedings for any relevant offence. A 'relevant offence' is an offence specified in a new Schedule 1A to the YJCEA 1999 (set out in Schedule 14 to the CAJA 2009). Similarly, on its coming into force, section 101 of the CAJA 2009 will introduce a new section 22A of the YJCEA 1999 which will make special provision for complainant witnesses aged over 18 in respect of sexual offences.   9.38

Special provision is made for applications which include information that the applicant thinks should not be disclosed to the other parties (rule 29.12). This will have particular importance where the application is for anonymity, or where an application for another measure relies on material the disclosure of which is contrary to the public interest. In those circumstances, the application is made in two parts, that which can be served on other parties and that which is provided only to the court, sets out the reasons why that part had been thus withheld (rule 29.12(2)), and which will be addressed during a private hearing from which, at the court's discretion, the other parties may be excluded (rule 29.12(3)).   9.39

(b) *Response to an application*
Once one party has applied for special measures, the other parties have the opportunity to object, in a form identified in rule 29.13. The opposition should state whether issue   9.40

---

[14] [2004] Crim LR 1034.

is taken with the witness's eligibility for the measures, with the effect of the measure on the quality of the evidence, or with the inhibiting effect the measure would have on the objecting party's ability to challenge the evidence (rule 29.13(4)). If it is necessary for the objecting party to rely on material that cannot be disclosed, the same procedure will be followed, in terms of a two-part application, as is described at paragraph 9.39 above (rule 29.13(3)).

(c) *The timetable*

9.41   The stages from the moment that a written application for a special measure is made by completing the relevant part of the form and its submissions to the court and other parties are as follows:

Step	Time	Rule
Submission of the application in writing and served on the court officer and each other party.	As soon as reasonably practical, and within 14 days of the defendant pleading not guilty.	29.3
Opposition to such an application to be completed in writing, including the reasons for opposition, and served on all parties.	14 days from receipt of the application.	29.13
The court shall decide the application without a hearing if no opposition has been received (r 29.8(b)), but should give its reasons for granting or refusing the measure sought in open court before the witness is called (r 29.4(2)).	After the time for opposition to the application has passed.	29.8
If opposition has been received, and a hearing has been requested (r 29.13(2)(c)), there will ordinarily be a hearing, either in public or in private.		29.8
The party seeking the measure should inform the witness of the outcome of the application, and how they will thus give evidence.	As soon as possible after the application has been decided.	29.4(1)

9.42   These time periods are subject to variation. The time in which a party can apply for special measures can be shortened or extended before or after the period has expired by a written application, served on all parties, and supported by a statement setting out the reasons why extra time is needed. Such applications are decided by a single justice or judge without the necessity for a hearing, and the decision is then communicated to the parties by the court (rule 29.5).

9.43   Unlike in its previous incarnations, the Rules now make no provision for the making of oral applications for special measures once the trial has started, or for the renewal of applications that have been refused. However, the court's discretion in this regard is nevertheless preserved by section 19(1) of the YJCEA 1999.

(d) *Procedure after the application has been decided*

9.44   Unless the court directs otherwise, the court officer will retain the application, and any other representations, or make arrangements for their alternative storage (rule 29.6).

9.45   Once an order for special measures has been made, it may be discharged or varied pursuant to section 20(2) of the YJCEA 1999, which allows such a change where there has been a material change of circumstances. Such an application is to be made in writing setting out the material change in circumstances, the reasons for the application, and indicating if a hearing is required (rule 29.11(2)). The application should be sent as soon as is practicable after the change to the court and the parties (rule 29.11(1)). Under the 2005 Rules provision was also made for the renewal of an application for measures that had been refused, where there was a change of circumstances. That is not replicated in the 2010 Rules.

Once an application has been made to vary or discharge an order, the procedure thereafter is the same as that which applies to fresh applications. Opposition to the application is to be communicated in the same way as opposition to an initial hearing (rule 29.13), and the hearing likewise conducted like a normal application (rule 29.8).   9.46

3. Specific measures

The general rules in Part 29 also addressed three specific measures, namely the use of live links, the use of video recordings, and the use of intermediaries.   9.47

(a) *Live links*

The use of a live link for the evidence of a witness is permitted by section 24 of the YJCEA 1999. In this context references to live links are references to 'a live television link or other arrangements whereby a witness, whilst absent from the courtroom or other place where the proceedings are being held, is able to see and hear a person there and to be heard and seen' by the judge, legal representatives, and interpreter for the defendant. Live links for vulnerable witnesses, pursuant to section 24, are distinct from links for witnesses who are overseas, which are dealt with below.   9.48

When applying for the use of a live link, using the prescribed form, under rule 29.10, the application must identify who will accompany the witness whilst they give evidence, and why that person is suitable to do so (rule 29.10(f)).   9.49

This rule is supplemented by the Practice Direction, even though paragraph III.29.1 continues to refer to the old Rules rather than to Part 29 of the new ones. The direction states that 'an increased degree of flexibility is now appropriate as to who can act as supporter of a witness giving evidence by live television link' (paragraph III.29.2). The judge is encouraged to direct who should accompany the witness in advance of the trial. The supporter should be 'completely independent' of, and have no previous knowledge of, the witness and should be trained in accordance with the relevant National Standards. The court usher should additionally be available to assist and to ensure that the judge's directions are complied with (paragraph III.29.3).   9.50

(b) *Video recordings*

The use of a video recording as evidence-in-chief of a witness is permitted by section 27 of the YJCEA 1999, where it is in the interests of justice to do so (section 27(2)). The conduct of such an interview is governed by Home Office guidance,[15] which sets out good practice for preparing for and conducting such interviews. The courts have made   9.51

---

[15] *Achieving Best Evidence in Criminal Proceedings: Guidance for Vulnerable or Intimidated Witnesses, including Children.*

clear that failure to comply with such guidance is a factor to be taken into account in deciding whether to permit such a video to be used as evidence at trial.[16] The test to be applied is that enunciated in *Hanton*,[17] namely 'could a reasonable jury properly directed be sure that the witness had given a credible and accurate account on the video tape, notwithstanding any breaches'.[18]

9.52   The rules in relation to video recorded evidence in chief are supplemented by paragraph IV.40 of the Practice Direction. The Practice Direction indicates the following:

(a) the court, when allowing a video recording to be used, under section 27(1), can direct that certain parts of it are to be excluded. The recording must then be edited in accordance with the court's ruling and the edited version then served on the court officer and on the parties (paragraph IV.40.2);

(b) where a video recording is adduced in Crown Court proceedings, it should be produced and proved by the interviewer or another witness who was present at the interview. Unless that person's statement is agreed, the party relying on the video must ensure that person can attend to give evidence at trial (paragraph IV.40.3);

(c) if at trial a problem with the editing of the video delays the proceedings, the court can consider making an order as to the costs wasted thereby (paragraph IV.40.4).

9.53   Where the application is made, using the prescribed form, under rule 29.1(2)(c), the application should identify the date and duration of the recording (rule 29.10(g)(i)). If the proposal is to show only part of the recorded interview, pursuant to the YJCEA 1999, section 27(2) and (6), the application must also specify which parts are to be adduced (rule 29.10(g)(ii)). The requirement in the 2005 Rules that the application for the use of a video recording should be accompanied by a statement of the circumstances in which the video recording was made is not reproduced in the 2010 Rules. However, the Practice Direction still envisages that a statement will be provided to produce and prove the video (paragraph IV.40.3). It is therefore reasonable to anticipate that a statement will accompany the video addressing matters relating to the time and location at which the video was made, the equipment used, and the personnel present.

9.54   Under the 2005 Rules there was a requirement, where the witness was assisted during the recorded interview by an intermediary, pursuant to section 29(6) of the YJCEA 1999, or by an aid to communication permitted under section 30, that details of this should be included in the statement of circumstances. These requirements are not reproduced in the 2010 Rules, but again the terms of the Practice Direction (paragraph IV.40.3) would suggest that it would be prudent for such detail still to be included.

9.55   Section 27 is not limited to the use of video recordings as evidence in chief by the prosecution, and this is demonstrated by the fact that rule 29.3 applies to any party seeking to take advantage of special measures. The concern raised when such special measures were introduced was that the defence would have to disclose the evidence of witnesses they might wish to call in advance, in contradistinction to the position of witnesses to whom the special measure provisions have no application.

---

[16] See *G v DPP* [1997] 2 Cr App R 78.
[17] [2005] EWCA Crim 2009.
[18] This approach was approved in *K* [2006] 2 Cr App R 175.

To overcome this concern, the 2005 Rules set out specific rules for defence applications, **9.56** which stated that the defence were not obliged to provide the recording to the prosecution until after the prosecution has closed its case. Those provisions are not replicated in the 2010 Rules. However, rule 29.12 does make provision for a party to withhold information relating to a special measures application from the other parties, and this provision may be of application to this situation, if the conditions there identified are met.

When section 137 of the CJA 2003 comes into effect, the court will be able to permit **9.57** a video recording of an interview with a witness (other than the accused) to be admitted as the evidence in chief of the witness in a wide range of circumstances. The court will be able to authorize such a video recording to replace the witness's evidence in chief provided that:

(a) the person claims to be a witness to the offence, or part of it, or to events closely connected with it; and

(b) the video recording of the statement was made at a time when the events were fresh in the witness's memory; and

(c) the offence is indictable-only, or is an either-way offence prescribed by order of the Home Secretary.

If the recording satisfies (a) to (c), then the court may admit it provided that: **9.58**

(i) the witness's recollection of events is likely to be significantly better at the time the recording was made than by the time of the trial; and

(ii) it is in the interests of justice to admit it, having regard to whether it is an early and reliable account from the witness, whether the quality is adequate, and the witness's own views about using the recording.

(c) *Intermediaries*

Section 29 of the YJCEA 1999 allows a witness to give evidence through an intermedi- **9.59** ary who will explain the questions and answers in so far as this is necessary for their comprehension. Under section 29(5), a person cannot act as an intermediary in a specific case unless he first makes a declaration. Rule 29.7 sets out the declaration required to be made by such an intermediary.

E. DEFENDANT'S EVIDENCE DIRECTIONS

Prior to 15 January 2006, the accused was specifically and comprehensibly excluded **9.60** from eligibility under either category (YJCEA 1999, sections 16(1) and 17(1)). This exclusion may have run counter to the thrust of the decision in *V v UK*[19] in respect of juvenile defendants and the spirit of the *Consolidated Criminal Practice Direction*, paragraph IV.39. Some steps were taken by the courts to ameliorate the harshness of this position, for example in *H (Special measures)*,[20] the Court of Appeal identified steps that a trial judge, in his discretion, might take to assist an accused with learning difficulties

---

[19] (2000) 30 EHRR 121. See *Blackstone's Criminal Practice 2011*, para **D23.53**.

[20] (2003) *The Times*, 15 April 2003.

to give evidence at trial. Since then, Parliament has also intervened to address access by a defendant to special measures in two important areas.

9.61   Section 47 of the Police and Justice Act 2007, which came into effect on 15 January 2007, imports new sections 33A to 33C into the YJCEA 1999.[21] Under these sections, a court may permit an accused to give his evidence via a live link (as defined for these purposes by section 33B) where to do so would enable him to participate more effectively in the proceedings as a witness where the accused is either under the age of 18 and his ability to participate is otherwise compromised by his intellectual ability or lack of social function (section 33A(4)) or where he is over 18 but suffering from a mental disorder which prevents his effective participation (section 33A(5)).

9.62   When it comes into force, section 104 of the CAJA 2009 will insert new sections 33BA and 33BB into the YJCEA 1999. Under section 33BA, the court may, on the accused's application, give a direction that provides for any examination of the accused to be conducted through an intermediary. The court may so direct where the accused is either under the age of 18 and his ability to participate effectively as a witness is compromised by his level of intellectual ability or lack of social function (section 33BA(5)); or where he is over 18 but suffering from a mental disorder which prevents his effective participation.

9.63   Provision is now made in Section 4 of Part 29 (rules 29.14 to 29.17) for applications for such measures. In summary:

(a)   the defence should submit an application, explaining how the measures sought meet the conditions for special measures set out in the YJCEA 1999 (rule 29.15.(a)). Those conditions, for the purposes of the use of a live link pursuant to section 33A are set out in section 33A(4) for defendants who are under 18 and section 33A(5) for defendants over that age. As with other live links,[22] the application should identify who will accompany the witness whilst they give evidence, and why that person is suitable to do so (rule 29.15(b));

(b)   although the specific rules for defendant's evidence directions are silent as to timetable, the note to these rules indicated that the general rules apply. It follows that such an application should be made as soon as is practicable, or within fourteen days of the defendant pleading not guilty (rule 29.3(a)), and served on the other parties and the court (rule 29.3(b));

(c)   once those defending have applied for measures for a defendant's evidence, the other parties have the opportunity to object, pursuant to rule 29.17. The opposition, which should be served on the court and other parties (rule 29.17(2)(a)) within fourteen days of the application (rule 29.17(2)(b)), should identify why it is contended that the conditions laid down in section 33A(4) or (5) are not satisfied (rule 29.17(3));

(d)   in the application and/or in any response to it, the parties have the right to ask for a hearing of the application (rule 29.15(c) and rule 29.17(2)(c)). The court may decide whether to make a defendant's evidence direction, following such a hearing (either in public or in private), or without a hearing if the fourteen days for

---

[21] See *Blackstone's Criminal Practice 2011*, para D14.105 for a discussion and para **D14.119** for the text.
[22] See r 29.10(f).

responding to an application has expired without a response having been submitted (rule 29.14);

(e) thereafter, a party may apply in writing for a variation or discharge of any defendant's evidence direction that the court has made (rule 29.16(1)(a)). The application, which should be served on the court and other parties (rule 29.16(1)(b)), is required to identify:

(i) for the purposes of a live link application, pursuant to section 33A(7), the application should identify why the link is no longer necessary in the interests of justice (rule 29.16(2)(a));

(ii) for the purposes of an intermediary, pursuant to section 33BB when it comes into force, the application should explain why the intermediary was no longer required or a variation is needed to secure a fair trial for the defendant (rule 29.16(2)(b)–(c));

(f) in making such an application, a request for a hearing can be made (rule 29.16(2)(d)). The same procedure for response by other parties to the application (rule 29.17) and adjudication of the application by the court (rule 19.14) as are described above are then engaged.

Clearly these rules will not come into full effect until sections 33BA and 33BB come into force. The Divisional Court has made clear in *R (C) v Sevenoaks Youth Court*[23] that courts are required, in the absence of such statutory powers, to use the combination of the principles underlying the Rules (especially rules 1.11 and 3.10) and their inherent powers to assist an accused through the use of such special measures as will ensure his comprehension of and participation in the proceedings (such as the provision of an intermediary). Given the considerable overlap between the terms of the general rules for special measures and the specific rules relating to defendant's evidence, it is reasonable to anticipate that the general rules can be used to make applications for intermediaries for defendants until the new provisions come into effect. 9.64

F. WITNESS ANONYMITY ORDERS

The 2005 Rules included no reference to the evidence of witnesses whose identity was concealed from the defendant and the public. At that time, the position was that identified by the Court of Appeal in *Davis*,[24] namely that a court could take measures to ensure witnesses remained anonymous. Because those measures were not regulated by the YJCEA 1999, Part 29 of the Rules did not address them. Since 2005, witness anonymity has undergone several significant revolutions. The House of Lords in *Davis*[25] made it clear that there was no common-law power to grant a witness anonymity, causing Parliament to intervene by passing the Criminal Evidence (Witness Anonymity) Act 2008.[26] This abolished the common-law rules and introduced a new procedure for the 9.65

---

[23] [2010] 1 All ER 735.
[24] [2006] 1 WLR 3130.
[25] [2008] 1 AC 1128.
[26] Which received Royal Assent on 22 July 2008.

making of witness anonymity orders, which was set out in the Consolidated Practice Direction.[27]

9.66   On 1 January 2010, the 2008 Act ceased to have effect and was replaced by Chapter 2 of Part 3 of the CAJA 2009.[28] Section 5 of Part 29 of the 2010 Rules (rules 29.18 to 29.22) set out the procedure for applications for witness anonymity orders pursuant to these new provisions. The repeal of the 2008 Act does not affect the continuation of a witness anonymity order made under that Act before 1 January 2010 (CAJA 2009, Schedule 22, paragraph 16(1)). An application made under section 3 of the 2008 Act which falls to be heard on or after 1 January 2010 is to be treated as an application made under section 87 of the CAJA 2009, and the conditions mentioned in section 88 of the CAJA 2009 must be satisfied in relation to it (Schedule 22, paragraph 16(2)). Rules 29.18 to 29.22 would appear to provide the procedure for applications within this transitional category.

9.67   In overview, a witness anonymity order protects the identity of the witness from disclosure in proceedings (CAJA 2009, section 86(1)), through the use of various measures that are identified in section 86(2). An application for a witness anonymity order may be made either by the prosecution or defence pursuant to CAJA 2009, section 87. Such orders may be sought in a magistrates' court, the Crown Court, and the Court of Appeal (section 97). Such an order will be granted where the criteria identified in CAJA 2009, section 88, are met.[29] These conditions address the necessity of the measures (condition A), the fact that the trial can still be fair to the accused (condition B), and the fact that the measures are in the interests of justice (condition C). The correct approach to these conditions is informed by section 89, which sets out relevant considerations, and by the decision of the Court of Appeal in *Mayers*.[30]

9.68   The procedure to be adopted in relation to applications under the CAJA 2009 is as follows:

(a)   the application, which should be served on all parties and which should not contain anything that might identify the witness (rule 29.19(1)), should specify the measures proposed, explain how those measures comply with section 88 and why no lesser measures will suffice and attach the required documentation (rule 29.19(1)(b)–(d));

(b)   this documentation is the statement of the witness whose anonymity is sought, any disclosure relating to that witness and a defence statement/other available particulars of the defence case (rule 29.19(1)(e)). The Court of Appeal in *Mayers* made clear that the prosecution's disclosure obligations in relation to an anonymous witness 'go much further than the ordinary duties of disclosure', adding that disclosure must be 'complete' and 'full and frank';

(c)   Where such an application is made by the defence, the court should then notify the DPP of it, unless the case has been brought by a public authority (rule 29.20). It is not clear what it is envisaged that the DPP should then do in response;

---

[27] As amended August 2008.
[28] Witness anonymity orders are dealt with in *Blackstone's Criminal Practice 2011*, para D14.120.
[29] See *Blackstone's Criminal Practice 2011*, para D14.122.
[30] [2009] 2 All ER 145.

(d) after an application has been made, the other parties are then afforded fourteen days to respond to the application (rule 29.22(2)). In *Mayers* the court stressed the importance, both to anonymity applications and to disclosure in relation to anonymous witnesses, of detailed defence statements. The court observed that 'the defence statement provides the benchmark against which the disclosure process must be examined'. Where the application has been made by the defence, and the response is thus from the prosecution, additional disclosure obligations arise at that stage (rule 29.22(6));

(e) an oral hearing will take place only where such a hearing has been sought either by the applicant (rule 29.19(1)(f)), or by a party responding to it (rule 29.22(2)(c)), or if the court considers that one is required (rule 29.18(1)). Otherwise, the decision may be reached without a hearing (rule 29.18(1)). However, the court cannot reach that decision to make a witness anonymity order before trial, without giving all parties the opportunity to make representations (rule 29.18(2)(a)). The same consideration applies to any appeal thereafter. After a trial, the witness himself is also to be afforded the chance to make representations (rule 29.18(2)(b)–(c));

(f) at the hearing of the application, the applicant should provide the court, but not the other parties, with the information redacted from the application, namely the witness statement, other evidence or other material relied on to establish that the section 88 criteria have been met (rule 29.19(2)(b)). At that stage, the applicant should also identify to the court the witness in question, unless, in the case of a prosecution witness, application is made for this not to happen, giving reasons why it is not possible to identify him (rule 29.19(2)(a)). If there is no such hearing, the applicant must reveal the witness's identity to the court before the witness gives evidence, again unless an application is made to the contrary (rule 29.19(4));

(g) any such hearing should normally take place in private, and can take place, in part, in the absence of the accused or his representative (rule 29.18.(1)). Such an *ex parte* hearing will, in any event, take place after the court has heard or received in writing the representations of the parties in relation to the application, so that the court can be addressed about, and give rigorous scrutiny to the confidential material additional to the application (rule 29.19(3));

(h) the court's overriding obligation is to ensure that the proceedings are fair (*Mayers*), and no order should be made without hearing representations of the parties, both before any material that is withheld from the other parties is heard by the court (rule 29.19(3)) and before a decision is made (rule 29.18.(2)).

Once a witness anonymity order has been made, section 91 of the CAJA 2009 permits 9.69 the variation or discharge of that order. This may occur either because the court varies or discharges the order of its own volition, in accordance with its duty to keep the order under review, or because one of the parties has requested discharge or variation. At this stage the parties include the witness himself (rule 29.21(1)), who should be notified of any application made after the trial and any appeal (rule 29.21(4)). The procedure for such an application is as follows:

(a) the application has to be in writing, and provided to the other parties (rule 29.21(1)), and should explain the reasons for the application (rule 29.21(2)). The application should not include material that might identify the witness;

(b) as with other applications, other parties may respond within fourteen days, indicating areas of disagreement (rule 29.22(5)). Either the applicant (rule 29.21(2)(c)), or any responding party (rule 29.22(2)(c)) may ask for a hearing;

(c) the procedure for the hearing of such an application should mirror that employed for the original application for an anonymity order (rule 29.18).

G. LIVE TELEVISION LINKS

1. Development of the use of live television links

9.70　The term 'live link' was defined in the glossary to the 2005 Rules in the following terms:

audio and/or video equipment set up in order to enable evidence to be given from outside the court room in which the case is being heard.

9.71　At paragraph 9.48, consideration was given to the use of live links as a special measure to enhance the quality of a vulnerable witness. Such live links, as is made clear by the definition provided for them in section 24(8) of the YJCEA 1999, were live television links to other rooms within the court building and their aim was to remove the witness from the stress of appearing in a public courtroom under the gaze of the public and, especially, of the defendant.

9.72　　Quite independent of that use of television links, section 32 of the Criminal Justice Act 1988 has provided for the use of television links for witnesses who are not only not in the same room as the remainder of the participants in the trial, but who are not in the same country.

9.73　　In its present form, section 32 states:

(1) A person other than the accused may give evidence through a live television link in proceedings to which subsection (1A) applies if—

(a) the witness is outside the United Kingdom;

. . .

but the evidence may not be so given without the leave of the court.

(1A) This subsection applies—

(a) to trials on indictment, appeals to the criminal division of the Court of Appeal and hearings of references under section 9 of the Criminal Appeal Act 1995. . .

9.74　This section came into force on 5 January 1989,[31] but only came into operation on 26 November 1990[32] when links were permitted in cases of murder, manslaughter, serious frauds, and cases initiated by a notice of transfer under section 4 of the Criminal Justice Act 1987. The availability of such links was considerably widened to any trial on indictment starting after 1 September 2004.[33] Such links are therefore now available at all trials in the Crown Court.

---

[31] SI 1988/2073.
[32] SI 1990/2084.
[33] SI 2004/1267.

2. The Rules

Part 30 of the Rules replaces rule 23B of the Crown Court Rules 1982 as the mechanism 9.75
by which application can now be made to the Crown Court for leave to call a witness via
a live television link. The 2010 Rules reproduce without alteration the 2005 Rules in
this regard. It should be remembered that such applications are not limited to the prosecution (rule 30.1(1)).

The application is to be made by completing a form specified in the Practice Direction 9.76
(rule 30.1(3)) which is to be served on the court officer and the other parties (rule
30.1(6)) within twenty-eight days of committal, the giving of notice of transfer, or the
service of the prosecution case following the sending of the defendant to the Crown
Court under section 51 (rule 30.1(4)). This period may be extended before or after it has
expired by written application to the court, setting out the reasons for the need for an
extension (rule 30.1(5)). This written application for an extension is likewise to be
provided to the other parties as well as the court (rule 30.1(6)).

The parties served with an application for a live link have twenty-eight days thereafter 9.77
to notify the applicant and the court officer whether or not he opposes the application,
and if so why, and whether he wishes to be present when the application is heard (rule
30.1(7)). After that twenty-eight day period has expired, the court will determine the
application, either with or without a hearing as appropriate (rule 30.1(8)). This hearing
will take place in chambers (rule 30.1(2)).

The court officer will then notify the parties of the court's decision. If leave is granted, 9.78
the notice will state the place and country from which the evidence will be given, and
the Crown Court at which the trial will take place (rule 30.1(9)(a), (b), and (d)). If the
witness is to be called by the prosecution, his statement will have been served and he
therefore will be named (rule 30.1(9)(c)).

The naming of the witness where he is to be called by the defence is a more compli- 9.79
cated matter because there has generally been no obligation on the defence to reveal
what witnesses they are to call. The two exceptions mentioned in rule 30.1(9)(c) are
where he is an alibi witness or an expert witness. In those situations the defence themselves are under obligations of disclosure by virtue of section 5(7) of the CPIA 1996,
which requires the details of an alibi witness to be included in the defence statement, and
section 81 of PACE 1984 which requires advance notice of expert evidence. In these two
situations the witness's name will therefore have been disclosed by the defence, and he
will be named in the court's notice of leave (rule 30.1.(9)(c)).

Rule 30.1(9)(c) fails in two respects to take into account the reforms of defence dis- 9.80
closure in two respects. First, since 4 April 2005, section 5 of the CPIA 1996 has been
amended by section 32 of the CJA 2003, so that the obligation to disclose details of alibi
is now to be found in section 6A(2) of that Act. The second change is that when section
34 of the CJA 2003 comes into force, the defendant will be obliged under a new section
6C of the CPIA 1996 to give notice of the details of witnesses he proposes to call. When
this occurs, the defence will be obliged to name all witnesses for whom a live link is
sought and this rule will need to be amended.

Rule 30.1(9) allows the court to place conditions on its grant of leave to call a witness 9.81
by live link. The conditions are as to who is to be present with the witness when he is
called, and who can answer the judge's questions on oath about the circumstances in
which the evidence is to be or has been given (rule 30.1(10)).

3. Links in the Court of Appeal

9.82   Section 32 allows for the use of live links not only in the Crown Court but in the Court of Appeal, in 'appeals to the criminal division of the Court of Appeal and hearings of references under section 9 of the Criminal Appeal Act 1995' (section 32(1A)(a)).[34]

4. The further expansion of the use of live links

9.83   In his review of the criminal justice system,[35] Sir Robin Auld recommended that expert witnesses should be permitted 'in appropriate cases to give evidence via one or other of these technologies [live link or internet link] at locations remote from the court and more convenient to them'. This recommendation was taken up and expanded by the Government and is now brought into effect by section 51 of the CJA 2003.

9.84   On 7 December 2007, section 51 of the CJA 2003 came into force in relation to certain sexual offences, and it has since been broadened to apply to any trial on indictment. Section 51 permits any witness other than the defendant to give evidence via a live link from another location in the United Kingdom, rather than just from overseas, and in any proceedings, rather than just those in the Crown Court and Court of Appeal. Section 55, which came into force on 29 January 2004, allows for rules to be prepared to deal with this large expansion in the use of live links, but this is an invitation that the Criminal Procedure Rules Committee has still not yet taken up.

H. RESTRICTIONS ON CROSS-EXAMINATION BY THE DEFENDANT IN PERSON

1. The relevant statutory provisions

9.85   Section 34 of the YJCEA 1999 prohibits cross-examination of the complainant by a defendant who is charged with a sexual offence.

9.86   This prohibition is extended by section 35 which prevents the defendant charged with an offence under Part 1 of the Sexual Offences Act 2003 (these include rape, sexual assault, child sex offences, sexual offences in relation to the mentally impaired, offences involving indecent images of children) or a variety of other offences which relate to children (listed in section 35(3)) from cross-examining the complainant or a child witness.

9.87   Section 36 allows the prosecution to apply for a similar prohibition in other cases, or for the court to order one of its own motion, where it would enhance the quality of the complainant's evidence and it will not be contrary to the interests of justice to make such an order.

---

[34] The rules for applying for a link in these circumstances are to be found in Part 68 of the Rules, which deals with appeals against sentence or conviction to the Court of Appeal, at rule 68.19. This is dealt with in Chapter 18 below.

[35] At chapter 11, para 148.

2. The rules as to securing legal representation

The rules, which have only been altered in one very small respect since 2005,[36] are aimed   9.88
at preventing both cross-examination by the defendant himself and unfairness being
caused to the defendant by this prohibition through the provision to him of legal
representation.

In any of the three situations set out in sections 34 to 36, the court is obliged to   9.89
explain to the defendant that he cannot cross-examine the relevant witness and should
obtain legal representation (rule 31.1(2)). This rule gives effect to the requirements of
section 38(2). The defendant then has seven days to notify the court, in writing
(rule 31.1(5)), of what action he has taken (rule 31.1(3)) and of the name of his legal
representatives, if any have been appointed (rule 31.1(4)). The court is then required
to inform the other parties of the details of the defendant's legal representative
(rule 31.1(6)).

The period of seven days can be extended when the court explains the position to the   9.90
defendant (rule 31.1(3)) or can be reduced in length if that explanation is given to him
less than seven days before the start of the trial (rule 31.1(7)). In any event, if no response
is received by the end of the relevant period, the court may extend the period either of
its own motion or at the defendant's request (rule 31.1(8)) for such period as it deems
appropriate (rule 31.1(10)). However, the court should allow all parties to make representations on the question before granting such an extension (rule 31.1(9)) and the
court should inform all parties of its decision in writing thereafter (rule 31.1(11)).

If either the court decides not to extend the period in which the defendant can give   9.91
notice of his having obtained legal representation, or he still fails to provide such notice
in the period of extension granted to him, the court is required by section 38(3) to consider appointing legal representation for him, and if it is so inclined, suitably qualified
counsel should be appointed to cross-examine the relevant witnesses (section 38(4)).
Where the court reaches this position, it should notify all parties of the details of the
relevant appointment (rule 31.2(1)).

Such an appointment ordinarily lasts until the end of the cross-examination of the   9.92
witness or witnesses to whom the section 34 to 36 prohibition applies (rule 31.2(1)).
However, the defendant may arrange for the legal representative appointed to cross-
examine any witness in relation to whom a section 34 to 36 prohibition exists (rule
31.3(1)). If this occurs, the defendant and his legal representative shall notify the court
of the fact, and the latter shall be treated as if the defendant had appointed counsel
rather than the court (that is under section 38(2)(a) rather than section 38(4)). The
court shall then investigate the matter (rule 31.3(3)).

Alternatively, the defendant may still appoint a legal representative of his choosing even   9.93
after the court has appointed one for him under section 38(4) (rule 31.3(4)), by notifying
the court of his intention to instruct someone and then, within the time allowed for the
purpose, of the details of the person he has instructed to act (rule 31.3(5)). The court shall
then discharge the order it made appointing someone itself to act for the defendant under
section 38(4) (rule 31.3(6)) and notify the parties of these facts (rule 31.3(7)).

---

[36] The change is to the title to r 31.4.

3. Application to prohibit cross-examination under section 36

9.94   Section 36 allows the prosecution to apply to the court that it should direct that the defendant should not be allowed to cross-examine a witness to whom sections 34 and 35 do not apply where it will improve the quality of the evidence and would not be contrary to the interests of justice.

9.95   Such an application should be sent to the court and to the parties (rule 31.4(1)), stating why, in his opinion, the requirements of section 36(2) are satisfied (rule 31.4(2)). On receipt by the court officer of this application, it shall be referred to the trial judge if the trial has started or to a judge who has been or may be designated to conduct the trial if it has not started (rule 1.4(3)).

9.96   If the application is received by the parties more than fourteen days before the trial, they then have fourteen days to respond to it (rule 31.4(4) and rule 31.4(6)(a)) and state the reasons for any opposition to the application (rule 31.4(5)). If the trial has started the time limit for a response will be set by the judge (rule 31.4(6)(b)), and if the trial is less than fourteen days away, the response must be provided before the trial starts (rule 31.4(6)(c)).

9.97   If the application is made before trial and is not contested, the court can determine the application on the papers (rule 31.4(7)(a)), and then notify the parties of its decision and reasons for it (rule 31.4(11)). If it is contested, the court should arrange a hearing (rule 31.4(7)(b)) and notify the parties of its listing (rule 31.4(9)). Such parties are thereafter entitled to attend and be heard at the hearing (rule 31.4(10)).

9.98   If the application is made after the trial has started, it may be made orally and the judge can make such directions as are necessary to deal with it (rule 31.4(8)). The prosecution will, however, have to justify why the application could not have been made earlier and provide the court with the reasons why the requirements of section 36(2) are satisfied (rule 31.4(2) and rule 31.4(12)).

10

INTERNATIONAL COOPERATION

A. INTRODUCTION

Increasingly, member states of the European Economic Authority are engaging in greater 10.01
cooperation in the prosecution of crime throughout Europe. Part 32 of the Rules provides a framework upon which the provisions of the Crime (International Co-operation)
Act 2003 can function.

B. NOTICE TO ACCOMPANY PROCESS

Under section 3(4)(b) of the Crime (International Co-operation) Act 2003 (concerning 10.02
general requirements for service of process) a notice must accompany any process served
outside the United Kingdom. By virtue of rule 32.1(6), process has the meaning given
by section 51(3) of the 2003 Act and thus means any summons or order issued by the
court. The requisite accompanying notice must state that the person required by the
process to appear as a party or attend as a witness, can obtain information about his
rights in connection therewith from the relevant authority. In addition it must give the
name and address of the 'relevant authority', along with the telephone and fax numbers
and email address of the relevant authority. It must also contain the name, telephone and
fax numbers and email address of a person at the relevant authority who can provide the
person who is the subject of the process with the necessary information about his rights
(r.32.1(1), (2), and (4)).

The relevant authority is identified by reference to rule 32.1(3). If the process is served 10.03
at the request of the prosecuting authority, then the relevant authority is the prosecuting
authority. If the process is served at the request of the defendant or the prosecutor in
the case of a private prosecution, the relevant authority is the court by which the process
is served.

With any process served outside the United Kingdom, translations of the information 10.04
required under this rule and any translation required under section 3(3)(b) of the 2003
Act must be sent by the justices' clerk or Crown Court officer (rule 32.1(5)).

10.05   By virtue of rule 32.2, a statement in a certificate given by or on behalf of the Secretary of State to the effect that process has been served on any person under section 4(1) of 2003 Act (concerning service of process otherwise than by post), including any description of the manner in which service was effected and the date on which process was served, is admissible as evidence of any those facts.

10.06   If a request is made for assistance under section 7 of the 2003 Act by a justice of the peace or a judge exercising the jurisdiction of the Crown Court, and that request is sent in accordance with section 8(1) of the 2003 Act, the justices' clerk or the Crown Court officer must send a copy of the letter of request to the Secretary of State as soon as practicable after the request has been made (rule 32.3).

C. HEARINGS

10.07   A court which is nominated to receive under section 15(1) of the 2003 Act may, by virtue of rule 32.4, determine who may appear or take part in the proceedings under Schedule 1 to the 2003 Act before the court and may decide whether a party to the proceedings is entitled to be legally represented. In addition it may direct that the public be excluded from those proceedings if it thinks it necessary to do so in the interests of justice.

10.08   Where a court is nominated under section 15(1) of the 2003 Act, the justices' clerk or Crown Court officer is required to enter certain details about the proceedings in the overseas record. The overseas records of a magistrates' court becomes part of the register of the court and may not be inspected by any person without the authorization of the Secretary of State or the leave of the court. The matters which must be entered concern details of the request in respect of which the notice under section 15(1) of the 2003 Act was given, the date on which, and place at which, the proceedings under Schedule 1 to the 2003 Act in respect of that request took place, the name of any witness who gave evidence at the proceedings in question, the name of any person who took part in the proceedings as a legal representative or an interpreter, whether a witness was required to give evidence on oath or (by virtue of section 5 of the Oaths Act 1978) after making a solemn affirmation, and whether the opportunity to cross-examine any witness was refused (rule 32.5).

10.09   A court may be nominated under section 30(3) or section 31(4) of the 2003 Act to hear witnesses in the United Kingdom through television links or to hear witnesses in the United Kingdom by telephone respectively. If it is so nominated then, by virtue of rule 32.6(2), where it appears to the justices' clerk or the Crown Court officer that the witness to be heard in the proceedings is likely to give evidence in a language other than English, he shall make arrangements for an interpreter to be present at the proceedings to translate what is said into English. Under rule 32.6(3), where it appears to the justices' clerk or the Crown Court officer that the witness to be heard in the relevant proceedings is likely to give evidence in a language other than that in which the proceedings of the court referred to as the external court (see sections 30(1) and 31(1) of the 2003 Act) will be conducted, he shall make arrangements for an interpreter to be present at the relevant proceedings to translate what is said into the language in which the proceedings of the external court will be conducted. If rules 32.6(2) cannot be complied with then the proceedings should be adjourned until an interpreter can attend (rule 32.6(4)).

In keeping with other provisions which pay due respect to the Welsh language, rule 32.6(2) and (4) do not apply when the court which hears the evidence is in Wales and understands Welsh.

If a court deals with evidence via a television under section 30(3) of the 2003 Act, the justices' clerk or Crown Court officer is required to enter a number of details in the overseas record. Those matters are the details of the request in respect of which the notice under section 30(3) of the 2003 Act was given, the date on which, and place at which, the proceedings under Part 1 of Schedule 2 to that Act in respect of that request took place, the technical conditions (including the type of equipment used) under which the proceedings took place, the name of the witness who gave evidence, the name of any person who took part in the proceedings as a legal representative or an interpreter and the language in which the evidence was given (rule 32.7(2)). As soon as practicable after the proceedings have taken place, the justices' clerk or Crown Court officer must send to the external authority that made the request a copy of an extract of the overseas record which relates to the proceedings that the request was concerned with (rule 32.7(3)).

10.10

If a court deals with evidence via telephone under section 31(4) of the 2003 Act, the justices' clerk or Crown Court officer is required to enter similar details in the overseas record to those required under rule 32.7(2) when the evidence is given over a television link. In this case the matters required to be entered are details of the request in respect of which the notice under section 31(4) of the 2003 Act was given, the date, time and place at which the proceedings under Part 2 of Schedule 2 to the 2003 Act took place, the name of the witness who gave evidence, the name of any interpreter who acted at the proceedings, and the language in which the evidence was given.

10.11

11

HEARSAY AND EXPERT EVIDENCE

A. INTRODUCTION

Parts 33 and 34 of the Rules address two areas in which evidence other than that of first-hand observations from personal knowledge may be permitted in criminal proceedings, namely expert opinion evidence and hearsay evidence. As with other areas in which the Rules address evidence, their purpose is not to identify tests for admissibility. Rather, they address the procedure by which applications to adduce such evidence may be made and regulated. In the case of hearsay this is purely a matter of procedure. In the case of expert evidence, it is more a matter of case management, and the court is expected to be far more interventionist than in the regulation of other types of evidence.   11.01

B. EXPERT EVIDENCE

The Rules themselves provide only a limited definition of what is meant by expert evidence, namely that contained in rule 33.1:   11.02

A reference to an 'expert' in this Part is a reference to a person who is required to give or prepare expert evidence for the purpose of criminal proceedings, including evidence required to determine fitness to plead or for the purpose of sentencing.

The approach adopted to the admissibility of expert evidence[1] and its definition remains that identified in the decision of the Court of Appeal in *R v Turner*.[2] Lawton LJ said:[3]   11.03

---

[1] More detailed analysis of the scope and admissibility of expert evidence than is appropriate here is to be found in *Blackstone's Criminal Practice 2011*, para F10.5.

[2] (1974) 60 Cr App R 80.

[3] Ibid, at 83.

The foundation of these rules [relating to opinion evidence] was laid by Lord Mansfield in Folkes v Chadd (1782) 3 Douglas KB 157 and was well laid. 'The opinion of scientific men upon unproven facts', he said, 'may be given by men of science within their own science'. An expert's opinion is admissible to furnish the Court with scientific information which is likely to be outside the experience and knowledge of a judge or jury. If on the proven facts a judge or jury can form their own conclusions without help, then the opinion of an expert is unnecessary. In such a case, if it is given dressed up in scientific jargon, it may make judgment more difficult. The fact that an expert witness has impressive scientific qualifications does not by that fact alone make his opinion on matters of human nature and behaviour within the limits of normality any more helpful than that of the jurors themselves; but there is a danger that they may think it does.

11.04   As the methods used in both the commission and detection of crime become ever more sophisticated, the scope for expert evidence in criminal proceedings has grown exponentially. This growth has the potential to impact significantly on the length and complexity of criminal proceedings. It is clear that the need for management of such evidence has been recognized by those who drafted the rules now contained in Part 33, which directly address the content of expert evidence and its presentation.

11.05   When the 2005 Rules came into force, no rules in relation to expert evidence were included in Part 33, which was left blank to allow for later insertion. The rules at that stage only addressed the disclosure of expert evidence, contained in Part 24 of the 2005 Rules, which simply constituted an amalgamation and restatement of the previous Rules.[4]

11.06   The rules now contained in Part 33 of the 2010 Rules came into effect on 5 October 2009.[5] At the same time that the new Part 33 was inserted, the old Part 24 of the Rules was omitted, with the result that Part 33 is now the only regulation of expert evidence to be found in the Rules.

1. The background to the Part 33 rules

11.07   To better understand what the rules now included in Part 33 are seeking to achieve it is of assistance to consider, albeit briefly, a number of reviews of various aspects of the use of expert witnesses that were available to the Rules Committee when Part 33 was drafted.

11.08   In his Review of the Criminal Courts of England and Wales, Lord Justice Auld made a series of recommendations in this regard, which, given his membership of the Criminal Procedure Rules Committee, are clearly relevant to the understanding of the rules. The key recommendations included the following:

262. Consideration should be given to concentrating in one self-governing professional body within England and Wales the role of setting, or overseeing the setting, of standards and of conduct for forensic scientists of all disciplines, the maintenance of a register of accreditation for them and the regulation of their compliance with its conditions of accreditation.

. . .

---

[4] The Magistrates' Courts (Advance Notice of Expert Evidence) Rules 1997 and the Crown Court (Advance Notice of Expert Evidence) Rules 1987.

[5] Inserted by the Criminal Procedure (Amendment) Rules 2009, SI 2009/2087, which represented an amendment of an earlier version inserted by Criminal Procedure (Amendment No 2) Rules 2006, SI 2006/2636.

264. The new Criminal Procedure Rules that I recommend should contain a rule in the same or similar terms to that in Part 35.3 of the Civil Procedure Rules that an expert witness's overriding duty is to the court.

. . .

266. Criminal courts' power to control the admission of experts' evidence should be formalised in the new Criminal Procedure Rules that I have recommended, and put on a similar footing to that for the Civil Courts as set out in the Civil Procedure Rules, Part 35, 1 and 4, namely by imposing upon them a duty, and declaring their power, to restrict expert evidence to that which is reasonably required to resolve any issue of importance in the proceedings.

267. Judges and magistrates should rigorously apply the test governing that power and duty, and the Court of Appeal should support them.

. . .

270. Where there is no issue, or one in which the parties are content that the matter should be resolved by a single expert, they should be encouraged to deal with it in that way, agreeing his report or a summary of it as part of the evidence in the case.

271. The prosecution and defence should normally arrange for their experts to discuss and jointly to identify at the earliest possible stage before the trial those issues on which they agree and those on which they do not agree, and to prepare a joint statement for use in evidence indicating the measure of their agreement and a summary of the reasons for their disagreement.

272. Failing such arrangement, the court should have power to direct such a discussion and identification of issues and preparation of a joint statement for use in evidence and to make any consequential directions as may be appropriate in each case.

Since Lord Justice Auld's Review, the House of Commons Science and Technology   11.09
Committee has produced a report, 'Forensic Science on Trial',[6] which echoed many of the Auld recommendations and called for the Criminal Procedure Rules Committee to address this area of evidence. This included the following recommendation for pre-trial meetings of experts:[7]

Pre-trial meetings to identify areas of agreement and disagreement between experts must be held as a matter of routine; it is a false economy not to allow enough time for full discussion at this stage. We trust that the Criminal Case Management Framework and Criminal Procedure Rules 2005 will help to ensure that this happens in the future . . . Effective use of pre-trial meetings should reduce the potential for juries to become confused by unnecessary adversarial questioning. It should also avert the collapse of trials due to a known but previously undisclosed piece of evidence being put forward mid-trial that causes the expert on the other side to change their view.

2. The status and content of expert report

The Auld Report's recommendation that the Rules should include 'a rule in the same or   11.10
similar terms to that in Part 35.3 of the Civil Procedure Rules that an expert witness's overriding duty is to the court' has been brought into effect by rule 33.2. This makes explicit the logical interpretation of rule 1.2(2) which requires 'anyone involved in any way with a criminal case' to abide by, and give effect to, the overriding objective of the rules. The expert

---

[6] Published on 29 March 2005.
[7] At para 152 of chapter 7 of their Report.

is therefore bound to help the just resolution of criminal cases by 'giving objective, unbiased opinion on matters within his expertise'. The expert's report is required to include a declaration that he understands and has applied this obligation (rule 33.3(i)).

11.11   This has important consequences. It means that the expert's overriding duty is to the court, rather than to the party instructing him (indeed rule 33.2(2) makes that explicit). It, further, underlines the obligation of an expert to provide an opinion adverse to his client if that is his opinion. This is illustrated in the case of *Puaca*.[8] In that case there were rival possible interpretations of a particular injury identified during post-mortem examination. The Court of Appeal was critical of the first pathologist, acting for the police, who failed to identify the rival interpretation of the injury, leaving it instead for a pathologist acting on behalf of the accused. In giving the judgment of the Court, Hooper LJ[9] quoted with approval the statement of principle of Cresswell J in *National Justice Compania Naviera SA v Prudential Assurance Co Ltd*:[10]

An expert witness should state the facts or assumptions on which his opinion is based. He should not omit to consider material facts which could detract from his concluded opinion.

11.12   Further, it obliges an expert to inform the other parties to the criminal proceedings if he changes his opinion (see rule 33.2(3)). As is discussed below, pre-trial meetings between experts are actively encouraged by the Rules, and if following such a meeting an expert comes to agree with a rival opinion rather than his own original report, he is obliged to say so, rather than just discretely withdrawing from the field. That said, this approach to expert evidence had already been identified as appropriate by the Court of Appeal in *Harris and others*.[11]

11.13   The contents of an expert's report are identified in rule 33.3. This should be read in conjunction with rule 27.2, which identifies that which all witness statements must contain. In other words, the expert report must include the normal declaration as to truth, whether at the beginning of the report, or in a statement exhibiting the report. In summary, the contents required from an expert's report relate to:

(a) his knowledge and the basis for his opinions (rule 33.3(a)–(d)). The expert is required to set out his qualifications, what he has read and taken into account, and make clear the distinction between that which is within his own knowledge, whether through tests or otherwise, and that which is reliant on others;

(b) his workings (rule 33.3(e)). The expert is required to set out what examinations and other work have taken place, what the results of those were, and what findings were reached;

(c) his opinion (rule 33.3(f)–(h)). If there is a range of opinion on an issue, the expert must identify the range and justify where his opinion falls, and where that opinion is subject to qualification, that must also be made clear. He must also provide a summary of his conclusions.

11.14   In effect, many of the matters now included in this list were included in the list of matters that a party relying on an expert was required to disclose under rule 24.1 of the 2005 Rules.

---

[8] [2006] Crim LR 341.
[9] Ibid, at para 32.
[10] [1993] 2 Lloyd's Rep 68.
[11] [2006] 1 Cr App R 5.

C. SERVICE OF EXPERT EVIDENCE

By section 81 of the PACE 1984, rules may require any party to proceedings before the **11.15** court to disclose to the other parties any expert evidence which he proposes to adduce. Part 33 now contains the rules that now apply under this power.

The Rules provide that, as soon as is practicable, any party intending to rely on expert **11.16** evidence (whether of fact or opinion) must, unless he has already done so, provide the other parties and the court with a written statement of any finding or opinion which he proposes to adduce by way of such evidence. On request, he must also supply a copy of the record of any 'observation, test, calculation or other procedure' on which the finding or opinion is based or, if it is more practicable, he must allow reasonable opportunity to examine such a record (rule 33.4(1)). The records to which this refers will in any event have been identified in the expert's report (in compliance with rule 33.3(e)). Such records and other evidence of examinations will be admissible pursuant to section 127 of the CJA 2003 and no notice under Part 34 of the Rules is required before such evidence may be adduced (see rule 34.2(1)).

This requirement largely mirrors the previous requirements as to disclosure of expert **11.17** evidence in rule 24.1 of the 2005 Rules, which itself sought to give effect to the observations of the Court of Appeal in *Ward*.[12] However, the definition of expert evidence in rule 33.1 (set out above) is wider than had previously been found in the 2005 Rules. Under rule 24.1 of the 2005 Rules, the requirements for disclosure of expert evidence did not apply to expert evidence that was to be adduced in relation to sentence. This clearly envisaged psychiatric or psychological expert opinion served, for example, to address the issue of the risk to members of the public of serious harm occasioned by the commission of further specified offences by the accused which the court is required to assess by the application of sections 225 and 226 of the CJA 2003. It is now clear that the Rules apply to expert evidence obtained in relation to sentence in the same way as to all other expert evidence.

Another significant change to the rules relating to the disclosure of expert evidence is **11.18** the omission from Part 33 of the 2010 Rules of any provision akin to rule 24.2 of the 2005 Rules. That provision had permitted a party to withhold evidence from the other parties if there was a risk that it might lead to the intimidation of the witness.

Once a report has been served, its author must be informed of this fact 'at once' **11.19** (rule 33.5).

1. Timetable

Unlike the position in relation to other types of evidence, including hearsay evidence, **11.20** which is addressed below, the Rules do not impose hard and fast deadlines for the service of expert evidence. In terms of timetable, rule 33.4(1) requires a party relying on expert evidence to serve it 'as soon as is practicable'. Where the expert evidence is to be relied on in support of another application, for example a submission that the accused is unfit to plead or an application to exclude the police interview of the accused because of his

---

[12] [1993] 96 Cr App R 1.

mental state, the evidence should be served at the same time as that application. Reference here to 'application' would logically also apply to a skeleton argument.

11.21   Although there is no specific deadline in the Rules, rule 33.9 affords the court the power to extend time limits for compliance with these Rules, even after their expiry. This is the standard form of words for the court's power to vary rule requirements which makes sense where deadlines are laid down but which appears of less immediate value in the present context. However, it makes more sense when it is read in conjunction with the court's case management powers (rule 3.5). The court has the power to impose, on a case-by-case basis, a deadline for the service of expert evidence as part of its wider management of the case. Rule 33.9 permits a party to seek, and the court to permit, an extension to such a deadline even after its expiry.

2. Breaches of the Rules

11.22   The flexibility of the timetable, and the court's power to vary such timetable as has been imposed in a particular case, means that failure to abide with a timetable for the service of expert evidence is unlikely to be significant. However, the Rules do envisage that failure to follow the rules in Part 33 can have consequences. Because the failures envisaged do not relate to the timetable, on this analysis, they must relate to a failure of an expert to comply with the requirements as to the content of his report (rule 33.3) and/or its disclosure (rule 33.4).

11.23   Failure to comply with the Rules means that the expert evidence will be admissible at trial only with leave of the court, or agreement of other parties (rule 33.4(2)). Again, the court retains the power to allow the evidence to be admitted even if details required by the Rules have been omitted (rule 33.9(1)(b)).

D. THE COURT'S ROLE IN RELATION TO EXPERT EVIDENCE

11.24   Under rule 3.2 it is the duty of the court to identify the real issues in a criminal trial, and that evidence is presented 'in the shortest and clearest way'. It is obvious that expert evidence, which by its nature can be both voluminous and complex, is a ripe area for the court to seek to comply with this duty by rigorous case management.

11.25   Reviews relating to expert evidence in criminal proceedings, such as the Auld Report quoted above, advocated the need for a meeting of rival experts, that is those instructed for the prosecution and defence 'to identify at the earliest possible stage before the trial those issues on which they agree and those on which they do not agree, and to prepare a joint statement for use in evidence indicating the measure of their agreement and a summary of the reasons for their disagreement'. Part 33 of the Rules gives effect to that recommendation.

11.26   Once an expert report has been served, the court may direct a meeting of experts to discuss the issues and to prepare a statement of those matters on which they do, and do not agree (rule 33.6(2)). Without the leave of the court it is only this statement that may be referred to in the proceedings (rule 33.6(3)); doubtless this is to encourage frank discussion at such a meeting of experts. The court is granted a sanction against the failure of the experts and the parties instructing them to comply with the requirement that a meeting be held and a statement as to the issues prepared. This sanction (pursuant to rule 33.6(4)) is that the court may prevent a party in default from relying on the expert in question.

The further step which the court may take to refine the issues and shorten the ambit of the expert evidence is to reduce the number of experts. Where several defendants give notice that they will seek to rely on expert opinion going to the same issue, the court may direct that only one expert should be instructed on their joint behalf (rule 33.7(1)).   11.27

Whether this is an appropriate step will, no doubt, depend on the nature of the case. If, for example, several defendants are running a 'cut-throat' defence blaming each other for the offence, it may be that the experts, whilst on the same issue, will be speaking from different positions. If such a single joint expert is instructed, each co-defendant can provide the expert with separate instructions (rule 33.8(1)), though these instructions must be sent not only to the expert but also to the co-defendants (rule 33.8(2)).   11.28

The court's role is not limited to deciding that a joint expert should be instructed. In addition, the court may do the following: 11.29

(a) where the defendants cannot agree as to who that expert should be, the court can make the choice for them, from a list they have either prepared or considered, or make directions as to how they are to reach agreement (rule 33.7(2));

(b) the court may give directions as to the examinations and tests that should be carried out (rule 33.7(3)(b));

(c) ordinarily, the co-defendants will be jointly and severally liable for the expert's fees and expenses (rule 33.8(5)). However, the court can give directions about the payment of the fees and expenses (rule 33.8(3)(a)) and can limit the amount that may be paid in this regard (rule 33.8(4)).

E. HEARSAY EVIDENCE

Chapter 2 of Part 11 of the CJA 2003 brings about a 'wholesale reform of the rule against hearsay'.[13] The rule itself is stated in section 114(1), namely that 'a statement not made in oral evidence in the proceedings is admissible as evidence of any matters stated if, but only if' one of the conditions in that subsection is met.   11.30

This is not the appropriate place to consider the details of the various gateways to the admissibility of hearsay evidence set out in Chapter 2 of Part 11 of the CJA 2003, which came into force on the same day as the Rules, 5 April 2005.[14]   11.31

The Rules come into play, however, because of section 132 of the CJA 2003. In so far as is relevant, this states: 11.32

(1) Rules of court may make such provision as appears to the appropriate authority to be necessary or expedient for the purposes of this Chapter; and the appropriate authority is the authority entitled to make the rules.

(2) The rules may make provision about the procedure to be followed and other conditions to be fulfilled by a party proposing to tender a statement in evidence under any provision of this Chapter.

---

[13] Blackstone's Guide to the Criminal Justice Act 2003 (Taylor, Wasik, and Leng), Chapter 9, p 143.
[14] These are analyzed in detail at para F16.1 of *Blackstone's Criminal Practice 2011*.

(3) The rules may require a party proposing to tender the evidence to serve on each party to the proceedings such notice, and such particulars of or relating to the evidence, as may be prescribed.

(4) The rules may provide that the evidence is to be treated as admissible by agreement of the parties if—

(a) a notice has been served in accordance with provision made under subsection (3), and

(b) no counter-notice in the prescribed form objecting to the admission of the evidence has been served by a party.

(5) If a party proposing to tender evidence fails to comply with a prescribed requirement applicable to it—

(a) the evidence is not admissible except with the court's leave;

(b) where leave is given the court or jury may draw such inferences from the failure as appear proper;

(c) the failure may be taken into account by the court in considering the exercise of its powers with respect to costs.

(6) In considering whether or how to exercise any of its powers under subsection (5) the court shall have regard to whether there is any justification for the failure to comply with the requirement.

(7) A person shall not be convicted of an offence solely on an inference drawn under subsection (5)(b).

(8) Rules under this section may—

(a) limit the application of any provision of the rules to prescribed circumstances;

(b) subject any provision of the rules to prescribed exceptions;

(c) make different provision for different cases or circumstances.

(9) Nothing in this section prejudices the generality of any enactment conferring power to make rules of court; and no particular provision of this section prejudices any general provision of it.

11.33 What the Rules seek to achieve is to give effect to section 132(2)–(4), above, in both the magistrates' court and the Crown Court (rule 34.1), by:

(a) setting out the procedure to be followed and the conditions to be fulfilled by a party to proceedings seeking to adduce evidence under Chapter 2, including the notices that have to be given;

(b) allowing that evidence to be admitted where there is no challenge to that notice (section 132(4)).

11.34 Section 132(5) envisages different application of the Rules in different situations. As originally drafted, the 2005 Rules applied equally to all the gateways to admissibility in the case of all parties, without limitations, variation, or differentiation according to different situations. Effect has now been given to section 132(5) by rule 34.2(1); this makes clear that the Rules only apply to certain forms of hearsay.

11.35 As a result, the rules in Part 34 apply to:

(a) section 114(1)(d) (evidence admissible in the interests of justice);

(b) section 116 (evidence where a witness is unavailable);

(c) section 121 (multiple hearsay).

11.36 Similarly, the rules do not apply to:

(a) section 117 (business and other documents);

(b) section 118 (preservation of certain common law categories of admissibility);

(c) section 119 (inconsistent statements);

(d) section 120 (other previous statements of a witness); or

(e) section 127 (expert evidence: preparatory work).

F. THE RULES FOR HEARSAY APPLICATIONS

The Rules, which apply equally to the Crown Court and magistrates' court (rule 4.1(a))   11.37
seek:

(a) to require that notice be served by a party seeking to adduce hearsay evidence before
they are allowed to adduce it (rule 34.2);

(b) to set out the timetable for the giving of notice or responding to it (rule 34.3);

(c) to set out the form of these documents.

1. Applications

As was the case with bad character, which is discussed in the next chapter, under the   11.38
2005 Rules an application to adduce hearsay evidence had to be made in writing within
fourteen days of committal, notice of transfer, or the service of the papers where the
defendant has been sent under section 51. The 2010 Rules no longer link the timing of
an application to the time when the defendant arrives in the Crown Court. That link
inevitably resulted in potentially unnecessary precautionary applications. Under the
2010 Rules, the prosecution is now not required to make a hearsay application until
after the accused has pleaded not guilty (rule 34.2(3)).

Similarly, the defence were required to make their application within fourteen days   11.39
of the purported completion of primary disclosure by the prosecution. This was a rather
arbitrary deadline, as there is no reason to imagine that defence hearsay applications
will be predicated by prosecution disclosure, as opposed to served prosecution evidence
or material already in the defendant's position. Under the 2010 Rules the defence
are simply required to make their application 'as soon as reasonably practicable' (rule
34.2(4)).

Again, as is the case with bad character applications under the new scheme, the 2010   11.40
Rules in relation to hearsay are drafted in a non-partisan fashion, in that they are designed
to be used in the same way by both the prosecution and the defence. This is a significant
alteration from the 2005 Rules, which identified the procedure and timetable for prosecution applications in a separate paragraph to those on behalf of a defendant and his
co-defendants.

The parties on whom notice of an application ought normally to be served may waive   11.41
service by informing the other parties and the court of that waiver (rule 34.2(5)).

2. Objection to hearsay

Under the 2005 Rules, it was envisaged that a party objecting to reliance on hearsay   11.42
evidence was only required to serve a notice to that effect in response to an application to
adduce that evidence. Under the 2010 Rules this is no longer the case, as is demonstrated

by rule 34.3(1) which states: 'This rule applies where a party objects to the introduction of hearsay evidence'; and by the timetable that rule 34.3 then sets out for when such objection is to be taken.

11.43   Under rule 34.3(2), a party opposing the introduction of hearsay evidence should apply to the court to exclude that evidence, by serving notice on the court and other parties within fourteen days of:

(a) receiving a notice served pursuant to rule 34.2 to adduce hearsay (rule 34.3(2)(c)(i));
(b) service of the evidence to which objection is taken (rule 34.3(2)(c)(ii));
(c) the defendant pleading not guilty (rule 34.3(2)(c)(iii)).

As will be appreciated, the order of these three events may well vary, for example the prosecution may serve its case before it serves a notice to adduce hearsay (especially as that notice is not required until after arraignment). This is catered for in the Rules, which indicate that the fourteen days runs from the 'latest' of the three events.

11.44   Where objection is taken, the court may determine the matter with or without a hearing (rule 34.3(3)(a)). It would appear from rule 34.3(3)(b) that the nature of the response to an application or the nature of the objection will determine whether a hearing is necessary.

11.45   Where no objection is received, the court may treat the evidence as admitted by agreement (rule 34.4). This accords with the route to admissibility of hearsay that is identified in CJA 2003, section 114(1)(c), which states that 'in criminal proceedings a statement not made in oral evidence in the proceedings is admissible as evidence of any matter stated if . . . (c) all parties to the proceedings agree to it being admissible. . .'. It also accords with section 132(4) of the CJA 2003, which states:

The rules may provide that the evidence is to be treated as admissible by agreement of the parties if—
(a) A notice has been served in accordance with provision made under subsection (3), and
(b) no counter-notice in the prescribed form objecting to the admission of the evidence has been served by a party.

11.46 However, it underlines the importance of a party objecting to hearsay evidence putting in a notice to say so, rather than leaving the matter until the case is listed for trial, or the evidence is about to be adduced.

3. Breach of the Rules

11.47 That importance is further underlined, in the clearest of terms, by section 132(5). This creates a number of sanctions for non-compliance with the Rules. These sanctions:

(a) require that the leave of the court is required to adduce evidence where the notice is late;
(b) allow the court or jury to draw such inferences, where leave is given for them to do so, with regard to the justifications advanced for the failure to comply with the Rules, from that failure as appear proper; although this cannot form the sole basis for a conviction;
(c) punish the failure in the apportionment of costs.

At the same time, however, it is possible for the court, on an application to do so or of   11.48
its own initiative, and the parties, in written form, to dispense with exact compliance
with the Rules, by:

(a) the court dispensing with the notice requirement entirely, or allowing it to be
    effected in additional ways. It may also shorten or extend the timetable, even after
    the prescribed periods have expired (rule 34.5(1));
(b) the party on whom the necessary notice needs to be served can waive that entitle-
    ment, by informing the court and the other parties of that waiver (rule 34.2(5)).

12

EVIDENCE OF BAD CHARACTER AND RELATING TO A COMPLAINANT'S SEXUAL BEHAVIOUR

A. INTRODUCTION

Parts 35 and 36 of the Rules address the procedural mechanisms by which evidence of   12.01
previous behaviour may be adduced in criminal proceedings. Part 35 deals with evidence
of previous misconduct either by a witness or other third party on the one hand or by
the defendant on the other. Part 36 deals with one specific category of witnesses, namely
complainants of sexual offences, and one specific category of previous misconduct,
namely previous sexual behaviour.

Both Parts of the Rules are concerned not with the tests to be applied to the granting   12.02
of an application to adduce such evidence, which are regulated by the Criminal Justice
Act 2003 (CJA 2003) in relation to bad character and the Youth Justice and Criminal
Evidence Act 1999 (YJCEA 1999) in relation to sexual behaviour, but with the mechanics
of the applications themselves, in terms of the notification of other parties and the time
in the course of proceedings when such an application should be made.

B. BAD CHARACTER EVIDENCE

Chapter 1 of Part 11 of the CJA 2003 achieved a thorough overhaul of the mechanism   12.03
of admissibility for evidence of bad character of defendants and of others. As with the
procedure relating to hearsay, another area in which Part 11 of the CJA 2003 wrought

significant change to the previous rules of admissibility, this is not the place for a detailed critique of the relevant provisions of the CJA 2003.[1]

12.04   In summary, however:

(a) The provisions relate to evidence of a person's bad character, which is defined by section 98 as 'evidence of, or of a disposition towards, misconduct on his part, other than evidence which (a) has to do with the alleged facts of the offence with which the defendant is charged, and (b) is evidence of misconduct in connection with the investigation or prosecution of that offence'. Section 112 of the CJA 2003 defines 'misconduct' as the commission of an offence or other reprehensible behaviour.

(b) CJA 2003, section 100, governs the admissibility of the bad character of a 'person other than the defendant'.

(c) Section 101 governs the admissibility of the defendant's bad character.

12.05   The purpose which the Rules seek to achieve is set out in CJA 2003, section 111. In so far as is relevant, this states:

(1) Rules of court may make such provision as appears to the appropriate authority to be necessary or expedient for the purposes of this Act; and the appropriate authority is the authority entitled to make the rules.

(2) The rules may, and, where the party in question is the prosecution, must, contain provision requiring a party who—
    (a) proposes to adduce evidence of a defendant's bad character, or
    (b) proposes to cross-examine a witness with a view to eliciting such evidence, to serve on the defendant such notice, and such particulars of or relating to the evidence, as may be prescribed.

(3) The rules may provide that the court or the defendant may, in such circumstances as may be prescribed, dispense with a requirement imposed by virtue of subsection (2).

(4) In considering the exercise of its powers with respect to costs, the court may take into account any failure by a party to comply with a requirement imposed by virtue of subsection (2) and not dispensed with by virtue of subsection (3).

(5) The rules may—
    (a) limit the application of any provision of the rules to prescribed circumstances;
    (b) subject any provision of the rules to prescribed exceptions;
    (c) make different provision for different cases or circumstances.

(6) Nothing in this section prejudices the generality of any enactment conferring power to make rules of court; and no particular provision of this section prejudices any general provision of it.

12.06   What the Rules seek to achieve is to give effect to section 111(2)–(3), above, in both the magistrates' court and the Crown Court (rule 35.1), by:

(a) setting out the procedure to be followed and the conditions to be fulfilled by a party to proceedings seeking to adduce evidence under Chapter 1, including the notices that have to be given;

(b) allowing the notice requirement to be dispensed with in certain circumstances.

---

[1] These provisions are considered at para F.12.1 of *Blackstone's Criminal Practice 2011*.

C. THE RULES

The Rules seek: 12.07

(a) to enunciate the requirement that notice must be served by a party seeking to adduce evidence of bad character before they are allowed to adduce it;
(b) to set out the timetable for the giving of notice or responding to it;
(c) to set out the form of these documents and the method of service.

The 2010 Rules are drafted in a non-partisan fashion, in that they are designed to be 12.08 used in the same way by both the prosecution and the defence. This is a significant alteration from the 2005 Rules, which identified the procedure and timetable for prosecution applications in a separate paragraph to those on behalf of a defendant and his co-defendants. The key difference between the procedure that the Rules impose on the prosecution and on the defence is the catalyst that initiates the procedure in each case, this is discussed at paragraph 12.14.

1. The content of the notice

The essential starting point is that the party wishing to adduce bad character evidence 12.09 has to give notice of that intention. To an extent the content of the application, naturally, varies according to whether it is an application to adduce the bad character of the defendant or another. Applications relating to non-defendants are covered by rule 35.3, and applications relating to defendants by rule 35.4. In fact in many respects the procedure is common to both types of application. Standard form notices are identified in the Practice Direction.

Rule 35.2(2) makes clear that the application must include the following: 12.10

(a) the facts of the misconduct relied on;
(b) an explanation of how those facts are to be proved; and
(c) an explanation of why the bad character is admissible.

As to the content of the notice, guidance has been given by the Court of Appeal in *R v* 12.11 *Hanson, Pickstone and Gilmore*,[2] where Rose LJ said:[3]

In cases of the kind we are considering, it is the Crown which begins the process of applying to adduce evidence of bad character. It must specify the relevant gateways. The form of application (BC2), prescribed by Rule 23E, inserted into the Crown Court Rules 1982 by Statutory Instrument 2004 No 2991 (L18) requires that the Crown set out 'a description of the bad character evidence and how it is to be adduced or elicited in the proceedings including the names of any relevant witnesses'. Form BC 3, similarly prescribed for the use of the defence, calls for particulars of why it is contended that the evidence ought not to be admitted. It follows from what we have already said that, in a conviction case the Crown needs to decide, at the time of giving notice of the application, whether it proposes to rely simply upon the fact of conviction or also upon the circumstances of it. The former may be enough when the circumstances of the conviction are sufficiently apparent from its description, to justify a finding that it can establish propensity, either to commit

---

[2] [2005] EWCA Crim 824.
[3] Ibid, at para 17.

an offence of the kind charged or to be untruthful and that the requirements of section 103(3) and 101(3) can, subject to any particular matter raised on behalf of the defendant, be satisfied. For example, a succession of convictions for dwelling-house burglary, where the same is now charged, may well call for no further evidence than proof of the fact of the convictions. But where, as will often be the case, the Crown needs and proposes to rely on the circumstances of the previous convictions, those circumstances and the manner in which they are to be proved must be set out in the application. There is a similar obligation of frankness upon the defendant, which will be reinforced by the general obligation contained in the new Criminal Procedure Rules to give active assistance to the court in its case management (see rule 3.3). Routine applications by defendants for disclosure of the circumstances of previous convictions are likely to be met by a requirement that the request be justified by identification of the reason why it is said that those circumstances may show the convictions to be inadmissible. We would expect the relevant circumstances of previous convictions generally to be capable of agreement, and that, subject to the trial judge's ruling as to admissibility, they will be put before the jury by way of admission. Even where the circumstances are genuinely in dispute, we would expect the minimum indisputable facts to be thus admitted. It will be very rare indeed for it to be necessary for the judge to hear evidence before ruling on admissibility under this Act.

12.12   Just as the notice must address the areas identified at rule 35.2(2), any response to the notice objecting to reliance on the bad character evidence is required to address those same criteria indicating in which respects the facts of the misconduct are disputed, and why the evidence is inadmissible. These matters are identified in relation to non-defendants' character at rule 35.3(4)(b) and in relation to defendants' character at rule 35.4(5)(c).

12.13   In most cases, where an application is made by the prosecution, the material that is to be used to prove the bad character will have been served as part of the evidence in the case. Proof of previous convictions will normally be achieved through a certificate of conviction. As the notes to rule 35.2 observe:

The fact that a person was convicted of an offence may be proved under—

(a) section 73 of the Police and Criminal Evidence Act 1984 (conviction in the United Kingdom or European Union); or

(b) section 7 of the Evidence Act 1851 (conviction outside the United Kingdom).

2. The timetable

12.14   It is in relation to timetable that the 2010 Rules concerning bad character have been most significantly revised from the 2005 scheme. In this respect the changes adopt the same approach as that introduced for hearsay evidence under the 2010 Rules, which were considered in the last chapter. Under both the old and new versions of the Rules, the procedure is predicated on proper disclosure of material that could form the basis for a bad character application having been provided. The clock does not begin to tick in relation to such an application until such disclosure. However, the 2010 Rules take a more realistic approach to disclosure as a trigger.

12.15   Under rule 35.2 of the 2005 Rules, the timing for applications on behalf of a defendant to adduce evidence of another's bad character was dictated by the time at which the prosecution complied with, or significantly purported to comply with, the obligation in CPIA 1996, section 3, to provide primary disclosure. The difficulty with that trigger was that there was no guarantee that primary disclosure would include such material. This was not necessarily due to a failure in the primary disclosure process, rather the need for disclosure in relation to a particular witness or other third party might not become clear until a defence statement was provided, for example. The 2010 Rules have adapted the procedure to recognize this, and now the timetable is dictated by the time at which the prosecution discloses the material on which the application is based.

A similarly realistic approach is also now taken in relation to the prosecution. Under the 2005 Rules, it had been required to make a bad character application against a defendant within fourteen days of the sending of the defendant to the Crown Court,[4] without knowing whether the defendant was to contest the case or not. This resulted in potentially unnecessary precautionary applications. Under the 2010 Rules, the prosecution is now not required to make a bad character application until after the defendant has pleaded not guilty.

12.16

In this context, the observations of the Vice President, Rose LJ, in *R v Bovell; R v Dowds*,[5] are germane to the disclosure required to allow the notice process to be effective. At paragraph 2, he said:

12.17

. . .it is necessary for all parties to have the appropriate information in relation to convictions and other evidence of bad character, whether in relation to the defendant or to some other person, in good time. That can only be achieved if the rules in relation to the giving of notice are complied with. It is worth mentioning that the basis of plea in relation to an earlier conviction may be relevant where it demonstrates differences from the way in which the prosecution initially put the case. In other words, a mere reference to the statement of a complainant in an earlier case may not provide the later court with the material needed to make a decision as to the admissibility of the earlier conviction.

Once the clock has started with the submission of an application, the stages of the process are the same in relation to each of the different forms of application, the time at which opposition to such a notice should be communicated, and the time at which the matter should be dealt with thereafter. The timetables for the different forms of application are as follows:

12.18

Party	Court	Time	Rule
Notice of an application to adduce evidence of a NON-DEFENDANT's bad character must be given:			
Either	Both Crown Court and magistrates' court	Prosecution: 'as soon reasonably practicable' Defence: 14 days after the prosecution have disclosed the material on which the application is based	35.3(3)
Opposition to such notice			
Both	Both	Within 14 days of receipt of the notice	35.3(4)
Notice of an application to adduce evidence of a DEFENDANT's bad character must be given:			
Prosecution	Both	14 days of the defendant pleading not guilty	35.4(3)
Co- defendant	Both	14 days after the prosecution have disclosed the material on which the application is based	35.4(4)
Opposition to such notice			
Defendant	Both	Within 14 days of receipt of the notice	35.4(5)

---

[4] 2005 Rules, r 35.4.
[5] [2005] EWCA Crim 1091.

3. The court's approach

12.19   The court is not required, or indeed expected, to act until after the conclusion of the above timetable. In other words, the court waits not only for the application but also any response to it. It should be noted that rule 35.3(5)(b) precludes a resolution of any application by the court until this fourteen days for the response of the other party has expired. Once that period has expired, the court may resolve the matter with or without a hearing (rule 35.3(5) for a non-defendant's character and rule 35.4(5) for a defendant's character). This underlines the importance of the timely submission of a written reply to an application, as the court is not even required to ensure the attendance of a responding party if they have had the opportunity to respond in writing (see rule 35.3(5)(b) and rule 35.4(5)(b) respectively).

12.20   Even if the application is adjudicated upon without a hearing, the court is required to announce the result of that adjudication in public (rule 35.5). This public pronouncement must include the court's reasons.

D. COMPLIANCE WITH THE RULES

12.21   The importance of compliance with these rules, and especially with these deadlines, is underlined in the clearest of terms by section 111(4). This is less severe in its terms than the comparable provision in the context of hearsay evidence, section 132(5). It does, however, allow the judge to punish the failure in the apportionment of costs. There are two issues that fall to be considered in this regard:

(a)   what power the court and/or parties have to vary or waive strict compliance with the procedure and/or timetable identified above; and

(b)   beyond the apportionment of costs, what the consequences of non-compliance actually are.

1. Variation and waiver of the Rules

12.22   It is possible for the court and the parties to dispense with exact compliance with the Rules.

12.23   The court's powers (set out in rule 35.6) are as follows:

(a)   it may shorten or extend the timetable, even after the prescribed periods have expired (rule 35.6(1)(a)). Its power to extent is predicated on an application being made by the relevant party for an extension (rule 35.6(2));

(b)   it may allow an application to be made other than in the form set out in the Practice Direction. This includes the making of an oral application without paper-based pre-shadowing (rule 35.6(1)(b));

(c)   it may permit an application to be made in relation to a defendant's bad character without notice (rule 35.6(1)(c)). Whilst the rules are silent on this point, it is reasonable to assume that this will relate to occasions when the prosecution (or a co-defendant) seeks to adduce evidence of character at the conclusion of a defendant's evidence in chief.

12.24   The position in relation to waiver is less clear-cut. On an application in relation to a non-defendant's bad character, the Rules do not permit any of the procedural steps to be waived by the other parties, as opposed to their being dispensed with by the court. The position is different in relation to applications to adduce the bad character of defendants. Under rule 35.4(7), the party on whom the necessary notice needs to be served can waive that entitlement, by informing the court and the other parties of that waiver.

2. Non-compliance

An important aspect of the exercise of the court's case management powers generally are the consequences of any failure of the parties to comply with time limits imposed by the Rules. Non-compliance with the rules relating to bad character applications has been the subject of consideration by the Court of Appeal on a number of occasions since the 2005 Rules came into force.   12.25

The proper approach to be adopted appears to be that identified in *Musone*,[6] where the Court of Appeal was concerned with whether the trial judge had correctly rejected the attempt by one accused to adduce evidence of the previous bad character of the other at a late stage—so late as to be in breach of the time limit for service of a notice of an application to adduce such evidence under rule 35.5.[7]   12.26

The court observed that the trial judge was entitled to exclude such evidence where he concluded that the applicant was deliberately manipulating the process so as to prevent the co-accused from dealing with the evidence properly. The court went on to make clear that it would be rare for a judge to exclude evidence of substantial probative value just because the time limits had not been complied with, but it would be proper to do so where such exclusion was the only means to ensure fairness.   12.27

The same approach was also adopted in cases such as *R (Robinson) v Sutton Coldfield Magistrates' Court*[8] and *Delay*,[9] namely that the court should consider whether the other parties have been prejudiced by the late notice of the application, and the reasons for the delay, before deciding whether evidence should be excluded as a consequence of the breach of the Rules.   12.28

E. RESTRICTIONS ON CROSS-EXAMINATION ON PREVIOUS SEXUAL HISTORY

Section 41 of the YJCEA 1999 prevents the defence adducing evidence of, or cross-examining the complainant about her previous sexual history without the court's leave. Such leave is only to be granted where: 12.29

(a) the evidence or questions relate to an issue in the case other than consent, or, where it is consent, it relates to behaviour at or about the time of the incident or which is probative because of its strong similarity to the incident (section 41(3));

---

[6] [2007] 1 WLR 2467.
[7] See also *Blackstone's Criminal Practice 2011*, para F12.33.
[8] [2006] 4 All ER 1029.
[9] (2006) 170 JP 581.

(b) the evidence or questions relate to evidence adduced by the prosecution or go no further than is necessary to rebut evidence adduced by the prosecution (section 41(5)); or

(c) refusal of leave would render any conviction unsafe (section 41(2)(b)).

12.30 The procedure for the making of an application for such leave is regulated by Part 36 of the Rules. These rules are of equal application to both the Crown Court and magistrates' court (rule 36.1).

1. Timing of an application

12.31 Under the 2005 Rules, application to adduce such evidence had to be made in writing within twenty-eight days of committal, notice of transfer, or the service of the papers where the defendant has been sent to the Crown Court under section 51. The 2010 Rules no longer link the timing of an application to the time when the defendant arrives in the Crown Court. Such a change was essential if the Rules were to apply not only to the Crown Court but also to the magistrates' court.

12.32 At first glance, the 2010 Rules in relation to the timing of applications to adduce evidence of previous sexual behaviour would appear to have been brought into line with the Rules in relation to bad character evidence, in that they now link the timing of such applications to disclosure by the prosecution. However, there is an interesting and illogical difference between the approach of the rules to the timing of applications under Parts 35 and 36 of the Rules. As was discussed at paragraph 12.14 above, the making of an application relating to other forms of 'bad character' on behalf of a defendant under Part 35 of the Rules was predicated on the prosecution providing disclosure of material relevant to the subject matter of that application. However, under rule 36.2(b), the deadline for applications relating to previous sexual behaviour refers not to disclosure of material relevant to that application in particular but to prosecution disclosure more generally, in the form of primary disclosure.

12.33 Whilst it is reasonable to assume that the prosecution would regard material relating to the previous sexual behaviour of a complainant as undermining its case or assisting that of the defence, and thus include it in primary disclosure, this would not necessarily follow. It is not clear what the rationale for the difference in timetabling is.

12.34 Another change from the 2005 Rules is the removal of the requirement (in 2005 Rules, rule 36.1(1)(b)) that an application which did not comply with the deadline should explain why that was not possible. However, as the court has the power to extend the time limit for the making of an application even after that time limit has expired (under rule 36.7), it is reasonable to assume that a late application will still address this issue.

12.35 A further change to the 2005 Rules which is of significance is the removal of the specific rules governing the making of an application to adduce previous sexual behaviour after a trial has started (these appeared in 2005 Rules, rule 36.1(13)–(14)). On the face of the Rules, therefore, the requirement that the defence apply in advance of the trial is absolute.

2. The application and response to it

12.36 The application should be made in writing (rule 36.2(a)) and served on the court and all other parties (rule 36.4). The application should include the following:

(a) the issue to which the previous behaviour is said to be relevant (rule 36.3(a));
(b) a summary of the evidence or questions in relation to which leave is sought (rule 36.3(b)). It should be noted that the 2005 rule requirement in addition for a summary of the documentation or other evidence submitted in support of the application (to be found in the 2005 Rules, rule 36.1(2)(c)) is not replicated in the 2010 Rules;
(c) a full explanation as to why the behaviour in question comes within section 41(3) or (5) (see paragraph 12.29 above) (rule 36.3(c));
(d) the application should also include details of any witness that it is proposed to call to give evidence about the matters summarized (rule 36.3(d)).

The other parties to the proceedings are given fourteen days from receipt to respond to an application (rule 36.5). Although the Rules are silent as to what such a reply should contain, it would seem logical, for example by comparison with the contents required in a response to a bad character application under Part 35 of the Rules, that the reply should address and counter the assertions in the application of relevance and/or the applicability of exceptions to the section 41 prohibition.   12.37

With one exception, which is discussed below, and in contrast to the 2005 Rules which identified the process by which the court should deal with an application made under Part 36, the 2010 Rules are silent as to how the court should deal with an application under rule 36.2. There is a hint, however, in the notes to rule 36.2 which states 'see part 3 for the court's general power to consider an application with or without a hearing or to give directions'. This is clearly a reference to rule 3.5, and thus it is reasonable to suppose that the court can, in relation to an application under rule 36.2, make such directions as it thinks appropriate, and decide on the matter with or without a hearing.   12.38

The one exception relates to special measures applications consequent on the granting of a rule 36.2 application. What is envisaged by the inclusion of rule 36.6 is that the prosecution may seek to make a special measures application, or make an application to vary an existing special measures direction, in relation to a complainant where either no measures have been sought or the measures that had been sought before the defence made their rule 36.2 application are no longer sufficient. For example, a complainant may need additional measures to help her give evidence, such as screens, when she knows that her previous behaviour is to be analyzed in cross-examination. Under rule 36.6, the prosecution is required to make such an application within fourteen days of the grant of the rule 36.2 application.   12.39

13

TRIAL AND SENTENCE IN A MAGISTRATES' COURT

A. INTRODUCTION

The 2005 version of the Rules differed substantially from the Rules now operative since 2010. The earlier Rules dealt with trial and sentence of adults in the magistrates' court and trial and sentence in the youth court separately, in Parts 37 and 38 respectively. The 2010 Rules now deal with trial and sentence in either venue in Part 37, whilst Part 38 now contains no rules. The new Rules are substantially revised and much simplified from those which went before them.   **13.01**

B. GENERAL

Rule 37.1 is comprised of a broad statement to the effect that the rule applies in a magistrates' court where the court tries a case and the defendant pleads guilty. If a defendant dealt with under this part is under 18, any reference to convicting the defendant is to be taken to include a reference to finding the defendant guilty of an offence. Equally any reference to sentence includes a reference to an order made on a finding of guilt. The use of such terminology in recognition of a person's youth is required by section 59 of the Children and Young Persons Act 1933 (CYPA 1933).   **13.02**

Unless the court directs otherwise the general rule is that any hearing must be in public. However, that general rule is subject to exceptions in that the court may exercise any power it has to order a hearing in private, impose reporting restrictions, or withhold information from the public. So far as youth court proceedings are concerned, persons who may be present (unless the court directs otherwise) are limited to the parties and   **13.03** their legal representatives, a defendant's parents, guardian or other supporting adult, a witness, anyone else directly concerned in the case, and a representative of a news-gathering or reporting organization (rule 37.2(1)).

13.04   At any hearing, unless it has already been done, either the justices' legal adviser or the court must read the allegation of the offence to the defendant. They must also explain the allegation, and what the procedure at the hearing will be in terms that can be under-stood by the defendant. They must ask whether the defendant has been advised about the credit available on sentence for a guilty plea and whether the defendant pleads guilty or not guilty. They must then take the defendant's plea (rule 37.2(2)). At any stage, the court may adjourn the hearing to the same or to another magistrates' court or (where the court is not a youth court and the defendant is under 18) to a youth court.

C. TRIAL

13.05   The procedure to be followed at trial, following the entering of a not guilty plea, or the refusal to enter a plea, or if in either case it appears to the court that there may be grounds to make a hospital order without convicting the defendant, is set out in rule 37.3.

13.06   If the defendant has already entered a plea of not guilty at a previous hearing, the first step to be taken is for the justices' legal adviser or the court to ask the defendant to confirm that plea (rule 37.3(2)).

13.07   The order of proceedings is then as follows. The prosecutor may, if he wishes, summarize the prosecution case by identifying the relevant law and facts. He must then introduce the evidence on which the prosecution case relies. When the prosecution case has concluded, the court may acquit the defendant on the ground that the prosecution evidence is insufficient for any reasonable court properly to convict. That course of action may be taken either on application by the defendant or of the court's own initia-tive but the court must not acquit unless the prosecutor has had an opportunity to make representations. If the defendant is not acquitted at that stage and the defence has a case to answer, the justices' legal adviser or the court must explain the defendant's right to give evidence. They must explain the potential effect of not doing so at all, or of refusing to answer a question while doing so. The legal adviser or court must also explain to the defendant that he may introduce evidence. All that explanation must be given in terms the defendant can understand. At the close of the defendant's evidence a party may introduce further admissible evidence such as rebuttal evidence. At the close of all the evidence, the prosecutor and defendant may make closing representations in support of their case. The prosecutor's right to make representations is limited to circumstances where the defendant is represented by a legal representative, or (whether he is represented or not) the defendant has introduced evidence other than his or her own (rule 37.3(1)–(3)).

13.08   The court has a discretion to refuse to receive any evidence or representations a party wants to introduce or make after that party's opportunity to do so under rule 37.3(3). The court must not receive any such evidence or representations after it has announced its verdict (rule 37.3(4)).

13.09   If the court convicts the defendant or makes a hospital order instead of doing so, it is obligatory that the court give sufficient reasons to explain its decision (rule 37.3(5)). If the court acquits the defendant, the court has a discretion whether or not to give an explanation of its decision and exercise any power it has to make a civil behaviour order (see paragraph 15.14) and/or a costs order (see Chapter 19) (rule 37.3(6)).

The procedure for calling a witness is governed by rule 37.4. It stipulates that a witness   13.10
waiting to give evidence (unless they are a party or an expert witness) must not wait inside the courtroom. A witness who gives evidence in the courtroom must do so from the witness box or any other place provided for the giving of evidence and a witness' address must not be announced unless it is relevant to an issue in the case (rule 37.4(1) and (2)). A witness must take an oath or affirm before they give evidence (unless legislation provides differently) (rule 37.4(3)). When a witness gives evidence, the order of questions is as follows. First, the party who calls a witness must ask questions in examination-in-chief, then every other party may ask questions in cross-examination. Following that, the party who called the witness may ask questions in re-examination. The Rules now also provide that, if legislation permits it, at any time while giving evidence, a witness may refer to a record of his recollection of events. The party who calls a witness, may ask that witness in examination-in-chief to adopt all or part of that record as part his evidence. Such a course is only allowed if the parties agree, and the court permits it. If the witness does adopt any part of that record, that part must be read aloud. Alternatively, if the court permits it, its contents may be summarized aloud (rule 37.4(4)). In addition to the parties, the justices' legal adviser or the court may ask a witness questions. If a defendant is unrepresented, they especially may ask any question necessary in the defendant's interests (rule 37.4(5)).

If a party introduces a written statement into evidence, he must read or summarize   13.11
aloud the parts of the statement which are relevant to the issues in the case (rule 37.5).

Any admission made by the parties must be recorded in writing unless the court   13.12
otherwise directs (rule 37.6).

D. GUILTY PLEAS

If a defendant enters a guilty plea and the court is satisfied that the plea is unequivocal,   13.13
then that defendant can be convicted without the court being required to receive any evidence (rule 37.7).

Rule 37.8 governs the procedure to be adopted for the receipt of guilty pleas in writ-   13.14
ing submitted without the need for the defendant to attend. The power arises under sections 12 and 12A of the MCA 1980 and applies to offences which are triable summarily only. Under section 12(1)(a) the Secretary of State may prescribe offences to which the rule does not apply but no such offences have been specified. The procedure can only be adopted in respect of defendants who are at least 16 years of age. The prosecutor must have served on the defendant the summons or requisition, the material on which the prosecutor relies to set out the facts of the offence and to provide information relevant to sentence, a notice that the procedure set out in this rule applies, and a notice for the defendant's use if the defendant wants to plead guilty without attending court. The prosecutor must also have served copies of those documents on the court officer, along with a certificate of service of those documents on the defendant (rule 37.8(1)). If a defendant wishes to plead guilty without attending court he must serve a notice of guilty plea on the court officer, and include with that notice any representations that he wants the court to consider before the hearing date specified in the summons or

requisition (rule 37.8(2)). A form for use in connection with this rule is set out in the Practice Direction. Any defendant must notify the court officer in writing before the hearing date if he wishes to withdraw his notice of guilty plea (rule 37.8(3)).

13.15   If a notice of guilty plea is served, the court may accept the plea on the hearing date. If it does so it must take account only of the material served by the prosecutor on the defendant under this rule along with any representations by the defendant (rule 37.8(4)). If the defendant is present at a hearing and has served a notice of guilty plea under rule 37.8(2) or pleads guilty there and then, the court may deal with the case in the same way as under rule 37.8(4) if the defendant consents (rule 37.8(5)).

13.16   If a defendant enters a guilty plea, he may apply to vacate that guilty plea. If he wishes to do so, the procedure in respect of any application is dealt with under rule 37.9. It stipulates that the defendant must make the application to do so as soon as practicable after becoming aware of the reasons for doing so and before sentence. The application must be in writing (unless the court otherwise directs) and it must be served on the court officer and the prosecutor. The application must contain an explanation of why it would be unjust not to allow the defendant to withdraw the guilty plea. In addition, it must identify any witness that the defendant wants to call along with any other proposed evidence. Importantly, rule 37.9(4) requires that it must also say whether the defendant waives legal professional privilege and stipulate any relevant name and date. Such relevant name would obviously include the name of any relevant legal representative and the date on which advice was given.

E. SENTENCE

13.17   The procedure to be followed in the exercise of the powers of the court on conviction is contained within rule 37.10. If the court convicts the defendant, the court may require a statement of the defendant's financial circumstances and a pre-sentence report. The court may also remit the defendant to a youth court for sentence where the defendant is under 18, and the convicting court is not itself a youth court. In some cases the court must take that course (rule 37.10(1) and (2)).

13.18   The sentencing procedure requires the prosecutor to summarize the prosecution case (if the sentencing court has not heard evidence), identify any offence to be taken into consideration in sentencing, and provide all information relevant to sentence. In addition, where it is likely to assist the court, the prosecutor must identify any other matter relevant to sentence, including the applicable legislation, aggravating and mitigating factor, and any guidelines issued by the Sentencing Guidelines Council, or guideline cases (rule 37.10(3)). The defendant is also required to provide information relevant to sentence. That information includes details of his financial circumstances (rule 37.10(4)).

13.19   If a defendant has pleaded guilty but wants to be sentenced on a different basis to that disclosed by the prosecution case, he must set out that basis in writing and identify what is in dispute. The court may then invite the parties to make representations about whether the dispute is material to sentence. If the court decides that the dispute between the parties is material, it will invite such further representations or evidence as it may require, and then decide the dispute.

13.20   Under rule 37.10(6) if a defendant wants the court to not exercise its power to endorse his licence or disqualify him from driving, he must introduce the evidence or information on which he relies. The prosecutor may then introduce evidence and the parties may make representations about the evidence or information from that which has been introduced by both sides.

By virtue of rule 37.10(7), before the court passes any sentence, it must allow the defendant to make representations and introduce any evidence which is relevant to sentence. If the defendant is under 18, the court must give the defendant's parents, guardian, or other supporting adult, if present, the same opportunity. In addition, the justices' legal adviser or the court must elicit any further information relevant to sentence. If the court requires more information, then under rule 37.10(8) it may exercise its power to adjourn the hearing. Any adjournment will be for three weeks if the defendant will be in custody during the adjournment or four weeks if he will not be. **13.21**

The general rule is that, when the court has taken into account all the evidence, information and any report(s) available, it will pass sentence there and then. It will also explain the sentence, the reasons for it, and its effect. That explanation will be in terms the defendant can understand. The court will also consider exercising any power it has to make a costs or other order (rule 37.10(9)) (see Chapter 19). However, the court must still adjourn the hearing if the case started with a summons or requisition, and the defendant is absent in circumstances where the court is considering passing a custodial sentence or imposing a disqualification (unless it has already adjourned the hearing to give the defendant an opportunity to attend). Additionally, the court would obviously not proceed to sentence there and then if it committed the defendant to the Crown Court for sentence or deferred sentence (which can be for a period of up to six months). **13.22**

F. MISCELLANEOUS

Rule 37.11 governs the procedure to be applied in all circumstances when a party is absent (save for when a defendant has served a notice of guilty plea under rule 37.8). If it is the prosecutor who is absent then, if the court has received evidence, it may proceed as if the prosecutor were present. In any other circumstances, the court may enquire into why it is that the prosecutor is not present, and if satisfied that there is no good reason for his absence may dismiss the allegation (rule 37.11(1) and (2)). **13.23**

The general rule where it is the defendant who is absent is that (unless a plea had already been entered) the court will proceed as if he were present, and had pleaded not guilty. The court must give reasons if it does not do so. The operation of that general rule is subject to a number of qualifications. First, the court must be satisfied that any summons or requisition was served on the defendant a reasonable time before the hearing. Secondly, where the case has previously been adjourned the court must be satisfied that defendant had reasonable notice of where and when it would resume. Thirdly, the operation of the general rule is subject to the limitations on passing sentence in the absence of the defendant (see rule 37.10). Fourthly, the general rule does not apply if the defendant is under 18. If a hearing does take place, it must be treated as having not taken place at all if it started with a summons or requisition, the defendant makes a statutory declaration of not having found out about the case until after the hearing began, and (unless the court extends the time limit) he serves that declaration on the court officer not more than twenty-one days after the date of finding out about the case (but the court has the power to extend that time limit) (rule 37.11(4)). **13.24**

13.25   If the defendant is absent and the court passes a custodial sentence, the court must exercise its power to issue a warrant for the defendant's arrest. In any other case, the court may issue a warrant if it does not apply the general rule (rule 37.11(4)).

13.26   Unless the court otherwise directs, rule 37.12 requires any party introducing a document into evidence, or otherwise relying on such a document in their case, to supply sufficient copies of the document for the other parties, the court and the justices' legal adviser.

13.27   Rule 37.13 provides a basic rule for where a trial will take place. That is that the hearing must take place in a courtroom provided by the Lord Chancellor, unless the court directs otherwise. An example of circumstances where the court might direct otherwise would be where a view of the place where the crime was alleged to have occurred was directed. In addition, rule 37.13(2) provides that if a hearing takes place in Wales, the Welsh language may be used by any party. Moreover, if it is practicable at least one member of the court must be Welsh-speaking.

13.28   The duties of a justices' legal adviser are governed by rule 37.14. Ordinarily a justices' legal adviser must attend at all proceedings. That need not be the case if the court includes a District Judge and that court directs that a justices' adviser need not be present. The justices' legal adviser is required to give legal advice to the court. If necessary he may give that advice to the members of the court outside the courtroom but he must inform the parties if that occurs (rule 37.14(1) and (2)). Further duties of a justices' legal adviser are that he must assist an unrepresented defendant and that he must assist the court by making a note of the substance of any oral evidence or representations (so as to assist the court to later recall that information), marking inadmissible parts of a statement, ensuring an adequate record is kept of the court's decisions (and the reasons for them), and making any announcement other than verdict or sentence (rule 37.14(3)). If the defendant has served a notice of guilty plea (see paragraph 13.14 above) a justices' legal adviser must read aloud to the court the material on which the prosecution relies and provide information relevant to sentence. If the court so directs, he may summarize any statement included in the prosecutor's material. He must also read aloud to the court any written representations by the defendant (rule 37.14(4)).

13.29   Finally in this Part, rule 37.15 sets out the duties of the court officer. First, unless the party was present when the new date for an adjourned hearing was fixed or the defendant has served a notice of guilty plea (see paragraph 13.14 above) and the adjournment is for not more than four weeks, the court officer is required to serve on each party notice of where and when an adjourned hearing will resume. If the reason for the adjournment was to postpone sentence, that reason must be included in any notice the court officer is required to serve. Secondly, the court officer must also (unless the court otherwise directs) make available to the parties any written report for sentence (see paragraph 13.17 above). Thirdly, where the court has ordered a defendant to provide information under section 25 of the RTOA 1988 (that information being the defendant's gender and date of birth), the court officer must serve notice of that order on the defendant unless the defendant was present when it was made. Fourthly, the court officer must serve any notice of guilty plea to which rule 37.8 applies, and any declaration served under rule 37.11 (to the effect that the defendant did not know about the case) on the prosecutor. Finally, the court officer must record in the magistrates' court register the court's reasons for not proceeding in the defendant's absence where the defendant did not know about the case. The court officer must also give the court any such other assistance as it requires.

14

TRIAL ON INDICTMENT, TAINTED ACQUITTALS, AND RETRIAL FOLLOWING ACQUITTAL FOR A SERIOUS OFFENCE

A. INTRODUCTION

Parts 39, 40, and 41 of the Rules make provision for trial on indictment, the recording of tainted acquittals under sections 54 to 57 of the Criminal Procedure and Investigations Act 1996 (CPIA 1996), and the new power, introduced by Part 10 of the Criminal Justice Act 2003 (CJA 2003), to order a retrial for a serious offence. 　14.01

B. PART 39— TRIAL ON INDICTMENT

Despite its title, the rules in Part 39 do not seek to regulate the overall conduct of trials on indictment. Under the 2005 Rules, the only provision within Part 39 was that which used to be rule 24 of the Crown Court Rules 1982. Rule 39.1 stipulates that, unless the defendant and prosecutor consent, a trial of a person committed by a magistrates' court shall not commence until at least fourteen days after committal. Equally, it should not commence any later than eight weeks after committal unless the court has made a contrary order. 　14.02

The 2010 Rules address two further areas, namely appeals against a refusal to excuse or defer jury service (rule 39.2) and applications on behalf of an accused to retract a guilty plea (rule 39.3). 　14.03

1. Appeal against refusal to excuse/defer

14.04   Under section 2 of the Juries Act 1974 (JA 1974), persons who are eligible to serve are summoned to attend for jury service. Those persons may apply to the appropriate officer of the Crown Court to be excused from attending, pursuant to section 9. Section 9(2) of the JA 1974 permits a juror discretionary excusal wherever he can show to the satisfaction of the appropriate officer that 'there is good reason why he should be excused from attending'. Section 9(2A) permits specific excusal for members of the armed forces.

14.05   Section 9A of the JA 1974 provides that, if a juror who has been summoned shows to the satisfaction of the appropriate officer that there is good reason why his attendance should be deferred, the officer shall vary the summons accordingly (section 9A(1)).

14.06   Section 9(3) of the JA 1974 provides that rules shall enable a juror refused excusal by an officer to appeal to the court against the refusal. A right of appeal is similarly created for a refusal to defer (section 9A(3)). The statutory provisions indicate that the Rules will regulate such appeals, and it is rule 39.2 that fulfils this role (rule 39.2(1)).

14.07   Such an appeal is initiated by the prospective juror giving notice of appeal to the appropriate court officer. That notice should be in writing, and should specify the reasons which it is submitted should permit the excusal or deferral of jury service (rule 39.2(4)). The court will not determine the appeal without giving the appellant the opportunity to be heard (rule 39.2(5)), and if, following that opportunity, the appeal is decided in the appellant's absence, he will be notified of the outcome by the court officer (rule 39.2(6)).

14.08   The appropriate court officer will be an officer of the Crown Court, by which such appeals will normally be heard (rule 39.2(2)), save that a High Court judge will hear appeals from those summoned to sit as jurors in the High Court in London, and the county court or the High Court sitting outside Greater London to which a juror has been summonsed, where that appeal has not been heard by the Crown Court in the interim (rule 39.2(3)).

2. Application to vacate a guilty plea

14.09   It has long been recognized that a judge has a discretion to allow the accused to withdraw a plea of guilty at any stage before sentence is passed. This was confirmed in *Plummer*.[1] In *Dodd*,[2] the Court of Appeal unhesitatingly accepted the three following propositions from counsel for the appellant, namely that: (a) the court has a discretion to allow a defendant to change a plea of guilty to one of not guilty at any time before sentence; (b) the discretion exists even where the plea of not guilty is unequivocal; and (c) the discretion must be exercised judicially. Ordinarily, a defendant will only be allowed to vacate a guilty plea where it can be shown that he pleaded guilty as a result of a genuine mistake or misunderstanding.

14.10   Rule 39.3 sets out the procedure by which such an application to change a defendant's plea from guilty to not guilty may be made. The application should be made as soon as possible, and must be before the defendant has been sentenced (rule 39.3(1)). This is

---

[1] [1902] 2 KB 339.
[2] (1981) 74 Cr App R 50, at 57.

because there is no conviction until sentence has been passed.[3] The application must be in writing (rule 39.3(2)), and served on the court and other parties to the proceedings (rule 39.3(3)).

The application must identify the reasons why it would be unjust for the guilty plea   14.11
to remain, and identify what evidence is to be called and, if so from whom (rule 39.3(2)). The reason such evidence will be required is that the court will be reluctant to vacate a guilty plea where the accused had indicated an intention to plead guilty, could not possibly have misunderstood the nature of a straightforward charge, and had unequivocally admitted guilt when the indictment was put to him, as was recognized in *McNally*.[4]

It will obviously be very difficult to convince the court that the guilty plea was entered   14.12
by a genuine mistake where the accused was legally represented at the time that the plea was entered. This was demonstrated in *Drew*,[5] where Lord Lane CJ said:[6]

. . .only rarely would it be appropriate for the trial judge to exercise his undoubted discretion in favour of an accused person wishing to change an unequivocal plea of guilty to one of not guilty. Particularly this is so in cases where, as here, the accused has throughout been advised by experienced counsel.

For this reason, in relation to the evidence that is to be adduced in support of an application to vacate, it is recognized that it may be necessary to waive legal professional privilege in relation to documents on which the accused will need to reply to establish such a genuine mistake (rule 39.3(2)(d)).

C. PART 40—TAINTED ACQUITTALS

The provisions of sections 54 to 57 of the CPIA 1996 allow a defendant to be retried for   14.13
an offence in the following circumstances:

(a) he must have been acquitted of the offence (section 54(1)(a));
(b) a person has been convicted of an administration of justice offence involving the interference or intimidation of a witness or potential witness (section 54(1)(b));
(c) the court that convicts for the administration of justice offence must certify that, but for that offence, there is a real possibility that the acquittal would not have happened (section 54(2)) and that it would not be contrary to the interests of justice to retry the person (section 54(5)); and
(d) the High Court must grant an order quashing the acquittal if it is satisfied that the requirements of section 55 are made out.[7]

---

[3] *S v Recorder of Manchester* [1971] AC 481.
[4] [1954] 1 WLR 933. The same approach was more recently adopted in *Revitt v DPP* [2006] 1 WLR 3172.
[5] [1985] 1 WLR 914.
[6] Ibid, at 923C.
[7] Those conditions are in essence, first, that it appears to the court likely that the acquittal would not have occurred but for the interference or intimidation; secondly, that it would not be contrary to the interests of justice to retry the acquitted person; thirdly, that the acquitted person has been given a reasonable opportunity to make written representations to the court; and fourthly, that it appears to the court that the conviction for the administration of justice offence will stand. See, generally, *Blackstone's Criminal Practice 2011*, para D12.33.

14.14   The rules contained within Part 40 set out the formalities associated with the tainted acquittal procedure. The 2010 Rules replicate with only limited alteration those included in Part 40 of the 2005 Rules, which themselves replicated without amendment those previously found in the Magistrates' Courts (Criminal Procedure and Investigations Act 1996) (Tainted Acquittals) Rules 1997 and the Crown Court (Criminal Procedure and Investigations Act 1996) (Tainted Acquittals) Rules 1997.

14.15   Where a person is convicted of a relevant offence under section 54(1) of the CPIA 1996, and it appears to the court that but for that offence there is a real possibility that the relevant acquittal would not have occurred, then the court should certify to that effect at any time following the conviction but no later than immediately after sentencing the person for the offence or committing the person to the Crown Court or remitting to the person to another magistrates' court or, in the case of a young person, remitting him to a youth court (rule 40.1). The form of certification made in the Crown Court should be as set out in the Practice Direction (rule 40.2).

14.16   Rule 40.3, which is the only rule within Part 40 to have been altered in the 2010 Rules, sets out requirements in relation to service of the certification. When a court makes such a certification,[8] then it should be served on the acquitted person as soon as practicable after it has been drawn up. It should also be served on the prosecutor of the trial which led to the relevant acquittal and, if the acquittal took place at a different court to the certifying court, then upon the relevant officer of that court.[9]

14.17   An entry concerning the certification must be made by the clerk of the magistrates' court or the Crown Court officer in the register of the conviction for the relevant administration of justice offence. The entry must specify the fact and date of certification, the name of the acquitted person, a description of the offence relating to the relevant acquittal, the date of the acquittal, and the court where the acquittal occurred (rule 40.4).

14.18   Similarly, if the court where the relevant acquittal took place is not the court which made the certification, the officer of the court where the acquittal took place must make an entry in the register specifying the fact and date of the certification, the name of the person who was the subject of the relevant conviction and a description of the relevant offence leading to the conviction. That entry must be made as soon as practicable after receipt of a copy of the certification. If the acquittal and certifying courts are one and the same, then the entry must be made as soon as practicable after the certification (rule 40.5).

14.19   The certifying court should display a copy of the relevant form containing the certification in a prominent place in the court premises as soon as practicable after the certification (rule 40.6). If the court where the relevant acquittal occurred is different to the court of certification, then it too must display a copy of the form containing a record of the certification in a prominent place in the court premises as soon as practicable after receiving a copy of the form (rule 40.6(2)). The notice must then be displayed for at least twenty-eight days from the date of certification or the receipt of the copy form (rule 40.6(3)).

---

[8] Pursuant to s 54(2) of the CPIA 1996.
[9] Methods of service are those identified in Part 4 of the Rules, see Chapter 4.

Once the High Court has decided either to quash the acquittal or not do so,[10] a note   14.20
to that effect must be made in the register of both the certifying court and the court
where the relevant acquittal occurred by the court officer as soon as practicable after
receipt of the appropriate notice (rule 40.7). In addition, both the certifying court and
the court where the acquittal occurred must display the notice in a prominent place in
the court premises for at least twenty-eight days as soon as practicable after receiving the
notice (rule 40.8).

D. PART 41—RETRIAL FOLLOWING ACQUITTAL FOR SERIOUS OFFENCE

Part 10 of the CJA 2003 introduced a controversial procedure for the potential retrial of   14.21
persons for an offence for which they had previously been acquitted, irrespective of
whether that acquittal was tainted. The Court of Appeal must now quash an acquittal
and order a retrial when it is satisfied that there is new and compelling evidence against
the acquitted person[11] and it is in the interests of justice to do so.[12] The power to quash
an acquittal and order a retrial of a person under the procedure is limited to specific,
qualifying offences.[13]

Part 41 of the Rules dictates the procedures to be followed if an application is to be   14.22
made under section 76 of the CJA 2003 ('a section 76 application') and deals with procedures for consequent orders relating to bail, reporting restrictions, the hearing of the
application, leave to arraign, abandonment of an application, and service of documents.

1. Section 76 applications

Rule 41.2 stipulates that any section 76 application made by a prosecutor must be in the   14.23
form set out in the Practice Direction and it must be served on the Registrar of the Court
of Appeal Criminal Division and the person who was previously acquitted. Wherever
practicable, the notice should be accompanied (rule 41.2(2)) by:

(a) relevant witness statements which are relied upon as forming the basis for the new
    and compelling evidence as well as the relevant witness statements from the original
    trial;
(b) any unused statements which (in accordance with the more general principles of
    disclosure) might reasonably be considered capable of undermining the section 76
    application or assisting the acquitted person's opposition to it;
(c) a copy of the indictment and the paper exhibits from the trial;

---

[10] Pursuant to s 55 of the CPIA 1996.
[11] Section 76 of the CJA 2003.
[12] Section 79 of the CJA 2003.
[13] Section 75(8) defines the qualifying offences as those listed in Part 1 of Sch 5 to the Act. They include
murder, rape, importation of class 'A' drugs, causing explosions, hostage-taking, and conspiracy to commit any
of the offences listed in that part of Sch 5. For a detailed exposition of the general scheme see *Blackstone's Guide
to the Criminal Justice Act 2003*, para 7.3.1 and *Blackstone's Criminal Practice 2011*, para. D12.34.

(d) copies of the transcript of the summing up and any other relevant transcripts from the trial; and

(e) any other documents relied upon in support of the section 76 application.

As soon as practicable after service of the notice on the acquitted person, the prosecutor must file a statement or certificate of service with the Registrar which exhibits a copy of the notice (rule 41.2(3)).

14.24   An acquitted person who wishes to contest a section 76 application must serve on the Registrar and the prosecutor a response in the form stipulated in the Practice Direction (rule 41.3). That response must indicate if he seeks an order under section 80(6) of the CJA 2003 for the production of any document, exhibit or other thing or an order for a witness to attend before the Court of Appeal (rule 41.3(1)(a)). The response must be served no later than twenty-eight days after receiving the notice of the section 76 application (rule 41.3(2)) but the Court of Appeal may extend that period either before or after it expires (rule 41.3(3)).

14.25   Should a party fail to make an application for an order under section 80(6) at the time of making a section 76 application or responding to one, or wish to make a further application, then the court may receive such an application no less than fourteen days before the date set for the hearing of the application (rule 41.4(4)). The notice of such an application must be in the required form set out in the Practice Direction, must be served on the Registrar and each party to the section 76 application (rule 41.4(2)) and the notice should stipulate the reasons why the order was not sought when the party had the opportunity when either making the application or answering it (rule 41.4(3)). If the Court of Appeal makes such an order by its own motion or at the request of the prosecutor then it should serve notice and the reasons for that order on all of the parties to the section 76 application (rule 41.4(5)).

2. Bail or custody

14.26   The scheme under the CJA 2003 allows for bail when a person is brought before the Crown Court pursuant to sections 88 or 89 of the Act.[14] Part 19 of the Rules, which deals with bail, therefore has application.[15] More particularly, rules 19.18, 19.22, and 19.23 apply (rule 41.5(1)) subject to a modification to rule 19.18 to the effect that the prosecutor must serve notice of the need for a hearing on the court officer (rule 41.5(2)). The court officer must forward a copy of any record made in pursuance of section 5(1) of the Bail Act 1976 to the Registrar (rule 41.5(4)).

14.27   Once a person is granted bail with conditions or remanded in custody before a section 76 application is made then, under section 88(6), if a section 76 application is not made within forty-two days of the remanding on bail with conditions or remanding into custody then the person must be given unconditional bail or released from custody on unconditional bail. Different time periods apply to other stages of the proceedings (see section 89(6)). Rule 41.6 requires that a prosecutor may apply to extend the relevant

---

[14] Section 88 deals with the determination of whether an acquitted person should be bailed or be in custody before a section 76 application is made and s 89 deals with the same decision before a hearing following a section 76 application.

[15] See Chapter 7.

period but only if the application is made before the expiry of the period and served on the Crown Court officer and the acquitted person. In addition, a prosecutor's application for a summons or warrant under section 89 (made when a person is not in custody) must be served on the acquitted person and the court officer (rule 41.6(2)).

Procedural provision is also made for the granting of bail or remand in custody under   14.28
section 90 of the CJA 2003 during the course of the hearing of a section 76 application. Rule 41.7 stipulates that the rules governing bail pending appeal[16] apply to an order made by the Court of Appeal during such a hearing.

3. Reporting restrictions

Section 82 of the CJA 2003 enables restrictions to be placed upon the reporting of any   14.29
matter which would give rise to a substantial risk of prejudice to the administration of justice in a retrial.[17] Rules 41.8 and 41.9 respectively lay down the procedure to be followed in an application for such an order by the DPP and any subsequent application by any party to revoke or vary the restrictions:

(a) an application by the DPP must be in the form set out in the Practice Direction and must be served on the Registrar (rule 41.8(1));
(b) the application must be served on the acquitted person (rule 41.8(1)) unless the Court of Appeal orders that it should not be served on him if notice of the section 76 application has not yet been served on him and the DPP sets out reasons why he should not receive notice of the application for reporting restrictions (rule 41.8(2)). Clearly one potential reason for not serving notice of the application on the acquitted person is that he might attempt to abscond or interfere with a witness if he was aware of the order sought; and
(c) if the Court of Appeal makes the order applied for by the DPP, or make such an order of its own motion, the Registrar must serve notice of it and the reasons for it upon all parties (rule 41.8(3)) unless the application has been made without notice to the acquitted person.[18]

If any party wants to revoke or vary an order made pursuant to section 82, then the   14.30
general rule (rule 41.9) is that a written application (a copy of which must be served on each of the parties) can be made to the Court of Appeal at any time after the order is made. In a similar fashion to the procedure in rule 41.8(2), if notice of a section 76 application has not yet been served on the acquitted person and the DPP sets out reasons why the acquitted person should not know of the application, then the Court of Appeal may order that service on the acquitted person should not be effected until notice of a section 76 application is served on that person (rule 41.9(3)). Except in those circumstances, if the Court of Appeal makes an order revoking or varying an order restricting publication, then notice and the reasons for the new order must be served on all the parties by the Registrar (rule 41.9(4)).

---

[16] Rules 68.7, 68.8, and 68.9, see Chapter 18.
[17] See *Blackstone's Criminal Practice 2011*, para D12.41.
[18] In accordance with r 41.8(2).

4. Management and adjudication of a section 76 application

14.31 The powers to be exercised in relation to a section 76 application by a single judge of the Court of Appeal or the Registrar are set out in rules 41.10 and 41.11 respectively. Under rule 41.10, the single judge may:

(a) order the production of any document, exhibit or thing in accordance with section 80(6)(a) of the CJA 2003;

(b) order any appropriate witness to attend for examination before the Court of Appeal;

(c) extend the time for the acquitted person to respond to a section 76 application;[19] and

(d) delay the requirement of service of a notice of application for restrictions on publication under rule 41.8, or variation to such an order under rule 41.9.[20]

14.32 The single judge may sit otherwise than in open court when exercising such powers (rule 41.10(2)) and, if he exercises any of his powers, the Registrar must serve notice of the single judge's decision on all parties (rule 41.10(3)). If the single judge refuses to exercise any of these powers, the disappointed party may renew the application to the full court, in the form set out in the Practice Direction (rule 41.12(1)), within fourteen days of that refusal, unless the Court of Appeal extends the period (rule 41.12(2)). If notice of such an application to renew is not served on the Registrar within the requisite period, it will be treated as refused (rule 41.12(3)).

14.33 The Registrar may exercise the same powers as a single judge (rule 41.11(2)) except that he may not delay the requirement of service of notice on the acquitted person of an application concerning restrictions on publication. When the Registrar exercises any of those powers, then he must give notice to all parties (rule 41.11(3)). In addition, the Registrar may require the Crown Court where the trial which led to the relevant acquittal took place to provide any assistance or information the Court of Appeal needs when dealing with a section 76 application (rule 41.11(1)). If the registrar refuses an application to exercise any of his powers under rule 41.11(2), a party may renew their application before the single judge, in the form set out in the Practice Direction, within fourteen days of that refusal, unless the Court of Appeal extends the period (rule 41.11(4)).

14.34 Rules 41.13 to 41.15 deal with procedural matters following the determination of a section 76 application. In summary:

(a) at the conclusion of the hearing of any section 76 application, the Court of Appeal may give or reserve its determination of the application (rule 41.13(1)). If the determination is reserved then notice of the determination should be served as soon as is practicable by the Registrar (rule 41.13(2));

(b) if the Court of Appeal orders a retrial under section 77 of the 2003 Act the Registrar must serve notice on the court officer at the Crown Court of the appropriate place for retrial as soon as is practicable (rule 41.13(3)).

---

[19] Application for extension for response pursuant to r 41.3, see para 14.24 above.
[20] See paras 14.29 and 14.30 above.

If a retrial is ordered, the defendant may not be arraigned any later than two months   14.35
after the date of the section 77 order without the leave of the Court of Appeal.[21] Further,
the Court of Appeal must not give such leave unless it is satisfied that the prosecutor has
acted with due expedition and there is good and sufficient cause for trial.[22] If a defendant has not been arraigned within this two-month period, he may apply to the Court
of Appeal to set aside the section 77 order for a retrial under section 84(4). Such an
application should be in the form set out in the Practice Direction, and served on the
Registrar and the prosecutor (rule 41.14). Similarly, if a prosecutor wishes to make an
application for leave to arraign a person more than two months after the section 77
order, it must be made in the form set out in the Practice Direction and must be served
on the Registrar and the acquitted person (rule 41.15).

A section 76 application may be abandoned by the prosecutor at any time before the   14.36
hearing of the application under rule 41.16. The notice of abandonment of the application must be made in the form set out in the Practice Direction and must be served on
the Registrar and the acquitted person (rule 41.16(1)). As soon as practicable after
receiving the notice, the Registrar should send a copy of it, endorsed with the date of
receipt, to the prosecutor and acquitted person (rule 41.16(2)).

In contrast to the 2005 Rules, there is no specific provision in Part 41 of the 2010   14.37
Rules addressing methods of service. This is because the service of documents is now
covered for all purposes by Part 4.

---

[21] Section 84(2) of the CJA 2003.
[22] Section 84(3) of the CJA 2003.

15

SENTENCING

A. INTRODUCTION

The section of the Rules dealing with sentencing in a magistrates' court or the Crown   15.01
Court is to be found in Parts 42 to 55. The rules set out the duties of court officers and
procedures to be followed in respect of various sentencing hearings. The 2010 Rules
contain substantial changes from the original Rules made in 2005 and those which operated before October 2010. Parts 43, 45, 47, 48, 49, 53, and 54 are now omitted and
replaced by the new rules in Part 42. In addition, the rules in Part 44 are now amended
so as to make them applicable in the Crown Court as well as the magistrates' court
and to take account of legislative changes. The rules in Part 52 are replaced with revised
and simplified rules concerning the enforcement of fines and other orders for payment.
Finally, there are amendments to Part 55 concerning road traffic penalties.

B. PART 42—SENTENCING PROCEDURE IN SPECIAL CASES

The new rule 42, operative from 4 October 2010, imposes a series of requirements on   15.02
courts when they pass particular sentences. Rule 42.1 requires a court to explain in its
sentencing remarks in certain circumstances why it has not chosen to follow a course
that was open to it. A court is thus now required to give such an explanation when it
does not follow a relevant guideline, does not make a reparation, compensation or travel
restriction order when it could have done so, or does not order where it could the activa-
tion of a suspended sentence, the endorsement of the offender's driving record, or the
disqualification from driving of the offender.

  If a court imposes a requirement when it passes a community sentence, youth reha-   15.03
bilitation order, or suspended sentence, or orders a defendant to meet with a supervisor,

the court must notify the defendant (and if the defendant is under 14, an appropriate adult) of the identity of the responsible officer or supervisor and how he may be contacted. The court must also notify the said responsible officer or supervisor (and if the defendant is under 14, the appropriate qualifying officer) of the defendant's name, address, telephone number, the offence(s) of which he was convicted, and the requirements imposed (rule 42.2(2)). Similarly, if the court imposes an electronic monitoring requirement, then it must inform the defendant (and an appropriate adult if the defendant is under 16) of the identity of the monitor (who may or may not be the responsible officer). The monitor must also be notified of the defendant's name, address, and phone number, the offence(s) of which he was convicted, the place(s) at which he is to be monitored, the period(s) during which he is to be monitored, and the name and contact details of the responsible officer (rule 42.2(3)).

15.04   If a defendant is required to notify the police of any information by virtue of any conviction, sentence, or order, the court must tell the defendant what it is that he has to notify and under what legislative provision (rule 42.3). Notification requirements can now be imposed under the Sexual Offences Act 2003 (SOA 2003) and the Counter Terrorism Act 2008.

15.05   Section 142 of the Magistrates' Courts Act 1980 (MCA 1980) allows a magistrates' court to vary or rescind a sentence or order it has imposed if it appears to be in the interest of justice to do so. Similarly, under section 155 of the Powers of Criminal Courts (Sentencing) Act 2000 (PCC(S)A 2000) the Crown Court may vary or rescind a sentence it has imposed within fifty-six days of its imposition (unless an application for permission to appeal against the sentence or order has been submitted). Under section 155(7) the Rules can extend that period of fifty-six days when a defendant tried separately on the same or related facts is sentenced or acquitted. Rule 42.4 governs the procedure to be followed for the court to consider varying or rescinding a sentence. The court may exercise its power of its own initiative or on application by one of the parties (rule 42.4(2)). Any application by a party must be in writing and must be served on the court officer and other parties as soon as practicable following the sentence or order or after the sentencing or acquittal of the other defendant. The application should explain why the sentence should be varied or rescinded, set out the proposed change to the sentence, and (if necessary) explain why the application is late (rule 42.4(3)). The court should not exercise its powers in the absence of the defendant unless it makes a variation proposed by him or he has had the opportunity to make representations at a hearing (rule 42.4(4)). The court may extend any time limit (even after it has expired) and may allow an application to be made orally (rule 42.4(5)).

15.06   If a defendant wishes a magistrates' court to vary or discharge a compensation order then, under rule 42.5, he must serve a written application on the magistrates' court officer (and serve a copy on the Crown Court officer if the order was made in the Crown Court) as soon as practicable after becoming aware of the grounds for doing so. The application must explain, as applicable, what civil court finding shows the injury, loss, or damage to be less than was thought when the order was made, the circumstances in which the beneficiary of the order has recovered the property lost, why a confiscation order means that the defendant cannot pay the order in full or the circumstances in which the defendant's means have been reduced substantially and unexpectedly and seem unlikely to increase for a considerable time (rule 42.5(2)). The court must serve a copy of the application on the beneficiary of the order (rule 42.5(3)). The court must not make the variation unless the defendant and the beneficiary have had the opportunity to make representations at a hearing. If the order was made in the Crown Court, the consent of the Crown Court is also necessary.

A court may remove a disqualification from keeping a dog under section 4(6) of the **15.07** Dangerous Dogs Act 1991 or remove a travel restriction on a person convicted of drug-trafficking under section 35 of the Criminal Justice and Police Act 2001. Rule 42.6 stipulates that a defendant who wishes the court to remove such a disqualification or restriction must serve a written application on the court officer no sooner than the date on which the court can first exercise the power which specifies the disqualification or restriction and explains why the defendant wishes the court to remove, revoke, or suspend it. The court officer must then serve a copy of the application on the chief officer of police for the local justice area.

Under section 148 of the PCCSA 2000, the court may order the return of stolen **15.08** property. Without waiting for a verdict any person seeking such an order must serve a written application on the court officer as soon as practicable. The application must specify the goods and explain why the applicant is entitled to them (rule 42.7(1) and (2)). The court must serve the application on each party and must not allow it unless each party has had the opportunity to make representations at a hearing (rule 42.7(3) and (4)). The court may vary any time limit and allow the application to be made orally (rule 42.7(5)).

Rule 42.8 governs the procedure when a court requests a medical examination of the **15.09** defendant or a report, or requests information about arrangements to be made when it is considering a hospital or guardianship order. Unless the court directs otherwise, as soon as practicable the court officer must serve a notice on each person from whom a report or information is requested. The notice must specify the power exercised by the court, the reason the court seeks a report or information, and must set out or summarize the relevant information available to the court.

Where the court orders the defendant's detention and treatment in a hospital or makes **15.10** a guardianship order, rule 42.9 stipulates that (unless the court directs otherwise) the court officer must serve on the hospital or guardian a record of the court's order. He must also serve such information as the court thinks fits to assist in the treatment of the defendant including information about his mental condition, his other circumstances, and the circumstances of the offence.

Rule 42.10 governs the procedure to be followed if the magistrates' court or Crown **15.11** Court convicts a defendant and has to send the case to another court or has to deal with an order made on another occasion or by another court. If the court commits or adjourns the case to another court for sentence, or for the defendant to be dealt with for breach of a deferred sentence, a conditional discharge or suspended sentence imposed by that other court, the court officer must, as soon as practicable, send specified relevant copy court records to the other court. Those include the certificate of conviction, the magistrates' court register entry, the record relating to bail, the note of evidence, any statement or other document introduced into evidence, any medical or other report, any representation order or application for such an order, and any interim driving disqualification (rule 42.10(2)(a)). If the court deals with a deferred sentence, conditional discharge, or suspended sentence imposed by another court or makes an order that another court is, or may be required to enforce, the court officer must as soon as practicable arrange the transmission from the convicting court to the other court the convicting court's order and the recording of the order at the other court (rule 42.10(2)(b)). In every case, the court officer must as soon as practicable inform the defendant (and the appropriate adult if the defendant is under 14) of the location of the other court (rule 42.10(2)(c)).

C. PART 44—BREACH, REVOCATION, AND AMENDMENT OF COMMUNITY AND OTHER ORDERS

15.12   Part 44 applies to proceedings concerned with failure to comply with orders under Schedules 3 (curfew and exclusion orders), 5 (attendance centre orders), 7 (supervision orders), and 8 (action plan and separation orders) to the PCC(S)A 2000; Schedule 8 (community orders) or 12 (suspended sentence orders) to the CJA 2003; Schedule 2 to the Criminal Justice and Immigration Act 2008 (youth rehabilitation orders) and the Schedule to the Street Offences Act 1959 (not yet in force). If the responsible officer or supervisor wants the court to deal with the defendant for failure to comply with an order, revoke or amend the order, or the court of its own initiative considers exercising any power it has to revoke or amend the order and summons the defendant to attend, then rules 7.2 to 7.4 (which concern the commencement of a prosecution) apply with necessary modifications as if the reference to an allegation of an offence included a reference to a failure to comply with the order. In addition, they apply as if reference to a prosecutor included reference to a responsible officer or supervisor (rule 44.2). If the application is made by defendant or a person affected, they must serve a written application, explaining why the order should be revoked or amended, on the court officer, the responsible officer or supervisor, and (as appropriate) the defendant or affected party (rule 44.3).

15.13   The procedure to be followed at a hearing following application by a responsible officer or supervisor is the same as that contained within Part 37 (save for rule 37.8). The rules in that Part apply as if a reference to an offence included a reference to a failure to comply, a reference to a verdict included a reference to the court's decision to exercise any power, and a reference to the sentence included the exercise of any such power.

D. PART 50—CIVIL BEHAVIOUR ORDERS AFTER CONVICTION OR FINDING

15.14   Part 50 deals with the procedures to be followed when a supplementary order of the kind detailed within the Part is made upon conviction. Numerous civil orders are now available to a sentencing court following a conviction or finding. On conviction, orders may be under section 14A of the Football Spectators Act 1989 (football banning orders), section 5 of the Protection from Harassment Act 1997 (restraining orders), sections 1C and 1D of the CDA 1998 (anti-social behaviour orders and interim anti-social behaviour orders), sections 8 and 9 of the CDA 1998 (parenting orders), section 104 of the SOA 2003 (sexual offences prevention orders), section 19 of the Serious Crime Act 2007 (serious crime prevention orders), section 6 of the Violent Crime Reduction Act 2006 (drinking banning orders). Upon a finding of not guilty by reason of insanity or disability a sexual offences prevention order may be made under section 104 of the SOA 2003. Following acquittal, a restraining order may be made under the Protection from Harassment Act 1997.

Save, in respect of an interim behaviour order, the court must not make a behaviour **15.15** order unless the person to whom it is directed has had an opportunity to consider what order is proposed and why. The person to whom it is directed must also have had the opportunity to make representations at a hearing. An interim behaviour order has no effect unless the person to whom it is directed is present when it is made or is handed a document recording the order not more than seven days after it is made (rule 50.2(1) and (2)). Where the court decides not to make, in circumstances where it could, a football banning order, a parenting order (after a person under 16 is convicted of disobeying an anti-social behaviour order), or a drinking banning order, the court must announce at a public hearing its reasons for not doing so (rule 50.2(3)).

If the prosecutor wants the court to make an anti-social behaviour order or a serious **15.16** crime prevention order, if the defendant is convicted, the prosecutor must serve a notice of intention to apply for such an order on the court officer, the defendant against whom the prosecutor wants the court to make the order, and any person on whom the order would be likely to have a significant adverse effect. The prosecutor must make such an application as soon as practicable and without waiting for the verdict (rule 50.3(2)). The notice must be in the form set out in the Practice Direction and must summarize the relevant facts, identify the evidence relied on by the prosecutor, attach any written statement that the prosecutor has not already served, and specify the order that the prosecutor wants the court to make (rule 50.3(3)). The defendant must then serve written notice of any evidence on which he relies on the court officer, and the prosecutor. The defendant must do so as soon as practicable and must not wait for the verdict. The defendant must identify in the notice any evidence and attach any written statement that has not already been served (rule 50.3(4)). Rule 50.3(5) stipulates that the rule does not apply to an application for an interim anti-social behaviour order.

Rule 50.4 sets out special rules relating to evidence when the court is considering **15.17** making particular orders of its own initiative. The orders in question are a football banning order, a restraining order, an anti-social behaviour order, or a drinking banning order. Under rule 50.4(2) a party who wants the court to take account of any particular evidence before making its decision must serve notice in writing on the court officer, and every other party. The notice must be served as soon as practicable, and the party must not wait for the verdict. He must identify the evidence and attach any written statement that has not already been served.

The procedure to deal with an application for variation or revocation of a behaviour **15.18** order is set out in rule 50.5. The court may vary or revoke a behaviour order if, first, the legislation under which it is made allows the court to do so and, secondly, one of a number of parties makes an application. The parties are the prosecutor, the person to whom the order is directed, any other person mentioned in the order, the relevant authority or responsible officer, the relevant chief officer of police, or the Director of Public Prosecutions (DPP) (rule 50.5(1)). Any application must be made in writing as soon as practicable after becoming aware of the grounds for doing so. The application must explain why the order should be varied or revoked. It must be served (along with any notice under rule 50.5 (3)) on the court officer and, as appropriate, any of the parties mentioned in rule 50.5(1). Rule 50.5(3) states that any party who wants the court to take account of any particular evidence before making its decision must serve notice in writing on the court officer, and anyone listed in rule 50.5(1) as appropriate. That service must also take place as soon as practicable and the notice must identify the evidence to be relied on and attach any written statement that has not already been served (rule 50.5(3)). The court need not hold a hearing to decide such an application but the court must not dismiss the application unless the applicant has had an opportunity to make representations at a hearing. Additionally the court should not allow an application under this rule unless everyone served with the application has had at least fourteen days in which to make representations, including representations about whether there should be a hearing (rule 50.5(4) and (5)). The application must be served by the court officer on any person the court directs. The court officer must also give notice of any hearing to the applicant and any other person who is required by this rule to be served (rule 50.5(6)).

15.19 Part 50 also makes provision for the receipt of hearsay evidence by the court when dealing with a relevant application. Rule 50.6 requires a party who wants to introduce hearsay evidence to serve a written notice on the court officer and every other party directly affected. The notice must explain that it is a notice of hearsay evidence, identify the proposed evidence, identify the person who made the hearsay statement or explain why if that person is not identified, and explain why the person will not give oral evidence. One notice is sufficient for several applications.

15.20 If a party wishes to cross-examine a witness whose evidence it is proposed will be introduced as hearsay, he must serve a written application with reasons, not more than seven days after service of the notice of hearsay evidence. The application must be served on the court officer, the party who served the original hearsay evidence notice, and every party on whom the hearsay evidence notice was served (rule 50.7(2)). The court does not need to hold a hearing in order to decide such an application (rule 50.7(3)). However, the court must not dismiss an application under this rule unless the applicant has had an opportunity to make representations at a hearing. Additionally, the court must not allow an application under this rule unless everyone served with the application has had at least seven days in which to make representations, including representations about whether there should be a hearing (rule 50.7(4)). Under rule 50.8, similar rules apply when a party wants to challenge the credibility or consistency of a person who made a statement which another party wants to introduce as hearsay. The party who wishes to make that challenge must serve a written notice of intention to do so on the court officer, and the party who served the notice of hearsay evidence. That notice must be served not more than seven days after service of the original hearsay evidence notice. The notice must identify any statement or other material on which that party relies (rule 50.8(2)). If such a notice is served, the party who served the hearsay notice may call that person to give oral evidence instead. If he decides to do that he must serve a notice of his intention to do so on the court officer and every party on whom he served the hearsay notice. That service must take place not more than seven days after service of the notice under rule 50.8(2).

15.21 Rule 50.9 allows the court to extend any time limit (even after its expiry) and allow an application to be made in any form, including orally.

E. PART 52—ENFORCEMENT OF FINES

15.22 Whilst there are currently no rules dealing with the making of fines, there are a great many that deal with their enforcement under Part 52. With effect from 4 October 2010, the rules in Part 52 are replaced with different rules intended to be simplified relative to those which previously operated.

Rule 52.1 stipulates the scope of Part 52. It applies where a magistrates' court can 15.23
enforce payment of a fine (or a penalty that legislation requires the court to treat as a
fine) or any other sum that a court has ordered to be paid following a conviction, or the
forfeiture of a surety (rule 52.1(1)). Rules 52.7 to 52.9 apply where the court, or a fines
officer, issues a warrant that requires someone to take control of goods or money belong-
ing to the defendant, remove and sell any such goods, and pay any such money, and any
proceeds of such a sale, to the court officer towards payment of a sum to which Part 52
applies (rule 52.1(2)). Rule 51.1(3) defines terms used in Part 52. 'Defendant' means
anyone liable to pay a sum to which Part 51 applies and 'payment terms' means by when,
and by what (if any) installments, such a sum must be paid.

The court must not exercise its enforcement powers unless the court officer has served 15.24
on the defendant any collection order or other notice of the obligation to pay, the payment terms, and how and where the defendant must pay in circumstances where the
defendant has failed to comply with the payment terms (rule 52.2).

Rule 52.3 concerns the duty to give a receipt when a payment is made. The duty arises 15.25
where the defendant makes a payment to the court officer specified in an order or notice
served under rule 52.2, another court officer, any custodian of the defendant, a supervisor appointed to encourage the defendant to pay, any responsible officer appointed
under a community sentence or a suspended sentence of imprisonment; or a person
executing a warrant to which rule 18.6 (warrants for arrest, detention or imprisonment
that cease to have effect on payment) or this Part applies. The person receiving the payment must give the defendant a receipt and as soon as practicable transmit the payment
to the court officer specified in an order or notice served under rule 52.2 (if the recipient
is not that court officer).

1. Appeal against the decision of the fines officer

Where a collection order is in force and a fines officer makes a decision under one of the 15.26
relevant paragraphs of Schedule 5 to the Courts Act 2003 paragraph 22 (Application to
fines officer for variation of order or attachment of earnings order), paragraph 31
(Application to fines officer for variation of reserve terms), or paragraph 37 (Functions
of fines officer in relation to defaulters: referral or further steps notice)) and the defendant wants to appeal against that decision then rule 52.4 sets out the procedure to be
followed. By virtue of rule 52.4(2), the defendant must (unless the court directs otherwise), serve a written appeal on the court officer not more than ten business days after
the decision. The appeal must explain why it is submitted that a different decision should
be made, and specify the different decision that the defendant proposes. The general rule
is that when a court decides such an application it will do so at a hearing; but it may do
so without a hearing.

If no collection order is in force, and the defendant wants the court to reduce 15.27
the amount of a fine or vary payment terms, the procedure for the application he makes
is set out in rule 52.5. He must serve a written application on the court officer. That
application must explain why the fine should be reduced or the terms of payment should
be varied. It must also set out any relevant circumstances which have not yet been
considered by the court.

Rule 52.6 governs the procedure to be followed when a person wishes to avoid a fine 15.28
after a penalty notice. Unless the court directs otherwise, a defendant who claims not to

be the person to whom the penalty notice was issued must serve a written claim on the court officer. The court officer is then required to notify the chief officer of police by whom the certificate was registered and refer the case to the court. The general rule is that where such a claim is made, the court will adjourn the enforcement for twenty-eight days and fix a hearing. However, the court has a discretion to make a different order. At any hearing which does follow the chief officer of police must introduce any evidence to contradict the defendant's claim.

15.29   Rules 52.7 to 52.9 deal with the issue and enforcement of warrants to take goods in enforcement of a fine. Rule 52.7 stipulates that a warrant must identify the person(s) to whom it is directed, the defendant against whom it was issued, the sum for which it was issued and the reason that sum is owed, the court or fines officer who issued it (unless that is otherwise recorded by the court officer) and the court office for the court or fines officer who issued it. When the warrant is received, the person to whom a warrant is directed must record on it the date and time of the receipt. As with warrants issued in compliance with Part 19 of the Rules, a warrant that contains an error is not invalid, as long as it was issued in respect of a lawful decision by the court or fines officer; and it contains enough information to identify that decision. The procedure for the execution of a warrant mirrors that under Part 19. It may be executed by any person to whom it is directed or anyone authorized to execute it by section 125, 125A, or 125B of the MCA 1980. Those sections deal with warrants, civilian enforcement officers, and execution by approved agencies respectively (rule 52.8(1)). The person who executes a warrant must explain the order or decision that the warrant was issued to enforce, the sum for which the warrant was issued, and any extra sum payable in connection with the execution of the warrant. That explanation must be given in terms the person can understand. The person executing the warrant must also, if he has it with him, show the defendant the warrant. If the defendant asks, the person executing the warrant must arrange for the defendant to see the warrant, if that person does not have it, and show the defendant any written statement of that person's authority required by section 125A or 125B of the MCA 1980. Unless the person executing the warrant removes those goods at once, the person must also clearly mark any goods that are taken under the warrant (rule 52.8(2)). There are certain goods which must not be removed under a warrant. They are clothes or bedding used by the defendant or by anyone living with the defendant and (unless the defendant is a corporation) tools, books, vehicles, or other equipment that the defendant needs to use in the defendant's employment, business, or vocation (rule 52.8(3)). If the person who executes the warrant takes household goods they must not be removed until the day of sale unless the defendant agrees or the court directs otherwise (rule 52.8(4)). The warrant ceases to have effect if any of the following occurs. First, if the sum for which it was issued and any extra sum payable in connection with its execution is paid to the person executing. Secondly, if those sums are offered to, but refused by, that person. Thirdly, if the person is shown a receipt given under rule 52.3 for the sum for which the warrant was issued, and is paid any extra sum payable in connection with its execution (rule 52.8(5)).

15.30   Rule 52.9 governs the sale of goods seized in pursuance of a warrant. It stipulates that they must be sold (unless the court directs otherwise) as soon as reasonably practicable after the expiry of five business days from the date of execution of the warrant and at a public auction (rule 52.9(1)). As soon as reasonably practicable after the sale has taken place, the person who executed the warrant must collect the proceeds of sale, deduct any sum payable in connection with the execution of the warrant, and pay the court officer specified in an order or notice served under rule 52.2 the sum for which the warrant was issued. He must then pay any balance remaining to the defendant; and deliver an account of those deductions and payments to the court officer

F. PART 55—ROAD TRAFFIC PENALTIES

The amendments to the Rules implemented on 4 October 2010 substantially revised Part 55 of the Rules. Whilst rule 55.5 remained unaltered, wholly new rules 55.1 to 55.4 were introduced, The rules were designed to provide a simplified procedure.   15.31

Rule 55.1 is concerned with an application to remove a disqualification from driving. A court may remove a disqualification under section 42 of the Road Traffic Offenders Act 1988 (RTOA 1988). A defendant who wants the court to exercise the power to remove a disqualification must make a written application. That application can be made no earlier than the date when the court can first exercise the power. The application must be served on the court officer and it must specify the disqualification that the defendant wants the court to remove, and explain why the court should take that course. Having received the application, the court officer must then serve a copy of the application on the local police.   15.32

The information which must be supplied when the court is required to endorse a defendant's driving record is governed by rule 55.2. Where the court convicts the defendant of an offence involving obligatory endorsement, and orders the endorsement of particulars of the conviction, any disqualification from driving that the court imposes, and the penalty points to be attributed to the offence, the court is required to notify particular matters to the Secretary of State as soon as practicable. Those details are the local justice area in which the court is acting, the dates of conviction and sentence, the offence, and the date on which it was committed, the sentence, and the date of birth, and sex, of the defendant, where those details are available. If the court disqualifies the defendant from driving for any other offence it must also inform the Secretary of State of the date and period of the disqualification, and the power under which the disqualification was made, exercised by the court. If the court suspends or removes a disqualification from driving, it must inform the Secretary of State of the date and period of the disqualification, the date and terms of the order for its suspension or removal, the power under which the court took the action, and where the court suspends the disqualification pending appeal, name of the court to which the defendant has appealed.   15.33

The procedure governing the making of a statutory declaration to avoid a financial penalty is dealt with by rule 55.3. A sum may be registered for enforcement as a fine after failure to comply with a fixed penalty notice under section 54(14), 55, 62(15), 63(16), 64, 70(17), and 71(18) of the RTOA 1988. If that occurs, the court officer must notify the defendant of the registration. If the defendant then makes a statutory declaration it has the effect that the fixed penalty notice, or any associated notice sent to the defendant as owner of the vehicle concerned, and the registration and any enforcement proceedings become void. Rule 55.3(2) provides that, unless the court extends the time limit, the defendant must serve that statutory declaration not more than twenty-one days after service of notice of the registration for enforcement. The court officer must then serve a copy of the statutory declaration on the person by whom the certificate was registered. He must   15.34

also cancel any endorsement on the defendant's driving record and on any counterpart licence. He must then notify the Secretary of State of any such cancellation.

15.35   Under sections 30A(21), 34A(22), and 34D(23) of the RTOA 1988 a court may reduce a road traffic penalty on condition that the defendant attend an approved course, or take part in an approved programme. Following an application by the defendant the court that made the order, or the defendant's local magistrates' court, may review a course or programme provider's decision that the defendant did not complete the course satisfactorily, or did not participate fully in the programme. Rule 55.4 governs the making of such an application by the defendant. The application must be in writing and made not more not more than twenty-eight days after the date by which the defendant was required to complete the course, or the giving of the certificate of failure fully to participate in the programme. The application must be served on the court officer. It must specify the course or programme and if the course provider has failed to give a certificate it must explain that. Where the court provider has refused to give a certificate it must explain why the defendant disagrees with the reasons for that decision. Where the programme provider has given a certificate, the defendant must explain why he disagrees with the reasons for that decision. The court officer must serve a copy of the application on the course or programme provider. The court must not determine the application unless the defendant, and the course or programme provider, each has had an opportunity to make representations at a hearing.

15.36   By virtue of section 56 of the Crime (International Co-operation) Act 2003 a foreign driving disqualification may be recognized in the United Kingdom. If the criteria under section 56 are met then under section 57, the appropriate minister may, and in some cases must, give the person concerned notice that he or she is disqualified in the United Kingdom, too, and for what period. Section 59 of the 2003 Act, allows a person subject to such a disqualification to appeal to a magistrates' court. The procedure for such an appeal is governed by rule 55.5. It stipulates that the appellant must serve an appeal notice on the court officer, at a magistrates' court in the local justice area in which the appellant lives; and the minister, at the address given in the disqualification notice. That notice appellant must be served within twenty-one days and must attach a copy of the disqualification notice. It must also explain which of the conditions in section 56 of the 2003 Act is not met, and why section 57 of the Act therefore does not apply. Finally, it must include any application to suspend the disqualification, under section 60 of the Act (rule 55.5(3) and (4)). The minister may serve a respondent's notice. He must do so if he wants to make representations to the court or is he directed to do so by the court.

15.37   Unless the court directs otherwise, the minister must serve any such respondent's notice not more than fourteen days after the appellant serves the appeal notice, or the minister is directed to serve a respondent's notice. The respondent's notice must identify the grounds of opposition on which the minister relies and summarize any relevant facts not already included in the disqualification and appeal notices. It must also identify any other document that the minister thinks the court will need to decide the appeal. Any such document must then be served with the notice (rule 55.5(5) and (6)). The general rule is that any appeal will be by way of a public hearing but it may do so without a hearing or at a private hearing (rule 55.5(7)). Following the determination of an appeal, the court officer must serve the minister a notice of the outcome of the appeal, notice of any suspension of the disqualification, and the appellant's driving licence (if it was surrendered to the court officer).

16

CONFISCATION

A. INTRODUCTION

Parts 56 to 61 of the Rules seek to regulate the various different aspects of the regime 16.01
that presently exist for the confiscation of the proceeds of criminal activity. In order to
understand these rules, it is necessary to understand the components of that regime.

For offences committed before 24 March 2003,[1] the appropriate legislation depends 16.02
on the type of offence. The confiscation of the proceeds of drug trafficking is subject to
the Drug Trafficking Act 1994 (DTA 1994). The confiscation of the proceeds of other
offending is subject to the Criminal Justice Act 1988 (CJA 1988). These two forms of
proceedings may collectively be described as old confiscation provisions. For offences
committed on or after 24 March 2003, the applicable confiscation provisions are those
of the Proceeds of Crime Act 2002 (POCA 2002).

At the time that the 2005 Rules were introduced, it was likely that there would have 16.03
been confiscation proceedings still in progress under the old confiscation provisions, and
thus a need for the Rules to address those provisions. Five years later, it seems unlikely
that there will be many such cases remaining. Despite this the old confiscation provisions are addressed in Part 56 of the Rules.

The remainder of the 2010 Rules provisions relating to confiscation deal with POCA 16.04
2002. This has been described as:

. . .a massive piece of legislation that comprehensively addresses the detection and recovery of
criminal property. There is now both a unified mandatory process of confiscation following a

---

[1] The date of the Proceeds of Crime Act 2002 (Commencement No 5, Transitional Provisions, Savings
and Amendments) Order 2003, SI 2003/333.

criminal conviction and a civil procedure for recovery of the proceeds of crime regardless of any criminal prosecution.[2]

16.05 In addition to rules of general application to the provisions of the 2002 Act, which are contained in Part 57 of the Rules, the areas of the POCA 2002 which are covered by the rules are:

(a) confiscation of the proceeds of crime (Part 58);
(b) restraint proceedings (Parts 59 and 61);
(c) receivership proceedings (Parts 60 and 61).

16.06 In each of these areas, the rules will be set in the relevant statutory context and addressed as they would arise chronologically in the proceedings. The 2005 Rules also included rules relating to financial investigations. These are not reproduced in the 2010 Rules, no doubt as a result of the insertion of the new Part dealing with investigation orders (Part 6).

B. CONFISCATION UNDER THE CRIMINAL JUSTICE 1988 AND THE DRUG TRAFFICKING ACT 1994

16.07 The notes to Part 56 of the 2010 Rules recognize that these rules will only have application to proceedings for offences committed before 24 March 2003. Unsurprisingly, the rules remain unchanged from the 2005 Rules. The context to the Part 56 rules is as follows:

(a) where a defendant has been convicted of one or more offences of drug trafficking,[3] the court should proceed from sentence to confiscation either if invited to do so by the prosecution or of its own motion (section 2(1) of the DTA 1994);
(b) similarly, where the defendant is convicted of an offence of the relevant description,[4] the court shall proceed to consider confiscation if written notice has been served by the prosecution requesting it, or it is minded to do so in any event (section 71(1) of the CJA 1988);
(c) the test to be applied in either case is the same,[5] namely:
   (i) whether the defendant has benefited from the relevant criminal conduct, and if so
   (ii) what amount is realizable from him.

1. Statements under section 73 or section 11

16.08 The next step, usually, is for the prosecution to serve a statement,[6] which identifies the matters relevant to whether and to what extent the defendant has benefited. The court can then order the defendant to serve a statement in response. Under rule 56.1, the

---

[2] *Blackstone's Guide to the Proceeds of Crime Act 2002* (Rees and Hall) Ch 1, p 3, para 1.1.4.
[3] Drug trafficking is defined by s 1 of the DTA 1994.
[4] As defined under s 71(9)(c) of the CJA 1988.
[5] Pursuant to ss 71(1A) and (1B) of the CJA 1988 and to ss 2(2) and (4) of the DTA 1994.
[6] Pursuant to either s 73 of the CJA 1988 or s 11 of the DTA 1994.

prosecutor or defendant, when serving their statement or response on the court, must also provide it to the other party (rule 56.1(1)).

Any statement served by the prosecution should include, in addition to the question 16.09
of whether and to what extent the defendant has benefited, the names of the defendant and the maker of the statement, the dates of conviction and of the statement (rule 56.1(2)). Any statement served by the defendant accepting the content of the prosecutor's statement should be served on the court as well as the prosecution (rule 56.1(3)).

2. Postponement

The court may postpone its determination of the application for confiscation to allow 16.10
more time for necessary information to be obtained, such postponement being limited to a period of six months from conviction unless exceptional circumstances exist to postpone it further.[7] Alternatively, the court can postpone its determination to await the outcome of an appeal against the defendant's conviction.

An application for a postponement may be made by either the prosecution or defence.[8] 16.11
In either event, the application must be in writing, and served on the other side as well as the court (rule 56.2(1)). The party on whom the application is served then has twenty-eight days to respond to the court and applicant, indicating whether or not it opposes the application (rule 56.2(2)). After that twenty-eight day period, the court shall determine the application, with or without a hearing (rule 56.2(3)).

3. Revision, discharge, or variation

There are provisions under both Acts which allow applications to be made to revise, vary, 16.12
or discharge orders made in relation to confiscation or to revisit findings made in relation to confiscation.

The key provisions[9] allowing for reassessment of an earlier resolution in relation to 16.13
confiscation can be summarized as follows:

(a) Section 13 of the DTA 1994 and section 74A of the CJA 1988 allow the prosecutor to apply for the court to proceed to confiscation[10] where material comes to light, which was not available at the time of sentence, which makes it appropriate to do so.

(b) Section 14 of the DTA 1994 and section 74B of the CJA 1988 allow the prosecutor to apply for a reassessment of a finding[11] that the defendant has not benefited from drug trafficking when further evidence comes to light.

(c) Section 15 of the DTA 1994 and section 74C of the CJA 1988 allow the prosecutor to apply for a reassessment of the finding[12] as to the amount to be recovered, where

---

[7] Pursuant s 72A of the CJA 1988 and s 3(1) of the DTA 1994.
[8] Under s 72A(5) of the CJA 1988 or s 3(5)(a) of the DTA 1994.
[9] The key provisions are ss 13–15 of the DTA 1994 and ss 74A–74C of the CJA 1988.
[10] Under s 2 of the DTA 1994 or s 71 of the CJA 1988.
[11] An assessment made under s 2(2) of the DTA 1994 or s 71(1A) of the CJA 1988.
[12] An assessment made under s 2(4) of the DTA 1994 or s 71(1B) of the CJA 1988.

he believes that the actual valuation of the defendant's assets is greater than their assessed value.

16.14　If the prosecutor wishes to make an application in any of these situations, they must apply in writing to the court, with a copy provided to the defendant (rule 56.3(1)), stating the name of the defendant, the details of his conviction, the date of the relevant order or finding in relation to confiscation, the grounds for the application, and the evidence that supports them (rule 56.3(2)).

16.15　To assist in the investigation into whether the defendant benefited from any criminal conduct, including drug trafficking, or into the extent of the proceeds of that conduct, the court can make orders for the production of material.[13] Where such an order has been made, any person affected by it may apply for it to be varied or discharged, and following a hearing the judge may vary or discharge the order (rule 56.4(1)).

16.16　The person affected who is seeking to vary or discharge the order must give the officer specified in the order at least forty-eight hours notice of the application, which must be in writing, indicating the time and place at which the application is to be made (rule 56.4(2)). This requirement may be dispensed with by a judge who is satisfied that there is good reason to seek the variation or discharge of the order more quickly than that (rule 56.4(3)).

16.17　Where an order is made for confiscation under either Act, a period of imprisonment should be fixed in default of payment. The prosecutor may apply to the court to increase that term.[14] Such application is to be made in writing (rule 56.5(2)), stating the details of the defendant and enforcement measures that have already been taken, the grounds for the application and including the confiscation order (rule 56.5(3)).

16.18　The Crown Court is then required to send copies of the application to the defendant and to the magistrates' court required to enforce payment of the order and inform the parties of the listing for the hearing (rule 56.5(4)). The court is also obliged to provide copies of any order it makes as a result of this application to the parties, the relevant magistrates' court, and any place of detention in which the defendant is being held (rule 56.5(5)).

16.19　Rule 56.6 deals with the notice that is to be given where a confiscation order made under section 19 of the DTA 1994 is cancelled under section 22(2) of that Act.

C. RULES APPLICABLE FOR ALL PROCEEDINGS UNDER THE PROCEEDS OF CRIME ACT 2002

16.20　This Part of the Rules addresses a range of procedural matters for the administration of the confiscation regime under POCA 2002. This includes such matters as the definitions of words, the calculation of timings, the procedures for registration of orders, the content of and service of statements and expert material, and proof of such service thereafter. As the title to Part 57 suggests, the rules apply not only to confiscation in criminal proceedings but to civil procedures for restraint and receivership.

---

[13] Under s 93H of the CJA 1988, s 55 of the DTA 1994, or issue of a production order under s 345 of the POCA 2002.

[14] Under s 75A(2) of the CJA 1988 and s 10(2) of the DTA 1994.

The 2005 version of these rules had been lifted unaltered from the Crown Court **16.21** (Confiscation, Restraint and Receivership) Rules 2003. The 2010 Rules in turn replicate their 2005 predecessors, save that a new rule 57.15 has been added, which is discussed below.

Rules 57.1 to 57.3 are definition provisions. Rule 57.1 defines terms as they are to **16.22** appear in the remaining rules that deal with the Proceeds of Crime Act 2002 and rules 57.2 and 57.3 deal with issues of timing, namely how periods which the rules allow for the completion of a task are to be calculated and what allowance is to be made for offices being closed on such deadline days.

1. Orders from Scotland or Northern Ireland

The Proceeds of Crime Act 2002 (Enforcement in different parts of the United Kingdom) **16.23** Order 2002[15] allows the enforcement in England and Wales of orders made in Northern Ireland or Scotland. The precondition to such enforcement is that the order is registered under article 6, which states as follows:

(1) Where an application for the registration of a Northern Ireland receivership order, a Northern Ireland restraint order, a Scottish administration order or a Scottish restraint order is made to the Crown Court in England and Wales, the Crown Court must direct that the order be registered in that court.
(2) Where the Crown Court has directed that an order be registered, it may make such order as it believes is appropriate for the purpose of—
  (a) ensuring that the order is effective; or
  (b) assisting an administrator appointed in pursuance of Part 3 of the Act or a receiver appointed in pursuance of Part 4 of the Act to exercise his functions.

Rules 57.4 to 57.6 give effect to this article. The application to register such a Scottish **16.24** or Northern Irish order is to be made in writing and accompanied by a statement which exhibits the relevant order and details the realizable property believed to be in England and Wales (rule 57.4(3)). Although the application to register can be made without notice (rule 57.4(2)), the applicant is obliged to give notice of the order, once registered, to those affected by it (rule 57.4(4)) and does not require the court's permission (which is generally required under rule 57.13(1)) to serve it outside England and Wales.

A person affected by such an order may apply to vary or set aside its registration (rule **16.25** 57.5(1)). Such an application is to be made in writing and supported by a witness statement (rule 57.5(2)), and both must be lodged with the court (rule 57.5(3)) and served on the person who applied to register the order at least seven days before the hearing of the application (rule 57.5(4)). Once the application has been served, the realization of property under the order is suspended until the matter is resolved (rule 57.5(5)).

The court is obliged to maintain a register of such orders, including the details of any **16.26** variation or setting aside of registration and of their execution (rule 57.6).

---

[15] SI 2002/3133.

2. Witness statements

16.27 Where the rules in relation to confiscation require that a witness statement be served, for example in support of orders to vary a confiscation order under rules 58.4 to 58.5 and 58.7, it must contain a statement of truth (rule 57.7(1)), namely a declaration by the maker of the statement that it is true to the best of their knowledge or belief in the same terms as are required for a statement served under section 9 of the CJA 1967 (rule 57.7(2)), which must be signed by the maker of the statement (rule 57.7(3)). If a witness statement does not include such a statement of truth, the court may rule it inadmissible (rule 57.7(4)).

16.28   A witness statement made in confiscation proceedings, when required by the rules, is only to be used for those proceedings (rule 57.8(1)) unless the rules provide otherwise, the maker or the Crown Court consents, or the content of the statement has been adduced in public (rule 57.8(2)).

3. Expert evidence

16.29 Where expert evidence is to be adduced in confiscation proceedings, it must be served as soon as possible on the other parties. This involves not only service of the statement but disclosure of any records or documents which relate to or support the opinions expressed in the statement (rule 57.9(1)). Failure to comply with this requirement can result in the exclusion of the evidence (rule 57.9(d)). This requirement can, however, be waived by one of the parties who may agree to be orally informed of the expert's opinion (rule 57.9(1)(c)).

16.30   Other than by waiver of the requirement to serve expert evidence under rule 57.9(1)(c), the other exception to the requirement arises where a party has reasonable grounds to believe that disclosure of the expert evidence would lead to the intimidation of the witness or otherwise interfere with justice (rule 57.10(1)). In this situation, the party must serve notice on the parties to state that the evidence is being withheld and why (rule 57.10(2)).

4. Evidence generally

16.31 In restraint and receivership proceedings, as regulated by Part 61 of the Rules, the court is required to give directions as to the evidence that may be called, defining the issues, the evidence necessary in relation to those issues, and the manner in which it may be given (rule 61.5(1)). As part of this process, the court may exclude otherwise admissible evidence (rule 61.5(2)), and restrict cross-examination (rule 61.5(3)). In relation to the admissibility of evidence it should be noted that the requirements of section 2(1) of the Civil Evidence Act 1995 (as to the service of a notice for hearsay evidence) do not apply to such proceedings (rule 61.8).

16.32   The presumption is that all evidence that is required will be adduced in writing (rule 61.6(1)). Any party may, however, apply to cross-examine such a witness (rule 61.6(2)) and in that event the witness' evidence may only be adduced if they attend for such cross-examination (rule 61.6(3)). To that end, a party may apply for a witness summons, either for the attendance of a witness or the production of a document, in the form set out in rule 28.3 (rule 61.7).

5. Service of documents

Ordinarily, the service of documents within the United Kingdom should be effected in accordance with rule 4.3,[16] and outside the United Kingdom under rule 32.1.[17] In receivership and restraint proceedings, however, the rules for service are those in rules 57.11 to 57.14. It should be noted that the newly inserted rule 57.15 makes these rules applicable to proceedings under the Proceeds of Crime Act 2002 (External Requests and Orders) Order 2005[18] as to other corresponding confiscation proceedings.   16.33

Documents are to be served by: 16.34

(a) personal delivery (rule 57.11(2)(a));
(b) posting them to the individual's last known or usual address (rule 57.11(2)(b)), which will be assumed to have arrived on the second business day thereafter (rule 57.11(3)(a));
(c) delivery by post, document exchange (DX) or (by agreement) fax on the individual's solicitor (rule 57.11(2)(c)), which in the case of post or DX will be assumed to have arrived on the second business day thereafter (rule 57.11(3)(a)–(b)) and in the case of fax on the same day unless sent after 4pm (rule 57.11(3)(c)).

These rules as to service can be ignored where the person affected by the order was in court when it was made (rule 57.11(4)) and can be varied to allow service by an alternative method on the application of a party (rule 57.12(1)) which is made with supporting evidence with or without notice (rule 57.12(2)). The order allowing the alternative method service must specify what it is and when it will be deemed to have been achieved (rule 57.12(3)).   16.35

Save for an order registered under rule 57.4, a document can only be served outside England and Wales with the court's permission (rule 57.13(1)). With such permission it can be served by any of the methods in paragraph 16.34 above (rule 57.13(2)) provided this is consistent with the law of the country in which it is being served (rule 57.13(3)).   16.36

Where a person on whom a document should have been served in relation to a hearing fails to attend that hearing, the court may only carry on if satisfied that service was achieved (rule 57.13(4)). To that end, on serving a document on such a person, the party serving the document must also serve a certificate on the court (rule 57.14(1)) which states the date and method of service (rule 57.14(2)). If the party was unable to serve the document, a certificate to that effect should also be provided (rule 57.14(3)).   16.37

D. RULES APPLICABLE TO CONFISCATION PROCEEDINGS UNDER THE PROCEEDS OF CRIME ACT 2002

Part 58 of the Rules regulates the conduct of such confiscation proceedings under POCA 2002 in the same way that section 56 regulated proceedings for offences committed   16.38

---

[16] See Chapter 3.
[17] See Chapter 9.
[18] SI 2005/3181.

before 24 March 2003. The 2010 version of the Rules are largely a repetition of the 2005 version, save that the references in the 2005 version to the Director of the Assets Recovery Agency have been removed to take account of the abolition of that agency.[19]

16.39   Where a defendant is liable to confiscation proceedings under section 6(2), the court should proceed with a view to confiscation either if invited to do so by the prosecution or of its own motion (section 6(3)). The test to be applied in either case is the same (pursuant to section 6(4)–(5)), namely:

(a) whether the defendant has a criminal lifestyle;[20]
(b) if so, whether he has benefited from this general criminal conduct;
(c) if not, whether the defendant has benefited from the relevant criminal conduct;
(d) in either situation, what amount is realizable from him.

1. Statements and disclosure under sections 16 to 18

16.40   The next step, usually, is for the prosecution to serve a statement of information under section 16, which identifies the matters relevant to whether the defendant has a criminal lifestyle, whether he has benefited either from that lifestyle or from specific conduct and, if so, by how much. The court can then order the defendant to serve a statement in response under section 17 or require the defence to provide such information as is specified in the order to assist in the confiscation proceedings.

16.41   Under rule 58.1, the prosecutor, when serving their statement on the court, must also provide it to the defence. Any such statement should include, in addition to the question of whether the defendant has benefited and if so by how much, the names of the defendant and the maker of the statement, the dates of conviction and of the statement (rule 58.1(2)).

16.42   Any statement served by the defendant under section 17 which indicates an acceptance of the content of the prosecutor's statement should be served on the court as well as the prosecution (rule 58.1(3)). Any information provided by the defence in compliance with an order made under section 18, must be provided in writing and copied to the prosecution (rule 58.1(4)).

2. Postponement

16.43   The court may postpone its determination of the application for confiscation to allow more time for necessary information to be obtained,[21] such postponement being limited to a period of two years' from conviction unless exceptional circumstances exist to postpone it further. Alternatively, the court can postpone its determination to await the outcome of an appeal against the defendant's conviction. The court may grant such a postponement without a hearing (rule 58.2).

---

[19] Pursuant to s 74 and Sch 8 to the Serious Crime Act 2007.
[20] Criminal lifestyle is defined in s 75 of the POCA 2002.
[21] Pursuant to s 14 of the POCA 2002.

3. Reconsideration, discharge, or variation

There are provisions under the Act which allow applications to be made for the recon- 16.44
sideration, variation, or discharge of orders made in relation of confiscation or findings
made in relation to confiscation proceedings.

The key provisions allowing for reconsideration of an earlier resolution in relation to 16.45
confiscation can be summarized as follows:

(a) Section 19 allows the prosecutor to apply for the court to proceed to confiscation
    under section 6 where material comes to light, which was not available at the time
    of conviction or the decision not to proceed to confiscation, which makes it appro-
    priate to do so, provided that the application is made within six years' of
    conviction.
(b) Section 20 allows the prosecutor to apply for a reassessment of a finding under sec-
    tion 6 that the defendant has not benefited from his criminal lifestyle or particular
    criminal conduct when further evidence comes to light within six years' of convic-
    tion which was not available at the time that the original assessment was made.
(c) Section 21 allows the prosecutor to apply within six years' of conviction for a reas-
    sessment of the finding under section 6 as to the amount to be recovered, where he
    believes that the actual valuation of the defendant's assets is greater than their assessed
    value.

If the prosecutor wishes to make an application in any of these situations, they must 16.46
apply in writing to the court (rule 58.3(1)), with a copy provided to the defendant
within seven days of the hearing (rule 58.3(4)), stating the name of the defendant,
the details of his conviction, the date of the relevant order or finding in relation to confiscation, the grounds for the application, and the evidence that supports them (rule
58.3(2)).

Where the amount assessed as realizable at the time that the order was made proves to 16.47
be incorrect, the provisions are as follows:

(a) Section 22 allows the prosecution or a receiver appointed under section 50 to apply
    to the court for a fresh valuation to be made of the defendant's realizable property.[22]
    An application for such a re-evaluation needs to be made in writing, supported by a
    witness statement (rule 58.4(2)) that complies with rule 57.7, lodged with the court
    (rule 58.4(3)) and served on the other parties (including the receiver where the appli-
    cation is not made by him) at least seven days before the hearing (rule 58.4(4)).
(b) Section 23 allows the defendant or a receiver[23] to apply for a re-evaluation of the
    amount that might be realized and, if this is less than the amount outstanding under
    the order, vary the order accordingly. Such an application is to be made in writing
    and supported by a witness statement (rule 58.5(2)) that complies with rule 57.7,
    lodged with the court (rule 58.5(3)) and served on the other parties (including the

---

[22] The 2005 Rules made reference to the appointment of a receiver under sections 50 or 52, the latter
provision was removed from the POCA 2002 by Sch 8, para 24, to the Serious Crime Act 2007, as a consequence of the abolition of the Asset Recovery Agency.

[23] A receiver in these circumstances is one appointed under s 50 of the POCA 2002 (see previous
footnote).

receiver where the application is not made by him) at least seven days before the hearing (rule 58.5(5)).

(c) Section 24 allows the justices' chief executive to apply for the discharge of an order under which less than £1,000 is outstanding. The court shall then carry out a re-evaluation of the amount that might be realized and, if this is less than the amount outstanding under the order, and it is inadequate for one of the reasons specified in section 24(4), it shall discharge the order. Section 25 allows for a similar application to be made where the amount outstanding is less than £50, without the need for either re-evaluation or specified reasons. Either application is to be made in writing (rule 58.6(2)) detailing the order, the amount outstanding, and grounds for the application. It should be served on the other parties (including the receiver where the application is not made by him) (rule 58.6(3)). The application will then be resolved without a hearing, unless one is requested by a party within seven days of service (rule 58.6(4)), and if the order is discharged all parties should be notified (rule 58.6(5)).

(d) Under section 28, where a defendant, whilst being prosecuted, absconds for a period of two years, and the prosecution apply to the court to do so, the court may proceed to make an order as to confiscation under section 6. If the defendant then ceases to be an absconder, he may apply to vary that order or to discharge it.[24] In each case the application should be made in writing and supported by a witness statement (rule 58.7(2) and rule 58.8(2)). In each case, details must be given of the order made, the circumstances in which the defendant ceased to be an absconder, whether he was convicted or, in the case of section 30, acquitted, and the grounds for the application. The application should be lodged with the court (rule 58.7(3) and rule 58.8(3)) and served on the other parties at least seven days before the hearing (rule 58.7(4) and rule 58.8(4)).[25]

4. Imprisonment in default

16.48   Where an order is made for confiscation under either Act, a period of imprisonment should be fixed in default of payment. The prosecutor may apply to the court to increase that term.[26] Such an application is to be made in writing (rule 58.9(1)), stating the details of the defendant, enforcement measures that have already been taken, the grounds for the application, and should include the confiscation order (rule 58.9(2)).

16.49   The Crown Court is then required to send copies of the application to the defendant and to the magistrates' court required to enforce payment of the order and inform the parties of the listing for the hearing (rule 58.9(3)). The court is also obliged to provide copies of any order it makes as a result of this application to the parties, the relevant

---

[24] Applications to vary are made pursuant to s 29 of the POCA 2002 and applications to discharge pursuant to s 30 of the POCA 2002.

[25] For the avoidance of doubt, r 58.7(4) in the 2010 Rules omits reference to the appointment of the Asset Recovery Agency under s 34 of the POCA 2002 because that provision was removed by para 18, Sch 8 to the Serious Crimes Act 2007. This also applies to other references to this provision elsewhere in the 2005 Rules.

[26] Under s 39(5) of the POCA 2002.

magistrates' court, and any place of detention in which the defendant is being held (rule 58.9(4)).

5. Compensation

Where a defendant is investigated or prosecuted but not ultimately convicted, there is serious default on the part of someone involved in the investigation but for which the investigation would not have carried on, and the applicant has suffered loss in consequence to the treatment of realizable property in his possession, he can apply for compensation.[27] Such an application should be made in writing, supported by a witness statement (rule 58.10(2)), and should be lodged with the court (rule 58.10(3)) and on the person in default and the person by whom the compensation would be payable (rule 58.10(4)) at least seven days before the hearing. 16.50

A similar application may be made for compensation where an order made in relation to an absconding defendant under section 28 has been varied under section 29 or discharged under section 30, and the applicant has suffered loss as a result of the original order.[28] Such an application should be made in writing, supported by a witness statement (rule 58.11(2)), and should be lodged with the court (rule 58.11(3)) and on the person in default and the person by whom the compensation would be payable (rule 58.11(4)) at least seven days before the hearing. 16.51

6. Seizure of money in a bank account

The magistrates' court can in particular circumstances[29] order a bank or building society to pay to the justices' clerk the amount payable under a confiscation order. The order should be directed to the relevant bank or building society, naming the person against whom the order was made, the account details, the amount to be paid, the person to whom it ought to be paid, and directing them to pay the amount in seven days, unless another period is fixed (rule 58.12(1)). 16.52

The order should be served on the relevant institution either by personal delivery or by posting it first class (rule 58.12(2)). If sent by post, it will be presumed to arrive on the second business day (rule 58.12(3)). 16.53

E. RESTRAINT PROCEEDINGS

The purpose of a restraint order is to freeze property that may later be the subject of a confiscation order. Such an order may be made where the circumstances enunciated in section 40 of the POCA 2002 apply, which have at their root a belief by those applying for the order that the person whose assets are to be frozen has benefited from criminal conduct. The order[30] prohibits anyone specified in the order from dealing with any 16.54

---

[27] Under s 72 of the POCA 2002.
[28] An application for compensation pursuant to s 73 of the POCA 2002.
[29] Under s 67(5) of the POCA 2002. The circumstances set out in subsections (1) to (4).
[30] The Restraint Order is made under s 41 of the POCA 2002.

realizable property held by him, unless that property is specifically excluded. Such an order may only be made on the application of the prosecution or those specified in section 42(2).

16.55 The rules in Part 59 of the 2010 Rules replicate those contained in the 2005 version, save for the addition of a new rule 59.6, which is discussed below. Part 59 should be read in conjunction with Part 61, which provides additional regulation in this area. Rule 59.2 addresses the content of such a restraint order. The order can include the following types of detail:

(a) The exclusion of property from the freezing effect of a restraint order is permitted by section 41(3) provided that it does not include provision for legal expenses under section 41(4). The order may therefore permit exceptions from the order for reasonable living expenses, and for purposes of carrying on a business (rule 59.2(1)). It also includes reasonable legal expenses (rule 59.2(1)) subject to section 41(4) (rule 59.2(2)). An exception to the order may be made subject to conditions (rule 59.2(3)).

(b) The order may be made subject to an undertaking by the applicant that he will pay the reasonable expenses incurred in complying with the order of someone other than the person who is prohibited from dealing with the property (rule 59.2(5)). However, it may not be made subject to an undertaking relating to damage sustained as a result of the order by the person who is prohibited from dealing with the property (rule 59.2(4)).

(c) The order must include a statement to the effect that disobedience to the order, whether by the person who is prohibited from dealing with the property or another, may be a contempt of court. It must also set out the potential consequences of such a contempt (rule 59.2(6)).

16.56 Where the order has been made without notice, copies of the order and the witness statement made in support of the application for it must be served on the defendant, any person who is prohibited from dealing with the property, and any person affected by the order (rule 59.2(8)).

16.57 Such an order has effect until it is varied or discharged (rule 59.2(7)). Such an application can be made either by someone affected by it (which can include someone prohibited from handling property under it) or by the person who applied for it originally.[31]

16.58 Where the application is made by someone affected by the order, their application must be in writing and supported by a witness statement which complies with rule 57.7 (rule 59.3(2)). The application must be lodged with the court (rule 59.3(3)) and served on the person who applied for the order and such persons as are prohibited by it (if not the maker of the application to vary or discharge) at least two days before the hearing unless the court directs otherwise (rule 59.3(4)).

16.59 Where the application is made by the original applicant the procedure varies according to whether it is an application to vary or to discharge.

16.60 If to vary:

(a) the application can be made without notice, if the application is urgent or there are reasons to believe that such notice would result in the dissipation of the property (rule 59.4(2));

---

[31] The application is pursuant to s 42(3) of the POCA 2002.

(b) otherwise, it should be made on notice to others concerned at least two days before the hearing unless the court directs otherwise (rule 59.4(5));

(c) in either case, the application, which must be lodged with the court (rule 59.4(4)), should be in writing and supported by a witness statement, which complies with rule 57.7, which sets out the grounds for the application and which provides the other details set out in rule 59.4(3);

(d) where such a variation has been granted, copies of the order and the supporting witness statement should be served on those affected by the order and the defendant (rule 59.4(6)).

If to discharge:
16.61

(a) the application may be made without notice (rule 59.5(2));

(b) it must be made in writing, stating the grounds for the application (rule 59.5(3)). It appears that no supporting statement is needed, no doubt because such applications will often be made where the proceedings in relation to which the order was obtained have come to an end;

(c) where such a discharge is granted, copies of the order and the supporting witness statement should be served on those affected by the order and the defendant (rule 59.5(4)).

Further rules that have an application to restraint proceedings, but which also have a relevance to receivership proceedings, are addressed below. If a person is accused of disobeying a restraint order, another party may apply to the court for this to be punished as a contempt of court. The rules that govern such an application are those contained in Part 62 of the Rules[32] (rule 59.6).
16.62

F. RECEIVERSHIP

Receivership proceedings follow on from the orders made in restraint proceedings dealt with above. The purpose of receivership is, in the context of the POCA 2002, twofold: first to ensure that either the restraint order or the ultimate confiscation order is effective, and that all property covered by it is taken from the control of the person who is prohibited from using it and secured, and, secondly, once seized it is managed properly.
16.63

To that end the Act provides for the appointment of management receivers,[33] whose job is to receive and manage the property that is the subject of a restraint order, and for the appointment of enforcement receivers,[34] whose job it is to secure all property encompassed by a confiscation order. As was noted in relation to Part 59 of the 2010 Rules, the abolition of the Assets Recovery Agency[35] has required amendment to the rules in Part 60 to remove references to a Director's Receiver appointed under section 52
16.64

---

[32] See Chapter 17 below.
[33] Pursuant to s 48 of the POCA 2002.
[34] Pursuant to s 50 of the POCA 2002.
[35] As a consequence of s 74(2) and Sch 8 to the Serious Crime Act 2007.

of the POCA 2002.[36] As with Part 59, this Part of the Rules should be read in conjunction with Part 61.

16.65   Part 60 of the Rules seeks to provide the procedural framework in which such receivers will operate. The rules mirror the stages of receivership proceedings, namely:

(a) the appointment of the receiver;
(b) the conferral of powers on the receiver;
(c) the variation or discharge of a receivership order;
(d) the regulation of the activities of the receiver.

16.66   At each of these stages, it should be noted that all applications should be made in writing and determined without a hearing unless the court directs otherwise. This creates an interesting problem of interpretation in the rules which require the applicant to give notice to others affected by the application two days or seven days before the date fixed for hearing[37] where there will in fact be no hearing normally. The scheme will therefore only work if dates are fixed for hearings which it is not anticipated will occur. If there actually is a hearing, it will take place in chambers (rule 61.4).

1. Appointment

16.67   Where, a restraint order has been made,[38] the applicant may apply for a management receiver to be appointed in relation to the realizable property under that order. Equally where the prosecutor applies for the appointment of an enforcement receiver for the enforcement of an unfulfilled confiscation order,[39] rule 60.1 applies to the appointment.

16.68   In each case, the application is made in writing, supported by a statement which complies with rule 60.1(3), both of which must be lodged with the court (rule 60.1(5)). In the case of an application for an enforcement receiver, a copy of the confiscation order which is to be enforced should also be attached (rule 60.1(4)).

16.69   The statement must give the grounds for the application, full details of the proposed receiver, and full details of the realizable property in relation to which the receiver will be acting. If the applicant is an accredited financial investigator, section 68(2) requires that he complete a declaration confirming that he falls within one of the categories of investigator set out in section 68(3). Any such declaration must also be included in the statement. In addition, if the receiver is not an employee of the Crown Prosecution Service,[40] reasons must be given if no security is to be given for the actions of the receiver (rule 60.1(3)(e)).[41]

16.70   The application may be made without notice where it is made in conjunction with an application for a restraint order (rule 60.1(2)(a)), which may be made without notice by

---

[36] Section 52 of the POCA 2002 is removed by para 24, Sch 8 to the Serious Crime Act 2007.
[37] See for example rr 59.3(4), 59.4(5), 60.1(6), and 60.3(3).
[38] Pursuant to s 48 of the POCA 2002.
[39] Under s 50 of the POCA 2002.
[40] Rule 60.1(3)(e) also refers to members of staff of the Revenue and Customs Prosecutions Office, but that office has now been subsumed into the CPS, and the rule therefore applies to anyone not from within the CPS.
[41] This is to take account of r 60.5, discussed below.

virtue of rule 59.1(2), or where either the application is urgent or there are reasons to believe that any notice would result in the dissipation of the property (rule 60.1(2)(b) and (c)). Otherwise, notice should be served on the defendant and those affected by the order at least seven days before the hearing, unless the court directs otherwise (rule 60.1(6)), and the same people need to be provided with copies of the order and supporting paperwork in the event that such an order is made.

2. Conferral of powers

Once a management receiver has been appointed under section 48, the court can order   16.71
that receiver should have such of the powers conferred by section 49 as it deems appropriate. This order is made as a result of an application by the person who applied for the restraint order.[42] Likewise, an enforcement receiver appointed under this section may have the powers set out in section 51 of the POCA 2002 conferred on him by court order. This order is made as a result of an application by the prosecutor.[43]

In each case, the application for the conferment of powers is to be made in writing,   16.72
supported by a statement which complies with rule 57.7 (rule 60.2(3)), both of which must be lodged with the court (rule 60.2(5)). In the case of an application in relation to an enforcement receiver, a copy of the confiscation order which is to be enforced should also be attached (rule 60.2(4)).

The statement must give the grounds for the application, full details of the realizable   16.73
property in relation to which the receiver will be acting. If the applicant is an accredited financial investigator, section 68(2) requires that he complete a declaration confirming that he falls within one of the categories of investigator set out in section 68(3). Any such declaration must also be included in the statement (rule 60.2(3)).

As with the making of the order of appointment, the application for conferral of   16.74
powers may be made without notice where it is made in conjunction with an application for a restraint order (rule 60.2(2)(a)), which may be made without notice by virtue of rule 59.1(2), or where either the application is urgent or there are reasons to believe that any notice would result in the dissipation of the property (rule 60.2(2)(b) and (c)). Otherwise, notice should be served on the defendant and those affected by the order at least seven days before the hearing, unless the court directs otherwise (rule 60.2(6)), and the same people need to be provided with copies of the order and supporting paperwork in the event that such an order is made (rule 60.2(7)).

Where the receiver appointed is not an employee of the Crown Prosecution Service[44]   16.75
the court may direct that he must give security or provide proof that he will be able to provide a security for any liability for his acts or omissions as a receiver before he is allowed to act (rule 60.5(2)). If the applicant is seeking to avoid giving security for the actions of the receiver whose appointment he seeks, reasons must be given (rule 60.1(3)(e)).

---

[42] Pursuant to s 49(1) of the POCA 2002.

[43] Pursuant to s 51(1) of the POCA 2002.

[44] Rule 60.5(1) also refers to members of staff of the Revenue and Customs Prosecutions Office, but that office has now been subsumed into the CPS, and the rule therefore applies to anyone not from within the CPS.

3. Application to vary or discharge

16.76 A receiver who has been appointed in accordance with the procedure above may apply to the court for directions as to how he may exercise his powers.[45] Similarly, anyone affected by his actions or proposed actions may apply to the court for such directions.[46] Additionally, the receiver, the person who sought his appointment, or anyone affected by his activities, may apply for the variation or discharge of the receivership order under section 63(1).

16.77 Any such application should be lodged with the court in writing (rule 60.3(2)) and served on those affected by it (who are listed) at least seven days before the hearing (rule 60.3(3)). The same persons will be provided with copies of any order the court makes as to variation or discharge (rule 60.3(4)).

16.78 Another way in which a receivership may be brought to an end is as a result of non-compliance by the receiver with any rule, practice direction, or other court direction. Where there is such non-compliance, the court may require the receiver to attend to explain himself (rule 60.8(1)) and if the court is not satisfied it may terminate his employment, reduce or disallow his remuneration, or order him to pay any party's costs (rule 60.8(2)).

16.79 The court may also terminate the appointment of a receiver if he fails to provide the security required under rule 60.5(2) (rule 60.5(3)).

16.80 Rule 78.1 allows the Crown Court to order costs on appeal from the magistrates' court. Where that occurs in the context of restraint or receivership proceedings, regard should be had to rule 61.19 which imports additional considerations and, under rule 61.20, further directions as to how such costs would be assessed. Any order to pay costs must be met in fourteen days (rule 61.21).

4. Regulation of the receiver's activities

16.81 The aim of the remaining provisions of the rules in this Part is to regulate the activities of the receiver to ensure that he is paid appropriately, handles monies provided to him appropriately, and keeps account of those monies correctly. The penalty for breaches in this area lies in the right of the court to terminate a receivership under rule 60.8.

16.82 Where monies have been paid to the receiver in relation to a confiscation order, but the monies paid exceed the amount owed, the receiver should seek the guidance of the court as to what he should do with that excess (rule 60.4(2)). The defence and any other person with an interest in property held by the receiver is entitled to at least seven days notice of such an application (rule 60.4(3)). Where the provisions for vesting of the sums in a trustee in bankruptcy apply (as set out in rule 60.4(5)), the court should make a declaration to that effect (rule 60.4(4)).

16.83 A receiver appointed by the court who is not an employee of the Crown Prosecution Service may only charge for his services if permitted to do so by the court, which has set out the basis upon which his remuneration is to be paid (rule 60.6(2)). The considerations which the court should take into account when determining the proper remuneration for

---

[45] Under s 62(2) of the POCA 2002.
[46] Under s 62(3) of the POCA 2002.

a receiver are set out in rule 60.6(3). The court may, alternatively, refer the calculation or proper remuneration to the taxing authority, which will the address the matter under rules 78.4 to 78.7 (rule 60.6(4)). The sources of that remuneration are then set out in rule 60.6(5)–(7).

A receiver appointed by the court may be required by the court to provide accounts   16.84 (rule 60.7(1)). Any party to the receivership proceedings can then apply to inspect those accounts (rule 60.7(2)). Having seen them, that party then has fourteen days to serve notice on the receiver specifying what objection he has to the accounts with reasons for that objection, and require the receiver either to accept that objection or to submit the accounts to examination (rule 60.7(3)). Within the fourteen days allowed to him, if the receiver decides to submit the accounts to examination, he should serve the accounts and the notice served under rule 60.7(3) on the court (rule 60.7(4)). If he fails to do this, any party to the proceedings may apply for such an examination of the accounts (rule 60.7(5)). The results of any such examination will be certified by the court (rule 60.7(6)).

Under both restraint orders and enforcement, power exists to levy distress against   16.85 realizable property and, where the order applies to a tenancy the landlord has a right of forfeiture by peaceful re-entry. However, under section 58(2) and (3) in relation to restraint proceedings, and section 59(2) and (3) in relation to enforcement receivers, before either action is taken the leave of the court is required. To obtain that leave, a written application has to be made to the court (rule 61.1(2)) and served on those specified within seven days (rule 61.1(3)).

Where there is a dispute as to whether property is realizable, the court can order the   16.86 disclosure of documents to assist (rule 61.9).

5. Documents

All orders made in the context of restraint and receivership will be drawn up by the court   16.87 unless the court orders one of the parties to do it, it is agreed that a party will do it, or it is a consent order (see below) (rule 61.15(1)). Where the drafting is entrusted to a party, the court may direct either that its terms are submitted for approval or that the order is checked by the court before it is sealed (rule 61.15(2)). Such an order must be lodged with the court within seven days (rule 61.15(3)).

Any order made in the context of restraint and receivership should state the name and   16.88 judicial title of the maker, and bear his seal and the date (rule 61.10(1)). The seal need not be genuine and can be electronic (rule 61.10(2)), but either form renders the document admissible without further proof (rule 61.10(3)). The court is, moreover, empowered to correct any mistake in any such order, and any party may apply for such a correction without notice (rule 61.12).

Where the parties have agreed the terms of an order (a consent order), any of them   16.89 may apply for judgment in those terms (rule 61.11(2)) and the court can make the order without a hearing (rule 61.11(3)), providing it complies with the content requirements of rule 61.11(4). Such a consent order does not require compliance with the other rules that relate to applications for such orders, which have been considered above (rule 61.11(5)).

Court documents may only be supplied from the court records with the court's   16.90 permission. An application for such permission needs to be made on notice to the parties (rule 61.13). The exception to this rule is that they may be provided to the judge presiding in proceedings for an offence in relation to which the restraint order was made, but its disclosure is limited to those proceedings (rule 61.14).

6. Legal representation

16.91 Rules 61.16 to 61.18 provide the rules which govern the method by which someone seeks to change from the solicitors who have been acting for him, or to appoint solicitors where he has been unrepresented hitherto (rule 61.16). They also provide for a solicitor to cease to act, and for the notices to be provided in those circumstances (rules 61.17 to 61.18).

17

CONTEMPT OF COURT

A. INTRODUCTION

The Rules originally devised and published in 2005 did not cover proceedings for con- 17.01
tempt of court. Part 62 of the 2010 Rules governs the procedure to deal with contempt
of court under section 45 of the Senior Courts Act 1981 (under which the Crown Court
has power to punish for contempt of court a person who disobeys its order) and under
section 18 of the CPIA 1996 (whereby a magistrates' court and the Crown Court can
punish for contempt of court the use of disclosed prosecution material in contravention
of section 17 of that Act. See Chapter 8, paragraph 20 *et seq* of this work for further
details). Chapter B14 of *Blackstone's Criminal Practice* provides in-depth coverage of the
law and practice relating to contempt of court.

B. SCOPE OF THE PART

Rule 62.1 stipulates that the rule governs the exercise of the court's powers under the two 17.02
statutory provisions identified above. The rule also defines a respondent for the purposes
of this part as being a person accused of contempt. In the absence of the respondent, the
court must not exercise its power to punish him for contempt unless he has had at least
fourteen days in which to make any representation and introduce any evidence (rule 62.2).

    A person who wants the court to exercise its power to punish the respondent for con- 17.03
tempt of court must serve a written application on the court officer. The application
must also be served on the respondent, as must notice of where and when the court will
hear the application. That must be not less than fourteen days after service (rule 62.3(1)).
The Practice Direction provides a form to be used for such an application. Part 4 of the
Rules requires that service be effected by handing the application to the respondent. The
written application must identify the respondent and stipulate that it is an application
for the respondent to be punished for contempt of court. It must make clear what the
applicant alleges against the respondent by containing sufficient details of the conduct
which is alleged to constitute contempt of court. The application must also include

a notice which warns the respondent of the court's powers of sentence (that is that the court can impose imprisonment, or a fine, or both, for contempt of court). It must also warn that the court has the power to deal with the application in the respondent's absence, if the respondent fails to attend the hearing (rule 62.3(2)).

17.04   If the court decides to impose a punishment it may suspend it for a period, or conditionally. If the respondent is absent when the court does that, the applicant must serve on the respondent notice of the terms of the court's order (rule 62.4).

17.05   If the court orders the imprisonment of the respondent for contempt, the respondent may apply to discharge that order. That application must be in writing and must be served on the court officer, and the applicant. The application must also explain why it is appropriate for the order to be discharged; and ask for a hearing, if he wants one.

C. RULES RELATING TO EVIDENCE

17.06   Part 62 also contains rules relating to the receipt of evidence at hearings. In provisions which are similar to those governing applications for civil behaviour orders under Part 50 of the Rules (see Chapter 15), rule 62.6 provides for the service of written statements and hearsay evidence in contempt proceedings. A copy of the statement, or notice of other hearsay, must be served on the court officer, and the other party. Any such notice by the applicant must be served with the application stipulated under rule 62.3. If it does not concern a written witness statement, that notice of hearsay must set out the evidence, or attach the document that contains it and identify the person who made the statement that is hearsay (rule 62.9). The respondent must serve any such notice no longer than seven days after receipt of the application (rule 62.6(1)). The entitlement to receive such a notice can be waived if a party wishes (rule 62.6(3)). By virtue of rule 62.7 a written witness statement served in accordance with rule 62.6 must contain a declaration by the person making it that it is true to the best of that person's knowledge and belief. If a false statement is made, the Crown Court has the power to punish the maker of the statement for contempt they did not honestly believe it to be true when they made it or caused it to be made. The Crown Court may exercise that power on its own initiative or may give permission for an application by a party. Any such application must then be in accordance with the other rules in Part 62 (rule 62.8).

17.07   If a party wishes to cross-examine the maker of a statement served in accordance with rule 62.6 then they must serve a written application on the court officer and the party who served the hearsay. That application must stipulate the reasons why they wish to cross-examine the maker of the statement. If a respondent wants to cross-examine such a person then any such application must be served not more than seven days after service of the hearsay by the applicant. If it is the applicant who wants to cross-examine a person then his application must be served not more than three days after service of the hearsay by the respondent (rule 62.9(1)–(4)). The court is not required to have a hearing in order to determine such an application but it must not dismiss the application unless the person making it has had an opportunity to make representations at a hearing.

17.08   Rule 62.10 governs the procedure for applying to challenge the credibility of a hearsay witness and any application to challenge the consistency of the person making the statement. The party who wishes to do so must serve a notice of the intention to do so on the court officer, and the party who served the hearsay. The notice must be in writing and must identify any statement or other material on which that party relies. If the application is made by the respondent the notice must be served not more than seven days after service of the hearsay by the applicant. If it is the applicant who wishes to make such an application then the notice must be served not more than three days after service of the hearsay by the respondent (rule 62.10(1)–(4)). The party who served the hearsay may decide to call that person to give oral evidence instead. If he does so then, as soon as practicable after the service of the notice under rule 69.10(2), he must serve a notice of intention to do so on the court officer and the other party.

As with many other parts of the Rules, the court may shorten or extend a time limit   17.09
under Part 62 even after it has expired. If a party wishes a time limit to be extended, he must make an application when he serves the relevant notice, statement, or application which requires the extension and must set out the reasons for the delay (rule 62.11).

18

APPEALS

A. INTRODUCTION

The Rules comprehensively cover procedure relating to appeals within the criminal justice system, ranging from appeals to the Crown Court from a magistrates' court through to a reference to the European Court. There have been significant changes to the rules relating to appeals since they were first introduced in 2005. Of principal importance is the creation of Part 65 which is comprised of a number of general rules applicable to all   18.01

appeals under Parts 66, 67, 68, 69, 70, and 74. Each of the rules in those Parts must be read in conjunction with Part 65. In addition, the more recent rules also see the conflation of the original Parts 69 and 70 (in which references by the Attorney General of a point of law or unduly lenient sentencing were respectively found) into a new Part 70 covering all references by the Attorney General. As with many other sections of the Rules, much of the original content of Parts 63 to 75 has been substantially revised and simplified in the current Rules.

B. PART 63—APPEAL TO THE CROWN COURT AGAINST CONVICTION OR SENTENCE

18.02 The procedure relating to appeal to the Crown Court against conviction or sentence is governed by Part 63. The Part applies to appeals by a defendant under section 108(1) of the Magistrates' Courts Act 1980 (appeal against conviction and sentence), section 45(1) of the Mental Health Act 1983 (appeal against hospital or guardianship order in the absence of conviction), paragraph 10 of Schedule 3 to the Powers of Criminal Courts (Sentencing) Act 2000 or paragraphs 9(8) or 13(5) of Schedule 8 to the Criminal Justice Act 2003 (where the magistrates' court revokes a community order and deals with the defendant in another way), section 10 of the Violent Crime Reduction Act 2006 (drinking banning orders), and section 42 of the Counter Terrorism Act 2008 (when the court decides that an offence has a terrorist connection for the purposes of sentence). Part 63 also covers appeals when the Criminal Cases Review Commission (CCRC) refers a defendant's case to the Crown Court under section 11 of the Criminal Appeal Act 1995. So far as appeals by the prosecution are concerned, it governs such appeals under section 14A(5A) of the Football Spectators Act 1989 (appeal against a failure to make a banning order), and section 147(3) of the Customs and Excise Management Act 1979 (appeal against any decision of the magistrates' court under any Act relating to customs and excise). Finally, Part 63 governs any appeal by a person under section 1 of the Magistrates' Courts (Appeals from Binding Over Orders) Act 1956, section 12(5) of the Contempt of Court Act 1981 (appeal against punishment for insulting a person in the proceedings or interrupting proceedings), regulation 3C or 3H of the Costs in Criminal Cases (General) Regulations 1986 (wasted costs against a legal representative or third party), or section 22 of the Football Spectators Act 1989 (appeal by any person aggrieved by the making of a football banning order). Greater coverage of the substantive law and practice relating to appeals to the Crown Court can be found at Chapter D28 of *Blackstone's Criminal Practice 2011*.

18.03 Rule 63.2 sets out the basic procedure for commencing an appeal under any provision governed by this rule. No later than twenty-one days after the decision to be appealed, written notice of appeal must be given to the court officer of the magistrates' court and any other parties to the appeal (rule 63.2(1)). An application may be made to extend the time period for serving the notice of appeal (before or after that time period expires), but it must be in writing, specifying why the application is late and must be served with the notice of appeal (rule 63.2(2)).

18.04 The form of the notice of appeal is governed by rule 63.3. The Practice Direction sets out a form for use in connection with such a notice. The notice should specify the conviction or finding of guilt, the sentence, or order (or failure to make an order) about which the appellant wants to appeal. It must also summarize the issues on appeal. If the appeal is concerned with conviction, it must list the prosecution witnesses whom the appellant will want to question if they are called to give oral evidence. It must also state the length of the trial in the magistrates' court and provide an estimate of how long the appeal is likely to last in the Crown Court. Any appeal against a finding that the appellant insulted someone or interrupted proceedings in the magistrates' court is required to attach the magistrates' court's written findings of fact and the appellant's response to those findings. Any notice of appeal must stipulate whether the appellant has asked the magistrates' court to reconsider the case and must include a list of the persons on whom the appellant has served the appeal notice.

If notice of appeal is given, the documents required to be sent to the Crown Court by the magistrates' court officer are set out in rule 63.4. In all cases, as soon as practicable the notice of appeal (and any accompanying application) must be sent to the Crown Court officer along with a copy of the relevant extract of the magistrates' court register and details of the parties including their addresses and any report used in sentencing. The magistrates' court officer is also required to keep any document or object exhibited in the proceedings in the magistrates' court (or arrange for it to be kept by some other appropriate person) until six weeks after the conclusion of those proceedings, or the conclusion of any proceedings in the Crown Court that begin within that six weeks. Within any time period stipulated by the Crown Court officer, he must also provide the Crown Court with any document, object, or information the Crown Court officer asks for. If, in accordance with rule 63.4, the court officer arranges for some other person to keep any exhibits, rule 63.5 stipulates that that person must keep any exhibit until six weeks after the conclusion of those proceedings, or the conclusion of any proceedings in the Crown Court that begin within that six weeks (unless the court otherwise directs). He must also furnish the Crown Court with any such exhibit the Crown Court officer asks for and must do so within the period stipulated by the Crown Court officer. **18.05**

Rule 63.6 governs the actions to be taken when the CCRC refers a case to the Crown Court. Under section 11 of the Criminal Appeal Act 1995, any appeal against conviction in the magistrates' court which is the subject of a reference by the CCRC must be dealt with by the Crown Court. Once the Crown Court officer receives notification of such a reference by the CCRC he must, as soon as practicable, serve the reference on the appellant, every other party, and the magistrates' court officer. The appellant may, if he wishes, serve an appeal notice on the Crown Court officer and every other party, no more than twenty-one days after the service of the reference. If he chooses not to do so, the Crown Court is required to treat the reference as the appeal notice. **18.06**

The procedure at any appeal hearing is set out in rule 63.7. The general rule is that an appeal or reference must be heard in public. However, that rule is not absolute and the Crown Court may order any hearing to be in private. Moreover, as would be expected, it must hold a hearing in private if it concerns a public interest ruling (rule 63.7(1)). In respect of any hearing, as much notice as reasonably practicable must be given by the Crown Court officer to the parties, any party's custodian, and any other person whom the Crown Court requires to be notified (rule 63.7(2)). Notice of any decision by the court must be served by the Crown Court officer on the parties, any other person whom the Crown Court requires to be served, and (where the decision determines an appeal) the magistrates' court officer and any party's custodian (rule 63.7(3)). That rule does not apply if the ruling concerns public interest immunity. In those circumstances **18.07** the Crown Court officer naturally must not (unless the court directs otherwise) give notice of the hearing to, or serve the decision on, anyone other than the prosecutor who applied for that ruling.

18.08   If an appellant wishes to abandon an appeal, either before or after the hearing of the appeal has commenced, then he must follow the procedure set out in rule 63.8. The appellant may abandon an appeal before the hearing commences without the Crown Court's permission. He is simply required to serve a notice of abandonment signed by him on the magistrates' court officer, the Crown Court officer, and every other party. There is a form set out in the Practice Direction for use in connection with such an abandonment. If the hearing of the appeal has commenced, the appeal may only be abandoned with the permission of the Crown Court. The court may award costs against him (see Chapter 19). If an appellant was on bail pending appeal prior to abandonment, then he must surrender to custody as directed by the magistrates' court officer. If there were conditions attached to his bail, then those conditions of bail apply until he surrenders.

18.09   As with many other sections of the Rules, the court has flexibility in its application of rule 63. In particular, under rule 63.9, the Crown Court may shorten or extend a time limit under this Part (even after that time limit has expired), allow an appellant to vary an appeal notice that he has served, direct that an appeal notice be served on any person, and allow an appeal notice or a notice of abandonment to be in a different form to one set out in the Practice Direction (or even be presented orally).

18.10   The general rule as to the composition of the court dealing with an appeal from the magistrates' court is that the Crown Court must comprise a judge of the High Court, a Circuit Judge or a Recorder, and no less than two and no more than four justices of the peace. None of those justices of the peace can have taken any part in the decision under appeal. Where any appeal is from a youth court the general rule is that each justice of the peace must be qualified to sit as a member of a youth court, and the court hearing the appeal must contain both a man and a woman. However, there are two possible sets of circumstances where the court may simply contain one justice of the peace and need not include both a man and a woman. Those are, first, if the presiding judge decides that the start of the appeal hearing would otherwise be delayed unreasonably, or, secondly, if one or more of the justices of the peace who started hearing the appeal is absent.

C. APPEAL TO THE HIGH COURT BY WAY OF CASE STATED

18.11   A person may apply to a magistrates' court to state a case under section 111(1) of the Magistrates' Courts Act 1980. Additional detail of the law and practice relating to applications under the section can be found at Chapter D28 of *Blackstone's Criminal Practice 2011*. According to rule 64.1, such an application must be made in writing, signed by the applicant or by someone else on his behalf, and must identify the issues of law or jurisdiction to be considered by the High Court. If the point for the High Court to consider is whether there was evidence on which the magistrates' court could come to its decision, then the application must specify the specific finding of fact which the applicant asserts cannot be supported. Any such application must be sent to the court officer of the magistrates' court which made the questioned decision.

18.12   If the justices decide to state a case, the court officer must send a draft case (containing the matters required in rule 64.6) to the applicant or his legal representative and a copy to the respondent or his legal representative within twenty-one days of receipt of the application (rule 64.2(1)). Within twenty-one days thereof, the parties must make written, signed representations on the draft case and they must be sent to the magistrates' court officer. If the magistrates' court refuses to state a case under section 111(5) of the Magistrates' Courts Act 1980 and are subsequently required to state a case by a mandatory order, then the same procedure commences analogously with a requirement that the magistrates' court officer send a draft case within twenty-one days of receipt of the mandatory order (rule 64.2).

Rule 64.3 dictates that within twenty-one days of the last day for the making of representations by the parties, the justices may make any amendments to the draft case that they see fit, having taken into account any representations made by the parties. Any two or more of the justices whose decision is questioned may state a case and it must be signed. It may be signed by them or, if they so direct, may be signed on their behalf by a justices' clerk. The case must then be sent forthwith to the applicant or his legal representative. Any statement required under rule 64.4 must also be sent with it.   **18.13**

A failure to comply with the time limits set out for the various participants to carry out certain tasks is not necessarily fatal to such an application: **18.14**

(a) If the court officer of the magistrates' court is unable to comply with the time limits set down in rule 64.2(1), then he must send the draft case as soon as practicable. When he does so, he must attach a statement of the delay and the reasons for it to the draft and final cases when they are sent to the appellant and his legal representative.
(b) If any of the parties request an extension of time for making any written representations on the draft case they must make it in writing with reasons for the application. If the justices' clerk allows the application, then he must give written notice to the party but must attach to the final case a statement giving the fact of and reasons for the extension when it is served on the applicant or his legal representative.
(c) If the justices cannot comply with the time limit for signing the final case, then they must do so as soon as practicable and the court officer must attach a statement setting out the delay and the reasons for it (rule 64.4).

The original rule 64.5 concerned the service of any of the documents in Part 64. It has now been revoked..   **18.15**

Rule 64.5 now governs the required content of a case stated by a magistrates' court. It must contain the facts found by the court and any questions of law or jurisdiction upon which the opinion of the High Court is sought. No statement of evidence is necessary unless one of the questions on which the opinion of the High Court is sought is whether there was evidence before the magistrates' court which would justify a particular finding of fact by that court. If there is such a question, then the particular finding of fact which it is claimed could not be supported by the evidence must be specified in the case.   **18.16**

An application to the Crown Court to state a case under section 28 of the Senior Courts Act 1981 follows a different procedure to that followed in relation to a magistrates' court and is set out in rule 64.6. Such an application must be made in writing to a court officer within twenty-one days of the decision which is to be questioned. The application must contain the grounds for making the application and a copy must be sent to the parties to the Crown Court proceedings at the same time. When the Crown Court officer receives the application, he must refer it forthwith to the judge of the Crown Court who made the decision and the judge, upon the receipt of the application,   **18.17** must then inform the Crown Court officer whether he has decided to state a case or not. The Crown Court officer must then give written notice to the applicant of the judge's decision. If the judge decides that the application is frivolous then he may refuse to state a case and, if the applicant requires it, he must ensure that a certificate setting out the reasons for the refusal be given to the applicant. If the judge decides to state a case, the following procedure must be followed:

(a) within twenty-one days of receiving the notice indicating that the judge is prepared to state a case, the applicant must prepare a draft case and send copies of it to the Crown Court officer and the other parties;

(b) within twenty-one days of receiving a copy of the draft case, each party must either:

(i) give written notice to the applicant and the Crown Court officer that he does not intend to take part in the High Court proceedings; or

(ii) send to the Crown Court officer a copy of the draft case indicating upon it in writing that he agrees with it; or

(iii) send to the Crown Court officer an alternative case that he has drafted and a copy of the applicant's case;

(c) the applicant's draft case and any alternative draft written by any other party must then be considered by the judge;

(d) the applicant may be required to enter into a recognizance, with or without sureties and in such sum as the Crown Court requires, before the case is stated and delivered to him;

(e) once the judge has received all the relevant documents set out in (b) or twenty-one days after each party has received a copy of the draft case (whichever is the sooner) then the judge must state and sign a case within fourteen days.

18.18   The stated case must contain a statement of the facts found by the Crown Court, the submissions of the parties and any authorities cited in support, the questioned decision of the Crown Court, and the question on which the opinion of the High Court is sought. Any time limit in this rule can be extended by the Crown Court either before or after it expires. If the Crown Court judge refuses to state a case and the High Court issues a mandatory order requiring him to do so then the same procedure as above applies from the date the mandatory order is issued.

D. APPEAL TO THE COURT OF APPEAL: GENERAL RULES

18.19   Part 65 of the Rules has been altered from the original Rules published in 2005. Whereas that Part previously contained rules relating to appeals related to preparatory hearings, it now contains a number of general rules applicable to appeals to the criminal division of the Court of Appeal under Parts 66 (appeals against any ruling at a preparatory hearing), 67 (appeals against rulings adverse to the prosecution), 68 (appeals against conviction or sentence), 69 (concerning reporting restrictions or public access), 70 (reference to the Court of Appeal on a point of law or unduly lenient sentencing), and 74 (reference to the Supreme Court) of the Rules.

18.20   Rule 65.2 governs the case management regime operating in the Court of Appeal. It stipulates that the court and the parties have the same duties and powers as under Part 3 of the Rules (see Chapter 2). Accordingly, subject to the directions of the court, the Registrar must fulfil the duty of active case management under rule 3.2. In fulfilling that duty he may exercise any of the powers of case management under the court's general powers of case management contained in rule 3.5, require a certificate of readiness under rule 3.9(3), and require a party to identify intentions and anticipated requirements under rule 3.10. In accordance with rule 3.4, the Registrar must also nominate a case progression officer.

The Registrar has a discretion to vary any requirements under this Part by virtue of   18.21
rule 65.3. The general rule is that the Registrar may shorten any time limit under this Part or extend it even after its expiry. However, that power is limited to the extent that its exercise must be consistent with other legislation. Thus, for example, the time limit for appealing under section 18 of the Criminal Appeal Act 1968 on an appeal against conviction or sentence under section 18 of the Criminal Appeal Act 1968 or against a contempt of court finding under section 18A of the same Act may be extended but not shortened. Equally, the time limit for seeking permission to refer a sentencing case under section 36 of the Criminal Justice Act 1988 may be neither extended nor shortened (see paragraph 18.75). The Registrar may also allow a party to vary any notice that that party has served, direct the service of a notice or application on any person and allow a notice or application to be in a different form than that specified in the Rules. The notice or application may even be permitted to be presented orally.

Rule 65.4 requires that any application for an extension of time to serve an applica-   18.22
tion or notice must be made at the same time as the service of the notice or application. The reasons for the application for an extension of time must be included.

If a party wishes to renew any application refused by the Registrar or a single judge,   18.23
the general rule by virtue of rule 65.5 is that he must renew the application in the form set out in the Practice Direction. The form must be signed by or on behalf of the applicant. If the applicant was present at the application, it must be served on the Registrar not more than fourteen days after the refusal of the application that the applicant wants to renew. If he was not, the renewal must be served no longer than fourteen days after the Registrar serves the refusal decision on the applicant. If the application is made under Parts 66, 67, or 69 the time limit of fourteen days under this rule is reduced to five days.

The general rule as to the procedure to be adopted in respect of whether hearings   18.24
are in public or private, as set out in rule 65.6, is similar to that under other Parts. The general rule is that any hearing of an application, including an application for permission to appeal and an appeal or reference must be in public. However, the court may order any hearing to be in private (rule 65.6(1)). Moreover, where a hearing concerns a public interest ruling, it must be in private unless the court otherwise directs (rule 65.6(2)). An appeal against an order restricting public access to a trial may be decided without a hearing but the court must announce its decision on such an appeal at a hearing in public (rule 65.6(3)). Similarly, an application to appeal or to refer a case to the Supreme Court may be decided without a hearing but the decision on such an application must be announced at a hearing in public (rule 65.6(4)). Finally, rule 65.6(5) provides that a judge of the Court of Appeal and the Registrar may exercise any of their powers at a hearing in public or in private, or without a hearing.

Rule 65.7 governs the procedure to be followed when notifying a party of any hearing   18.25
or decision. Mirroring rules in other Parts, as much notice as reasonably practicable of

any hearing must be given by the Registrar to the parties, any party's custodian, and any other person whom the court requires to be notified. If the appeal is under Parts 66, 67, or 69 then such notice must also be given to the Crown Court officer. Notice of every decision must also be served by the Registrar on the parties, any other person whom the court requires to be served, and (where the decision determines an appeal or application for permission to appeal) the Crown Court officer and any party's custodian. An important qualification to that general rule is that (unless the court differently directs) where the hearing or decision is about a public interest ruling, the Registrar must not give notice of, or serve the decision on anyone other than the prosecutor who applied for the ruling.

18.26   Rule 65.8 sets out the duties of a Crown Court officer in respect of any appeal to the Court of Appeal. Those duties are as follows. First, the Crown Court officer must provide the Registrar with any document, object, or information which the Registrar asks for and within the period required by the Registrar (rule 65.8(1)). He must also arrange for the recording of the proceedings in the Crown Court and if the Registrar or anyone else (subject to the restrictions in rule 65.9(2)—see paragraph 18.27) wants a transcript, he must arrange it. He must also arrange for any exhibit from the Crown Court proceedings to be kept there (or kept by some other appropriate person) until six weeks after the conclusion of the proceedings (rule 65.8(2)). Under rule 65.10, similar rules apply to a person required to keep the exhibit. On any appeal to the Court of Appeal against ruling at a preparatory hearing under Part 66, a transcript or note of each order or ruling against which the appellant wants to appeal and the decision by the Crown Court judge on any application for permission to appeal must be served as soon as practicable by the Crown Court officer on the appellant (rule 65.8(3)). On any appeal to the Court of Appeal against a ruling adverse to prosecution under Part 67, a transcript or note of each ruling against which the appellant wants to appeal, the decision by the Crown Court judge on any application for permission to appeal, and the decision by the Crown Court judge on any request to expedite the appeal must, as soon as practicable, be served by the Crown Court officer on the appellant (rule 65.8(4)). On any appeal to the Court of Appeal about conviction or sentence under Part 68 the appeal notice and any accompanying application that the appellant serves on the Crown Court officer, any Crown Court judge's certificate that the case is fit for appeal, the decision on any application at the Crown Court centre for bail pending appeal, such of the Crown Court case papers as the Registrar requires and such transcript of the Crown Court proceedings as the Registrar requires must be served on the Registrar by the Crown Court officer as soon as practicable (rule 65.8(5)). Finally, on any appeal to the Court of Appeal regarding reporting or public access under Part 69, where an order is made restricting public access to a trial, the Crown Court officer must immediately notify the Registrar of that order if the appellant has given advance notice of intention to appeal. As soon as practicable, he must also provide the applicant for that order with a transcript or note of the application (rule 65.8(6)).

18.27   Rule 65.9 places duties on the transcriber of proceedings. It provides that he must provide the Registrar with any transcript for which the Registrar asks within the period the Registrar specifies. He must also, unless the court otherwise directs, provide anyone else with any transcript that person asks for in accordance with the transcription arrangements made by the Crown Court officer and contingent on payment of any charge fixed by the Treasury for the transcript. That is subject to the qualification that any transcript of a public interest hearing must only be provided to the Registrar unless it is otherwise directed.

For the purposes of proceedings in the Court of Appeal, rule 65.11 provides that, on payment of any charge fixed by the Treasury, the Registrar must provide a party with a copy of any document or transcript held by the Registrar for those proceedings, or allow a party to inspect such a document or transcript. In keeping with the duties imposed on a transcriber under rule 65.9, the Registrar must not provide a copy or allow the inspection of a document provided only for the court and the Registrar, or a transcript of a public interest ruling, or of an application for such a ruling. 18.28

If an appellant seeks a declaration of incompatibility between a legislative provision and the European Convention on Human Rights, or raises an issue which the Registrar thinks may give rise to such a declaration, the procedure to be followed is set out in rule 65.12. The Registrar must serve notice on the relevant person named in the list published under section 17(1) of the Crown Proceedings Act 1947 or (if it is not clear who is the relevant person is) the Treasury Solicitor. The legislation affected, the Convention right concerned, the parties to the appeal, and any other information or document that the Registrar thinks relevant must be specified in the notice or other accompanying documents. If a person who has a right to become a party to the appeal under the 1998 Act wants to exercise that right he must serve notice on the Registrar, and the other parties. The notice must specify what conclusion he invites the court to reach on the question of incompatibility, and also specify each ground for that invitation. The arguments in support must also be concisely outlined (rule 65.12(1) to (4)). No declaration of incompatibility must be made by the court less than twenty-one days after the Registrar served the relevant notice or without giving any person with the right to become a party an opportunity to make representations at a hearing. 18.29

The procedure for an appellant wishing to abandon an appeal or ground of appeal is set out in rules 65.13 and 65.14. Rule 65.13 governs the abandoning of an appeal. If an appellant wants to abandon an application to the court for permission to appeal, or an appeal before the hearing has commenced he may do so without the court's permission by serving a notice of abandonment on the Registrar, and any respondent. The notice of abandonment must be in the form set out in the Practice Direction. If the hearing has commenced, the appellant or applicant may only abandon the application or appeal with the court's permission. Following receipt of the notice of abandonment, the Registrar must date it and serve such a dated copy on the appellant, the appellant's custodian (if any), the Crown Court officer, and any other person on whom the appellant or the Registrar served the appeal notice. He must also treat the application or appeal as if it had been refused or dismissed by the Court of Appeal. If an appellant wishes to reinstate an application or appeal after he has abandoned it, he must serve a written and reasoned application on the Registrar. It should be noted that it is only in exceptional circumstances where the Court of Appeal takes the view that, in effect, the abandonment was a nullity that the court will allow such a reinstatement. 18.30

Rule 65.14 provides that if a party wishes to abandon a ground of appeal identified in an appeal notice or a ground of opposition identified in a respondent's notice, then written notice must be given before the hearing of the ground to the Registrar and every other party. 18.31

E. APPEAL TO THE COURT OF APPEAL AGAINST RULING AT PREPARATORY HEARING

18.32   Section 9(11) of the Criminal Justice Act 1987 (serious or complex fraud cases), section 35(1) of the Criminal Procedure and Investigations Act 1996 (other complex, serious, or long cases), and section 47(1) of the CJA 2003 (jury tampering) provide for interlocutory appeals to the Court of Appeal pursuant to a preparatory hearing. Such interlocutory appeals are dealt with in detail in *Blackstone's Criminal Practice 2011* at Chapter D14. Appeals of this type were originally governed by Part 65 of the Rules. They have now been revised and simplified and included at Part 66.

18.33   Notice of appeal to the Court of Appeal must be served on the Registrar, the Crown Court officer, and all parties to the preparatory hearing affected by the order or ruling to be appealed (rule 66.2(1)). It must be served no later than five business days after the date of the decision to be appealed or, if an application is made to the judge of the Crown Court for leave to appeal, no later than five business days after the determination or withdrawal of that application (rule 66.2(2)). Under rule 66.3, the notice of appeal must be in the form set out in the Practice Direction (formerly Form 1A(1) for a CJA 1987 appeal or Form 5312 for a CPIA 1996 appeal). The notice of appeal must:

(a) specify each order or ruling that is to be the subject of appeal;
(b) identify each ground of appeal on which the appellant relies, numbering them consecutively (if there is more than one) and concisely outlining each argument in support;
(c) summarize the relevant facts and identify any relevant authorities.

The notice must also include or attach any application for permission to appeal (if the appellant needs the court's permission), any extension of time within which to serve the appeal notice, and any application for a direction to attend in person a hearing that the appellant could attend by live link (if the appellant is in custody). Any such application must be supported with reasons. The notice must also include a list of those on whom the appellant has served the appeal notice. Attached to the notice must be a transcript or note of each order or ruling against which the appellant wants to appeal, along with all relevant skeleton arguments considered by the Crown Court judge, any written application for permission to appeal that the appellant made to the Crown Court judge, a transcript or note of the decision by the Crown Court judge on any application for permission to appeal, and any other document or thing that the appellant thinks the court will need to decide the appeal (rule 66.4).

18.34   Rule 66.4 sets out the requirements imposed on a person making an application to the Crown Court for leave to appeal. It requires that an application for leave to the judge of the Crown Court who made the decision to be appealed should be made orally, immediately after the order. Alternatively an application may be made within two days of the relevant decision. Unless the application for leave is made on the same occasion that the relevant decision is given, then the appellant must make an application in writing and it must be served on the Crown Court officer and all the parties directly affected by the decision. The written application must include the same information as the notice of appeal.

18.35   Any party who receives an appeal notice may serve a respondent's notice under rule 66.5. He must serve such a notice if he wishes to make representations on the appeal or if the court directs him to do so. The notice must be in the form set out in the Practice Direction (rule 66.5(4)) and it must be served on the Registrar, the appellant, the Crown Court officer and any other party who was served with an appellant's notice. The respondent's notice must be served no more than five business days after the appellant served the appeal notice or the respondent is directed to serve the notice (rule 66.5(3)). The notice must state the date on which he received the appellant's notice, and identify each ground of opposition on which he relies. He must number those grounds consecutively and concisely outline each argument in support, identifying the ground of appeal to which each relates. He must also summarize any relevant facts not already summarized in the appeal notice and identify any relevant authorities. If he wishes to apply for an extension of time within which to serve the respondent's notice or (if the respondent is in custody) a direction to attend in person any hearing that the respondent could attend by live link, he must include or attach any such application with supporting reasons. Finally, he must identify any other document or thing that the respondent thinks the court will need to decide the appeal.

The powers of a single judge of the Court of Appeal are set out in rule 66.6. The single judge may give permission to appeal and exercise any other powers of a single judge under section 31 of the Criminal Appeal Act 1968, section 49 of the CJA 2003, or the Rules. 18.36

Any application refused by a single judge or the Registrar must be renewed no later than five business days after the decision under rule 66.7. 18.37

By virtue of rule 66.8, any party in custody has a right to attend a public hearing but the court or Registrar may direct that they attend by a live link. 18.38

F. APPEAL TO THE COURT OF APPEAL AGAINST RULING ADVERSE TO THE PROSECUTION

The CJA 2003 introduced new provision for appeals by the prosecution against rulings of the Crown Court in relation to trial on indictment. *Blackstone's Criminal Practice 2011*, Chapter D15 gives a detailed explanation of the operation of the scheme to which this Part applies. 18.39

1. General

Part 67 of the Rules sets out a system of procedural rules designed to supplement the provisions within the 2003 Act. Rule 66.1 defines an 'appellant' for the purposes of the Part as being a prosecutor. 18.40

If a prosecutor decides to appeal under this Part, then in accordance with rule 67.2, he must tell the judge of the court immediately following the relevant ruling or on expiry of the time allowed for consideration of whether to appeal. Under rule 67.2(2), if the appellant requires time to consider whether to appeal he must immediately ask the Crown Court judge for that time. Generally, the judge should allow until the next business day for the decision to be made. Under section 58(7) of the CJA 2003, if an appeal concerns a ruling that there is no case to answer, the prosecutor may also appeal against earlier rulings. By virtue of section 58(8) of the same Act, the appellant must agree that if the appeal is unsuccessful or permission is not granted, the defendant will be acquitted. 18.41

That the order of events set out in the statute and Rules must be followed was emphasized in *C, M and H*[1] and *LSA*.[2]

18.42   Under rule 67.3, the appellant must serve an appeal notice on the Crown Court officer, the Registrar, and every defendant directly affected by the ruling against which the appellant wants to appeal. If the judge expedites the appeal, the notice must be served no later than the next business day after informing the Crown Court judge of the decision to appeal. If the judge does not expedite the appeal, the notice must be served no later than five days after informing the Crown Court judge of his decision to appeal.

18.43   The appeal notice which is served must be in the form set out in the Practice Direction (rule 67.4(1)). Moreover, it must specify each ruling to be challenged by the appellant and identify every ground of appeal on which the appellant relies. If there is more than one ground, they must be numbered consecutively and each argument in support must be concisely outlined. The notice must also summarize the relevant facts and identify any relevant authorities. Any application for permission to appeal (if the appellant needs the court's permission), for an extension of time within which to serve the appeal notice, for expedition of the appeal, or for revocation of a direction expediting the appeal must be attached and the reasons for making such an application must be set out. In addition, the notice must include a list of those on whom the appellant has served the appeal notice. Attached to the notice must be a transcript or note of each ruling against which the appellant wants to appeal, all relevant skeleton arguments considered by the Crown Court judge, any written application for permission to appeal that the appellant made to the Crown Court judge, a transcript or note of the decision by the Crown Court judge on any application for permission to appeal, a transcript or note of the decision by the Crown Court judge on any request to expedite the appeal, and any other document or thing that the appellant thinks the court will need to decide the appeal. Finally, the appellant must attach a form of respondent's notice. That is provided so that any defendant served with the appeal notice may complete it if he wants to do so (rule 67.4(2)).

18.44   By virtue of section 57(4) of the CJA 2003, any appellant needs the Court of Appeal's permission to appeal if he does not have the permission of the Crown Court judge. Rule 67.5 sets out the requirements imposed on a prosecutor making an application to the Crown Court for leave to appeal. It requires that an application for leave to the judge of the Crown Court who made the decision to be appealed should be made orally, with reasons, immediately after the order. Alternatively an application may be made within the time allowed by the judge to consider appealing. Unless the application for leave is made on the same occasion that the relevant decision is given, then the appellant must make an application in writing and it must be served on the Crown Court officer and all the defendants directly affected by the decision. The written application must include the same information as the notice of appeal. The Crown Court judge must allow any defendant who is affected an opportunity to make representations. The general rule is that the decision on permission must be made by the judge on the same day as the application.

18.45   A Crown Court judge has the power to expedite an appeal under section 59 of the CJA 2003. An appellant who wishes the judge to exercise the power must ask the court to do so on telling the judge of the appeal and must give reasons for doing so (rule 67.6(1)).

---

[1] [2009] EWCA Crim 2614.
[2] [2009] EWCA Crim 1034.

Every defendant who is affected must be allowed to make representations and the judge may revoke a direction expediting the appeal unless the appellant has served the appeal notice (rule 67.6(2) and (3)).

The notice to be served by the respondent is dealt with in rule 67.7. Any party who   18.46
receives an appeal notice may serve a respondent's notice under rule 67.7(1). He must serve such a notice if he wishes to make representations on the appeal or if the court directs him to do so. The notice must be in the form set out in the Practice Direction (rule 67.7(4)) and it must be served on the Registrar, the appellant, the Crown Court officer, and any other party who was served with an appellant's notice. If the Crown Court judge expedites the appeal, the respondent's notice must be served no later than the next day. If the judge does not expedite the appeal, it must be served no more than five business days after the appellant served the appeal notice or the respondent is directed to serve the notice (rule 67.5(3)). The notice must state the date on which he received the appellant's notice, and identify each ground of opposition on which he relies. He must number them consecutively and concisely outline each argument in support, identifying the ground of appeal to which each relates. He must also summarize any relevant facts not already summarized in the appeal notice and identify any relevant authorities. If he wishes to apply for an extension of time within which to serve the respondent's notice or (if the respondent is in custody) a direction to attend in person any hearing that the respondent could attend by live link, he must include or attach any such application with supporting reasons. Finally, he must identify any other document or thing that the respondent thinks the court will need to decide the appeal.

2. Orders for disclosure

Procedures for dealing with appeals against an order to disclose material in the posses-   18.47
sion of the prosecutor are set out in rule 67.8. Any notice of appeal or written application for permission to appeal against a public interest ruling must not be served on any defendant directly affected by the hearing if the appellant thinks that to do so would reveal something that he takes the view should not be disclosed (rule 67.8(1)). Moreover, if the appellant thinks he would in effect reveal something that ought not to be disclosed if he included the material, or an indication of the sort of material, that was the subject of the ruling he must not include it (rule 67.8(2)). When the appellant serves an appeal notice on the Registrar, he must also serve an annex. That annex must be marked to show that its contents are only for the court and the Registrar and contain whatever the appellant has omitted from the appeal notice. Reasons for the omission of the material must be given in the annex, as (if it is appropriate) must reasons why the appellant has not served the appeal notice.

3. Procedure subsequent to application

Rule 67.9 sets out the powers of a single judge in relation to such appeals. The single   18.48
judge may:

(a) give permission to appeal under section 57(4) of the 2003 Act;
(b) revoke a decision by the trial judge to expedite an appeal; and
(c) (upon abandonment of the appeal) order the acquittal of the defendant along with his release (if necessary) and the payment of his costs.

The single judge may also exercise any other powers conferred on him by any other legislation and the Rules.

18.49   By virtue of rule 67.10, any application refused by a single judge or the Registrar must be renewed no later than five business days after the decision.

18.50   Under rule 66.8, any party in custody has a right to attend a public hearing but the court or Registrar may direct that they attend by a live link.

G. PART 68—APPEAL TO THE COURT OF APPEAL ABOUT CONVICTION OR SENTENCE

18.51   Part 68 has been substantially revised and simplified since the original Rules were published in 2005. That process has been greatly assisted by the inclusion of the general rules relating to appeal at Part 65.

18.52   Rule 68.1 sets out the large number of provisions to which Part 68 applies. They are where:[3]

(a) a *defendant* wants to appeal under—
    (i) Part 1 of the Criminal Appeal Act 1968, or
    (ii) paragraph 14 of Schedule 22 to the Criminal Justice Act 2003 [appeal against the minimum term imposed on a life sentence],
    (iii) section 42 of the Counter Terrorism Act 2008 [appeal against a decision of the Crown Court that an offence has a terrorist connection];
(b) the Criminal Cases Review Commission refers a case to the Court of Appeal under section 9 of the Criminal Appeal Act 1995;
(c) a *prosecutor* wants to appeal to the Court of Appeal under section 14A(5A) of the Football Spectators Act 1989 [appeal against a failure by the Crown Court to make a football banning order];
(d) a *party* wants to appeal under section 74(8) of the Serious Organised Crime and Police Act 2005 [appeal against a review by a Crown Court judge of a sentence that was reduced because the defendant assisted the investigator or prosecutor];
(e) a person found in contempt of court wants to appeal under section 13 of the Administration of Justice Act 1960 and section 18A of the Criminal Appeal Act 1968; or
(f) a person wants to appeal to the Court of Appeal under—
    (i) section 24 of the Serious Crime Act 2007 [appeal to the Court of Appeal against a decision of the Crown Court in relation to a serious crime prevention order], or
    (ii) regulation 3C or 3H of The Costs in Criminal Cases (General) Regulations 1986 [appeal against a wasted costs order].

Rule 68.1(2) stipulates that an 'appellant' for the purposes of this Part is a reference to any party or person described above. Additional coverage of the law and practice in respect of appeals about conviction and sentence can be found at Chapters D25 and D26 of *Blackstone's Criminal Practice 2011*.

18.53   The procedure governing the service of an appeal notice are set out at rule 68.2. The general rule as to service is contained in rule 68.2(1). The appellant must serve the appeal notice on the Crown Court officer at the Crown Court centre where the relevant

---

[3] Emphasis added.

conviction, verdict, finding, sentence, order, or failure to make an order about which the appellant wants to appeal occurred. That service must take place not more than twenty-eight days after the matter which is to be appealed occurred, or, in respect of a wasted or third party costs order, twenty-one days after the order. However, an appellant must serve an appeal notice if the appeal is against a minimum term review decision under paragraph 14 of Schedule 22 to the Criminal Justice Act 2003, or the CCRC refers the case to the court the appeal notice must be served on the Registrar. So far as a referral by the Commission is concerned, the time limits for service in respect of a referral of sentence is twenty-eight days after a decision to refer, or after the Registrar serves notice, that the Commission has referred a sentence. In respect of a conviction, it is fifty-six days after the Registrar serves notice that the Commission has referred the conviction.

The required form of the appeal notice is set out in rule 68.3. The appeal notice which is served must be in the form set out in the Practice Direction (rule 67.4(1)). Moreover, it must specify the conviction, verdict, finding, sentence, order or failure to make an order to be challenged by the appellant and identify every ground of appeal on which the appellant relies. If there is more than one ground, they must be numbered consecutively and each argument in support must be concisely outlined. The notice must identify any transcript the appellant is of the view will be relevant to the court on any appeal against conviction, and any sentencing powers of the Crown Court if the appeal concerns sentence. If the appeal is by way of reference by the CCRC, the notice must explain the relationship between each ground of appeal and the reasons for referral. The notice must also summarize the relevant facts and identify any relevant authorities. Any application for permission to appeal (if the appellant needs the court's permission), an extension of time within which to serve the appeal notice, bail pending appeal, a direction to attend in person, the introduction of evidence, a witness order or a special measures direction for a witness or the appellant must be attached and the reasons for making such an application must be set out. In addition, the notice must identify any other document or thing that the appellant is of the view that the court will need to decide the appeal. **18.54**

Rule 68.4 deals with the circumstances whereby a judge may certify that a case is fit for appeal. A judge may do so under sections 1(2), 11(1A), 12(b), 15(2)(b), or 16A(2)(b) of the Criminal Appeal Act 1968. He may also do so under section 81(1B) of the Senior Courts Act 1981, under section 14A(5B) of the Football Spectators Act 1989, or under section 24(4) of the Serious Crime Act 2007. Any oral application by the appellant for such a certificate should be made and supported with reasons, immediately after the conviction, verdict, finding, sentence, order, or failure to make an order about which the appellant wants to appeal. Any application in writing must be served on the Crown Court officer not more than fourteen days after the relevant event which is proposed to be the subject of the appeal. A written application must include the same information as an appeal notice but with any necessary adaptations. **18.55**

By virtue of rule 68.5, any reference by the CCRC must be served on the appellant by the Registrar. If the appellant does not serve an appeal notice himself, the court must treat the reference as the appeal notice. **18.56**

The procedure governing the role of a respondent's notice under Part 68 is governed by rule 68.6. Rule 68.6(1) stipulates that the Registrar may serve an appeal notice on any person directly affected by the appeal and must do so if the CCRC refers a conviction, finding, or sentence to the court. Any party who receives an appeal notice may serve a respondent's notice under rule 68.6(2). He must serve such a notice if he wishes to make **18.57** representations on the appeal or if the court directs him to do so. The notice must be in the form set out in the Practice Direction (rule 68.6(5)) and it must be served on the Registrar, the appellant, the Crown Court officer, and any other party who was served with an appellant's notice. The party must serve the respondent's notice no more than fourteen days after the Registrar served the appeal notice or there is a direction to serve the relevant notice. The notice must state the date on which he received the appellant's notice, and identify each ground of opposition on which he relies. He must number them consecutively and concisely outline each argument in support, identifying the ground of appeal to which each relates. He must identify the relevant sentencing powers of the Crown Court if sentence is a subject of the appeal. He must also summarize any relevant facts not already summarized in the appeal notice and identify any relevant authorities. If he wishes to apply for an extension of time within which to serve the respondent's notice, or bail pending appeal, or (if the respondent is in custody) a direction to attend in person any hearing that the respondent could attend by live link, or to introduce evidence, or a witness order, or special measures, he must include or attach any such application with supporting reasons. Finally, he must identify any other document or thing that he thinks the court will need to decide the appeal.

18.58   In respect of the introduction of evidence in Part 68, Parts 29 (special measures directions), 30 (use of live television link other than for vulnerable witnesses), 34 (hearsay evidence), 35 (evidence of bad character), and 36 (evidence of a complainant's previous sexual behaviour) apply with such adaptations as the court or Registrar may direct. That is so by virtue of rule 68.7. The general rule is that if a respondent opposes an appellant's application, he must do so in the respondent's notice, setting out his reasons. If the objection is by the appellant to an application by the respondent, then he must serve reasoned notice on the Registrar and respondent no more than fourteen days after service of the respondent's notice. The court or Registrar may then give directions without a hearing.

18.59   An appellant may be granted bail pending appeal or retrial. The appellant or respondent may serve an application about bail pending appeal or retrial in the form set out in the Practice Direction under rule 68.8. It should be served on the Registrar and the other party. The court must not decide the application without giving the other party an opportunity to make representations (whether about bail generally or about any conditions or surety).

18.60   The detailed procedure governing the granting of bail with conditions are set out in rule 68.9.

18.61   Under rule 68.10, if bail pending appeal or retrial is granted subject to a surety and the party fails to surrender to custody as required, the Registrar must notify the surety and prosecutor of a hearing to determine whether the recognizance will be forfeited. The court must not order the forfeiture of any such sum less than seven days after the notice of the hearing is given and without giving the surety an opportunity to make representations at a hearing.

18.62   The general rule is that a person in custody is entitled to attend a public hearing. That general rule does not apply if the hearing is one which is preliminary or incidental to an appeal. Such a hearing includes the hearing of an application for permission to appeal. It equally does not apply if the person is in custody pursuant to a verdict of not guilty by reason of insanity, or a finding of disability (rule 68.11).

Rule 68.12 governs the procedure where the court may vary an order on appeal con- 18.63
cerning sentence which was made in a party's absence. That may occur if the court did
not take account of a relevant matter because of the party's absence. The party which
seeks such a variation must make a reasoned, written application. If the party was represented at the appeal hearing, the application must be served on the Registrar no more
than seven days after the decision. If he was not so represented, it must be served no
more than seven days after the Registrar serves the decision.

If an appellant subject to an order under section 37(1) of the Mental Health Act 1983 18.64
(detention in hospital on conviction), or an order under section 5(2) of the Criminal
Procedure (Insanity) Act 1964 (detention in hospital on finding of insanity or disability)
has been released on bail pending appeal and the court subsequently refuses permission to
appeal, dismisses the appeal, or affirms the order under appeal then by virtue of rule 68.13
the court must give appropriate directions for the appellant's readmission to hospital. If
necessary, directions must also be given about temporary detention pending readmission.

Section 8 of the Criminal Appeal Act 1968 requires that, following the quashing of a 18.65
conviction and an order for retrial, the defendant must be arraigned no more than two
months after the date on which the conviction was quashed. If a prosecutor wants a
defendant to be arraigned more than two months after the court ordered a retrial under
section 7 of the Criminal Appeal Act 1968 or a defendant wants such an order set aside
after two months have passed since it was made, rule 68.14 requires that the party apply
in writing, with reasons, and serve the application on the Registrar and the other party.

H. APPEAL TO THE COURT OF APPEAL AGAINST ORDER RESTRICTING REPORTING OR PUBLIC ACCESS

An application for leave to appeal against an order restricting publication under section 18.66
159(a), (aa), or (c) of the Criminal Justice Act 1988 is governed by Part 69. In respect of
an order restricting public access to a trial, such an application must be made the next
business day after the order. In respect of an order restricting the reporting of the trial, it
must be made no later than ten business days after the date of the order. The application
must be served on the Registrar, the Crown Court officer where the order was made, the
parties, and any other person directly affected by the order (rule 69.2(1)).

The appeal notice which is served must be in the form set out in the Practice Direction 18.67
(rule 69.3(1)). Moreover, it must specify the order to be challenged by the appellant and
identify every ground of appeal on which the appellant relies. If there is more than one
ground, they must be numbered consecutively and each argument in support must be
concisely outlined. The notice must also summarize the relevant facts and identify any
relevant authorities. Any application for permission to appeal (which is necessary in any
appeal under this Part and is governed by section 31(2)(b) of the Criminal Appeal Act
1968), for an extension of time within which to serve the appeal notice, for a direction
to attend in person, to introduce evidence, for a witness order, and a list of those on
whom the appellant has served the appeal notice must be attached. The reasons for
making any such application must be set out. In addition, the notice must attach any
other document or thing that the appellant is of the view that the court will need to
decide the appeal (rule 69.3(2)).

18.68   Where an appellant wishes to appeal against an order restricting public access to a trial, rule 69.4 provides that he may serve advance written notice of intention to appeal against any such order that may be made. That advance notice must be served no later than five business days after the Crown Court officer displays notice of the application for the order. It must be served on the Crown Court officer, the Registrar, the parties, and any other person who will be directly affected by the order against which the appellant intends to appeal (if it is made). Such an advance notice must include the same information as an appeal notice (with the appropriate adaptations) and the court must treat it as the appeal notice if the order is made.

18.69   In addition, if an appellant wishes to appeal against an order restricting public access to a trial, rule 69.5 requires him to serve on the Registrar a transcript or note of the application for the order and any other document or thing that that party thinks the court will need to decide the appeal. Those items must be served as soon as practicable after the appellant serves the appeal notice or (where the appellant served advance notice of intention to appeal) the order.

18.70   The procedure relating to the service of a respondent's notice under Part 69 is set out in rule 69.6. It provides that any party who receives an appeal notice may serve a respondent's notice under rule 69.6(2). He must serve such a notice if he wishes to make representations on the appeal or if the court directs him to do so. The notice must be in the form set out in the Practice Direction (rule 68.6(5)) and it must be served on the Registrar, the appellant, the Crown Court officer, the parties, and any other party who was served with an appellant's notice. The party must serve the respondent's notice no more than three business days after the appellant serves the appeal notice or there is a direction to serve the relevant notice. The notice must state the date on which he received the appellant's notice, and identify each ground of opposition on which he relies. He must number them consecutively and concisely outline each argument in support, identifying the ground of appeal to which each relates. He must also summarize any relevant facts not already summarized in the appeal notice and identify any relevant authorities. If he wishes to apply for an extension of time within which to serve the respondent's notice, or (if the respondent is in custody) a direction to attend in person any hearing that the respondent could attend by live link, or to introduce evidence, he must include or attach any such application with supporting reasons. Finally, he must identify any other document or thing that he thinks the court will need to decide the appeal.

18.71   If a party wishes to renew any application refused by a judge or the Registrar then he must do so within five business days of the decision (rule 69.7).

18.72   By virtue of rule 69.8, the court's permission is required for any evidence to be introduced.

18.73   Under rule 69.9, any party in custody has a right to attend a public hearing but the court or Registrar may direct that they attend by a live link.

I. PART 70—REFERENCE TO THE COURT OF APPEAL OF POINT OF LAW OR UNDULY LENIENT SENTENCING

18.74   The original version of the Rules dealt separately with the two types of reference under Parts 69 and 70 respectively. Part 70 is now substantially revised and simplified to cover a reference by the Attorney General of a point of law under section 36 of the CJA 1972 or a sentencing case under section 36 of the CJA 1988. Chapter D27 of *Blackstone's Criminal Practice 2011* provides further detail on the reference procedure governed by Part 70.

If the Attorney General wishes to make such a reference, he must serve any notice of reference, any application for permission to refer a sentencing case on the Registrar. If a notice of reference of a point of law is served, the Attorney must also give the Registrar details of the defendant affected, the date and place of the relevant Crown Court decision, and the relevant verdict and sentencing (rule 70.2(1)). The Attorney General must serve an application for permission to refer a sentencing case not more than twenty-eight days after the last of the sentences in that case (rule 70.2(2)). By virtue of paragraph 1 of Schedule 3 to the CJA 1988, that time limit may be neither extended nor shortened. **18.75**

The form of notice of reference is prescribed by rule 70.3. A notice of reference and an application for permission to refer a sentencing case must be in the appropriate form set out in the Practice Direction, giving the year and number (rule 70.3(1)). A notice of reference of a point of law must specify the point of law in issue and indicate the opinion that the Attorney General invites the court to give. It must also identify each ground on which that invitation is based. If there is more than one, they must be numbered consecutively. Each argument in support must be concisely outlined. The application must exclude any reference to the defendant's name and any other reference that may identify the defendant, must summarize the relevant facts and must identify any relevant authorities (rule 70.3(2)). Any application for permission to refer a sentencing case must provide details of the defendant affected, the date and place of the relevant Crown Court decision, and the relevant verdict and sentencing. It must also explain why that sentencing appears to the Attorney General unduly lenient. It must concisely outline each argument in support of that view and include the necessary application for permission to refer the case to the court (rule 70.3(3)). Any notice of reference of a sentencing case must include the same details and explanation as the application for permission to refer the case, must summarize the relevant facts, and must identify any relevant authorities (rule 70.3(4)). If the court gives the Attorney General permission to refer a sentencing case, it may treat the application for permission as the notice of reference (rule 70.3(5)). **18.76**

The Registrar must inform the defendant of the proceedings by serving on him any notice of reference and any application for permission to refer a sentencing case (rule 70.4(1)). If the Attorney General refers a point of law, the Registrar must give the defendant notice that the outcome of the reference will not make any difference to the outcome of the trial. He must also give the defendant notice that he may serve a respondent's notice (rule 70.4(2)). If the Attorney General applies for permission to refer a sentencing case, the Registrar must give the defendant notice that the outcome of the reference may result in a more severe sentence and that he may serve a respondent's notice (rule 70.4(3)). **18.77**

The procedure governing any such respondent's notice is set out at rule 70.5. A defendant who has a reference or an application for permission to refer a sentencing case served on him by the Registrar may serve a respondent's notice under rule 70.5. He must serve such a notice if he wishes to make representations on the appeal or if the court directs him to do so. The notice must be served on the Registrar and the Attorney General (rule 70.5(2)). Where the Attorney General refers a point of law, the defendant must serve the respondent's notice no more than twenty-eight days after the Registrar serves the reference or there is a direction to do so. If the application is for permission to refer a sentencing case, the corresponding time limit for the service of the respondent's notice is fourteen days (rule 70.5(3)). If the respondent's notice is concerned with a **18.78**

191

reference of a point of law, it must identify each ground of opposition on which he relies. The defendant must number them consecutively and concisely outline each argument in support, identifying the Attorney General's ground to which each relates. He must also summarize any relevant facts not already summarized and identify any relevant authorities. If he wishes to apply for an extension of time within which to serve the respondent's notice, or (if the respondent is in custody) a direction to attend in person any hearing that the respondent could attend by live link, or permission to attend a hearing the respondent does not have a right to attend he must include or attach any such application with supporting reasons (rule 70.5(4)). If the Attorney General applies for permission to refer a sentencing case, the respondent's notice must say if the respondent wants to make representations at the hearing of the application or reference. It must also include or attach any application for an extension of time within which to serve the respondent's notice, permission to attend a hearing that the respondent does not have a right to attend, or (if the respondent is in custody) a direction to attend in person a hearing that the respondent could attend by live link. Any such application must be supported by reasons.

18.79   If the Attorney General wants to vary or withdraw a notice of reference, or an application for permission to refer a sentencing case, before any hearing of the reference or application, he may do so without the court's permission by serving notice on the Registrar, and the defendant. However, if any such hearing has commenced, he may only vary or withdraw that notice or application with the court's permission (rule 70.6).

18.80   A respondent's right to be present at a relevant hearing is dealt with in rule 70.7. The general rule is that a person in custody is entitled to attend a public hearing. That general rule does not apply if the hearing is one which is preliminary or incidental to a reference. Such a hearing includes the hearing of an application for permission to refer a sentencing case. The court or Registrar may direct that a respondent is to attend the hearing via live link.

18.81   Upon a reference of a point of law, rule 70.8 dictates that the court must prevent anyone from identifying the defendant during the proceedings unless the defendant permits it.

J. PART 71—APPEAL TO THE COURT OF APPEAL UNDER THE PROCEEDS OF CRIME ACT 2002—GENERAL RULES

18.82   Part 71 deals with issues of general procedure in respect of an appeal to the Court of Appeal under the Proceeds of Crime Act 2002.

18.83   By rule 71.1, any application to extend the time period allowed for serving notice of an application for leave to appeal under Part 2 of the 2002 Act must state the grounds for the application and must be included in the notice of appeal. Any extension of the period allowed under this Part or Parts 72 or 73, or by the Proceeds of Crime Act 2002 (Appeals under Part 2) Order 2003, cannot be made by agreement between the parties.

18.84   Many of the rules which relate to appeals under Part 65 apply equally, but modified as necessary, to appeals under this Part. Upon appeal under Part 2 of the 2002 Act, rule 71.2 dictates that, if an application is made for, first, a witness to attend or the evidence of a witness to be received by the court pursuant to article 7 of the Proceeds of

Crime Act (Appeals under Part 2) Order 2003, or, secondly, an application is made by the defendant for leave to be present at proceedings where such leave is needed pursuant to article 6 of the same 2003 order, then rule 68.3(2)(h) applies.

The forms required under the Practice Direction may be modified accordingly. If a witness is required to attend for examination pursuant to an appeal under Part 2 of the 2002 Act, then, by virtue of rule 71.2, the form set out in the Practice Direction may be modified accordingly. Moreover, just as rule 65.11 (see paragraph 18.28) governs the supply of documentary and other exhibits under the Criminal Appeal Act 1968, so it does under the 2002 Act (rule 71.4).   18.85

Rules 65.6 (see paragraph 18.24) and 65.5 (see paragraph 18.23), concerning the exercise of the court's power to grant leave and the renewal of an application for leave to the court respectively, also apply under this Part with any necessary modifications to the form (rule 71.6 and rule 71.7).   18.86

Under rule 71.5, the Registrar may require the Crown Court to provide the Court of Appeal with any information or assistance it requires for the purposes of determining such an appeal. When a single judge or the court has determined an appeal under this Part, then rule 71.8 requires that the Registrar must serve notice of the determination on all the parties to the proceedings as soon as is practicable. If the proceedings concerned section 31 of the 2002 Act, then the Registrar must also serve notice, as soon as is practicable, on the Crown Court officer and the officer of any magistrates' court responsible for the enforcement of any confiscation order made by the Crown Court.   18.87

According to rule 71.9, the rules under Part 65 relating to making a record of proceedings at trial (rule 65.8(2)(a) and (b)), and preparation of transcripts (rule 65.9), also apply under this Part.   18.88

Rule 71.10 governs the procedure associated with an application for leave to appeal to the Supreme Court under this Part. Any such application must be made either orally, after the relevant decision of the Court of Appeal, or in writing, served on the Registrar, in the form set out in the Practice Direction. Such an application may be abandoned by written notice to the Registrar at any time before it is heard by the Court of Appeal. Rules 65.5 and 65.6 (see paragraphs 18.23 and 18.24 respectively) apply accordingly to the exercise of powers under article 15 of the Proceeds of Crime Act 2002 (Appeals under Part 2) Order 2003. The form required for rule 65.5 may be modified as necessary.   18.89

Rule 71.11 under the old rules has now been removed.   18.90

K. PART 72—APPEAL TO THE COURT OF APPEAL UNDER THE PROCEEDS OF CRIME ACT 2002—PROSECUTOR'S APPEAL REGARDING CONFISCATION

Section 31 of the 2002 Act provides for appeals by the prosecution against any order made. If such an application is to be made then rule 72.1 requires that the notice of appeal must be in the form set out in the Practice Direction (formerly Form 1) and must be served on the Crown Court officer and the defendant. The notice served on the defendant must be accompanied by a respondent's notice set out in the stipulated form in the Practice Direction (formerly Form 2), which is for the defendant to complete, and a further notice informing him that the confiscation order may be increased by the   18.91

Court of Appeal or it may make a confiscation order itself or it may require the Crown Court to conduct another confiscation hearing.

18.92   The defendant must also be informed by that notice of any right he has to be present at the appeal hearing. He must also be invited to serve notice on the Registrar if he wishes to apply for leave to be present at the hearing or wishes to make any submissions to the Court of Appeal at the hearing, and also whether he wishes to be present in person or by means of a legal representative. The notice must also draw the provisions of rule 71.4 (see paragraph 18.98) to the attention of the defendant and advise the defendant to consult a solicitor as soon as possible. The appellant must then serve a notice of service on the Crown Court officer stating that he has served the notice in accordance with rule 72.1 or he must set out why it is that he has been unable to serve it.

18.93   If a defendant wishes to oppose the application then he must, under rule 72.2(2), serve notice to that effect within fourteen days of receipt of the appellant's notice on the Registrar and the appellant. That notice must be in the form set out in the Practice Direction (formerly Form 2) and must stipulate the date on which the notice was received, must summarize his response to the arguments of the appellant, and must specify any authorities he proposes to cite. The time for the giving of notice may be extended by the Registrar, a single judge, or the Court of Appeal. If the Registrar refuses an application for such an extension, the application may be renewed to a single judge and, if the applicant fails there, he may renew the application to the full court.

18.94   An appeal by the prosecutor may be amended or abandoned in accordance with rule 72.3. An appeal may be amended or abandoned without leave at any time before the hearing and with the leave of the court once the hearing has begun. Notice must be served on the Registrar. If the appeal is abandoned, then the appellant must also send a copy of the notice abandoning the appeal to the defendant, the Crown Court officer, and the magistrates' court required to enforce the order. Any abandoned appeal is treated as if it was refused or dismissed by the Court of Appeal. If the appellant serves a notice of amendment, he must send a copy of it to the defendant.

L. PART 73—APPEAL TO THE COURT OF APPEAL UNDER THE PROCEEDS OF CRIME ACT 2002—RESTRAINT OR RECEIVERSHIP ORDERS

18.95   Rule 73.1 stipulates that if a person applies for leave to appeal to the Court of Appeal under section 43 or section 65 of the 2002 Act, then it will only be given where the Court of Appeal considers that the appeal would have a real prospect of success or there is some other compelling reason why the appeal should be heard. If leave is given, the order for leave may limit the issues to be heard and may be made subject to conditions.

18.96   By virtue of rule 73.2, any application for leave under this Part must be by way of notice in the form set out in the Practice Direction (formerly Form 3) and must be served on the Crown Court officer. The appellant (unless the Registrar, single judge, or court directs otherwise) must serve the notice of appeal on each respondent (together with a respondent's notice), any person holding property which is relevant to the appeal and realizable, and any other person affected by the appeal. That notice must be served as soon as practicable and no later than seven days after the notice of appeal is served on the Crown Court officer. The appellant's notice of appeal must be accompanied by the following documents:

(a) four copies of the notice of appeal for the Court of Appeal;
(b) four copies of any skeleton argument;
(c) one sealed copy and four unsealed copies of any order being appealed;
(d) four copies of any witness statement or affidavit in support of the application for leave to appeal;
(e) four copies of a suitable record of the reasons for judgment of the Crown Court; and
(f) four copies of the bundle of documents used in the Crown Court proceedings from which the appeal lies.

If it is not possible to serve all of those documents, then the appellant must indicate which documents have not yet been served and why they are not currently available. In addition the appellant must provide a certificate of service to the Crown Court officer. That certificate of service must state that he has served the notice of appeal on each respondent and give full details of each respondent. If he has not done so then the certificate must explain why he has not done so.

18.97 If a respondent seeks leave to appeal from the Court of Appeal or asks the Court of Appeal to uphold the decision of the Crown Court for reasons different from, or additional to, those given by the Crown Court, he must serve a respondent's notice of appeal. The respondent's notice must be in the form set out in the Practice Direction (formerly Form 4). If the respondent is seeking leave to appeal to the Court of Appeal, then that must be stipulated in the notice. The notice must be served no more than fourteen days after the respondent is notified that the Court of Appeal has given leave to the appellant, or the respondent is notified that the application for leave and the appeal are to be heard together. The respondent's notice must also be served by him (unless the Registrar, single judge, or Court of Appeal directs otherwise) on the appellant and any other respondent as soon as practicable and within seven days of its service on the Registrar (rule 73.3).

18.98 By virtue of rule 73.4, an appellant may amend or abandon any notice of appeal without leave at any time before the hearing. If the hearing has begun, the Court of Appeal must give leave. Notice must be served on the Registrar. If the appellant serves a notice abandoning the appeal, he must send a copy of it to each respondent. Under rule 73.5, an appeal under this Part does not stay the decision or order of the Crown Court.

18.99 Any notice served under rule 73.2 (see paragraph 18.96) may be struck out in whole or in part by the Court of Appeal. Equally, the Court of Appeal may impose or vary conditions upon which an appeal may be brought (rule 73.6(1)). The Court of Appeal will only exercise either of those powers where there is a compelling reason for doing so and, if a party was present at the hearing at which leave was given, he may not later ask the court to impose or vary conditions on which the appeal is brought (rule 73.6(3)).

18.100 Rule 73.7 provides that ordinarily any hearing under this Part will be limited to a review of the Crown Court decision. However, if the court thinks it necessary in the interests of justice, it may hold a full rehearing. The court will allow an appeal when the decision of the Crown Court was either wrong, or unjust because of a serious irregularity of a procedural or other kind in the Crown Court proceedings. The Court of Appeal may draw any justified inference of fact from the evidence and a party may not rely on any matter not contained in his notice of appeal without the leave of the court.

M. PART 74—APPEAL OR REFERENCE TO THE SUPREME COURT

18.101   Part 74 governs the procedure concerned with either an appeal or reference to the Supreme Court. It is therefore concerned with an application for a retrial following acquittal (see Part 41), appeal against a ruling at a preparatory hearing (Part 66), appeal against a ruling adverse to the prosecution (Part 67), appeal against conviction or sentence (Part 68), or a reference of a point law or an unduly lenient sentence (Part 70). The rules in Part 65 also apply. Chapter D29 of *Blackstone's Criminal Practice 2011* contains further information on the law and procedure governing this appeal process.

18.102   Rule 74.2 stipulates that an application for permission to appeal or refer must be made orally to the Court of Appeal immediately after the court gives the reasons for its decision or in writing. If it is in writing, it must be served on the Registrar and every other party no later than fourteen days after the court gives the reasons on a sentencing reference under Part 70, or twenty-eight days after the court gives such reasons in any other case. If in writing, it must also be in the form set out in the Practice Direction (rule 74.2(5)). Any application for permission to appeal or to refer a sentencing case must identify the point of law of general public importance that the appellant wants the court to certify is involved in the decision. It must also set out the give reasons why that point of law ought to be considered by the Supreme Court, and the court ought to give permission to appeal. So far as an application to refer a point of law is concerned, it must also set out the reasons why that point ought to be considered by the Supreme Court. Any application for an extension of time within which to make the application for permission, or for a reference, or bail pending appeal, or (if the appellant is in custody) permission to attend any hearing in the Supreme Court must be included in or attached to the application for permission.

18.103   A defendant can be detained pending a prosecution appeal to the Supreme Court under section 37 of the Criminal Appeal Act 1968 or article 19 of the Serious Organised Crime and Police Act 2005 (Appeals under Section 74) Order 2006. Under rule 74.3, if an application for permission to appeal is made to the Court of Appeal, the court must decide whether a person who would have been detained but for the decision of the court should be ordered to be detained. The court must also decide any application for permission to attend any hearing in the Supreme Court, or for a representation order or for bail pending appeal. If bail is considered then Rules 68.8 (application for bail pending appeal or retrial), 68.9 (conditions of bail pending appeal or re-trial), and 68.10 (forfeiture of a recognizance given as a condition of bail) apply to that consideration.

N. PART 75—REQUEST TO THE EUROPEAN COURT FOR A PRELIMINARY RULING

18.104   Article 267 of the Treaty on the Functioning of the European Union, provides that a court of a Member State may request the Court of Justice of the European Union (the European Court) to give a preliminary ruling concerning the interpretation of the Treaty on European Union, or of the Treaty on the Functioning of the European Union, or on the validity and interpretation of acts of the institutions, bodies, offices, or agencies of

the Union if the court considers that a decision on the question is ne
to give judgment. Part 75 governs the procedure for making such a re
detail as to the law and practice relevant to this procedure can be fo
of *Blackstone's Criminal Practice 2011*.

The submission of the request may be ordered by the court on i
application by a party. The court may give directions for the preparation o.
such a request (rule 75.2(1)). In any request the court must include the identity of th.
court making the request, the identity of the parties, and state whether a party is in
custody. The request must also include a succinct statement of the question on which
the court seeks the ruling of the European Court, a succinct statement of any opinion
on the answer that the court may have expressed in any judgment that it has delivered,
along with a summary of the nature and history of the proceedings, including the salient
facts and an indication of whether those facts are proved, admitted, or assumed. In addition the relevant rules of national law, a summary of the relevant contentions of the
parties, an indication of the provisions of European Union law that the European Court
is asked to interpret, and an explanation of why a ruling of the European Court is
requested must be set out. The request must be expressed in terms that are readily trans-
latable into other languages and the request must be set out in a schedule to the order
(rule 75.2(2)).

The order for the submission of the request must be served on the Senior Master   18.106
of the Queen's Bench Division of the High Court by the court officer. When that is done
the Senior Master will submit the request to the European Court. That service will not
take place (unless the court otherwise directs) until the period allowed for any appeal
against the order has been exceeded, and any appeal against the order has been determined (rule 75.3).

The general rule if the court orders the submission of a request is that it will adjourn   18.107
or postpone any further hearing. However under rule 75.4, it may otherwise direct.

19
COSTS

A. INTRODUCTION

The 2005 Rules dealt with any provisions as to costs in Part 78. The rules relating to costs have now been substantially revised and simplified and placed into Part 76 of the Rules. They cover most circumstances in which an order as to costs can be made in criminal proceedings, but regard should also be had to other relevant provisions. Those provisions include the Criminal Costs Practice Direction along with Part 68 of the Rules which relates to appeals against costs orders made in the Crown Court under sections 18 and 19(1) of the Prosecution of Offences Act 1985. Moreover, Parts 63 and 68 contain rules about appeals against costs orders made under section 19B of the Prosecution of Offences Act 1985 (provision for award of costs against third parties) and regulation 3F of the Costs in Criminal Cases (General) Regulations 1986. In respect of costs in restraint or receivership proceedings under Part 2 of the Proceeds of Crime Act 2002, regard should be had to rules 61.19 to 61.22 in Chapter 17. For detailed coverage of the law and practice in respect of costs, regard may be had to Chapter D30 of *Blackstone's Criminal Practice 2011*.   19.01

B. GENERAL

Rule 76.1 sets out the statutory costs provisions to which Part 76 applies. They are: 19.02

(a) Part II of the Prosecution of Offences Act 1985 and Part II, IIA or IIB of the Costs in Criminal Cases (General) Regulations 1986;
(b) section 109 of the Magistrates' Courts Act 1980;
(c) section 52 of the Senior Courts Act 1981 and rule 76.6;
(d) section 8 of the Bankers' Books Evidence Act 1879;

(e) section 2C(8) of the Criminal Procedure (Attendance of Witnesses) Act 1965;
(f) section 36(5) of the Criminal Justice Act 1972;
(g) section 159(5) and Schedule 3, paragraph 11, to the Criminal Justice Act 1988;
(h) section 14H(5) of the Football Spectators Act 1989; or
(i) Part 3 of the Serious Crime Act 2007 (Appeals under Section 24) Order 2008.

19.03 Rule 76.1 also defines the term 'costs' for the purposes of this Part. They are defined as the fees payable to a legal representative, any disbursements paid by a legal representative, and any other expenses incurred in connection with the case.

19.04 General rules about orders for costs are set out in rule 76.2. Unless each party and any other person directly affected is present or has had an opportunity to attend, or make representations, the court should not make an order for costs (rule 76.2(1)). The court may make such an order with or without a hearing and any hearing may be in public or private (rule 76.2(2)). The court must have regard to all the circumstances, including the conduct of all the parties and any costs order already made when deciding what, if any, order as to costs to make (rule 76.2(3)). If such an order is made the court must specify who must, or must not, pay what, to whom. Where the court has a choice of powers under which to make the order, it must identify the legislation under which the order is made (rule 76.2(4)). If the court refuses an application for a costs order or rejects representations opposing a costs order, it must give reasons (rule 76.2(5)). The general rule is that any order for costs made by the court will be for an amount that is sufficient reasonably to compensate the recipient for any costs which are actually, reasonably and properly incurred, and are of a reasonable amount. However, the court may decide to order the payment of a proportion of that amount, a stated amount less than that amount, costs from or until a certain date only, costs relating only to particular steps taken, or costs relating only to a distinct part of the case (rule 76.2(6)). The factors which are relevant when making an assessment as to costs are stated to include the conduct of all the parties, the particular complexity of the matter or the difficulty or novelty of the questions raised. They also include the skill, effort, specialized knowledge and responsibility involved, the time spent on the case, the place where and the circumstances in which work or any part of it was done, and any direction or observations by the court that made the costs order (rule 76.2(7)). The court may order a party to pay costs to be assessed under rule 76.11. If it does so it may order that party to pay an amount on account (rule 76.2(8)). Unless the court orders otherwise, any order for the payment of costs takes effect when the amount is assessed (rule 76.2(9)).

19.05 Rule 76.3 stipulates that, even after it has expired, the court may extend a time limit for serving an application or representations under this Part. The court may consider any application or representations which are made in a different form to one set out in the Practice Direction, or even made orally. If a party requires an extension of time, he must make an appropriate application when he serves the application or representations for which it is needed. When he makes that application, he must explain the delay.

C. COSTS OUT OF CENTRAL FUNDS

19.06 Rule 76.4 concerns the award by a court of costs from central funds. The circumstances in which an order for the payment of costs out of central funds can be made are as follows.

For a defendant they are either following acquittal, or where a prosecution does not proceed, or where the Crown Court allows any part of a defendant's appeal from a magistrates' court, or where the Court of Appeal allows any part of a defendant's appeal from the Crown Court, or where the Court of Appeal decides a prosecutor's appeal under Part 66 (appeal to the Court of Appeal against ruling at preparatory hearing) or Part 67 (appeal to the Court of Appeal against ruling adverse to prosecution), or where the Court of Appeal decides a reference by the Attorney General under Part 70 (reference to the Court of Appeal of point of law or unduly lenient sentence), or where the Court of Appeal decides an appeal by someone other than the defendant about a serious crime prevention order. For a private prosecutor, costs out of central funds may be awarded to the private prosecutor in respect of proceedings concerning an offence that is triable either way or triable on indictment only. Costs out of central funds may also be awarded to a person adversely affected by a serious crime prevention order in a case where the Court of Appeal allows an appeal by that person about that order, or decides an appeal about that order by someone else.

When dealing with an appeal, the court can make an award of costs out of central 19.07 funds in respect of costs incurred in a court that made the decision under appeal. Equally, at a retrial, the court may award costs incurred at the initial trial and on any appeal. However, such costs may not include any funded by the Legal Services Commission (rule 76.4(2)). An order may be made by the court on its own initiative or following an application by the person who incurred the costs (rule 74.6(3)). Any application must be made as soon as practicable. If the applicant wants the court to direct an assessment, it must outline the type of costs and the amount claimed. If the applicant wants the court to assess the amount itself, it must specify the amount claimed (rule 76.4(4)). As a general rule, the court will make an order. However, the court may decline to make a defendant's costs order if, for example, the defendant is convicted of at least one offence, or the defendant's conduct led the prosecutor reasonably to think the prosecution case stronger than it was. In addition, the court may decline to make a prosecutor's costs order if, for example, the prosecution was started or continued unreasonably (rule 76.4(5), (6)). If the court makes an order it may direct an assessment under regulations 4 to 12 of the Costs in Criminal Cases (General) Regulations 1986, or articles 21 to 28 of the Serious Crime Act 2007 (Appeals under Section 24) Order 2008, whichever is applicable. Alternatively, if the recipient agrees, it may assess the amount itself. In a case in which it decides not to allow an amount that is reasonably sufficient to compensate the recipient for expenses properly incurred in the proceedings, it must assess the amount itself.

D. PAYMENT OF COSTS BY ONE PARTY TO ANOTHER

The procedure governing the award of costs to the prosecutor following conviction or 19.08 sentence is governed by rule 76.5. It applies whether the defendant is convicted or found guilty, dealt with in the Crown Court after committal for sentence, or dealt with for breach of a sentence. Such an order can be made on the court's own initiative or following a prosecution application by the prosecutor. Any application by the prosecution must be made as soon as practicable and must specify the amount claimed. If the court is satisfied that the defendant can pay, the general rule is that it will make the order. However, the court has a discretion to refuse to make the order. Any representations by the defendant opposing the application must be made as soon as practicable. The court itself assesses the amount to be paid.

19.09 Costs following an appeal are dealt with in rule 76.6. It applies in the magistrates' court, Crown Court, and Court of Appeal and has effect when the court can order a party to pay another person's costs on an appeal, or an application for permission to appeal. In the magistrates' court the court can order an appellant to pay a respondent's costs on abandoning an appeal to the Crown Court. So far as the Crown Court is concerned, it can order the defendant to pay the prosecutor's costs on dismissing a defendant's appeal against conviction or sentence, under section 108 of the Magistrates' Courts Act 1980, or where the magistrates' court makes a hospital order or guardianship order without convicting the defendant, under section 45 of the Mental Health Act 1983. The Crown Court can also order a party to pay another party's costs on deciding any other appeal governed by Part 63. Rule 76.6(1)(b) also specifically authorizes the Crown Court to order a party to pay another party's costs on an appeal to that court, except on an appeal under section 108 of the Magistrates' Courts Act 1980 or section 45 of the Mental Health Act 1983. The Court of Appeal has various powers as to costs. It can order the defendant to pay another person's costs on dismissing a defendant's appeal or application in respect of a ruling at a preparatory hearing (see Part 66 of the Rules at Chapter 18), or following appeal to the Court of Appeal in respect of conviction or sentence (see Part 68 of the Rules at Chapter 18), or upon an appeal or reference to the Supreme Court (see Part 74 of the Rules at Chapter 18). The Court of Appeal may also make an order as to costs to be paid by the defendant on allowing a prosecutor's appeal against a ruling adverse to the prosecution (see Part 76 of the Rules at Chapter 18), may order the appellant to pay another person's costs on dismissing an appeal or application by a person affected by a serious crime prevention order, and may order one party to pay another party's costs on deciding an appeal regarding reporting or public access restriction (see Part 69 of the Rules at Chapter 18).

19.10 In contrast to rule 76.4 (see paragraph 19.07 above), costs for this rule include not only costs incurred in the court that made the decision under appeal but also costs funded by the Legal Services Commission (rule 76.6(2)). Any order from the court may be of its own initiative or on application by the person who incurred the costs (rule 76.6(3)). Any application for such an order must be made as soon as practicable and must be notified to every other party. The application must specify the amount claimed, and against whom the amount is claimed. Where a notice of abandonment is served by an appellant abandoning an appeal to the Crown Court, the application for costs must be in writing and must be made not more than fourteen days after the notice of abandonment is served. The application must then be served on the appellant and the Crown Court officer (rule 76.6(4)). Any representations in opposition to an application for costs under this rule must be made as soon as practicable. If the application for costs followed an abandonment of an appeal to the Crown Court written representations of opposition must be served on the applicant, and on the Crown Court officer, not more than seven days after the application was served (rule 76.6(5)). If the application followed the abandonment of an appeal to the Crown Court, the Crown Court officer may submit the application to the Crown Court or serve it on the magistrates' court officer. By virtue of rule 76.7, if the court makes an order in circumstances where the appellant abandons an appeal to the Crown Court, or the Crown Court decides an appeal (except an appeal under section 108 of the Magistrates' Courts Act 1980 or section 45 of the Mental Health Act 1983) or the Court of Appeal decides an appeal regarding reporting or public access restriction, the court may either assess the amount to be paid itself or direct an assessment under rule 76.11 (see paragraph 19.17 below) (rule 76.6(7)). In any other case where a court makes an order, it must assess the amount (rule 76.6(8)).

The procedure governing orders as to costs when the court decides an application for   19.11
the production in evidence of a copy of a bank record, or a magistrates' court, or the Crown Court decides an application to terminate a football banning order, or the Crown Court allows an application to withdraw a witness summons, is to be found in rule 76.7. Any order by the court may be made of its own initiative or following an application by the party which incurred the costs. Any application must be made as soon as practicable, all other parties must be notified and the amount claimed against whom must be specified in the application. Representations in opposition to the application must be made as soon as practicable. If the court makes an order it may either assess the amount to be paid itself or direct an assessment under rule 76.11 (see paragraph 19.17 below).

Rule 76.8 applies where the court can order a party to pay another party's costs   19.12
incurred as a result of an unnecessary or improper act or omission. As with rule 76.6, for the purposes of this rule costs include costs funded by the Legal Services Commission (rule 76.8(2)). The court may make an order as to costs in respect of behaviour by a party on its own initiative or on application by the party who incurred the costs which are the subject of the order (rule 76.8(3)). Any application pursuant to rule 76.8(3) must be in writing and served on the court officer and any other party as soon as is practicable after the applicant becomes aware of the grounds for doing so. The application must specify the party by whom costs should be paid, the relevant act or omission, the reasons why that act or omission meets the criteria for making an order, the amount claimed, and those on whom the application has been served (rule 76.8(4)). If the court is considering making an order of its own initiative, it must identify the party against whom it proposes making the order. It must also specify the relevant act or omission, the reasons why that act or omission meets the criteria for making an order, and the amount involved (with the assistance of the party which incurred the costs) (rule 76.8(5)). Any representations in opposition to the application must be made as soon as practicable. If they are in response to an application by a party, they must be written representations and must be served on the applicant and on the court officer not more than seven days after it was served (rule 76.8(6)). The court must assess the amount of any order it makes itself (rule 76.8(7)).

E. OTHER COSTS ORDERS

Rule 76.9 deals with costs against legal representatives. It applies where a party has   19.13
incurred costs because of an improper, unreasonable, or negligent act or omission by a legal or other representative or representative's employee, or it has become unreasonable for that party to have to pay the costs because of such an act or omission occurring after those costs were incurred. In either case, it can be ordered that the representative responsible pay such costs, or the payment of costs to that representative be prohibited (r 76.9(1)). Costs can include any amounts expended by the Legal Services Commission

(rule 76.9(2)). An order may be made by the court of its own initiative or following an application by the party who incurred such costs (rule 76.9(3)). Any application must be in writing and made as soon as practicable after the applicant becomes aware of the grounds for making it (rule 76.9(4)). It must be served on the court officer, the representative allegedly responsible, all other parties and any other person directly affected. In addition, the application must specify the representative responsible, the relevant act or omission, the reasons why that act or omission meets the criteria for making an order, the amount claimed, and those on whom the application has been served (rule 76.9(5)). A form of application to use in connection with this rule is set out in the Criminal Costs Practice Direction. If the court is considering making an order of its own initiative, it must identify the representative against whom it proposes making that order. It must also specify the alleged act or omission leading to the consideration of making an order, the reasons why that act or omission meets the criteria for making an order, and the amount of any prospective order (with the assistance of the other party) (rule 76.9(6)).

19.14   Any representations from the representative who wishes to oppose the order must be made as soon as practicable. If those representations are in reply to an application, they must be served on the applicant and on the court officer in writing not more than seven days after the application was served. The general rule is that any order the court makes will be made without waiting until the end of the case, but the court may postpone making the order. The court must assess the amount to be paid (rule 76.9(7)). An alternative to making an order is for the court to make adverse observations about the representative's conduct for use in any assessment where a party's costs are either to be funded by the Legal Services Commission, or paid out of central funds or there is to be an assessment under rule 76.11.

19.15   Similar provisions apply under rule 76.10 when there has been serious misconduct by a person who is not a party but is a person whom the court can order to pay a party's costs (costs are taken to include costs funded by the Legal Services Commission under this rule). An order as to costs can be made under this rule by the court of its own initiative or following an application by the party who incurred the costs (rule 76.10(3)). Any application from a party must be in writing and must be made as soon as practicable after the party has become aware of the grounds for making it. It must be served on the court officer, the person allegedly responsible, all other parties, and any other person directly affected. The application must specify the person allegedly responsible, the relevant misconduct, the reasons why the criteria for making an order are met, the amount claimed, and those on whom the application has been served (rule 76.10(4)). A form of application to be used in connection with this rule is set out in the Criminal Costs Practice Direction. If the court is considering making an order on its own initiative, it must identify the person against whom it proposes making the order. It must also specify the relevant misconduct, the reasons why the criteria for making an order are met, and the amount of costs involved (with the assistance of the relevant party) (rule 76.10(5)).

19.16   Any representations opposing the application must be made as soon as practicable. If those representations follow an application, they must be in writing and served on the applicant and on the court officer not more than seven days after the application was served (rule 76.9(6)). The general rule is that, if a court makes any such order, it will do so at the end of the case, but it may do so earlier. The court must assess the amount of the order itself.

F. ASSESSMENT OF COSTS

Rule 76.11 governs the procedure when a court directs an assessment of costs under rule 61.20 (see Chapter 17), rule 76.6 (see paragraph 19.09 above) or rule 76.7 (see paragraph 19.12 above). Any such assessment must be carried out by the relevant assessing authority. If the direction was given by a magistrates' court or Crown Court, the relevant assessing authority is the court officer. The relevant assessing authority is the Registrar of Criminal Appeals, where the direction was given by the Court of Appeal (rule 76.11(2)). The party in whose favour the court made the costs order is known as the applicant for the purposes of this rule. The applicant must make an application in writing for an assessment. That application is required to be in any form required by the assessing authority. The application must be served, no more than three months after the costs order, on the assessing authority, and the respondent (the party against whom the costs order was made) (rule 76.11(3)). Any application must be detailed. It must summarize the work done and specify each item of work done, giving the date, time taken, and amount claimed, as well as any disbursements or expenses, including the fees of any advocate. It must also specify any circumstances which the applicant wants the assessing authority to take particular account of. The applicant must also supply receipts or other evidence of the amount claimed, as well as any other information or document for which the assessing authority asks and within such period as that authority may require (rule 76.11(4)).   **19.17**

If a respondent wishes to make representations about the amount claimed they must be in writing and must be served on the assessing authority, and the applicant, not more than twenty-one days after service of the application (rule 76.11(5)). If it seems likely that it would help with the assessment, the assessing authority must obtain any other information or document. Any doubt on the part of the assessing authority about what should be allowed should be resolved in favour of the defendant. The assessing authority should serve the assessment on the parties (rule 76.11(6)). Any party who wants the amount allowed to be re-assessed must make a written application to the assessing authority in any form required by that authority. That application must be served on the assessing authority and the other party not more than twenty-one days after service of the assessment. The application must explain the objections to the assessment, supply any additional supporting information or document, and ask for a hearing, if that party wants one. If a party wishes to make representations about an application for re-assessment they must be in writing and he must serve the representations on the assessing authority and the other party, not more than twenty-one days after service of the application. He must also ask for a hearing, if he wants one. If either party does ask for a hearing, the assessing authority must arrange one, whether in public or in private. If no such request is made, it may proceed to re-assessment with or without a hearing and re-assess the amount allowed on the initial assessment, taking into account the reasons for disagreement with that amount and any other representations. It may maintain, increase or decrease the amount allowed on the assessment. It must serve the re-assessment on the parties. If, no more than twenty-one days after the re-assessment either party asks for reasons for the re-assessment, the assessing authority must serve written reasons on the parties (rule 76.11(7)). Even after a time limit under this rule has expired, it may be   **19.18** extended by the assessing authority, or (if the assessing authority declines to do so) by the Senior Costs Judge (rule 76.11(8)).

19.19   If a re-assessment by an assessing authority is disputed by either party, they may appeal against it. The procedure for doing so is governed by rule 76.12. Not more than twenty-one days after service of the written reasons for the re-assessment, the party wishing to appeal must serve an appeal notice on the Senior Costs Judge, the other party, and the assessing authority. He must explain the objections to the re-assessment. Along with the appeal notice, he must serve on the Senior Costs Judge the applications for assessment and re-assessment, any other information or document considered by the assessing authority, the assessing authority's written reasons for the re-assessment, and any other information or document for which a costs judge asks, within such period as the judge may require. If he wishes to have one, he must also ask for a hearing (rule 76.12(1) and (2)). A form for use in respect of such an appeal is set out in the Criminal Costs Practice Direction. Any party who wishes to make representations about an appeal must serve those representations in writing on the Senior Costs Judge, and the applicant. Those representations must be served no more than twenty-one days after service of the appeal notice. If that party wishes a hearing to take place, he must ask for one (rule 76.12(3)). Unless a costs judge otherwise directs, the parties may rely only on the objections to the amount allowed on the initial assessment and any other representations and material considered by the assessing authority (rule 76.12(4)).

19.20   If either party asks for one, a costs judge must arrange a hearing, in public or in private. Unless such a request is made, he may determine an appeal with or without a hearing. In considering his determination, he may consult the assessing authority and/or the court which made the costs order, and he may obtain any other information or document. The costs judge must reconsider the amount allowed by the assessing authority. He must take into account the objections to the re-assessment and any other representations. He may maintain, increase, or decrease the amount allowed on the re-assessment. He may also make provision for the costs incurred by either party to the appeal. He must then serve reasons for the decision on the parties, and the assessing authority (rule 76.12(5)). Any time limit under this rule may be extended by a costs judge even after it has expired (rule 76.12(6)).

19.21   The final opportunity for appeal is to a High Court judge. The procedure to be adopted for an appeal to a High Court judge from a decision of a costs judge is set out in rule 76.13. If a party wishes to appeal, they may do so only if a costs judge certifies that a point of principle of general importance was involved in the decision by the costs judge. An application for such a certificate must be in writing and must be served on the costs judge and the other party no later than twenty-one days after service of the Senior Cost Judge's decision (rule 76.13(1) and (2)). If the certificate is granted, the party must appeal to a judge of the High Court attached to the Queen's Bench Division as if it were an appeal from the decision of a master under Part 52 of the Civil Procedure Rules 1998. They must serve the appeal no later than twenty-one days after service of the costs judge's certificate (rule 76.13(3)). A time limit under this rule can be extended by a High Court judge even after it has expired. The High Court judge has the same powers and duties as a costs judge under rule 76.12 and may hear the appeal with one or more assessors (rule 76.13(4)).

Appendix 1 Criminal Procedure Rules 2010 (SI 2010 No. 60, as amended by the Criminal Procedure (Amendment) Rules 2010 (SI 2010 No. 1921))

CRIMINAL PROCEDURE RULES 2010 (SI 2010 NO. 60), AS AMENDED BY THE CRIMINAL PROCEDURE (AMENDMENT) RULES 2010 (SI 2010 NO. 1921)

PART 1   THE OVERRIDING OBJECTIVE

The overriding objective

1.1   (1) The overriding objective of this new code is that criminal cases be dealt with justly.

(2) Dealing with a criminal case justly includes—

(a) acquitting the innocent and convicting the guilty;

(b) dealing with the prosecution and the defence fairly;

(c) recognising the rights of a defendant, particularly those under Article 6 of the European Convention on Human Rights;

(d) respecting the interests of witnesses, victims and jurors and keeping them informed of the progress of the case;

(e) dealing with the case efficiently and expeditiously;

(f) ensuring that appropriate information is available to the court when bail and sentence are considered; and

(g) dealing with the case in ways that take into account—

(i) the gravity of the offence alleged,

(ii) the complexity of what is in issue,

(iii) the severity of the consequences for the defendant and others affected, and

(iv) the needs of other cases.

The duty of the participants in a criminal case

1.2   (1) Each participant, in the conduct of each case, must—

(a) prepare and conduct the case in accordance with the overriding objective;

(b) comply with these Rules, practice directions and directions made by the court; and

(c) at once inform the court and all parties of any significant failure (whether or not that participant is responsible for that failure) to take any procedural step required by these Rules, any practice direction or any direction of the court. A failure is significant if it might hinder the court in furthering the overriding objective.

(2) Anyone involved in any way with a criminal case is a participant in its conduct for the purposes of this rule.

The application by the court of the overriding objective

1.3   The court must further the overriding objective in particular when—

(a) exercising any power given to it by legislation (including these Rules);

(b) applying any practice direction; or

(c) interpreting any rule or practice direction.

PART 2   UNDERSTANDING AND APPLYING THE RULES

When the Rules apply

2.1   (1) In general, the Criminal Procedure Rules apply—

(a) in all criminal cases in magistrates' courts and in the Crown Court; and

(b) in all cases in the criminal division of the Court of Appeal.

(2) If a rule applies only in one or two of those courts, the rule makes that clear.

(3) The Rules apply on and after 5th April, 2010, but unless the court otherwise directs they do not affect—

(a) a right or duty existing under the Criminal Procedure Rules 2005; or

(b) the application of Part 29, Part 34 or Part 35 of the Criminal Procedure Rules 2005 in a case in which an application or notice under the Part has been served before that date.

Definitions

2.2 (1) In these Rules, unless the context makes it clear that something different is meant:

'business day' means any day except Saturday, Sunday, Christmas Day, Boxing Day, Good Friday, Easter Monday or a bank holiday;

'court' means a tribunal with jurisdiction over criminal cases. It includes a judge, recorder, District Judge (Magistrates' Courts), lay justice and, when exercising their judicial powers, the Registrar of Criminal Appeals, a justices' clerk or assistant clerk;

'court officer' means the appropriate member of the staff of a court;

'justices' legal adviser' means a justices' clerk or an assistant to a justices' clerk;

'live link' means an arrangement by which a person can see and hear, and be seen and heard by, the court when that person is not in court;

'Practice Direction' means the Lord Chief Justice's Consolidated Criminal Practice Direction, as amended, and 'Criminal Costs Practice Direction' means the Lord Chief Justice's Practice Direction (Costs in Criminal Proceedings), as amended ; and

'public interest ruling' means a ruling about whether it is in the public interest to disclose prosecution material under sections 3(6), 7A(8) or 8(5) of the Criminal Procedure and Investigations Act 1996.

(2) Definitions of some other expressions are in the rules in which they apply.

References to Acts of Parliament and to Statutory Instruments

2.3 In these Rules, where a rule refers to an Act of Parliament or to subordinate legislation by title and year, subsequent references to that Act or to that legislation in the rule are shortened: so, for example, after a reference to the Criminal Procedure and Investigations Act 1996 that Act is called 'the 1996 Act'; and after a reference to the Criminal Procedure and Investigations Act 1996 (Defence Disclosure Time Limits) Regulations 1997 those Regulations are called 'the 1997 Regulations'.

The glossary

2.4 The glossary at the end of the Rules is a guide to the meaning of certain legal expressions used in them.

Representatives

2.5 (1) Under these Rules, unless the context makes it clear that something different is meant, anything that a party may or must do may be done—

(a) by a legal representative on that party's behalf;

(b) by a person with the corporation's written authority, where that party is a corporation;

(c) with the help of a parent, guardian or other suitable supporting adult where that party is a defendant—

(i) who is under 18, or

(ii) whose understanding of what the case involves is limited.

(2) Anyone with a prosecutor's authority to do so may, on that prosecutor's behalf—

(a) serve on the magistrates' court officer, or present to a magistrates' court, an information under section 1 of the Magistrates' Courts Act 1980; or

(b) issue a written charge and requisition under section 29 of the Criminal Justice Act 2003.

PART 3   CASE MANAGEMENT

The scope of this Part

3.1   This Part applies to the management of each case in a magistrates' court and in the Crown Court (including an appeal to the Crown Court) until the conclusion of that case.

The duty of the court

3.2   (1) The court must further the overriding objective by actively managing the case.
(2) Active case management includes—
    (a) the early identification of the real issues;
    (b) the early identification of the needs of witnesses;
    (c) achieving certainty as to what must be done, by whom, and when, in particular by the early setting of a timetable for the progress of the case;
    (d) monitoring the progress of the case and compliance with directions;
    (e) ensuring that evidence, whether disputed or not, is presented in the shortest and clearest way;
    (f) discouraging delay, dealing with as many aspects of the case as possible on the same occasion, and avoiding unnecessary hearings;
    (g) encouraging the participants to co-operate in the progression of the case; and
    (h) making use of technology.
(3) The court must actively manage the case by giving any direction appropriate to the needs of that case as early as possible.

The duty of the parties

3.3   Each party must—
    (a) actively assist the court in fulfilling its duty under rule 3.2, without or if necessary with a direction; and
    (b) apply for a direction if needed to further the overriding objective.

Case progression officers and their duties

3.4   (1) At the beginning of the case each party must, unless the court otherwise directs—
    (a) nominate an individual responsible for progressing that case; and
    (b) tell other parties and the court who he is and how to contact him.
(2) In fulfilling its duty under rule 3.2, the court must where appropriate—
    (a) nominate a court officer responsible for progressing the case; and
    (b) make sure the parties know who he is and how to contact him.
(3) In this Part a person nominated under this rule is called a case progression officer.
(4) A case progression officer must—
    (a) monitor compliance with directions;
    (b) make sure that the court is kept informed of events that may affect the progress of that case;
    (c) make sure that he can be contacted promptly about the case during ordinary business hours;
    (d) act promptly and reasonably in response to communications about the case; and
    (e) if he will be unavailable, appoint a substitute to fulfil his duties and inform the other case progression officers.

The court's case management powers

3.5   (1) In fulfilling its duty under rule 3.2 the court may give any direction and take any step actively to manage a case unless that direction or step would be inconsistent with legislation, including these Rules.
(2) In particular, the court may—
    (a) nominate a judge, magistrate or justices' legal adviser to manage the case;
    (b) give a direction on its own initiative or on application by a party;
    (c) ask or allow a party to propose a direction;

(d) for the purpose of giving directions, receive applications and representations by letter, by telephone or by any other means of electronic communication, and conduct a hearing by such means;

(e) give a direction without a hearing;

(f) fix, postpone, bring forward, extend or cancel a hearing;

(g) shorten or extend (even after it has expired) a time limit fixed by a direction;

(h) require that issues in the case should be determined separately, and decide in what order they will be determined; and

(i) specify the consequences of failing to comply with a direction.

(3) A magistrates' court may give a direction that will apply in the Crown Court if the case is to continue there.

(4) The Crown Court may give a direction that will apply in a magistrates' court if the case is to continue there.

(5) Any power to give a direction under this Part includes a power to vary or revoke that direction.

(6) If a party fails to comply with a rule or a direction, the court may

(a) fix, postpone, bring forward, extend, cancel or adjourn a hearing;

(b) exercise its powers to make a costs order; and

(c) impose such other sanction as may be appropriate.

Application to vary a direction

3.6 (1) A party may apply to vary a direction if—

(a) the court gave it without a hearing;

(b) the court gave it at a hearing in his absence; or

(c) circumstances have changed.

(2) A party who applies to vary a direction must—

(a) apply as soon as practicable after he becomes aware of the grounds for doing so; and

(b) give as much notice to the other parties as the nature and urgency of his application permits.

Agreement to vary a time limit fixed by a direction

3.7 (1) The parties may agree to vary a time limit fixed by a direction, but only if—

(a) the variation will not—

(i) affect the date of any hearing that has been fixed, or

(ii) significantly affect the progress of the case in any other way;

(b) the court has not prohibited variation by agreement; and

(c) the court's case progression officer is promptly informed.

(2) The court's case progression officer must refer the agreement to the court if he doubts the condition in paragraph (1)(a) is satisfied.

Case preparation and progression

3.8 (1) At every hearing, if a case cannot be concluded there and then the court must give directions so that it can be concluded at the next hearing or as soon as possible after that.

(2) At every hearing the court must, where relevant—

(a) if the defendant is absent, decide whether to proceed nonetheless;

(b) take the defendant's plea (unless already done) or if no plea can be taken then find out whether the defendant is likely to plead guilty or not guilty;

(c) set, follow or revise a timetable for the progress of the case, which may include a timetable for any hearing including the trial or (in the Crown Court) the appeal;

(d) in giving directions, ensure continuity in relation to the court and to the parties' representatives where that is appropriate and practicable; and

(e) where a direction has not been complied with, find out why, identify who was responsible, and take appropriate action.

(3) In order to prepare for a trial in the Crown Court, the court must conduct a plea and case management hearing unless the circumstances make that unnecessary.

(4) In order to prepare for the trial, the court must take every reasonable step to encourage and to facilitate the attendance of witnesses when they are needed.

Readiness for trial or appeal

3.9 (1) This rule applies to a party's preparation for trial or appeal, and in this rule and rule 3.10 trial includes any hearing at which evidence will be introduced.

(2) In fulfilling his duty under rule 3.3, each party must—
  (a) comply with directions given by the court;
  (b) take every reasonable step to make sure his witnesses will attend when they are needed;
  (c) make appropriate arrangements to present any written or other material; and
  (d) promptly inform the court and the other parties of anything that may—
    (i) affect the date or duration of the trial or appeal, or
    (ii) significantly affect the progress of the case in any other way.

(3) The court may require a party to give a certificate of readiness.

Conduct of a trial or an appeal

3.10 In order to manage the trial or an appeal—
  (a) the court must establish, with the active assistance of the parties, what are the disputed issues;
  (b) must consider setting a timetable that—
    (i) takes account of those issues and any timetable proposed by a party, and
    (ii) may limit the duration of any stage of the hearing;
  (c) may require a party to identify—
    (i) which witnesses that party wants to give evidence in person,
    (ii) the order in which that party wants those witnesses to give their evidence,
    (iii) whether that party requires an order compelling the attendance of a witness,
    (iv) what arrangements are desirable to facilitate the giving of evidence by a witness,
    (v) what arrangements are desirable to facilitate the participation of any other person, including the defendant,
    (vi) what written evidence that party intends to introduce,
    (vii) what other material, if any, that person intends to make available to the court in the presentation of the case,
    (viii) whether that party intends to raise any point of law that could affect the conduct of the trial or appeal, and
  (d) may limit—
    (i) the examination, cross-examination or re-examination of a witness, and
    (ii) the duration of any stage of the hearing.

Case management forms and records

3.11 (1) The case management forms set out in the Practice Direction must be used, and where there is no form then no specific formality is required.

(2) The court must make available to the parties a record of directions given.

PART 4   SERVICE OF DOCUMENTS

When this Part applies

4.1 The rules in this Part apply to the service of every document in a case to which these Rules apply, subject to any special rules in other legislation (including other Parts of these Rules) or in the Practice Direction.

Methods of service

4.2 A document may be served by any of the methods described in rules 4.3 to 4.6 (subject to rule 4.7), or in rule 4.8.

Service by handing over a document

4.3   (1) A document may be served on—

    (a) an individual by handing it to him or her;

    (b) a corporation by handing it to a person holding a senior position in that corporation;

    (c) an individual or corporation who is legally represented in the case by handing it to that representative;

    (d) the prosecution by handing it to the prosecutor or to the prosecution representative;

    (e) the court officer by handing it to a court officer with authority to accept it at the relevant court office; and

    (f) the Registrar of Criminal Appeals by handing it to a court officer with authority to accept it at the Criminal Appeal Office.

    (2) If an individual is 17 or under, a copy of a document served under paragraph (1)(a) must be handed to his or her parent, or another appropriate adult, unless no such person is readily available.

Service by leaving or posting a document

4.4   (1) A document may be served by leaving it at the appropriate address for service under this rule or by sending it to that address by first class post or by the equivalent of first class post.

    (2) The address for service under this rule on—

    (a) an individual is an address where it is reasonably believed that he or she will receive it;

    (b) a corporation is its principal office, and if there is no readily identifiable principal office then any place where it carries on its activities or business;

    (c) an individual or corporation who is legally represented in the case is that representative's office;

    (d) the prosecution is the prosecutor's office;

    (e) the court officer is the relevant court office; and

    (f) the Registrar of Criminal Appeals is the Criminal Appeal Office, Royal Courts of Justice, Strand, London WC2A 2LL.

Service through a document exchange

4.5   A document may be served by document exchange (DX) where—

    (a) the writing paper of the person to be served gives a DX box number; and

    (b) that person has not refused to accept service by DX.

Service by fax, e-mail or other electronic means

4.6   (1) A document may be served by fax, e-mail or other electronic means where—

    (a) the person to be served has given a fax, e-mail or other electronic address; and

    (b) that person has not refused to accept service by that means.

    (2) Where a document is served under this rule the person serving it need not provide a paper copy as well.

Documents that must be served only by handing them over, leaving or posting them

4.7   (1) The documents listed in paragraph (2) may be served—

    (a) on an individual, only under rule 4.3(1)(a) (handing over) or rule 4.4(1) and (2)(a) (leaving or posting); and

    (b) on a corporation only under rule 4.3(1)(b) (handing over) or rule 4.4(1) and (2)(b) (leaving or posting).

    (2) Those documents are—

    (a) a summons, requisition or witness summons;

    (b) notice of an order under section 25 of the Road Traffic Offenders Act 1988;

    (c) a notice of registration under section 71(6) of that Act;

    (d) a notice of discontinuance under section 23(4) of the Prosecution of Offences Act 1985;

    (e) notice under rule 37.3(1) of the date, time and place to which the trial of an information has been adjourned, where it was adjourned in the defendant's absence;

    (f) a notice of fine or forfeited recognizance required by rule 52.1(1);

    (g) notice under section 86 of the Magistrates' Courts Act 1980 of a revised date to attend a means inquiry;

    (h) notice of a hearing to review the postponement of the issue of a warrant of commitment under section 77(6) of the Magistrates' Courts Act 1980;

    (i) a copy of the minute of a magistrates' court order required by rule 52.7(1);

    (j) an invitation to make observations or attend a hearing under rule 53.1(2) on the review of a compensation order under section 133 of the Powers of Criminal Courts (Sentencing) Act 2000;

    (k) any notice or document served under Part 19.

(3) An application under rule 62.3 for the court to punish for contempt of court may be served—

    (a) on an individual, only under rule 4.3(1)(a) (by handing it to him or her);

    (b) on a corporation, only under rule 4.3(1)(b) (by handing it to a person holding a senior position in that corporation).

Service by person in custody

4.8 (1) A person in custody may serve a document by handing it to the custodian addressed to the person to be served.

    (2) The custodian must—

    (a) endorse it with the time and date of receipt;

    (b) record its receipt; and

    (c) forward it promptly to the addressee.

Service by another method

4.9 (1) The court may allow service of a document by a method other than those described in rules 4.3 to 4.6 and in rule 4.8.

    (2) An order allowing service by another method must specify—

    (a) the method to be used; and

    (b) the date on which the document will be served.

Date of service

4.10 (1) A document served under rule 4.3 or rule 4.8 is served on the day it is handed over.

    (2) Unless something different is shown, a document served on a person by any other method is served—

    (a) in the case of a document left at an address, on the next business day after the day on which it was left;

    (b) in the case of a document sent by first class post or by the equivalent of first class post, on the second business day after the day on which it was posted or despatched;

    (c) in the case of a document served by document exchange, on the second business day after the day on which it was left at the addressee's DX or at a correspondent DX;

    (d) in the case of a document transmitted by fax, e-mail or other electronic means, on the next business day after it was transmitted; and

    (e) in any case, on the day on which the addressee responds to it if that is earlier.

    (3) Unless something different is shown, a document produced by a court computer system is to be taken as having been sent by first class post or by the equivalent of first class post to the addressee on the business day after the day on which it was produced.

    (4) Where a document is served on or by the court officer, 'business day' does not include a day on which the court office is closed.

Proof of service

4.11   The person who serves a document may prove that by signing a certificate explaining how and when it was served.

Court's power to give directions about service

4.12   (1) The court may specify the time as well as the date by which a document must be—
           (a) served under rule 4.3 or rule 4.8; or
           (b) transmitted by fax, e-mail or other electronic means if it is served under rule 4.6.
        (2) The court may treat a document as served if the addressee responds to it even if it was not served in accordance with the rules in this Part.

Part 5   Forms and Court Records
Section 1: Forms

Forms

5.1   The forms set out in the Practice Direction and in the Criminal Costs Practice Direction shall be used as appropriate in connection with the rules to which they apply.

Magistrates' court forms in Welsh

5.2   (1) Subject to the provisions of this rule, the Welsh language forms set out in the Practice Direction or forms to the like effect may be used in connection with proceedings in magistrates' courts in Wales.
        (2) Both a Welsh form and an English form may be used in the same document.
        (3) When only a Welsh form set out in the Practice Direction accompanying this rule, or only the corresponding English form, is used in connection with proceedings in magistrates' courts in Wales, there shall be added the following words in Welsh and English:
                'Darperir y ddogfen hon yn Gymraeg/Saesneg os bydd arnoch ei heisiau. Dylech wneud cais yn ddioed i (Glerc Llys yr Ynadon) (rhodder yma'r cyfeiriad)..............
                ....
                This document will be provided in Welsh/English if you require it. You should apply immediately to (the Justices' Clerk to the Magistrates' Court) (address)........
                ....
                (If a person other than a justices' clerk is responsible for sending or giving the document, insert that person's name instead.)
        (4) The justices' clerk or other person responsible for the service of a form bearing the additional words set out in paragraph (3) above shall, if any person upon whom the form is served so requests, provide him with the corresponding English or Welsh form.
        (5) In this rule any reference to serving a document shall include the sending, giving or other delivery of it.
        (6) In the case of a discrepancy between an English and Welsh text the English text shall prevail.

Signature of magistrates' court forms by justices' clerk

5.3   (1) This rule applies where a form for use in connection with a magistrates' court provides for its signature.
        (2) Unless other legislation otherwise requires, signature may be by any written or electronic authentication of the form by, or with the authority of, the signatory.

Section 2: Court Records

Magistrates' court register

5.4   (1) A magistrates' court officer shall keep a register in which there shall be entered—
           (a) a minute or memorandum of every adjudication of the court; and
           (b) a minute or memorandum of every other proceeding or thing required by these Rules or any other enactment to be so entered.

(2) The register may be stored in electronic form on the court computer system and entries in the register shall include, where relevant, the following particulars—

   (a) the name of the informant, complainant or applicant;

   (b) the name and date of birth (if known) of the defendant or respondent;

   (c) the nature of offence, matter of complaint or details of the application;

   (d) the date of offence or matter of complaint;

   (e) the plea or consent to order; and

   (f) the minute of adjudication.

(3) Particulars of any entry relating to a decision about bail or the reasons for any such decisions or the particulars of any certificate granted under section 5(6A) of the Bail Act 1976 may be made in a book separate from that in which the entry recording the decision itself is made, but any such separate book shall be regarded as forming part of the register.

(4) Where, by virtue of section 128(3A) of the Magistrates' Courts Act 1980, an accused gives his consent to the hearing and determination in his absence of any application for his remand on an adjournment of the case under sections 5, 10(1) or 18(4) of that Act, the court shall cause the consent of the accused, and the date on which it was notified to the court, to be entered in the register.

(5) Where any consent mentioned in paragraph (4) is withdrawn, the court shall cause the withdrawal of the consent and the date on which it was notified to the court to be entered in the register.

(6) On the summary trial of an information the accused's plea shall be entered in the register.

(7) Where a court tries any person summarily in any case in which he may be tried summarily only with his consent, the court shall cause his consent to be entered in the register and, if the consent is signified by a person representing him in his absence, the court shall cause that fact also to be entered in the register.

(8) Where a person is charged before a magistrates' court with an offence triable either way the court shall cause the entry in the register to show whether he was present when the proceedings for determining the mode of trial were conducted and, if they were conducted in his absence, whether they were so conducted by virtue of section 18(3) of the 1980 Act (disorderly conduct on his part) or by virtue of section 23(1) of that Act (consent signified by person representing him).

(9) In any case to which section 22 of the 1980 Act (certain offences triable either way to be tried summarily if value involved is small) applies, the court shall cause its decision as to the value involved or, as the case may be, the fact that it is unable to reach such a decision to be entered in the register.

(10) Where a court has power under section 53(3) of the 1980 Act to make an order with the consent of the defendant without hearing evidence, the court shall cause any consent of the defendant to the making of the order to be entered in the register.

(11) In the case of conviction or dismissal, the register shall clearly show the nature of the offence of which the accused is convicted or, as the case may be, the nature of the offence charged in the information that is dismissed.

(12) An entry of a conviction in the register shall state the date of the offence.

(13) Where a court is required under section 130(3) of the Powers of Criminal Courts (Sentencing) Act 2000 to give reasons for not making a compensation order the court shall cause the reasons given to be entered in the register.

(14) Where a court passes a custodial sentence, the court shall cause a statement of whether it obtained and considered a pre-sentence report before passing sentence to be entered in the register.

(15) Every register shall be open to inspection during reasonable hours by any justice of the peace, or any person authorised in that behalf by a justice of the peace or the Lord Chancellor.

(16) A record of summary conviction or order made on complaint required for an appeal or other legal purpose may be in the form of certified extract from the court register.

(17) Such part of the register as relates to proceedings in a youth court may be recorded separately and stored in electronic form on the court computer system.

Registration of endorsement of licence under section 57 of the Road Traffic Offenders Act 1988

5.5   A magistrates' court officer or justices' clerk who, as a fixed penalty clerk within the meaning of section 69(4) of the Road Traffic Offenders Act 1988, endorses a driving licence under section 57(3) or (4) of that Act (endorsement of licences without hearing) shall register the particulars of the endorsement in a record separate from the register kept under rule 6.1 but any such record shall be regarded as forming part of the register.

Registration of certificate issued under section 70 of the Road Traffic Offenders Act 1988

5.6   A magistrates' court officer shall register receipt of a registration certificate issued under section 70 of the Road Traffic Offenders Act 1988 (sum payable in default of fixed penalty to be enforced as a fine) in a record separate from the register kept under rule 6.1 but any such record shall be regarded as forming part of the register.

Proof of proceedings in magistrates' courts

5.7   The register of a magistrates' court, or an extract from the register certified by the magistrates' court officer as a true extract, shall be available for admission in any legal proceedings as evidence of the proceedings of the court entered in the register.

Part 6   Investigation Orders

Section 1: Understanding and Applying this Part

When this Part applies

6.1   (1) Sections 2 and 3 of this Part apply where, for the purposes of a terrorist investigation—
           (a) a Circuit judge can make, vary or discharge—
               (i)   an order for the production of, or for giving access to, material, or for a statement of its location, under paragraphs 5 and 10 of Schedule 5 to the Terrorism Act 2000,
               (ii) an explanation order, under paragraphs 10 and 13 of Schedule 5 to the 2000 Act,
               (iii) a customer information order, under paragraphs 1 and 4 of Schedule 6 to the 2000 Act;
           (b) a Circuit judge can make, and the Crown Court can vary or discharge, an account monitoring order, under paragraphs 2 and 4 of Schedule 6A to the 2000 Act.
        (2) Sections 2 and 4 of this Part apply where, for the purposes of a confiscation investigation or a money laundering investigation, a Crown Court judge can make, and the Crown Court can vary or discharge—
           (a) a production order, under sections 345 and 351 of the Proceeds of Crime Act 2002;
           (b) an order to grant entry, under sections 347 and 351 of the 2002 Act;
           (c) a disclosure order, under sections 357 and 362 of the 2002 Act;
           (d) a customer information order, under sections 363 and 369 of the 2002 Act;
           (e) an account monitoring order, under sections 370 and 375 of the 2002 Act.

Meaning of 'court', 'applicant' and 'respondent'

6.2   In this Part—
           (a) a reference to the 'court' includes a reference to any judge who can exercise a power to which this Part applies;
           (b) 'applicant' means any person who can apply for an order to which this Part applies; and
           (c) 'respondent' means a person against whom such an order is sought or made.

Section 2: General Rules

Exercise of court's powers

6.3   (1) The court must determine an application for an order—
           (a) at a hearing (which will be in private unless the court otherwise directs); and
           (b) in the applicant's presence.

(2) The court must not determine such an application in the absence of the respondent or any other person affected, unless—
    (a) the absentee has had at least 2 business days in which to make representations; or
    (b) the court is satisfied that—
        (i) the applicant cannot identify or contact the absentee,
        (ii) it would prejudice the investigation if the absentee were present, or
        (iii) it would prejudice the investigation to adjourn or postpone the application so as to allow the absentee to attend.
(3) The court may determine an application to vary or discharge an order—
    (a) at a hearing (which will be in private unless the court otherwise directs), or without a hearing; and
    (b) in the absence of—
        (i) the applicant,
        (ii) the respondent,
        (iii) any other person affected by the order.

Court's power to vary requirements under this Part

6.4   (1) The court may—
    (a) shorten or extend (even after it has expired) a time limit under this Part;
    (b) dispense with a requirement for service under this Part (even after service was required); and
    (c) consider an application made orally instead of in writing.
    (2) A person who wants an extension of time must—
    (a) apply when serving the application for which it is needed; and
    (b) explain the delay.

Custody of documents

6.5   Unless the court otherwise directs, the court officer may—
    (a) keep a written application; or
    (b) arrange for the whole or any part to be kept by some other appropriate person, subject to any conditions that the court may impose.

Section 3: orders under the Terrorism Act 2000

Application for an order under the Terrorism Act 2000

6.6   (1) This rule applies where an applicant wants the court to make one of the orders listed in rule 6.1(1).
    (2) The applicant must—
    (a) apply in writing;
    (b) serve the application on—
        (i) the court officer, and
        (ii) the respondent (unless the court otherwise directs);
    (c) identify the respondent;
    (d) give the information required by whichever of rules 6.7 to 6.10 applies; and
    (e) serve any order made on the respondent.

Content of application for a production etc. order

6.7   As well as complying with rule 6.6, an applicant who wants the court to make an order for the production of, or access to, material, or for a statement of its location, must—
    (a) describe that material;
    (b) explain why the applicant thinks the material is—
        (i) in the respondent's possession, custody or power, or
        (ii) likely to be so within 28 days of the order;
    (c) explain how the material constitutes or contains excluded material or special procedure material;

(d) confirm that none of the material is expected to be subject to legal privilege;

(e) explain why the material is likely to be of substantial value to the investigation;

(f) explain why it is in the public interest for the material to be produced, or for the applicant to be given access to it, having regard to—

    (i) the benefit likely to accrue to the investigation if it is obtained, and

    (ii) the circumstances in which the respondent has the material, or is expected to have it; and

(g) propose—

    (i) the terms of the order, and

    (ii) the period within which it should take effect.

Content of application for an explanation order

6.8   As well as complying with rule 6.6, an applicant who wants the court to make an explanation order must—

(a) identify the material that the applicant wants the respondent to explain;

(b) confirm that the explanation is not expected to infringe legal privilege; and

(c) propose—

    (i) the terms of the order, and

    (ii) the period within which it should take effect, if 7 days from the date of the order would not be appropriate.

Content of application for a customer information order

6.9   As well as complying with rule 6.6, an applicant who wants the court to make a customer information order must—

(a) explain why it is desirable for the purposes of the investigation to trace property said to be terrorist property within the meaning of the Terrorism Act 2000;

(b) explain why the order will enhance the effectiveness of the investigation; and

(c) propose the terms of the order.

Content of application for an account monitoring order

6.10   As well as complying with rule 6.6, an applicant who wants the court to make an account monitoring order must—

(a) specify—

    (i) the information sought,

    (ii) the period during which the applicant wants the respondent to provide that information (to a maximum of 90 days), and

    (iii) where, when and in what manner the applicant wants the respondent to provide that information;

(b) explain why it is desirable for the purposes of the investigation to trace property said to be terrorist property within the meaning of the Terrorism Act 2000;

(c) explain why the order will enhance the effectiveness of the investigation; and

(d) propose the terms of the order.

Application to vary or discharge an order

6.11   (1) This rule applies where one of the following wants the court to vary or discharge an order listed in rule 6.1(1)—

(a) an applicant;

(b) the respondent; or

(c) a person affected by the order.

(2) That applicant, respondent or person affected must—

(a) apply in writing as soon as practicable after becoming aware of the grounds for doing so;

(b) serve the application on—

    (i) the court officer, and

    (ii) the respondent, applicant, or any person known to be affected, as applicable;

(c) explain why it is appropriate for the order to be varied or discharged;

(d) propose the terms of any variation; and

(e) ask for a hearing, if one is wanted, and explain why it is needed.

Application containing information withheld from a respondent or other person

6.12 (1) This rule applies where—

    (a) an applicant serves on a respondent or other person an application for one of the orders listed in rule 6.1(1), or for the variation or discharge of such an order; and

    (b) the application includes information that the applicant thinks ought not be revealed to that recipient.

(2) The applicant must—

    (a) omit that information from the part of the application that is served on the respondent or other person;

    (b) mark the other part, to show that it is only for the court; and

    (c) in that other part, explain why the applicant has withheld it.

(3) A hearing of an application to which this rule applies may take place, wholly or in part, in the absence of the respondent and any other person.

(4) At a hearing of an application to which this rule applies—

    (a) the general rule is that the court will receive, in the following sequence—

        (i) representations first by the applicant and then by the respondent and any other person, in the presence of them all, and then

        (ii) further representations by the applicant, in the others' absence; but

    (b) the court may direct other arrangements for the hearing.

Application to punish for contempt of court

6.13 (1) This rule applies where a person is accused of disobeying—

    (a) a production etc. order made under paragraph 5 of Schedule 5 to the Terrorism Act 2000;

    (b) an explanation order made under paragraph 13 of that Schedule; or

    (c) an account monitoring order made under paragraph 2 of Schedule 6A to that Act.

(2) An applicant who wants the court to exercise its power to punish that person for contempt of court must comply with the rules in Part 62 (Contempt of court).

Section 4: orders under the Proceeds of Crime Act 2002

Application for an order under the Proceeds of Crime Act 2002

6.14 (1) This rule applies where an applicant wants the court to make one of the orders listed in rule 6.1(2).

(2) The applicant must—

    (a) apply in writing;

    (b) serve the application on—

        (i) the court officer, and

        (ii) the respondent (unless the court otherwise directs);

    (c) identify—

        (i) the respondent, and

        (ii) the person the subject of the confiscation or money laundering investigation;

    (d) explain why the applicant thinks the person under investigation has—

        (i) benefited from criminal conduct, in the case of a confiscation investigation, or

        (ii) committed a money laundering offence, in the case of a money laundering investigation;

    (e) give the additional information required by whichever of rules 6.15 to 6.19 applies; and

    (f) serve any order made on each respondent.

Content of application for a production order

6.15   As well as complying with rule 6.14, an applicant who wants the court to make an order for the production of, or access to, material, must—
   (a) describe that material;
   (b) explain why the applicant thinks the material is in the respondent's possession or control;
   (c) confirm that none of the material is—
        (i) expected to be subject to legal privilege, or
        (ii) excluded material;
   (d) explain why the material is likely to be of substantial value to the investigation;
   (e) explain why it is in the public interest for the material to be produced, or for the applicant to be given access to it, having regard to—
        (i) the benefit likely to accrue to the investigation if it is obtained, and
        (ii) the circumstances in which the respondent has the material; and
   (f) propose—
        (i) the terms of the order, and
        (ii) the period within which it should take effect, if 7 days from the date of the order would not be appropriate.

Content of application for an order to grant entry

6.16   An applicant who wants the court to make an order to grant entry must—
   (a) specify the premises to which entry is sought;
   (b) explain why the order is needed; and
   (c) propose the terms of the order.

Content of application for a disclosure order

6.17   As well as complying with rule 6.14, an applicant who wants the court to make a disclosure order must—
   (a) describe in general terms the information that the applicant wants the respondent to provide;
   (b) confirm that none of the information is—
        (i) expected to be subject to legal privilege, or
        (ii) excluded material;
   (c) explain why the information is likely to be of substantial value to the investigation;
   (d) explain why it is in the public interest for the information to be provided, having regard to the benefit likely to accrue to the investigation if it is obtained; and
   (e) propose the terms of the order.

Content of application for a customer information order

6.18   As well as complying with rule 6.14, an applicant who wants the court to make a customer information order must—
   (a) explain why customer information about the person under investigation is likely to be of substantial value to that investigation;
   (b) explain why it is in the public interest for the information to be provided, having regard to the benefit likely to accrue to the investigation if it is obtained; and
   (c) propose the terms of the order.

Content of application for an account monitoring order

6.19   As well as complying with rule 6.14, an applicant who wants the court to make an account monitoring order for the provision of account information must—
   (a) specify—
        (i) the information sought,
        (ii) the period during which the applicant wants the respondent to provide that information (to a maximum of 90 days), and
        (iii) when and in what manner the applicant wants the respondent to provide that information;

(b) explain why the information is likely to be of substantial value to the investigation;

(c) explain why it is in the public interest for the information to be provided, having regard to the benefit likely to accrue to the investigation if it is obtained; and

(d) propose the terms of the order.

Application to vary or discharge an order

6.20 (1) This rule applies where one of the following wants the court to vary or discharge an order listed in rule 6.1(2)—

(a) an applicant;

(b) the respondent; or

(c) a person affected by the order.

(2) That applicant, respondent or person affected must—

(a) apply in writing as soon as practicable after becoming aware of the grounds for doing so;

(b) serve the application on—

(i) the court officer, and

(ii) the respondent, applicant, or any person known to be affected, as applicable;

(c) explain why it is appropriate for the order to be varied or discharged;

(d) propose the terms of any variation; and

(e) ask for a hearing, if one is wanted, and explain why it is needed.

Application containing information withheld from a respondent or other person

6.21 (1) This rule applies where—

(a) an applicant serves on a respondent or other person an application for one of the orders listed in rule 6.1(2), or for the variation or discharge of such an order; and

(b) the application includes information that the applicant thinks ought not be revealed to that recipient.

(2) The applicant must—

(a) omit that information from the part of the application that is served on the respondent or other person;

(b) mark the other part, to show that it is only for the court; and

(c) in that other part, explain why the applicant has withheld it.

(3) A hearing of an application to which this rule applies may take place, wholly or in part, in the absence of the respondent and any other person.

(4) At a hearing of an application to which this rule applies—

(a) the general rule is that the court will receive, in the following sequence—

(i) representations first by the applicant and then by the respondent and any other person, in the presence of them all, and then

(ii) further representations by the applicant, in the others' absence; but

(b) the court may direct other arrangements for the hearing.

Application to punish for contempt of court

6.22 (1) This rule applies where a person is accused of disobeying—

(a) a production order made under section 345 of the Proceeds of Crime Act 2002; or

(b) an account monitoring order made under section 370 of that Act.

(2) An applicant who wants the court to exercise its power to punish that person for contempt of court must comply with the rules in Part 62 (contempt of court).

SECTION 5: ORDERS UNDER THE CORONERS AND JUSTICE ACT 2009

Exercise of court's powers

6.23 (1) The court may determine an application for an investigation anonymity order, and any appeal against the refusal of such an order—

(a) at a hearing (which will be in private unless the court otherwise directs); or

(b) without a hearing.

(2) The court must determine an application to discharge an investigation anonymity order, and any appeal against the decision on such an application—

    (a) at a hearing (which will be in private unless the court otherwise directs); and

    (b) in the presence of the person specified in the order, unless—

        (i) that person applied for the discharge of the order,

        (ii) that person has had an opportunity to make representations, or

        (iii) the court is satisfied that it is not reasonably practicable to communicate with that person.

(3) The court may consider an application or an appeal made orally instead of in writing.

Application for an investigation anonymity order

6.24 (1) This rule applies where an applicant wants a magistrates' court to make an investigation anonymity order.

    (2) The applicant must—

    (a) apply in writing;

    (b) serve the application on the court officer;

    (c) identify the person to be specified in the order, unless—

        (i) the applicant wants the court to determine the application at a hearing, or

        (ii) the court otherwise directs;

    (d) explain how the proposed order meets the conditions prescribed by section 78 of the Coroners and Justice Act 2009;

    (e) say if the applicant intends to appeal should the court refuse the order;

    (f) attach any material on which the applicant relies; and

    (g) propose the terms of the order.

    (3) At any hearing of the application, the applicant must—

    (a) identify to the court the person to be specified in the order, unless—

        (i) the applicant has done so already, or

        (ii) the court otherwise directs; and

    (b) unless the applicant has done so already, inform the court if the applicant intends to appeal should the court refuse the order.

Application to discharge an investigation anonymity order

6.25 (1) This rule applies where one of the following wants a magistrates' court to discharge an investigation anonymity order—

    (a) an applicant; or

    (b) the person specified in the order.

    (2) That applicant or the specified person must—

    (a) apply in writing as soon as practicable after becoming aware of the grounds for doing so;

    (b) serve the application on—

        (i) the court officer, and as applicable

        (ii) the applicant for the order, and

        (iii) the specified person;

    (c) explain—

        (i) what material circumstances have changed since the order was made, or since any previous application was made to discharge it, and

        (ii) why it is appropriate for the order to be discharged; and

    (d) attach—

        (i) a copy of the order, and

        (ii) any material on which the applicant relies.

    (3) A party must inform the court if that party intends to appeal should the court discharge the order.

Appeal

6.26 (1) This rule applies where one of the following ('the appellant') wants to appeal to the Crown Court—

     (a) the applicant for an investigation anonymity order, where a magistrates' court has refused to make the order;

     (b) a party to an application to discharge such an order, where a magistrates' court has decided that application.

    (2) The appellant must—

     (a) serve on the Crown Court officer a copy of the application to the magistrates' court; and

     (b) where the appeal concerns a discharge decision, notify each other party,

    not more that 21 days after the decision against which the appellant wants to appeal.

    (3) The Crown Court must hear the appeal without justices of the peace.

PART 7   STARTING A PROSECUTION IN A MAGISTRATES' COURT

When this Part applies

7.1 (1) This part applies in a magistrates' court where—

     (a) a prosecutor wants the court to issue a summons or warrant under section 1 of the Magistrates' Courts Act 1980;

     (b) a public prosecutor—

       (i) wants the court to issue a warrant under section 1 of the Magistrates' Courts Act 1980, or

       (ii) issues a written charge and requisition under section 29 of the Criminal Justice Act 2003; or

     (c) a person who is in custody is charged with an offence.

    (2) In this Part, 'public prosecutor' means one of those public prosecutors listed in section 29 of the Criminal Justice Act 2003.

Information and written charge

7.2 (1) A prosecutor who wants the court to issue a summons must—

     (a) serve an information in writing on the court officer; or

     (b) unless other legislation prohibits this, present an information orally to the court, with a written record of the allegation that it contains.

    (2) A prosecutor who wants the court to issue a warrant must—

     (a) serve on the court officer—

       (i) an information in writing, or

       (ii) a copy of a written charge that has been issued; or

     (b) present to the court either of those documents.

    (3) A public prosecutor who issues a written charge must notify the court officer immediately.

    (4) A single document may contain—

     (a) more than one information; or

     (b) more than one written charge.

    (5) Where an offence can be tried only in a magistrates' court, then unless other legislation otherwise provides—

     (a) a prosecutor must serve an information on the court officer or present it to the court; or

     (b) a public prosecutor must issue a written charge,

    not more than 6 months after the offence alleged.

    (6) Where an offence can be tried in the Crown Court then—

     (a) a prosecutor must serve an information on the court officer or present it to the court; or

     (b) a public prosecutor must issue a written charge,

    within any time limit that applies to that offence.

Allegation of offence in information or charge

7.3   (1) An allegation of an offence in an information or charge must contain—
      (a) a statement of the offence that—
         (i) describes the offence in ordinary language, and
         (ii) identifies any legislation that creates it; and
      (b) such particulars of the conduct constituting the commission of the offence as to make clear what the prosecutor alleges against the defendant.
  (2) More than one incident of the commission of the offence may be included in the allegation if those incidents taken together amount to a course of conduct having regard to the time, place or purpose of commission.

Summons, warrant and requisition

7.4   (1) The court may issue or withdraw a summons or warrant—
      (a) without giving the parties an opportunity to make representations; and
      (b) without a hearing, or at a hearing in public or in private.
  (2) A summons, warrant or requisition may be issued in respect of more than one offence.
  (3) A summons or requisition must—
      (a) contain notice of when and where the defendant is required to attend the court;
      (b) specify each offence in respect of which it is issued; and
      (c) in the case of a summons, identify—
         (i) the court that issued it, unless that is otherwise recorded by the court officer,
         (ii) the court office for the court that issued it; and
      (d) in the case of a requisition, identify the person under whose authority it is issued.
  (4) A summons may be contained in the same document as an information.
  (5) A requisition may be contained in the same document as a written charge.
  (6) Where the court issues a summons—
      (a) the prosecutor must—
         (i) serve it on the defendant, and
         (ii) notify the court officer; or
      (b) the court officer must—
         (i) serve it on the defendant, and
         (ii) notify the prosecutor.
  (7) Where a public prosecutor issues a requisition that prosecutor must—
      (a) serve on the defendant—
         (i) the requisition, and
         (ii) the written charge; and
      (b) serve a copy of each on the court officer.
  (8) Unless it would be inconsistent with other legislation, a replacement summons or requisition may be issued without a fresh information or written charge where the one replaced—
      (a) was served by leaving or posting it under rule 4.7 (documents that must be served only by handing them over, leaving or posting them); but
      (b) is shown not to have been received by the addressee.
  (9) A summons or requisition issued to a defendant under 18 may require that defendant's parent or guardian to attend the court with the defendant, or a separate summons or requisition may be issued for that purpose.

PART 8   OBJECTING TO THE DISCONTINUANCE OF PROCEEDINGS IN A MAGISTRATES' COURT

Time for objecting

8.1   The period within which an accused person may give notice under section 23(7) of the Prosecution of Offences Act 1985 that he wants proceedings against him to continue is 35 days from the date when the proceedings were discontinued under that section.

Form of notice

8.2　Notice under section 23(3), (4) or (7) of the Prosecution of Offences Act 1985 shall be given in writing and shall contain sufficient particulars to identify the particular offence to which it relates.

Duty of Director of Public Prosecutions

8.3　On giving notice under section 23(3) or (4) of the Prosecution of Offences Act 1985 the Director of Public Prosecutions shall inform any person who is detaining the accused person for the offence in relation to which the notice is given that he has given such notice and of the effect of the notice.

Duty of magistrates' court

8.4　On being given notice under section 23(3) of the Prosecution of Offences Act 1985 in relation to an offence for which the accused person has been granted bail by a court, a magistrates' court officer shall inform—
(a) any sureties of the accused; and
(b) any persons responsible for securing the accused's compliance with any conditions of bail that he has been given such notice and of the effect of the notice.

PART 9

[This part currently contains no rules.]

PART 10　COMMITTAL FOR TRIAL

Restrictions on reports of committal proceedings

10.1　(1) Except in a case where evidence is, with the consent of the accused, to be tendered in his absence under section 4(4)(b) of the Magistrates' Courts Act 1980 (absence caused by ill health), a magistrates' court acting as examining justices shall before admitting any evidence explain to the accused the restrictions on reports of committal proceedings imposed by section 8 of that Act and inform him of his right to apply to the court for an order removing those restrictions.
(2) Where a magistrates' court has made an order under section 8(2) of the 1980 Act removing restrictions on the reports of committal proceedings, such order shall be entered in the register.
(3) Where the court adjourns any such proceedings to another day, the court shall, at the beginning of any adjourned hearing, state that the order has been made.

Committal for trial without consideration of the evidence

10.2　(1) This rule applies to committal proceedings where the accused has a solicitor acting for him in the case and where the court has been informed that all the evidence falls within section 5A(2) of the Magistrates' Courts Act 1980.
(2) A magistrates' court inquiring into an offence in committal proceedings to which this rule applies shall cause the charge to be written down, if this has not already been done, and read to the accused and shall then ascertain whether he wishes to submit that there is insufficient evidence to put him on trial by jury for the offence with which he is charged.
(3) If the court is satisfied that the accused or, as the case may be, each of the accused does not wish to make such a submission as is referred to in paragraph (2) it shall, after receiving any written evidence falling within section 5A(3) of the 1980 Act, determine whether or not to commit the accused for trial without consideration of the evidence, and where it determines not to so commit the accused it shall proceed in accordance with rule 10.3.

Consideration of evidence at committal proceedings

10.3　(1) This rule does not apply to committal proceedings where under section 6(2) of the Magistrates' Courts Act of 1980 a magistrates' court commits a person for trial without consideration of the evidence.

(2) A magistrates' court inquiring into an offence as examining justices, having ascertained—
   (a) that the accused has no legal representative acting for him in the case; or
   (b) that the accused's legal representative has requested the court to consider a submission that there is insufficient evidence to put the accused on trial by jury for the offence with which he is charged, as the case may be,
   shall permit the prosecutor to make an opening address to the court, if he so wishes, before any evidence is tendered.

(3) After such opening address, if any, the court shall cause evidence to be tendered in accordance with sections 5B(4), 5C(4), 5D(5) and 5E(3) of the 1980 Act, that is to say by being read out aloud, except where the court otherwise directs or to the extent that it directs that an oral account be given of any of the evidence.

(4) The court may view any exhibits produced before the court and may take possession of them.

(5) After the evidence has been tendered the court shall hear any submission which the accused may wish to make as to whether there is sufficient evidence to put him on trial by jury for any indictable offence.

(6) The court shall permit the prosecutor to make a submission—
   (a) in reply to any submission made by the accused in pursuance of paragraph (5); or
   (b) where the accused has not made any such submission but the court is nevertheless minded not to commit him for trial.

(7) After hearing any submission made in pursuance of paragraph (5) or (6) the court shall, unless it decides not to commit the accused for trial, cause the charge to be written down, if this has not already been done, and, if the accused is not represented by counsel or a solicitor, shall read the charge to him and explain it in ordinary language.

Objection to committal statements being read at trial

10.4 (1) This rule applies where—
   (a) a written statement is admitted as evidence in committal proceedings;
   (b) under Schedule 2 to the Criminal Procedure and Investigations Act 1996, the statement may be introduced in evidence at trial; and
   (c) a party wants to object to that.

(2) Such a party must serve notice of objection—
   (a) on each other party and on the Crown Court officer;
   (b) not more than 14 days after the defendant is committed for trial.

(3) A prosecutor who introduces a written statement in committal proceedings must serve with it on the defendant a notice—
   (a) of the right to object, and of the time limit; and
   (b) that if the defendant does not object, the prosecutor may decide not to call the witness to give evidence in person at trial, but to rely on the written statement instead.

(4) The magistrates' court that commits the defendant for trial must remind the defendant of that right to object.

(5) The Crown Court may extend the time limit under this rule, even after it has expired.

Material to be sent to court of trial

10.5 (1) As soon as practicable after the committal of any person for trial, and in any case within 4 days from the date of his committal (not counting Saturdays, Sundays, Good Friday, Christmas Day or Bank Holidays), the magistrates' court officer shall, subject to the provisions of section 7 of the Prosecution of Offences Act 1985 (which relates to the sending of documents and things to the Director of Public Prosecutions), send to the Crown Court officer—
   (a) the information, if it is in writing;
   (b)
      (i) the evidence tendered in accordance with section 5A of the Magistrates' Courts Act 1980 and, where any of that evidence consists of a copy of a

deposition or documentary exhibit which is in the possession of the court, any such deposition or documentary exhibit, and

(ii) a certificate to the effect that that evidence was so tendered;

(c) any notification by the prosecutor under section 5D(2) of the 1980 Act regarding the admissibility of a statement under section 23 or 24 of the Criminal Justice Act 1988 (first hand hearsay; business documents);

(d) a copy of the record made in pursuance of section 5 of the Bail Act 1976 relating to the grant or withholding of bail in respect of the accused on the occasion of the committal;

(e) any recognizance entered into by any person as surety for the accused together with a statement of any enlargement thereof under section 129(4) of the 1980 Act;

(f) a list of the exhibits produced in evidence before the justices or treated as so produced;

(g) such of the exhibits referred to in paragraph (1)(f) as have been retained by the justices;

(h) the names and addresses of any interpreters engaged for the defendant for the purposes of the committal proceedings, together with any telephone numbers at which they can be readily contacted, and details of the languages or dialects in connection with which they have been so engaged;

(i) if the committal was under section 6(2) of the 1980 Act (committal for trial without consideration of the evidence), a statement to that effect;

(j) if the magistrates' court has made an order under section 8(2) of the 1980 Act (removal of restrictions on reports of committal proceedings), a statement to that effect;

(k) the certificate of the examining justices as to the costs of the prosecution under the Costs in Criminal Cases (General) Regulations 1986;

(l) if any person under the age of 18 is concerned in the committal proceedings, a statement whether the magistrates' court has given a direction under section 39 of the Children and Young Persons Act 1933 (prohibition of publication of certain matter in newspapers);

(m) a copy of any representation order previously made in the case;

(n) a copy of any application for a representation order previously made in the case which has been refused; and

(o) any documents relating to an appeal by the prosecution against the granting of bail.

(2) The period of 4 days specified in paragraph (1) may be extended in relation to any committal for so long as the Crown Court officer directs, having regard to the length of any document mentioned in that paragraph or any other relevant circumstances.

PART 11   TRANSFER FOR TRIAL OF SERIOUS FRAUD CASES OR CASES INVOLVING CHILDREN

Interpretation of this part

11.1 (1) In this Part:

'notice of transfer' means a notice referred to in section 4(1) of the Criminal Justice Act 1987 or section 53(1) of the Criminal Justice Act 1991.

(2) Where this Part requires a document to be given or sent, or a notice to be communicated in writing, it may, with the consent of the addressee, be sent by electronic communication.

(3) Electronic communication means a communication transmitted (whether from one person to another, from one device to another or from a person to a device or vice versa)—

(a) by means of an electronic communications network (within the meaning of the Communications Act 2003); or

(b) by other means but while in an electronic form.

Transfer on bail

11.2 (1) Where a person in respect of whom notice of transfer has been given—

    (a) is granted bail under section 5(3) or (7A) of the Criminal Justice Act 1987 by the magistrates' court to which notice of transfer was given; or

    (b) is granted bail under paragraph 2(1) or (7) of Schedule 6 to the Criminal Justice Act 1991 by the magistrates' court to which notice of transfer was given,

the magistrates' court officer shall give notice thereof in writing to the governor of the prison or remand centre to which the said person would have been committed by that court if he had been committed in custody for trial.

(2) Where notice of transfer is given under section 4(1) of the 1987 Act in respect of a corporation the magistrates' court officer shall give notice thereof to the governor of the prison to which would be committed a male over 21 committed by that court in custody for trial.

Notice where person removed to hospital

11.3 Where a transfer direction has been given by the Secretary of State under section 47 or 48 of the Mental Health Act 1983 in respect of a person remanded in custody by a magistrates' court and, before the direction ceases to have effect, notice of transfer is given in respect of that person, the magistrates' court officer shall give notice thereof in writing—

    (a) to the governor of the prison to which that person would have been committed by that court if he had been committed in custody for trial; and

    (b) to the managers of the hospital where he is detained.

Variation of arrangements for bail

11.4 (1) A person who intends to make an application to a magistrates' court under section 3(8) of the Bail Act 1976 as that subsection has effect under section 3(8A) of that Act shall give notice thereof in writing to the magistrates' court officer, and to the designated authority or the defendant, as the case may be, and to any sureties concerned.

(2) Where, on an application referred to in paragraph (1), a magistrates' court varies or imposes any conditions of bail, the magistrates' court officer shall send to the Crown Court officer a copy of the record made in pursuance of section 5 of the 1976 Act relating to such variation or imposition of conditions.

Documents to be sent to the Crown Court

11.5 As soon as practicable after a magistrates' court to which notice of transfer has been given has discharged the functions reserved to it under section 4(1) of the Criminal Justice Act 1987 or section 53(3) of the Criminal Justice Act 1991, the magistrates' court officer shall send to the Crown Court officer—

    (a) a list of the names, addresses and occupations of the witnesses;

    (b) a copy of the record made in pursuance of section 5 of the Bail Act 1976 relating to the grant of withholding of bail in respect of the accused;

    (c) any recognizance entered into by any person as surety for the accused together with a statement of any enlargement thereof;

    (d) a copy of any representation order previously made in the case; and

    (e) a copy of any application for a representation order previously made in the case which has been refused.

PART 12   SENDING FOR TRIAL

Documents to be sent to the Crown Court

12.1 (1) As soon as practicable after any person is sent for trial (pursuant to section 51 of the Crime and Disorder Act 1998), and in any event within 4 days from the date on which he is sent (not counting Saturdays, Sundays, Good Friday, Christmas Day or Bank Holidays), the magistrates' court officer shall, subject to section 7 of the Prosecution of

Offences Act 1985 (which relates to the sending of documents and things to the Director of Public Prosecutions), send to the Crown Court officer—

(a) the information, if it is in writing;

(b) the notice required by section 51(7) of the 1998 Act;

(c) a copy of the record made in pursuance of section 5 of the Bail Act 1976 relating to the granting or withholding of bail in respect of the accused on the occasion of the sending;

(d) any recognizance entered into by any person as surety for the accused together with any enlargement thereof under section 129(4) of the Magistrates' Courts Act 1980;

(e) the names and addresses of any interpreters engaged for the defendant for the purposes of the appearance in the magistrates' court, together with any telephone numbers at which they can be readily contacted, and details of the languages or dialects in connection with which they have been so engaged;

(f) if any person under the age of 18 is concerned in the proceedings, a statement whether the magistrates' court has given a direction under section 39 of the Children and Young Persons Act 1933 (prohibition of publication of certain matter in newspapers);

(g) a copy of any representation order previously made in the case;

(h) a copy of any application for a representation order previously made in the case which has been refused; and

(i) any documents relating to an appeal by the prosecution against the granting of bail.

(2) The period of 4 days specified in paragraph (1) may be extended in relation to any sending for trial for so long as the Crown Court officer directs, having regard to any relevant circumstances.

Time for first appearance of accused sent for trial

12.2 A Crown Court officer to whom notice has been given under section 51(7) of the Crime and Disorder Act 1998, shall list the first Crown Court appearance of the person to whom the notice relates in accordance with any directions given by the magistrates' court.

PART 13 DISMISSAL OF CHARGES TRANSFERRED
OR SENT TO THE CROWN COURT

Interpretation of this Part

13.1 In this Part:

'notice of transfer' means a notice referred to in section 4(1) of the Criminal Justice Act 1987 or section 53(1) of the Criminal Justice Act 1991; and

'the prosecution' means the authority by or on behalf of whom notice of transfer was given under the 1987 or 1991 Acts, or the authority by or on behalf of whom documents were served under paragraph 1 of Schedule 3 to the Crime and Disorder Act 1998.

Written notice of oral application for dismissal

13.2 (1) Where notice of transfer has been given under the Criminal Justice Act 1987 or the Criminal Justice Act 1991, or a person has been sent for trial under the Crime and Disorder Act 1998, and the person concerned proposes to apply orally—

(a) under section 6(1) of the 1987 Act;

(b) under paragraph 5(1) of Schedule 6 to the 1991 Act; or

(c) under paragraph 2(1) of Schedule 3 to the 1998 Act

for any charge in the case to be dismissed, he shall give notice of his intention in writing to the Crown Court officer at the place specified by the notice of transfer under the 1987 or 1991 Acts or the notice given under section 51(7) of the 1998 Act as the proposed place of trial. Notice of intention to make an application under the 1987 or 1991 Acts shall be in the form set out in the Practice Direction.

(2) Notice of intention to make an application shall be given—
  (a) in the case of an application to dismiss charges transferred under the 1987 Act, not later than 28 days after the day on which notice of transfer was given;
  (b) in the case of an application to dismiss charges transferred under the 1991 Act, not later than 14 days after the day on which notice of transfer was given; and
  (c) in the case of an application to dismiss charges sent under the 1998 Act, not later than 14 days after the day on which the documents were served under paragraph 1 of Schedule 3 to that Act,
and a copy of the notice shall be given at the same time to the prosecution and to any person to whom the notice of transfer relates or with whom the applicant for dismissal is jointly charged.

(3) The time for giving notice may be extended, either before or after it expires, by the Crown Court, on an application made in accordance with paragraph (4).

(4) An application for an extension of time for giving notice shall be made in writing to the Crown Court officer, and a copy thereof shall be given at the same time to the prosecution and to any other person to whom the notice of transfer relates or with whom the applicant for dismissal is jointly charged. Such an application made in proceedings under the 1987 or 1991 Acts shall be in the form set out in the Practice Direction.

(5) The Crown Court officer shall give notice in the form set out in the Practice Direction of the judge's decision on an application under paragraph (3)—
  (a) to the applicant for dismissal;
  (b) to the prosecution; and
  (c) to any other person to whom the notice of transfer relates or with whom the applicant for dismissal is jointly charged.

(6) A notice of intention to make an application under section 6(1) of the 1987 Act, paragraph 5(1) of Schedule 6 to the 1991 Act or paragraph 2(1) of Schedule 3 to the 1998 Act shall be accompanied by a copy of any material on which the applicant relies and shall—
  (a) specify the charge or charges to which it relates;
  (b) state whether the leave of the judge is sought under section 6(3) of the 1987 Act, paragraph 5(4) of Schedule 6 to the 1991 Act or paragraph 2(4) of Schedule 3 to the 1998 Act to adduce oral evidence on the application, indicating what witnesses it is proposed to call at the hearing; and
  (c) in the case of a transfer under the 1991 Act, confirm in relation to each such witness that he is not a child to whom paragraph 5(5) of Schedule 6 to that Act applies.

(7) Where leave is sought from the judge for oral evidence to be given on an application, notice of his decision, indicating what witnesses are to be called if leave is granted, shall be given in writing by the Crown Court officer to the applicant for dismissal, the prosecution and to any other person to whom the notice of transfer relates or with whom the applicant for dismissal is jointly charged. Notice of a decision in proceedings under the 1987 or 1991 Acts shall be in the form set out in the Practice Direction.

(8) Where an application for dismissal under section 6(1) of the 1987 Act, paragraph 5(1) of Schedule 6 to the 1991 Act or paragraph 2(1) of Schedule 3 to the 1998 Act is to be made orally, the Crown Court officer shall list the application for hearing before a judge of the Crown Court and the prosecution shall be given the opportunity to be represented at the hearing.

Written application for dismissal

13.3 (1) Application may be made for dismissal under section 6(1) of the Criminal Justice Act 1987, paragraph 5(1) of Schedule 6 to the Criminal Justice Act 1991 or paragraph 2(1) of Schedule 3 to the Crime and Disorder Act 1998 without an oral hearing. Such an application shall be in writing, and in proceedings under the 1987 or 1991 Acts shall be in the form set out in the Practice Direction.

(2) The application shall be sent to the Crown Court officer and shall be accompanied by a copy of any statement or other document, and identify any article, on which the applicant for dismissal relies.

(3) A copy of the application and of any accompanying documents shall be given at the same time to the prosecution and to any other person to whom the notice of transfer relates or with whom the applicant for dismissal is jointly charged.

(4) A written application for dismissal shall be made—

    (a) not later than 28 days after the day on which notice of transfer was given under the 1987 Act;

    (b) not later than 14 days after the day on which notice of transfer was given under the 1991 Act; or

    (c) not later than 14 days after the day on which documents required by paragraph 1 of Schedule 3 to the 1998 Act were served

unless the time for making the application is extended, either before or after it expires, by the Crown Court; and rule 13.2(4) and (5) shall apply for the purposes of this paragraph as if references therein to giving notice of intention to make an oral application were references to making a written application under this rule.

Prosecution reply

13.4 (1) Not later than seven days from the date of service of notice of intention to apply orally for the dismissal of any charge contained in a notice of transfer or based on documents served under paragraph 1 of Schedule 3 to the Crime and Disorder Act 1998, the prosecution may apply to the Crown Court under section 6(3) of the Criminal Justice Act 1987, paragraph 5(4) of Schedule 6 to the Criminal Justice Act 1991 or paragraph 2(4) of Schedule 3 to the 1998 Act for leave to adduce oral evidence at the hearing of the application, indicating what witnesses it is proposed to call.

(2) Not later than seven days from the date of receiving a copy of an application for dismissal under rule 13.3, the prosecution may apply to the Crown Court for an oral hearing of the application.

(3) An application under paragraph (1) or (2) shall be served on the Crown Court officer in writing and, in the case of an application under paragraph (2), shall state whether the leave of the judge is sought to adduce oral evidence and, if so, shall indicate what witnesses it is proposed to call. Where leave is sought to adduce oral evidence under paragraph 5(4) of Schedule 6 to the 1991 Act, the application should confirm in relation to each such witness that he is not a child to whom paragraph 5(5) of that Schedule applies. Such an application in proceedings under the 1987 or 1991 Acts shall be in the form set out in the Practice Direction.

(4) Notice of the judge's determination upon an application under paragraph (1) or (2), indicating what witnesses (if any) are to be called shall be served in writing by the Crown Court officer on the prosecution, on the applicant for dismissal and on any other party to whom the notice of transfer relates or with whom the applicant for dismissal is jointly charged. Such a notice in proceedings under the 1987 or 1991 Acts shall be in the form set out in the Practice Direction.

(5) Where, having received the material specified in rule 13.2 or, as the case may be, rule 13.3, the prosecution proposes to adduce in reply thereto any written comments or any further evidence, the prosecution shall serve any such comments, copies of the statements or other documents outlining the evidence of any proposed witnesses, copies of any further documents and, in the case of an application to dismiss charges transferred under the 1991 Act, copies of any video recordings which it is proposed to tender in evidence, on the Crown Court officer not later than 14 days from the date of receiving the said material, and shall at the same time serve copies thereof on the applicant for dismissal and any other person to whom the notice of transfer relates or with whom the applicant is jointly charged. In the case of a defendant acting in person, copies of video recordings need not be served but shall be made available for viewing by him.

(6) The time for—

    (a) making an application under paragraph (1) or (2) above; or

    (b) serving any material on the Crown Court officer under paragraph (5) above may be extended, either before or after it expires, by the Crown Court, on an application made in accordance with paragraph (7) below.

(7) An application for an extension of time under paragraph (6) above shall be made in writing and shall be served on the Crown Court officer, and a copy thereof shall be served at the same time on to the applicant for dismissal and on any other person to whom the notice of transfer relates or with whom the applicant for dismissal is jointly charged. Such an application in proceedings under the 1987 or 1991 Acts shall be in the form set out in the Practice Direction.

Determination of applications for dismissal

13.5 (1) A judge may grant leave for a witness to give oral evidence on an application for dismissal notwithstanding that notice of intention to call the witness has not been given in accordance with the foregoing provisions of this Part.

(2) Where an application for dismissal is determined otherwise than at an oral hearing, the Crown Court officer shall as soon as practicable, send to all the parties to the case written notice of the outcome of the application. Such a notice in proceedings under the 1987 and 1991 Acts shall be in the form set out in the Practice Direction.

Part 14 The Indictment

Service and signature of indictment

14.1 (1) The prosecutor must serve a draft indictment on the Crown Court officer not more than 28 days after—

(a) service on the defendant and on the Crown Court officer of copies of the documents containing the evidence on which the charge or charges are based, in a case where the defendant is sent for trial;

(b) a High Court judge gives permission to serve a draft indictment;

(c) the Court of Appeal orders a retrial; or

(d) the committal or transfer of the defendant for trial.

(2) The Crown Court may extend the time limit, even after it has expired.

(3) Unless the Crown Court otherwise directs, the court officer must—

(a) sign, and add the date of receipt on, the indictment; and

(b) serve a copy of the indictment on all parties.

Form and content of indictment

14.2 (1) An indictment must be in one of the forms set out in the Practice Direction and must contain, in a paragraph called a 'count'—

(a) a statement of the offence charged that—

(i) describes the offence in ordinary language, and

(ii) identifies any legislation that creates it; and

(b) such particulars of the conduct constituting the commission of the offence as to make clear what the prosecutor alleges against the defendant.

(2) More than one incident of the commission of the offence may be included in a count if those incidents taken together amount to a course of conduct having regard to the time, place or purpose of commission.

(3) An indictment may contain more than one count if all the offences charged—

(a) are founded on the same facts; or

(b) form or are a part of a series of offences of the same or a similar character.

(4) The counts must be numbered consecutively.

(5) An indictment may contain—

(a) any count charging substantially the same offence as one—

(i) specified in the notice of the offence or offences for which the defendant was sent for trial,

(ii) on which the defendant was committed for trial, or

(iii) specified in the notice of transfer given by the prosecutor; and

(b) any other count based on the prosecution evidence already served which the Crown Court may try.

PART 15   PREPARATORY HEARINGS IN CASES OF SERIOUS FRAUD AND OTHER COMPLEX OR LENGTHY CASES IN THE CROWN COURT

Application for a preparatory hearing

15.1   (1) A party who wants the court to order a preparatory hearing under section 7(2) of the Criminal Justice Act 1987 or under section 29(4) of the Criminal Procedure and Investigations Act 1996 must—

(a) apply in the form set out in the Practice Direction;

(b) include a short explanation of the reasons for applying; and

(c) serve the application on the court officer and all other parties.

(2) A prosecutor who wants the court to order that—

(a) the trial will be conducted without a jury under section 43 or section 44 of the Criminal Justice Act 2003; or

(b) the trial of some of the counts included in the indictment will be conducted without a jury under section 17 of the Domestic Violence, Crime and Victims Act 2004,

must apply under this rule for a preparatory hearing, whether or not the defendant has applied for one.

Time for applying for a preparatory hearing

15.2   (1) A party who applies under rule 15.1 must do so not more than 28 days after—

(a) the committal of the defendant;

(b) the consent to the preferment of a bill of indictment in relation to the case;

(c) the service of a notice of transfer; or

(d) where a person is sent for trial, the service of copies of the documents containing the evidence on which the charge or charges are based.

(2) A prosecutor who applies under rule 15.1 because he wants the court to order a trial without a jury under section 44 of the Criminal Justice Act 2003 (jury tampering) must do so as soon as reasonably practicable where the reasons do not arise until after that time limit has expired.

(3) The court may extend the time limit, even after it has expired.

Representations concerning an application

15.3   (1) A party who wants to make written representations concerning an application made under rule 15.1 must—

(a) do so within 7 days of receiving a copy of that application; and

(b) serve those representations on the court officer and all other parties.

(2) A defendant who wants to oppose an application for an order that the trial will be conducted without a jury under section 43 or section 44 of the Criminal Justice Act 2003 must serve written representations under this rule, including a short explanation of the reasons for opposing that application.

Determination of an application

15.4   (1) Where an application has been made under rule 15.1(2), the court must hold a preparatory hearing.

(2) Other applications made under rule 15.1 should normally be determined without a hearing.

(3) The court officer must serve on the parties in the case, in the form set out in the Practice Direction—

(a) notice of the determination of an application made under rule 15.1; and

(b) an order for a preparatory hearing made by the court of its own initiative, including one that the court is required to make.

Orders for disclosure by prosecution or defence

15.5 (1) Any disclosure order under section 9 of the Criminal Justice Act 1987, or section 31 of the Criminal Procedure and Investigations Act 1996, must identify any documents that are required to be prepared and served by the prosecutor under that order.

(2) A disclosure order under either of those sections does not require a defendant to disclose who will give evidence, except to the extent that disclosure is required—

(a) by section 6A(2) of the 1996 Act (disclosure of alibi); or

(b) by Part 33 of these Rules (disclosure of expert evidence).

(3) The court officer must serve notice of the order, in the relevant form set out in the Practice Direction, on the parties.

PART 16 RESTRICTIONS ON REPORTING AND PUBLIC ACCESS

Application for a reporting direction under section 46(6) of the Youth Justice and Criminal Evidence Act 1999

16.1 (1) An application for a reporting direction made by a party to any criminal proceedings, in relation to a witness in those proceedings, must be made in the form set out in the Practice Direction or orally under rule 16.3.

(2) If an application for a reporting direction is made in writing, the applicant shall send that application to the court officer and copies shall be sent at the same time to every other party to those proceedings.

Opposing an application for a reporting direction under section 46(6) of the Youth Justice and Criminal Evidence Act 1999

16.2 (1) If an application for a reporting direction is made in writing, any party to the proceedings who wishes to oppose that application must notify the applicant and the court officer in writing of his opposition and give reasons for it.

(2) A person opposing an application must state in the written notification whether he disputes that the—

(a) witness is eligible for protection under section 46 of the Youth Justice and Criminal Evidence Act 1999; or

(b) granting of protection would be likely to improve the quality of the evidence given by the witness or the level of co-operation given by the witness to any party to the proceedings in connection with that party's preparation of its case.

(3) The notification under paragraph (1) must be given within five business days of the date the application was served on him unless an extension of time is granted under rule 16.6.

Urgent action on an application under section 46(6) of the Youth Justice and Criminal Evidence Act 1999

16.3 (1) The court may give a reporting direction under section 46 of the Youth Justice and Criminal Evidence Act 1999 in relation to a witness in those proceedings, notwithstanding that the five business days specified in rule 16.2(3) have not expired if—

(a) an application is made to it for the purposes of this rule; and

(b) it is satisfied that, due to exceptional circumstances, it is appropriate to do so.

(2) Any party to the proceedings may make the application under paragraph (1) whether or not an application has already been made under rule 16.1.

(3) An application under paragraph (1) may be made orally or in writing.

(4) If an application is made orally, the court may hear and take into account representations made to it by any person who in the court's view has a legitimate interest in the application before it.

(5) The application must specify the exceptional circumstances on which the applicant relies.

Excepting direction under section 46(9) of the Youth Justice and Criminal Evidence Act 1999

16.4 (1) An application for an excepting direction under section 46(9) of the Youth Justice and Criminal Evidence Act 1999 (a direction dispensing with restrictions imposed by a reporting direction) may be made by—

(a) any party to those proceedings; or

(b) any person who, although not a party to the proceedings, is directly affected by a reporting direction given in relation to a witness in those proceedings.

(2) If an application for an excepting direction is made, the applicant must state why—

(a) the effect of a reporting direction imposed places a substantial and unreasonable restriction on the reporting of the proceedings; and

(b) it is in the public interest to remove or relax those restrictions.

(3) An application for an excepting direction may be made in writing, pursuant to paragraph (4), at any time after the commencement of the proceedings in the court or orally at a hearing of an application for a reporting direction.

(4) If the application for an excepting direction is made in writing it must be in the form set out in the Practice Direction and the applicant shall send that application to the court officer and copies shall be sent at the same time to every party to those proceedings.

(5) Any person served with a copy of an application for an excepting direction who wishes to oppose it, must notify the applicant and the court officer in writing of his opposition and give reasons for it.

(6) The notification under paragraph (5) must be given within five business days of the date the application was served on him unless an extension of time is granted under rule 16.6.

Variation or revocation of a reporting or excepting direction under section 46 of the Youth Justice and Criminal Evidence Act 1999

16.5 (1) An application for the court to—

(a) revoke a reporting direction; or

(b) vary or revoke an excepting direction,

may be made to the court at any time after the commencement of the proceedings in the court.

(2) An application under paragraph (1) may be made by a party to the proceedings in which the direction was issued, or by a person who, although not a party to those proceedings, is in the opinion of the court directly affected by the direction.

(3) An application under paragraph (1) must be made in writing and the applicant shall send that application to the officer of the court in which the proceedings commenced, and at the same time copies of the application shall be sent to every party or, as the case may be, every party to the proceedings.

(4) The applicant must set out in his application the reasons why he seeks to have the direction varied or, as the case may be, revoked.

(5) Any person served with a copy of an application who wishes to oppose it, must notify the applicant and the court officer in writing of his opposition and give reasons for it.

(6) The notification under paragraph (5) must be given within five business days of the date the application was served on him unless an extension of time is granted under rule 16.6.

Application for an extension of time in proceedings under section 46 of the Youth Justice and Criminal Evidence Act 1999

16.6 (1) An application may be made in writing to extend the period of time for notification under rule 16.2(3), rule 16.4(6) or rule 16.5(6) before that period has expired.

(2) An application must be accompanied by a statement setting out the reasons why the applicant is unable to give notification within that period.

(3) An application must be sent to the court officer and a copy of the application must be sent at the same time to the applicant.

Decision of the court on an application under section 46 of the Youth Justice and Criminal Evidence Act 1999

16.7 (1) The court may—

(a) determine any application made under rules 16.1 and rules 16.3 to 16.6 without a hearing; or

(b) direct a hearing of any application.

(2) The court officer shall notify all the parties of the court's decision as soon as reasonably practicable.

(3) If a hearing of an application is to take place, the court officer shall notify each party to the proceedings of the time and place of the hearing.

(4) A court may hear and take into account representations made to it by any person who in the court's view has a legitimate interest in the application before it.

Proceedings sent or transferred to the Crown Court with direction under section 46 of the Youth Justice and Criminal Evidence Act 1999 in force

16.8 Where proceedings in which reporting directions or excepting directions have been ordered are sent or transferred from a magistrates' court to the Crown Court, the magistrates' court officer shall forward copies of all relevant directions to the Crown Court officer at the place to which the proceedings are sent or transferred.

Hearings in camera and applications under section 46 of the Youth Justice and Criminal Evidence Act 1999

16.9 If in any proceedings, a prosecutor or defendant has served notice under rule 16.10 of his intention to apply for an order that all or part of a trial be held in camera, any application under this Part relating to a witness in those proceedings need not identify the witness by name and date of birth.

Application to hold a Crown Court trial in camera

16.10 (1) Where a prosecutor or a defendant intends to apply for an order that all or part of a trial be held in camera for reasons of national security or for the protection of the identity of a witness or any other person, he shall not less than 7 days before the date on which the trial is expected to begin serve a notice in writing to that effect on the Crown Court officer and the prosecutor or the defendant as the case may be.

(2) On receiving such notice, the court officer shall forthwith cause a copy thereof to be displayed in a prominent place within the precincts of the Court.

(3) An application by a prosecutor or a defendant who has served such a notice for an order that all or part of a trial be heard in camera shall, unless the Court orders otherwise, be made in camera, after the defendant has been arraigned but before the jury has been sworn and, if such an order is made, the trial shall be adjourned until whichever of the following shall be appropriate—

(a) 24 hours after the making of the order, where no application for leave to appeal from the order is made; or

(b) after the determination of an application for leave to appeal, where the application is dismissed; or

(c) after the determination of the appeal, where leave to appeal is granted.

Crown Court hearings in chambers

16.11 (1) The criminal jurisdiction of the Crown Court specified in the following paragraph may be exercised by a judge of the Crown Court sitting in chambers.

(2) The said jurisdiction is—

(a) hearing applications for bail;

(b) issuing a summons or warrant;

(c) hearing any application relating to procedural matters preliminary or incidental to criminal proceedings in the Crown Court, including applications relating to legal aid;

(d) jurisdiction under rules 12.2 (listing first appearance of accused sent for trial), 28.3 (application for witness summons), 63.9(a) (extending time for appeal against decision of magistrates' court), and 64.7 (application to state case for consideration of High Court);

(e) hearing an application under section 41(2) of the Youth Justice and Criminal Evidence Act 1999 (evidence of complainant's previous sexual history);

(f) hearing applications under section 22(3) of the Prosecution of Offences Act 1985 (extension or further extension of custody time limit imposed by regulations made under section 22(1) of that Act);

(g) hearing an appeal brought by an accused under section 22(7) of the 1985 Act against a decision of a magistrates' court to extend, or further extend, such a time limit, or brought by the prosecution under section 22(8) of the same Act against a decision of a magistrates' court to refuse to extend, or further extend, such a time limit;

(h) hearing appeals under section 1 of the Bail (Amendment) Act 1993 (against grant of bail by magistrates' court); and

(i) hearing appeals under section 16 of the Criminal Justice Act 2003 (against condition of bail imposed by magistrates' court).

PART 17   EXTRADITION

Refusal to make an order of committal

17.1 (1) Where a magistrates' court refuses to make an order of committal in relation to a person in respect of the offence or, as the case may be, any of the offences to which the authority to proceed relates and the state, country or colony seeking the surrender of that person immediately informs the court that it intends to make an application to the court to state a case for the opinion of the High Court, if the magistrates' court makes an order in accordance with section 10(2) of the Extradition Act 1989 releasing that person on bail, the court officer shall forthwith send a copy of that order to the Administrative Court Office.

(2) Where a magistrates' court refuses to make an order of committal in relation to a person in respect of the offence or, as the case may be, any of the offences to which the authority to proceed relates and the state, country or colony seeking his surrender wishes to apply to the court to state a case for the opinion of the High Court under section 10(1) of the 1989 Act, such application must be made to the magistrates' court within the period of 21 days following the day on which the court refuses to make the order of committal unless the court grants a longer period within which the application is to be made.

(3) Such an application shall be made in writing and shall identify the question or questions of law on which the opinion of the High Court is sought.

(4) Within 21 days after receipt of an application to state a case under section 10(1) of the 1989 Act, the magistrates' court officer shall send a draft case to the solicitor for the state, country or colony and to the person whose surrender is sought or his solicitor and shall allow each party 21 days within which to make representations thereon; within 21 days after the latest day on which such representations may be made the court of committal shall, after considering any such representations and making such adjustments, if any, to the draft case as it thinks fit, state and sign the case which the court officer shall forthwith send to the solicitor for the state, country or colony.

Notice of waiver

17.2 (1) A notice given under section 14 of, or paragraph 9 of Schedule 1 to, the Extradition Act 1989 (notice of waiver under the simplified procedure) shall be in the form set out in the Practice Direction or a form to the like effect.

(2) Such a notice shall be signed in the presence of the Senior District Judge (Chief Magistrate) or another District Judge (Magistrates' Courts) designated by him for the purposes of the Act, a justice of the peace or a justices' clerk.

(3) Any such notice given by a person in custody shall be delivered to the Governor of the prison in whose custody he is.

(4) If a person on bail gives such notice he shall deliver it to, or send it by post in a registered letter or by recorded delivery service addressed to, the Secretary of State for the Home Department, c/o Extradition Section, Home Office, 5th Floor, Fry Building, 2 Marsham Street, London SW1P 4DF.

Notice of consent

17.3 (1) A person arrested in pursuance of a warrant under section 8 of or paragraph 5 of Schedule 1 to the Extradition Act 1989 may at any time consent to his return; and where such consent is given in accordance with the following provisions of this rule, the Senior District Judge (Chief Magistrate) or another District Judge (Magistrates' Courts) designated by him for the purposes of the Act may order the committal for return of that person in accordance with section 14(2) of that Act or, as the case may be, paragraph 9(2) of Schedule 1 to the Act.

(2) A notice of consent for the purposes of this rule shall be given in the form set out in the Practice Direction and shall be signed in the presence of the Senior District Judge (Chief Magistrate) or another District Judge (Magistrates' Courts) designated by him for the purposes of the 1989 Act.

Notice of consent (parties to 1995 Convention)

17.4 (1) This rule applies as between the United Kingdom and states other than the Republic of Ireland that are parties to the Convention drawn up on the basis of Article 31 of the Treaty on European Union on Simplified Extradition Procedures between the Member States of the European Union, in relation to which section 14A of the Extradition Act 1989 applies by virtue of section 34A and Schedule 1A of that Act.

(2) Notice of consent for the purposes of section 14A(3) of the 1989 Act shall be given in the form set out in the Practice Direction and shall be signed in the presence of the Senior District Judge (Chief Magistrate) or another District Judge (Magistrates' Courts) designated by him for the purposes of that Act.

(3) A Senior District Judge (Chief Magistrate) or another District Judge (Magistrates' Courts) designated by him for the purposes of the Act may order the committal for return of a person if he gives consent under section 14A of the 1989 Act in accordance with paragraph (2) above before he is committed under section 9 of that Act.

Consent to early removal to Republic of Ireland

17.5 (1) A notice given under section 3(1)(a) of the Backing of Warrants (Republic of Ireland) Act 1965 (consent to surrender earlier than is otherwise permitted) shall be signed in the presence of a justice of the peace or a justices' clerk.

(2) Any such notice given by a person in custody shall be delivered to the Governor of the prison in whose custody he is.

(3) If a person on bail gives such notice, he shall deliver it to, or send it by post in a registered letter or by recorded delivery service addressed to, the police officer in charge of the police station specified in his recognizance.

(4) Any such notice shall be attached to the warrant ordering the surrender of that person.

Bail pending removal to Republic of Ireland

17.6 (1) The person taking the recognizance of a person remanded on bail under section 2(1) or 4(3) of the Backing of Warrants (Republic of Ireland) Act 1965 shall furnish a copy of the recognizance to the police officer in charge of the police station specified in the recognizance.

(2) The court officer for a magistrates' court which ordered a person to be surrendered and remanded him on bail shall deliver to, or send by post in a registered letter or by

recorded delivery service addressed to, the police officer in charge of the police station specified in the recognizance the warrant ordering the person to be surrendered.

(3) The court officer for a magistrates' court which refused to order a person to be delivered under section 2 of the 1965 Act but made an order in accordance with section 2A(2) of that Act releasing that person on bail, upon the chief officer of police immediately informing the court that he intended to make an application to the court to state a case for the opinion of the High Court, shall forthwith send a copy of that order to the Administrative Court Office.

Delivery of warrant issued in Republic of Ireland

17.7 (1) The court officer for a magistrates' court which ordered a person to be surrendered under section 2(1) of the Backing of Warrants (Republic of Ireland) Act 1965 shall deliver to, or send by post in a registered letter or by recorded delivery service addressed to—

(a) if he is remanded in custody under section 5(1)(a) of the 1965 Act, the prison Governor to whose custody he is committed;

(b) if he is remanded on bail under section 5(1)(b) of the 1965 Act, the police officer in charge of the police station specified in the recognizance; or

(c) if he is committed to the custody of a constable pending the taking from him of a recognizance under section 5(1) of the 1965 Act, the police officer in charge of the police station specified in the warrant of commitment,

the warrant of arrest issued by a judicial authority in the Republic of Ireland and endorsed in accordance with section 1 of the 1965 Act.

(2) The Governor or police officer to whom the said warrant of arrest is delivered or sent shall arrange for it to be given to the member of the police force of the Republic into whose custody the person is delivered when the person is so delivered.

Verification of warrant etc. issued in Republic of Ireland

17.8 (1) A document purporting to be a warrant issued by a judicial authority in the Republic of Ireland shall, for the purposes of section 7(a) of the Backing of Warrants (Republic of Ireland) Act 1965, be verified by a certificate purporting to be signed by a judicial authority, a clerk of a court or a member of the police force of the Republic and certifying that the document is a warrant and is issued by a judge or justice of a court or a peace commissioner.

(2) A document purporting to be a copy of a summons issued by a judicial authority in the Republic shall, for the purposes of section 7(a) of the 1965 Act, be verified by a certificate purporting to be signed by a judicial authority, a clerk of a court or a member of the police force of the Republic and certifying that the document is a true copy of such a summons.

(3) A deposition purporting to have been made in the Republic, or affidavit or written statement purporting to have been sworn therein, shall, for the purposes of section 7(c) of the 1965 Act, be verified by a certificate purporting to be signed by the person before whom it was sworn and certifying that it was so sworn.

Application to state a case where court declines to order removal to Republic of Ireland

17.9 (1) Where a magistrates' court refuses to make an order in relation to a person under section 2 of the Backing of Warrants (Republic of Ireland) Act 1965, any application to the court under section 2A(1) of that Act to state a case for the opinion of the High Court on any question of law arising in the proceedings must be made to the court by the chief officer of police within the period of 21 days following the day on which the order was refused, unless the court grants a longer period within which the application is to be made.

(2) Such an application shall be made in writing and shall identify the question or questions of law on which the opinion of the High Court is sought.

Draft case where court declines to order removal to Republic of Ireland

17.10 Within 21 days after receipt of an application to state a case under section 2A(1) of the Backing of Warrants (Republic of Ireland) Act 1965, the magistrates' court officer shall send a draft case to the applicant or his solicitor and to the person to whom the warrant relates or his solicitor and shall allow each party 21 days within which to make representations thereon; within 21 days after the latest day on which such representations may be made the court shall, after considering such representations and making such adjustments, if any, to the draft case as it thinks fit, state and sign the case which the court officer shall forthwith send to the applicant or his solicitor.

Forms for proceedings for removal to Republic of Ireland

17.11 Where a requirement is imposed by the Backing of Warrants (Republic of Ireland) Act 1965 for the use of a form, and an appropriate form is contained in the Practice Direction, that form shall be used.

PART 18   WARRANTS FOR ARREST, DETENTION OR IMPRISONMENT

When this Part applies

18.1 (1) This Part applies where the court can issue a warrant for arrest, detention or imprisonment.

(2) In this Part, 'defendant' means anyone against whom such a warrant is issued.

Terms of a warrant for arrest

18.2 A warrant for arrest must require the person(s) to whom it is directed to arrest the defendant and—

(a) bring the defendant to a court—
 (i) specified in the warrant, or
 (ii) required or allowed by law; or

(b) release the defendant on bail (with conditions or without) to attend court at a date, time and place—
 (i) specified in the warrant, or
 (ii) to be notified by the court.

Terms of a warrant for detention or imprisonment

18.3 (1) A warrant for detention or imprisonment must—

(a) require the person(s) to whom it is directed to—
 (i) arrest the defendant,
 (ii) take the defendant to any place specified in the warrant, and
 (iii) deliver the defendant to the custodian of that place; and

(b) require that custodian to keep the defendant in custody, as ordered by the court, until in accordance with the law—
 (i) the defendant is delivered to the appropriate court or place, or
 (ii) the defendant is released.

(2) Where a magistrates' court remands a defendant to police detention under section 128(7) or section 136 of the Magistrates' Courts Act 1980, or to customs detention under section 152 of the Criminal Justice Act 1988, the warrant it issues must—

(a) be directed, as appropriate, to—
 (i) a constable, or
 (ii) an officer of Her Majesty's Revenue and Customs; and

(b) require that constable or officer to keep the defendant in custody—
 (i) for a period (not exceeding the maximum permissible) specified in the warrant, or
 (ii) until in accordance with the law the defendant is delivered to the appropriate court or place.

Information to be included in a warrant

18.4   (1) A warrant must identify—
        (a) the person(s) to whom it is directed;
        (b) the defendant against whom it was issued;
        (c) the reason for its issue;
        (d) the court that issued it, unless that is otherwise recorded by the court officer; and
        (e) the court office for the court that issued it.
     (2) A warrant for detention or imprisonment must contain a record of any decision by the court under—
        (a) section 23 of the Children and Young Persons Act 1969 (remand to local authority accommodation);
        (b) section 80 of the Magistrates' Courts Act 1980 (application of money found on defaulter to satisfy sum adjudged); or
        (c) section 82(1) or (4) of the 1980 Act (conditions for issue of a warrant).
     (3) A warrant that contains an error is not invalid, as long as—
        (a) it was issued in respect of a lawful decision by the court; and
        (b) it contains enough information to identify that decision.

Execution of a warrant

18.5   (1) A warrant may be executed—
        (a) by any person to whom it is directed; or
        (b) if the warrant was issued by a magistrates' court, by anyone authorised to do so by section 125 (warrants), 125A (civilian enforcement officers) or 125B (execution by approved enforcement agency) of the Magistrates' Courts Act 1980.
     (2) The person who executes a warrant must—
        (a) explain, in terms the defendant can understand, what the warrant requires, and why;
        (b) show the defendant the warrant, if that person has it; and
        (c) if the defendant asks—
           (i) arrange for the defendant to see the warrant, if that person does not have it, and
           (ii) show the defendant any written statement of that person's authority required by section 125A or 125B of the 1980 Act.
     (3) The person who executes a warrant of arrest that requires the defendant to be released on bail must—
        (a) make a record of—
           (i) the defendant's name,
           (ii) the reason for the arrest,
           (iii) the defendant's release on bail, and
           (iv) when and where the warrant requires the defendant to attend court; and
        (b) serve the record on—
           (i) the defendant, and
           (ii) the court officer.
     (4) The person who executes a warrant of detention or imprisonment must—
        (a) take the defendant—
           (i) to any place specified in the warrant, or
           (ii) if that is not immediately practicable, to any other place at which the defendant may be lawfully detained (and the warrant then has effect as if it specified that place);
        (b) obtain a receipt from the custodian; and
        (c) notify the court officer that the defendant has been taken to that place.

Warrants that cease to have effect on payment

18.6 (1) This rule applies to a warrant issued by a magistrates' court under any of the following provisions of the Magistrates' Courts Act 1980—

(a) section 76 (enforcement of sums adjudged to be paid);

(b) section 83 (process for securing attendance of offender);

(c) section 86 (power of magistrates' court to fix day for appearance of offender at means inquiry, etc.);

(d) section 136 (committal to custody overnight at police station for non-payment of sum adjudged by conviction).

(2) The warrant no longer has effect if—

(a) the sum in respect of which the warrant was issued is paid to the person executing it;

(b) that sum is offered to, but refused by, that person; or

(c) that person is shown a receipt for that sum given by—

(i) the court officer, or

(ii) the authority to which that sum is due.

Warrant issued when the court office is closed

18.7 (1) This rule applies where the court issues a warrant when the court office is closed.

(2) The applicant for the warrant must, not more than 72 hours later, serve on the court officer—

(a) a copy of the warrant; and

(b) any written material that was submitted to the court.

Part 19   Bail in Magistrates' Courts and the Crown Court

Application to a magistrates' court to vary conditions of bail

19.1 (1) An application under section 43B(1) of the Magistrates' Courts Act of 1980 or section 47(1E) of the Police and Criminal Evidence Act 1984, to vary conditions of police bail shall—

(a) be made in writing;

(b) contain a statement of the grounds upon which it is made;

(c) specify the offence with which the applicant was charged before his release on bail;

(d) where the applicant has been bailed following charge, specify the offence with which he was charged and, in any other case, specify the offence under investigation;

(e) specify the name and address of any surety provided by the applicant before his release on bail to secure his surrender to custody; and

(f) specify the address at which the applicant would reside, if the court imposed a condition of residence.

(2) Any such application shall be sent to the court officer for—

(a) the magistrates' court appointed by the custody officer as the court before which the applicant has a duty to appear; or

(b) if no such court has been appointed, a magistrates' court acting for the local justice area in which the police station at which the applicant was granted bail or at which the conditions of his bail were varied, as the case may be, is situated.

(3) The court officer to whom an application is sent under paragraph (2) above shall serve not less than 24 hours' notice in writing of the date, time and place fixed for the hearing of the application on—

(a) the applicant;

(b) the prosecutor or, if the applicant has not been charged, the chief officer of police or other investigator, together with a copy of the application; and

(c) any surety in connection with bail in criminal proceedings granted to, or the conditions of which were varied by a custody officer in relation to, the applicant.

(4) The time fixed for the hearing shall be not later than 72 hours after receipt of the application. In reckoning for the purposes of this paragraph any period of 72 hours, no account shall be taken of Christmas Day, Boxing Day, Good Friday, any bank holiday, or any Saturday or Sunday.

(5) A party who wants a magistrates' court to vary or to impose conditions of bail under section 3(8) of the Bail Act 1976, must—

    (a) serve notice, not less than 24 hours before the hearing at which that party intends to apply, on—

        (i) the court officer, and

        (ii) the other party; and

    (b) in that notice—

        (i) specify the variation or conditions proposed, and

        (ii) explain the reasons.

(6) If the magistrates' court hearing an application under section 43B(1) of the 1980 Act or section 47(1E) of the 1984 Act discharges or enlarges any recognizance entered into by any surety or increases or reduces the amount in which that person is bound, the court officer shall forthwith give notice thereof to the applicant and to any such surety.

(7) The court may—

    (a) vary or waive a time limit under paragraph (3) or (5) of this rule; and

    (b) allow a notice to be—

        (i) in a different form to one set out in the Practice Direction, or

        (ii) given orally.

Application to a magistrates' court to reconsider grant of police bail

19.2 (1) The appropriate court for the purposes of section 5B of the Bail Act 1976 in relation to the decision of a constable to grant bail shall be—

    (a) the magistrates' court appointed by the custody officer as the court before which the person to whom bail was granted has a duty to appear; or

    (b) if no such court has been appointed, a magistrates' court acting for the local justice area in which the police station at which bail was granted is situated.

(2) An application under section 5B(1) of the 1976 Act shall—

    (a) be made in writing;

    (b) contain a statement of the grounds on which it is made;

    (c) specify the offence which the proceedings in which bail was granted were connected with, or for;

    (d) specify the decision to be reconsidered (including any conditions of bail which have been imposed and why they have been imposed);

    (e) specify the name and address of any surety provided by the person to whom the application relates to secure his surrender to custody; and

    (f) contain a notice of the powers available to the court under section 5B of the 1976 Act.

(3) The court officer to whom an application is sent under paragraph (2) above shall serve notice in writing of the date, time and place fixed for the hearing of the application on—

    (a) the prosecutor who made the application;

    (b) the person to whom bail was granted, together with a copy of the application; and

    (c) any surety specified in the application

(4) The time fixed for the hearing shall be not later than 72 hours after receipt of the application. In reckoning for the purpose of this paragraph any period of 72 hours, no account shall be taken of Christmas Day, Good Friday, any bank holiday or any Sunday.

(5) [Revoked.]

(6) At the hearing of an application under section 5B of the 1976 Act the court shall consider any representations made by the person affected (whether in writing or orally) before taking any decision under that section with respect to him; and, where the

person affected does not appear before the court, the court shall not take such a decision unless it is proved to the satisfaction of the court, on oath or in the manner set out by rule 4.11, that the notice required to be given under paragraph (3) of this rule was served on him before the hearing.

(7) Where the court proceeds in the absence of the person affected in accordance with paragraph (6)—

(a) if the decision of the court is to vary the conditions of bail or impose conditions in respect of bail which has been granted unconditionally, the court officer shall notify the person affected;

(b) if the decision of the court is to withhold bail, the order of the court under section 5B(5)(b) of the 1976 Act (surrender to custody) shall be signed by the justice issuing it or state his name and be authenticated by the signature of the clerk of the court.

Notice of change of time for appearance before magistrates' court

19.3 Where—

(a) a person has been granted bail under the Police and Criminal Evidence Act 1984 subject to a duty to appear before a magistrates' court and the court before which he is to appear appoints a later time at which he is to appear; or

(b) a magistrates' court further remands a person on bail under section 129 of the Magistrates' Courts Act 1980 in his absence,

it shall give him and his sureties, if any, notice thereof.

Directions by a magistrates' court as to security, etc

19.4 Where a magistrates' court, under section 3(5) or (6) of the Bail Act 1976, imposes any requirement to be complied with before a person's release on bail, the court may give directions as to the manner in which and the person or persons before whom the requirement may be complied with.

Requirements to be complied with before release on bail granted by a magistrates' court

19.5 (1) Where a magistrates' court has fixed the amount in which a person (including any surety) is to be bound by a recognizance, the recognizance may be entered into—

(a) in the case of a surety where the accused is in a prison or other place of detention, before the governor or keeper of the prison or place as well as before the persons mentioned in section 8(4)(a) of the Bail Act 1976;

(b) in any other case, before a justice of the peace, a justices' clerk, a magistrates' court officer, a police officer who either is of the rank of inspector or above or is in charge of a police station or, if the person to be bound is in a prison or other place of detention, before the governor or keeper of the prison or place; or

(c) where a person other than a police officer is authorised under section 125A or 125B of the Magistrates' Courts Act 1980 to execute a warrant of arrest providing for a recognizance to be entered into by the person arrested (but not by any other person), before the person executing the warrant.

(2) The court officer for a magistrates' court which has fixed the amount in which a person (including any surety) is to be bound by a recognizance or, under section 3(5), (6) or (6A) of the 1976 Act imposed any requirement to be complied with before a person's release on bail or any condition of bail shall issue a certificate showing the amount and conditions, if any, of the recognizance, or as the case may be, containing a statement of the requirement or condition of bail; and a person authorised to take the recognizance or do anything in relation to the compliance with such requirement or condition of bail shall not be required to take or do it without production of such a certificate as aforesaid.

(3) If any person proposed as a surety for a person committed to custody by a magistrates' court produces to the governor or keeper of the prison or other place of detention in

which the person so committed is detained a certificate to the effect that he is accept-able as a surety, signed by any of the justices composing the court or the clerk of the court and signed in the margin by the person proposed as surety, the governor or keeper shall take the recognizance of the person so proposed.

(4) Where the recognizance of any person committed to custody by a magistrates' court or of any surety of such a person is taken by any person other than the court which com-mitted the first-mentioned person to custody, the person taking the recognizance shall send it to the court officer for that court:
Provided that, in the case of a surety, if the person committed has been committed to the Crown Court for trial or under any of the enactments mentioned in rule 43.1(1), the person taking the recognizance shall send it to the Crown Court officer.

Notice to governor of prison, etc, where release from custody is ordered by a magistrates' court

19.6 Where a magistrates' court has, with a view to the release on bail of a person in custody, fixed the amount in which he or any surety of such a person shall be bound or, under section 3(5), (6) or (6A) of the Bail Act 1976, imposed any requirement to be complied with before his release or any condition of bail—

(a) the magistrates' court officer shall give notice thereof to the governor or keeper of the prison or place where that person is detained by sending him such a certificate as is mentioned in rule 19.5(2); and

(b) any person authorised to take the recognizance of a surety or do anything in relation to the compliance with such requirement shall, on taking or doing it, send notice thereof by post to the said governor or keeper and, in the case of a recognizance of a surety, shall give a copy of the notice to the surety.

Release when notice received by governor of prison that recognizances have been taken or requirements complied with

19.7 Where a magistrates' court has, with a view to the release on bail of a person in custody, fixed the amount in which he or any surety of such a person shall be bound or, under section 3(5) or (6) of the Bail Act 1976, imposed any requirement to be complied with before his release and given notice thereof in accordance with this Part to the governor or keeper of the prison or place where that person is detained, the governor or keeper shall, when satisfied that the recognizances of all sureties required have been taken and that all such requirements have been complied with, and unless he is in custody for some other cause, release him.

Notice from a magistrates' court of enlargement of recognizances

19.8 (1) If a magistrates' court before which any person is bound by a recognizance to appear enlarges the recognizance to a later time under section 129 of the Magistrates' Courts Act 1980 in his absence, it shall give him and his sureties, if any, notice thereof.

(2) If a magistrates' court, under section 129(4) of the 1980 Act, enlarges the recognizance of a surety for a person committed for trial on bail, it shall give the surety notice thereof.

Further remand by a youth court

19.9 Where a child or young person has been remanded, and the period of remand is extended in his absence in accordance with section 48 of the Children and Young Persons Act 1933, notice shall be given to him and his sureties (if any) of the date at which he will be required to appear before the court.

Notes of argument in magistrates' court bail hearings

19.10 Where a magistrates' court hears full argument as to bail, the clerk of the court shall take a note of that argument.

Bail records to be entered in register of magistrates' court

19.11 Any record required by section 5 of the Bail Act 1976 to be made by a magistrates' court (together with any note of reasons required by section 5(4) to be included and the particulars set out in any certificate granted under section 5(6A)) shall be made by way of an entry in the register.

Notification of bail decision by magistrate after arrest while on bail

19.12   Where a person who has been released on bail and is under a duty to surrender into the custody of a court is brought under section 7(4)(a) of the Bail Act 1976 before a justice of the peace, the justice shall cause a copy of the record made in pursuance of section 5 of that Act relating to his decision under section 7(5) of that Act in respect of that person to be sent to the court officer for that court:

Provided that this rule shall not apply where the court is a magistrates' court acting for the same local justice area as that for which the justice acts.

Transfer of remand hearings

19.13   (1) Where a magistrates' court, under section 130(1) of the Magistrates' Courts Act 1980, orders that an accused who has been remanded in custody be brought up for any subsequent remands before an alternate magistrates' court, the court officer for the first-mentioned court shall, as soon as practicable after the making of the order and in any case within 2 days thereafter (not counting Sundays, Good Friday, Christmas Day or bank holidays), send to the court officer for the alternate court—

(a) a statement indicating the offence or offences charged;

(b) a copy of the record made by the first-mentioned court in pursuance of section 5 of the Bail Act 1976 relating to the withholding of bail in respect of the accused when he was last remanded in custody;

(c) a copy of any representation order previously made in the same case;

(d) a copy of any application for a representation order;

(e) if the first-mentioned court has made an order under section 8(2) of the 1980 Act (removal of restrictions on reports of committal proceedings), a statement to that effect.

(f) a statement indicating whether or not the accused has a solicitor acting for him in the case and has consented to the hearing and determination in his absence of any application for his remand on an adjournment of the case under sections 5, 10(1) and 18(4) of the 1980 Act together with a statement indicating whether or not that consent has been withdrawn;

(g) a statement indicating the occasions, if any, on which the accused has been remanded under section 128(3A) of the 1980 Act without being brought before the first-mentioned court; and

(h) if the first-mentioned court remands the accused under section 128A of the 1980 Act on the occasion upon which it makes the order under section 130(1) of that Act, a statement indicating the date set under section 128A(2) of that Act.

(2) Where the first-mentioned court is satisfied as mentioned in section 128(3A) of the 1980 Act, paragraph (1) shall have effect as if for the words 'an accused who has been remanded in custody be brought up for any subsequent remands before' there were substituted the words 'applications for any subsequent remands of the accused be made to'.

(3) The court officer for an alternate magistrates' court before which an accused who has been remanded in custody is brought up for any subsequent remands in pursuance of an order made as aforesaid shall, as soon as practicable after the order ceases to be in force and in any case within 2 days thereafter (not counting Sundays, Good Friday, Christmas Day or bank holidays), send to the court officer for the magistrates' court which made the order—

(a) a copy of the record made by the alternate court in pursuance of section 5 of the 1976 Act relating to the grant or withholding of bail in respect of the accused when he was last remanded in custody or on bail;

(b) a copy of any representation order made by the alternate court;

(c) a copy of any application for a representation order made to the alternate court;

(d) if the alternate court has made an order under section 8(2) of the 1980 Act (removal of restrictions on reports of committal proceedings), a statement to that effect;

(e) a statement indicating whether or not the accused has a solicitor acting for him in the case and has consented to the hearing and determination in his absence of any application for his remand on an adjournment of the case under sections 5, 10(1) and 18(4) of the 1980 Act together with a statement indicating whether or not that consent has been withdrawn; and

(f) a statement indicating the occasions, if any, on which the accused has been remanded by the alternate court under section 128(3A) of the 1980 Act without being brought before that court.

(4) Where the alternate court is satisfied as mentioned in section 128(3A) of the 1980 Act paragraph (2) above shall have effect as if for the words 'an accused who has been remanded in custody is brought up for any subsequent remands' there shall be substituted the words 'applications for the further remand of the accused are to be made'.

Notice of further remand in certain cases

19.14 Where a transfer direction has been given by the Secretary of State under section 47 of the Mental Health Act 1983 in respect of a person remanded in custody by a magistrates' court and the direction has not ceased to have effect, the court officer shall give notice in writing to the managers of the hospital where he is detained of any further remand under section 128 of the Magistrates' Courts Act 1980.

Cessation of transfer direction

19.15 Where a magistrates' court directs, under section 52(5) of the Mental Health Act 1983, that a transfer direction given by the Secretary of State under section 48 of that Act in respect of a person remanded in custody by a magistrates' court shall cease to have effect, the court officer shall give notice in writing of the court's direction to the managers of the hospital specified in the Secretary of State's direction and, where the period of remand has not expired or the person has been committed to the Crown Court for trial or to be otherwise dealt with, to the Governor of the prison to which persons of the sex of that person are committed by the court if remanded in custody or committed in custody for trial.

Lodging an appeal against a grant of bail by a magistrates' court

19.16 (1) Where the prosecution wishes to exercise the right of appeal, under section 1 of the Bail (Amendment) Act 1993, to a judge of the Crown Court against a decision to grant bail, the oral notice of appeal must be given to the justices' clerk and to the person concerned, at the conclusion of the proceedings in which such bail was granted and before the release of the person concerned.

(2) When oral notice of appeal is given, the justices' clerk shall announce in open court the time at which such notice was given.

(3) A record of the prosecution's decision to appeal and the time the oral notice of appeal was given shall be made in the register and shall contain the particulars set out.

(4) Where an oral notice of appeal has been given the court shall remand the person concerned in custody by a warrant of commitment.

(5) On receipt of the written notice of appeal required by section 1(5) of the 1993 Act, the court shall remand the person concerned in custody by a warrant of commitment, until the appeal is determined or otherwise disposed of.

(6) A record of the receipt of the written notice of appeal shall be made in the same manner as that of the oral notice of appeal under paragraph (3).

(7) If, having given oral notice of appeal, the prosecution fails to serve a written notice of appeal within the two hour period referred to in section 1(5) of the 1993 Act the justices' clerk shall, as soon as practicable, by way of written notice (served by a court officer) to the persons in whose custody the person concerned is, direct the release of the person concerned on bail as granted by the magistrates' court and subject to any conditions which it imposed.

(8) If the prosecution serves notice of abandonment of appeal on a court officer, the justices' clerk shall, forthwith, by way of written notice (served by the court officer) to the governor of the prison where the person concerned is being held, or the person responsible for any other establishment where such a person is being held, direct his release on bail as granted by the magistrates' court and subject to any conditions which it imposed.

(9) A court officer shall record the prosecution's failure to serve a written notice of appeal, or its service of a notice of abandonments.

(10) Where a written notice of appeal has been served on a magistrates' court officer, he shall provide as soon as practicable to a Crown Court officer a copy of that written notice, together with—

(a) the notes of argument made by the court officer for the court under rule 19.10; and

(b) a note of the date, or dates, when the person concerned is next due to appear in the magistrates' court, whether he is released on bail or remanded in custody by the Crown Court.

(11) References in this rule to 'the person concerned' are references to such a person within the meaning of section 1 of the 1993 Act.

Crown Court procedure on appeal against grant of bail by a magistrates' court

19.17 (1) This rule shall apply where the prosecution appeals under section 1 of the Bail (Amendment) Act 1993 against a decision of a magistrates' court granting bail and in this rule 'the person concerned' has the same meaning as in that Act.

(2) The written notice of appeal required by section 1(5) of the 1993 Act shall be in the form set out in the Practice Direction and shall be served on—

(a) the magistrates' court officer; and

(b) the person concerned.

(3) The Crown Court officer shall enter the appeal and give notice of the time and place of the hearing to—

(a) the prosecution;

(b) the person concerned or his legal representative; and

(c) the magistrates' court officer.

(4) The person concerned shall be entitled to be present at the hearing of the appeal.

(5) Where a person concerned has not been able to instruct a solicitor to represent him at the appeal, he may give notice to the Crown Court requesting that the Official Solicitor shall represent him at the appeal, and the court may, if it thinks fit, assign the Official Solicitor to act for the person concerned accordingly.

(6) At any time after the service of written notice of appeal under paragraph (2), the prosecution may abandon the appeal by giving notice in writing in the form set out in the Practice Direction.

(7) The notice of abandonment required by the preceding paragraph shall be served on—

(a) the person concerned or his legal representative;

(b) the magistrates' court officer; and

(c) the Crown Court officer.

(8) Any record required by section 5 of the Bail Act 1976 (together with any note of reasons required by subsection (4) of that section to be included) shall be made by way of an entry in the file relating to the case in question and the record shall include the following particulars, namely—

(a) the effect of the decision;

(b) a statement of any condition imposed in respect of bail, indicating whether it is to be complied with before or after release on bail; and

(c) where bail is withheld, a statement of the relevant exception to the right to bail (as provided in Schedule 1 to the 1976 Act) on which the decision is based.

(9) The Crown Court officer shall, as soon as practicable after the hearing of the appeal, give notice of the decision and of the matters required by the preceding paragraph to be recorded to—

    (a) the person concerned or his legal representative;

    (b) the prosecution;

    (c) the police;

    (d) the magistrates' officer; and

    (e) the governor of the prison or person responsible for the establishment where the person concerned is being held.

(10) Where the judge hearing the appeal grants bail to the person concerned, the provisions of rule 19.18(9) (informing the Court of any earlier application for bail) and rule 19.22 (conditions attached to bail granted by the Crown Court) shall apply as if that person had applied to the Crown Court for bail.

(11) The notices required by paragraphs (3), (5), (7) and (9) of this rule may be served under rule 4.6 (service by fax, e-mail or other electronic means) and the notice required by paragraph (3) may be given by telephone.

Applications to the Crown Court relating to bail

19.18 (1) This rule applies where an application to the Crown Court relating to bail is made otherwise than during the hearing of proceedings in the Crown Court.

    (2) Subject to paragraph (7) below, notice in writing of intention to make such an application to the Crown Court shall, at least 24 hours before it is made, be given to the prosecutor and if the prosecution is being carried on by the Crown Prosecution Service, to the appropriate Crown Prosecutor or, if the application is to be made by the prosecutor or a constable under section 3(8) of the Bail Act 1976, to the person to whom bail was granted.

    (3) On receiving notice under paragraph (2), the prosecutor or appropriate Crown Public Prosecutor or, as the case may be, the person to whom bail was granted shall—

        (a) notify the Crown Court officer and the applicant that he wishes to be represented at the hearing of the application;

        (b) notify the Crown Court officer and the applicant that he does not oppose the application; or

        (c) give to the Crown Court officer, for the consideration of the Crown Court, a written statement of his reasons for opposing the application, at the same time sending a copy of the statement to the applicant.

    (4) A notice under paragraph (2) shall be in the form set out in the Practice Direction or a form to the like effect, and the applicant shall give a copy of the notice to the Crown Court officer.

    (5) Except in the case of an application made by the prosecutor or a constable under section 3(8) of the 1976 Act, the applicant shall not be entitled to be present on the hearing of his application unless the Crown Court gives him leave to be present.

    (6) Where a person who is in custody or has been released on bail desires to make an application relating to bail and has not been able to instruct a solicitor to apply on his behalf under the preceding paragraphs of this rule, he may give notice in writing to the Crown Court of his desire to make an application relating to bail, requesting that the Official Solicitor shall act for him in the application, and the Court may, if it thinks fit, assign the Official Solicitor to act for the applicant accordingly.

    (7) Where the Official Solicitor has been so assigned the Crown Court may, if it thinks fit, dispense with the requirements of paragraph (2) and deal with the application in a summary manner.

    (8) Any record required by section 5 of the 1976 Act (together with any note of reasons required by section 5(4) to be included) shall be made by way of an entry in the file

relating to the case in question and the record shall include the following particulars, namely—

(a) the effect of the decision;

(b) a statement of any condition imposed in respect of bail, indicating whether it is to be complied with before or after release on bail;

(c) where conditions of bail are varied, a statement of the conditions as varied; and

(d) where bail is withheld, a statement of the relevant exception to the right to bail (as provided in Schedule 1 to the 1976 Act) on which the decision is based.

(9) Every person who makes an application to the Crown Court relating to bail shall inform the Court of any earlier application to the High Court or the Crown Court relating to bail in the course of the same proceedings.

Notice to governor of prison of committal on bail

19.19 (1) Where the accused is committed or sent for trial on bail, a magistrates' court officer shall give notice thereof in writing to the governor of the prison to which persons of the sex of the person committed or sent are committed or sent by that court if committed or sent in custody for trial and also, if the person committed or sent is under 21, to the governor of the remand centre to which he would have been committed or sent if the court had refused him bail.

(2) Where a corporation is committed or sent for trial, a magistrates' court officer shall give notice thereof to the governor of the prison to which would be committed or sent a man committed or sent by that court in custody for trial.

Notices on committal of person subject to transfer direction

19.20 Where a transfer direction has been given by the Secretary of State under section 48 of the Mental Health Act 1983 in respect of a person remanded in custody by a magistrates' court and, before the direction ceases to have effect, that person is committed or sent for trial, a magistrates' court officer shall give notice—

(a) to the governor of the prison to which persons of the sex of that person are committed or sent by that court if committed or sent in custody for trial; and

(b) to the managers of the hospital where he is detained.

Variation of arrangements for bail on committal to the Crown Court

19.21 Where a magistrates' court has committed or sent a person on bail to the Crown Court for trial or under any of the enactments mentioned in rule 43.1(1) and subsequently varies any conditions of the bail or imposes any conditions in respect of the bail, the magistrates' court officer shall send to the Crown Court officer a copy of the record made in pursuance of section 5 of the Bail Act 1976 relating to such variation or imposition of conditions.

Conditions attached to bail granted by the Crown Court

19.22 (1) Where the Crown Court grants bail, the recognizance of any surety required as a condition of bail may be entered into before an officer of the Crown Court or, where the person who has been granted bail is in a prison or other place of detention, before the governor or keeper of the prison or place as well as before the persons specified in section 8(4) of the Bail Act 1976.

(2) Where the Crown Court under section 3(5) or (6) of the 1976 Act imposes a requirement to be complied with before a person's release on bail, the Court may give directions as to the manner in which and the person or persons before whom the requirement may be complied with.

(3) A person who, in pursuance of an order made by the Crown Court for the grant of bail, proposes to enter into a recognizance or give security must, unless the Crown Court otherwise directs, give notice to the prosecutor at least 24 hours before he enters into the recognizance or gives security as aforesaid.

(4) Where, in pursuance of an order of the Crown Court, a recognizance is entered into or any requirement imposed under section 3(5) or (6) of the 1976 Act is complied with

(being a requirement to be complied with before a person's release on bail) before any person, it shall be his duty to cause the recognizance or, as the case may be, a statement of the requirement to be transmitted forthwith to the court officer; and a copy of the recognizance or statement shall at the same time be sent to the governor or keeper of the prison or other place of detention in which the person named in the order is detained, unless the recognizance was entered into or the requirement was complied with before such governor or keeper.

(5) Where, in pursuance of section 3(5) of the 1976 Act, security has been given in respect of a person granted bail with a duty to surrender to the custody of the Crown Court and either—

(a) that person surrenders to the custody of the Court; or

(b) that person having failed to surrender to the custody of the Court, the Court decides not to order the forfeiture of the security,

the court officer shall as soon as practicable give notice of the surrender to custody or, as the case may be, of the decision not to forfeit the security to the person before whom the security was given.

Estreat of recognizances in respect of person bailed to appear before the Crown Court

19.23 (1) Where a recognizance has been entered into in respect of a person granted bail to appear before the Crown Court and it appears to the Court that a default has been made in performing the conditions of the recognizance, other than by failing to appear before the Court in accordance with any such condition, the Court may order the recognizance to be estreated.

(2) Where the Crown Court is to consider making an order under paragraph (1) for a recognizance to be estreated, the court officer shall give notice to that effect to the person by whom the recognizance was entered into indicating the time and place at which the matter will be considered; and no such order shall be made before the expiry of 7 days after the notice required by this paragraph has been given.

Forfeiture of recognizances in respect of person bailed to appear before the Crown Court

19.24 (1) Where a recognizance is conditioned for the appearance of an accused before the Crown Court and the accused fails to appear in accordance with the condition, the Court shall declare the recognizance to be forfeited.

(2) Where the Crown Court declares a recognizance to be forfeited under paragraph (1), the court officer shall issue a summons to the person by whom the recognizance was entered into requiring him to appear before the Court at a time and place specified in the summons to show cause why the Court should not order the recognizance to be estreated.

(3) At the time specified in the summons the Court may proceed in the absence of the person by whom the recognizance was entered into if it is satisfied that he has been served with the summons.

Grant of bail subject to a condition of residence

19.25 (1) The defendant must notify the prosecutor of the address at which the defendant would reside if released on bail with a condition of residence –

(a) as soon as practicable after the institution of proceedings, unless already done; and

(b) as soon as practicable after any change of that address.

(2) The prosecutor must help the court to assess the suitability of an address proposed as a condition of residence.

Grant of bail subject to electronic monitoring requirements

19.26 (1) This rule applies where the court imposes electronic monitoring requirements (where available) as a condition of bail.

(2) The court officer must—

    (a) inform the person responsible for the monitoring ('the monitor') of—

        (i) the defendant's name, and telephone number (if available),

        (ii) the offence or offences with which the defendant is charged,

        (iii) details of the place at which the defendant's presence must be monitored,

        (iv) the period or periods during which the defendant's presence at that place must be monitored, and

        (v) if fixed, the date on which the defendant must surrender to custody;

    (b) inform the defendant and, where the defendant is under 16, an appropriate adult, of the monitor's name, and the means by which the monitor may be contacted; and

    (c) notify the monitor of any subsequent—

        (i) variation or termination of the electronic monitoring requirements, or

        (ii) fixing or variation of the date on which the defendant must surrender to custody.

Grant of bail subject to accommodation or support requirements

19.27 (1) This rule applies where the court imposes as a condition of bail a requirement (where available) that the defendant must—

    (a) reside in accommodation provided for that purpose by, or on behalf of, a public authority;

    (b) receive bail support provided by, or on behalf of, a public authority.

    (2) The court officer must—

    (a) inform the person responsible for the provision of any such accommodation or support ('the service provider') of—

        (i) the defendant's name, and telephone number (if available),

        (ii) the offence or offences with which the defendant is charged,

        (iii) details of the requirement,

        (iv) any other bail condition, and

        (v) if fixed, the date on which the defendant must surrender to custody;

    (b) inform the defendant and, where the defendant is under 16, an appropriate adult, of—

        (i) the service provider's name, and the means by which the service provider may be contacted, and

        (ii) the address of any accommodation in which the defendant must reside; and

    (c) notify the service provider of any subsequent—

        (i) variation or termination of the requirement,

        (ii) variation or termination of any other bail condition, and

        (iii) fixing or variation of the date on which the defendant must surrender to custody.

PART 20   CUSTODY TIME LIMITS

Appeal to the Crown Court against a decision of a magistrates' court in respect of a custody time limit

20.1 (1) This rule applies—

    (a) to any appeal brought by an accused, under section 22(7) of the Prosecution of Offences Act 1985, against a decision of a magistrates' court to extend, or further extend, a custody time limit imposed by regulations made under section 22(1) of the 1985 Act; and

    (b) to any appeal brought by the prosecution, under section 22(8) of the 1985 Act, against a decision of a magistrates' court to refuse to extend, or further extend, such a time limit.

    (2) An appeal to which this rule applies shall be commenced by the appellant's giving notice in writing of appeal—

    (a) to the court officer for the magistrates' court which took the decision;

(b) if the appeal is brought by the accused, to the prosecutor and, if the prosecution is to be carried on by the Crown Prosecution Service, to the appropriate Crown Prosecutor;

(c) if the appeal is brought by the prosecution, to the accused; and

(d) to the Crown Court officer.

(3) The notice of an appeal to which this rule applies shall state the date on which the custody time limit applicable to the case is due to expire and, if the appeal is brought by the accused under section 22(7) of the 1985 Act, the date on which the custody time limit would have expired had the court decided not to extend or further extend that time limit.

(4) On receiving notice of an appeal to which this rule applies, the Crown Court officer shall enter the appeal and give notice of the time and place of the hearing to—

(a) the appellant;

(b) the other party to the appeal; and

(c) the court officer for the magistrates' court which took the decision.

(5) Without prejudice to the power of the Crown Court to give leave for an appeal to be abandoned, an appellant may abandon an appeal to which this rule applies by giving notice in writing to any person to whom notice of the appeal was required to be given by paragraph (2) of this rule not later than the third day preceding the day fixed for the hearing of the appeal:

Provided that, for the purpose of determining whether notice was properly given in accordance with this paragraph, there shall be disregarded any Saturday and Sunday and any day which is specified to be a bank holiday in England and Wales under section 1(1) of the Banking and Financial Dealings Act 1971.

PART 21   INITIAL DETAILS OF THE PROSECUTION CASE

When this Part applies

21.1   (1) This Part applies in a magistrates' court, where the offence is one that can be tried in a magistrates' court.

(2) The court may direct that, for a specified period, this Part will not apply—

(a) to any case in that court; or

(b) to any specified category of case.

Providing initial details of the prosecution case

21.2   The prosecutor must provide initial details of the prosecution case by—

(a) serving those details on the court officer; and

(b) making those details available to the defendant,

at, or before, the beginning of the day of the first hearing.

Content of initial details

21.3   Initial details of the prosecution case must include—

(a) a summary of the evidence on which that case will be based; or

(b) any statement, document or extract setting out facts or other matters on which that case will be based; or

(c) any combination of such a summary, statement, document or extract; and

(d) the defendant's previous convictions.

PART 22   DISCLOSURE

When this Part applies

22.1   This Part applies—

(a) in a magistrates' court and in the Crown Court;

(b) where Parts I and II of the Criminal Procedure and Investigations Act 1996 apply.

Prosecution disclosure

22.2   (1) This rule applies in the Crown Court where, under section 3 of the Criminal Procedure and Investigations Act 1996, the prosecutor—

      (a) discloses prosecution material to the defendant; or

      (b) serves on the defendant a written statement that there is no such material to disclose.

    (2) The prosecutor must at the same time so inform the court officer.

Prosecutor's application for public interest ruling

22.3   (1) This rule applies where—

      (a) without a court order, the prosecutor would have to disclose material; and

      (b) the prosecutor wants the court to decide whether it would be in the public interest to disclose it.

    (2) The prosecutor must—

      (a) apply in writing for such a decision; and

      (b) serve the application on—

         (i) the court officer,

         (ii) any person who the prosecutor thinks would be directly affected by disclosure of the material, and

         (iii) the defendant, but only to the extent that serving it on the defendant would not disclose what the prosecutor thinks ought not be disclosed.

    (3) The application must—

      (a) describe the material, and explain why the prosecutor thinks that—

         (i) it is material that the prosecutor would have to disclose,

         (ii) it would not be in the public interest to disclose that material, and

         (iii) no measure such as the prosecutor's admission of any fact, or disclosure by summary, extract or edited copy, adequately would protect both the public interest and the defendant's right to a fair trial;

      (b) omit from any part of the application that is served on the defendant anything that would disclose what the prosecutor thinks ought not be disclosed (in which case, paragraph (4) of this rule applies); and

      (c) explain why, if no part of the application is served on the defendant.

    (4) Where the prosecutor serves only part of the application on the defendant, the prosecutor must—

      (a) mark the other part, to show that it is only for the court; and

      (b) in that other part, explain why the prosecutor has withheld it from the defendant.

    (5) Unless already done, the court may direct the prosecutor to serve an application on—

      (a) the defendant;

      (b) any other person who the court considers would be directly affected by the disclosure of the material.

    (6) The court must determine the application at a hearing which—

      (a) will be in private, unless the court otherwise directs; and

      (b) if the court so directs, may take place, wholly or in part, in the defendant's absence.

    (7) At a hearing at which the defendant is present—

      (a) the general rule is that the court will receive, in the following sequence—

         (i) representations first by the prosecutor and any other person served with the application, and then by the defendant, in the presence of them all, and then

         (ii) further representations by the prosecutor and any such other person in the defendant's absence; but

      (b) the court may direct other arrangements for the hearing.

(8) The court may only determine the application if satisfied that it has been able to take adequate account of—
(a) such rights of confidentiality as apply to the material; and
(b) the defendant's right to a fair trial.

(9) Unless the court otherwise directs, the court officer—
(a) must not give notice to anyone other than the prosecutor—
  (i) of the hearing of an application under this rule, unless the prosecutor served the application on that person, or
  (ii) of the court's decision on the application;
(b) may—
  (i) keep a written application or representations, or
  (ii) arrange for the whole or any part to be kept by some other appropriate person, subject to any conditions that the court may impose.

Defence disclosure

22.4 The defendant must serve any defence statement given under the Criminal Procedure and Investigations Act 1996 on—
(a) the court officer; and
(b) the prosecutor.

Defendant's application for prosecution disclosure

22.5 (1) This rule applies where the defendant—
(a) has served a defence statement given under the Criminal Procedure and Investigations Act 1996; and
(b) wants the court to require the prosecutor to disclose material.

(2) The defendant must serve an application on—
(a) the court officer; and
(b) the prosecutor.

(3) The application must—
(a) describe the material that the defendant wants the prosecutor to disclose;
(b) explain why the defendant thinks there is reasonable cause to believe that—
  (i) the prosecutor has that material, and
  (ii) it is material that the Criminal Procedure and Investigations Act 1996 requires the prosecutor to disclose; and
(c) ask for a hearing, if the defendant wants one, and explain why it is needed.

(4) The court may determine an application under this rule—
(a) at a hearing, in public or in private; or
(b) without a hearing.

(5) The court must not require the prosecutor to disclose material unless the prosecutor—
(a) is present; or
(b) has had at least 14 days in which to make representations.

Review of public interest ruling

22.6 (1) This rule applies where the court has ordered that it is not in the public interest to disclose material that the prosecutor otherwise would have to disclose, and—
(a) the defendant wants the court to review that decision; or
(b) the Crown Court reviews that decision on its own initiative.

(2) Where the defendant wants the court to review that decision, the defendant must—
(a) serve an application on—
  (i) the court officer, and
  (ii) the prosecutor; and
(b) in the application—
  (i) describe the material that the defendant wants the prosecutor to disclose, and
  (ii) explain why the defendant thinks it is no longer in the public interest for the prosecutor not to disclose it.

(3) The prosecutor must serve any such application on any person who the prosecutor thinks would be directly affected if that material were disclosed.

(4) The prosecutor, and any such person, must serve any representations on—

    (a) the court officer; and

    (b) the defendant, unless to do so would in effect reveal something that either thinks ought not be disclosed.

(5) The court may direct—

    (a) the prosecutor to serve any such application on any person who the court considers would be directly affected if that material were disclosed;

    (b) the prosecutor and any such person to serve any representations on the defendant.

(6) The court must review a decision to which this rule applies at a hearing which—

    (a) will be in private, unless the court otherwise directs; and

    (b) if the court so directs, may take place, wholly or in part, in the defendant's absence.

(7) At a hearing at which the defendant is present—

    (a) the general rule is that the court will receive, in the following sequence—

        (i) representations first by the defendant, and then by the prosecutor and any other person served with the application, in the presence of them all, and then

        (ii) further representations by the prosecutor and any such other person in the defendant's absence; but

    (b) the court may direct other arrangements for the hearing.

(8) The court may only conclude a review if satisfied that it has been able to take adequate account of—

    (a) such rights of confidentiality as apply to the material; and

    (b) the defendant's right to a fair trial.

Defendant's application to use disclosed material

22.7 (1) This rule applies where a defendant wants the court's permission to use disclosed prosecution material—

    (a) otherwise than in connection with the case in which it was disclosed; or

    (b) beyond the extent to which it was displayed or communicated publicly at a hearing.

(2) The defendant must serve an application on—

    (a) the court officer; and

    (b) the prosecutor.

(3) The application must—

    (a) specify what the defendant wants to use or disclose; and

    (b) explain why.

(4) The court may determine an application under this rule—

    (a) at a hearing, in public or in private; or

    (b) without a hearing.

(5) The court must not permit the use of such material unless—

    (a) the prosecutor has had at least 28 days in which to make representations; and

    (b) the court is satisfied that it has been able to take adequate account of any rights of confidentiality that may apply to the material.

Unauthorised use of disclosed material

22.8 (1) This rule applies where a person uses disclosed prosecution material in contravention of section 17 of the Criminal Procedure and Investigations Act 1996.

(2) The court may exercise its power to punish such a person for contempt of court—

    (a) on an application by—

        (i) the prosecutor, or

        (ii) any person directly affected by the disclosure of the material; or

    (b) on its own initiative.

(3) An applicant who wants the court to exercise that power must comply with the rules in Part 62 (Contempt of court).

(4) The court must not exercise its power to forfeit material used in contempt of court unless—

(a) the prosecutor; and

(b) any other person directly affected by the disclosure of the material,

is present, or has had at least 14 days in which to make representations.

(5) The provisions of Schedule 3 to the Contempt of Court Act 1981 apply to a magistrates' court's exercise of the power to which this rule applies.

Court's power to vary requirements under this Part

22.9 The court may—

(a) shorten or extend (even after it has expired) a time limit under this Part;

(b) allow a defence statement to be in a different written form to one set out in the Practice Direction, as long as it contains what the Criminal Procedure and Investigations Act 1996 requires;

(c) allow an application under this Part to be in a different form to one set out in the Practice Direction, or to be presented orally; and

(d) specify the period within which—

(i) any application under this Part must be made, or

(ii) any material must be disclosed, on an application to which rule 22.5 applies (defendant's application for prosecution disclosure).

PART 23

[This part currently contains no rules.]

PART 24

[This part currently contains no rules.]

PART 25

[This part currently contains no rules.]

PART 26

[This part currently contains no rules.]

PART 27 WITNESS STATEMENTS

When this part applies

27.1 This Part applies where a party wants to introduce a written statement in evidence under section 9 of the Criminal Justice Act 1967.

Content of written statement

27.2 (1) The statement must contain—

(a) at the beginning—

(i) the witness' name, and

(ii) the witness' age, if under 18;

(b) a declaration by the witness that—

(i) it is true to the best of the witness' knowledge and belief, and

(ii) the witness knows that if it is introduced in evidence, then it would be an offence wilfully to have stated in it anything that the witness knew to be false or did not believe to be true;

(c) if the witness cannot read the statement, a signed declaration by someone else that that person read it to the witness; and

(d) the witness' signature.

Reference to exhibit

27.3 Where the statement refers to a document or object as an exhibit—

(a) the statement must contain such a description of that exhibit as to identify it clearly; and

(b) the exhibit must be labelled or marked correspondingly, and the label or mark signed by the maker of the statement.

Written statement in evidence

27.4 (1) A party who wants to introduce in evidence a written statement must—

(a) before the hearing at which that party wants to do so, serve a copy of the statement on—

(i) the court officer, and

(ii) each other party; and

(b) at or before that hearing, serve the statement itself on the court officer.

(2) If that party relies on only part of the statement, that party must mark the copy in such a way as to make that clear.

(3) A prosecutor must serve on a defendant, with the copy of the statement, a notice—

(a) of the right within 7 days of service to object to the introduction of the statement in evidence instead of the witness giving evidence in person; and

(b) that if the defendant does not object in time, the court—

(i) can nonetheless require the witness to give evidence in person, but

(ii) may decide not to do so.

(4) The court may exercise its power to require the witness to give evidence in person—

(a) on application by any party; or

(b) on its own initiative.

(5) A party entitled to receive a copy of a statement may waive that entitlement by so informing—

(a) the party who would have served it; and

(b) the court.

PART 28 WITNESS SUMMONSES, WARRANTS AND ORDERS

When this Part applies

28.1 (1) This Part applies in magistrates' courts and in the Crown Court where—

(a) a party wants the court to issue a witness summons, warrant or order under—

(i) section 97 of the Magistrates' Courts Act 1980,

(ii) section 2 of the Criminal Procedure (Attendance of Witnesses) Act 1965, or

(iii) section 7 of the Bankers' Books Evidence Act 1879;

(b) the court considers the issue of such a summons, warrant or order on its own initiative as if a party had applied; or

(c) one of those listed in rule 28.7 wants the court to withdraw such a summons, warrant or order.

(2) A reference to a 'witness' in this Part is a reference to a person to whom such a summons, warrant or order is directed.

Issue etc. of summons, warrant or order with or without a hearing

28.2 (1) The court may issue or withdraw a witness summons, warrant or order with or without a hearing.

(2) A hearing under this Part must be in private unless the court otherwise directs.

Application for summons, warrant or order: general rules

28.3 (1) A party who wants the court to issue a witness summons, warrant or order must apply as soon as practicable after becoming aware of the grounds for doing so.

    (2) The party applying must—

        (a) identify the proposed witness;

        (b) explain—

            (i) what evidence the proposed witness can give or produce,

            (ii) why it is likely to be material evidence, and

            (iii) why it would be in the interests of justice to issue a summons, order or warrant as appropriate.

    (3) The application may be made orally unless—

        (a) rule 28.5 applies; or

        (b) the court otherwise directs.

Written application: form and service

28.4 (1) An application in writing under rule 28.3 must be in the form set out in the Practice Direction, containing the same declaration of truth as a witness statement.

    (2) The party applying must serve the application—

        (a) in every case, on the court officer and as directed by the court; and

        (b) as required by rule 28.5, if that rule applies.

Application for summons to produce a document, etc.: special rules

28.5 (1) This rule applies to an application under rule 28.3 for a witness summons requiring the proposed witness—

        (a) to produce in evidence a document or thing; or

        (b) to give evidence about information apparently held in confidence,

    that relates to another person.

    (2) The application must be in writing in the form required by rule 28.4.

    (3) The party applying must serve the application—

        (a) on the proposed witness, unless the court otherwise directs; and

        (b) on one or more of the following, if the court so directs—

            (i) a person to whom the proposed evidence relates,

            (ii) another party.

    (4) The court must not issue a witness summons where this rule applies unless—

        (a) everyone served with the application has had at least 14 days in which to make representations, including representations about whether there should be a hearing of the application before the summons is issued; and

        (b) the court is satisfied that it has been able to take adequate account of the duties and rights, including rights of confidentiality, of the proposed witness and of any person to whom the proposed evidence relates.

    (5) This rule does not apply to an application for an order to produce in evidence a copy of an entry in a banker's book.

Application for summons to produce a document, etc.: court's assessment of relevance and confidentiality

28.6 (1) This rule applies where a person served with an application for a witness summons requiring the proposed witness to produce in evidence a document or thing objects to its production on the ground that—

        (a) it is not likely to be material evidence; or

        (b) even if it is likely to be material evidence, the duties or rights, including rights of confidentiality, of the proposed witness or of any person to whom the document or thing relates outweigh the reasons for issuing a summons.

(2) The court may require the proposed witness to make the document or thing available for the objection to be assessed.

(3) The court may invite—

(a) the proposed witness or any representative of the proposed witness; or

(b) a person to whom the document or thing relates or any representative of such a person,

to help the court assess the objection.

Application to withdraw a summons, warrant or order

28.7 (1) The court may withdraw a witness summons, warrant or order if one of the following applies for it to be withdrawn—

(a) the party who applied for it, on the ground that it no longer is needed;

(b) the witness, on the grounds that—

(i) he was not aware of any application for it, and

(ii) he cannot give or produce evidence likely to be material evidence, or

(iii) even if he can, his duties or rights, including rights of confidentiality, or those of any person to whom the evidence relates outweigh the reasons for the issue of the summons, warrant or order; or

(c) any person to whom the proposed evidence relates, on the grounds that—

(i) he was not aware of any application for it, and

(ii) that evidence is not likely to be material evidence, or

(iii) even if it is, his duties or rights, including rights of confidentiality, or those of the witness outweigh the reasons for the issue of the summons, warrant or order.

(2) A person applying under the rule must—

(a) apply in writing as soon as practicable after becoming aware of the grounds for doing so, explaining why he wants the summons, warrant or order to be withdrawn; and

(b) serve the application on the court officer and as appropriate on—

(i) the witness,

(ii) the party who applied for the summons, warrant or order, and

(iii) any other person who he knows was served with the application for the summons, warrant or order.

(3) Rule 28.6 applies to an application under this rule that concerns a document or thing to be produced in evidence.

Court's power to vary requirements under this Part

28.8 (1) The court may—

(a) shorten or extend (even after it has expired) a time limit under this Part; and

(b) where a rule or direction requires an application under this Part to be in writing, allow that application to be made orally instead.

(2) Someone who wants the court to allow an application to be made orally under paragraph (1)(b) of this rule must—

(a) give as much notice as the urgency of his application permits to those on whom he would otherwise have served an application in writing; and

(b) in doing so explain the reasons for the application and for wanting the court to consider it orally.

PART 29   MEASURES TO ASSIST A WITNESS OR
DEFENDANT TO GIVE EVIDENCE

SECTION 1: UNDERSTANDING AND APPLYING THIS PART

When this Part applies

29.1. This Part applies—
  (a) where the court can give a direction (a 'special measures direction'), under section 19 of the Youth Justice and Criminal Evidence Act 1999, on an application or on its own initiative, for any of the following measures—
    (i) preventing a witness from seeing the defendant (section 23 of the 1999 Act),
    (ii) allowing a witness to give evidence by live link (section 24 of the 1999 Act),
    (iii) hearing a witness' evidence in private (section 25 of the 1999 Act),
    (iv) dispensing with the wearing of wigs and gowns (section 26 of the 1999 Act),
    (v) admitting video recorded evidence (sections 27 and 28 of the 1999 Act),
    (vi) questioning a witness through an intermediary (section 29 of the 1999 Act),
    (vii) using a device to help a witness communicate (section 30 of the 1999 Act);
  (b) where the court can vary or discharge such a direction, under section 20 of the 1999 Act;
  (c) where the court can give, vary or discharge a direction (a 'defendant's evidence direction') for a defendant to give evidence—
    (i) by live link, under section 33A of the 1999 Act, or
    (ii) through an intermediary, under sections 33BA and 33BB of the 1999 Act;
  (d) where the court can—
    (i) make a witness anonymity order, under section 86 of the Coroners and Justice Act 2009, or
    (ii) vary or discharge such an order, under section 91, 92 or 93 of the 2009 Act;
  (e) where the court can give or discharge a direction (a 'live link direction'), on an application or on its own initiative, for a witness to give evidence by live link under—
    (i) section 32 of the Criminal Justice Act 1988, or
    (ii) sections 51 and 52 of the Criminal Justice Act 2003;
  (f) where the court can exercise any other power it has to give, vary or discharge a direction for a measure to help a witness give evidence.

Meaning of 'witness'

29.2. In this Part, 'witness' means anyone (other than a defendant) for whose benefit an application, direction or order is made.

SECTION 2: GENERAL RULES

Making an application for a direction or order

29.3. A party who wants the court to exercise its power to give or make a direction or order must—
  (a) apply in writing—
    (i) as soon as reasonably practicable, and in any event
    (ii) not more than 14 days after the defendant pleads not guilty; and
  (b) serve the application on—
    (i) the court officer, and
    (ii) each other party.

Decisions and reasons

29.4 (1) A party who wants to introduce the evidence of a witness who is the subject of an application, direction or order must—
  (a) inform the witness of the court's decision as soon as reasonably practicable; and
  (b) explain to the witness the arrangements that as a result will be made for him or her to give evidence.

(2) The court must announce, at a hearing in public before the witness gives evidence, the reasons for a decision—

(a) to give, make, vary or discharge a direction or order; or

(b) to refuse to do so.

Court's power to vary requirements under this Part

29.5 (1) The court may—

(a) shorten or extend (even after it has expired) a time limit under this Part; and

(b) allow an application or representations to be made in a different form to one set out in the Practice Direction, or to be made orally.

(2) A person who wants an extension of time must—

(a) apply when serving the application or representations for which it is needed; and

(b) explain the delay.

Custody of documents

29.6. Unless the court otherwise directs, the court officer may—

(a) keep a written application or representations; or

(b) arrange for the whole or any part to be kept by some other appropriate person, subject to any conditions that the court may impose.

Declaration by intermediary

29.7 (1) This rule applies where—

(a) a video recorded interview with a witness is conducted through an intermediary;

(b) the court directs the examination of a witness or defendant through an intermediary.

(2) An intermediary must make a declaration—

(a) before such an interview begins;

(b) before the examination begins (even if such an interview with the witness was conducted through the same intermediary).

(3) The declaration must be in these terms—

'I solemnly, sincerely and truly declare [*or* I swear by Almighty God] that I will well and faithfully communicate questions and answers and make true explanation of all matters and things as shall be required of me according to the best of my skill and understanding.'

SECTION 3: SPECIAL MEASURES DIRECTIONS

Exercise of court's powers

29.8 The court may decide whether to give, vary or discharge a special measures direction—

(a) at a hearing, in public or in private, or without a hearing;

(b) in a party's absence, if that party—

(i) applied for the direction, variation or discharge, or

(ii) has had at least 14 days in which to make representations.

Special measures direction for a young witness

29.9 (1) This rule applies where, under section 21 or section 22 of the Youth Justice and Criminal Evidence Act 1999, the primary rule requires the court to give a direction for a special measure to assist a child witness or a qualifying witness—

(a) on an application, if one is made; or

(b) on the court's own initiative, in any other case.

(2) A party who wants to introduce the evidence of such a witness must as soon as reasonably practicable—

(a) notify the court that the witness is eligible for assistance;

(b) provide the court with any information that the court may need to assess the witness' views, if the witness does not want the primary rule to apply; and

      (c) serve any video recorded evidence on—
          (i)   the court officer, and
          (ii) each other party.

Content of application for a special measures direction

29.10 An applicant for a special measures direction must—

    (a) explain how the witness is eligible for assistance;

    (b) explain why special measures would be likely to improve the quality of the witness' evidence;

    (c) propose the measure or measures that in the applicant's opinion would be likely to maximise so far as practicable the quality of that evidence;

    (d) report any views that the witness has expressed about—
        (i)   his or her eligibility for assistance,
        (ii) the likelihood that special measures would improve the quality of his or her evidence, and
        (iii) the measure or measures proposed by the applicant;

    (e) in a case in which a child witness or a qualifying witness does not want the primary rule to apply, provide any information that the court may need to assess the witness' views;

    (f) in a case in which the applicant proposes that the witness should give evidence by live link—
        (i)   identify someone to accompany the witness while the witness gives evidence,
        (ii) name that person, if possible, and
        (iii) explain why that person would be an appropriate companion for the witness, including the witness' own views;

    (g) in a case in which the applicant proposes the admission of video recorded evidence, identify—
        (i)   the date and duration of the recording,
        (ii) which part the applicant wants the court to admit as evidence, if the applicant does not want the court to admit all of it;

    (h) attach any other material on which the applicant relies; and

    (i) if the applicant wants a hearing, ask for one, and explain why it is needed.

Application to vary or discharge a special measures direction

29.11 (1) A party who wants the court to vary or discharge a special measures direction must—

    (a) apply in writing, as soon as reasonably practicable after becoming aware of the grounds for doing so; and

    (b) serve the application on—
        (i)   the court officer, and
        (ii) each other party.

  (2) The applicant must—

    (a) explain what material circumstances have changed since the direction was given (or last varied, if applicable);

    (b) explain why the direction should be varied or discharged; and

    (c) ask for a hearing, if the applicant wants one, and explain why it is needed.

Application containing information withheld from another party

29.12 (1) This rule applies where—

    (a) an applicant serves an application for a special measures direction, or for its variation or discharge; and

    (b) the application includes information that the applicant thinks ought not be revealed to another party.

  (2) The applicant must—

    (a) omit that information from the part of the application that is served on that other party;

    (b) mark the other part to show that, unless the court otherwise directs, it is only for the court; and

    (c) in that other part, explain why the applicant has withheld that information from that other party.

  (3) Any hearing of an application to which this rule applies—

    (a) must be in private, unless the court otherwise directs; and

    (b) if the court so directs, may be, wholly or in part, in the absence of a party from whom information has been withheld.

  (4) At any hearing of an application to which this rule applies—

    (a) the general rule is that the court will receive, in the following sequence—

       (i) representations first by the applicant and then by each other party, in all the parties' presence, and then

      (ii) further representations by the applicant, in the absence of a party from whom information has been withheld; but

    (b) the court may direct other arrangements for the hearing.

Representations in response

29.13 (1) This rule applies where a party wants to make representations about—

    (a) an application for a special measures direction;

    (b) an application for the variation or discharge of such a direction; or

    (c) a direction, variation or discharge that the court proposes on its own initiative.

  (2) Such a party must—

    (a) serve the representations on—

       (i) the court officer, and

      (ii) each other party;

    (b) do so not more than 14 days after, as applicable—

       (i) service of the application, or

      (ii) notice of the direction, variation or discharge that the court proposes; and

    (c) ask for a hearing, if that party wants one, and explain why it is needed.

  (3) Where representations include information that the person making them thinks ought not be revealed to another party, that person must—

    (a) omit that information from the representations served on that other party;

    (b) mark the information to show that, unless the court otherwise directs, it is only for the court; and

    (c) with that information include an explanation of why it has been withheld from that other party.

  (4) Representations against a special measures direction must explain—

    (a) why the witness is not eligible for assistance; or

    (b) if the witness is eligible for assistance, why—

       (i) no special measure would be likely to improve the quality of the witness' evidence,

      (ii) the proposed measure or measures would not be likely to maximise so far as practicable the quality of the witness' evidence, or

      (iii) the proposed measure or measures might tend to inhibit the effective testing of that evidence.

  (5) Representations against the variation or discharge of a special measures direction must explain why it should not be varied or discharged.

Section 4: Defendant's Evidence Directions

Exercise of court's powers

29.14 The court may decide whether to give, vary or discharge a defendant's evidence direction—

    (a) at a hearing, in public or in private, or without a hearing;

(b) in a party's absence, if that party—
    (i) applied for the direction, variation or discharge, or
    (ii) has had at least 14 days in which to make representations.

Content of application for a defendant's evidence direction

29.15 An applicant for a defendant's evidence direction must—
    (a) explain how the proposed direction meets the conditions prescribed by the Youth Justice and Criminal Evidence Act 1999;
    (b) in a case in which the applicant proposes that the defendant give evidence by live link—
        (i) identify a person to accompany the defendant while the defendant gives evidence, and
        (ii) explain why that person is appropriate;
    (c) ask for a hearing, if the applicant wants one, and explain why it is needed.

Application to vary or discharge a defendant's evidence direction

29.16 (1) A party who wants the court to vary or discharge a defendant's evidence direction must—
    (a) apply in writing, as soon as reasonably practicable after becoming aware of the grounds for doing so; and
    (b) serve the application on—
        (i) the court officer, and
        (ii) each other party.
    (2) The applicant must—
    (a) on an application to discharge a live link direction, explain why it is in the interests of justice to do so;
    (b) on an application to discharge a direction for an intermediary, explain why it is no longer necessary in order to ensure that the defendant receives a fair trial;
    (c) on an application to vary a direction for an intermediary, explain why it is necessary for the direction to be varied in order to ensure that the defendant receives a fair trial; and
    (d) ask for a hearing, if the applicant wants one, and explain why it is needed.

Representations in response

29.17 (1) This rule applies where a party wants to make representations about—
    (a) an application for a defendant's evidence direction;
    (b) an application for the variation or discharge of such a direction; or
    (c) a direction, variation or discharge that the court proposes on its own initiative.
    (2) Such a party must—
    (a) serve the representations on—
        (i) the court officer, and
        (ii) each other party;
    (b) do so not more than 14 days after, as applicable—
        (i) service of the application, or
        (ii) notice of the direction, variation or discharge that the court proposes; and
    (c) ask for a hearing, if that party wants one, and explain why it is needed.
    (3) Representations against a direction, variation or discharge must explain why the conditions prescribed by the Youth Justice and Criminal Evidence Act 1999 are not met.

SECTION 5: WITNESS ANONYMITY ORDERS

Exercise of court's powers

29.18 (1) The court may decide whether to make, vary or discharge a witness anonymity order—
    (a) at a hearing (which will be in private, unless the court otherwise directs), or without a hearing (unless any party asks for one);
    (b) in the absence of a defendant.

(2) The court must not exercise its power to make, vary or discharge a witness anonymity order, or to refuse to do so—

  (a) before or during the trial, unless each party has had an opportunity to make representations;

  (b) on an appeal by the defendant to which applies Part 63 (appeal to the Crown Court) or Part 68 (appeal to the Court of Appeal about conviction or sentence), unless in each party's case—

    (i) that party has had an opportunity to make representations, or

    (ii) the appeal court is satisfied that it is not reasonably practicable to communicate with that party;

  (c) after the trial and any such appeal are over, unless in the case of each party and the witness—

    (i) each has had an opportunity to make representations, or

    (ii) the court is satisfied that it is not reasonably practicable to communicate with that party or witness.

Content and conduct of application for a witness anonymity order

29.19 (1) An applicant for a witness anonymity order must—

  (a) include in the application nothing that might reveal the witness' identity;

  (b) describe the measures proposed by the applicant;

  (c) explain how the proposed order meets the conditions prescribed by section 88 of the Coroners and Justice Act 2009;

  (d) explain why no measures other than those proposed will suffice, such as—

    (i) an admission of the facts that would be proved by the witness,

    (ii) an order restricting public access to the trial,

    (iii) reporting restrictions, in particular under section 46 of the Youth Justice and Criminal Evidence Act 1999 or under section 39 of the Children and Young Persons Act 1933,

    (iv) a direction for a special measure under section 19 of the Youth Justice and Criminal Evidence Act 1999,

    (v) introduction of the witness' written statement as hearsay evidence, under section 116 of the Criminal Justice Act 2003, or

    (vi) arrangements for the protection of the witness;

  (e) attach to the application—

    (i) a witness statement setting out the proposed evidence, edited in such a way as not to reveal the witness' identity,

    (ii) where the prosecutor is the applicant, any further prosecution evidence to be served, and any further prosecution material to be disclosed under the Criminal Procedure and Investigations Act 1996, similarly edited, and

    (iii) any defence statement that has been served, or as much information as may be available to the applicant that gives particulars of the defence; and

  (f) ask for a hearing, if the applicant wants one.

(2) At any hearing of the application, the applicant must—

  (a) identify the witness to the court, unless at the prosecutor's request the court otherwise directs; and

  (b) present to the court, unless it otherwise directs—

    (i) the unedited witness statement from which the edited version has been prepared,

    (ii) where the prosecutor is the applicant, the unedited version of any further prosecution evidence or material from which an edited version has been prepared, and

    (iii) such further material as the applicant relies on to establish that the proposed order meets the conditions prescribed by section 88 of the 2009 Act.

(3) At any such hearing—
    (a) the general rule is that the court will receive, in the following sequence—
        (i) representations first by the applicant and then by each other party, in all the parties' presence, and then
        (ii) information withheld from a defendant, and further representations by the applicant, in the absence of any (or any other) defendant; but
    (b) the court may direct other arrangements for the hearing.
(4) Before the witness gives evidence, the applicant must identify the witness to the court—
    (a) if not already done;
    (b) without revealing the witness' identity to any other party or person; and
    (c) unless at the prosecutor's request the court otherwise directs.

Duty of court officer to notify the Director of Public Prosecutions

29.20 The court officer must notify the Director of Public Prosecutions of an application, unless the prosecutor is, or acts on behalf of, a public authority.

Application to vary or discharge a witness anonymity order

29.21 (1) A party who wants the court to vary or discharge a witness anonymity order, or a witness who wants the court to do so when the case is over, must—
    (a) apply in writing, as soon as reasonably practicable after becoming aware of the grounds for doing so; and
    (b) serve the application on—
        (i) the court officer, and
        (ii) each other party.
(2) The applicant must—
    (a) explain what material circumstances have changed since the order was made (or last varied, if applicable);
    (b) explain why the order should be varied or discharged, taking account of the conditions for making an order; and
    (c) ask for a hearing, if the applicant wants one.
(3) Where an application includes information that the applicant thinks might reveal the witness' identity, the applicant must—
    (a) omit that information from the application that is served on a defendant;
    (b) mark the information to show that it is only for the court and the prosecutor (if the prosecutor is not the applicant); and
    (c) with that information include an explanation of why it has been withheld.
(4) Where a party applies to vary or discharge a witness anonymity order after the trial and any appeal are over, the party who introduced the witness' evidence must serve the application on the witness.

Representations in response

29.22 (1) This rule applies where a party or, where the case is over, a witness, wants to make representations about—
    (a) an application for a witness anonymity order;
    (b) an application for the variation or discharge of such an order; or
    (c) a variation or discharge that the court proposes on its own initiative.
(2) Such a party or witness must—
    (a) serve the representations on—
        (i) the court officer, and
        (ii) each other party;
    (b) do so not more than 14 days after, as applicable—
        (i) service of the application, or
        (ii) notice of the variation or discharge that the court proposes; and
    (c) ask for a hearing, if that party or witness wants one.

(3) Where representations include information that the person making them thinks might reveal the witness' identity, that person must—
    (a) omit that information from the representations served on a defendant;
    (b) mark the information to show that it is only for the court (and for the prosecutor, if relevant); and
    (c) with that information include an explanation of why it has been withheld.

(4) Representations against a witness anonymity order must explain why the conditions for making the order are not met.

(5) Representations against the variation or discharge of such an order must explain why it would not be appropriate to vary or discharge it, taking account of the conditions for making an order.

(6) A prosecutor's representations in response to an application by a defendant must include all information available to the prosecutor that is relevant to the conditions and considerations specified by sections 88 and 89 of the Coroners and Justice Act 2009.

Section 6: Live Link Directions

Exercise of court's powers

29.23 The court may decide whether to give, vary or discharge a live link direction—
    (a) at a hearing, in public or in private, or without a hearing;
    (b) in a party's absence, if that party—
        (i) applied for the direction, variation or discharge, or
        (ii) has had at least 14 days in which to make representations.

Content of application for a live link direction

29.24. An applicant for a live link direction must—
    (a) unless the court otherwise directs, identify the place from which the witness will give evidence;
    (b) if that place is in the United Kingdom, explain why it would be in the interests of the efficient or effective administration of justice for the witness to give evidence by live link;
    (c) if the applicant wants the witness to be accompanied by another person while giving evidence—
        (i) name that person, if possible, and
        (ii) explain why it is appropriate for the witness to be accompanied;
    (d) ask for a hearing, if the applicant wants one, and explain why it is needed.

Application to discharge a live link direction

29.25 (1) A party who wants the court to discharge a live link direction must—
    (a) apply in writing, as soon as reasonably practicable after becoming aware of the grounds for doing so; and
    (b) serve the application on—
        (i) the court officer, and
        (ii) each other party.

(2) The applicant must—
    (a) explain what material circumstances have changed since the direction was given;
    (b) explain why it is in the interests of justice to discharge the direction; and
    (c) ask for a hearing, if the applicant wants one, and explain why it is needed.

Representations in response

29.26 (1) This rule applies where a party wants to make representations about—
    (a) an application for a live link direction;
    (b) an application for the discharge of such a direction; or
    (c) a direction or discharge that the court proposes on its own initiative.

(2) Such a party must—
   (a) serve the representations on—
      (i) the court officer, and
      (ii) each other party;
   (b) do so not more than 14 days after, as applicable—
      (i) service of the application, or
      (ii) notice of the direction or discharge that the court proposes; and
   (c) ask for a hearing, if that party wants one, and explain why it is needed.
(3) Representations against a direction or discharge must explain, as applicable, why the conditions prescribed by the Criminal Justice Act 1988 or the Criminal Justice Act 2003 are not met.

PART 30

[Omitted with effect 4 October 2010 and replaced by rr. 29.23 to 29.26 (SI 2010/1921).]

PART 31   RESTRICTION ON CROSS-EXAMINATION BY A DEFENDANT ACTING IN PERSON

Restrictions on cross-examination of witness

31.1 (1) This rule and rules 31.2 and 31.3 apply where an accused is prevented from cross-examining a witness in person by virtue of section 34, 35 or 36 of the Youth Justice and Criminal Evidence Act 1999.
   (2) The court shall explain to the accused as early in the proceedings as is reasonably practicable that he—
      (a) is prevented from cross-examining a witness in person; and
      (b) should arrange for a legal representative to act for him for the purpose of cross-examining the witness.
   (3) The accused shall notify the court officer within 7 days of the court giving its explanation, or within such other period as the court may in any particular case allow, of the action, if any, he has taken.
   (4) Where he has arranged for a legal representative to act for him, the notification shall include details of the name and address of the representative.
   (5) The notification shall be in writing.
   (6) The court officer shall notify all other parties to the proceedings of the name and address of the person, if any, appointed to act for the accused.
   (7) Where the court gives its explanation under paragraph (2) to the accused either within 7 days of the day set for the commencement of any hearing at which a witness in respect of whom a prohibition under section 34, 35 or 36 of the 1999 Act applies may be cross-examined or after such a hearing has commenced, the period of 7 days shall be reduced in accordance with any directions issued by the court.
   (8) Where at the end of the period of 7 days or such other period as the court has allowed, the court has received no notification from the accused it may grant the accused an extension of time, whether on its own motion or on the application of the accused.
   (9) Before granting an extension of time, the court may hold a hearing at which all parties to the proceedings may attend and be heard.
   (10) Any extension of time shall be of such period as the court considers appropriate in the circumstances of the case.
   (11) The decision of the court as to whether to grant the accused an extension of time shall be notified to all parties to the proceedings by the court officer.

Appointment of legal representative by the court

31.2 (1) Where the court decides, in accordance with section 38(4) of the Youth Justice and Criminal Evidence Act 1999, to appoint a qualified legal representative, the court officer shall notify all parties to the proceedings of the name and address of the representative.

(2) An appointment made by the court under section 38(4) of the 1999 Act shall, except to such extent as the court may in any particular case determine, terminate at the conclusion of the cross-examination of the witness or witnesses in respect of whom a prohibition under section 34, 35 or 36 of the 1999 Act applies.

Appointment arranged by the accused

31.3 (1) The accused may arrange for the qualified legal representative, appointed by the court under section 38(4) of the Youth Justice and Criminal Evidence Act 1999, to be appointed to act for him for the purpose of cross-examining any witness in respect of whom a prohibition under section 34, 35 or 36 of the 1999 Act applies.

(2) Where such an appointment is made—

    (a) both the accused and the qualified legal representative appointed shall notify the court of the appointment; and

    (b) the qualified legal representative shall, from the time of his appointment, act for the accused as though the arrangement had been made under section 38(2)(a) of the 1999 Act and shall cease to be the representative of the court under section 38(4).

(3) Where the court receives notification of the appointment either from the qualified legal representative or from the accused but not from both, the court shall investigate whether the appointment has been made, and if it concludes that the appointment has not been made, paragraph (2)(b) shall not apply.

(4) An accused may, notwithstanding an appointment by the court under section 38(4) of the 1999 Act, arrange for a legal representative to act for him for the purpose of cross-examining any witness in respect of whom a prohibition under section 34, 35 or 36 of the 1999 Act applies.

(5) Where the accused arranges for, or informs the court of his intention to arrange for, a legal representative to act for him, he shall notify the court, within such period as the court may allow, of the name and address of any person appointed to act for him.

(6) Where the court is notified within the time allowed that such an appointment has been made, any qualified legal representative appointed by the court in accordance with section 38(4) of the 1999 Act shall be discharged.

(7) The court officer shall, as soon as reasonably practicable after the court receives notification of an appointment under this rule or, where paragraph (3) applies, after the court is satisfied that the appointment has been made, notify all the parties to the proceedings—

    (a) that the appointment has been made;

    (b) where paragraph (4) applies, of the name and address of the person appointed; and

    (c) that the person appointed by the court under section 38(4) of the 1999 Act has been discharged or has ceased to act for the court.

Prohibition on cross-examination of witness

31.4 (1) An application by the prosecutor for the court to give a direction under section 36 of the Youth Justice and Criminal Evidence Act 1999 in relation to any witness must be sent to the court officer and at the same time a copy thereof must be sent by the applicant to every other party to the proceedings.

(2) In his application the prosecutor must state why, in his opinion—

    (a) the evidence given by the witness is likely to be diminished if cross-examination is undertaken by the accused in person;

    (b) the evidence would be improved if a direction were given under section 36(2) of the 1999 Act; and

    (c) it would not be contrary to the interests of justice to give such a direction.

(3) On receipt of the application the court officer must refer it—

    (a) if the trial has started, to the court of trial; or

(b) if the trial has not started when the application is received—
    (i) to the judge or court designated to conduct the trial, or
    (ii) if no judge or court has been designated for that purpose, to such judge or court designated for the purposes of hearing that application.

(4) Where a copy of the application is received by a party to the proceedings more than 14 days before the date set for the trial to begin, that party may make observations in writing on the application to the court officer, but any such observations must be made within 14 days of the receipt of the application and be copied to the other parties to the proceedings.

(5) A party to whom an application is sent in accordance with paragraph (1) who wishes to oppose the application must give his reasons for doing so to the court officer and the other parties to the proceedings.

(6) Those reasons must be notified—
    (a) within 14 days of the date the application was served on him, if that date is more than 14 days before the date set for the trial to begin;
    (b) if the trial has begun, in accordance with any directions issued by the court; or
    (c) if neither paragraph (6)(a) nor (b) applies, before the date set for the trial to begin.

(7) Where the application made in accordance with paragraph (1) is made before the date set for the trial to begin and—
    (a) is not contested by any party to the proceedings, the court may determine the application without a hearing;
    (b) is contested by a party to the proceedings, the court must direct a hearing of the application.

(8) Where the application is made after the trial has begun—
    (a) the application may be made orally; and
    (b) the court may give such directions as it considers appropriate to deal with the application.

(9) Where a hearing of the application is to take place, the court officer shall notify each party to the proceedings of the time and place of the hearing.

(10) A party notified in accordance with paragraph (9) may be present at the hearing and be heard.

(11) The court officer must, as soon as possible after the determination of an application made in accordance with paragraph (1), give notice of the decision and the reasons for it to all the parties to the proceedings.

(12) A person making an oral application under paragraph (8)(a) must—
    (a) give reasons why the application was not made before the trial commenced; and
    (b) provide the court with the information set out in paragraph (2).

PART 32   INTERNATIONAL CO-OPERATION

Notice required to accompany process served outside the United Kingdom and translations

32.1 (1) The notice which by virtue of section 3(4)(b) of the Crime (International Co-operation) Act 2003 (general requirements for service of process) must accompany any process served outside the United Kingdom must give the information specified in paragraphs (2) and (4) below.

(2) The notice must—
    (a) state that the person required by the process to appear as a party or attend as a witness can obtain information about his rights in connection therewith from the relevant authority; and
    (b) give the particulars specified in paragraph (4) about that authority.

(3) The relevant authority where the process is served—
    (a) at the request of the prosecuting authority, is that authority; or
    (b) at the request of the defendant or the prosecutor in the case of a private prosecution, is the court by which the process is served.

(4) The particulars referred to in paragraph (2) are—

    (a) the name and address of the relevant authority, together with its telephone and fax numbers and e-mail address; and

    (b) the name of a person at the relevant authority who can provide the information referred to in paragraph (2)(a), together with his telephone and fax numbers and e-mail address.

(5) The justices' clerk or Crown Court officer must send, together with any process served outside the United Kingdom—

    (a) any translation which is provided under section 3(3)(b) of the 2003 Act; and

    (b) any translation of the information required to be given by this rule which is provided to him.

(6) In this rule 'process' has the same meaning as in section 51(3) of the 2003 Act.

Proof of service outside the United Kingdom

32.2 (1) A statement in a certificate given by or on behalf of the Secretary of State—

    (a) that process has been served on any person under section 4(1) of the Crime (International Co-operation) Act 2003 (service of process otherwise than by post);

    (b) of the manner in which service was effected; and

    (c) of the date on which process was served;

    shall be admissible as evidence of any facts so stated.

  (2) In this rule 'process' has the same meaning as in section 51(3) of the 2003 Act.

Supply of copy of notice of request for assistance abroad

32.3 Where a request for assistance under section 7 of the Crime (International Co-operation) Act 2003 is made by a justice of the peace or a judge exercising the jurisdiction of the Crown Court and is sent in accordance with section 8(1) of the 2003 Act, the justices' clerk or the Crown Court officer shall send a copy of the letter of request to the Secretary of State as soon as practicable after the request has been made.

Persons entitled to appear and take part in proceedings before a nominated court, and exclusion of public

32.4 A court nominated under section 15(1) of the Crime (International Co-operation) Act 2003 (nominating a court to receive evidence) may—

    (a) determine who may appear or take part in the proceedings under Schedule 1 to the 2003 Act before the court and whether a party to the proceedings is entitled to be legally represented; and

    (b) direct that the public be excluded from those proceedings if it thinks it necessary to do so in the interests of justice.

Record of proceedings to receive evidence before a nominated court

32.5 (1) Where a court is nominated under section 15(1) of the Crime (International Co-operation) Act 2003 the justices' clerk or Crown Court officer shall enter in an overseas record—

    (a) details of the request in respect of which the notice under section 15(1) of the 2003 Act was given;

    (b) the date on which, and place at which, the proceedings under Schedule 1 to the 2003 Act in respect of that request took place;

    (c) the name of any witness who gave evidence at the proceedings in question;

    (d) the name of any person who took part in the proceedings as a legal representative or an interpreter;

    (e) whether a witness was required to give evidence on oath or (by virtue of section 5 of the Oaths Act 1978) after making a solemn affirmation; and

    (f) whether the opportunity to cross-examine any witness was refused.

(2) When the court gives the evidence received by it under paragraph 6(1) of Schedule 1 to the 2003 Act to the court or authority that made the request or to the territorial authority for forwarding to the court or authority that made the request, the justices' clerk or Crown Court officer shall send to the court, authority or territorial authority (as the case may be) a copy of an extract of so much of the overseas record as relates to the proceedings in respect of that request.

Interpreter for the purposes of proceedings involving a television or telephone link

32.6　(1) This rule applies where a court is nominated under section 30(3) (hearing witnesses in the UK through television links) or section 31(4) (hearing witnesses in the UK by telephone) of the Crime (International Co-operation) Act 2003.

(2) Where it appears to the justices' clerk or the Crown Court officer that the witness to be heard in the proceedings under Part 1 or 2 of Schedule 2 to the 2003 Act ('the relevant proceedings') is likely to give evidence in a language other than English, he shall make arrangements for an interpreter to be present at the proceedings to translate what is said into English.

(3) Where it appears to the justices' clerk or the Crown Court officer that the witness to be heard in the relevant proceedings is likely to give evidence in a language other than that in which the proceedings of the court referred to in section 30(1) or, as the case may be, 31(1) of the 2003 Act ('the external court') will be conducted, he shall make arrangements for an interpreter to be present at the relevant proceedings to translate what is said into the language in which the proceedings of the external court will be conducted.

(4) Where the evidence in the relevant proceedings is either given in a language other than English or is not translated into English by an interpreter, the court shall adjourn the proceedings until such time as an interpreter can be present to provide a translation into English.

(5) Where a court in Wales understands Welsh—

(a) paragraph (2) does not apply where it appears to the justices' clerk or Crown Court officer that the witness in question is likely to give evidence in Welsh;

(b) paragraph (4) does not apply where the evidence is given in Welsh; and

(c) any translation which is provided pursuant to paragraph (2) or (4) may be into Welsh instead of English.

Record of television link hearing before a nominated court

32.7　(1) This rule applies where a court is nominated under section 30(3) of the Crime (International Co-operation) Act 2003.

(2) The justices' clerk or Crown Court officer shall enter in an overseas record—

(a) details of the request in respect of which the notice under section 30(3) of the 2003 Act was given;

(b) the date on which, and place at which, the proceedings under Part 1 of Schedule 2 to that Act in respect of that request took place;

(c) the technical conditions, such as the type of equipment used, under which the proceedings took place;

(d) the name of the witness who gave evidence;

(e) the name of any person who took part in the proceedings as a legal representative or an interpreter; and

(f) the language in which the evidence was given.

(3) As soon as practicable after the proceedings under Part 1 of Schedule 2 to the 2003 Act took place, the justices' clerk or Crown Court officer shall send to the external authority that made the request a copy of an extract of so much of the overseas record as relates to the proceedings in respect of that request.

Record of telephone link hearing before a nominated court

32.8 (1) This rule applies where a court is nominated under section 31(4) of the Crime (International Co-operation) Act 2003.

(2) The justices' clerk or Crown Court officer shall enter in an overseas record—

(a) details of the request in respect of which the notice under section 31(4) of the 2003 Act was given;

(b) the date, time and place at which the proceedings under Part 2 of Schedule 2 to the 2003 Act took place;

(c) the name of the witness who gave evidence;

(d) the name of any interpreter who acted at the proceedings; and

(e) the language in which the evidence was given.

Overseas record

32.9 (1) The overseas records of a magistrates' court shall be part of the register (within the meaning of section 150(1) of the Magistrates' Courts Act 1980).

(2) The overseas records of any court shall not be open to inspection by any person except—

(a) as authorised by the Secretary of State; or

(b) with the leave of the court.

Overseas freezing orders

32.10 (1) This rule applies where a court is nominated under section 21(1) of the Crime (International Co-operation) Act 2003 to give effect to an overseas freezing order.

(2) Where the Secretary of State serves a copy of such an order on the court officer—

(a) the general rule is that the court will consider the order no later than the next business day;

(b) exceptionally, the court may consider the order later than that, but not more than 5 business days after service.

(3) The court must not consider the order unless—

(a) it is satisfied that the chief officer of police for the area in which the evidence is situated has had notice of the order; and

(b) that chief officer of police has had an opportunity to make representations, at a hearing if that officer wants.

(4) The court may consider the order—

(a) without a hearing; or

(b) at a hearing, in public or in private.

PART 33   EXPERT EVIDENCE

Reference to expert

33.1 A reference to an 'expert' in this Part is a reference to a person who is required to give or prepare expert evidence for the purpose of criminal proceedings, including evidence required to determine fitness to plead or for the purpose of sentencing.

Expert's duty to the court

33.2 (1) An expert must help the court to achieve the overriding objective by giving objective, unbiased opinion on matters within his expertise.

(2) This duty overrides any obligation to the person from whom he receives instructions or by whom he is paid.

(3) This duty includes an obligation to inform all parties and the court if the expert's opinion changes from that contained in a report served as evidence or given in a statement.

Content of expert's report

33.3 (1) An expert's report must—

(a) give details of the expert's qualifications, relevant experience and accreditation;

(b) give details of any literature or other information which the expert has relied on in making the report;

(c) contain a statement setting out the substance of all facts given to the expert which are material to the opinions expressed in the report or upon which those opinions are based;

(d) make clear which of the facts stated in the report are within the expert's own knowledge;

(e) say who carried out any examination, measurement, test or experiment which the expert has used for the report and—

  (i) give the qualifications, relevant experience and accreditation of that person,

  (ii) say whether or not the examination, measurement, test or experiment was carried out under the expert's supervision, and

  (iii) summarise the findings on which the expert relies;

(f) where there is a range of opinion on the matters dealt with in the report—

  (i) summarise the range of opinion, and

  (ii) give reasons for his own opinion;

(g) if the expert is not able to give his opinion without qualification, state the qualification;

(h) contain a summary of the conclusions reached;

(i) contain a statement that the expert understands his duty to the court, and has complied and will continue to comply with that duty; and

(j) contain the same declaration of truth as a witness statement.

(2) Only sub-paragraphs (i) and (j) of rule 33.3(1) apply to a summary by an expert of his conclusions served in advance of that expert's report.

Service of expert evidence

33.4 (1) A party who wants to introduce expert evidence must—

  (a) serve it on—

    (i) the court officer, and

    (ii) each other party;

  (b) serve it—

    (i) as soon as practicable, and in any event

    (ii) with any application in support of which that party relies on that evidence; and

  (c) if another party so requires, give that party a copy of, or a reasonable opportunity to inspect—

    (i) a record of any examination, measurement, test or experiment on which the expert's findings and opinion are based, or that were carried out in the course of reaching those findings and opinion, and

    (ii) anything on which any such examination, measurement, test or experiment was carried out.

(2) A party may not introduce expert evidence if that party has not complied with this rule, unless—

  (a) every other party agrees; or

  (b) the court gives permission.

Expert to be informed of service of report

33.5 A party who serves on another party or on the court a report by an expert must, at once, inform that expert of that fact.

Pre-hearing discussion of expert evidence

33.6 (1) This rule applies where more than one party wants to introduce expert evidence.

(2) The court may direct the experts to—

  (a) discuss the expert issues in the proceedings; and

  (b) prepare a statement for the court of the matters on which they agree and disagree, giving their reasons.

(3) Except for that statement, the content of that discussion must not be referred to without the court's permission.

Failure to comply with directions

[The former r. 33.7 was not reproduced in the new part 33 having effect from 5 October 2009.]

Court's power to direct that evidence is to be given by a single joint expert

33.7 (1) Where more than one defendant wants to introduce expert evidence on an issue at trial, the court may direct that the evidence on that issue is to be given by one expert only.
   (2) Where the co-defendants cannot agree who should be the expert, the court may—
      (a) select the expert from a list prepared or identified by them; or
      (b) direct that the expert be selected in another way.

Instructions to a single joint expert

33.8 (1) Where the court gives a direction under rule 33.7 for a single joint expert to be used, each of the co-defendants may give instructions to the expert.
   (2) When a co-defendant gives instructions to the expert he must, at the same time, send a copy of the instructions to the other co-defendant(s).
   (3) The court may give directions about—
      (a) the payment of the expert's fees and expenses; and
      (b) any examination, measurement, test or experiment which the expert wishes to carry out.
   (4) The court may, before an expert is instructed, limit the amount that can be paid by way of fees and expenses to the expert.
   (5) Unless the court otherwise directs, the instructing co-defendants are jointly and severally liable for the payment of the expert's fees and expenses.

Court's power to vary requirements under this Part

33.9 (1) The court may—
      (a) extend (even after it has expired) a time limit under this Part;
      (b) allow the introduction of expert evidence which omits a detail required by this Part.
   (2) A party who wants an extension of time must—
      (a) apply when serving the expert evidence for which it is required; and
      (b) explain the delay.

PART 34   HEARSAY EVIDENCE

When this Part applies

34.1 This Part applies—
   (a) in a magistrates' court and in the Crown Court;
   (b) where a party wants to introduce hearsay evidence, within the meaning of section 114 of the Criminal Justice Act 2003.

Notice to introduce hearsay evidence

34.2 (1) This rule applies where a party wants to introduce hearsay evidence for admission under any of the following sections of the Criminal Justice Act 2003—
      (a) section 114(1)(d) (evidence admissible in the interests of justice);
      (b) section 116 (evidence where a witness is unavailable);
      (c) section 121 (multiple hearsay).
   (2) That party must—
      (a) serve notice on—
         (i) the court officer, and
         (ii) each other party;
      (b) in the notice—
         (i) identify the evidence that is hearsay,

       (ii)   set out any facts on which that party relies to make the evidence admissible,

       (iii) explain how that party will prove those facts if another party disputes them, and

       (iv) explain why the evidence is admissible; and

   (c) attach to the notice any statement or other document containing the evidence that has not already been served.

(3) A prosecutor who wants to introduce such evidence must serve the notice not more than 14 days after the defendant pleads not guilty.

(4) A defendant who wants to introduce such evidence must serve the notice as soon as reasonably practicable.

(5) A party entitled to receive a notice under this rule may waive that entitlement by so informing—

   (a) the party who would have served it; and

   (b) the court.

Opposing the introduction of hearsay evidence

34.3 (1) This rule applies where a party objects to the introduction of hearsay evidence.

     (2) That party must—

   (a) apply to the court to determine the objection;

   (b) serve the application on—

       (i)   the court officer, and

       (ii) each other party;

   (c) serve the application as soon as reasonably practicable, and in any event not more than 14 days after—

       (i)   service of notice to introduce the evidence under rule 34.2,

       (ii) service of the evidence to which that party objects, if no notice is required by that rule, or

       (iii) the defendant pleads not guilty

      whichever of those events happens last; and

   (d) in the application, explain—

       (i)   which, if any, facts set out in a notice under rule 34.2 that party disputes,

       (ii) why the evidence is not admissible,

       (iii) any other objection to the application.

     (3) The court—

   (a) may determine an application—

       (i)   at a hearing, in public or in private, or

       (ii) without a hearing;

   (b) must not determine the application unless the party who served the notice—

       (i)   is present, or

       (ii) has had a reasonable opportunity to respond;

   (c) may adjourn the application; and

   (d) may discharge or vary a determination where it can do so under—

       (i)   section 8B of the Magistrates' Courts Act 1980 (ruling at pre-trial hearing in a magistrates' court), or

       (ii) section 9 of the Criminal Justice Act 1987, or section 31 or 40 of the Criminal Procedure and Investigations Act 1996 (ruling at preparatory or other pre-trial hearing in the Crown Court).

Unopposed hearsay evidence

34.4 (1) This rule applies where—

   (a) a party has served notice to introduce hearsay evidence under rule 34.2; and

   (b) no other party has applied to the court to determine an objection to the introduction of the evidence.

     (2) The court will treat the evidence as if it were admissible by agreement.

Court's power to vary requirements under this Part

34.5 (1) The court may—
    (a) shorten or extend (even after it has expired) a time limit under this Part;
    (b) allow an application or notice to be given in a different form to one set out in the Practice Direction, or to be made or given orally; or
    (c) dispense with the requirement for notice to introduce hearsay evidence.
    (2) A party who wants an extension of time must—
    (a) apply when serving the application or notice for which it is needed; and
    (b) explain the delay.

PART 35   Evidence of Bad Character

When this Part applies

35.1 This Part applies—
    (a) in a magistrates' court and in the Crown Court;
    (b) where a party wants to introduce evidence of bad character, within the meaning of section 98 of the Criminal Justice Act 2003.

Content of application or notice

35.2 (1) A party who wants to introduce evidence of bad character must—
    (a) make an application under rule 35.3, where it is evidence of a non-defendant's bad character;
    (b) give notice under rule 35.4, where it is evidence of a defendant's bad character; and
    (2) An application or notice must—
    (a) set out the facts of the misconduct on which that party relies,
    (b) explain how that party will prove those facts (whether by certificate of conviction, other official record, or other evidence), if another party disputes them, and
    (c) explain why the evidence is admissible.

Application to introduce evidence of a non-defendant's bad character

35.3 (1) This rule applies where a party wants to introduce evidence of the bad character of a person other than the defendant.
    (2) That party must serve an application to do so on—
    (a) the court officer; and
    (b) each other party.
    (3) The applicant must serve the application—
    (a) as soon as reasonably practicable; and in any event
    (b) not more than 14 days after the prosecutor discloses material on which the application is based (if the prosecutor is not the applicant).
    (4) A party who objects to the introduction of the evidence must—
    (a) serve notice on—
        (i) the court officer, and
        (ii) each other party
    not more than 14 days after service of the application; and
    (b) in the notice explain, as applicable—
        (i) which, if any, facts of the misconduct set out in the application that party disputes,
        (ii) what, if any, facts of the misconduct that party admits instead,
        (iii) why the evidence is not admissible, and
        (iv) any other objection to the application.
    (5) The court—
    (a) may determine an application—
        (i) at a hearing, in public or in private, or
        (ii) without a hearing;

(b) must not determine the application unless each party other than the applicant—
   (i)   is present, or
   (ii) has had at least 14 days in which to serve a notice of objection;
(c) may adjourn the application; and
(d) may discharge or vary a determination where it can do so under—
   (i)   section 8B of the Magistrates' Courts Act 1980 (ruling at pre-trial hearing in a magistrates' court), or
   (ii) section 9 of the Criminal Justice Act 1987, or section 31 or 40 of the Criminal Procedure and Investigations Act 1996 (ruling at preparatory or other pre-trial hearing in the Crown Court).

Notice to introduce evidence of a defendant's bad character

35.4 (1) This rule applies where a party wants to introduce evidence of a defendant's bad character.
      (2) That party must serve notice on—
         (a) the court officer; and
         (b) each other party.
      (3) A prosecutor who wants to introduce such evidence must serve the notice not more than 14 days after the defendant pleads not guilty.
      (4) A co-defendant who wants to introduce such evidence must serve the notice—
         (a) as soon as reasonably practicable; and in any event
         (b) not more than 14 days after the prosecutor discloses material on which the notice is based.
      (5) A party who objects to the introduction of the evidence must—
         (a) apply to the court to determine the objection;
         (b) serve the application on—
            (i) the court officer, and
            (ii) each other party
            not more than 14 days after service of the notice; and
         (c) in the application explain, as applicable—
            (i)   which, if any, facts of the misconduct set out in the notice that party disputes,
            (ii) what, if any, facts of the misconduct that party admits instead,
            (iii) why the evidence is not admissible,
            (iv) why it would be unfair to admit the evidence, and
            (v)   any other objection to the notice.
      (6) The court—
         (a) may determine an application—
            (i) at a hearing, in public or in private, or
            (ii) without a hearing;
         (b) must not determine the application unless the party who served the notice—
            (i) is present, or
            (ii) has had a reasonable opportunity to respond;
         (c) may adjourn the application; and
         (d) may discharge or vary a determination where it can do so under—
            (i) section 8B of the Magistrates' Courts Act 1980 (ruling at pre-trial hearing in a magistrates' court), or
            (ii) section 9 of the Criminal Justice Act 1987, or section 31 or 40 of the Criminal Procedure and Investigations Act 1996 (ruling at preparatory or other pre-trial hearing in the Crown Court).
      (7) A party entitled to receive a notice may waive that entitlement by so informing—
         (a) the party who would have served it; and
         (b) the court.

Reasons for decisions

35.5   The court must announce at a hearing in public (but in the absence of the jury, if there is one) the reasons for a decision—
(a) to admit evidence as evidence of bad character, or to refuse to do so; or
(b) to direct an acquittal or a retrial under section 107 of the Criminal Justice Act 2003.

Court's power to vary requirements under this Part

35.6   (1) The court may—
(a) shorten or extend (even after it has expired) a time limit under this Part;
(b) allow an application or notice to be in a different form to one set out in the Practice Direction, or to be made or given orally;
(c) dispense with a requirement for notice to introduce evidence of a defendant's bad character.
(2) A party who wants an extension of time must—
(a) apply when serving the application or notice for which it is needed; and
(b) explain the delay.

PART 36   EVIDENCE OF A COMPLAINANT'S PREVIOUS SEXUAL BEHAVIOUR

When this Part applies

36.1   This Part applies in magistrates' courts and in the Crown Court where a defendant wants to—
(a) introduce evidence; or
(b) cross-examine a witness
about a complainant's sexual behaviour despite the prohibition in section 41 of the Youth Justice and Criminal Evidence Act 1999.

Application for permission to introduce evidence or cross-examine

36.2   The defendant must apply for permission to do so—
(a) in writing; and
(b) not more than 28 days after the prosecutor has complied or purported to comply with section 3 of the Criminal Procedure and Investigations Act 1996 (disclosure by prosecutor).

Content of application

36.3   The application must—
(a) identify the issue to which the defendant says the complainant's sexual behaviour is relevant;
(b) give particulars of—
(i) any evidence that the defendant wants to introduce, and
(ii) any questions that the defendant wants to ask;
(c) identify the exception to the prohibition in section 41 of the Youth Justice and Criminal Evidence Act 1999 on which the defendant relies; and
(d) give the name and date of birth of any witness whose evidence about the complainant's sexual behaviour the defendant wants to introduce.

Service of application

36.4   The defendant must serve the application on the court officer and all other parties.

Reply to application

36.5   A party who wants to make representations about an application under rule 36.2 must—
(a) do so in writing not more than 14 days after receiving it; and
(b) serve those representations on the court officer and all other parties.

Application for special measures

36.6 If the court allows an application under rule 36.2 then—

(a) a party may apply not more than 14 days later for a special measures direction or for the variation of an existing special measures direction; and

(b) the court may shorten the time for opposing that application.

Court's power to vary requirements under this Part

36.7 The court may shorten or extend (even after it has expired) a time limit under this Part.

PART 37   TRIAL AND SENTENCE IN A MAGISTRATES' COURT

When this Part applies

37.1 (1) This Part applies in a magistrates' court where—

(a) the court tries a case; or

(b) the defendant pleads guilty.

(2) Where the defendant is under 18, in this Part—

(a) a reference to convicting the defendant includes a reference to finding the defendant guilty of an offence; and

(b) a reference to sentence includes a reference to an order made on a finding of guilt.

General rules

37.2 (1) Where this Part applies—

(a) the general rule is that the hearing must be in public; but

(b) the court may exercise any power it has to—

(i) impose reporting restrictions,

(ii) withhold information from the public, or

(iii) order a hearing in private; and

(c) unless the court otherwise directs, only the following may attend a hearing in a youth court—

(i) the parties and their legal representatives,

(ii) a defendant's parents, guardian or other supporting adult,

(iii) a witness,

(iv) anyone else directly concerned in the case, and

(v) a representative of a news-gathering or reporting organisation.

(2) Unless already done, the justices' legal adviser or the court must—

(a) read the allegation of the offence to the defendant;

(b) explain, in terms the defendant can understand (with help, if necessary)—

(i) the allegation, and

(ii) what the procedure at the hearing will be;

(c) ask whether the defendant has been advised about the potential effect on sentence of a guilty plea;

(d) ask whether the defendant pleads guilty or not guilty; and

(e) take the defendant's plea.

(3) The court may adjourn the hearing—

(a) at any stage, to the same or to another magistrates' court; or

(b) to a youth court, where the court is not itself a youth court and the defendant is under 18.

Procedure on plea of not guilty

37.3 (1) This rule applies—

(a) if the defendant has—

(i) entered a plea of not guilty, or

(ii) not entered a plea; or

(b) if, in either case, it appears to the court that there may be grounds for making a hospital order without convicting the defendant.

(2) If a not guilty plea was taken on a previous occasion, the justices' legal adviser or the court must ask the defendant to confirm that plea.

(3) In the following sequence—

    (a) the prosecutor may summarise the prosecution case, identifying the relevant law and facts;

    (b) the prosecutor must introduce the evidence on which the prosecution case relies;

    (c) at the conclusion of the prosecution case, on the defendant's application or on its own initiative, the court—

        (i) may acquit on the ground that the prosecution evidence is insufficient for any reasonable court properly to convict, but

        (ii) must not do so unless the prosecutor has had an opportunity to make representations;

    (d) the justices' legal adviser or the court must explain, in terms the defendant can understand (with help, if necessary)—

        (i) the right to give evidence, and

        (ii) the potential effect of not doing so at all, or of refusing to answer a question while doing so;

    (e) the defendant may introduce evidence;

    (f) a party may introduce further evidence if it is then admissible (for example, because it is in rebuttal of evidence already introduced);

    (g) the prosecutor may make final representations in support of the prosecution case, where—

        (i) the defendant is represented by a legal representative, or

        (ii) whether represented or not, the defendant has introduced evidence other than his or her own; and

    (h) the defendant may make final representations in support of the defence case.

(4) Where a party wants to introduce evidence or make representations after that party's opportunity to do so under paragraph (3), the court—

    (a) may refuse to receive any such evidence or representations; and

    (b) must not receive any such evidence or representations after it has announced its verdict.

(5) If the court—

    (a) convicts the defendant; or

    (b) makes a hospital order instead of doing so,

   it must give sufficient reasons to explain its decision.

(6) If the court acquits the defendant, it may—

    (a) give an explanation of its decision; and

    (b) exercise any power it has to make—

        (i) a civil behaviour order,

        (ii) a costs order.

Evidence of a witness in person

37.4   (1) This rule applies where a party wants to introduce evidence by calling a witness to give that evidence in person.

    (2) Unless the court otherwise directs—

    (a) a witness waiting to give evidence must not wait inside the courtroom, unless that witness is—

        (i) a party, or

        (ii) an expert witness;

    (b) a witness who gives evidence in the courtroom must do so from the place provided for that purpose; and

    (c) a witness' address must not be announced unless it is relevant to an issue in the case.

(3) Unless other legislation otherwise provides, before giving evidence a witness must take an oath or affirm.

(4) In the following sequence—

    (a) the party who calls a witness must ask questions in examination-in-chief;

    (b) every other party may ask questions in cross-examination;

    (c) the party who called the witness may ask questions in re-examination;

    (d) at any time while giving evidence, a witness may refer to a record of that witness' recollection of events, if other legislation so permits;

    (e) the party who calls a witness, in examination-in-chief may ask that witness to adopt all or part of such a record as part of that witness' evidence, but only if—

        (i) the parties agree, and

        (ii) the court so permits;

    (f) if the witness adopts any part of such a record—

        (i) that part must be read aloud, or

        (ii) with the court's permission, its contents may be summarised aloud.

(5) The justices' legal adviser or the court may—

    (a) ask a witness questions; and in particular

    (b) where the defendant is not represented, ask any question necessary in the defendant's interests.

Evidence by written statement

37.5 (1) This rule applies where a party introduces in evidence the written statement of a witness.

    (2) The party introducing the statement must read or summarise aloud those parts that are relevant to the issues in the case.

Evidence by admission

37.6 (1) This rule applies where—

    (a) a party introduces in evidence a fact admitted by another party; or

    (b) parties jointly admit a fact.

    (2) Unless the court otherwise directs, a written record must be made of the admission.

Procedure on plea of guilty

37.7 (1) This rule applies if—

    (a) the defendant pleads guilty; and

    (b) the court is satisfied that the plea represents a clear acknowledgement of guilt.

    (2) The court may convict the defendant without receiving evidence.

Written guilty plea: special rules

37.8 (1) This rule applies where—

    (a) the offence alleged—

        (i) can be tried only in a magistrates' court, and

        (ii) is not one specified under section 12(1)(a) of the Magistrates' Courts Act 1980;

    (b) the defendant is at least 16 years old;

    (c) the prosecutor has served on the defendant—

        (i) the summons or requisition,

        (ii) the material on which the prosecutor relies to set out the facts of the offence and to provide information relevant to sentence,

        (iii) a notice that the procedure set out in this rule applies, and

        (iv) a notice for the defendant's use if the defendant wants to plead guilty without attending court; and

    (d) the prosecutor has served on the court officer—

        (i) copies of those documents, and

        (ii) a certificate of service of those documents on the defendant.

(2) A defendant who wants to plead guilty without attending court must, before the hearing date specified in the summons or requisition—

    (a) serve a notice of guilty plea on the court officer; and

    (b) include with that notice any representations that the defendant wants the court to consider on that date.

(3) A defendant who wants to withdraw such a notice must notify the court officer in writing before the hearing date.

(4) The court may accept such a guilty plea on the hearing date, and if it does so must take account only of—

    (a) the material served by the prosecutor on the defendant under this rule; and

    (b) any representations by the defendant.

(5) With the defendant's agreement, the court may deal with the case in the same way as under paragraph (4) where the defendant—

    (a) is present; and

    (b) has served a notice of guilty plea under paragraph (2); or

    (c) pleads guilty there and then.

Application to withdraw a guilty plea

37.9 (1) This rule applies where the defendant wants to withdraw a guilty plea.

    (2) The defendant must apply to do so—

        (a) as soon as practicable after becoming aware of the reasons for doing so; and

        (b) before sentence.

    (3) Unless the court otherwise directs, the application must be in writing and the defendant must serve it on—

        (a) the court officer; and

        (b) the prosecutor.

    (4) The application must—

        (a) explain why it would be unjust not to allow the defendant to withdraw the guilty plea;

        (b) identify—

            (i) any witness that the defendant wants to call, and

            (ii) any other proposed evidence; and

        (c) say whether the defendant waives legal professional privilege, giving any relevant name and date.

Procedure if the court convicts

37.10 (1) This rule applies if the court convicts the defendant.

    (2) The court—

        (a) may exercise its power to require—

            (i) a statement of the defendant's financial circumstances,

            (ii) a pre-sentence report; and

        (b) may (and in some circumstances must) remit the defendant to a youth court for sentence where—

            (i) the defendant is under 18, and

            (ii) the convicting court is not itself a youth court.

    (3) The prosecutor must—

        (a) summarise the prosecution case, if the sentencing court has not heard evidence;

        (b) identify any offence to be taken into consideration in sentencing;

        (c) provide information relevant to sentence; and

        (d) where it is likely to assist the court, identify any other matter relevant to sentence, including—

            (i) aggravating and mitigating factors,

            (ii) the legislation applicable, and

            (iii) any sentencing guidelines or guideline cases.

(4) The defendant must provide information relevant to sentence, including details of financial circumstances.

(5) Where the defendant pleads guilty but wants to be sentenced on a different basis to that disclosed by the prosecution case—

    (a) the defendant must set out that basis in writing, identifying what is in dispute;

    (b) the court may invite the parties to make representations about whether the dispute is material to sentence; and

    (c) if the court decides that it is a material dispute, the court will—

        (i) invite such further representations or evidence as it may require, and

        (ii) decide the dispute.

(6) Where the court has power to order the endorsement of the defendant's driving licence, or power to order the disqualification of the defendant from holding or obtaining one—

    (a) if other legislation so permits, a defendant who wants the court not to exercise that power must introduce the evidence or information on which the defendant relies;

    (b) the prosecutor may introduce evidence; and

    (c) the parties may make representations about that evidence or information.

(7) Before the court passes sentence—

    (a) the court must—

        (i) give the defendant an opportunity to make representations and introduce evidence relevant to sentence, and

        (ii) where the defendant is under 18, give the defendant's parents, guardian or other supporting adult, if present, such an opportunity as well; and

    (b) the justices' legal adviser or the court must elicit any further information relevant to sentence that the court may require.

(8) If the court requires more information, it may exercise its power to adjourn the hearing for not more than—

    (a) 3 weeks at a time, if the defendant will be in custody; or

    (b) 4 weeks at a time.

(9) When the court has taken into account all the evidence, information and any report available, the general rule is that the court will—

    (a) pass sentence there and then;

    (b) explain the sentence, the reasons for it, and its effect, in terms the defendant can understand (with help, if necessary); and

    (c) consider exercising any power it has to make a costs or other order.

(10) Despite the general rule—

    (a) the court must adjourn the hearing if—

        (i) the case started with a summons or requisition, and the defendant is absent, and

        (ii) the court considers passing a custodial sentence, or

        (iii) the court considers imposing a disqualification (unless it has already adjourned the hearing to give the defendant an opportunity to attend);

    (b) the court may exercise any power it has to—

        (i) commit the defendant to the Crown Court for sentence (and in some cases it must do so), or

        (ii) defer sentence for up to 6 months.

Procedure where a party is absent

37.11 (1) This rule—

    (a) applies where a party is absent; but

    (b) does not apply where the defendant has served a notice of guilty plea under rule 37.8 (written guilty plea: special rules).

(2) Where the prosecutor is absent, the court may—

    (a) if it has received evidence, deal with the case as if the prosecutor were present; and

(b) in any other case—
   (i) enquire into the reasons for the prosecutor's absence, and
   (ii) if satisfied there is no good reason, exercise its power to dismiss the allegation.
(3) Where the defendant is absent—
   (a) the general rule is that the court will proceed as if the defendant—
       (i) were present, and
       (ii) had pleaded not guilty (unless a plea already has been taken)
       and the court must give reasons if it does not do so; but
   (b) the general rule does not apply if the defendant is under 18;
   (c) the general rule is subject to the court being satisfied that—
       (i) any summons or requisition was served on the defendant a reasonable time
            before the hearing, or
       (ii) in a case in which the hearing has been adjourned, the defendant had reason-
            able notice of where and when it would resume;
   (d) the general rule is subject also to rule 37.10(10)(a) (restrictions on passing sentence
       in the defendant's absence); and
   (e) the hearing must be treated as if it had not taken place at all if—
       (i)   the case started with a summons or requisition,
       (ii) the defendant makes a statutory declaration of not having found out about
             the case until after the hearing began, and
       (iii) the defendant serves that declaration on the court officer not more than 21
             days after the date of finding out about the case, unless the court extends that
             time limit.
(4) Where the defendant is absent, the court—
   (a) must exercise its power to issue a warrant for the defendant's arrest, if it passes a
       custodial sentence; and
   (b) may exercise its power to do so in any other case, if it does not apply the general
       rule in paragraph (3)(a) of this rule about proceeding in the defendant's absence.

Provision of documents for the court

37.12 (1) This rule applies where a party—
   (a) introduces in evidence any document; or
   (b) relies on any other document in the presentation of that party's case.
   (2) Unless the court otherwise directs, that party must supply sufficient copies of such a
       document for—
   (a) each other party;
   (b) the court; and
   (c) the justices' legal adviser.

Place of trial

37.13 (1) Unless the court otherwise directs, the hearing must take place in a courtroom pro-
          vided by the Lord Chancellor.
   (2) Where the hearing takes place in Wales—
   (a) any party or witness may use the Welsh language; and
   (b) if practicable, at least one member of the court must be Welsh-speaking.

Duty of justices' legal adviser

37.14 (1) A justices' legal adviser must attend, unless the court—
   (a) includes a District Judge (Magistrates' Courts); and
   (b) otherwise directs.
   (2) A justices' legal adviser must—
   (a) give the court legal advice; and
   (b) if necessary, attend the members of the court outside the courtroom to give such
       advice; but

    (c) inform the parties of any such advice given outside the courtroom.

(3) A justices' legal adviser must—

    (a) assist an unrepresented defendant;

    (b) assist the court by—

        (i) making a note of the substance of any oral evidence or representations, to help the court recall that information,

        (ii) if the court rules inadmissible part of a written statement introduced in evidence, marking that statement in such a way as to make that clear,

        (iii) ensuring that an adequate record is kept of the court's decisions and the reasons for them, and

        (iv) making any announcement, other than of the verdict or sentence.

(4) Where the defendant has served a notice of guilty plea to which rule 37.8 (written guilty plea: special rules) applies, a justices' legal adviser must read aloud to the court—

    (a) the material on which the prosecutor relies to set out the facts of the offence and to provide information relevant to sentence (or summarise any written statement included in that material, if the court so directs); and

    (b) any written representations by the defendant.

Duty of court officer

37.15 The court officer must—

    (a) serve on each party notice of where and when an adjourned hearing will resume, unless—

        (i) the party was present when that was arranged, or

        (ii) the defendant has served a notice of guilty plea to which rule 37.8 applies, and the adjournment is for not more than 4 weeks;

    (b) if the reason for the adjournment was to postpone sentence, include that reason in any such notice to the defendant;

    (c) unless the court otherwise directs, make available to the parties any written report to which rule 37.10 applies;

    (d) where the court has ordered a defendant to provide information under section 25 of the Road Traffic Offenders Act 1988, serve on the defendant notice of that order unless the defendant was present when it was made;

    (e) serve on the prosecutor—

        (i) any notice of guilty plea to which rule 37.8 applies, and

        (ii) any declaration served under rule 37.11(3)(e) that the defendant did not know about the case;

    (f) record in the magistrates' court register the court's reasons for not proceeding in the defendant's absence where rule 37.11(3)(a) applies; and

    (g) give the court such other assistance as it requires.

Part 38   [empty]

[There are currently no rules in this part]

Part 39   Trial on Indictment

Time limits for beginning of trials

39.1 The periods set out for the purposes of section 77(2)(a) and (b) of the Senior Courts Act 1981 shall be 14 days and 8 weeks respectively and accordingly the trial of a person committed by a magistrates' court—

    (a) shall not begin until the expiration of 14 days beginning with the date of his committal, except with his consent and the consent of the prosecution; and

    (b) shall, unless the Crown Court has otherwise ordered, begin not later than the expiration of 8 weeks beginning with the date of his committal.

Appeal against refusal to excuse from jury service or to defer attendance

39.2 (1) A person summoned under the Juries Act 1974 for jury service may appeal in accordance with the provisions of this rule against any refusal of the appropriate court officer to excuse him under section 9(2), or to defer his attendance under section 9A(1), of that Act.

(2) Subject to paragraph (3), an appeal under this rule shall be heard by the Crown Court.

(3) Where the appellant is summoned under the 1974 Act to attend before the High Court in Greater London the appeal shall be heard by a judge of the High Court and where the appellant is summoned under that Act to attend before the High Court outside Greater London or before a county court and the appeal has not been decided by the Crown Court before the day on which the appellant is required by the summons to attend, the appeal shall be heard by the court before which he is summoned to attend.

(4) An appeal under this rule shall be commenced by the appellant's giving notice of appeal to the appropriate court officer of the Crown Court or the High Court in Greater London, as the case may be, and such notice shall be in writing and shall specify the matters upon which the appellant relies as providing good reason why he should be excused from attending in pursuance of the summons or why his attendance should be deferred.

(5) The court shall not dismiss an appeal under this rule unless the appellant has been given an opportunity of making representations.

(6) Where an appeal under this rule is decided in the absence of the appellant, the appropriate court officer of the Crown Court or the High Court in Greater London, as the case may be, shall notify him of the decision without delay.

Application to change a plea of guilty

39.3 (1) The defendant must apply as soon as practicable after becoming aware of the grounds for making an application to change a plea of guilty, and may only do so before the final disposal of the case, by sentence or otherwise.

(2) Unless the court otherwise directs, the application must be in writing and it must—

(a) set out the reasons why it would be unjust for the guilty plea to remain unchanged;

(b) indicate what, if any, evidence the defendant wishes to call;

(c) identify any proposed witness; and

(d) indicate whether legal professional privilege is waived, specifying any material name and date.

(3) The defendant must serve the written application on—

(a) the court officer; and

(b) the prosecutor.

Part 40 Tainted Acquittals

Time of certification

40.1 Where a person is convicted of an offence as referred to in section 54(1)(b) of the Criminal Procedure and Investigations Act 1996 and it appears to the court before which the conviction has taken place that the provisions of section 54(2) are satisfied, the court shall make the certification referred to in section 54(2) at any time following conviction but no later than—

(a) immediately after the court sentences or otherwise deals with that person in respect of the offence; or

(b) where the court, being a magistrates' court, commits that person to the Crown Court, or remits him to another magistrates' court, to be dealt with in respect of the offence, immediately after he is so committed or remitted, as the case may be; or

(c) where that person is a child or young person and the court, being the Crown Court, remits him to a youth court to be dealt with in respect of the offence, immediately after he is so remitted.

Form of certification in the Crown Court

40.2   A certification referred to in section 54(2) of the Criminal Procedure and Investigations Act 1996 by the Crown Court shall be drawn up in the form set out in the Practice Direction.

Service of a copy of the certification

40.3   (1)   Where a magistrates' court or the Crown Court makes a certification as referred to in section 54(2) of the Criminal Procedure and Investigations Act 1996, the court officer shall, as soon as practicable after the drawing up of the form, serve a copy on the acquitted person referred to in the certification, on the prosecutor in the proceedings which led to the acquittal, and, where the acquittal has taken place before a court other than, or at a different place to, the court where the certification has been made, on—

(a)   the clerk of the magistrates' court before which the acquittal has taken place; or

(b)   the Crown Court officer at the place where the acquittal has taken place.

(2) to (4) [Revoked.]

Entry in register or records in relation to the conviction which occasioned certification

40.4   A clerk of a magistrates' court or an officer of a Crown Court which has made a certification under section 54(2) of the Criminal Procedure and Investigations Act 1996 shall enter in the register or records, in relation to the conviction which occasioned the certification, a note of the fact that certification has been made, the date of certification, the name of the acquitted person referred to in the certification, a description of the offence of which the acquitted person has been acquitted, the date of the acquittal, and the name of the court before which the acquittal has taken place.

Entry in the register or records in relation to the acquittal

40.5   The court officer of the court before which an acquittal has taken place shall, as soon as practicable after receipt of a copy of a form recording a certification under section 54(2) of the Criminal Procedure and Investigations Act 1996 relating to the acquittal, enter in the register or records a note that the certification has been made, the date of the certification, the name of the court which has made the certification, the name of the person whose conviction occasioned the making of the certification, and a description of the offence of which that person has been convicted. Where the certification has been made by the same court as the court before which the acquittal has occurred, sitting at the same place, the entry shall be made as soon as practicable after the making of the certification. In the case of an acquittal before a magistrates' court the entry in the register shall be signed by the clerk of the court.

Display of copy certification form

40.6   (1)   Where a court makes a certification as referred to in section 54(2) of the Criminal Procedure and Investigations Act 1996, the court officer shall, as soon as practicable after the drawing up of the form, display a copy of that form at a prominent place within court premises to which place the public has access.

(2)   Where an acquittal has taken place before a court other than, or at a different place to, the court which has made the certification under section 54(2) of the 1996 Act in relation to the acquittal, the court officer at the court where the acquittal has taken place shall, as soon as practicable after receipt of a copy of the form recording the certification, display a copy of it at a prominent place within court premises to which place the public has access.

(3)   The copy of the form referred to in paragraph (1), or the copy referred to in paragraph (2), shall continue to be displayed as referred to, respectively, in those paragraphs at least until the expiry of 28 days from, in the case of paragraph (1), the day on which the certification was made, or, in the case of paragraph (2), the day on which the copy form was received at the court.

Entry in the register or records in relation to decision of High Court

40.7 (1) The court officer at the court where an acquittal has taken place shall, on receipt from the Administrative Court Office of notice of an order made under section 54(3) of the Criminal Procedure and Investigations Act 1996 quashing the acquittal, or of a decision not to make such an order, enter in the register or records, in relation to the acquittal, a note of the fact that the acquittal has been quashed by the said order, or that a decision has been made not to make such an order, as the case may be.

(2) The court officer of the court which has made a certification under section 54(2) of the 1996 Act shall, on receipt from the Administrative Court Office of notice of an order made under section 54(3) of that Act quashing the acquittal referred to in the certification, or of a decision not to make such an order, enter in the register or records, in relation to the conviction which occasioned the certification, a note that the acquittal has been quashed by the said order, or that a decision has been made not to make such an order, as the case may be.

(3) The entries in the register of a magistrates' court referred to, respectively, in paragraphs (1) and (2) above shall be signed by the magistrates' court officer.

Display of copy of notice received from High Court

40.8 (1) Where the court officer of a court which has made a certification under section 54(2) of the Criminal Procedure and Investigations Act 1996 or before which an acquittal has occurred to which such a certification refers, receives from the Administrative Court Office notice of an order quashing the acquittal concerned, or notice of a decision not to make such an order, he shall, as soon as practicable after receiving the notice, display a copy of it at a prominent place within court premises to which place the public has access.

(2) The copy notice referred to in paragraph (1) shall continue to be displayed as referred to in that paragraph at least until the expiry of 28 days from the day on which the notice was received at the court.

Part 41   Retrial Following Acquittal for Serious Offence

Interpretation

41.1 In this Part:

'business day' means any day other than a Saturday, Sunday, Christmas Day, Good Friday or a bank holiday under the Banking and Financial Dealings Act 1971, in England and Wales; and

'section 76 application' means an application made by a prosecutor under section 76(1) or (2) of the Criminal Justice Act 2003.

Notice of a section 76 application

41.2 (1) A prosecutor who wants to make a section 76 application must serve notice of that application in the form set out in the Practice Direction on the Registrar and the acquitted person.

(2) That notice shall, where practicable, be accompanied by—

(a) relevant witness statements which are relied upon as forming new and compelling evidence of guilt of the acquitted person as well as any relevant witness statements from the original trial;

(b) any unused statements which might reasonably be considered capable of undermining the section 76 application or of assisting an acquitted person's application to oppose that application under rule 41.3;

(c) a copy of the indictment and paper exhibits from the original trial;

(d) copies of the transcript of the summing up and any other relevant transcripts from the original trial; and

(e) any other documents relied upon to support the section 76 application.

(3) The prosecutor must, as soon as practicable after service of that notice on the acquitted person, file with the Registrar a witness statement or certificate of service which exhibits a copy of that notice.

Response of the acquitted person

41.3 (1) An acquitted person who wants to oppose a section 76 application must serve a response in the form set out in the Practice Direction on the Registrar and the prosecutor which—

  (a) indicates if he is also seeking an order under section 80(6) of the Criminal Justice Act 2003 for—

    (i) the production of any document, exhibit or other thing, or

    (ii) a witness to attend for examination and to be examined before the Court of Appeal; and

  (b) exhibits any relevant documents.

(2) The acquitted person must serve that response not more than 28 days after receiving notice under rule 41.2.

(3) The Court of Appeal may extend the period for service under paragraph (2), either before or after that period expires.

Examination of witnesses or evidence by the Court of Appeal

41.4 (1) Prior to the hearing of a section 76 application, a party may apply to the Court of Appeal for an order under section 80(6) of the Criminal Justice Act 2003 for—

  (a) the production of any document, exhibit or other thing; or

  (b) a witness to attend for examination and to be examined before the Court of Appeal.

(2) An application under paragraph (1) must be in the form set out in the Practice Direction and must be sent to the Registrar and a copy sent to each party to the section 76 application.

(3) An application must set out the reasons why the order was not sought from the Court when—

  (a) the notice was served on the Registrar under rule 41.2, if the application is made by the prosecutor; or

  (b) the response was served on the Registrar under rule 41.3, if the application is made by the acquitted person.

(4) An application must be made at least 14 days before the day of the hearing of the section 76 application.

(5) If the Court of Appeal makes an order under section 80(6) of the 2003 Act on its own motion or on application from the prosecutor, it must serve notice and reasons for that order on all parties to the section 76 application.

Bail or custody hearings in the Crown Court

41.5 (1) Rules 19.18, 19.22 and 19.23 shall apply where a person is to appear or be brought before the Crown Court pursuant to sections 88 or 89 of the Criminal Justice Act 2003 (with the modification as set out in paragraph (2)), as if they were applications under rule 19.18(1).

(2) Substitute the following for Rule 19.18:

  'Where a person is to appear or be brought before the Crown Court pursuant to sections 88 or 89 of the Criminal Justice Act 2003, the prosecutor must serve notice of the need for such a hearing on the court officer.'

(3) Where a person is to appear or be brought before the Crown Court pursuant to sections 88 or 89 of the 2003 Act the Crown Court may order that the person shall be released from custody on entering into a recognizance, with or without sureties, or giving other security before—

  (a) the Crown Court officer; or

  (b) any other person authorised by virtue of section 119(1) of the Magistrates' Courts Act 1980 to take a recognizance where a magistrates' court having power to take

291

the recognizance has, instead of taking it, fixed the amount in which the principal and his sureties, if any, are to be bound.

(4) The court officer shall forward to the Registrar a copy of any record made in pursuance of section 5(1) of the Bail Act 1976.

Further provisions regarding bail and custody in the Crown Court

41.6 (1) The prosecutor may only apply to extend or further extend the relevant period before it expires and that application must be served on the Crown Court officer and the acquitted person.

(2) A prosecutor's application for a summons or a warrant under section 89(3)(a) or (b) of the Criminal Justice Act 2003 must be served on the court officer and the acquitted person.

Bail or custody orders in the Court of Appeal

41.7 Rules 68.8 and 68.9 shall apply to bail or custody orders made in the Court of Appeal under section 90 of the Criminal Justice Act 2003 as if they were orders made pursuant to an application under rule 68.7.

Application for restrictions on publication

41.8 (1) An application by the Director of Public Prosecutions, under section 82 of the Criminal Justice Act 2003, for restrictions on publication must be in the form set out in the Practice Direction and be served on the Registrar and the acquitted person.

(2) If notice of a section 76 application has not been given and the Director of Public Prosecution has indicated that there are reasons why the acquitted person should not be notified of the application for restrictions on publication, the Court of Appeal may order that service on the acquitted person is not to be effected until notice of a section 76 application is served on that person.

(3) If the Court of Appeal makes an order for restrictions on publication of its own motion or on application of the Director of Public Prosecutions, the Registrar must serve notice and reasons for that order on all parties, unless paragraph (2) applies.

Variation or revocation of restrictions on publication

41.9 (1) A party who wants to vary or revoke an order for restrictions on publication, under section 82(7) of the Criminal Justice Act 2003, may apply to the Court of Appeal in writing at any time after that order was made.

(2) A copy of the application to vary or revoke shall be sent to all parties to the section 76 application unless paragraph (3) applies.

(3) If the application to vary or revoke is made by the Director of Public Prosecutions and—

(a) the notice of a section 76 application has not been given under rule 41.2; and

(b) the Director of Public Prosecutions has indicated that there are reasons why the acquitted person should not be notified of an application for restrictions on publication, the Court of Appeal may order that service on the acquitted person is not to be effected until notice of a section 76 application is served on that person.

(4) If the Court of Appeal varies or revokes an order for restrictions on publication of its own motion or on application, it must serve notice and reasons for that order on all parties, unless paragraph (3) applies.

Powers exercisable by a single judge of the Court of Appeal

41.10 (1) The following powers under the Criminal Justice Act 2003 and under this Part may be exercised by a single judge in the same manner as they may be exercised by the Court of Appeal and subject to the same provisions, namely to—

(a) order the production of any document, exhibit or thing under section 80(6)(a) of the 2003 Act;

(b) order any witness who would be a compellable witness in proceedings pursuant to an order or declaration made on the application to attend for examination and be examined before the Court of Appeal under section 80(6)(b) of the 2003 Act;

(c) extend the time for service under rule 41.3(2); and

(d) delay the requirement of service on the acquitted person of an application for restrictions on publication under rules 41.8(2) and 41.9(3).

(2) A single judge may, for the purposes of exercising any of the powers specified in paragraph (1), sit in such place as he appoints and may sit otherwise than in open court.

(3) Where a single judge exercises one of the powers set out in paragraph (1), the Registrar must serve notice of the single judge's decision on all parties to the section 76 application.

Powers exercisable by the Registrar

41.11 (1) The Registrar may require the Crown Court at the place of original trial to provide the Court of Appeal with any assistance or information which it may require for the purposes of exercising its jurisdiction under Part 10 of the Criminal Justice Act 2003 or this Part.

(2) The following powers may be exercised by the Registrar in the same manner as the Court of Appeal and subject to the same provisions

(a) order the production of any document, exhibit or thing under section 80(6)(a) of the 2003 Act;

(b) order any witness who would be a compellable witness in proceedings pursuant to an order or declaration made on the application to attend for examination and be examined before the Court of Appeal under section 80(6)(b) of the 2003 Act; and

(c) extend the time for service under rule 41.3(2).

(3) Where the Registrar exercises one of the powers set out in paragraph (2) the Registrar must serve notice of that decision on all parties to the section 76 application.

(4) Where the Registrar has refused an application to exercise any of the powers referred to in paragraph (2), the party making the application may have it determined by a single judge by serving a renewal in the form set out in the Practice Direction within 14 days of the day on which notice of the Registrar's decision is served on the party making the application, unless that period is extended by the Court of Appeal.

Determination by full court

41.12 (1) Where a single judge has refused an application to exercise any of the powers referred to in rule 41.10, the applicant may have that application determined by the Court of Appeal by serving a notice of renewal in the form set out in the Practice Direction.

(2) A notice under paragraph (1) must be served on the Registrar within 14 days of the day on which notice of the single judge's decision is served on the party making the application, unless that period is extended by the Court of Appeal.

(3) If a notice under paragraph (1) is not served on the Registrar within the period specified in paragraph (2) or such extended period as the Court of Appeal has allowed, the application shall be treating as having been refused by the Court of Appeal.

Notice of the determination of the application

41.13 (1) The Court of Appeal may give its determination of the section 76 application at the conclusion of the hearing.

(2) If determination is reserved, the Registrar shall as soon as practicable, serve notice of the determination on the parties to the section 76 application.

(3) If the Court of Appeal orders under section 77 of the Criminal Justice Act 2003 that a retrial take place, the Registrar must as soon as practicable, serve notice on the Crown Court officer at the appropriate place of retrial.

Notice of application to set aside order for retrial

41.14 (1) If an acquitted person has not been arraigned before the end of 2 months after the date of an order under section 77 of the Criminal Justice Act 2003 he may apply in the form set out in the Practice Direction to the Court of Appeal to set aside the order.

(2) An application under paragraph (1) must be served on the Registrar and the prosecutor.

Leave to arraign

41.15 (1) If the acquitted person has not been arraigned before the end of 2 months after the date of an order under section 77 of the Criminal Justice Act 2003, the prosecutor may apply in the form set out in the Practice Direction to the Court of Appeal for leave to arraign.

(2) An application under paragraph (1) must be served on the Registrar and the acquitted person.

Abandonment of the application

41.16 (1) A section 76 application may be abandoned by the prosecutor before the hearing of that application by serving a notice in the form set out in the Practice Direction on the Registrar and the acquitted person.

(2) The Registrar must, as soon as practicable, after receiving a notice under paragraph (1) send a copy of it endorsed with the date of receipt to the prosecutor and acquitted person.

PART 42   SENTENCING PROCEDURES IN SPECIAL CASES

Reasons for deciding not to follow a guideline or make an order

42.1 (1) This rule applies where the court decides—

(a) not to follow a relevant sentencing guideline;

(b) not to make, where it could—

(i) a reparation order (unless it passes a custodial or community sentence),

(ii) a compensation order, or

(iii) a travel restriction order;

(c) not to order, where it could—

(i) that a suspended sentence of imprisonment is to take effect,

(ii) the endorsement of the defendant's driving record, or

(iii) the defendant's disqualification from driving, for the usual minimum period or at all.

(2) The court must explain why it has not done so, when it explains the sentence that it has passed.

Requirements of community sentence, etc.

42.2 (1) This rule applies where the court—

(a) imposes a requirement in connection with—

(i) a community sentence,

(ii) a youth rehabilitation order, or

(iii) a suspended sentence of imprisonment; or

(b) orders the defendant to attend meetings with a supervisor.

(2) The court officer must—

(a) notify the defendant and, where the defendant is under 14, an appropriate adult, of—

(i) the requirement or requirements imposed, and

(ii) the name of the responsible officer or supervisor, and the means by which that person may be contacted; and

(b) notify the responsible officer or supervisor, and, where the defendant is under 14, the appropriate qualifying officer (if that is not the responsible officer), of—

(i) the defendant's name, address and telephone number (if available),

(ii) the offence or offences of which the defendant was convicted, and

(iii) the requirement or requirements imposed.

(3) If the court imposes an electronic monitoring requirement, the monitor of which is not the responsible officer, the court officer must—

    (a) notify the defendant and, where the defendant is under 16, an appropriate adult, of the monitor's name, and the means by which the monitor may be contacted; and

    (b) notify the monitor of—

        (i) the defendant's name, address and telephone number (if available),

        (ii) the offence or offences of which the defendant was convicted,

        (iii) the place or places at which the defendant's presence must be monitored,

        (iv) the period or periods during which the defendant's presence there must be monitored, and

        (v) the responsible officer's name, and the means by which that officer may be contacted.

Defendant's duty to notify information to police

42.3 (1) This rule applies where, on a conviction, sentence or order, legislation requires the defendant to notify information to the police.

    (2) The court must tell the defendant that notification requirements apply, and under what legislation.

Variation of sentence

42.4 (1) This rule—

    (a) applies where a magistrates' court or the Crown Court can vary or rescind a sentence or order; and

    (b) authorises the Crown Court, in addition to its other powers, to do so within the period of 56 days beginning with another defendant's acquittal or sentencing where—

        (i) defendants are tried separately in the Crown Court on the same or related facts alleged in one or more indictments, and

        (ii) one is sentenced before another is acquitted or sentenced.

    (2) The court may exercise its power—

    (a) on application by a party; or

    (b) on its own initiative.

    (3) A party who wants the court to exercise that power must—

    (a) apply in writing as soon as reasonably practicable after—

        (i) the sentence or order that that party wants the court to vary or rescind, or

        (ii) where paragraph (1)(b) applies, the other defendant's acquittal or sentencing;

    (b) serve the application on—

        (i) the court officer, and

        (ii) each other party; and

    (c) in the application—

        (i) explain why the sentence should be varied or rescinded,

        (ii) specify the variation that the applicant proposes, and

        (iii) if the application is late, explain why.

    (4) The court must not exercise its power in the defendant's absence unless—

    (a) the court makes a variation proposed by the defendant; or

    (b) the defendant has had an opportunity to make representations at a hearing (whether or not the defendant in fact attends).

    (5) The court may—

    (a) extend (even after it has expired) the time limit under paragraph (3), unless the court's power to vary or rescind the sentence cannot be exercised; and

    (b) allow an application to be made orally.

Application to vary or discharge a compensation order

42.5 (1) This rule applies where a magistrates' court can vary or discharge a compensation order on application by the defendant.

    (2) A defendant who wants the court to exercise that power must—

        (a) apply in writing as soon as practicable after becoming aware of the grounds for doing so;

        (b) serve the application on the magistrates' court officer;

        (c) where the compensation order was made in the Crown Court, serve a copy of the application on the Crown Court officer; and

        (d) in the application, specify the compensation order that the defendant wants the court to vary or discharge and explain (as applicable)—

            (i) what civil court finding shows that the injury, loss or damage was less than it had appeared to be when the order was made,

            (ii) in what circumstances the person for whose benefit the order was made has recovered the property for the loss of which it was made,

            (iii) why a confiscation order makes the defendant now unable to pay compensation in full, or

            (iv) in what circumstances the defendant's means have been reduced substantially and unexpectedly, and why they seem unlikely to increase for a considerable period.

    (3) The court officer must serve a copy of the application on the person for whose benefit the compensation order was made.

    (4) The court must not vary or discharge the compensation order unless—

        (a) the defendant, and the person for whose benefit it was made, each has had an opportunity to make representations at a hearing (whether or not either in fact attends); and

        (b) where the order was made in the Crown Court, the Crown Court has notified its consent.

Application to remove, revoke or suspend a disqualification or restriction

42.6 (1) This rule applies where, on application by the defendant, the court can remove, revoke or suspend a disqualification or restriction included in a sentence (except a disqualification from driving).

    (2) A defendant who wants the court to exercise such a power must—

        (a) apply in writing, no earlier than the date on which the court can exercise the power;

        (b) serve the application on the court officer; and

        (c) in the application—

            (i) specify the disqualification or restriction, and

            (ii) explain why the defendant wants the court to remove, revoke or suspend it.

    (3) The court officer must serve a copy of the application on the chief officer of police for the local justice area.

Application for a restitution order by the victim of a theft

42.7 (1) This rule applies where, on application by the victim of a theft, the court can order a defendant to give that person goods obtained with the proceeds of goods stolen in that theft.

    (2) A person who wants the court to exercise that power if the defendant is convicted must—

        (a) apply in writing as soon as practicable (without waiting for the verdict);

        (b) serve the application on the court officer; and

        (c) in the application—

            (i) identify the goods, and

            (ii) explain why the applicant is entitled to them.

(3) The court officer must serve a copy of the application on each party.

(4) The court must not determine the application unless the applicant and each party has had an opportunity to make representations at a hearing (whether or not each in fact attends).

(5) The court may—

    (a) extend (even after it has expired) the time limit under paragraph (2); and

    (b) allow an application to be made orally.

Requests for medical reports, etc.

42.8 (1) This rule applies where the court—

    (a) requests a medical examination of the defendant and a report; or

    (b) requires information about the arrangements that could be made for the defendant where the court is considering—

        (i) a hospital order, or

        (ii) a guardianship order.

(2) Unless the court otherwise directs, the court officer must, as soon as practicable, serve on each person from whom a report or information is sought a note that—

    (a) specifies the power exercised by the court;

    (b) explains why the court seeks a report or information from that person; and

    (c) sets out or summarises any relevant information available to the court.

Information to be supplied on admission to hospital or guardianship

42.9 (1) This rule applies where the court—

    (a) orders the defendant's detention and treatment in hospital; or

    (b) makes a guardianship order.

(2) Unless the court otherwise directs, the court officer must, as soon as practicable, serve on (as applicable) the hospital or the guardian—

    (a) a record of the court's order;

    (b) such information as the court has received that appears likely to assist in treating or otherwise dealing with the defendant, including information about—

        (i) the defendant's mental condition,

        (ii) the defendant's other circumstances, and

        (iii) the circumstances of the offence.

Information to be supplied on committal for sentence, etc.

42.10 (1) This rule applies where a magistrates' court or the Crown Court convicts the defendant and—

    (a) commits or adjourns the case to another court—

        (i) for sentence, or

        (ii) for the defendant to be dealt with for breach of a deferred sentence, a conditional discharge, or a suspended sentence of imprisonment, imposed by that other court;

    (b) deals with a deferred sentence, a conditional discharge, or a suspended sentence of imprisonment, imposed by another court; or

    (c) makes an order that another court is, or may be, required to enforce.

(2) Unless the convicting court otherwise directs, the court officer must, as soon as practicable—

    (a) where paragraph (1)(a) applies, arrange the transmission from the convicting to the other court of relevant copy court records and other relevant documents, including any—

        (i) certificate of conviction,

        (ii) magistrates' court register entry,

        (iii) record relating to bail,

        (iv) note of evidence,

　　　　(v)　statement or other document introduced in evidence,
　　　　(vi)　medical or other report,
　　　　(vii)　representation order or application for such order, and
　　　　(viii) interim driving disqualification;
　　(b)　where paragraph (1)(b) or (c) applies, arrange—
　　　　(i)　the transmission from the convicting to the other court of notice of the convicting court's order, and
　　　　(ii)　the recording of that order at the other court;
　　(c)　in every case, notify the defendant and, where the defendant is under 14, an appropriate adult, of the location of the other court.

PART 43

[Omitted with effect 4 October 2010 and replaced by part 42 (SI 2010/1921).]

PART 44　BREACH, REVOCATION AND AMENDMENT OF COMMUNITY AND OTHER ORDERS

When this Part applies

44.1　This Part applies where—
　　(a)　the person responsible for a defendant's compliance with an order to which applies—
　　　　(i)　Schedule 3, 5, 7 or 8 to the Powers of Criminal Courts (Sentencing) Act 2000,
　　　　(ii)　Schedule 8 or 12 to the Criminal Justice Act 2003,
　　　　(iii)　Schedule 2 to the Criminal Justice and Immigration Act 2008,
　　　　(iv)　or the Schedule to the Street Offences Act 1959
　　　　wants the court to deal with that defendant for failure to comply;
　　(b)　one of the following wants the court to exercise any power it has to revoke or amend such an order—
　　　　(i)　the responsible officer or supervisor,
　　　　(ii)　the defendant, or
　　　　(iii)　where the legislation allows, a person affected by the order; or
　　(c)　the court considers exercising on its own initiative any power it has to revoke or amend such an order.

Application by responsible officer or supervisor

44.2　(1)　This rule applies where—
　　(a)　the responsible officer wants the court to—
　　　　(i)　deal with a defendant for failure to comply with an order to which this Part applies, or
　　　　(ii)　revoke or amend such an order; or
　　(b)　the court considers exercising on its own initiative any power it has to—
　　　　(i)　revoke or amend such an order, and
　　　　(ii)　summon the defendant to attend for that purpose.
　　(2)　Rules 7.2 to 7.4, which deal, among other things, with starting a prosecution in a magistrates' court by information and summons, apply—
　　(a)　as if—
　　　　(i)　a reference in those rules to an allegation of an offence included a reference to an allegation of failure to comply with an order to which this Part applies, and
　　　　(ii)　a reference to the prosecutor included a reference to the responsible officer or supervisor; and
　　(b)　with the necessary consequential modifications.

Application by defendant or person affected

44.3 (1) This rule applies where—
    (a) the defendant wants the court to exercise any power it has to revoke or amend an order to which this Part applies; or
    (b) where the legislation allows, a person affected by such an order wants the court to exercise any such power.

  (2) That defendant, or person affected, must—
    (a) apply in writing, explaining why the order should be revoked or amended; and
    (b) serve the application on—
      (i) the court officer,
      (ii) the responsible officer or supervisor, and
      (iii) as appropriate, the defendant or the person affected.

Procedure on application by responsible officer or supervisor

44.4 (1) Except for rule 37.8, the rules in Part 37, which deal with the procedure at a trial in a magistrates' court, apply—
    (a) as if—
      (i) a reference in those rules to an allegation of an offence included a reference to an allegation of failure to comply with an order to which this Part applies,
      (ii) a reference to the court's verdict included a reference to the court's decision to revoke or amend such an order, or to exercise any other power it has to deal with the defendant, and
      (iii) a reference to the court's sentence included a reference to the exercise of any such power; and
    (b) with the necessary consequential modifications.

  (2) The court officer must serve on each party any order revoking or amending an order to which this Part applies.

Part 45

[Omitted with effect 4 October 2010 and replaced by part 42 (SI 2010/1921).]

Part 46

[There are currently no rules in this part.]

Part 47

[Omitted with effect 4 October 2010 andreplaced by part 42 (SI 2010/1921).]

Part 48

[Omitted with effect 4 October 2010 and replaced by part 42 (SI 2010/1921).]

Part 49

[Omitted with effect 4 October 2010 and replaced by part 42. (SI 2010/1921).]

Part 50   Civil Behaviour Orders after Verdict or Finding

When this Part applies

50.1 (1) This Part applies in magistrates' courts and in the Crown Court where the court could decide to make, vary or revoke a civil order—
    (a) under a power that the court can exercise after reaching a verdict or making a finding, and
    (b) that requires someone to do, or not do, something.

(2) A reference to a 'behaviour order' in this Part is a reference to any such order.

(3) A reference to 'hearsay evidence' in this Part is a reference to evidence consisting of hearsay within the meaning of section 1(2) of the Civil Evidence Act 1995.

Behaviour orders: general rules

50.2 (1) The court must not make a behaviour order unless the person to whom it is directed has had an opportunity—

(a) to consider what order is proposed and why; and

(b) to make representations at a hearing (whether or not that person in fact attends).

(2) That restriction does not apply to making an interim behaviour order, but such an order has no effect unless the person to whom it is directed—

(a) is present when it is made; or

(b) is handed a document recording the order not more than 7 days after it is made.

(3) Where the court decides not to make, where it could—

(a) a football banning order;

(b) a parenting order, after a person under 16 is convicted of disobeying an anti-social behaviour order; or

(c) a drinking banning order,

the court must announce, at a hearing in public, the reasons for its decision.

Application for behaviour order: special rules

50.3 (1) This rule applies where a prosecutor wants the court to make—

(a) an anti-social behaviour order; or

(b) a serious crime prevention order,

if the defendant is convicted.

(2) The prosecutor must serve a notice of intention to apply for such an order on—

(a) the court officer;

(b) the defendant against whom the prosecutor wants the court to make the order; and

(c) any person on whom the order would be likely to have a significant adverse effect,

as soon as practicable (without waiting for the verdict).

(3) The notice must be in the form set out in the Practice Direction and must—

(a) summarise the relevant facts;

(b) identify the evidence on which the prosecutor relies in support;

(c) attach any written statement that the prosecutor has not already served; and

(d) specify the order that the prosecutor wants the court to make.

(4) The defendant must then—

(a) serve written notice of any evidence on which the defendant relies on—

(i) the court officer, and

(ii) the prosecutor,

as soon as practicable (without waiting for the verdict); and

(b) in the notice, identify that evidence and attach any written statement that has not already been served.

(5) This rule does not apply to an application for an interim anti-social behaviour order.

Evidence to assist the court: special rules

50.4 (1) This rule applies where the court indicates that it may make on its own initiative—

(a) a football banning order;

(b) a restraining order;

(c) an anti-social behaviour order; or

(d) a drinking banning order.

(2) A party who wants the court to take account of any particular evidence before making that decision must—

(a) serve notice in writing on—

(i) the court officer, and

      (ii) every other party,
      as soon as practicable (without waiting for the verdict); and
  (b) in that notice identify that evidence and attach any written statement that has not already been served.

Application to vary or revoke behaviour order

50.5 (1) The court may vary or revoke a behaviour order if—
    (a) the legislation under which it is made allows the court to do so; and
    (b) one of the following applies—
        (i) the prosecutor,
        (ii) the person to whom the order is directed,
        (iii) any other person mentioned in the order,
        (iv) the relevant authority or responsible officer,
        (v) the relevant Chief Officer of Police, or
        (vi) the Director of Public Prosecutions.
  (2) A person applying under this rule must—
    (a) apply in writing as soon as practicable after becoming aware of the grounds for doing so, explaining—
        (i) what material circumstances have changed since the order was made, and
        (ii) why the order should be varied or revoked as a result;
    (b) serve the application on—
        (i) the court officer,
        (ii) as appropriate, the prosecutor or defendant,
        (iii) any other person listed in paragraph (1)(b), if the court so directs.
  (3) A party who wants the court to take account of any particular evidence before making its decision must, as soon as practicable—
    (a) serve notice in writing on—
        (i) the court officer,
        (ii) as appropriate, the prosecutor or defendant, and
        (ii) as appropriate, anyone listed in paragraph (1)(b) on whom the court directed the application to be served; and
    (b) in that notice identify the evidence and attach any written statement that has not already been served.
  (4) The court may decide an application under this rule with or without a hearing.
  (5) But the court must not—
    (a) dismiss an application under this rule unless the applicant has had an opportunity to make representations at a hearing (whether or not the applicant in fact attends); or
    (b) allow an application under this rule unless everyone required to be served, by this rule or by the court, has had at least 14 days in which to make representations, including representations about whether there should be a hearing.
  (6) The court officer must—
    (a) serve the application on any person, if the court so directs; and
    (b) give notice of any hearing to—
        (i) the applicant, and
        (ii) any person required to be served, by this rule or by the court.

Notice of hearsay evidence

50.6 (1) A party who wants to introduce hearsay evidence must—
    (a) serve notice in writing on—
        (i) the court officer, and
        (ii) every other party directly affected; and
    (b) in that notice—
        (i) explain that it is a notice of hearsay evidence,
        (ii) identify that evidence,

         (iii) identify the person who made the statement which is hearsay, or explain why if that person is not identified, and

         (iv) explain why that person will not be called to give oral evidence.

    (2) A party may serve one notice under this rule in respect of more than one statement and more than one witness.

Cross-examination of maker of hearsay statement

50.7 (1) This rule applies where a party wants the court's permission to cross-examine a person who made a statement which another party wants to introduce as hearsay.

    (2) The party who wants to cross-examine that person must—

        (a) apply in writing, with reasons, not more than 7 days after service of the notice of hearsay evidence; and

        (b) serve the application on—

            (i) the court officer,

           (ii) the party who served the hearsay evidence notice, and

         (iii) every party on whom the hearsay evidence notice was served.

    (3) The court may decide an application under this rule with or without a hearing.

    (4) But the court must not—

        (a) dismiss an application under this rule unless the applicant has had an opportunity to make representations at a hearing (whether or not the applicant in fact attends); or

        (b) allow an application under this rule unless everyone served with the application has had at least 7 days in which to make representations, including representations about whether there should be a hearing.

Credibility and consistency of maker of hearsay statement

50.8 (1) This rule applies where a party wants to challenge the credibility or consistency of a person who made a statement which another party wants to introduce as hearsay.

    (2) The party who wants to challenge the credibility or consistency of that person must—

        (a) serve a written notice of intention to do so on—

            (i) the court officer, and

           (ii) the party who served the notice of hearsay evidence

      not more than 7 days after service of that hearsay evidence notice; and

        (b) in the notice, identify any statement or other material on which that party relies.

    (3) The party who served the hearsay notice—

        (a) may call that person to give oral evidence instead; and

        (b) if so, must serve a notice of intention to do so on—

            (i) the court officer, and

           (ii) every party on whom he served the hearsay notice

      not more than 7 days after service of the notice under paragraph (2).

Court's power to vary requirements under this Part

50.9 The court may—

    (a) shorten a time limit or extend it (even after it has expired);

    (b) allow a notice or application to be given in a different form, or presented orally.

PART 51

[This part currently contains no rules.]

PART 52   ENFORCEMENT OF FINES AND OTHER ORDERS FOR PAYMENT

When this Part applies

52.1 (1) This Part applies where a magistrates' court can enforce payment of—

        (a) a fine, or a penalty that legislation requires the court to treat as a fine; or

(b) any other sum that a court has ordered to be paid—
    (i) on a conviction, or
    (ii) on the forfeiture of a surety.
(2) Rules 52.7 to 52.9 apply where the court, or a fines officer, issues a warrant that requires someone to—
    (a) take control of goods or money belonging to the defendant;
    (b) remove and sell any such goods; and
    (c) pay any such money, and any proceeds of such a sale, to the court officer towards payment of a sum to which this Part applies.
(3) In this Part—
    (a) 'defendant' means anyone liable to pay a sum to which this Part applies;
    (b) 'payment terms' means by when, and by what (if any) instalments, such a sum must be paid.

Exercise of court's powers

52.2. The court must not exercise its enforcement powers unless—
    (a) the court officer has served on the defendant any collection order or other notice of—
        (i) the obligation to pay,
        (ii) the payment terms, and
        (iii) how and where the defendant must pay; and
    (b) the defendant has failed to comply with the payment terms.

Duty to give receipt

52.3 (1) This rule applies where the defendant makes a payment to—
    (a) the court officer specified in an order or notice served under rule 52.2;
    (b) another court officer;
    (c) any—
        (i) custodian of the defendant,
        (ii) supervisor appointed to encourage the defendant to pay, or
        (iii) responsible officer appointed under a community sentence or a suspended sentence of imprisonment; or
    (d) a person executing a warrant to which rule 18.6 (warrants for arrest, detention or imprisonment that cease to have effect on payment) or this Part applies.
(2) The person receiving the payment must—
    (a) give the defendant a receipt; and
    (b) as soon as practicable transmit the payment to the court officer specified in an order or notice served under rule 52.2, if the recipient is not that court officer.

Appeal against decision of fines officer

52.4 (1) This rule applies where—
    (a) a collection order is in force;
    (b) a fines officer makes a decision under one of these paragraphs of Schedule 5 to the Courts Act 2003—
        (i) paragraph 22 (Application to fines officer for variation of order or attachment of earnings order, etc.),
        (ii) paragraph 31 (Application to fines officer for variation of reserve terms), or
        (iii) paragraph 37 (Functions of fines officer in relation to defaulters: referral or further steps notice); and
    (c) the defendant wants to appeal against that decision.
(2) Unless the court otherwise directs, the defendant must—
    (a) appeal in writing not more than 10 business days after the decision;
    (b) serve the appeal on the court officer; and

       (c) in the appeal—
          (i)   explain why a different decision should be made, and
          (ii) specify the decision that the defendant proposes.
    (3) Where the court determines an appeal—
       (a) the general rule is that it will do so at a hearing; but
       (b) it may do so without a hearing.

Application to reduce a fine or vary payment terms

52.5 (1) This rule applies where—
       (a) no collection order is in force; and
       (b) the defendant wants the court to—
          (i)   reduce the amount of a fine, or
          (ii) vary payment terms.
    (2) Unless the court otherwise directs, the defendant must—
       (a) apply in writing;
       (b) serve the application on the court officer; and
       (c) in the application, explain—
          (i)   what relevant circumstances have not yet been considered by the court, and
          (ii) why the fine should be reduced, or the payment terms varied.

Claim to avoid fine after penalty notice

52.6 (1) This rule applies where—
       (a) a chief officer of police serves on the magistrates' court officer a certificate registering, for enforcement as a fine, a sum payable by a defendant after failure to comply with a penalty notice; and
       (b) the court or a fines officer enforces the fine.
    (2) A defendant who claims not to be the person to whom the penalty notice was issued must, unless the court otherwise directs—
       (a) make that claim in writing; and
       (b) serve it on the court officer.
    (3) The court officer must—
       (a) notify the chief officer of police by whom the certificate was registered; and
       (b) refer the case to the court.
    (4) Where such a claim is made—
       (a) the general rule is that the court will adjourn the enforcement for 28 days and fix a hearing; but
       (b) the court may make a different order.
    (5) At any such hearing, the chief officer of police must introduce any evidence to contradict the defendant's claim.

Information to be included in a warrant to take goods, etc.

52.7 (1) A warrant must identify—
       (a) the person(s) to whom it is directed;
       (b) the defendant against whom it was issued;
       (c) the sum for which it was issued and the reason that sum is owed;
       (d) the court or fines officer who issued it, unless that is otherwise recorded by the court officer; and
       (e) the court office for the court or fines officer who issued it.
    (2) A person to whom a warrant is directed must record on it the date and time at which it is received.
    (3) A warrant that contains an error is not invalid, as long as—
       (a) it was issued in respect of a lawful decision by the court or fines officer; and
       (b) it contains enough information to identify that decision.

Part 53

Execution of a warrant to take goods, etc.

52.8   (1) A warrant may be executed by—
      (a) any person to whom it is directed; or
      (b) anyone authorised to do so by section 125 (warrants), 125A (civilian enforcement officers) or 125B (execution by approved enforcement agency) of the Magistrates' Courts Act 1980.
  (2) The person who executes a warrant must—
      (a) explain, in terms the defendant can understand—
         (i) the order or decision that the warrant was issued to enforce,
         (ii) the sum for which the warrant was issued, and
         (iii) any extra sum payable in connection with the execution of the warrant;
      (b) show the defendant the warrant, if that person has it;
      (c) if the defendant asks—
         (i) arrange for the defendant to see the warrant, if that person does not have it, and
         (ii) show the defendant any written statement of that person's authority required by section 125A or 125B of the 1980 Act; and
      (d) clearly mark any goods that are taken under the warrant, unless that person removes those goods at once.
  (3) These goods must not be taken under the warrant—
      (a) clothes or bedding used by the defendant or by anyone living with the defendant;
      (b) tools, books, vehicles or other equipment that the defendant needs to use in the defendant's employment, business or vocation, unless the defendant is a corporation.
  (4) Unless the court otherwise directs, or the defendant otherwise agrees, if the person who executes the warrant takes household goods they must not be removed until the day of sale.
  (5) The warrant no longer has effect if—
      (a) there is paid to the person executing it the sum for which it was issued and any extra sum payable in connection with its execution;
      (b) those sums are offered to, but refused by, that person; or
      (c) that person—
         (i) is shown a receipt given under rule 52.3 for the sum for which the warrant was issued, and
         (ii) is paid any extra sum payable in connection with its execution.

Sale of goods taken under a warrant

52.9   (1) Unless the court otherwise directs or the defendant otherwise agrees, goods taken under a warrant must be sold—
      (a) at public auction; and
      (b) as soon as reasonably practicable after the expiry of 5 business days from the date of execution of the warrant.
  (2) After a sale, the person who executed the warrant must, as soon as reasonably practicable—
      (a) collect the proceeds of sale;
      (b) deduct any sum payable in connection with the execution of the warrant;
      (c) pay the court officer specified in an order or notice served under rule 52.2 the sum for which the warrant was issued;
      (d) pay any balance remaining to the defendant; and
      (e) deliver an account of those deductions and payments to the court officer.

PART 53

[Omitted with effect 4 October 2010 and replaced by part 42 (SI 2010/1921).]

PART 54

[Omitted with effect 4 October 2010 and replaced by part 42 (SI 2010 No. 1921).]

PART 55   ROAD TRAFFIC PENALTIES

Application to remove a disqualification from driving

55.1 (1) This rule applies where, on application by the defendant, the court can remove a disqualification from driving.

(2) A defendant who wants the court to exercise that power must—

(a) apply in writing, no earlier than the date on which the court can exercise the power;

(b) serve the application on the court officer; and

(c) in the application—

(i) specify the disqualification that the defendant wants the court to remove, and

(ii) explain why.

(3) The court officer must serve a copy of the application on the chief officer of police for the local justice area.

Information to be supplied on order for endorsement of driving record, etc.

55.2 (1) This rule applies where the court—

(a) convicts the defendant of an offence involving obligatory endorsement, and orders there to be endorsed on the defendant's driving record and on any counterpart licence—

(i) particulars of the conviction,

(ii) particulars of any disqualification from driving that the court imposes, and

(iii) the penalty points to be attributed to the offence;

(b) disqualifies the defendant from driving for any other offence; or

(c) suspends or removes a disqualification from driving.

(2) The court officer must, as soon as practicable, serve on the Secretary of State notice that includes details of—

(a) where paragraph (1)(a) applies—

(i) the local justice area in which the court is acting,

(ii) the dates of conviction and sentence,

(iii) the offence, and the date on which it was committed,

(iv) the sentence, and

(v) the date of birth, and sex, of the defendant, where those details are available;

(b) where paragraph (1)(b) applies—

(i) the date and period of the disqualification,

(ii) the power exercised by the court;

(c) where paragraph (1)(c) applies—

(i) the date and period of the disqualification,

(ii) the date and terms of the order for its suspension or removal,

(iii) the power exercised by the court, and

(iv) where the court suspends the disqualification pending appeal, the court to which the defendant has appealed.

Statutory declaration to avoid fine after fixed penalty notice

55.3 (1) This rule applies where—

(a) a chief officer of police, or the Secretary of State, serves on the magistrates' court officer a certificate registering, for enforcement as a fine, a sum payable by a defendant after failure to comply with a fixed penalty notice;

(b) the court officer notifies the defendant of the registration; and

    (c) the defendant makes a statutory declaration with the effect that—

        (i) the fixed penalty notice, or any associated notice sent to the defendant as owner of the vehicle concerned, and

        (ii) the registration and any enforcement proceedings

        become void.

(2) The defendant must serve that statutory declaration not more than 21 days after service of notice of the registration, unless the court extends that time limit.

(3) The court officer must—

    (a) serve a copy of the statutory declaration on the person by whom the certificate was registered,

    (b) cancel any endorsement on the defendant's driving record and on any counterpart licence, and

    (c) notify the Secretary of State of any such cancellation.

Application for declaration about a course or programme certificate decision

55.4 (1) This rule applies where the court can declare unjustified—

    (a) a course provider's failure or refusal to give a certificate of the defendant's satisfactory completion of an approved course; or

    (b) a programme provider's giving of a certificate of the defendant's failure fully to participate in an approved programme.

(2) A defendant who wants the court to exercise that power must—

    (a) apply in writing, not more than 28 days after—

        (i) the date by which the defendant was required to complete the course, or

        (ii) the giving of the certificate of failure fully to participate in the programme;

    (b) serve the application on the court officer; and

    (c) in the application, specify the course or programme and explain (as applicable)—

        (i) that the course provider has failed to give a certificate,

        (ii) where the course provider has refused to give a certificate, why the defendant disagrees with the reasons for that decision, or

        (iii) where the programme provider has given a certificate, why the defendant disagrees with the reasons for that decision.

(3) The court officer must serve a copy of the application on the course or programme provider.

(4) The court must not determine the application unless the defendant, and the course or programme provider, each has had an opportunity to make representations at a hearing (whether or not either in fact attends).

Appeal against recognition of foreign driving disqualification

55.5 (1) This rule applies where—

    (a) a minister gives a disqualification notice under section 57 of the Crime (International Co-operation) Act 2003; and

    (b) the person to whom it is given wants to appeal under section 59 of the Act to a magistrates' court.

(2) That person ('the appellant') must serve an appeal notice on—

    (a) the court officer, at a magistrates' court in the local justice area in which the appellant lives; and

    (b) the minister, at the address given in the disqualification notice.

(3) The appellant must serve the appeal notice within the period for which section 59 of the 2003 Act provides.

(4) The appeal notice must—

    (a) attach a copy of the disqualification notice;

    (b) explain which of the conditions in section 56 of the 2003 Act is not met, and why section 57 of the Act therefore does not apply; and

    (c) include any application to suspend the disqualification, under section 60 of the Act.

(5) The minister may serve a respondent's notice, and must do so if—
    (a) the minister wants to make representations to the court; or
    (b) the court so directs.
(6) The minister must—
    (a) unless the court otherwise directs, serve any such respondent's notice not more than 14 days after—
        (i) the appellant serves the appeal notice, or
        (ii) a direction to do so;
    (b) in any such respondent's notice—
        (i) identify the grounds of opposition on which the minister relies,
        (ii) summarise any relevant facts not already included in the disqualification and appeal notices, and
        (iii) identify any other document that the minister thinks the court will need to decide the appeal (and serve any such document with the notice).
(7) Where the court determines an appeal—
    (a) the general rule is that it will do so at a hearing (which will be in public, unless the court otherwise directs); but
    (b) it may do so without a hearing.
(8) The court officer must serve on the minister—
    (a) notice of the outcome of the appeal; and
    (b) notice of any suspension of the disqualification; and
    (c) the appellant's driving licence, if surrendered to the court officer.

PART 56   CONFISCATION PROCEEDINGS UNDER THE CRIMINAL JUSTICE ACT 1988 AND THE DRUG TRAFFICKING ACT 1994

Statements etc., relevant to making confiscation orders

56.1   (1) Where a prosecutor or defendant—
    (a) tenders to a magistrates' court any statement or other document under section 73 of the Criminal Justice Act 1988 in any proceedings in respect of an offence listed in Schedule 4 to that Act; or
    (b) tenders to the Crown Court any statement or other document under section 11 of the Drug Trafficking Act 1994 or section 73 of the 1988 Act in any proceedings in respect of a drug trafficking offence or in respect of an offence to which Part VI of the 1988 Act applies,
he must serve a copy as soon as practicable on the defendant or the prosecutor, as the case may be.
  (2) Any statement tendered by the prosecutor to the magistrates' court under section 73 of the 1988 Act or to the Crown Court under section 11(1) of the 1994 Act or section 73(1A) of the 1988 Act shall include the following particulars—
    (a) the name of the defendant;
    (b) the name of the person by whom the statement is made and the date on which it was made;
    (c) where the statement is not tendered immediately after the defendant has been convicted, the date on which and the place where the relevant conviction occurred; and
    (d) such information known to the prosecutor as is relevant to the determination as to whether or not the defendant has benefited from drug trafficking or relevant criminal conduct and to the assessment of the value of his proceeds of drug trafficking or, as the case may be, benefit from relevant criminal conduct.
  (3) Where, in accordance with section 11(7) of the 1994 Act or section 73(1C) of the 1988 Act, the defendant indicates the extent to which he accepts any allegation contained within the prosecutor's statement, if he indicates the same in writing to the prosecutor, he must serve a copy of that reply on the court officer.
  (4) Expressions used in this rule shall have the same meanings as in the 1994 Act or, where appropriate, the 1988 Act.

Postponed determinations

56.2 (1) Where an application is made by the defendant or the prosecutor—
    (a) to a magistrates' court under section 72A(5)(a) of the Criminal Justice Act 1988 asking the court to exercise its powers under section 72A(4) of that Act; or
    (b) to the Crown Court under section 3(5)(a) of the Drug Trafficking Act 1994 asking the Court to exercise its powers under section 3(4) of that Act, or under section 72A(5)(a) of the 1988 Act asking the court to exercise its powers under section 72A(4) of the 1988 Act,
    the application must be made in writing and a copy must be served on the prosecutor or the defendant, as the case may be.

    (2) A party served with a copy of an application under paragraph (1) shall, within 28 days of the date of service, notify the applicant and the court officer, in writing, whether or not he proposes to oppose the application, giving his reasons for any opposition.

    (3) After the expiry of the period referred to in paragraph (2), the court shall determine whether an application under paragraph (1) is to be dealt with—
    (a) without a hearing; or
    (b) at a hearing at which the parties may be represented.

Confiscation orders—revised assessments

56.3 (1) Where the prosecutor makes an application under section 13, 14 or 15 of the Drug Trafficking Act 1994 or section 74A, 74B or 74C of the Criminal Justice Act 1988, the application must be in writing and a copy must be served on the defendant.

    (2) The application must include the following particulars—
    (a) the name of the defendant;
    (b) the date on which and the place where any relevant conviction occurred;
    (c) the date on which and the place where any relevant confiscation order was made or, as the case may be, varied;
    (d) the grounds on which the application is made; and
    (e) an indication of the evidence available to support the application.

Application to the Crown Court to discharge or vary order to make material available

56.4 (1) Where an order under section 93H of the Criminal Justice Act 1988 (order to make material available) or section 55 of the Drug Trafficking Act 1994 (order to make material available) has been made by the Crown Court, any person affected by it may apply in writing to the court officer for the order to be discharged or varied, and on hearing such an application a circuit judge may discharge the order or make such variations to it as he thinks fit.

    (2) Subject to paragraph (3), where a person proposes to make an application under paragraph (1) for the discharge or variation of an order, he shall give a copy of the application, not later than 48 hours before the making of the application—
    (a) to a constable at the police station specified in the order; or
    (b) to the office of the appropriate officer who made the application, as specified in the order,
    in either case together with a notice indicating the time and place at which the application for discharge or variation is to be made.

    (3) A circuit judge may direct that paragraph (2) need not be complied with if he is satisfied that the person making the application has good reason to seek a discharge or variation of the order as soon as possible and it is not practicable to comply with that paragraph.

    (4) In this rule:
    'constable' includes a person commissioned by the Commissioners for Her Majesty's Revenue and Customs;
    'police station' includes a place for the time being occupied by Her Majesty's Revenue and Customs.

Application to the Crown Court for increase in term of imprisonment in default of payment

56.5 (1) This rule applies to applications made, or that have effect as made, to the Crown Court under section 10 of the Drug Trafficking Act 1994 and section 75A of the Criminal Justice Act 1988 (interest on sums unpaid under confiscation orders).

(2) Notice of an application to which this rule applies to increase the term of imprisonment or detention fixed in default of payment of a confiscation order by a person ('the defendant') shall be made by the prosecutor in writing to the court officer.

(3) A notice under paragraph (2) shall—
   (a) state the name and address of the defendant;
   (b) specify the grounds for the application;
   (c) give details of the enforcement measures taken, if any; and
   (d) include a copy of the confiscation order.

(4) On receiving a notice under paragraph (2), the court officer shall—
   (a) forthwith send to the defendant and the magistrates' court required to enforce payment of the confiscation order under section 140(1) of the Powers of Criminal Courts (Sentencing) Act 2000, a copy of the said notice; and
   (b) notify in writing the applicant and the defendant of the date, time and place appointed for the hearing of the application.

(5) Where the Crown Court makes an order pursuant to an application mentioned in paragraph (1) above, the court officer shall send forthwith a copy of the order—
   (a) to the applicant;
   (b) to the defendant;
   (c) where the defendant is at the time of the making of the order in custody, to the person having custody of him; and
   (d) to the magistrates' court mentioned in paragraph (4)(a).

Drug trafficking—compensation on acquittal in the Crown Court

56.6 Where a Crown Court cancels a confiscation order under section 22(2) of the Drug Trafficking Act 1994, the court officer shall serve notice to that effect on the High Court and on the magistrates' court which has responsibility for enforcing the order.

Part 57 Proceeds of Crime Act 2002: Rules Applicable to all Proceedings

Interpretation

57.1 In this Part and in Parts 58, 59, 60 and 61:
'business day' means any day other than a Saturday, Sunday, Christmas Day or Good Friday, or a bank holiday under the Banking and Financial Dealings Act 1971, in England and Wales;
'document' means anything in which information of any description is recorded;
'hearsay evidence' means evidence consisting of hearsay within the meaning of section 1(2) of the Civil Evidence Act 1995;
'restraint proceedings' means proceedings under sections 42 and 58(2) and (3) of the Proceeds of Crime Act 2002;
'receivership proceedings' means proceedings under sections 48, 49, 50, 51, 54(4), 59(2) and (3), 62 and 63 of the 2002 Act;
'witness statement' means a written statement signed by a person which contains the evidence, and only that evidence, which that person would be allowed to give orally; and
words and expressions used have the same meaning as in Part 2 of the 2002 Act.

Calculation of time

57.2 (1) This rule shows how to calculate any period of time for doing any act which is specified by this Part and Parts 58, 59, 60 and 61 for the purposes of any proceedings under Part 2 of the Proceeds of Crime Act 2002 or by an order of the Crown Court in restraint proceedings or receivership proceedings.

(2) A period of time expressed as a number of days shall be computed as clear days.

(3) In this rule 'clear days' means that in computing the number of days—

    (a) the day on which the period begins; and

    (b) if the end of the period is defined by reference to an event, the day on which that event occurs are not included.

(4) Where the specified period is five days or less and includes a day which is not a business day that day does not count.

Court office closed

57.3 When the period specified by this Part or Parts 58, 59, 60 and 61, or by an order of the Crown Court under Part 2 of the Proceeds of Crime Act 2002, for doing any act at the court office falls on a day on which the office is closed, that act shall be in time if done on the next day on which the court office is open.

Application for registration of Scottish or Northern Ireland Order

57.4 (1) This rule applies to an application for registration of an order under article 6 of the Proceeds of Crime Act 2002 (Enforcement in different parts of the United Kingdom) Order 2002.

(2) The application may be made without notice.

(3) The application must be in writing and may be supported by a witness statement which must—

    (a) exhibit the order or a certified copy of the order; and

    (b) to the best of the witness's ability, give full details of the realisable property located in England and Wales in respect of which the order was made and specify the person holding that realisable property.

(4) If the court registers the order, the applicant must serve notice of the registration on—

    (a) any person who holds realisable property to which the order applies; and

    (b) any other person whom the applicant knows to be affected by the order.

(5) The permission of the Crown Court under rule 57.13 is not required to serve the notice outside England and Wales.

Application to vary or set aside registration

57.5 (1) An application to vary or set aside registration of an order under article 6 of the Proceeds of Crime Act 2002 (Enforcement in different parts of the United Kingdom) Order 2002 may be made to the Crown Court by—

    (a) any person who holds realisable property to which the order applies; and

    (b) any other person affected by the order.

(2) The application must be in writing and may be supported by a witness statement.

(3) The application and any witness statement must be lodged with the Crown Court.

(4) The application must be served on the person who applied for registration at least seven days before the date fixed by the court for hearing the application, unless the Crown Court specifies a shorter period.

(5) No property in England and Wales may be realised in pursuance of the order before the Crown Court has decided the application.

Register of orders

57.6 (1) The Crown Court must keep, under the direction of the Lord Chancellor, a register of the orders registered under article 6 of the Proceeds of Crime Act 2002 (Enforcement in different parts of the United Kingdom) Order 2002.

(2) The register must include details of any variation or setting aside of a registration under rule 57.5 and of any execution issued on a registered order.

(3) If the person who applied for registration of an order which is subsequently registered notifies the Crown Court that the court which made the order has varied or discharged the order, details of the variation or discharge, as the case may be, must be entered in the register.

Statements of truth

57.7 (1) Any witness statement required to be served by this Part or by Parts 58, 59, 60 or 61 must be verified by a statement of truth contained in the witness statement.

(2) A statement of truth is a declaration by the person making the witness statement to the effect that the witness statement is true to the best of his knowledge and belief and that he made the statement knowing that, if it were tendered in evidence, he would be liable to prosecution if he wilfully stated in it anything which he knew to be false or did not believe to be true.

(3) The statement of truth must be signed by the person making the witness statement.

(4) If the person making the witness statement fails to verify the witness statement by a statement of truth, the Crown Court may direct that it shall not be admissible as evidence.

Use of witness statements for other purposes

57.8 (1) Except as provided by this rule, a witness statement served in proceedings under Part 2 of the Proceeds of Crime Act 2002 may be used only for the purpose of the proceedings in which it is served.

(2) Paragraph (1) does not apply if and to the extent that—

(a) the witness gives consent in writing to some other use of it;

(b) the Crown Court gives permission for some other use; or

(c) the witness statement has been put in evidence at a hearing held in public.

Expert evidence

57.9 (1) A party to proceedings under Part 2 of the Proceeds of Crime Act 2002 who wishes to adduce expert evidence (whether of fact or opinion) in the proceedings must, as soon as practicable—

(a) serve on the other parties a statement in writing of any finding or opinion which he proposes to adduce by way of such evidence; and

(b) serve on any party who requests it in writing, a copy of (or if it appears to the party proposing to adduce the evidence to be more practicable, a reasonable opportunity to examine)—

(i) the record of any observation, test, calculation or other procedure on which the finding or opinion is based, and

(ii) any document or other thing or substance in respect of which the observation, test, calculation or other procedure mentioned in paragraph (1)(b)(i) has been carried out.

(c) A party may serve notice in writing waiving his right to be served with any of the matters mentioned in paragraph (1) and, in particular, may agree that the statement mentioned in paragraph (1)(a) may be given to him orally and not served in writing.

(d) If a party who wishes to adduce expert evidence in proceedings under Part 2 of the 2002 Act fails to comply with this rule he may not adduce that evidence in those proceedings without the leave of the court, except where rule 57.10 applies.

Exceptions to procedure for expert evidence

57.10 (1) If a party has reasonable grounds for believing that the disclosure of any evidence in compliance with rule 57.9 might lead to the intimidation, or attempted intimidation, of any person on whose evidence he intends to rely in the proceedings, or otherwise to the course of justice being interfered with, he shall not be obliged to comply with those requirements in relation to that evidence, unless the Crown Court orders otherwise.

(2) Where, in accordance with paragraph (1), a party considers that he is not obliged to comply with the requirements imposed by rule 57.9 with regard to any evidence in relation to any other party, he must serve notice in writing on that party stating—

(a) that the evidence is being withheld; and

(b) the reasons for withholding the evidence.

Service of documents

57.11 (1) Part 4 and rule 32.1 (notice required to accompany process served outside the United Kingdom and translations) shall not apply in restraint proceedings and receivership proceedings.

(2) Where this Part or Parts 58, 59, 60 or 61 requires service of a document, then, unless the Crown Court directs otherwise, the document may be served by any of the following methods—

(a) in all cases, by delivering the document personally to the party to be served;

(b) if no solicitor is acting for the party to be served by delivering the document at, or by sending it by first class post to, his residence or his last-known residence; or

(c) if a solicitor is acting for the party to be served—

(i) by delivering the document at, or sending it by first class post to, the solicitor's business address, or

(ii) where the solicitor's business address includes a numbered box at a document exchange, by leaving the document at that document exchange or at a document exchange which transmits documents on every business day to that document exchange, or

(iii) if the solicitor has indicated that he is willing to accept service by facsimile transmission, by sending a legible copy of the document by facsimile transmission to the solicitor's office.

(3) A document shall, unless the contrary is proved, be deemed to have been served—

(a) in the case of service by first class post, on the second business day after posting;

(b) in the case of service in accordance with paragraph (2)(c)(ii), on the second business day after the day on which it is left at the document exchange; and

(c) in the case of service in accordance with paragraph (2)(c)(iii), where it is transmitted on a business day before 4 p.m., on that day and in any other case, on the next business day.

(4) An order made in restraint proceedings or receivership proceedings may be enforced against the defendant or any other person affected by it notwithstanding that service of a copy of the order has not been effected in accordance with this rule if the Crown Court is satisfied that the person had notice of the order by being present when the order was made.

Service by an alternative method

57.12 (1) Where it appears to the Crown Court that there is a good reason to authorise service by a method not otherwise permitted by rule 57.11, the court may make an order permitting service by an alternative method.

(2) An application for an order permitting service by an alternative method—

(a) must be supported by evidence; and

(b) may be made without notice.

(3) An order permitting service by an alternative method must specify—

(a) the method of service; and

(b) the date when the document will be deemed to be served.

Service outside the jurisdiction

57.13 (1) Where this Part requires a document to be served on someone who is outside England and Wales, it may be served outside England and Wales with the permission of the Crown Court.

(2) Where a document is to be served outside England and Wales it may be served by any method permitted by the law of the country in which it is to be served.

(3) Nothing in this rule or in any court order shall authorise or require any person to do anything in the country where the document is to be served which is against the law of that country.

(4) Where this Part requires a document to be served a certain period of time before the date of a hearing and the recipient does not appear at the hearing, the hearing must not take place unless the Crown Court is satisfied that the document has been duly served.

Certificates of service

57.14 (1) Where this Part requires that the applicant for an order in restraint proceedings or receivership proceedings serve a document on another person, the applicant must lodge a certificate of service with the Crown Court within seven days of service of the document.

(2) The certificate must state—
(a) the method of service;
(b) the date of service; and
(c) if the document is served under rule 57.12, such other information as the court may require when making the order permitting service by an alternative method.

(3) Where a document is to be served by the Crown Court in restraint proceedings and receivership proceedings and the court is unable to serve it, the court must send a notice of non-service stating the method attempted to the party who requested service.

External requests and orders

57.15 (1) The rules in this Part and in Parts 59 to 61 and 71 apply with the necessary modifications to proceedings under the Proceeds of Crime Act 2002 (External Requests and Orders) Order 2005 in the same way that they apply to corresponding proceedings under Part 2 of the Proceeds of Crime Act 2002.

(2) This table shows how provisions of the 2005 Order correspond with provisions of the 2002 Act.

Article of the Proceeds of Crime Act 2002 (External Requests and Orders) Order 2005	Section of the Proceeds of Crime Act 2002
8	41
9	42
10	43
11	44
15	48
16	49
17	58
23	31
27	50
28	51
41	62
42	63
44	65
45	66

PART 58   PROCEEDS OF CRIME ACT 2002: RULES APPLICABLE ONLY TO CONFISCATION PROCEEDINGS

Statements in connection with confiscation orders

58.1 (1) When the prosecutor or the Director is required, under section 16 of the Proceeds of Crime Act 2002, to give a statement to the Crown Court, the prosecutor or the

Director, as the case may be, must also, as soon as practicable, serve a copy of the statement on the defendant.

(2) Any statement given to the Crown Court by the prosecutor under section 16 of the 2002 Act must, in addition to the information required by the 2002 Act, include the following information—

    (a) the name of the defendant;

    (b) the name of the person by whom the statement is made and the date on which it is made; and

    (c) where the statement is not given to the Crown Court immediately after the defendant has been convicted, the date on which and the place where the relevant conviction occurred.

(3) Where, under section 17 of the 2002 Act, the Crown Court orders the defendant to indicate the extent to which he accepts each allegation in a statement given by the prosecutor, the defendant must indicate this in writing to the prosecutor and must give a copy to the Crown Court.

(4) Where the Crown Court orders the defendant to give to it any information under section 18 of the 2002 Act, the defendant must provide the information in writing and must, as soon as practicable, serve a copy of it on the prosecutor.

Postponement of confiscation proceedings

58.2 The Crown Court may grant a postponement under section 14(1)(b) of the Proceeds of Crime Act 2002 without a hearing.

Application for reconsideration

58.3 (1) This rule applies where the prosecutor makes an application under section 19, 20 or 21 of the Proceeds of Crime Act 2002.

(2) The application must be in writing and give details of—

    (a) the name of the defendant;

    (b) the date on which and the place where any relevant conviction occurred;

    (c) the date on which and the place where any relevant confiscation order was made or varied;

    (d) the grounds for the application; and

    (e) an indication of the evidence available to support the application.

(3) The application must be lodged with the Crown Court.

(4) The application must be served on the defendant at least seven days before the date fixed by the court for hearing the application, unless the Crown Court specifies a shorter period.

Application for new calculation of available amount

58.4 (1) This rule applies where the prosecutor or a receiver makes an application under section 22 of the Proceeds of Crime Act 2002 for a new calculation of the available amount.

(2) The application must be in writing and may be supported by a witness statement.

(3) The application and any witness statement must be lodged with the Crown Court.

(4) The application and any witness statement must be served on—

    (a) the defendant;

    (b) the receiver, if the prosecutor is making the application and a receiver has been appointed under section 50 of the 2002 Act; and

    (c) the prosecutor, if the receiver is making the application,

at least seven days before the date fixed by the court for hearing the application, unless the Crown Court specifies a shorter period.

Variation of confiscation order due to inadequacy of available amount

58.5 (1) This rule applies where the defendant or a receiver makes an application under section 23 of the Proceeds of Crime Act 2002 for the variation of a confiscation order.

(2) The application must be in writing and may be supported by a witness statement.

(3) The application and any witness statement must be lodged with the Crown Court.

(4) The application and any witness statement must be served on—

(a) the prosecutor;

(b) the defendant, if the receiver is making the application; and

(c) the receiver, if the defendant is making the application and a receiver has been appointed under section 50 of the 2002 Act,

at least seven days before the date fixed by the court for hearing the application, unless the Crown Court specifies a shorter period.

Application by magistrates' court officer to discharge confiscation order

58.6 (1) This rule applies where a magistrates' court officer makes an application under section 24 or 25 of the Proceeds of Crime Act 2002 for the discharge of a confiscation order.

(2) The application must be in writing and give details of—

(a) the confiscation order;

(b) the amount outstanding under the order; and

(c) the grounds for the application.

(3) The application must be served on—

(a) the defendant;

(b) the prosecutor; and

(c) any receiver appointed under section 50 of the 2002 Act.

(4) The Crown Court may determine the application without a hearing unless a person listed in paragraph (3) indicates, within seven days after the application was served on him, that he would like to make representations.

(5) If the Crown Court makes an order discharging the confiscation order, the court must, at once, send a copy of the order to—

(a) the magistrates' court officer who applied for the order;

(b) the defendant;

(c) the prosecutor; and

(d) any receiver appointed under section 50 of the 2002 Act.

Application for variation of confiscation order made against an absconder

58.7 (1) This rule applies where the defendant makes an application under section 29 of the Proceeds of Crime Act 2002 for the variation of a confiscation order made against an absconder.

(2) The application must be in writing and supported by a witness statement which must give details of—

(a) the confiscation order made against an absconder under section 6 of the 2002 Act as applied by section 28 of the 2002 Act;

(b) the circumstances in which the defendant ceased to be an absconder;

(c) the defendant's conviction of the offence or offences concerned; and

(d) the reason why he believes the amount required to be paid under the confiscation order was too large.

(3) The application and witness statement must be lodged with the Crown Court.

(4) The application and witness statement must be served on the prosecutor at least seven days before the date fixed by the court for hearing the application, unless the Crown Court specifies a shorter period.

Application for discharge of confiscation order made against an absconder

58.8 (1) This rule applies if the defendant makes an application under section 30 of the Proceeds of Crime Act 2002 for the discharge of a confiscation order.

(2) The application must be in writing and supported by a witness statement which must give details of—

(a) the confiscation order made under section 28 of the 2002 Act;

    (b) the date on which the defendant ceased to be an absconder;

    (c) the acquittal of the defendant if he has been acquitted of the offence concerned; and

    (d) if the defendant has not been acquitted of the offence concerned—

        (i) the date on which the defendant ceased to be an absconder,

        (ii) the date on which the proceedings taken against the defendant were instituted and a summary of steps taken in the proceedings since then, and

        (iii) any indication given by the prosecutor that he does not intend to proceed against the defendant.

(3) The application and witness statement must be lodged with the Crown Court.

(4) The application and witness statement must be served on the prosecutor at least seven days before the date fixed by the court for hearing the application, unless the Crown Court specifies a shorter period.

(5) If the Crown Court orders the discharge of the confiscation order, the court must serve notice on the magistrates' court responsible for enforcing the order.

Application for increase in term of imprisonment in default

58.9 (1) This rule applies where the prosecutor makes an application under section 39(5) of the Proceeds of Crime Act 2002 to increase the term of imprisonment in default of payment of a confiscation order.

(2) The application must be made in writing and give details of—

    (a) the name and address of the defendant;

    (b) the confiscation order;

    (c) the grounds for the application; and

    (d) the enforcement measures taken, if any.

(3) On receipt of the application, the court must—

    (a) at once, send to the defendant and the magistrates' court responsible for enforcing the order, a copy of the application; and

    (b) fix a time, date and place for the hearing and notify the applicant and the defendant of that time, date and place.

(4) If the Crown Court makes an order increasing the term of imprisonment in default, the court must, at once, send a copy of the order to—

    (a) the applicant;

    (b) the defendant;

    (c) where the defendant is in custody at the time of the making of the order, the person having custody of the defendant; and

    (d) the magistrates' court responsible for enforcing the order.

Compensation—general

58.10 (1) This rule applies to an application for compensation under section 72 of the Proceeds of Crime Act 2002.

(2) The application must be in writing and may be supported by a witness statement.

(3) The application and any witness statement must be lodged with the Crown Court.

(4) The application and any witness statement must be served on—

    (a) the person alleged to be in default; and

    (b) the person or authority by whom the compensation would be payable under section 72(9) or 302(7A) of the 2002 Act (or if the compensation is payable out of a police fund under section 72(9)(a) or 302(7A), the chief officer of the police force concerned),

at least seven days before the date fixed by the court for hearing the application, unless the Crown Court directs otherwise.

Compensation—confiscation order made against absconder

58.11 (1) This rule applies to an application for compensation under section 73 of the Proceeds of Crime Act 2002.

(2) The application must be in writing and supported by a witness statement which must give details of—

    (a) the confiscation order made under section 28 of the 2002 Act;

    (b) the variation or discharge of the confiscation order under section 29 or 30 of the 2002 Act;

    (c) the realisable property to which the application relates; and

    (d) the loss suffered by the applicant as result of the confiscation order.

(3) The application and witness statement must be lodged with the Crown Court.

(4) The application and witness statement must be served on the prosecutor at least seven days before the date fixed by the court for hearing the application, unless the Crown Court specifies a shorter period.

Payment of money in bank or building society account in satisfaction of confiscation order

58.12 (1) An order under section 67 of the Proceeds of Crime Act 2002 requiring a bank or building society to pay money to a magistrates' court officer ('a payment order') shall—

    (a) be directed to the bank or building society in respect of which the payment order is made;

    (b) name the person against whom the confiscation order has been made;

    (c) state the amount which remains to be paid under the confiscation order;

    (d) state the name and address of the branch at which the account in which the money ordered to be paid is held and the sort code of that branch, if the sort code is known;

    (e) state the name in which the account in which the money ordered to be paid is held and the account number of that account, if the account number is known;

    (f) state the amount which the bank or building society is required to pay to the court officer under the payment order;

    (g) give the name and address of the court officer to whom payment is to be made; and

    (h) require the bank or building society to make payment within a period of seven days beginning on the day on which the payment order is made, unless it appears to the court that a longer or shorter period would be appropriate in the particular circumstances.

(2) The payment order shall be served on the bank or building society in respect of which it is made by leaving it at, or sending it by first class post to, the principal office of the bank or building society.

(3) A payment order which is served by first class post shall, unless the contrary is proved, be deemed to have been served on the second business day after posting.

(4) In this rule 'confiscation order' has the meaning given to it by section 88(6) of the Proceeds of Crime Act 2002.

PART 59 PROCEEDS OF CRIME ACT 2002: RULES APPLICABLE ONLY TO RESTRAINT PROCEEDINGS

Application for restraint order

59.1 (1) This rule applies where the prosecutor or an accredited financial investigator makes an application for a restraint order under section 42 of the Proceeds of Crime Act 2002.

(2) The application may be made without notice.

(3) The application must be in writing and supported by a witness statement which must—

    (a) give the grounds for the application;

    (b) to the best of the witness's ability, give full details of the realisable property in respect of which the applicant is seeking the order and specify the person holding that realisable property;

    (c) give the grounds for, and full details of, any application for an ancillary order under section 41(7) of the 2002 Act for the purposes of ensuring that the restraint order is effective; and

(d) where the application is made by an accredited financial investigator, include a statement that he has been authorised to make the application under section 68 of the 2002 Act.

Restraint orders

59.2 (1) The Crown Court may make a restraint order subject to exceptions, including, but not limited to, exceptions for reasonable living expenses and reasonable legal expenses, and for the purpose of enabling any person to carry on any trade, business or occupation.

(2) But the Crown Court must not make an exception for legal expenses where this is prohibited by section 41(4) of the Proceeds of Crime Act 2002.

(3) An exception to a restraint order may be made subject to conditions.

(4) The Crown Court must not require the applicant for a restraint order to give any undertaking relating to damages sustained as a result of the restraint order by a person who is prohibited from dealing with realisable property by the restraint order.

(5) The Crown Court may require the applicant for a restraint order to give an undertaking to pay the reasonable expenses of any person, other than a person who is prohibited from dealing with realisable property by the restraint order, which are incurred in complying with the restraint order.

(6) A restraint order must include a statement that disobedience of the order, either by a person to whom the order is addressed, or by another person, may be contempt of court and the order must include details of the possible consequences of being held in contempt of court.

(7) Unless the Crown Court directs otherwise, a restraint order made without notice has effect until the court makes an order varying or discharging the restraint order.

(8) The applicant for a restraint order must—

(a) serve copies of the restraint order and of the witness statement made in support of the application on the defendant and any person who is prohibited from dealing with realisable property by the restraint order; and

(b) notify any person whom the applicant knows to be affected by the restraint order of the terms of the restraint order.

Application for discharge or variation of restraint order by person affected by order

59.3 (1) This rule applies where a person affected by a restraint order makes an application to the Crown Court under section 42(3) of the Proceeds of Crime Act 2002 to discharge or vary the restraint order or any ancillary order made under section 41(7) of the Act.

(2) The application must be in writing and may be supported by a witness statement.

(3) The application and any witness statement must be lodged with the Crown Court.

(4) The application and any witness statement must be served on the person who applied for the restraint order and any person who is prohibited from dealing with realisable property by the restraint order (if he is not the person making the application) at least two days before the date fixed by the court for hearing the application, unless the Crown Court specifies a shorter period.

Application for variation of restraint order by the person who applied for the order

59.4 (1) This rule applies where the applicant for a restraint order makes an application under section 42(3) of the Proceeds of Crime Act 2002 to the Crown Court to vary the restraint order or any ancillary order made under section 41(7) of the 2002 Act (including where the court has already made a restraint order and the applicant is seeking to vary the order in order to restrain further realisable property).

(2) The application may be made without notice if the application is urgent or if there are reasonable grounds for believing that giving notice would cause the dissipation of realisable property which is the subject of the application.

(3) The application must be in writing and must be supported by a witness statement which must—

   (a) give the grounds for the application;

   (b) where the application is for the inclusion of further realisable property in the order give full details, to the best of the witness's ability, of the realisable property in respect of which the applicant is seeking the order and specify the person holding that realisable property; and

   (c) where the application is made by an accredited financial investigator, include a statement that he has been authorised to make the application under section 68 of the 2002 Act.

(4) The application and witness statement must be lodged with the Crown Court.

(5) Except where, under paragraph (2), notice of the application is not required to be served, the application and witness statement must be served on any person who is prohibited from dealing with realisable property by the restraint order at least 2 days before the date fixed by the court for hearing the application, unless the Crown Court specifies a shorter period.

(6) If the court makes an order for the variation of a restraint order, the applicant must serve copies of the order and of the witness statement made in support of the application on—

   (a) the defendant;

   (b) any person who is prohibited from dealing with realisable property by the restraint order (whether before or after the variation); and

   (c) any other person whom the applicant knows to be affected by the order.

Application for discharge of a restraint order by the person who applied for the order

59.5 (1) This rule applies where the applicant for a restraint order makes an application under section 42(3) of the Proceeds of Crime Act 2002 to discharge the order or any ancillary order made under section 41(7) of the 2002 Act.

   (2) The application may be made without notice.

   (3) The application must be in writing and must state the grounds for the application.

   (4) If the court makes an order for the discharge of a restraint order, the applicant must serve copies of the order on—

   (a) the defendant;

   (b) any person who is prohibited from dealing with realisable property by the restraint order (whether before or after the discharge); and

   (c) any other person whom the applicant knows to be affected by the order.

Application to punish for contempt of court

59.6 (1) This rule applies where a person is accused of disobeying a restraint order.

   (2) An applicant who wants the Crown Court to exercise its power to punish that person for contempt of court must comply with the rules in Part 62 (Contempt of court).

PART 60 PROCEEDS OF CRIME ACT 2002: RULES APPLICABLE ONLY TO RECEIVERSHIP PROCEEDINGS

Application for appointment of a management or an enforcement receiver

60.1 (1) This rule applies to an application for the appointment of a management receiver under section 48(1) of the Proceeds of Crime Act 2002 and an application for the appointment of an enforcement receiver under section 50(1) of the 2002 Act.

   (2) The application may be made without notice if—

   (a) the application is joined with an application for a restraint order under rule 59.1;

   (b) the application is urgent; or

   (c) there are reasonable grounds for believing that giving notice would cause the dissipation of realisable property which is the subject of the application.

(3) The application must be in writing and must be supported by a witness statement which must—

(a) give the grounds for the application;

(b) give full details of the proposed receiver;

(c) to the best of the witness's ability, give full details of the realisable property in respect of which the applicant is seeking the order and specify the person holding that realisable property;

(d) where the application is made by an accredited financial investigator, include a statement that he has been authorised to make the application under section 68 of the 2002 Act; and

(e) if the proposed receiver is not a person falling within section 55(8) of the 2002 Act and the applicant is asking the court to allow the receiver to act—

(i) without giving security, or

(ii) before he has given security or satisfied the court that he has security in place,

explain the reasons why that is necessary.

(4) Where the application is for the appointment of an enforcement receiver, the applicant must provide the Crown Court with a copy of the confiscation order made against the defendant.

(5) The application and witness statement must be lodged with the Crown Court.

(6) Except where, under paragraph (2), notice of the application is not required to be served, the application and witness statement must be lodged with the Crown Court and served on—

(a) the defendant;

(b) any person who holds realisable property to which the application relates; and

(c) any other person whom the applicant knows to be affected by the application,

at least seven days before the date fixed by the court for hearing the application, unless the Crown Court specifies a shorter period.

(7) If the court makes an order for the appointment of a receiver, the applicant must serve copies of the order and of the witness statement made in support of the application on—

(a) the defendant;

(b) any person who holds realisable property to which the order applies; and

(c) any other person whom the applicant knows to be affected by the order.

Application for conferral of powers on a management receiver or an enforcement receiver

60.2 (1) This rule applies to an application for the conferral of powers on a management receiver under section 49(1) of the Proceeds of Crime Act 2002 or an enforcement receiver under section 51(1) of the 2002 Act.

(2) The application may be made without notice if the application is to give the receiver power to take possession of property and—

(a) the application is joined with an application for a restraint order under rule 59.1;

(b) the application is urgent; or

(c) there are reasonable grounds for believing that giving notice would cause the dissipation of the property which is the subject of the application.

(3) The application must be made in writing and supported by a witness statement which must—

(a) give the grounds for the application;

(b) give full details of the realisable property in respect of which the applicant is seeking the order and specify the person holding that realisable property; and

(c) where the application is made by an accredited financial investigator, include a statement that he has been authorised to make the application under section 68 of the 2002 Act.

(4) Where the application is for the conferral of powers on an enforcement receiver or Director's receiver, the applicant must provide the Crown Court with a copy of the confiscation order made against the defendant.

(5) The application and witness statement must be lodged with the Crown Court.

(6) Except where, under paragraph (2), notice of the application is not required to be served, the application and witness statement must be served on—

(a) the defendant;

(b) any person who holds realisable property in respect of which a receiver has been appointed or in respect of which an application for a receiver has been made;

(c) any other person whom the applicant knows to be affected by the application; and

(d) the receiver (if one has already been appointed), at least seven days before the date fixed by the court for hearing the application, unless the Crown Court specifies a shorter period.

(7) If the court makes an order for the conferral of powers on a receiver, the applicant must serve copies of the order on—

(a) the defendant;

(b) any person who holds realisable property in respect of which the receiver has been appointed; and

(c) any other person whom the applicant knows to be affected by the order.

Applications for discharge or variation of receivership orders, and applications for other orders

60.3 (1) This rule applies to applications under section 62(3) of the Proceeds of Crime Act 2002 for orders (by persons affected by the action of receivers) and applications under section 63(1) of the 2002 Act for the discharge or variation of orders relating to receivers.

(2) The application must be made in writing and lodged with the Crown Court.

(3) The application must be served on the following persons (except where they are the person making the application)—

(a) the person who applied for appointment of the receiver;

(b) the defendant;

(c) any person who holds realisable property in respect of which the receiver has been appointed;

(d) the receiver; and

(e) any other person whom the applicant knows to be affected by the application, at least seven days before the date fixed by the court for hearing the application, unless the Crown Court specifies a shorter period.

(4) If the court makes an order for the discharge or variation of an order relating to a receiver under section 63(2) of the 2002 Act, the applicant must serve copies of the order on any persons whom he knows to be affected by the order.

Sums in the hands of receivers

60.4 (1) This rule applies where the amount payable under a confiscation order has been fully paid and any sums remain in the hands of an enforcement receiver or Director's receiver.

(2) The receiver must make an application to the Crown Court for directions as to the distribution of the sums in his hands.

(3) The application and any evidence which the receiver intends to rely on in support of the application must be served on—

(a) the defendant; and

(b) any other person who held (or holds) interests in any property realised by the receiver,

at least seven days before the date fixed by the court for hearing the application, unless the Crown Court specifies a shorter period.

(4) If any of the provisions listed in paragraph (5) (provisions as to the vesting of funds in a trustee in bankruptcy) apply, then the Crown Court must make a declaration to that effect.

(5) These are the provisions—
  (a) section 31B of the Bankruptcy (Scotland) Act 1985;
  (b) section 306B of the Insolvency Act 1986; and
  (c) article 279B of the Insolvency (Northern Ireland) Order 1989.

Security

60.5 (1) This rule applies where the Crown Court appoints a receiver under section 48, 50 or 52 of the Proceeds of Crime Act 2002 and the receiver is not a person falling within section 55(8) of the 2002 Act (and it is immaterial whether the receiver is a permanent or temporary member of staff or on secondment).

(2) The Crown Court may direct that before the receiver begins to act, or within a specified time, he must either—
  (a) give such security as the Crown Court may determine; or
  (b) file with the Crown Court and serve on all parties to any receivership proceedings evidence that he already has in force sufficient security,
to cover his liability for his acts and omissions as a receiver.

(3) The Crown Court may terminate the appointment of a receiver if he fails to—
  (a) give the security; or
  (b) satisfy the court as to the security he has in force, by the date specified.

Remuneration

60.6 (1) This rule applies where the Crown Court appoints a receiver under section 48, 50 or 52 of the Proceeds of Crime Act 2002 and the receiver is not a person falling within section 55(8) of the 2002 Act (and it is immaterial whether the receiver is a permanent or temporary member or he is on secondment from elsewhere).

(2) The receiver may only charge for his services if the Crown Court—
  (a) so directs; and
  (b) specifies the basis on which the receiver is to be remunerated.

(3) Unless the Crown Court orders otherwise, in determining the remuneration of the receiver, the Crown Court shall award such sum as is reasonable and proportionate in all the circumstances and which takes into account—
  (a) the time properly given by him and his staff to the receivership;
  (b) the complexity of the receivership;
  (c) any responsibility of an exceptional kind or degree which falls on the receiver in consequence of the receivership;
  (d) the effectiveness with which the receiver appears to be carrying out, or to have carried out, his duties, and
  (e) the value and nature of the subject matter of the receivership.

(4) The Crown Court may refer the determination of a receiver's remuneration to be ascertained by the taxing authority of the Crown Court and rules 76.11 to 76.14 shall have effect as if the taxing authority was ascertaining costs.

(5) A receiver appointed under section 48 of the 2002 Act is to receive his remuneration by realising property in respect of which he is appointed, in accordance with section 49(2)(d) of the 2002 Act.

(6) A receiver appointed under section 50 of the 2002 Act is to receive his remuneration by applying to the magistrates' court officer for payment under section 55(4)(b) of the 2002 Act.

(7) A receiver appointed under section 52 of the 2002 Act is to receive his remuneration by applying to the Director for payment under section 57(4)(b) of the 2002 Act.

Accounts

60.7 (1) The Crown Court may order a receiver appointed under section 48, 50 or 52 of the Proceeds of Crime Act 2002 to prepare and serve accounts.

(2) A party to receivership proceedings served with such accounts may apply for an order permitting him to inspect any document in the possession of the receiver relevant to those accounts.

(3) Any party to receivership proceedings may, within 14 days of being served with the accounts, serve notice on the receiver—
  (a) specifying any item in the accounts to which he objects;
  (b) giving the reason for such objection; and
  (c) requiring the receiver within 14 days of receipt of the notice, either—
    (i) to notify all the parties who were served with the accounts that he accepts the objection, or
    (ii) if he does not accept the objection, to apply for an examination of the accounts in relation to the contested item.

(4) When the receiver applies for the examination of the accounts he must at the same time lodge with the Crown Court—
  (a) the accounts; and
  (b) a copy of the notice served on him under this section of the rule.

(5) If the receiver fails to comply with paragraph (3)(c) of this rule, any party to receivership proceedings may apply to the Crown Court for an examination of the accounts in relation to the contested item.

(6) At the conclusion of its examination of the accounts the court will certify the result.

Non-compliance by receiver

60.8 (1) If a receiver appointed under section 48, 50 or 52 of the Proceeds of Crime Act 2002 fails to comply with any rule, practice direction or direction of the Crown Court, the Crown Court may order him to attend a hearing to explain his non-compliance.

(2) At the hearing, the Crown Court may make any order it considers appropriate, including—
  (a) terminating the appointment of the receiver;
  (b) reducing the receiver's remuneration or disallowing it altogether; and
  (c) ordering the receiver to pay the costs of any party.

PART 61   PROCEEDS OF CRIME ACT 2002: RULES APPLICABLE TO RESTRAINT AND RECEIVERSHIP PROCEEDINGS

Distress and forfeiture

61.1 (1) This rule applies to applications under sections 58(2) and (3) and 59(2) and (3) of the Proceeds of Crime Act 2002 for leave of the Crown Court to levy distress against property or exercise a right of forfeiture by peaceable re-entry in relation to a tenancy, in circumstances where the property or tenancy is the subject of a restraint order or a receiver has been appointed in respect of the property or tenancy.

(2) The application must be made in writing to the Crown Court.

(3) The application must be served on—
  (a) the person who applied for the restraint order or the order appointing the receiver; and
  (b) any receiver appointed in respect of the property or tenancy,
  at least seven days before the date fixed by the court for hearing the application, unless the Crown Court specifies a shorter period.

Joining of applications

61.2 An application for the appointment of a management receiver or enforcement receiver under rule 60.1 may be joined with—
  (a) an application for a restraint order under rule 59.1; and
  (b) an application for the conferral of powers on the receiver under rule 60.2.

Applications to be dealt with in writing

61.3 Applications in restraint proceedings and receivership proceedings are to be dealt with without a hearing, unless the Crown Court orders otherwise.

Business in chambers

61.4 Restraint proceedings and receivership proceedings may be heard in chambers.

Power of court to control evidence

61.5 (1) When hearing restraint proceedings and receivership proceedings, the Crown Court may control the evidence by giving directions as to—
(a) the issues on which it requires evidence;
(b) the nature of the evidence which it requires to decide those issues; and
(c) the way in which the evidence is to be placed before the court.
(2) The court may use its power under this rule to exclude evidence that would otherwise be admissible.
(3) The court may limit cross-examination in restraint proceedings and receivership proceedings.

Evidence of witnesses

61.6 (1) The general rule is that, unless the Crown Court orders otherwise, any fact which needs to be proved in restraint proceedings or receivership proceedings by the evidence of a witness is to be proved by their evidence in writing.
(2) Where evidence is to be given in writing under this rule, any party may apply to the Crown Court for permission to cross-examine the person giving the evidence.
(3) If the Crown Court gives permission under paragraph (2) but the person in question does not attend as required by the order, his evidence may not be used unless the court gives permission.

Witness summons

61.7 (1) Any party to restraint proceedings or receivership proceedings may apply to the Crown Court to issue a witness summons requiring a witness to—
(a) attend court to give evidence; or
(b) produce documents to the court.
(2) Rule 28.3 applies to an application under this rule as it applies to an application under section 2 of the Criminal Procedure (Attendance of Witnesses) Act 1965.

Hearsay evidence

61.8 Section 2(1) of the Civil Evidence Act 1995 (duty to give notice of intention to rely on hearsay evidence) does not apply to evidence in restraint proceedings and receivership proceedings.

Disclosure and inspection of documents

61.9 (1) This rule applies where, in the course of restraint proceedings or receivership proceedings, an issue arises as to whether property is realisable property.
(2) The Crown Court may make an order for disclosure of documents.
(3) Part 31 of the Civil Procedure Rules 1998 as amended from time to time shall have effect as if the proceedings were proceedings in the High Court.

Court documents

61.10 (1) Any order which the Crown Court issues in restraint proceedings or receivership proceedings must—
(a) state the name and judicial title of the person who made it;
(b) bear the date on which it is made; and
(c) be sealed by the Crown Court.
(2) The Crown Court may place the seal on the order—
(a) by hand; or
(b) by printing a facsimile of the seal on the order whether electronically or otherwise.
(3) A document purporting to bear the court's seal shall be admissible in evidence without further proof.

Consent orders

61.11 (1) This rule applies where all the parties to restraint proceedings or receivership proceedings agree the terms in which an order should be made.

(2) Any party may apply for a judgment or order in the terms agreed.

(3) The Crown Court may deal with an application under paragraph (2) without a hearing.

(4) Where this rule applies—

(a) the order which is agreed by the parties must be drawn up in the terms agreed;

(b) it must be expressed as being 'By Consent'; and

(c) it must be signed by the legal representative acting for each of the parties to whom the order relates or by the party if he is a litigant in person.

(5) Where an application is made under this rule, then the requirements of any other rule as to the procedure for making an application do not apply.

Slips and omissions

61.12 (1) The Crown Court may at any time correct an accidental slip or omission in an order made in restraint proceedings or receivership proceedings.

(2) A party may apply for a correction without notice.

Supply of documents from court records

61.13 (1) No document relating to restraint proceedings or receivership proceedings may be supplied from the records of the Crown Court for any person to inspect or copy unless the Crown Court grants permission.

(2) An application for permission under paragraph (1) must be made on notice to the parties to the proceedings.

Disclosure of documents in criminal proceedings

61.14 (1) This rule applies where—

(a) proceedings for an offence have been started in the Crown Court and the defendant has not been either convicted or acquitted on all counts; and

(b) an application for a restraint order under section 42(1) of the Proceeds of Crime Act 2002 has been made.

(2) The judge presiding at the proceedings for the offence may be supplied from the records of the Crown Court with documents relating to restraint proceedings and any receivership proceedings.

(3) Such documents must not otherwise be disclosed in the proceedings for the offence.

Preparation of documents

61.15 (1) Every order in restraint proceedings or receivership proceedings will be drawn up by the Crown Court unless—

(a) the Crown Court orders a party to draw it up;

(b) a party, with the permission of the Crown Court, agrees to draw it up; or

(c) the order is made by consent under rule 61.10.

(2) The Crown Court may direct that—

(a) an order drawn up by a party must be checked by the Crown Court before it is sealed; or

(b) before an order is drawn up by the Crown Court, the parties must lodge an agreed statement of its terms.

(3) Where an order is to be drawn up by a party—

(a) he must lodge it with the Crown Court no later than seven days after the date on which the court ordered or permitted him to draw it up so that it can be sealed by the Crown Court; and

(b) if he fails to lodge it within that period, any other party may draw it up and lodge it.

(4) Nothing in this rule shall require the Crown Court to accept a document which is illegible, has not been duly authorised, or is unsatisfactory for some other similar reason.

Change of solicitor

61.16 (1) This rule applies where—

    (a) a party for whom a solicitor is acting in restraint proceedings or receivership proceedings wants to change his solicitor;

    (b) a party, after having represented himself in such proceedings, appoints a solicitor to act on his behalf (except where the solicitor is appointed only to act as an advocate for a hearing); or

    (c) a party, after having been represented by a solicitor in such proceedings, intends to act in person.

  (2) Where this rule applies, the party or his solicitor (where one is acting) must—

    (a) lodge notice of the change at the Crown Court; and

    (b) serve notice of the change on every other party and, where paragraph (1)(a) or (c) applies, on the former solicitor.

  (3) The notice lodged at the Crown Court must state that notice has been served as required by paragraph (2)(b).

  (4) Subject to paragraph (5), where a party has changed his solicitor or intends to act in person, the former solicitor will be considered to be the party's solicitor unless and until—

    (a) notice is served in accordance with paragraph (2); or

    (b) the Crown Court makes an order under rule 61.17 and the order is served as required by paragraph (3) of that rule.

  (5) Where the certificate of a LSC funded client is revoked or discharged—

    (a) the solicitor who acted for that person will cease to be the solicitor acting in the proceedings as soon as his retainer is determined under regulation 4 of the Community Legal Service (Costs) Regulations 2000; and

    (b) if that person wishes to continue, where he appoints a solicitor to act on his behalf paragraph (2) will apply as if he had previously represented himself in the proceedings.

  (6) 'Certificate' in paragraph (5) means a certificate issued under the Funding Code (approved under section 9 of the Access to Justice Act 1999) and 'LSC funded client' means an individual who receives services funded by the Legal Services Commission as part of the Community Legal Service within the meaning of Part I of the 1999 Act.

Application by solicitor for declaration that solicitor has ceased to act

61.17 (1) A solicitor may apply to the Crown Court for an order declaring that he has ceased to be the solicitor acting for a party to restraint proceedings or receivership proceedings.

  (2) Where an application is made under this rule—

    (a) notice of the application must be given to the party for whom the solicitor is acting, unless the Crown Court directs otherwise; and

    (b) the application must be supported by evidence.

  (3) Where the Crown Court makes an order that a solicitor has ceased to act, the solicitor must serve a copy of the order on every party to the proceedings.

Application by other party for declaration that solicitor has ceased to act

61.18 (1) Where—

    (a) a solicitor who has acted for a party to restraint proceedings or receivership proceedings—

      (i) has died,

      (ii) has become bankrupt,

      (iii) has ceased to practise, or

      (iv) cannot be found, and

    (b) the party has not given notice of a change of solicitor or notice of intention to act in person as required by rule 61.16,

any other party may apply to the Crown Court for an order declaring that the solicitor has ceased to be the solicitor acting for the other party in the proceedings.

(2) Where an application is made under this rule, notice of the application must be given to the party to whose solicitor the application relates unless the Crown Court directs otherwise.

(3) Where the Crown Court makes an order under this rule, the applicant must serve a copy of the order on every other party to the proceedings.

Order for costs

61.19 (1) This rule applies where the Crown Court is deciding whether to make an order for costs in restraint proceedings or receivership proceedings.

(2) The court has discretion as to—

  (a) whether costs are payable by one party to another;

  (b) the amount of those costs; and

  (c) when they are to be paid.

(3) If the court decides to make an order about costs—

  (a) the general rule is that the unsuccessful party will be ordered to pay the costs of the successful party; but

  (b) the court may make a different order.

(4) In deciding what order (if any) to make about costs, the court must have regard to all of the circumstances, including—

  (a) the conduct of all the parties; and

  (b) whether a party has succeeded on part of an application, even if he has not been wholly successful.

(5) The orders which the court may make include an order that a party must pay—

  (a) a proportion of another party's costs;

  (b) a stated amount in respect of another party's costs;

  (c) costs from or until a certain date only;

  (d) costs incurred before proceedings have begun;

  (e) costs relating to particular steps taken in the proceedings;

  (f) costs relating only to a distinct part of the proceedings; and

  (g) interest on costs from or until a certain date, including a date before the making of an order.

(6) Where the court would otherwise consider making an order under paragraph (5)(f), it must instead, if practicable, make an order under paragraph (5)(a) or (c).

(7) Where the court has ordered a party to pay costs, it may order an amount to be paid on account before the costs are assessed.

Assessment of costs

61.20 (1) Where the Crown Court has made an order for costs in restraint proceedings or receivership proceedings it may either—

  (a) make an assessment of the costs itself; or

  (b) order assessment of the costs under rule 76.11.

(2) In either case, the Crown Court or the assessing authority, as the case may be, must—

  (a) only allow costs which are proportionate to the matters in issue; and

  (b) resolve any doubt which it may have as to whether the costs were reasonably incurred or reasonable and proportionate in favour of the paying party.

(3) The Crown Court or the assessing authority, as the case may be, is to have regard to all the circumstances in deciding whether costs were proportionately or reasonably incurred or proportionate and reasonable in amount.

(4) In particular, the Crown Court or the assessing authority must give effect to any orders which have already been made.

(5) The Crown Court or the assessing authority must also have regard to—

  (a) the conduct of all the parties, including in particular, conduct before, as well as during, the proceedings;

  (b) the amount or value of the property involved;

    (c) the importance of the matter to all the parties;
    (d) the particular complexity of the matter or the difficulty or novelty of the questions raised;
    (e) the skill, effort, specialised knowledge and responsibility involved;
    (f) the time spent on the application; and
    (g) the place where and the circumstances in which work or any part of it was done.

Time for complying with an order for costs

61.21 (1) A party to restraint proceedings or receivership proceedings must comply with an order for the payment of costs within 14 days of—
    (a) the date of the order if it states the amount of those costs;
    (b) if the amount of those costs is decided later under rule 76.11, the date of the assessing authority's decision; or
    (c) in either case, such later date as the Crown Court may specify.

Application of costs rules

61.22 Rules 61.19, 61.20 and 61.21 do not apply to the assessment of costs in proceedings to the extent that section 11 of the Access to Justice Act 1999 applies and provisions made under that Act make different provision.

PART 62   CONTEMPT OF COURT

When this Part applies

62.1 (1) This Part applies—
    (a) in the Crown Court, where a person is accused of disobeying—
        (i) an order of the Crown Court, or
        (ii) any other order, where legislation allows that person to be punished as if that were an order of the Crown Court;
    (b) in magistrates' courts and in the Crown Court, where a person is accused of contempt of court under section 18 of the Criminal Procedure and Investigations Act 1996.
  (2) In this Part, 'respondent' means any such accused person.

Exercise of court's power to punish for contempt of court

62.2 The court must not exercise its power to punish the respondent for contempt of court in the respondent's absence, unless the respondent has had at least 14 days in which to—
  (a) make any representations; and
  (b) introduce any evidence.

Application to punish for contempt of court

62.3 (1) A person who wants the court to exercise its power to punish the respondent for contempt of court must—
    (a) apply in writing and serve the application on the court officer; and
    (b) serve on the respondent—
        (i) the application, and
        (ii) notice of where and when the court will hear the application (not less than 14 days after service).
  (2) The application must—
    (a) identify the respondent;
    (b) explain that it is an application for the respondent to be punished for contempt of court;
    (c) contain such particulars of the conduct constituting contempt of court as to make clear what the applicant alleges against the respondent; and

    (d) include a notice warning the respondent that the court—
        (i)   can impose imprisonment, or a fine, or both, for contempt of court, and
        (ii) may deal with the application in the respondent's absence, if the respondent does not attend the hearing of the application.

Notice of suspension of punishment

62.4 (1) This rule applies where—
    (a) the court exercises its power to suspend a punishment it imposes for contempt of court—
        (i)   for a period, or
        (ii) conditionally; and
    (b) the respondent is absent when the court does so.
    (2) The applicant must serve on the respondent notice of the terms of the court's order.

Application to discharge an order for imprisonment

62.5 (1) This rule applies where—
    (a) the court has ordered the respondent's imprisonment for contempt of court; and
    (b) the respondent wants the court to discharge that order.
    (2) The respondent must—
    (a) apply in writing;
    (b) serve the application on—
        (i)   the court officer, and
        (ii) the applicant who applied for the respondent's punishment;
    (c) explain why it is appropriate for the order to be discharged; and
    (d) ask for a hearing, if the respondent wants one.

Introduction of written witness statement or other hearsay

62.6 (1) A party who wants to introduce in evidence the written statement of a witness, or other hearsay, must—
    (a) serve a copy of the statement, or notice of other hearsay, on—
        (i)   the court officer, and
        (ii) the other party; and
    (b) serve the copy or notice—
        (i)   when serving the application under rule 62.3, in the case of the applicant, or
        (ii) not more than 7 days after service of that application, in the case of the respondent.
    (2) Such service is notice of that party's intention to introduce in evidence that written witness statement, or other hearsay, unless that party otherwise indicates when serving it.
    (3) A party entitled to receive such notice may waive that entitlement by so informing the court officer and the party who would have given it.

Content of written witness statement

62.7 (1) This rule applies to a written witness statement served under rule 62.6.
    (2) Such a written witness statement must contain a declaration by the person making it that it is true to the best of that person's knowledge and belief.

False statements

62.8 (1) In the Crown Court, the court can punish for contempt of court a person who makes, or causes to be made, a false statement in such a written witness statement without an honest belief in its truth.
    (2) The Crown Court may exercise its power to punish that person for contempt of court—
    (a) on an application by a party, with the court's permission; or
    (b) on its own initiative.

(3) A person who wants the court to exercise that power must comply with the rules in this Part.

Content of notice of other hearsay

62.9 (1) This rule applies to a notice of hearsay, other than a written witness statement, served under rule 62.6.

(2) Such a notice must—

(a) set out the evidence, or attach the document that contains it; and

(b) identify the person who made the statement that is hearsay.

Cross-examination of maker of written witness statement or other hearsay

62.10 (1) This rule applies where a party wants the court's permission to cross-examine the maker of a written witness statement, or other hearsay statement, served under rule 62.6.

(2) The party who wants to cross-examine that person must—

(a) apply in writing, with reasons; and

(b) serve the application on—

(i) the court officer, and

(ii) the party who served the hearsay.

(3) A respondent who wants to cross-examine such a person must apply to do so not more than 7 days after service of the hearsay by the applicant.

(4) An applicant who wants to cross-examine such a person must apply to do so not more than 3 days after service of the hearsay by the respondent.

(5) The court—

(a) may decide an application under this rule without a hearing; but

(b) must not dismiss such an application unless the person making it has had an opportunity to make representations at a hearing.

Credibility and consistency of maker of written witness statement or other hearsay

62.11 (1) This rule applies where a party wants to challenge the credibility or consistency of the maker of a written witness statement, or other hearsay statement, served under rule 62.6.

(2) The party who wants to challenge the credibility or consistency of that person must—

(a) serve a written notice of intention to do so on—

(i) the court officer, and

(ii) the party who served the hearsay; and

(b) in it, identify any statement or other material on which that party relies.

(3) A respondent who wants to challenge such a person's credibility or consistency must serve such a notice not more than 7 days after service of the hearsay by the applicant.

(4) An applicant who wants to challenge such a person's credibility or consistency must serve such a notice not more than 3 days after service of the hearsay by the respondent.

(5) The party who served the hearsay—

(a) may call that person to give oral evidence instead; and

(b) if so, must serve a notice of intention to do so on—

(i) the court officer, and

(ii) the other party

as soon as practicable after service of the notice under paragraph (2).

R Court's power to vary requirements under this Part

62.12 (1) The court may shorten or extend (even after it has expired) a time limit under this Part.

(2) A person who wants an extension of time must—

(a) apply when serving the statement, notice or application for which it is needed; and

(b) explain the delay.

PART 63 APPEAL TO THE CROWN COURT

When this Part applies

63.1 (1) This part applies where—
- (a) a defendant wants to appeal under—
  - (i) section 108 of the Magistrates' Courts Act 1980,
  - (ii) section 45 of the Mental Health Act 1983,
  - (iii) paragraph 10 of schedule 3 to the Powers of Criminal Courts (Sentencing) Act 2000, or paragraphs 9(8) or 13(5) of Schedule 8 to the Criminal Justice Act 2003;
- (b) the Criminal Cases Review Commission refers a defendant's case to the Crown Court under section 11 of the Criminal Appeal Act 1995;
- (c) a prosecutor wants to appeal under—
  - (i) section 14A(5A) of the Football Spectators Act 1989, or
  - (ii) section 147(3) of the Customs and Excise Management Act 1979; or
- (d) a person wants to appeal under—
  - (i) section 1 of the Magistrates' Courts (Appeals from Binding Over Orders) Act 1956,
  - (ii) section 12(5) of the Contempt of Court Act 1981,
  - (iii) regulation 3C or 3H of the Costs in Criminal Cases (General) Regulations 1986, or
  - (iv) section 22 of the Football Spectators Act 1989.

(2) A reference to an 'appellant' in this part is a reference to such a party or person.

Service of appeal notice

63.2 (1) An appellant must serve an appeal notice on—
- (a) the magistrates' court officer; and
- (b) every other party.

(2) The appellant must serve the appeal notice—
- (a) as soon after the decision appealed against as the appellant wants; but
- (b) not more than 21 days after—
  - (i) sentence or the date sentence is deferred, whichever is earlier, if the appeal is against conviction or against a finding of guilt,
  - (ii) sentence, if the appeal is against sentence, or
  - (iii) the order or failure to make an order about which the appellant wants to appeal, in any other case.

(3) The appellant must—
- (a) serve with the appeal notice any application for an extension of the time limit under this rule; and
- (b) in that application, explain why the appeal notice is late.

Form of appeal notice

63.3 The appeal notice must be in writing and must—
- (a) specify—
  - (i) the conviction or finding of guilt,
  - (ii) the sentence, or
  - (iii) the order, or the failure to make an order
  about which the appellant wants to appeal;
- (b) summarise the issues;
- (c) in an appeal against conviction—
  - (i) identify the prosecution witnesses whom the appellant will want to question if they are called to give oral evidence, and
  - (ii) say how long the trial lasted in the magistrates' court and how long the appeal is likely to last in the Crown Court;

(d) in an appeal against a finding that the appellant insulted someone or interrupted proceedings in the magistrates' court, attach—
    (i) the magistrates' court's written findings of fact, and
    (ii) the appellant's response to those findings;
(e) say whether the appellant has asked the magistrates' court to reconsider the case; and
(f) include a list of those on whom the appellant has served the appeal notice.

Duty of magistrates' court officer

63.4 The magistrates' court officer must—
(a) as soon as practicable serve on the Crown Court officer—
    (i) the appeal notice and any accompanying application served by the appellant,
    (ii) details of the parties including their addresses,
    (iii) a copy of each magistrates' court register entry relating to the decision under appeal and to any application for bail pending appeal, and
    (iv) any report received for the purposes of sentencing;
(b) keep any document or object exhibited in the proceedings in the magistrates' court, or arrange for it to be kept by some other appropriate person, until—
    (i) 6 weeks after the conclusion of those proceedings, or
    (ii) the conclusion of any proceedings in the Crown Court that begin within that 6 weeks; and
(c) provide the Crown Court with any document, object or information for which the Crown Court officer asks, within such period as the Crown Court officer may require.

Duty of person keeping exhibit

63.5 A person who, under arrangements made by the magistrates' court officer, keeps a document or object exhibited in the proceedings in the magistrates' court must—
(a) keep that exhibit until—
    (i) 6 weeks after the conclusion of those proceedings, or
    (ii) the conclusion of any proceedings in the Crown Court that begin within that 6 weeks, unless the magistrates' court or the Crown Court otherwise directs; and
(b) provide the Crown Court with any such document or object for which the Crown Court officer asks, within such period as the Crown Court officer may require.

Reference by the Criminal Cases Review Commission

63.6 (1) The Crown Court officer must, as soon as practicable, serve a reference by the Criminal Cases Review Commission on—
    (a) the appellant;
    (b) every other party; and
    (c) the magistrates' court officer.
(2) The appellant may serve an appeal notice on—
    (a) the Crown Court officer; and
    (b) every other party,
    not more than 21 days later.
(3) The Crown Court must treat the reference as the appeal notice if the appellant does not serve an appeal notice.

Hearings and decisions

63.7 (1) The Crown Court as a general rule must hear in public an appeal or reference to which this part applies, but—
    (a) may order any hearing to be in private; and
    (b) where a hearing is about a public interest ruling, must hold that hearing in private.
(2) The Crown Court officer must give as much notice as reasonably practicable of every hearing to—
    (a) the parties;
    (b) any party's custodian; and
    (c) any other person whom the Crown Court requires to be notified.

(3) The Crown Court officer must serve every decision on—
   (a) the parties;
   (b) any other person whom the Crown Court requires to be served; and
   (c) the magistrates' court officer and any party's custodian, where the decision determines an appeal.
(4) But where a hearing or decision is about a public interest ruling, the Crown Court officer must not—
   (a) give notice of that hearing to; or
   (b) serve that decision on,
   anyone other than the prosecutor who applied for that ruling, unless the court otherwise directs.

Abandoning an appeal

63.8 (1) The appellant—
   (a) may abandon an appeal without the Crown Court's permission, by serving a notice of abandonment on—
      (i) the magistrates' court officer,
      (ii) the Crown Court officer, and
      (iii) every other party
      before the hearing of the appeal begins; but
   (b) after the hearing of the appeal begins, may only abandon the appeal with the Crown Court's permission.
(2) A notice of abandonment must be signed by or on behalf of the appellant.
(3) Where an appellant who is on bail pending appeal abandons an appeal—
   (a) the appellant must surrender to custody as directed by the magistrates' court officer; and
   (b) any conditions of bail apply until then.

Court's power to vary requirements under this Part

63.9 The Crown Court may—
   (a) shorten or extend (even after it has expired) a time limit under this Part;
   (b) allow an appellant to vary an appeal notice that that appellant has served;
   (c) direct that an appeal notice be served on any person;
   (d) allow an appeal notice or a notice of abandonment to be in a different form to one set out in the Practice Direction, or to be presented orally.

Constitution of the Crown Court

63.10 On the hearing of an appeal—
   (a) the general rule is that the Crown Court must comprise—
      (i) a judge of the High Court, a Circuit judge or a Recorder, and
      (ii) no less than two and no more than four justices of the peace, none of whom took part in the decision under appeal; and
   (b) if the appeal is from a youth court—
      (i) each justice of the peace must be qualified to sit as a member of a youth court, and
      (ii) the Crown Court must include a man and a woman; but
   (c) the Crown Court may include only one justice of the peace and need not include both a man and a woman if—
      (i) the presiding judge decides that otherwise the start of the appeal hearing will be delayed unreasonably, or
      (ii) one or more of the justices of the peace who started hearing the appeal is absent.

PART 64   APPEAL TO THE HIGH COURT BY WAY OF CASE STATED

Application to a magistrates' court to state a case

64.1   (1)   An application under section 111(1) of the Magistrates' Courts Act 1980 shall be made in writing and signed by or on behalf of the applicant and shall identify the question or questions of law or jurisdiction on which the opinion of the High Court is sought.

(2)   Where one of the questions on which the opinion of the High Court is sought is whether there was evidence on which the magistrates' court could come to its decision, the particular finding of fact made by the magistrates' court which it is claimed cannot be supported by the evidence before the magistrates' court shall be specified in such application.

(3)   Any such application shall be sent to a court officer for the magistrates' court whose decision is questioned.

Consideration of a draft case by a magistrates' court

64.2   (1)   Within 21 days after receipt of an application made in accordance with rule 64.1, a court officer for the magistrates' court whose decision is questioned shall, unless the justices refuse to state a case under section 111(5) of the Magistrates' Courts Act 1980, send a draft case in which are stated the matters required under rule 64.6 (content of case stated) to the applicant or his legal representative and shall send a copy thereof to the respondent or his legal representative.

(2)   Within 21 days after receipt of the draft case under paragraph (1), each party may make representations thereon. Any such representations shall be in writing and signed by or on behalf of the party making them and shall be sent to the magistrates' court officer.

(3)   Where the justices refuse to state a case under section 111(5) of the 1980 Act and they are required by a mandatory order of the High Court under section 111(6) to do so, this rule shall apply as if in paragraph (1)—

(a)   for the words 'receipt of an application made in accordance with rule 64.1' there were substituted the words 'the date on which a mandatory order under section 111(6) of the 1980 Act is made'; and

(b)   the words 'unless the justices refuse to state a case under section 111(5) of the 1980 Act' were omitted.

Preparation and submission of final case to a magistrates' court

64.3   (1)   Within 21 days after the latest day on which representations may be made under rule 64.2, the justices whose decision is questioned shall make such adjustments, if any, to the draft case prepared for the purposes of that rule as they think fit, after considering any such representations, and shall state and sign the case.

(2)   A case may be stated on behalf of the justices whose decision is questioned by any 2 or more of them and may, if the justices so direct, be signed on their behalf by the justices' clerk.

(3)   Forthwith after the case has been stated and signed a court officer for the court shall send it to the applicant or his legal representative, together with any statement required by rule 64.4.

Extension of time limits by a magistrates' court

64.4   (1)   If a magistrates' court officer is unable to send to the applicant a draft case under rule 64.2(1) within the time required by that paragraph, he shall do so as soon as practicable thereafter and the provisions of that rule shall apply accordingly; but in that event a court officer shall attach to the draft case, and to the final case when it is sent to the applicant or his legal representative under rule 64.3(3), a statement of the delay and the reasons for it.

(2) If a magistrates' court officer receives an application in writing from or on behalf of the applicant or the respondent for an extension of the time within which representations on the draft case may be made under rule 64.2(2), together with reasons in writing for it, the justices' clerk may, by notice in writing sent to the applicant, or respondent as the case may be, by the magistrates' court officer, extend the time and the provisions of that paragraph and of rule 64.3 shall apply accordingly; but in that event the court officer shall attach to the final case, when it is sent to the applicant or his legal representative under rule 64.3(3), a statement of the extension and the reasons for it.

(3) If the justices are unable to state a case within the time required by rule 64.3(1), they shall do so as soon as practicable thereafter and the provisions of that rule shall apply accordingly; but in that event a court officer shall attach to the final case, when it is sent to the applicant or his legal representative under rule 64.3(3), a statement of the delay and the reasons for it.

Content of case stated by a magistrates' courts

64.5 (1) A case stated by the magistrates' court shall state the facts found by the court and the question or questions of law or jurisdiction on which the opinion of the High Court is sought.

(2) Where one of the questions on which the opinion of the High Court is sought is whether there was evidence on which the magistrates' court could come to its decision, the particular finding of fact which it is claimed cannot be supported by the evidence before the magistrates' court shall be specified in the case.

(3) Unless one of the questions on which the opinion of the High Court is sought is whether there was evidence on which the magistrates' court could come to its decision, the case shall not contain a statement of evidence.

Application to the Crown Court to state a case

64.6 (1) An application under section 28 of the Senior Courts Act 1981 to the Crown Court to state a case for the opinion of the High Court shall be made in writing to a court officer within 21 days after the date of the decision in respect of which the application is made.

(2) The application shall state the ground on which the decision of the Crown Court is questioned.

(3) After making the application, the applicant shall forthwith send a copy of it to the parties to the proceedings in the Crown Court.

(4) On receipt of the application, the Crown Court officer shall forthwith send it to the judge who presided at the proceedings in which the decision was made.

(5) On receipt of the application, the judge shall inform the Crown Court officer as to whether or not he has decided to state a case and that officer shall give notice in writing to the applicant of the judge's decision.

(6) If the judge considers that the application is frivolous, he may refuse to state a case and shall in that case, if the applicant so requires, cause a certificate stating the reasons for the refusal to be given to him.

(7) If the judge decides to state a case, the procedure to be followed shall, unless the judge in a particular case otherwise directs, be the procedure set out in paragraphs (8) to (12) of this rule.

(8) The applicant shall, within 21 days of receiving the notice referred to in paragraph (5), draft a case and send a copy of it to the Crown Court officer and to the parties to the proceedings in the Crown Court.

(9) Each party to the proceedings in the Crown Court shall, within 21 days of receiving a copy of the draft case under paragraph (8), either—

(a) give notice in writing to the applicant and the Crown Court officer that he does not intend to take part in the proceedings before the High Court;

(b) indicate in writing on the copy of the draft case that he agrees with it and send the copy to a court officer; or

     (c) draft an alternative case and send it, together with the copy of the applicant's case, to the Crown Court officer.

(10) The judge shall consider the applicant's draft case and any alternative draft case sent to the Crown Court officer under paragraph (9)(c).

(11) If the Crown Court so orders, the applicant shall, before the case is stated and delivered to him, enter before the Crown Court officer into a recognizance, with or without sureties and in such sum as the Crown Court considers proper, having regard to the means of the applicant, conditioned to prosecute the appeal without delay.

(12) The judge shall state and sign a case within 14 days after either—

     (a) the receipt of all the documents required to be sent to a court officer under paragraph (9); or

     (b) the expiration of the period of 21 days referred to in that paragraph,

     whichever is the sooner.

(13) A case stated by the Crown Court shall state the facts found by the Crown Court, the submissions of the parties (including any authorities relied on by the parties during the course of those submissions), the decision of the Crown Court in respect of which the application is made and the question on which the opinion of the High Court is sought.

(14) Any time limit referred to in this rule may be extended either before or after it expires by the Crown Court.

(15) If the judge decides not to state a case but the stating of a case is subsequently required by a mandatory order of the High Court, paragraphs (7) to (14) shall apply to the stating of the case save that—

     (a) in paragraph (7) the words 'If the judge decides to state a case' shall be omitted; and

     (b) in paragraph (8) for the words 'receiving the notice referred to in paragraph (5)' there shall be substituted the words 'the day on which the mandatory order was made'.

Part 65   Appeal to the Court of Appeal: General Rules

When this Part applies

65.1 (1) This Part applies to all applications, appeals and references to the Court of Appeal to which Parts 66, 67, 68, 69, 70 and 74 apply.

    (2) In this Part and in those, unless the context makes it clear that something different is meant—

    'court' means the Court of Appeal or any judge of that court;

    'Registrar' means the Registrar of Criminal Appeals or a court officer acting with the Registrar's authority.

Case management in the Court of Appeal

65.2 (1) The court and the parties have the same duties and powers as under Part 3 (case management).

    (2) The Registrar—

     (a) must fulfil the duty of active case management under rule 3.2; and

     (b) in fulfilling that duty may exercise any of the powers of case management under—

      (i) rule 3.5 (the court's general powers of case management),

      (ii) rule 3.9(3) (requiring a certificate of readiness), and

      (iii) rule 3.10 (requiring a party to identify intentions and anticipated requirements)

     subject to the directions of the court.

    (3) The Registrar must nominate a case progression officer under rule 3.4.

Power to vary requirements

65.3 The court or the Registrar may—

    (a) shorten a time limit or extend it (even after it has expired) unless that is inconsistent with other legislation;

    (b) allow a party to vary any notice that that party has served;

(c) direct that a notice or application be served on any person;

(d) allow a notice or application to be in a different form, or presented orally.

Application for extension of time

65.4   A person who wants an extension of time within which to serve a notice or make an application must—

(a) apply for that extension of time when serving that notice or making that application; and

(b) give the reasons for the application for an extension of time.

Renewing an application refused by a judge or the Registrar

65.5   (1) This rule applies where a party with the right to do so wants to renew—

(a) to a judge of the Court of Appeal an application refused by the Registrar; or

(b) to the Court of Appeal an application refused by a judge of that court.

(2) That party must—

(a) renew the application in the form set out in the Practice Direction, signed by or on behalf of the applicant;

(b) serve the renewed application on the Registrar not more than 14 days after—

(i) the refusal of the application that the applicant wants to renew; or

(ii) the Registrar serves that refusal on the applicant, if the applicant was not present in person or by live link when the original application was refused.

Hearings

65.6   (1) The general rule is that the Court of Appeal must hear in public—

(a) an application, including an application for permission to appeal; and

(b) an appeal or reference,

but it may order any hearing to be in private.

(2) Where a hearing is about a public interest ruling that hearing must be in private unless the court otherwise directs.

(3) Where the appellant wants to appeal against an order restricting public access to a trial, the court—

(a) may decide without a hearing—

(i) an application, including an application for permission to appeal; and

(ii) an appeal; but

(b) must announce its decision on such an appeal at a hearing in public.

(4) Where the appellant wants to appeal or to refer a case to the Supreme Court the court—

(a) may decide without a hearing an application—

(i) for permission to appeal or to refer a sentencing case, or

(ii) to refer a point of law; but

(b) must announce its decision on such an application at a hearing in public.

(5) A judge of the Court of Appeal and the Registrar may exercise any of their powers—

(a) at a hearing in public or in private; or

(b) without a hearing.

Notice of hearings and decisions

65.7   (1) The Registrar must give as much notice as reasonably practicable of every hearing to—

(a) the parties;

(b) any party's custodian;

(c) any other person whom the court requires to be notified; and

(d) the Crown Court officer, where Parts 66, 67 or 69 apply.

(2) The Registrar must serve every decision on—

(a) the parties;

(b) any other person whom the court requires to be served; and

    (c) the Crown Court officer and any party's custodian, where the decision determines an appeal or application for permission to appeal.

(3) But where a hearing or decision is about a public interest ruling, the Registrar must not—

    (a) give notice of that hearing to; or

    (b) serve that decision on,

anyone other than the prosecutor who applied for that ruling, unless the court otherwise directs.

Duty of Crown Court officer

65.8 (1) The Crown Court officer must provide the Registrar with any document, object or information for which the Registrar asks within such period as the Registrar may require.

    (2) Unless the Crown Court otherwise directs, where someone may appeal to the Court of Appeal the Crown Court officer must—

        (a) arrange for the recording of the proceedings in the Crown Court;

        (b) arrange for the transcription of such a recording if—

            (i) the Registrar wants such a transcript, or

            (ii) anyone else wants such a transcript (but that is subject to the restrictions in rule 65.9(2)); and

        (c) arrange for any document or object exhibited in the proceedings in the Crown Court to be kept there, or kept by some other appropriate person, until 6 weeks after the conclusion of those proceedings.

    (3) Where Part 66 applies (appeal to the Court of Appeal against ruling at preparatory hearing), the Crown Court officer must as soon as practicable serve on the appellant a transcript or note of—

        (a) each order or ruling against which the appellant wants to appeal; and

        (b) the decision by the Crown Court judge on any application for permission to appeal.

    (4) Where Part 67 applies (appeal to the Court of Appeal against ruling adverse to prosecution), the Crown Court officer must as soon as practicable serve on the appellant a transcript or note of—

        (a) each ruling against which the appellant wants to appeal;

        (b) the decision by the Crown Court judge on any application for permission to appeal; and

        (c) the decision by the Crown Court judge on any request to expedite the appeal.

    (5) Where Part 68 applies (appeal to the Court of Appeal about conviction or sentence), the Crown Court officer must as soon as practicable serve on the Registrar—

        (a) the appeal notice and any accompanying application that the appellant serves on the Crown Court officer;

        (b) any Crown Court judge's certificate that the case is fit for appeal;

        (c) the decision on any application at the Crown Court centre for bail pending appeal;

        (d) such of the Crown Court case papers as the Registrar requires; and

        (e) such transcript of the Crown Court proceedings as the Registrar requires.

    (6) Where Part 69 applies (appeal to the Court of Appeal regarding reporting or public access) and an order is made restricting public access to a trial, the Crown Court officer must—

        (a) immediately notify the Registrar of that order, if the appellant has given advance notice of intention to appeal; and

        (b) as soon as practicable provide the applicant for that order with a transcript or note of the application.

Duty of person transcribing proceedings in the Crown Court

65.9 (1) A person who transcribes a recording of proceedings in the Crown Court under arrangements made by the Crown Court officer must provide the Registrar with any transcript for which the Registrar asks within such period as the Registrar may require.

(2) Unless the Crown Court otherwise directs, such a person—
- (a) must not provide anyone else with a transcript of a public interest ruling or of an application for such a ruling;
- (b) subject to that, must provide anyone else with any transcript for which that person asks—
  - (i) in accordance with the transcription arrangements made by the Crown Court officer, and
  - (ii) on payment by that person of any charge fixed by the Treasury.

Duty of person keeping exhibit

65.10 A person who under arrangements made by the Crown Court officer keeps a document or object exhibited in the proceedings in the Crown Court must—
- (a) keep that exhibit until—
  - (i) 6 weeks after the conclusion of the Crown Court proceedings, or
  - (ii) the conclusion of any appeal proceedings that begin within that 6 weeks,

  unless the court, the Registrar or the Crown Court otherwise directs; and
- (b) provide the Registrar with any such document or object for which the Registrar asks within such period as the Registrar may require.

Registrar's duty to provide copy documents for appeal or reference

65.11 Unless the court otherwise directs, for the purposes of an appeal or reference—
- (a) the Registrar must—
  - (i) provide a party with a copy of any document or transcript held by the Registrar for such purposes, or
  - (ii) allow a party to inspect such a document or transcript,

  on payment by that party of any charge fixed by the Treasury; but
- (b) the Registrar must not provide a copy or allow the inspection of—
  - (i) a document provided only for the court and the Registrar, or
  - (ii) a transcript of a public interest ruling or of an application for such a ruling.

Declaration of incompatibility with a Convention right

65.12 (1) This rule applies where a party—
- (a) wants the court to make a declaration of incompatibility with a Convention right under section 4 of the Human Rights Act 1998; or
- (b) raises an issue that the Registrar thinks may lead the court to make such a declaration.

(2) The Registrar must serve notice on—
- (a) the relevant person named in the list published under section 17(1) of the Crown Proceedings Act 1947; or
- (b) the Treasury Solicitor, if it is not clear who is the relevant person.

(3) That notice must include or attach details of—
- (a) the legislation affected and the Convention right concerned;
- (b) the parties to the appeal; and
- (c) any other information or document that the Registrar thinks relevant.

(4) A person who has a right under the 1998 Act to become a party to the appeal must—
- (a) serve notice on—
  - (i) the Registrar, and
  - (ii) the other parties,

  if that person wants to exercise that right; and
- (b) in that notice—
  - (i) indicate the conclusion that that person invites the court to reach on the question of incompatibility, and
  - (ii) identify each ground for that invitation, concisely outlining the arguments in support.

(5) The court must not make a declaration of incompatibility—
    (a) less than 21 days after the Registrar serves notice under paragraph (2); and
    (b) without giving any person who serves a notice under paragraph (4) an opportunity to make representations at a hearing.

Abandoning an appeal

65.13 (1) This rule applies where an appellant wants to—
    (a) abandon—
        (i) an application to the court for permission to appeal, or
        (ii) an appeal; or
    (b) reinstate such an application or appeal after abandoning it.
(2) The appellant—
    (a) may abandon such an application or appeal without the court's permission by serving a notice of abandonment on—
        (i) the Registrar, and
        (ii) any respondent
    before any hearing of the application or appeal; but
    (b) at any such hearing, may only abandon that application or appeal with the court's permission.
(3) A notice of abandonment must be in the form set out in the Practice Direction, signed by or on behalf of the appellant.
(4) On receiving a notice of abandonment the Registrar must—
    (a) date it;
    (b) serve a dated copy on—
        (i) the appellant,
        (ii) the appellant's custodian, if any,
        (iii) the Crown Court officer, and
        (iv) any other person on whom the appellant or the Registrar served the appeal notice; and
    (c) treat the application or appeal as if it had been refused or dismissed by the Court of Appeal.
(5) An appellant who wants to reinstate an application or appeal after abandoning it must—
    (a) apply in writing, with reasons; and
    (b) serve the application on the Registrar.

Abandoning a ground of appeal or opposition

65.14 (1) This rule applies where a party wants to abandon—
    (a) a ground of appeal identified in an appeal notice; or
    (b) a ground of opposition identified in a respondent's notice.
(2) Such a party must give written notice to—
    (a) the Registrar; and
    (b) every other party,
    before any hearing at which that ground will be considered by the court.

PART 66   APPEAL TO THE COURT OF APPEAL AGAINST RULING AT PREPARATORY HEARING

When this Part applies

66.1 (1) This Part applies where a party wants to appeal under—
    (a) section 9(11) of the Criminal Justice Act 1987 or section 35(1) of the Criminal Procedure and Investigations Act 1996; or
    (b) section 47(1) of the Criminal Justice Act 2003.
(2) A reference to an 'appellant' in this Part is a reference to such a party.

Service of appeal notice

66.2 (1) An appellant must serve an appeal notice on—
  (a) the Crown Court officer;
  (b) the Registrar; and
  (c) every party directly affected by the order or ruling against which the appellant wants to appeal.
(2) The appellant must serve the appeal notice not more than 5 business days after—
  (a) the order or ruling against which the appellant wants to appeal; or
  (b) the Crown Court judge gives or refuses permission to appeal.

Form of appeal notice

66.3 (1) An appeal notice must be in the form set out in the Practice Direction.
(2) The appeal notice must—
  (a) specify each order or ruling against which the appellant wants to appeal;
  (b) identify each ground of appeal on which the appellant relies, numbering them consecutively (if there is more than one) and concisely outlining each argument in support;
  (c) summarise the relevant facts;
  (d) identify any relevant authorities;
  (e) include or attach any application for the following, with reasons—
    (i) permission to appeal, if the appellant needs the court's permission,
    (ii) an extension of time within which to serve the appeal notice,
    (iii) a direction to attend in person a hearing that the appellant could attend by live link, if the appellant is in custody;
  (f) include a list of those on whom the appellant has served the appeal notice; and
  (g) attach—
    (i) a transcript or note of each order or ruling against which the appellant wants to appeal,
    (ii) all relevant skeleton arguments considered by the Crown Court judge,
    (iii) any written application for permission to appeal that the appellant made to the Crown Court judge,
    (iv) a transcript or note of the decision by the Crown Court judge on any application for permission to appeal, and
    (v) any other document or thing that the appellant thinks the court will need to decide the appeal.

Crown Court judge's permission to appeal

66.4 (1) An appellant who wants the Crown Court judge to give permission to appeal must—
  (a) apply orally, with reasons, immediately after the order or ruling against which the appellant wants to appeal; or
  (b) apply in writing and serve the application on—
    (i) the Crown Court officer, and
    (ii) every party directly affected by the order or ruling not more than 2 business days after that order or ruling.
(2) A written application must include the same information (with the necessary adaptations) as an appeal notice.

Respondent's notice

66.5 (1) A party on whom an appellant serves an appeal notice may serve a respondent's notice, and must do so if—
  (a) that party wants to make representations to the court; or
  (b) the court so directs.
(2) Such a party must serve the respondent's notice on—
  (a) the appellant;
  (b) the Crown Court officer;

        (c) the Registrar; and

        (d) any other party on whom the appellant served the appeal notice.

   (3) Such a party must serve the respondent's notice not more than 5 business days after—

        (a) the appellant serves the appeal notice; or

        (b) a direction to do so.

   (4) The respondent's notice must be in the form set out in the Practice Direction.

   (5) The respondent's notice must—

        (a) give the date on which the respondent was served with the appeal notice;

        (b) identify each ground of opposition on which the respondent relies, numbering them consecutively (if there is more than one), concisely outlining each argument in support and identifying the ground of appeal to which each relates;

        (c) summarise any relevant facts not already summarised in the appeal notice;

        (d) identify any relevant authorities;

        (e) include or attach any application for the following, with reasons—

           (i) an extension of time within which to serve the respondent's notice,

           (ii) a direction to attend in person any hearing that the respondent could attend by live link, if the respondent is in custody;

        (f) identify any other document or thing that the respondent thinks the court will need to decide the appeal.

Powers of Court of Appeal judge

66.6   A judge of the Court of Appeal may give permission to appeal as well as exercising the powers given by other legislation (including these Rules).

Renewing applications

66.7   Rule 65.5 (renewing an application refused by a judge or the Registrar) applies with a time limit of 5 business days.

Right to attend hearing

66.8   (1) A party who is in custody has a right to attend a hearing in public.

      (2) The court or the Registrar may direct that such a party is to attend a hearing by live link.

PART 67   APPEAL TO THE COURT OF APPEAL AGAINST
RULING ADVERSE TO THE PROSECUTION

When this Part applies

67.1   (1) This Part applies where a prosecutor wants to appeal under section 58(2) of the Criminal Justice Act 2003.

      (2) A reference to an 'appellant' in this Part is a reference to such a prosecutor.

Decision to appeal

67.2   (1) An appellant must tell the Crown Court judge of any decision to appeal—

        (a) immediately after the ruling against which the appellant wants to appeal; or

        (b) on the expiry of the time to decide whether to appeal allowed under paragraph (2).

      (2) If an appellant wants time to decide whether to appeal—

        (a) the appellant must ask the Crown Court judge immediately after the ruling; and

        (b) the general rule is that the judge must not require the appellant to decide there and then but instead must allow until the next business day.

Service of appeal notice

67.3   (1) An appellant must serve an appeal notice on—

        (a) the Crown Court officer;

        (b) the Registrar; and

        (c) every defendant directly affected by the ruling against which the appellant wants to appeal.

(2) The appellant must serve the appeal notice not later than—

    (a) the next business day after telling the Crown Court judge of the decision to appeal, if the judge expedites the appeal; or

    (b) 5 business days after telling the Crown Court judge of that decision, if the judge does not expedite the appeal.

Form of appeal notice

67.4 (1) An appeal notice must be in the form set out in the Practice Direction.

    (2) The appeal notice must—

        (a) specify each ruling against which the appellant wants to appeal;

        (b) identify each ground of appeal on which the appellant relies, numbering them consecutively (if there is more than one) and concisely outlining each argument in support;

        (c) summarise the relevant facts;

        (d) identify any relevant authorities;

        (e) include or attach any application for the following, with reasons—

            (i) permission to appeal, if the appellant needs the court's permission,

            (ii) an extension of time within which to serve the appeal notice,

            (iii) expedition of the appeal, or revocation of a direction expediting the appeal;

        (f) include a list of those on whom the appellant has served the appeal notice;

        (g) attach—

            (i) a transcript or note of each ruling against which the appellant wants to appeal,

            (ii) all relevant skeleton arguments considered by the Crown Court judge,

            (iii) any written application for permission to appeal that the appellant made to the Crown Court judge,

            (iv) a transcript or note of the decision by the Crown Court judge on any application for permission to appeal,

            (v) a transcript or note of the decision by the Crown Court judge on any request to expedite the appeal, and

            (vi) any other document or thing that the appellant thinks the court will need to decide the appeal; and

        (h) attach a form of respondent's notice for any defendant served with the appeal notice to complete if that defendant wants to do so.

Crown Court judge's permission to appeal

67.5 (1) An appellant who wants the Crown Court judge to give permission to appeal must—

        (a) apply orally, with reasons, immediately after the ruling against which the appellant wants to appeal; or

        (b) apply in writing and serve the application on—

            (i) the Crown Court officer, and

            (ii) every defendant directly affected by the ruling

    on the expiry of the time allowed under rule 67.2 to decide whether to appeal.

    (2) A written application must include the same information (with the necessary adaptations) as an appeal notice.

    (3) The Crown Court judge must allow every defendant directly affected by the ruling an opportunity to make representations.

    (4) The general rule is that the Crown Court judge must decide whether or not to give permission to appeal on the day that the application for permission is made.

Expediting an appeal

67.6 (1) An appellant who wants the Crown Court judge to expedite an appeal must ask, giving reasons, on telling the judge of the decision to appeal.

(2) The Crown Court judge must allow every defendant directly affected by the ruling an opportunity to make representations.

(3) The Crown Court judge may revoke a direction expediting the appeal unless the appellant has served the appeal notice.

Respondent's notice

67.7 (1) A defendant on whom an appellant serves an appeal notice may serve a respondent's notice, and must do so if—

    (a) the defendant wants to make representations to the court; or

    (b) the court so directs.

(2) Such a defendant must serve the respondent's notice on—

    (a) the appellant;

    (b) the Crown Court officer;

    (c) the Registrar; and

    (d) any other defendant on whom the appellant served the appeal notice.

(3) Such a defendant must serve the respondent's notice—

    (a) not later than the next business day after—

        (i) the appellant serves the appeal notice, or

        (ii) a direction to do so

    if the Crown Court judge expedites the appeal; or

    (b) not more than 5 business days after—

        (i) the appellant serves the appeal notice, or

        (ii) a direction to do so

    if the Crown Court judge does not expedite the appeal.

(4) The respondent's notice must be in the form set out in the Practice Direction.

(5) The respondent's notice must—

    (a) give the date on which the respondent was served with the appeal notice;

    (b) identify each ground of opposition on which the respondent relies, numbering them consecutively (if there is more than one), concisely outlining each argument in support and identifying the ground of appeal to which each relates;

    (c) summarise any relevant facts not already summarised in the appeal notice;

    (d) identify any relevant authorities;

    (e) include or attach any application for the following, with reasons—

        (i) an extension of time within which to serve the respondent's notice,

        (ii) a direction to attend in person any hearing that the respondent could attend by live link, if the respondent is in custody;

    (f) identify any other document or thing that the respondent thinks the court will need to decide the appeal.

Public interest ruling

67.8 (1) This rule applies where the appellant wants to appeal against a public interest ruling.

(2) The appellant must not serve on any defendant directly affected by the ruling—

    (a) any written application to the Crown Court judge for permission to appeal; or

    (b) an appeal notice

    if the appellant thinks that to do so in effect would reveal something that the appellant thinks ought not be disclosed.

(3) The appellant must not include in an appeal notice—

    (a) the material that was the subject of the ruling; or

    (b) any indication of what sort of material it is

    if the appellant thinks that to do so in effect would reveal something that the appellant thinks ought not be disclosed.

(4) The appellant must serve on the Registrar with the appeal notice an annex—

    (a) marked to show that its contents are only for the court and the Registrar;

  (b) containing whatever the appellant has omitted from the appeal notice, with reasons; and

  (c) if relevant, explaining why the appellant has not served the appeal notice.

 (5) Rules 67.5(3) and 67.6(2) do not apply.

Powers of Court of Appeal judge

67.9 A judge of the Court of Appeal may—

  (a) give permission to appeal;

  (b) revoke a Crown Court judge's direction expediting an appeal; and

  (c) where an appellant abandons an appeal, order a defendant's acquittal, his release from custody and the payment of his costs,

 as well as exercising the powers given by other legislation (including these Rules).

Renewing applications

67.10 Rule 65.5 (renewing an application refused by a judge or the Registrar) applies with a time limit of 5 business days.

Right to attend hearing

67.11 (1) A respondent who is in custody has a right to attend a hearing in public.

 (2) The court or the Registrar may direct that such a respondent is to attend a hearing by live link.

PART 68 APPEAL TO THE COURT OF APPEAL ABOUT
CONVICTION OR SENTENCE

When this Part applies

68.1 (1) This Part applies where—

  (a) a defendant wants to appeal under—

   (i) Part 1 of the Criminal Appeal Act 1968, or

   (ii) paragraph 14 of Schedule 22 to the Criminal Justice Act 2003,

   (iii) section 42 of the Counter-Terrorism Act 2008;

  (b) the Criminal Cases Review Commission refers a case to the Court of Appeal under section 9 of the Criminal Appeal Act 1995;

  (c) a prosecutor wants to appeal to the Court of Appeal under section 14A(5A) of the Football Spectators Act 1989;

  (d) a party wants to appeal under section 74(8) of the Serious Organised Crime and Police Act 2005;

  (e) a person found to be in contempt of court wants to appeal under section 13 of the Administration of Justice Act 1960 and section 18A of the Criminal Appeal Act 1968; or

  (f) a person wants to appeal to the Court of Appeal under—

   (i) section 24 of the Serious Crime Act 2007, or

   (ii) regulation 3C or 3H of the Costs in Criminal Cases (General) Regulations 1986.

 (2) A reference to an 'appellant' in this Part is a reference to such a party or person.

Service of appeal notice

68.2 (1) The general rule is that an appellant must serve an appeal notice—

  (a) on the Crown Court officer at the Crown Court centre where there occurred—

   (i) the conviction, verdict, or finding,

   (ii) the sentence, or

   (iii) the order, or the failure to make an order

  about which the appellant wants to appeal; and

  (b) not more than—

   (i) 28 days after that occurred, or

      (ii)   21 days after the order, in a case in which the appellant appeals against a wasted or third party costs order.

  (2) But an appellant must serve an appeal notice—

    (a) on the Registrar instead where—

      (i)   the appeal is against a minimum term review decision under paragraph 14 of Schedule 22 to the Criminal Justice Act 2003, or

      (ii) the Criminal Cases Review Commission refers the case to the court; and

    (b) not more than—

      (i)   28 days after such a decision, or after the Registrar serves notice that the Commission has referred a sentence, or

      (ii) 56 days after the Registrar serves notice that the Commission has referred a conviction.

Form of appeal notice

68.3 (1) An appeal notice must be in the form set out in the Practice Direction.

  (2) The appeal notice must—

    (a) specify—

      (i)   the conviction, verdict, or finding,

      (ii) the sentence, or

      (iii) the order, or the failure to make an order

    about which the appellant wants to appeal;

    (b) identify each ground of appeal on which the appellant relies, numbering them consecutively (if there is more than one) and concisely outlining each argument in support;

    (c) identify the transcript that the appellant thinks the court will need, if the appellant wants to appeal against a conviction;

    (d) identify the relevant sentencing powers of the Crown Court, if sentence is in issue;

    (e) where the Criminal Cases Review Commission refers a case to the court, explain how each ground of appeal relates (if it does) to the reasons for the reference;

    (f) summarise the relevant facts;

    (g) identify any relevant authorities;

    (h) include or attach any application for the following, with reasons—

      (i)   permission to appeal, if the appellant needs the court's permission,

      (ii) an extension of time within which to serve the appeal notice,

      (iii) bail pending appeal,

      (iv) a direction to attend in person a hearing that the appellant could attend by live link, if the appellant is in custody,

      (v) the introduction of evidence, including hearsay evidence and evidence of bad character,

      (vi) an order requiring a witness to attend court,

      (vii) a direction for special measures for a witness,

      (viii) a direction for special measures for the giving of evidence by the appellant;

      (ix) identify any other document or thing that the appellant thinks the court will need to decide the appeal.

Crown Court judge's certificate that case is fit for appeal

68.4 (1) An appellant who wants the Crown Court judge to certify that a case is fit for appeal must—

    (a) apply orally, with reasons, immediately after there occurs—

      (i)   the conviction, verdict, or finding,

      (ii) the sentence, or

      (iii) the order, or the failure to make an order

    about which the appellant wants to appeal; or

   (b) apply in writing and serve the application on the Crown Court officer not more than 14 days after that occurred.

  (2) A written application must include the same information (with the necessary adaptations) as an appeal notice.

Reference by Criminal Cases Review Commission

68.5 (1) The Registrar must serve on the appellant a reference by the Criminal Cases Review Commission.

  (2) The court must treat that reference as the appeal notice if the appellant does not serve such a notice under rule 68.2.

Respondent's notice

68.6 (1) The Registrar—

   (a) may serve an appeal notice on any party directly affected by the appeal; and

   (b) must do so if the Criminal Cases Review Commission refers a conviction, verdict, finding or sentence to the court.

  (2) Such a party may serve a respondent's notice, and must do so if—

   (a) that party wants to make representations to the court; or

   (b) the court or the Registrar so directs.

  (3) Such a party must serve the respondent's notice on—

   (a) the appellant;

   (b) the Registrar; and

   (c) any other party on whom the Registrar served the appeal notice.

  (4) Such a party must serve the respondent's notice not more than 14 days after the Registrar serves—

   (a) the appeal notice; or

   (b) a direction to do so.

  (5) The respondent's notice must be in the form set out in the Practice Direction.

  (6) The respondent's notice must—

   (a) give the date on which the respondent was served with the appeal notice;

   (b) identify each ground of opposition on which the respondent relies, numbering them consecutively (if there is more than one), concisely outlining each argument in support and identifying the ground of appeal to which each relates;

   (c) identify the relevant sentencing powers of the Crown Court, if sentence is in issue;

   (d) summarise any relevant facts not already summarised in the appeal notice;

   (e) identify any relevant authorities;

   (f) include or attach any application for the following, with reasons—

    (i) an extension of time within which to serve the respondent's notice,

    (ii) bail pending appeal,

    (iii) a direction to attend in person a hearing that the respondent could attend by live link, if the respondent is in custody,

    (iv) the introduction of evidence, including hearsay evidence and evidence of bad character,

    (v) an order requiring a witness to attend court,

    (vi) a direction for special measures for a witness; and

   (g) identify any other document or thing that the respondent thinks the court will need to decide the appeal.

Adaptation of rules about introducing evidence

68.7 (1) The following Parts apply with such adaptations as the court or the Registrar may direct—

   (a) Part 29 (special measures directions);

   (b) Part 30 (use of live television link other than for vulnerable witnesses);

(c) Part 34 (hearsay evidence);
(d) Part 35 (evidence of bad character); and
(e) Part 36 (evidence of a complainant's previous sexual behaviour).

(2) But the general rule is that—

    (a) a respondent who opposes an appellant's application to which one of those Parts applies must do so in the respondent's notice, with reasons;

    (b) an appellant who opposes a respondent's application to which one of those Parts applies must serve notice, with reasons, on—

        (i) the Registrar, and

        (ii) the respondent

    not more than 14 days after service of the respondent's notice; and

    (c) the court or the Registrar may give directions with or without a hearing.

Application for bail pending appeal or retrial

68.8 (1) This rule applies where a party wants to make an application to the court about bail pending appeal or retrial.

    (2) That party must serve an application in the form set out in the Practice Direction on—

    (a) the Registrar, unless the application is with the appeal notice; and

    (b) the other party.

    (3) The court must not decide such an application without giving the other party an opportunity to make representations, including representations about any condition or surety proposed by the applicant.

Conditions of bail pending appeal or retrial

68.9 (1) This rule applies where the court grants a party bail pending appeal or retrial subject to any condition that must be met before that party is released.

    (2) The court may direct how such a condition must be met.

    (3) The Registrar must serve a certificate in the form set out in the Practice Direction recording any such condition and direction on—

    (a) that party;

    (b) that party's custodian; and

    (c) any other person directly affected by any such direction.

    (4) A person directly affected by any such direction need not comply with it until the Registrar serves that person with that certificate.

    (5) Unless the court otherwise directs, if any such condition or direction requires someone to enter into a recognizance it must be—

    (a) in the form set out in the Practice Direction and signed before—

        (i) the Registrar,

        (ii) the custodian, or

        (iii) someone acting with the authority of the Registrar or custodian;

    (b) copied immediately to the person who enters into it; and

    (c) served immediately by the Registrar on the appellant's custodian or vice versa, as appropriate.

    (6) Unless the court otherwise directs, if any such condition or direction requires someone to make a payment, surrender a document or take some other step—

    (a) that payment, document or step must be made, surrendered or taken to or before—

        (i) the Registrar,

        (ii) the custodian, or

        (iii) someone acting with the authority of the Registrar or custodian;

    (b) the Registrar or the custodian, as appropriate, must serve immediately on the other a statement that the payment, document or step has been made, surrendered or taken, as appropriate.

(7) The custodian must release the appellant where it appears that any condition ordered by the court has been met.

(8) For the purposes of section 5 of the Bail Act 1976 (record of decision about bail), the Registrar must keep a copy of—

   (a) any certificate served under paragraph (3);

   (b) a notice of hearing given under rule 65.7(1); and

   (c) a notice of the court's decision served under rule 65.7(2).

(9) Where the court grants bail pending retrial the Registrar must serve on the Crown Court officer copies of the documents kept under paragraph (8).

Forfeiture of a recognizance given as a condition of bail

68.10 (1) This rule applies where—

   (a) the court grants a party bail pending appeal or retrial; and

   (b) the bail is subject to a condition that that party provides a surety to guarantee that he will surrender to custody as required; but

   (c) that party does not surrender to custody as required.

(2) The Registrar must serve notice on—

   (a) the surety; and

   (b) the prosecutor

of the hearing at which the court may order the forfeiture of the recognizance given by that surety.

(3) The court must not forfeit a surety's recognizance—

   (a) less than 7 days after the Registrar serves notice under paragraph (2); and

   (b) without giving the surety an opportunity to make representations at a hearing.

Right to attend hearing

68.11 A party who is in custody has a right to attend a hearing in public unless—

   (a) it is a hearing preliminary or incidental to an appeal, including the hearing of an application for permission to appeal; or

   (b) that party is in custody in consequence of—

      (i) a verdict of not guilty by reason of insanity, or

      (ii) a finding of disability.

Power to vary determination of appeal against sentence

68.12 (1) This rule applies where the court decides an appeal affecting sentence in a party's absence.

(2) The court may vary such a decision if it did not take account of something relevant because that party was absent.

(3) A party who wants the court to vary such a decision must—

   (a) apply in writing, with reasons;

   (b) serve the application on the Registrar not more than 7 days after—

      (i) the decision, if that party was represented at the appeal hearing, or

      (ii) the Registrar serves the decision, if that party was not represented at that hearing.

Directions about re-admission to hospital on dismissal of appeal

68.13 (1) This rule applies where—

   (a) an appellant subject to—

      (i) an order under section 37(1) of the Mental Health Act 1983 (detention in hospital on conviction), or

      (ii) an order under section 5(2) of the Criminal Procedure (Insanity) Act 1964 (detention in hospital on finding of insanity or disability) has been released on bail pending appeal; and

    (b) the court—
        (i) refuses permission to appeal,
        (ii) dismisses the appeal, or
        (iii) affirms the order under appeal.
(2) The court must give appropriate directions for the appellant's—
    (a) re-admission to hospital; and
    (b) if necessary, temporary detention pending re-admission.

Renewal or setting aside of order for retrial

68.14 (1) This rule applies where—
    (a) a prosecutor wants a defendant to be arraigned more than 2 months after the court ordered a retrial under section 7 of the Criminal Appeal Act 1968; or
    (b) a defendant wants such an order set aside after 2 months have passed since it was made.
(2) That party must apply in writing, with reasons, and serve the application on—
    (a) the Registrar;
    (b) the other party.

PART 69   APPEAL TO THE COURT OF APPEAL REGARDING REPORTING OR PUBLIC ACCESS RESTRICTIONS

When this Part applies

69.1 (1) This Part applies where a person directly affected by an order to which section 159(1) of the Criminal Justice Act 1988 applies wants to appeal against that order.
(2) A reference to an 'appellant' in this Part is a reference to such a party.

Service of appeal notice

69.2 (1) An appellant must serve an appeal notice on—
    (a) the Crown Court officer;
    (b) the Registrar;
    (c) the parties; and
    (d) any other person directly affected by the order against which the appellant wants to appeal.
(2) The appellant must serve the appeal notice not later than—
    (a) the next business day after an order restricting public access to the trial;
    (b) 10 business days after an order restricting reporting of the trial.

Form of appeal notice

69.3 (1) An appeal notice must be in the form set out in the Practice Direction.
(2) The appeal notice must—
    (a) specify the order against which the appellant wants to appeal;
    (b) identify each ground of appeal on which the appellant relies, numbering them consecutively (if there is more than one) and concisely outlining each argument in support;
    (c) summarise the relevant facts;
    (d) identify any relevant authorities;
    (e) include or attach, with reasons—
        (i) an application for permission to appeal,
        (ii) any application for an extension of time within which to serve the appeal notice,
        (iii) any application for a direction to attend in person a hearing that the appellant could attend by live link, if the appellant is in custody,
        (iv) any application for permission to introduce evidence, and
        (v) a list of those on whom the appellant has served the appeal notice; and
    (f) attach any document or thing that the appellant thinks the court will need to decide the appeal.

Advance notice of appeal against order restricting public access

69.4 (1) This rule applies where the appellant wants to appeal against an order restricting public access to a trial.

   (2) The appellant may serve advance written notice of intention to appeal against any such order that may be made.

   (3) The appellant must serve any such advance notice—

   (a) on—

   (i) the Crown Court officer,

   (ii) the Registrar,

   (iii) the parties, and

   (iv) any other person who will be directly affected by the order against which the appellant intends to appeal, if it is made; and

   (b) not more than 5 business days after the Crown Court officer displays notice of the application for the order.

   (4) The advance notice must include the same information (with the necessary adaptations) as an appeal notice.

   (5) The court must treat that advance notice as the appeal notice if the order is made.

Duty of applicant for order restricting public access

69.5 (1) This rule applies where the appellant wants to appeal against an order restricting public access to a trial.

   (2) The party who applied for the order must serve on the Registrar—

   (a) a transcript or note of the application for the order; and

   (b) any other document or thing that that party thinks the court will need to decide the appeal.

   (3) That party must serve that transcript or note and any such other document or thing as soon as practicable after—

   (a) the appellant serves the appeal notice; or

   (b) the order, where the appellant served advance notice of intention to appeal.

Respondent's notice on appeal against reporting restriction

69.6 (1) This rule applies where the appellant wants to appeal against an order restricting the reporting of a trial.

   (2) A person on whom an appellant serves an appeal notice may serve a respondent's notice, and must do so if—

   (a) that person wants to make representations to the court; or

   (b) the court so directs.

   (3) Such a person must serve the respondent's notice on—

   (a) the appellant;

   (b) the Crown Court officer;

   (c) the Registrar;

   (d) the parties; and

   (e) any other person on whom the appellant served the appeal notice.

   (4) Such a person must serve the respondent's notice not more than 3 business days after—

   (a) the appellant serves the appeal notice; or

   (b) a direction to do so.

   (5) The respondent's notice must be in the form set out in the Practice Direction.

   (6) The respondent's notice must—

   (a) give the date on which the respondent was served with the appeal notice;

   (b) identify each ground of opposition on which the respondent relies, numbering them consecutively (if there is more than one), concisely outlining each argument in support and identifying the ground of appeal to which each relates;

   (c) summarise any relevant facts not already summarised in the appeal notice;

   (d) identify any relevant authorities;

    (e) include or attach any application for the following, with reasons—
        (i) an extension of time within which to serve the respondent's notice,
        (ii) a direction to attend in person any hearing that the respondent could attend by live link, if the respondent is in custody,
        (iii) permission to introduce evidence; and
    (f) identify any other document or thing that the respondent thinks the court will need to decide the appeal.

Renewing applications

69.7   Rule 65.5 (renewing an application refused by a judge or the Registrar) applies with a time limit of 5 business days.

Right to introduce evidence

69.8   No person may introduce evidence without the court's permission.

Right to attend hearing

69.9   (1) A party who is in custody has a right to attend a hearing in public of an appeal against an order restricting the reporting of a trial.

        (2) The court or the Registrar may direct that such a party is to attend a hearing by live link.

Part 70   Reference to the Court of Appeal of Point of Law or Unduly Lenient Sentencing

When this Part applies

70.1   This Part applies where the Attorney General wants to—
    (a) refer a point of law to the Court of Appeal under section 36 of the Criminal Justice Act 1972; or
    (b) refer a sentencing case to the Court of Appeal under section 36 of the Criminal Justice Act 1988.

Service of notice of reference and application for permission

70.2   (1) The Attorney General must—
        (a) serve on the Registrar—
            (i) any notice of reference, and
            (ii) any application for permission to refer a sentencing case; and
        (b) with a notice of reference of a point of law, give the Registrar details of—
            (i) the defendant affected,
            (ii) the date and place of the relevant Crown Court decision, and
            (iii) the relevant verdict and sentencing.

        (2) The Attorney General must serve an application for permission to refer a sentencing case not more than 28 days after the last of the sentences in that case.

Form of notice of reference and application for permission

70.3   (1) A notice of reference and an application for permission to refer a sentencing case must be in the appropriate form set out in the Practice Direction, giving the year and number.

        (2) A notice of reference of a point of law must—
        (a) specify the point of law in issue and indicate the opinion that the Attorney General invites the court to give;
        (b) identify each ground for that invitation, numbering them consecutively (if there is more than one) and concisely outlining each argument in support;
        (c) exclude any reference to the defendant's name and any other reference that may identify the defendant;
        (d) summarise the relevant facts; and
        (e) identify any relevant authorities.

(3) An application for permission to refer a sentencing case must—
    (a) give details of—
        (i)   the defendant affected,
        (ii) the date and place of the relevant Crown Court decision, and
        (iii) the relevant verdict and sentencing;
    (b) explain why that sentencing appears to the Attorney General unduly lenient, concisely outlining each argument in support; and
    (c) include the application for permission to refer the case to the court.

(4) A notice of reference of a sentencing case must—
    (a) include the same details and explanation as the application for permission to refer the case;
    (b) summarise the relevant facts; and
    (c) identify any relevant authorities.

(5) Where the court gives the Attorney General permission to refer a sentencing case, it may treat the application for permission as the notice of reference.

Registrar's notice to defendant

70.4 (1) The Registrar must serve on the defendant—
    (a) a notice of reference;
    (b) an application for permission to refer a sentencing case.

    (2) Where the Attorney General refers a point of law, the Registrar must give the defendant notice that—
    (a) the outcome of the reference will not make any difference to the outcome of the trial; and
    (b) the defendant may serve a respondent's notice.

    (3) Where the Attorney General applies for permission to refer a sentencing case, the Registrar must give the defendant notice that—
    (a) the outcome of the reference may make a difference to that sentencing, and in particular may result in a more severe sentence; and
    (b) the defendant may serve a respondent's notice.

Respondent's notice

70.5 (1) A defendant on whom the Registrar serves a reference or an application for permission to refer a sentencing case may serve a respondent's notice, and must do so if—
    (a) the defendant wants to make representations to the court; or
    (b) the court so directs.

    (2) Such a defendant must serve the respondent's notice on—
    (a) the Attorney General; and
    (b) the Registrar.

    (3) Such a defendant must serve the respondent's notice—
    (a) where the Attorney General refers a point of law, not more than 28 days after—
        (i) the Registrar serves the reference, or
        (ii) a direction to do so;
    (b) where the Attorney General applies for permission to refer a sentencing case, not more than 14 days after—
        (i) the Registrar serves the application, or
        (ii) a direction to do so.

    (4) Where the Attorney General refers a point of law, the respondent's notice must—
    (a) identify each ground of opposition on which the respondent relies, numbering them consecutively (if there is more than one), concisely outlining each argument in support and identifying the Attorney General's ground or reason to which each relates;
    (b) summarise any relevant facts not already summarised in the reference;

      (c) identify any relevant authorities; and

      (d) include or attach any application for the following, with reasons—

         (i) an extension of time within which to serve the respondent's notice,

         (ii) permission to attend a hearing that the respondent does not have a right to attend,

         (iii) a direction to attend in person a hearing that the respondent could attend by live link, if the respondent is in custody.

(5) Where the Attorney General applies for permission to refer a sentencing case, the respondent's notice must—

      (a) say if the respondent wants to make representations at the hearing of the application or reference; and

      (b) include or attach any application for the following, with reasons—

         (i) an extension of time within which to serve the respondent's notice,

         (ii) permission to attend a hearing that the respondent does not have a right to attend,

         (iii) a direction to attend in person a hearing that the respondent could attend by live link, if the respondent is in custody.

Variation or withdrawal of notice of reference or application for permission

70.6 (1) This rule applies where the Attorney General wants to vary or withdraw—

      (a) a notice of reference; or

      (b) an application for permission to refer a sentencing case.

  (2) The Attorney General—

      (a) may vary or withdraw the notice or application without the court's permission by serving notice on—

         (i) the Registrar, and

         (ii) the defendant

      before any hearing of the reference or application; but

      (b) at any such hearing, may only vary or withdraw that notice or application with the court's permission.

Right to attend hearing

70.7 (1) A respondent who is in custody has a right to attend a hearing in public unless it is a hearing preliminary or incidental to a reference, including the hearing of an application for permission to refer a sentencing case.

  (2) The court or the Registrar may direct that such a respondent is to attend a hearing by live link.

Anonymity of defendant on reference of point of law

70.8 Where the Attorney General refers a point of law, the court must not allow anyone to identify the defendant during the proceedings unless the defendant gives permission.

PART 71 APPEAL TO THE COURT OF APPEAL UNDER THE PROCEEDS OF CRIME ACT 2002: GENERAL RULES

Extension of time

71.1 (1) An application to extend the time limit for giving notice of application for leave to appeal under Part 2 of the Proceeds of Crime Act 2002 must—

      (a) be included in the notice of appeal; and

      (b) state the grounds for the application.

  (2) The parties may not agree to extend any date or time limit set by this Part, Part 72 or Part 73, or by the Proceeds of Crime Act 2002 (Appeals under Part 2) Order 2003.

Other applications

71.2   Rules 68.3(2)(h) (form of appeal notice) shall apply in relation to an application—
   (a) by a party to an appeal under Part 2 of the Proceeds of Crime Act 2002 that, under
        article 7 of the Proceeds of Crime Act 2002 (Appeals under Part 2) Order 2003, a wit-
        ness be ordered to attend or that the evidence of a witness be received by the Court of
        Appeal; or
   (b) by the defendant to be given leave by the court to be present at proceedings for which
        leave is required under article 6 of the 2003 Order,
   as they apply in relation to applications under Part I of the Criminal Appeal Act 1968 and
   the form in which rules 68.15 and 68.26 require notice to be given may be modified as
   necessary.

Examination of witness by court

71.3   Rule 65.7 (notice of hearings and decisions) shall apply in relation to an order of the court
        under article 7 of the Proceeds of Crime Act 2002 (Appeals under Part 2) Order 2003 to
        require a person to attend for examination as it applies in relation to such an order of the
        court under Part I of the Criminal Appeal Act 1968.

Supply of documentary and other exhibits

71.4   Rule 65.11 (supply of documentary and other exhibits) shall apply in relation to an appel-
        lant or respondent under Part 2 of the Proceeds of Crime Act 2002 as it applies in relation
        to an appellant and respondent under Part I of the Criminal Appeal Act 1968.

Registrar's power to require information from court of trial

71.5   The Registrar may require the Crown Court to provide the Court of Appeal with any
        assistance or information which they may require for the purposes of exercising their juris-
        diction under Part 2 of the Proceeds of Crime Act 2002, the Proceeds of Crime Act 2002
        (Appeals under Part 2) Order 2003, this Part or Parts 72 and 73.

Hearing by single judge

71.6   Rule 65.6(5) (hearings) applies in relation to a judge exercising any of the powers referred
        to in article 8 of the Proceeds of Crime Act 2002 (Appeals under Part 2) Order 2003
        or the powers in rules 72.2(3) and (4) (respondent's notice), 73.2(2) (notice of appeal) and
        73.3(6) (respondent's notice), as it applies in relation to a judge exercising the powers
        referred to in section 31(2) of the Criminal Appeal Act 1968.

Determination by full court

71.7   Rule 65.5 (renewing an application refused by a single judge or the registrar) shall
        apply where a single judge has refused an application by a party to exercise in his favour any
        of the powers listed in article 8 of the Proceeds of Crime Act 2002 (Appeals under Part 2)
        Order 2003 or the power in rule 72.2(3) or (4) as it applies where the judge has refused to
        exercise the powers referred to in section 31(2) of the Criminal Appeal Act 1968.

Notice of determination

71.8   (1) This rule applies where a single judge or the Court of Appeal has determined an appli-
             cation or appeal under the Proceeds of Crime Act 2002 (Appeals under Part 2) Order
             2003 or under Part 2 of the Proceeds of Crime Act 2002.
        (2) The Registrar must, as soon as practicable, serve notice of the determination on all of
             the parties to the proceedings.
        (3) Where a single judge or the Court of Appeal has disposed of an application for leave to
             appeal or an appeal under section 31 of the 2002 Act, the registrar must also, as soon as
             practicable, serve the order on a court officer of the court of trial and any magistrates' court
             responsible for enforcing any confiscation order which the Crown Court has made.

Record of proceedings and transcripts

71.9 Rule 65.8(2)(a) and (b) (duty of Crown Court officer—arranging recording of proceedings in Crown Court and arranging transcription) and rule 65.9 (duty of person transcribing proceedings in the Crown Court) apply in relation to proceedings in respect of which an appeal lies to the Court of Appeal under Part 2 of the Proceeds of Crime Act 2002 as they apply in relation to proceedings in respect of which an appeal lies to the Court of Appeal under Part I of the Criminal Appeal Act 1968.

Appeal to Supreme Court

71.10 (1) An application to the Court of Appeal for leave to appeal to the Supreme Court under Part 2 of the Proceeds of Crime Act 2002 must be made—
    (a) orally after the decision of the Court of Appeal from which an appeal lies to the Supreme Court; or
    (b) in the form set out in the Practice Direction, in accordance with article 12 of the Proceeds of Crime Act 2002 (Appeals under Part 2) Order 2003 and served on the Registrar.

    (2) The application may be abandoned at any time before it is heard by the Court of Appeal by serving notice in writing on the Registrar.

    (3) Rule 65.6(5) (hearings) applies in relation to a single judge exercising any of the powers referred to in article 15 of the 2003 Order, as it applies in relation to a single judge exercising the powers referred to in section 31(2) of the Criminal Appeal Act 1968.

    (4) Rules 65.5 (renewing an application refused by a judge or the registrar) applies where a single judge has refused an application by a party to exercise in his favour any of the powers listed in article 15 of the 2003 Order as they apply where the judge has refused to exercise the powers referred to in section 31(2) of the 1968 Act.

    (5) The form in which rule 65.5(2) requires an application to be made may be modified as necessary.

PART 72 APPEAL TO THE COURT OF APPEAL UNDER PROCEEDS OF CRIME ACT 2002: PROSECUTOR'S APPEAL REGARDING CONFISCATION

Notice of appeal

72.1 (1) Where an appellant wishes to apply to the Court of Appeal for leave to appeal under section 31 of the Proceeds of Crime Act 2002, he must serve a notice of appeal in the form set out in the Practice Direction on—
    (a) the Crown Court officer; and
    (b) the defendant.

    (2) When the notice of the appeal is served on the defendant, it must be accompanied by a respondent's notice in the form set out in the Practice Direction for the defendant to complete and a notice which—
    (a) informs the defendant that the result of an appeal could be that the Court of Appeal would increase a confiscation order already imposed on him, make a confiscation order itself or direct the Crown Court to hold another confiscation hearing;
    (b) informs the defendant of any right he has under article 6 of the Proceeds of Crime Act 2002 (Appeals under Part 2) Order 2003 to be present at the hearing of the appeal, although he may be in custody;
    (c) invites the defendant to serve notice on the registrar if he wishes—
      (i) to apply to the Court of Appeal for leave to be present at proceedings for which leave is required under article 6 of the 2003 Order, or
      (ii) to present any argument to the Court of Appeal on the hearing of the application or, if leave is given, the appeal, and whether he wishes to present it in person or by means of a legal representative;

     (d) draws to the defendant's attention the effect of rule 71.4 (supply of documentary and other exhibits); and

     (e) advises the defendant to consult a solicitor as soon as possible.

  (3) The appellant must provide a Crown Court officer with a certificate of service stating that he has served the notice of appeal on the defendant in accordance with paragraph (1) or explaining why he has been unable to effect service.

Respondent's notice

72.2 (1) This rule applies where a defendant is served with a notice of appeal under rule 72.1.

  (2) If the defendant wishes to oppose the application for leave to appeal, he must, not later than 14 days after the date on which he received the notice of appeal, serve on the Registrar and on the appellant a notice in the form set out in the Practice Direction—

     (a) stating the date on which he received the notice of appeal;

     (b) summarising his response to the arguments of the appellant; and

     (c) specifying the authorities which he intends to cite.

  (3) The time for giving notice under this rule may be extended by the Registrar, a single judge or by the Court of Appeal.

  (4) Where the Registrar refuses an application under paragraph (3) for the extension of time, the defendant shall be entitled to have his application determined by a single judge.

  (5) Where a single judge refuses an application under paragraph (3) or (4) for the extension of time, the defendant shall be entitled to have his application determined by the Court of Appeal.

Amendment and abandonment of appeal

72.3 (1) The appellant may amend a notice of appeal served under rule 72.1 or abandon an appeal under section 31 of the Proceeds of Crime Act 2002—

     (a) without the permission of the Court at any time before the Court of Appeal have begun hearing the appeal; and

     (b) with the permission of the Court after the Court of Appeal have begun hearing the appeal, by serving notice in writing on the Registrar.

  (2) Where the appellant serves a notice abandoning an appeal under paragraph (1), he must send a copy of it to—

     (a) the defendant;

     (b) a court officer of the court of trial; and

     (c) the magistrates' court responsible for enforcing any confiscation order which the Crown Court has made.

  (3) Where the appellant serves a notice amending a notice of appeal under paragraph (1), he must send a copy of it to the defendant.

  (4) Where an appeal is abandoned under paragraph (1), the application for leave to appeal or appeal shall be treated, for the purposes of section 85 of the 2002 Act (conclusion of proceedings), as having been refused or dismissed by the Court of Appeal.

PART 73 APPEAL TO THE COURT OF APPEAL UNDER POCA 2002: RESTRAINT OR RECEIVERSHIP ORDERS

Leave to appeal

73.1 (1) Leave to appeal to the Court of Appeal under section 43 or section 65 of the Proceeds of Crime Act 2002 will only be given where—

     (a) the Court of Appeal considers that the appeal would have a real prospect of success; or

     (b) there is some other compelling reason why the appeal should be heard.

  (2) An order giving leave may limit the issues to be heard and be made subject to conditions.

Notice of appeal

73.2 (1) Where an appellant wishes to apply to the Court of Appeal for leave to appeal under section 43 or 65 of the Proceeds of Crime Act 2002 Act, he must serve a notice of appeal in the form set out in the Practice Direction on the Crown Court officer.

(2) Unless the Registrar, a single judge or the Court of Appeal directs otherwise, the appellant must serve the notice of appeal, accompanied by a respondent's notice in the form set out in the Practice Direction for the respondent to complete, on—

(a) each respondent;

(b) any person who holds realisable property to which the appeal relates; and

(c) any other person affected by the appeal,

as soon as practicable and in any event not later than 7 days after the notice of appeal is served on a Crown Court officer.

(3) The appellant must serve the following documents with his notice of appeal—

(a) four additional copies of the notice of appeal for the Court of Appeal;

(b) four copies of any skeleton argument;

(c) one sealed copy and four unsealed copies of any order being appealed;

(d) four copies of any witness statement or affidavit in support of the application for leave to appeal;

(e) four copies of a suitable record of the reasons for judgment of the Crown Court; and

(f) four copies of the bundle of documents used in the Crown Court proceedings from which the appeal lies.

(4) Where it is not possible to serve all of the documents referred to in paragraph (3), the appellant must indicate which documents have not yet been served and the reasons why they are not currently available.

(5) The appellant must provide a Crown Court officer with a certificate of service stating that he has served the notice of appeal on each respondent in accordance with paragraph (2) and including full details of each respondent or explaining why he has been unable to effect service.

Respondent's notice

73.3 (1) This rule applies to an appeal under section 43 or 65 of the Proceeds of Crime Act 2002.

(2) A respondent may serve a respondent's notice on the Registrar.

(3) A respondent who—

(a) is seeking leave to appeal from the Court of Appeal; or

(b) wishes to ask the Court of Appeal to uphold the decision of the Crown Court for reasons different from or additional to those given by the Crown Court,

must serve a respondent's notice on the Registrar.

(4) A respondent's notice must be in the form set out in the Practice Direction and where the respondent seeks leave to appeal to the Court of Appeal it must be requested in the respondent's notice.

(5) A respondent's notice must be served on the Registrar not later than 14 days after—

(a) the date the respondent is served with notification that the Court of Appeal has given the appellant leave to appeal; or

(b) the date the respondent is served with notification that the application for leave to appeal and the appeal itself are to be heard together.

(6) Unless the Registrar, a single judge or the Court of Appeal directs otherwise, the respondent serving a respondent's notice must serve the notice on the appellant and any other respondent—

(a) as soon as practicable; and

(b) in any event not later than seven days,

after it is served on the Registrar.

Amendment and abandonment of appeal

73.4   (1) The appellant may amend a notice of appeal served under rule 73.2 or abandon an appeal under section 43 or 65 of the Proceeds of Crime Act 2002—

(a) without the permission of the Court at any time before the Court of Appeal have begun hearing the appeal; and

(b) with the permission of the Court after the Court of Appeal have begun hearing the appeal,

by serving notice in writing on the Registrar.

(2) Where the appellant serves a notice under paragraph (1), he must send a copy of it to each respondent.

Stay

73.5   Unless the Court of Appeal or the Crown Court orders otherwise, an appeal under section 43 or 65 of the Proceeds of Crime Act 2002 shall not operate as a stay of any order or decision of the Crown Court.

Striking out appeal notices and setting aside or imposing conditions on leave to appeal

73.6   (1) The Court of Appeal may—

(a) strike out the whole or part of a notice of appeal served under rule 73.2; or

(b) impose or vary conditions upon which an appeal under section 43 or 65 of the Proceeds of Crime Act 2002 may be brought.

(2) The Court of Appeal will only exercise its powers under paragraph (1) where there is a compelling reason for doing so.

(3) Where a party is present at the hearing at which leave to appeal was given, he may not subsequently apply for an order that the Court of Appeal exercise its powers under paragraph (1)(b).

Hearing of appeals

73.7   (1) This rule applies to appeals under section 43 or 65 of the Proceeds of Crime Act 2002.

(2) Every appeal will be limited to a review of the decision of the Crown Court unless the Court of Appeal considers that in the circumstances of an individual appeal it would be in the interests of justice to hold a re-hearing.

(3) The Court of Appeal will allow an appeal where the decision of the Crown Court was—

(a) wrong; or

(b) unjust because of a serious procedural or other irregularity in the proceedings in the Crown Court.

(4) The Court of Appeal may draw any inference of fact which it considers justified on the evidence.

(5) At the hearing of the appeal a party may not rely on a matter not contained in his notice of appeal unless the Court of Appeal gives permission.

PART 74   APPEAL OR REFERENCE TO THE SUPREME COURT

When this Part applies

74.1   (1) This Part applies where—

(a) a party wants to appeal to the Supreme Court after—

(i) an application to the Court of Appeal to which Part 41 applies (retrial following acquittal for serious offence), or

(ii) an appeal to the Court of Appeal to which applies Part 66 (appeal to the Court of Appeal against ruling at preparatory hearing), Part 67 (appeal to the Court of Appeal against ruling adverse to prosecution), or Part 68 (appeal to the Court of Appeal about conviction or sentence); or

(b) a party wants to refer a case to the Supreme Court after a reference to the Court of Appeal to which Part 70 applies (reference to the Court of Appeal of point of law or unduly lenient sentencing).

(2) A reference to an 'appellant' in this Part is a reference to such a party.

Application for permission or reference

74.2 (1) An appellant must—

    (a) apply orally to the Court of Appeal—

        (i) for permission to appeal or to refer a sentencing case, or

        (ii) to refer a point of law

    immediately after the court gives the reasons for its decision; or

    (b) apply in writing and serve the application on the Registrar and every other party not more than—

        (i) 14 days after the court gives the reasons for its decision if that decision was on a sentencing reference to which Part 70 applies (Attorney General's reference of sentencing case), or

        (ii) 28 days after the court gives those reasons in any other case.

(2) An application for permission to appeal or to refer a sentencing case must—

    (a) identify the point of law of general public importance that the appellant wants the court to certify is involved in the decision; and

    (b) give reasons why—

        (i) that point of law ought to be considered by the Supreme Court, and

        (ii) the court ought to give permission to appeal.

(3) An application to refer a point of law must give reasons why that point ought to be considered by the Supreme Court.

(4) An application must include or attach any application for the following, with reasons—

    (a) an extension of time within which to make the application for permission or for a reference,

    (b) bail pending appeal,

    (c) permission to attend any hearing in the Supreme Court, if the appellant is in custody.

(5) A written application must be in the form set out in the Practice Direction.

Determination of detention pending appeal, etc.

74.3 On an application for permission to appeal the Court of Appeal must—

    (a) decide whether to order the detention of a defendant who would have been liable to be detained but for the decision of the court; and

    (b) determine any application for—

        (i) bail pending appeal,

        (ii) permission to attend any hearing in the Supreme Court, or

        (iii) a representation order.

Bail pending appeal

74.4 Rules 68.8 (Application for bail pending appeal or retrial), 68.9 (Conditions of bail pending appeal or re-trial) and 68.10 (Forfeiture of a recognizance given as a condition of bail) apply.

Part 75   Request to the European Court for a Preliminary Ruling

When this Part applies

75.1 This Part applies where the court can request the Court of Justice of the European Union ('the European Court') to give a preliminary ruling, under Article 267 of the Treaty on the Functioning of the European Union.

Preparation of request

75.2 (1) The court may—

    (a) make an order for the submission of a request—

        (i) on application by a party, or

        (ii) on its own initiative;

    (b) give directions for the preparation of the terms of such a request.

    (2) The court must—

    (a) include in such a request—

        (i) the identity of the court making the request,

        (ii) the parties' identities,

        (iii) a statement of whether a party is in custody,

        (iv) a succinct statement of the question on which the court seeks the ruling of the European Court,

        (v) a succinct statement of any opinion on the answer that the court may have expressed in any judgment that it has delivered,

        (vi) a summary of the nature and history of the proceedings, including the salient facts and an indication of whether those facts are proved, admitted or assumed,

        (vii) the relevant rules of national law,

        (viii) a summary of the relevant contentions of the parties,

        (ix) an indication of the provisions of European Union law that the European Court is asked to interpret, and

        (x) an explanation of why a ruling of the European Court is requested;

    (b) express the request in terms that can be translated readily into other languages; and

    (c) set out the request in a schedule to the order.

Submission of request

75.3 (1) The court officer must serve the order for the submission of the request on the Senior Master of the Queen's Bench Division of the High Court.

    (2) The Senior Master will—

    (a) submit the request to the European Court; but

    (b) unless the court otherwise directs, postpone the submission of the request until—

        (i) the time for any appeal against the order has expired, and

        (ii) any appeal against the order has been determined.

Postponement of case pending request

75.4 Where the court orders the submission of a request—

    (a) the general rule is that it will adjourn or postpone any further hearing; but

    (b) it may otherwise direct.

Part 76 Costs

Section 1: General

When this Part applies

76.1 (1) This Part applies where the court can make an order about costs under—

    (a) Part II of the Prosecution of Offences Act 1985 and Part II, IIA or IIB of The Costs in Criminal Cases (General) Regulations 1986;

    (b) section 109 of the Magistrates' Courts Act 1980;

    (c) section 52 of the Senior Courts Act 1981 and rule 76.6;

    (d) section 8 of the Bankers Books Evidence Act 1879;

    (e) section 2C(8) of the Criminal Procedure (Attendance of Witnesses) Act 1965;

    (f) section 36(5) of the Criminal Justice Act 1972;

(g) section 159(5) and Schedule 3, paragraph 11, of the Criminal Justice Act 1988;

(h) section 14H(5) of the Football Spectators Act 1989; or

(i) Part 3 of The Serious Crime Act 2007 (Appeals under Section 24) Order 2008.

(2) In this Part, 'costs' means—

(a) the fees payable to a legal representative;

(b) the disbursements paid by a legal representative; and

(c) any other expenses incurred in connection with the case.

Costs orders: general rules

76.2 (1) The court must not make an order about costs unless each party and any other person directly affected—

(a) is present; or

(b) has had an opportunity—

(i) to attend, or

(ii) to make representations.

(2) The court may make an order about costs—

(a) at a hearing in public or in private; or

(b) without a hearing.

(3) In deciding what order, if any, to make about costs, the court must have regard to all the circumstances, including—

(a) the conduct of all the parties; and

(b) any costs order already made.

(4) If the court makes an order about costs, it must—

(a) specify who must, or must not, pay what, to whom; and

(b) identify the legislation under which the order is made, where there is a choice of powers.

(5) The court must give reasons if it—

(a) refuses an application for a costs order; or

(b) rejects representations opposing a costs order.

(6) If the court makes an order for the payment of costs—

(a) the general rule is that it will be for an amount that is sufficient reasonably to compensate the recipient for costs—

(i) actually, reasonably and properly incurred, and

(ii) reasonable in amount; but

(b) the court may order the payment of—

(i) a proportion of that amount,

(ii) a stated amount less than that amount,

(iii) costs from or until a certain date only,

(iv) costs relating only to particular steps taken, or

(v) costs relating only to a distinct part of the case.

(7) On an assessment of the amount of costs, relevant factors include—

(a) the conduct of all the parties;

(b) the particular complexity of the matter or the difficulty or novelty of the questions raised;

(c) the skill, effort, specialised knowledge and responsibility involved;

(d) the time spent on the case;

(e) the place where and the circumstances in which work or any part of it was done; and

(f) any direction or observations by the court that made the costs order.

(8) If the court orders a party to pay costs to be assessed under rule 76.11, it may order that party to pay an amount on account.

(9) An order for the payment of costs takes effect when the amount is assessed, unless the court exercises any power it has to order otherwise.

Court's power to vary requirements under Sections 2, 3 and 4

76.3 (1) The court may—
- (a) extend a time limit for serving an application or representations under section 2, 3 or 4 of this Part, even after it has expired; and
- (b) consider an application or representations—
  - (i) made in a different form to one set out in the Practice Direction, or
  - (ii) made orally instead of in writing.
(2) A person who wants an extension of time must—
- (a) apply when serving the application or representations for which it is needed; and
- (b) explain the delay.

Section 2: Costs Out of Central Funds

Costs out of central funds

76.4 (1) This rule applies where the court can order the payment of costs out of central funds.
(2) In this rule, costs—
- (a) include—
  - (i) on an appeal, costs incurred in the court that made the decision under appeal, and
  - (ii) at a retrial, costs incurred at the initial trial and on any appeal; but
- (b) do not include costs funded by the Legal Services Commission.
(3) The court may make an order—
- (a) on application by the person who incurred the costs; or
- (b) on its own initiative.
(4) Where a person wants the court to make an order that person must—
- (a) apply as soon as practicable; and
- (b) outline the type of costs and the amount claimed, if that person wants the court to direct an assessment; or
- (c) specify the amount claimed, if that person wants the court to assess the amount itself.
(5) The general rule is that the court will make an order, but —
- (a) the court may decline to make a defendant's costs order if, for example—
  - (i) the defendant is convicted of at least one offence, or
  - (ii) the defendant's conduct led the prosecutor reasonably to think the prosecution case stronger than it was; and
- (b) the court may decline to make a prosecutor's costs order if, for example, the prosecution was started or continued unreasonably.
(6) If the court makes an order—
- (a) it may direct an assessment under, as applicable—
  - (i) regulations 4 to 12 of The Costs in Criminal Cases (General) Regulations 1986, or
  - (ii) articles 21 to 28 of The Serious Crime Act 2007 (Appeals under Section 24) Order 2008;
- (b) it may assess the amount itself, if the recipient agrees; and
- (c) it must assess the amount itself, in a case in which it decides not to allow an amount that is reasonably sufficient to compensate the recipient for expenses properly incurred in the proceedings.

Section 3: Payment of Costs by One Party to Another

Costs on conviction and sentence

76.5 (1) This rule applies where the court can order a defendant to pay the prosecutor's costs if the defendant is—
- (a) convicted or found guilty;
- (b) dealt with in the Crown Court after committal for sentence there; or
- (c) dealt with for breach of a sentence.

(2) The court may make an order—
  (a) on application by the prosecutor; or
  (b) on its own initiative.
(3) Where the prosecutor wants the court to make an order—
  (a) the prosecutor must—
    (i) apply as soon as practicable, and
    (ii) specify the amount claimed; and
  (b) the general rule is that the court will make an order if it is satisfied that the defendant can pay; but
  (c) the court may decline to do so.
(4) A defendant who wants to oppose an order must make representations as soon as practicable.
(5) If the court makes an order, it must assess the amount itself.

Costs on appeal
76.6 (1) This rule—
  (a) applies where a magistrates' court, the Crown Court or the Court of Appeal can order a party to pay another person's costs on an appeal, or an application for permission to appeal;
  (b) authorises the Crown Court, in addition to its other powers, to order a party to pay another party's costs on an appeal to that court, except on an appeal under—
    (i) section 108 of the Magistrates' Courts Act 1980, or
    (ii) section 45 of the Mental Health Act 1983.
(2) In this rule, costs include—
  (a) costs incurred in the court that made the decision under appeal; and
  (b) costs funded by the Legal Services Commission.
(3) The court may make an order—
  (a) on application by the person who incurred the costs; or
  (b) on its own initiative.
(4) A person who wants the court to make an order must—
  (a) apply as soon as practicable;
  (b) notify each other party;
  (c) specify—
    (i) the amount claimed, and
    (ii) against whom; and
  (d) where an appellant abandons an appeal to the Crown Court by serving a notice of abandonment—
    (i) apply in writing not more than 14 days later, and
    (ii) serve the application on the appellant and on the Crown Court officer.
(5) A party who wants to oppose an order must—
  (a) make representations as soon as practicable; and
  (b) where the application was under paragraph (4)(d), serve written representations on the applicant, and on the Crown Court officer, not more than 7 days after it was served.
(6) Where the application was under paragraph (4)(d), the Crown Court officer may—
  (a) submit it to the Crown Court; or
  (b) serve it on the magistrates' court officer, for submission to the magistrates' court.
(7) If the court makes an order, it may direct an assessment under rule 76.11, or assess the amount itself where—
  (a) the appellant abandons an appeal to the Crown Court;
  (b) the Crown Court decides an appeal, except an appeal under—
    (i) section 108 of the Magistrates' Courts Act 1980, or
    (ii) section 45 of the Mental Health Act 1983; or

(c) the Court of Appeal decides an appeal to which Part 69 applies (appeal to the Court of Appeal regarding reporting or public access restriction).

(8) If the court makes an order in any other case, it must assess the amount itself.

Costs on an application

76.7 (1) This rule applies where the court can order a party to pay another person's costs in a case in which—

    (a) the court decides an application for the production in evidence of a copy of a bank record;

    (b) a magistrates' court or the Crown Court decides an application to terminate a football banning order; or

    (c) the Crown Court allows an application to withdraw a witness summons.

(2) The court may make an order—

    (a) on application by the person who incurred the costs; or

    (b) on its own initiative.

(3) A person who wants the court to make an order must—

    (a) apply as soon as practicable;

    (b) notify each other party; and

    (c) specify—

        (i) the amount claimed, and

        (ii) against whom.

(4) A party who wants to oppose an order must make representations as soon as practicable.

(5) If the court makes an order, it may direct an assessment under rule 76.11, or assess the amount itself.

Costs resulting from unnecessary or improper act, etc.

76.8 (1) This rule applies where the court can order a party to pay another party's costs incurred as a result of an unnecessary or improper act or omission by or on behalf of the first party.

(2) In this rule, costs include costs funded by the Legal Services Commission.

(3) The court may make an order—

    (a) on application by the party who incurred such costs; or

    (b) on its own initiative.

(4) A party who wants the court to make an order must—

    (a) apply in writing as soon as practicable after becoming aware of the grounds for doing so;

    (b) serve the application on—

        (i) the court officer (or, in the Court of Appeal, the Registrar), and

        (ii) each other party;

    (c) in that application specify—

        (i) the party by whom costs should be paid,

        (ii) the relevant act or omission,

        (iii) the reasons why that act or omission meets the criteria for making an order,

        (iv) the amount claimed, and

        (v) those on whom the application has been served.

(5) Where the court considers making an order on its own initiative, it must—

    (a) identify the party against whom it proposes making the order; and

    (b) specify—

        (i) the relevant act or omission,

        (ii) the reasons why that act or omission meets the criteria for making an order, and

        (iii) with the assistance of the party who incurred the costs, the amount involved.

(6) A party who wants to oppose an order must—
   (a) make representations as soon as practicable; and
   (b) in reply to an application, serve written representations on the applicant and on the court officer (or Registrar) not more than 7 days after it was served.
(7) If the court makes an order, it must assess the amount itself.

SECTION 4: OTHER COSTS ORDERS

Costs against a legal representative

76.9 (1) This rule applies where—
   (a) a party has incurred costs—
      (i) as a result of an improper, unreasonable or negligent act or omission by a legal or other representative or representative's employee, or
      (ii) which it has become unreasonable for that party to have to pay because of such an act or omission occurring after those costs were incurred; and
   (b) the court can—
      (i) order the representative responsible to pay such costs, or
      (ii) prohibit the payment of costs to that representative.

PART 77   RECOVERY OF DEFENCE COSTS ORDERS

[No rules are contained under this part. It is omitted with effect
5 October 2009 (SI 2009/ 2087.]

PART 78   COSTS ORDERS AGAINST THE PARTIES

[Omitted with effect 5 October 2009 (SI 2009 No. 2087). See part 76.]

Glossary
This glossary is a guide to the meaning of certain legal expressions as used in these rules.

Expression	Meaning
account monitoring order	an order requiring certain types of financial institution to provide certain information held by them relating to a customer for the purposes of an investigation
action plan order	a type of community sentence requiring a child or young person to comply with a three month plan relating to his actions and whereabouts and to comply with the directions of a responsible officer (e.g. probation officer)
admissible evidence	evidence allowed in proceedings (not all evidence introduced by the parties may be allowable in court)
adduce	to introduce (in evidence)
adjourn	to suspend or delay the hearing of a case
advance information	information about the case against an accused, to which the accused may be entitled before he or she enters a plea
affidavit	a written, sworn statement of evidence
affirmation	a non-religious alternative to the oath sworn by someone about to give evidence in court or swearing a statement
appellant	person who is appealing against a decision of the court
arraign	to put charges to the defendant in open court in the Crown Court
arraignment	the formal process of putting charges to the defendant in the Crown Court which consists of three parts: (1) calling him to the bar by name, (2) putting the charges to him by reading from the indictment and (3) asking him whether he pleads guilty or not guilty

Expression	Meaning
authorities	judicial decisions or opinions of authors of repute used as grounds of statements of law
bill of indictment	a written accusation of a crime against one or more persons—a criminal trial in the Crown Court cannot start without a valid indictment
in camera (trial)	trial in private
case stated	an appeal to the High Court against the decision of a magistrates' court on the basis that the decision was wrong in law or in excess of the magistrates' jurisdiction
in chambers	non-trial hearing in private
committal	sending someone to a court (usually from a magistrates' court to the Crown Court) or to prison
committal for sentence	procedure whereby a person convicted in a magistrates' court is sent to the Crown Court for sentencing when the sentencing powers of the magistrates' court are not considered sufficient
committal proceedings	preliminary hearing in a magistrates' court before a case is sent to be tried before a jury in the Crown Court
compellable witness	a witness who can be forced to give evidence against an accused (not all witnesses are compellable)
compensation order	an order that a convicted person must pay compensation for loss or damage caused by the convicted person
complainant	a person who makes a formal complaint. In relation to an offence of rape or other sexual offences the complainant is the person against whom the offence is alleged to have been committed
complaint	document used to start certain types of proceedings in a magistrates' court, or the process of using such a document to start proceedings
conditional discharge	an order which does not impose any immediate punishment on a person convicted of an offence, subject to the condition that he does not commit an offence in a specified period
confiscation order	an order that private property be taken into possession by the state
Convention right	a right under the European Convention on Human Rights
costs	the expenses involved in a court case, including the fees of the solicitors and barristers and of the court
counsel	a barrister
cross examination	questioning of a witness by a party other than the party who called the witness
custody time limit	the maximum period, as set down in statute, for which a person may be kept in custody before being brought to trial—these maximum periods may only be extended by an order of the judge
customer information order	an order requiring a financial institution to provide certain information held by them relating to a customer for the purposes of an investigation into the proceeds of crime
declaration of incompatibility	a declaration by a court that a piece of UK legislation is incompatible with the provisions of the European Convention on Human Rights
deferred sentence	a sentence which is determined after a delay to allow the court to assess any change in the person's conduct or circumstances after his or her conviction
deposition	written record of a witness' written evidence
distress warrant	court order giving the power to seize goods from a debtor to pay his debts
estreatment (of recognizance)	forfeiture

Expression	Meaning
evidence in chief	the evidence given by a witness for the party who called him
examining justice	a magistrate carrying out his or her function of checking that a case appears on the face of the prosecution case papers to exist against an accused before the case is put forward for trial in the Crown Court—see committal and sending for trial
exhibit	a document or thing presented as evidence in court
forfeiture by peaceable re-entry	the re-possession by a landlord of premises occupied by tenants
guardianship order	an order appointing someone to take charge of a child's affairs and property
hearsay evidence	oral or written statements made by someone who is not a witness in the case but which the court is asked to accept as proving what they say—this expression is defined further by rule 34.1 for the purposes of Part 34, and by rule 57.1 for the purposes of Parts 57–61
hospital order	an order that an offender be admitted to and detained in a specified hospital
indictment	the document containing the formal charges against a defendant—a trial in the Crown Court cannot start without this
informant	someone who lays an information
information	statement by which a magistrate is informed of the offence for which a summons or warrant is required—the procedure by which this statement is brought to the magistrates' attention is known as laying an information
intermediary	a person who asks a witness (particularly a child) questions posed by the cross-examining legal representative
inter partes	a hearing where both parties attend and can make submissions
justice of the peace	a magistrate, either a lay magistrate or a District Judge (Magistrates' Courts);
justices' clerk	post in the magistrates' court of person who has various powers and duties in a magistrates' court, including giving advice to the magistrates on law and procedure
leave of the court	permission granted by the court
leave to appeal	permission granted to appeal the decision of a court
letter of request	letter issued to a foreign court asking a judge to take the evidence of some person within that court's jurisdiction
to levy distress	to seize property from a debtor or a wrongdoer
local justice area	an area established for the purposes of the administration of magistrates' courts
mandatory order	order from the Divisional Court of the Queen's Bench Division ordering a body (such as a magistrates' court) to do something (such as rehear a case)
nominated court	a court nominated to take evidence pursuant to a request by a foreign court
notice of transfer	procedure used in cases of serious and complex fraud, and in certain cases involving child witnesses, whereby the prosecution can, without seeking judicial approval, have the case sent direct to the Crown Court without the need to have the accused committed for trial
offence triable only summarily	an offence which can be tried only in a magistrates' court
in open court	in a courtroom which is open to the public
order restricting discharge	an order restricting the discharge from hospital of patients who have been sent there for psychiatric treatment
parenting order	an order which can be made in certain circumstances where a child has been convicted of an offence which may require parents of the offender to comply with certain requirements including attendance of counselling or guidance sessions

Expression	Meaning
party	a person or organisation directly involved in a criminal case, either as prosecutor or defendant
prefer, preferment	to bring or lay a charge or indictment
preparatory hearing	a hearing forming part of the trial sometimes used in long and complex cases to settle various issues without requiring the jury to attend
realisable property	property which can be sold for money
receiver	a person appointed with certain powers in respect of the property and affairs of a person who has obtained such property in the course of criminal conduct and who has been convicted of an offence—there are various types of receiver (management receiver, director's receiver, enforcement receiver)
receivership order	an order that a person's assets be put into the hands of an official with certain powers and duties to deal with that property
recognizance	formal undertaking to pay the Crown a specified sum if an accused fails to surrender to custody
register	the formal records kept by a magistrates' court
to remand	to send a person away when a case is adjourned until another date—the person may be remanded on bail (when he can leave, subject to conditions) or in custody
reparation order	an order made against a child or young person who has been convicted of an offence, requiring him or her to make specific reparations to the victim or to the community at large
representation order	an order authorising payment of legal aid for a defendant
requisition	a document issued under section 29 of the Criminal Justice Act 2003 requiring a person to appear before a magistrates' court to answer a written charge;
respondent	the other party (to the appellant) in a case which is the subject of an appeal
restraint order	an order prohibiting a person from dealing with any realisable property held by him
seal	a formal mark which the court puts on a document to indicate that the document has been issued by the court
security	money deposited to ensure that the defendant attends court
sending for trial	procedure whereby indictable offences are transferred to the Crown Court without the need for a committal hearing in the magistrates' court
skeleton argument	a document prepared by a party or their legal representative, setting out the basis of the party's argument, including any arguments based on law—the court may require such documents to be served on the court and on the other party prior to a trial
special measures	measures which can be put in place to provide protection and/or anonymity to a witness (e.g. a screen separating witness from the accused)
statutory declaration	a declaration made before a Commissioner for Oaths in a prescribed form
to stay	to halt proceedings, apart from taking any steps allowed by the Rules or the terms of the stay — proceedings may be continued if a stay is lifted
summons	a document signed by a magistrate after an information is laid before him which sets out the basis of the accusation against the accused and the time and place when he must appear
surety	a person who guarantees that a defendant will attend court
suspended sentence	sentence which takes effect only if the offender commits another offence punishable with imprisonment within the specified period
supervision order	an order placing a person who has been given a suspended sentence under the supervision of a local officer

Expression	Meaning
tainted acquittal	an acquittal affected by interference with a witness or a juror
taxing authority	a body which assesses costs
territorial authority	the UK authority which has power to do certain things in connection with co-operation with other countries and international organisations in relation to the collection of or hearing of evidence etc
transfer direction (mental health)	a direction that a person who is serving a sentence of imprisonment who is suffering from a mental disorder be transferred to a hospital and be detained there for treatment
warrant of arrest	court order to arrest a person
warrant of commitment	court order sending someone to prison
warrant of distress	court order giving the power to seize goods from a debtor to pay his debts
warrant of detention	a court order authorising someone's detention
wasted costs order	an order that a barrister or solicitor is not to be paid fees that they would normally be paid by the Legal Services Commission
witness	a person who gives evidence, either by way of a written statement or orally in court
witness summons	a document served on a witness requiring him or her to attend court to give evidence
written charge	a document issued by a public prosecutor under section 29 of the Criminal Justice Act 2003 which institutes criminal proceedings by charging a person with an offence;
youth court	magistrates' courts exercising jurisdiction over offences committed by and other matters related to, children and young persons.

Appendix 2   The Consolidated Criminal Practice Direction

This is a consolidation, with some amendments, of existing Practice Directions, Practice Statements and Practice Notes as they affect proceedings in the Court of Appeal (Criminal Division), the Crown Court and the magistrates' courts, with the exception of the Practice Directions which relate to costs. Practice Directions relating to costs are consolidated in the Practice Direction on Costs in Criminal Proceedings, handed down on 18 May 2004.

The following Practice Directions are included by way of cross-reference only:
(a)   The Practice Direction relating to References to the European Court of Justice by the Court of Appeal and the High Court under Article 177 of the European Communities Treaty [1999] 1 WLR 260; [1999] 1 Cr App R 452.
(b)   The Practice Direction relating to Devolution Issues [1999] 1 WLR 1592; [1999] 3 All ER 466; [1999] 2 Cr App R 486.
(c)   The Practice Direction (Court of Appeal (Civil Division)) [1999] 1 WLR 1027; [1999] 2 All ER 490, paragraph 9 (relating to the availability of judgments given in the Court of Appeal and the High Court) and paragraph 10.1 (relating to the citation of judgments in court).

Guidelines issued by the Attorney General are not included.

Also excluded is the guidance given by the Court of Appeal (Civil Division) in *C v S (Money Laundering: Discovery of Documents) (Practice Direction)* [1991] 1 WLR 1551, which deals with the conflict which can arise between the interests of the state in combating crime on the one hand and, on the other hand, the entitlement of private bodies to obtain redress from the courts and the principles that justice should be administered in public and that a party should know the case advanced against him, should have the opportunity to reply to it and should know the reasons for the decision of the court. Though arising from crime, this was civil litigation.

Reference should also be made to the following Civil Procedure Practice Directions:
(a)   Such parts of the Practice Direction—Addition and Substitution of Parties, supplementary to CPR Part 19, as may apply where a defendant makes a claim for a declaration of incompatibility in accordance with section 4 of the Human Rights Act 1998.
(b)   The Practice Direction—Court Sittings, supplementary to CPR Part 39.

This consolidation is not a comprehensive statement of the practice and procedure of the criminal courts. For this reference must be made to the relevant Acts and Rules to which this Direction is supplementary and to the Attorney General's guidelines.

A list of the Practice Directions which are consolidated *for the purpose of criminal proceedings* is at Appendix A. Where appropriate, these Practice Directions have been brought up to date. Any changes were of a relatively minor nature.

The consolidation does not affect proceedings in the Court of Appeal (Civil Division) or in any division of the High Court. So, for example, in the Family Division, reference should still be made to such directions, etc as affect proceedings there. Some criminal cases come before the Administrative Court. These form a small part of the work of that court and are not affected by this consolidation. The Administrative Court Office has a list of the relatively few Practice Directions which apply there.

This Practice Direction is divided into the following Parts:

Part I   Directions of General Application

Part II   Further Directions applying in the Court of Appeal (Criminal Division)

Part III   Further Directions applying in the Crown Court and in magistrates' courts

Part IV   Further Directions applying in the Crown Court

Part V   Further Directions applying in magistrates' courts

Annex A   List of Practice Directions, Practice Notes and Practice Statements included in this consolidation [omitted].

Annex B   List of Practice Directions, Practice Notes and Practice Statements not included in this consolidation, but no longer applicable in criminal proceedings [omitted].

Annex C   Form of words recommended for use in explanations for the imposition of custodial sentences.

Annex D   Forms for use in criminal proceedings [omitted].

Annex E   Forms to facilitate case management [omitted]

NOTE: Throughout this document words connoting the masculine include the feminine.

Part I Directions of General Application

I.1. Court dress

I.1.1 In magistrates' courts, advocates appear without robes or wigs. In all other courts, Queen's Counsel wear a short wig and a silk (or stuff) gown over a court coat, junior counsel wear a short wig and stuff gown with bands. Solicitors and other advocates authorised under the Courts and Legal Services Act 1990 wear a black solicitor's gown with bands; they may wear short wigs in circumstances where they would be worn by Queen's or junior counsel.

I.1.2 High Court Judges hearing criminal cases shall wear the winter criminal robe year-round. Scarlet summer robes are no longer issued or worn.

I.2. Unofficial tape recording of proceedings

I.2.1 Section 9 of the Contempt of Court Act 1981 contains provisions governing the unofficial use of tape recorders in court. Section 9(1) provides that it is a contempt of court (a) to use in court, or bring into court for use, any tape recorder or other instrument for recording sound, except with the leave of the Court; (b) to publish a recording of legal proceedings made by means of any such instrument, or any recording derived directly or indirectly from it, by playing it in the hearing of the public or any section of the public, or to dispose of it or any recording so derived, with a view to such publication; (c) to use any such recording in contravention of any conditions of leave granted under paragraph (a). These provisions do not apply to the making or use of sound recordings for purposes of official transcripts of the proceedings, upon which the Act imposes no restriction whatever.

I.2.2 The discretion given to the Court to grant, withhold or withdraw leave to use tape recorders or to impose conditions as to the use of the recording is unlimited, but the following factors may be relevant to its exercise: (a) the existence of any reasonable need on the part of the applicant for leave, whether a litigant or a person connected with the press or broadcasting, for the recording to be made; (b) the risk that the recording could be used for the purpose of briefing witnesses out of court; (c) any possibility that the use of the recorder would disturb the proceedings or distract or worry any witnesses or other participants.

I.2.3 Consideration should always be given whether conditions as to the use of a recording made pursuant to leave should be imposed. The identity and role of the applicant for leave and the nature of the subject matter of the proceedings may be relevant to this.

I.2.4 The particular restriction imposed by section 9(1)(b) applies in every case, but may not be present to the mind of every applicant to whom leave is given. It may therefore be desirable on occasion for this provision to be drawn to the attention of those to whom leave is given.

I.2.5 The transcript of a permitted recording is intended for the use of the person given leave to make it and is not intended to be used as, or to compete with, the official transcript mentioned in section 9(4).

I.3. Restrictions on reporting proceedings

I.3.1 Under section 4(2) of the Contempt of Court Act 1981 a court may, where it appears necessary for avoiding a substantial risk of prejudice to the administration of justice in the proceedings before it or in any others pending or imminent, order that publication of any report of the proceedings or part thereof be postponed for such time as the court thinks necessary for that purpose. Section 11 of the Act provides that a court may prohibit the publication of any name or other matter in connection with the proceedings before it which it has allowed to be withheld from the public.

I.3.2 When considering whether to make such an order there is nothing which precludes the court from hearing a representative of the press. Indeed it is likely that the court will wish to do so.

I.3.3 It is necessary to keep a permanent record of such orders for later reference. For this purpose all orders made under section 4(2) must be formulated in precise terms having regard to the decision in *R v Horsham Justices ex parte Farquharson* [1982] QB 762; 76 Cr App R 87, and orders under both sections must be committed to writing either by the judge personally or by the clerk of the court under the judge's directions. An order must state (a) its precise scope, (b) the time at which it shall cease to have effect, if appropriate, and (c) the specific purpose of making the order. Courts will normally give notice to the press in some form that an order has been made under either section of the Act and the court staff should be prepared to answer any enquiry about a specific case, but it is, and will remain, the responsibility of those reporting cases, and their editors, to ensure that no breach of any orders occurs and the onus rests on them to make enquiry in any case of doubt.

I.4. Availability of judgments given in the Court of Appeal and the High Court

I.4.1 Reference should be made to paragraph 9 of Practice Direction (Court of Appeal (Civil Division)) [1999] 1 WLR 1027; [1999] 2 All ER 490.

I.5. Wards of court

I.5.1 Where a child has been interviewed by the police in connection with contemplated criminal proceedings and the child subsequently becomes a ward of court, no leave of the wardship court is required for the child to be called as a witness in those proceedings. Where, however, the police desire to interview a child who is already a ward of court, application must, other than in the exceptional cases referred to in paragraph I.5.3, be made to the wardship court, on summons and on notice to all parties, for leave for the police to do so. Where, however, a party may become the subject of a criminal investigation and it is considered necessary for the ward to be interviewed without that party knowing that the police are making inquiries, the application for leave may be made ex parte to a judge without notice to that party. Notice, should, where practicable, be given to the reporting officer.

I.5.2 Where leave is given the order should, unless some special reason requires the contrary, give leave for any number of interviews which may be required by the prosecution or the police. If it is desired to conduct any interview beyond what has been permitted by the order, a further application should be made.

I.5.3 The exceptional cases are those where the police need to deal with complaints or alleged offences concerning wards and it is appropriate, if not essential, for action to be taken straight away without the prior leave of the wardship court. Typical examples may be: (a) serious offences against the ward, such as rape, where medical examination and the collection of scientific evidence ought to be carried out promptly; (b) where the ward is suspected by the police of having committed a criminal act and the police wish to interview him about it; (c) where the police wish to interview the ward as a potential witness. The list is not exhaustive; there will inevitably be other instances where immediate action is appropriate. In such cases the police should notify the parent or foster parent with whom the ward is living or other 'appropriate adult' within the Code of Practice for the Detention, Treatment and Questioning of Persons by Police Officers, so that that adult has the opportunity of being present when the police interview the child. Additionally, if practicable, the reporting officer (if one has been appointed) should be notified and invited to attend the police interview or to nominate a third party to attend on his behalf. A record of the interview or a copy of any statement made by the ward should be supplied to the reporting officer. Where the ward has been interviewed without the reporting officer's knowledge, he should be informed at the earliest opportunity. So too, if it be the case that the police wish to conduct further interviews. The wardship court should be appraised of the situation at the earliest possible opportunity thereafter by the reporting officer, the parent, foster parent (through the local authority) or other responsible adult.

I.5.4 No evidence or documents in the wardship proceedings or information about the proceedings should be disclosed in the criminal proceedings without leave of the wardship court.

I.6. Spent convictions

I.6.1 The effect of section 4(1) of the Rehabilitation of Offenders Act 1974 is that a person who has become a rehabilitated person for the purpose of the Act in respect of a conviction (known as a 'spent' conviction) shall be treated for all purposes in law as a person who has not committed or been charged with or prosecuted for or convicted of or sentenced for the offence or offences which were the subject of that conviction.

I.6.2 Section 4(1) of the 1974 Act does not apply, however, to evidence given in criminal proceedings: section 7(2)(a). Convictions are often disclosed in such criminal proceedings. When the Bill was before the House of Commons on 28 June 1974 the hope was expressed that the Lord Chief Justice would issue a Practice Direction for the guidance of the Crown Court with a view to reducing disclosure of spent convictions to a minimum and securing uniformity of approach. The direction is set out in the following paragraphs. The same approach should be adopted in all courts of criminal jurisdiction.

I.6.3 During the trial of a criminal charge, reference to previous convictions (and therefore to spent convictions) can arise in a number of ways. The most common is when the character of the accused or a witness is sought to be attacked by reference to his criminal record, but there are, of course, cases where previous convictions are relevant and admissible as, for instance, to prove system.

I.6.4 It is not possible to give general directions which will govern all these different situations, but it is recommended that both court and advocates should give effect to the general intention of Parliament by never referring to a spent conviction when such reference can reasonably be avoided.

I.6.5 After a verdict of guilty the court must be provided with a statement of the defendant's record for the purposes of sentence. The record supplied should contain all previous convictions, but those which are spent should, so far as practicable, be marked as such.

I.6.6 No one should refer in open court to a spent conviction without the authority of the judge, which authority should not be given unless the interests of justice so require.

I.6.7 When passing sentence the judge should make no reference to a spent conviction unless it is necessary to do so for the purpose of explaining the sentence to be passed.

I.7. Explanations for the imposition of custodial sentences

I.7.1 The practical effect of custodial sentences imposed by the courts is almost entirely governed by statutory provisions. Those statutory provisions, changed by Parliament from time to time, are not widely understood by the general public. It is desirable that when sentence is passed the practical effect of the sentence should be understood by the defendant, any victim and any member of the public who is present in court or reads a full report of the proceedings.

I.7.2 Whenever a custodial sentence is imposed on an offender the court should explain the practical effect of the sentence in addition to complying with existing statutory requirements.

This will be no more than an explanation; the sentence will be that pronounced by the court.

I.7.3 Sentencers should give the explanation in terms of their own choosing, taking care to ensure that the explanation is clear and accurate. No form of words is prescribed. Annexed to this Practice Direction are short statements which may, adapted as necessary, be of value as models (see Annex C). These statements are based on the statutory provisions in force on 1 January 1998 and will, of course, require modification if those provisions are materially amended.

I.7.4 Sentencers will continue to give such explanation as they judge necessary of ancillary orders relating to matters such as disqualification, compensation, confiscation, costs and so on.

I.7.5 The power of the Secretary of State to release a prisoner early under supervision is not part of the sentence. The judge is therefore not required in his sentencing remarks to provide an explanation of this power. However, in explaining the effect of custodial sentences the judge should not say anything which conflicts with the existence of this power.

I.8. Words to be used when passing sentence

I.8.1 Where a court passes on a defendant more than one term of imprisonment the court should state in the presence of the defendant whether the terms are to be concurrent or consecutive. Should this not be done the court clerk should ask the court, before the defendant leaves court, to do so.

I.8.2 If a prisoner is, at the time of sentence, already serving two or more consecutive terms of imprisonment and the court intends to increase the total period of imprisonment, it should use the expression 'consecutive to the total period of imprisonment to which you are already subject' rather than 'at the expiration of the term of imprisonment you are now serving', lest the prisoner be not then serving the last of the terms to which he is already subject.

I.9. Substitution of suspended sentences for immediate custodial sentences

I.9.1 Where an appellate court substitutes a suspended sentence of imprisonment for one having immediate effect, the court should have in mind any period the appellant has spent in custody. If the court is of the opinion that it would be fair to do so, an approximate adjustment to the term of the suspended sentence should be made. Whether or not the court makes such adjustment, it should state that it had that period in mind. The court should further indicate that the operational period of suspension runs from the date the court passes the suspended sentence.

I.10. References to the European Court of Justice

I.10.1 These are the subject of Practice Direction: References to the European Court of Justice by the Court of Appeal and the High Court under Article 177 of the EC Treaty [1999] 1 WLR 260; [1999] 1 Cr App R 452, to which reference should be made.

I.11. Devolution issues

I.11.1 These are the subject of Practice Direction: (Supreme Court) (Devolution Issues) [1999] 1 WLR 1592; [1999] 3 All ER 466; [1999] 2 Cr App R 486, to which reference should be made.

I.12. Preparation of judgments: neutral citation

I.12.1 Since 11 January 2001 every judgment of the Court of Appeal, and of the Administrative Court, and since 14 January 2002 every judgment of the High Court, has been prepared and issued as approved with single spacing, paragraph numbering (in the margins) and no page numbers. In courts with more than one judge the paragraph numbering continues sequentially through each judgment and does not start again at the beginning of each judgment. Indented paragraphs are not numbered. A unique reference number is given to each judgment. For judgments of the Court of Appeal this number is given by the official shorthand writers. For judgments of the High Court it is provided by the Mechanical Recording Department at the Royal Courts of Justice. Such a number will also be furnished, on request to the Mechanical Recording Department, Royal Courts of Justice, Strand, London WC2A 2LL (Tel: 020 7947 7771), to High Court judgments delivered outside London.

I.12.2 Each Court of Appeal judgment starts with the year, followed by EW (for England and Wales), then CA (for Court of Appeal), followed by Civ or Crim and finally the sequential number. For example *Smith v Jones* [2001] EWCA Civ 10.

I.12.3 In the High Court, represented by HC, the number comes before the divisional abbreviation and, unlike Court of Appeal judgments, the latter is bracketed: (Ch), (Pat), (QB), (Admin), (Comm), (Admlty), (TCC) or (Fam) as appropriate. For example, [2002] EWHC 123 (Fam) or [2002] EWHC 124 (QB) or [2002] EWHC 125 (Ch).

I.12.4 This 'neutral citation', as it is called, is the official number attributed to the judgment and must always be used at least once when the judgment is cited in a later judgment. Once the judgment is reported this neutral citation appears in front of the familiar citation from the law reports series. Thus: *Smith v Jones* [2001] EWCA Civ 10; [2001] QB 124; [2001] 2 All ER 364, etc.

I.12.5 Paragraph numbers are referred to in square brackets. When citing a paragraph from a High Court judgment it is unnecessary to include the descriptive word in brackets: (Admin), (QB) or whatever. When citing a paragraph from a Court of Appeal judgment, however, Civ or Crim is included. If it is desired to cite more than one paragraph of a judgment each numbered paragraph should be enclosed with a square bracket. Thus paragraph 59 in *Green v White* [2002] EWHC 124 (QB) would be cited: *Green v White* [2002] EWHC 124 at [59]; paragraphs 30–35 in *Smith v Jones* would be *Smith v Jones* [2001] EWCA Civ 10 at [30]–[35]; similarly, where a number of paragraphs are cited: *Smith v Jones* [2001] EWCA Civ 10 at [30], [35] and [40–43].

I.12.6 If a judgment is cited more than once in a later judgment it is helpful if only one abbreviation is used, e.g. *Smith v Jones* or Smith's case, but preferably not both (in the same judgment).

I.13. Bail: failure to surrender and trials in absence

I.13.1 The following directions take effect immediately.

I.13.2 The failure of the defendants to comply with the terms of their bail by not surrendering can undermine the administration of justice. It can disrupt proceedings. The resulting delays impact on victims, witnesses and other court users and also waste costs. A defendant's failure to surrender affects not only the case with which he is concerned, but also the courts' ability to administer justice more generally by damaging the confidence of victims, witnesses and the public in the effectiveness of the court system and the judiciary. It is therefore most important that defendants who are granted bail appreciate the significance of the obligation to surrender to custody in accordance with the terms of their bail and that courts take appropriate action if they fail to do so.

I.13.3 There are at least three courses of action for the courts to consider taking:—

[A] imposing penalties for the failure to surrender;

[B] revoking bail or imposing more stringent bail conditions; and

[C] conducting trials in the absence of the defendant.

Penalties for Failure to Surrender

I.13.4 A defendant who commits a section 6(1) or section 6(2) Bail Act 1976 offence commits an offence that stands apart from the proceedings in respect of which bail was granted. The seriousness of the offence can be reflected by an appropriate penalty being imposed for the Bail Act offence.

I.13.5 The common practice at present of courts automatically deferring disposal of a section 6(1) or section 6(2) Bail Act 1976 offence (failure to surrender) until the conclusion of the proceedings in respect of which bail was granted should no longer be followed. Instead, courts should now deal with defendants as soon as is practicable. In deciding what is practicable, the Court must take into account when the proceedings in respect of which bail was granted are expected to conclude, the seriousness of the offence for which the defendant is already being prosecuted, the type of penalty that might be imposed for the breach of bail and the original offence as well as any other relevant circumstances. If there is no good reason for postponing dealing with the breach until after the trial, the breach should be dealt with as soon as practicable. If the disposal of the breach of bail is deferred, then it is still necessary to consider imposing a separate penalty at the trial and the sentence for the breach of the bail should usually be custodial and consecutive to any other custodial sentence (as to which see I.13.13). In addition, bail should usually be revoked in the meantime (see I.13.14 to 16). In the case of offences which cannot, or are unlikely to, result in a custodial sentence, trial in the absence of the defendant may be a pragmatic sensible response to the situation (see I.13.17 to I.13.19). This is not a penalty for the Bail Act offence and a penalty may also be imposed for the Bail Act offence.

Initiating proceedings—bail granted by a police officer

I.13.6 When a person has been granted bail by a police officer to attend court and subsequently fails to surrender to custody, the decision whether to initiate proceedings for a section 6(1) or section 6(2) offence will be for the police/prosecutor.

I.13.7 The offence in this form is a summary offence and should be initiated as soon as practicable after the offence arises in view of the six month time limit running from the failure to surrender. It should be dealt with on the first appearance after arrest, unless an adjournment is necessary, as it will be relevant in considering whether to grant bail again.

Initiating proceedings—bail granted by a court

I.13.8 When a person has been granted bail by a court and subsequently fails to surrender to custody, on arrest that person should normally be brought as soon as appropriate before the court at which the proceedings in respect of which bail was granted are to be heard. (The six months time limit does not apply where bail was granted by the court.) Should the defendant commit another offence outside the jurisdiction of the bail court, the Bail Act offence should, where practicable, be dealt with by the new court at the same time as the new offence. If impracticable, the defendant may, if this is appropriate, be released formally on bail by the new court so that the warrant may be executed for his attendance before the first court in respect of the substantive and Bail Act offences.

I.13.9 Given that bail was granted by a court, it is more appropriate that the court itself should initiate the proceedings by its own motion. The court will be invited to take proceedings by the prosecutor, if the prosecutor considers proceedings are appropriate.

Conduct of proceedings

I.13.10 Proceedings under section 6 Bail Act 1976 may be conducted either as a summary offence or as a criminal contempt of court. Where the court is invited to take proceedings by the prosecutor, the prosecutor will conduct the proceedings and, if the matter is contested, call the evidence. Where the court initiates proceedings without such an invitation the same role can be played by the prosecutor at the request of the court, where this is practicable.

I.13.11 The burden of proof is on the defendant to prove that he had reasonable cause for his failure to surrender to custody (s 6(3) Bail Act 1976).

Proceedings to be progressed to disposal as soon as is practicable

I.13.12 If the court decides to proceed, the section 6 Bail Act offence should be concluded as soon as practicable.

Sentencing for a Bail Act offence

I.13.13 In principle, a custodial sentence for the offence of failing to surrender should be ordered to be served consecutively to any other sentence imposed at the same time for another offence unless there are circumstances that make this inappropriate (see *White & McKinnon*).

Relationship between the Bail Act Offence and Further Remands on Bail or in Custody

I.13.14 When a defendant has been convicted of a Bail Act offence, the court should review the remand status of the defendant, including the conditions of that bail, in respect of the main proceedings for which bail had been granted.

I.13.15 Failure by the defendant to surrender or a conviction for failing to surrender to bail in connection with the main proceedings will be significant factors weighing against the re-granting of bail or, in the case of offences which do not normally give rise to a custodial sentence, in favour of trial in the absence of the offender.

I.13.16 Whether or not an immediate custodial sentence has been imposed for the Bail Act offence, the court may, having reviewed the defendant's remand status, also remand the defendant in custody in the main proceedings.

Trials in Absence

I.13.17 A defendant has a right, in general, to be present and to be represented at his trial. However, a defendant may choose not to exercise those rights by voluntarily absenting himself and failing to instruct his lawyers adequately so that they can represent him and, in the case of proceedings before the magistrates' court, there is an express statutory power to hear trials in the defendant's absence (s11 of the Magistrates' Courts Act 1980). In such circumstances, the court has discretion whether the trial should take place in his/her absence.

I.13.18 The court must exercise its discretion to proceed in the absence of the defendant with the utmost care and caution. The overriding concern must be to ensure that such a trial is as fair as circumstances permit and leads to a just outcome.

I.13.19 Due regard should be had to the judgment of Lord Bingham in *R* v *Jones* [2003] AC 1, [2002] 2 AER 113 in which Lord Bingham identified circumstances to be taken into account before proceeding, which include: the conduct of the defendant, the disadvantage to the defendant, public interest, the effect of any delay and whether the attendance of the defendant could be secured at a later hearing. Other relevant considerations are the seriousness of the offence and likely outcome if the defendant is found guilty. If the defendant is only likely to be fined for a summary offence this can be relevant since the costs that a defendant might otherwise be ordered to pay as a result of an adjournment could be disproportionate. In the case of summary proceedings the fact that there can be an appeal that is a complete rehearing is also relevant, as is the power to re-open the case under s 142 of the Magistrates' Courts Act 1980.

I.14. Forms

I.14.1 This Practice Direction supplements Part 5 (forms) of the Criminal Procedure Rules.

I.14.2 The forms set out in Annex D, or forms to that effect, are to be used in the criminal courts on or after 4th April 2005, when the Criminal Procedure Rules come into force. Almost all are identical to those in use before that date, and accordingly a form in use before that date which corresponds with one set out in Annex D may still be used in connection with the rule to which it applies.

I.14.3 The table at the beginning of Annex D lists the forms set out in that Annex and—
- shows the rule in connection with which each form applies
- describes each form
- in the case of a form in use before the Criminal Procedure Rules came into force, shows the legislation by which the form was prescribed and by what number (if any) it was known.

I.15. Witness anonymity orders

I.15.1 This direction supplements Part 29 of the Criminal Procedure Rules, which governs the procedure to be followed on an application for a witness anonymity order. The court's power to make such an order is conferred by the Coroners and Justice Act 2009 (in this direction, 'the Act'). The court's power to give case management directions is conferred by Part 3 of the Criminal Procedure Rules. Section 87 of the Act provides specific relevant powers and obligations.

Case management

I.15.2 Where such an application is proposed, with the parties' active assistance the court should set a realistic timetable, in accordance with the duties imposed by rules 3.2 and 3.3. Where possible, the trial judge should determine the application, and any hearing should be attended by the parties' trial advocates.

Service of evidence and disclosure of prosecution material pending an application

I.15.3 Where the prosecutor proposes an application for a witness anonymity order it is not necessary for that application to have been determined before the proposed evidence is served. In most cases an early indication of what that evidence will be if an order is made will be consistent with a party's duties under rules 1.2 and 3.3. The prosecutor should serve with the other prosecution evidence a witness statement setting out the proposed evidence, redacted in such a way as to prevent disclosure of the witness' identity, as permitted by section 87(4) of the Act. Likewise the prosecutor should serve with other prosecution material disclosed under the Criminal Procedure and Investigations Act 1996 any such material appertaining to the witness, similarly redacted.

The application

I.15.4 An application for a witness anonymity order should be made as early as possible and within the period for which rule 29.3 provides. The application must comply with the requirements of that rule and with those of rule 29.19. In accordance with rules 1.2 and 3.3, the applicant must provide the court with all available information relevant to the considerations to which the Act requires a court to have regard.

I.15.5 The application (to be served on all parties and on the court) must comply with rule 29.19(1).

I.15.6 Other, confidential, information that supports the application, including the identity of the witness, must be presented separately to the court in accordance with rule 29.19(2).t

I.15.7 Such information will be received by the court in accordance with rule 29.19(3).

Response to the application

I.15.8 A party upon whom an application for a witness anonymity order is served should serve a response on the other parties and on the court within 14 days: rule 29.2. That period may be extended or shortened in the court's discretion: rule 29.5.

I.15.9 To avoid the risk of injustice a respondent must actively assist the court. If not already done, a respondent defendant should serve a defence statement under section 5 or 6 of the Criminal Procedure and Investigations Act 1996, so that the court is fully informed of what is in issue. The prosecutor's continuing duty to disclose material under section 7A of the Criminal Procedure and Investigations Act 1996 may be engaged by a defendant's application for a witness anonymity order. Therefore a prosecutor's response should include confirmation that that duty has been considered. Nothing disclosed under the 1996 Act by a respondent prosecutor to a respondent defendant should contain anything that might reveal the witness' identity. A respondent prosecutor should provide an applicant defendant and the court with all available information relevant to the considerations to which the Act requires a court to have regard, whether or not that information falls to be disclosed under the 1996 Act: rule 29.22(6).

Determination of the application

I.15.10 All parties must have an opportunity to make oral representations to the court on an application for a witness anonymity order: section 87(6) of the Act. However, a hearing may not be needed if none is sought: rule 29.18(1)(a). Where, for example, the witness is an investigator who is recognisable by the defendant but known only by an assumed name, and there is no likelihood that the witness' credibility will be in issue, then the court may indicate a provisional decision and invite representations within a defined period, usually 14 days, including representations about whether there should be a hearing. In such a case, where the parties do not object the court may make an order without a hearing. Or where the court provisionally considers an application to be misconceived, an applicant may choose to withdraw it without requiring a hearing. Where the court directs a hearing of the application then it should allow adequate time for service of the representations in response.

I.15.11 The hearing of an application for a witness anonymity order usually should be in private: rule 29.18(1)(a). The court has power to hear a party in the absence of a defendant and that defendant's representatives: section 87(7) of the Act and rule 29.18(1)(b). In the Crown Court, a recording of the proceedings will be made, in accordance with rule 65.8(2). The Crown Court officer must treat such a recording in the same way as the recording of an application for a public interest ruling. It must be kept in secure conditions, and the arrangements made by the Crown Court officer for any transcription must impose restrictions that correspond with those under rule 65.9(2)(a).

I.15.12 At a hearing the court will proceed in accordance with rule 29.19(3).

I.15.13 Where confidential supporting information is presented to the court before the last stage of the hearing, the court may prefer not to read that information until that last stage.

I.15.14 The court may adjourn the hearing at any stage, and should do so if its duty under rule 3.2 so requires.

I.15.15 On a prosecutor's application, the court is likely to be assisted by the attendance of a senior investigator or other person of comparable authority who is familiar with the case.

I.15.16 During the last stage of the hearing it is essential that the court test thoroughly the information supplied in confidence in order to satisfy itself that the conditions prescribed by the Act are met. At that stage, if the court concludes that this is the only way in which it can satisfy itself as to a relevant condition or consideration, exceptionally it may invite the applicant to present the proposed witness to be questioned by the court. Any such questioning should be carried out at such a time, and the witness brought to the court in such a way, as to prevent disclosure of his or her identity.

I.15.17 The court may ask the Attorney General to appoint special counsel to assist. However, it must be kept in mind that, 'Such an appointment will always be exceptional, never automatic; a course of last and never first resort. It should not be ordered unless and until the trial judge is satisfied that no other course will adequately meet the overriding requirement of fairness to the defendant': *R v H* [2004] 2 AC 134, at paragraph 22. Whether to accede to such a request is a matter for the Attorney General, and adequate time should be allowed for the consideration of such a request.

I.15.18 Following a hearing the court should announce its decision on an application for a witness anonymity order in the parties' presence and in public: rule 29.4(2). The court should give such reasons as it is possible to give without revealing the witness' identity. In the Crown Court, the court will be conscious that reasons given in public may be reported and reach the jury. Consequently, the court should ensure that nothing in its decision or its reasons could undermine any warning it may give jurors under section 90(2) of the Act. A record of the reasons must be kept. In the Crown Court, the announcement of those reasons will be recorded.

Order

I.15.19 Where the court makes a witness anonymity order it is essential that the measures to be taken are clearly specified in a written record of that order approved by the court and issued on its behalf. An order made in a magistrates' court must be recorded in the court register, in accordance with rule 5.4.

I.15.20 Self-evidently, the written record of the order must not disclose the identity of the witness to whom it applies. However, it is essential that there be maintained some means of establishing a clear correlation between witness and order, and especially where in the same proceedings witness anonymity orders are made in respect of more than one witness, specifying different measures in respect of each. Careful preservation of the application for the order, including the confidential information presented to the court, ordinarily will suffice for this purpose.

Discharge or variation of the order

I.15.21 Section 91 of the Act allows the court to discharge or vary a witness anonymity order: on application, if there has been a material change of circumstances since the order was made or since any previous variation of it; or on its own initiative. Rule 29.21 allows the parties to apply for the variation of a pre-trial direction where circumstances have changed.

I.15.22 The court should keep under review the question of whether the conditions for making an order are met. In addition, consistently with the parties' duties under rules 1.2 and 3.3, it is incumbent on each, and in particular on the applicant for the order, to keep the need for it under review.

I.15.23 Where the court considers the discharge or variation of an order, the procedure that it adopts should be appropriate to the circumstances. As a general rule, that procedure should approximate to the procedure for determining an application for an order. The court may need to hear further representations by the applicant for the order in the absence of a respondent defendant and that defendant's representatives.

Retention of confidential material

I.15.24 If retained by the court, confidential material must be stored in secure conditions by the court officer. Alternatively, subject to such directions as the court may give, such material may be committed to the safe keeping of the applicant or any other appropriate person in exercise of the powers conferred by rule 29.6. If the material is released to any such person, the court should ensure that it will be available to the court at trial.

PART II FURTHER DIRECTIONS APPLYING IN THE COURT OF APPEAL (CRIMINAL DIVISION)

II.1. Appeals against sentence—the provision of notice to the prosecution

II.1.1 The Registrar of Criminal Appeals will notify the relevant prosecution authority in the event that:

(a) leave to appeal against sentence is granted by the single Judge; or

(b) the single Judge or the Registrar refers an application for leave to appeal against sentence to the Full Court for determination; or

(c) the Registrar becomes aware that Counsel for the applicant will be appearing at a renewed application for leave to appeal against sentence.

II.1.2 The Prosecution will have 7 days from the grant of leave by the single Judge or the referral by the Registrar to notify the Registrar if they wish to be represented at the hearing OR to request sight of the grounds of appeal and/or any comments made by the single Judge when granting leave or referring the case to the Full Court. Upon such a request, the prosecution will have a further 7 days from receipt to notify the Registrar if they wish to be represented at the hearing.

II.1.3 Occasionally, for example, where the single Judge fixes a hearing date at short notice, the Registrar may have to foreshorten the period specified in II.1.2 above.

II.1.4 In relation to (c) in paragraph II.1.1, the prosecution will have 72 hours or, if the case is listed, 48 hours, to notify the Registrar that they wish to be represented at the hearing. Should the prosecution require sight of the grounds of appeal and the single Judge's comments, such a request should be made as expeditiously as possible.

II.1.5 If the prosecution wishes to be represented at any hearing, the notification should include details of Counsel instructed, a time estimate and an indication whether a skeleton argument will be lodged no later than 14 days before the hearing (or such shorter period as may be necessary). If a skeleton argument is to be lodged, it must be served on the Court and the applicant/appellant.

II.1.6 An application by the prosecution to remove a case from the list for Counsel's convenience, or to allow further preparation time, will rarely be granted.

II.1.7 There may be occasions when the Court of Appeal Criminal Division will grant leave to appeal to an unrepresented applicant and proceed forthwith with the appeal in the absence of the appellant and Counsel. In those circumstances there will be no opportunity to notify the prosecution.

II.1.8 As a Court of Review, the Court of Appeal Criminal Division would expect the prosecution to have raised any specific matters of relevance with the sentencing Judge in the first instance.

II.1.9 When the prosecution attend a hearing as a result of this Practice Direction, the prosecution should not volunteer assistance in relation to any unrepresented applicant.

II.1.10 This Direction will come into force as from 10 November 2003.

II.1.11 The Prosecution are already invited to appear and respond, as a matter of course, in appeals against Confiscation Orders and where the Court is considering issuing sentencing guidelines. This practice will continue without change.

II.1.12 This Practice Direction replaces the existing protocol whereby the prosecution were responsible for lodging a letter of interest with the Registrar of Criminal Appeals via the Crown Court.

II.2. Listing of appeals against conviction and sentence in the CACD

II.2.1 Arrangements for the fixing of dates for the hearing of appeals will be made by the Criminal Appeal Office Listing Officer, under the superintendence of the Registrar of Criminal Appeals who may give such directions as he deems necessary.

II.2.2 Where possible, regard will be had to an advocate's existing commitments. However, in relation to the listing of appeals, the Court of Appeal takes precedence over all lower courts, including the Crown Court. Wherever practicable a lower court will have regard to this principle when making arrangements to release an advocate to appear in the Court of Appeal. In case of difficulty the lower court should communicate with the Registrar. In general an advocate's commitment in a lower court will not be regarded as a good reason for failing to accept a date proposed for a hearing in the Court of Appeal.

II.2.3 The copy of the Criminal Appeal Office summary provided to advocates will contain the summary writer's time estimate for the whole hearing including delivery of judgment. The Listing Officer will rely on that estimate unless the advocate for the appellant or the Crown provides a different time estimate to the Listing Officer, in writing, within 7 days of the receipt of the summary by the advocate. Where the time estimate is considered by an advocate to be inadequate, or where the estimate has been altered because, for example, a ground of appeal has been abandoned, it is the duty of the advocate to inform the Court promptly, in which event the Registrar will reconsider the time estimate and inform the parties accordingly.

II.2.4 In furtherance of the Court's aim of continuing to improve the service provided to appellants and respondents the following target times will be set for the hearing of appeals. Target times will run from the receipt of the appeal by the Listing Officer, as being ready for hearing. These arrangements will apply to appeals so received on and after 22nd March 2004.

II.2.5

Nature of appeal	From receipt by listing officer to fixing of hearing date	From fixing of hearing date to hearing	Total time from receipt by listing officer to hearing
Sentence Appeal	14 days	14 days	28 days
Conviction Appeal	21 days	42 days	63 days
Conviction Appeal where witness to attend	28 days	52 days	80 days

II.2.6 Where legal vacations impinge these periods may be extended. Where expedition is required, the Registrar may direct that these periods be abridged.

II.2.7 'Appeal' includes an application for leave to appeal which requires an oral hearing.

II.13. Mode of addressing the court

II.13.1 Judges of the Court of Appeal and of the High Court are addressed as 'My Lord' or 'My Lady'; so are Circuit Judges sitting as judges of the High Court under section 9 of the Supreme Court Act 1981.

II.14. Notices of appeal and of applications for leave to appeal

II.14.1 These are to be served on the Crown Court at the centre where the proceedings took place. The Crown Court will forward them to the Criminal Appeal Office together with the trial documents and any others which may be required.

II.15. Grounds of appeal

II.15.1 Advocates should not settle grounds or support them with written advice unless they consider that they are properly arguable. Grounds should be carefully drafted and properly particularised. Advocates should not assume that the Court will entertain any ground of appeal not set out and properly particularised. Should leave to amend the grounds be granted it is most unlikely that further grounds will be entertained.

II.15.2 A copy of the advocate's positive advice about the merits should be attached as part of the grounds.

II.16. Loss of time

II.16.1 Both the Court and the single judge have power in their discretion to direct that part of the time during which an applicant is in custody after putting in his notice of application for leave to appeal should not count towards sentence. Those who contemplate putting in such a notice and their legal advisers should bear this in mind. It is important that those contemplating an appeal should seek advice and should remember that it is useless to appeal without grounds and that grounds should be substantial and particularised and not a mere formula. Where an application devoid of merit has been refused by the single judge and a direction for loss of time has been made, the Full Court, on renewal of the application, may direct that additional time shall be lost if it, once again, thinks it right so to exercise its discretion in all the circumstances of the case.

II.17. Skeleton arguments

II.17.1 In all appeals against conviction a skeleton argument from the advocate for the appellant is to be lodged with the Registrar of Criminal Appeals and served on the prosecuting authority within 14 days of receipt by the advocate of the notification of the grant of leave to appeal against conviction or such longer period as the Registrar or the Court may direct. The skeleton may refer to an advice, which should be annexed with an indication of which parts of it are relied upon, and should include any additional arguments to be advanced.

II.17.2 The advocate for the prosecuting authority should lodge with the Registrar and the advocate for the appellant his skeleton argument within 14 days of the receipt of the skeleton argument for the appellant or such longer (or, in exceptional cases, shorter) period as the Registrar or the Court may direct.

II.17.3 Practitioners should ensure that, where reliance is placed upon unreported cases in skeleton arguments, short head notes are included.

II.17.4 Advocates should ensure that the correct Criminal Appeal Office number appears at the beginning of their skeleton arguments and that their names are at the end.

II.17.5 A skeleton argument should contain a numbered list of the points the advocate intends to argue, grouped under each ground of appeal, and stated in no more than one or two sentences. It should be as succinct as possible, the object being to identify each point, not to argue it or elaborate on it. Each listed point should be followed by full references to the material to which the advocate will refer in support of it, i.e. the relevant passages in the transcripts, authorities, etc. It should also contain anything the advocate would expect to be taken down by the Court during the hearing, such as propositions of law, chronologies, etc. If more convenient, these can be annexed to the skeletons rather than included in it. For points of law, the skeleton should state the point and cite the principal authority or authorities in support with reference to the passages where the principle is enunciated. Chronologies should, if possible, be agreed with the opposing advocate before the hearing. Respondents' skeletons should follow the same principles.

II.18. Criminal Appeal Office summaries

II.18.1 To assist the Court the Criminal Appeal Office prepares summaries of the cases coming before it. These are entirely objective and do not contain any advice about how the Court should deal with the case or any view about its merits. They consist of two Parts.

II.18.2 Part I, which is provided to all of the advocates in the case, generally contains (a) particulars of the proceedings in the Crown Court, including representation and details of any co-accused, (b) particulars of the proceedings in the Court of Appeal (Criminal Division), (c) the facts of the case, as drawn from the transcripts, advice of the advocates, witness statements and/or the exhibits, (d) the submissions and rulings, summing up and sentencing remarks. Should an advocate not want any factual material in his advice taken into account this should be stated in the advice.

II.18.3 The contents of the summary are a matter for the professional judgment of the writer, but an advocate wishing to suggest any significant alteration to Part I should write to the Registrar of Criminal Appeals. If the Registrar does not agree, the summary and the letter will be put to the Court for decision. The Court will not generally be willing to hear oral argument about the content of the summary.

II.18.4 Advocates may show Part I of the summary to their professional or lay clients (but to no one else) if they believe it would help to check facts or formulate arguments, but summaries are not to be copied or reproduced without the permission of the Criminal Appeal Office; permission for this will not normally be given in cases involving children or sexual offences or where the Crown Court has made an order restricting reporting.

II.18.5 Unless a judge of the High Court or the Registrar of Criminal Appeals gives a direction to the contrary in any particular case involving material of an explicitly salacious or sadistic nature, Part I will also be supplied to appellants who seek to represent themselves before the full court or who renew to the full court their applications for leave to appeal against conviction or sentence.

II.18.6 Part II, which is supplied to the Court alone, contains (a) a summary of the grounds of appeal and (b) in appeals against sentence (and applications for such leave), summaries of the antecedent histories of the parties and of any relevant pre-sentence, medical or other reports.

II.18.7 All of the source material is provided to the Court and advocates are able to draw attention to anything in it which may be of particular relevance.

II.19. Citation of judgments in court

II.19.1 Reference should be made to paragraph 10.1 of Practice Direction (Court of Appeal (Civil Division)) [1999] 1 WLR 1027; [1999] 2 All ER 490.

II.20. Citation of Hansard

II.20.1 Where any party intends to refer to the reports of Parliamentary proceedings as reported in the Official Reports of either House of Parliament ('Hansard') in support of any such argument as is permitted by the decisions in *Pepper* v *Hart* [1993] AC 593 and *Pickstone* v *Freeman* [1989] AC 66 or otherwise he must, unless the Court otherwise directs, serve upon all other parties and the Court copies of any such extract together with a brief summary of the argument intended to be based upon such extract. No other report of Parliamentary proceedings may be cited.

II.20.2 Unless the Court otherwise directs, service of the extract and summary of the argument shall be effected not less than 5 clear working days before the first day of the hearing, whether or not it has a fixed date. Advocates must keep themselves informed as to the state of the lists where no fixed date has been given. Service on the Court shall be effected by sending three copies to the Registrar of Criminal Appeals, Room C212, Royal Courts of Justice, Strand, London WC2A 2LL. If any party fails to do so the Court may make such order (relating to costs or otherwise) as is in all the circumstances appropriate.

PART III FURTHER DIRECTIONS APPLYING IN THE
CROWN COURT AND MAGISTRATES' COURTS

III.21.1 Classification of Crown Court business and allocation to Crown Court Centres

Classification

III.21.1 For the purposes of trial in the Crown Court offences are classified as follows:

Class 1: (a) Misprision of treason and treason felony; (b) Murder; (c) Genocide; (d) Torture, hostage-taking and offences under the War Crimes Act 1991; (e) An offence under the Official Secrets Acts; (f) Manslaughter; (g) Infanticide; (h) Child destruction; (i) Abortion (section 58 of the Offences against the Person Act 1861); (j) Sedition; (k) An offence under section 1 of the Geneva Conventions Act 1957; (l) Mutiny; (m) Piracy; (n) Soliciting, incitement, attempt or conspiracy to commit any of the above offences.

Class 2: (a) Rape; (b) Sexual intercourse with a girl under 13; (c) Incest with a girl under 13; (d) Assault by penetration; (e) Causing a person to engage in sexual activity, where penetration is involved; (f) Rape of a child under 13; (g) Assault of a child under 13 by penetration; (h) Causing or inciting a child under 13 to engage in sexual activity, where penetration is involved; (i) Sexual activity with a person with a mental disorder, where penetration is involved; (j) Inducement to procure sexual activity with a mentally disordered person where penetration is involved; (k) Paying for sexual services of a child where child is under 13 and penetration is involved; (l) Committing an offence with intent to commit a sexual offence, where the offence is kidnapping or false imprisonment; (m) Soliciting, incitement, attempt or conspiracy to commit any of the above offences.

Class 3: All other offences not listed in classes 1 or 2.

III.21.2 The magistrates' court, upon either committing a person for trial under section 6 of the Magistrates' Courts Act 1980, or sending a person under section 51 of the Crime and Disorder Act 1998, shall:

(a) if the offence or any of the offences is included in Class 1, specify the most convenient location of the Crown Court where a High Court Judge, or, where a Circuit Judge duly authorised by the Lord Chief Justice to try class 1 cases, regularly sits.

(b) if the offence or any of the offences is included in Class 2, specify the most convenient location of the Crown Court where a Judge duly authorised to try Class 2 regularly sits. These courts on each Circuit will be identified by the Presiding Judges, with the concurrence of the Lord Chief Justice.

(c) where an offence is in Class 3 the magistrates' court shall specify the most convenient location of the Crown Court.

Where a case is transferred under section 4 of the Criminal Justice Act 1987 or section 53 of the Criminal Justice Act 1991, the authority shall, in specifying the proposed place of trial in the notice of transfer, comply with the provisions of this paragraph.

III.21.3 In selecting the most convenient location of the Crown Court the justices shall have regard to the considerations referred to in section 7 of the Magistrates' Courts Act 1980 and section 51(10) of the Crime and Disorder Act 1998 and the location or locations of the Crown Court designated by a Presiding Judge as the location to which cases should normally be committed from their court.

III.21.4 Where on one occasion a person is committed in respect of a number of offences all the committals shall be to the same location of the Crown Court and that location shall be the one where a High Court Judge regularly sits if such a location is appropriate for any of the offences.

Committals following breach

III.21.5 Where, in the Crown Court, a community order or an order for conditional discharge has been made, or a suspended sentence has been passed, and the offender is subsequently found or alleged to be in breach before a magistrates' court which decides to commit the offender to the Crown Court, he shall be committed in accordance with paragraphs III.21.6, III.21.7 or III.21.8

III.21.6 He shall be committed to the location of the Crown Court where the order was made or the suspended sentence was passed, unless it is inconvenient, impracticable or inappropriate to do so in all the circumstances.

III.21.7 If, for whatever reason, he is not so committed and the order was made or sentence passed by a High Court Judge, he shall be committed to the most convenient location of the Crown Court where a High Court Judge regularly sits.

III.21.8 In all other cases he shall be committed to the most convenient location of the Crown Court.

III.21.9 In selecting the most convenient location of the Crown Court, the justices shall have regard to the locations of the Crown Court designated by a Presiding Judge as the locations to which cases should normally be committed from their court.

Notice of transfer in cases of serious or complex fraud

III.21.10 Where a notice of transfer is served under section 4 of the Criminal Justice Act 1987 the proposed place of trial to be specified in the notice shall be one of the Crown Court centres designated by the Senior Presiding Judge.

Notice of transfer in child witness cases

III.21.11 Where a notice of transfer is served under section 53 of the Criminal Justice Act 1991 (child witness cases) the proposed place of trial to be specified in accordance with paragraph 1(1) of schedule 6 to the Act shall be a Crown Court centre which is equipped with live television link facilities.

III.22. Applications for evidence to be given in Welsh

III.22.1 If a defendant in a court in England asks to give or call evidence in the Welsh language the case should not be transferred to Wales. In ordinary circumstances interpreters can be provided on request.

III.23. Use of the Welsh language in courts in Wales

III.23.1 The purpose of this direction is to reflect the principle of the Welsh Language Act 1993 that in the administration of justice in Wales the English and Welsh languages should be treated on a basis of equality.

General

III.23.2 It is the responsibility of the legal representatives in every case in which the Welsh language may be used by any witness or party or in any document which may be placed before the court to inform the court of that fact so that appropriate arrangements can be made for the listing of the case.

III.23.3 If the possible use of the Welsh language is known at the time of committal, transfer or appeal to the Crown Court, the court should be informed immediately after committal or transfer or when the notice of appeal is lodged. Otherwise the court should be informed as soon as possible use of the Welsh language becomes known.

III.23.4 If costs are incurred as a result of failure to comply with these directions, a wasted costs order may be made against the defaulting party and/or his legal representatives.

III.23.5 The law does not permit the selection of jurors in a manner which enables the court to discover whether a juror does or does not speak Welsh or to secure a jury whose members are bilingual to try a case in which the Welsh language may be used.

Plea and directions hearings

III.23.6 An advocate in a case in which the Welsh language may be used must raise that matter at the plea and directions hearing and endorse details of it on the judge's questionnaire so that appropriate directions may be given for the progress of the case.

Listing

III.23.7 The listing officer, in consultation with the resident judge, should ensure that a case in which the Welsh language may be used is listed (a) wherever practicable before a Welsh speaking judge, and (b) in a court in Wales with simultaneous translation facilities.

Interpreters

III.23.8 Whenever an interpreter is needed to translate evidence from English into Welsh or from Welsh into English, the court manager in whose court the case is to be heard shall ensure that the attendance is secured of an interpreter whose name is included in the list of approved court interpreters.

Jurors

III.23.9 The jury bailiff when addressing the jurors at the start of their period of jury service shall inform them that each juror may take an oath or affirm in Welsh or English as he wishes.

III.23.10 After the jury has been selected to try a case, and before it is sworn, the court officer swearing in the jury shall inform the jurors in open court that each juror may take an oath or affirm in Welsh or English as he wishes.

Witnesses

III.23.11 When each witness is called the court officer administering the oath or affirmation shall inform the witness that he may be sworn or affirm Welsh or English as he wishes.

Opening/closing of courts

III.23.12 Unless it is not reasonably practicable to do so, the opening and closing of the court should be performed in Welsh and English.

Role of liaison judge

III.23.13 If any question or problem arises concerning the implementation of paragraphs III.23.1–III.23.12, contact should in the first place be made with the liaison judge for Welsh language matters on circuit.

III.24. Evidence by written statement

III.24.1 Where the prosecution proposes to tender written statements in evidence either under sections 5A and 5B of the Magistrates' Courts Act 1980 or section 9 of the Criminal Justice Act 1967 it will frequently be not only proper, but also necessary for the orderly presentation of the evidence, for certain statements to be edited. This will occur either because a witness has made more than one statement whose contents should conveniently be reduced into a single, comprehensive statement or where a statement contains inadmissible, prejudicial or irrelevant material. Editing of statements should in all circumstances be done by a Crown Prosecutor (or by a legal representative, if any, of the prosecutor if the case is not being conducted by the Crown Prosecution Service) and not by a police officer.

Composite statements

III.24.2 A composite statement giving the combined effect of two or more earlier statements or settled by a person referred to in paragraph III.24.1 must be prepared in compliance with the requirements of sections 5A and 5B of the 1980 Act or section 9 of the 1967 Act as appropriate and must then be signed by the witness.

Editing single statements

III.24.3 There are two acceptable methods of editing single statements.

(a) By marking *copies* of the statement in a way which indicates the passages on which the prosecution will not rely. This merely indicates that the prosecution will not seek to adduce the evidence so marked. The *original signed statement* to be tendered to the court is not marked in any way. The marking on the copy statement is done by lightly striking out the passages to be edited so that what appears beneath can still be read, or by bracketing, or by a combination of both. It is not permissible to produce a photocopy with the deleted material obliterated, since this would be contrary to the requirement that the defence and the court should be served with copies of the signed original statement. Whenever the striking out/bracketing method is used, it will assist if the following words appear at the foot of the frontispiece or index to any bundle of copy statements to be tendered: 'The prosecution does not propose to adduce evidence of those passages of the attached copy statements which have been struck out and/or bracketed (nor will it seek to do so at the trial unless a notice of further evidence is served).'

(b) By obtaining a fresh statement, signed by the witness, which omits the offending material, applying the procedure in paragraph III.24.2.

III.24.4 In most cases where a single statement is to be edited, the striking out/bracketing method will be the more appropriate, but the taking of a fresh statement is preferable in the following circumstances:

(a) When a police (or other investigating) officer's statement contains details of interviews with more suspects than are eventually charged, a fresh statement should be prepared and signed omitting all details of interview with those not charged except, insofar as it is relevant, for the bald fact that a certain named person was interviewed at a particular time, date and place.

(b) When a suspect is interviewed about more offences than are eventually made the subject of committal charges, a fresh statement should be prepared and signed omitting all questions and answers about the uncharged offences unless either they might appropriately be taken into consideration or evidence about those offences is admissible on the charges preferred, such as evidence of system. It may, however, be desirable to replace the omitted questions and answers with a phrase such as: 'After referring to some other matters, I then said . . .', so as to make it clear that part of the interview has been omitted.

(c) A fresh statement should normally be prepared and signed if the only part of the original on which the prosecution is relying is only a small proportion of the whole, although it remains desirable to use the alternative method if there is reason to believe that the defence might itself wish to rely, in mitigation or for any other purpose, on at least some of those parts which the prosecution does not propose to adduce.

(d) When the passages contain material which the prosecution is entitled to withhold from disclosure to the defence.

III.24.5 Prosecutors should also be aware that, where statements are to be tendered under section 9 of the 1967 Act in the course of *summary* proceedings, there will be a need to prepare fresh statements excluding inadmissible or prejudicial material rather than using the striking out or bracketing method.

III.24.6 None of the above principles applies, in respect of committal proceedings, to documents which are exhibited (including statements under caution and signed contemporaneous notes). Nor do they apply to oral statements of a defendant which are recorded in the witness statements of interviewing police officers, except in the circumstances referred to in paragraph III.24.4(b). All this material should remain in its original state in the committal bundles, any editing being left to prosecuting counsel at the Crown Court (after discussion with defence counsel and, if appropriate, the trial judge).

III.24.7 Whenever a fresh statement is taken from a witness, a copy of the earlier, unedited statement(s) of that witness will be given to the defence in accordance with the Attorney General's guidelines on the disclosure of unused material (*Practice Note* [1982] 1 All ER 734) unless there are grounds under paragraph 6 of the guidelines for withholding such disclosure.

III.25. Bail during trial

III.25.1 Paragraphs III.25.2 to III.25.5 are to be read subject to the Bail Act 1976, especially section 4.

III.25.2 Once a trial has begun the further grant of bail, whether during the short adjournment or overnight, is in the discretion of the trial judge. It may be a proper exercise of this discretion to refuse bail during the short adjournment if the accused cannot otherwise be segregated from witnesses and jurors.

III.25.3 An accused who was on bail while on remand should not be refused overnight bail during the trial unless in the opinion of the judge there are positive reasons to justify this refusal. Such reasons are likely to be:

(a)   that a point has been reached where there is a real danger that the accused will abscond, either because the case is going badly for him, or for any other reason;

(b)   that there is a real danger that he may interfere with witnesses or jurors.

III.25.4 There is no universal rule of practice that bail shall not be renewed when the summing-up has begun. Each case must be decided in the light of its own circumstances and having regard to the judge's assessment from time to time of the risks involved.

III.25.5 Once the jury has returned a verdict a further renewal of bail should be decided in the light of the gravity of the offence and the likely sentence to be passed in all the circumstances of the case.

III.26. Facts to be stated on pleas of guilty

III.26.1 To enable the press and the public to know the circumstances of an offence of which an accused has been convicted and for which he is to be sentenced, in relation to each offence to which an accused has pleaded guilty the prosecution shall state those facts in open court before sentence is imposed.

III.27. Antecedents

Standard for the provision of information of antecedents in the Crown Court and magistrates' courts

III.27.1 In the Crown Court the police will provide brief details of the circumstances of the last three similar convictions and/or of convictions likely to be of interest to the court, the latter being judged on a case by case basis. This information should be provided separately and attached to the antecedents as set out below.

III.27.2 Where the current alleged offence could constitute a breach of an existing community order, e.g. community rehabilitation order, and it is known that that order is still in force then, to enable the court to consider the possibility of revoking that order, details of the circumstances of the offence leading to the community order should be included in the antecedents as set out below.

Preparation of antecedents and standard formats to be used

III.27.3 In magistrates' courts and the Crown Court:

Personal details and summary of convictions and cautions—Police National Computer ['PNC'] Court/Defence/Probation Summary Sheet;

Previous convictions—PNC Court/Defence/Probation printout, supplemented by Form MG16 if the police force holds convictions not shown on PNC;

Recorded cautions—PNC Court/Defence/Probation printout, supplemented by Form MG17 if the police force holds cautions not shown on PNC.and, in addition, in the Crown Court:

Circumstances of the last three similar convictions;

Circumstances of offence leading to a community order still in force;

Form MG(c). The detail should be brief and include the date of the offence.

Provision of antecedents to the court and parties
Crown Court

III.27.4 The Crown Court antecedents will be prepared by the police immediately following committal proceedings, including committals for sentence, transfers under section 4 of the Criminal Justice Act 1987 or section 53 of the Criminal Justice Act 1991 or upon receipt of a notice of appeal, excluding non-imprisonable motoring offences.

III.27.5 Seven copies of the antecedents will be prepared in respect of each defendant. Two copies are to be provided to the Crown Prosecution Service ['CPS'] direct, the remaining five to be sent to the Crown Court. The court will send one copy to the defence and one to the Probation Service. The remaining copies are for the court's use. Where following conviction a custodial order is made one copy is to be attached to the order sent to the prison.

III.27.6 The antecedents must be provided, as above, within 21 days of committal or transfer in each case. Any points arising from them are to be raised with the police by the defence solicitor as soon as possible and, where there is time, at least seven days before the hearing date so that the matter can be resolved prior to that hearing.

III.27.7 Seven days before the hearing date the police will check the record of convictions. Details of any additional convictions will be provided using the standard format above. These will be provided as above and attached to the documents already supplied. Details of any additional outstanding cases will also be provided at this stage.

Magistrates' courts

III.27.8 The magistrates' court antecedents will be prepared by the police and submitted to the CPS with the case file.

III.27.9 Five copies of the antecedents will be prepared in respect of each defendant and provided to the CPS who will be responsible for distributing them to others at the sentencing hearing. Normally two copies will be provided to the court, one to the defence and one to the Probation Service when appropriate. Where following conviction a custodial order is made, one of the court's copies is to be attached to the order sent to the prison.

III.27.10 In instances where antecedents have been provided to the court some time before the hearing the police will, if requested to do so by the CPS, check the record of convictions. Details of any additional convictions will be provided using the standard format above. These will be provided as above and attached to the documents already supplied. Details of any additional outstanding cases will also be provided at this stage.

III.27.11 The above arrangements whereby the police provide the antecedents to the CPS for passing on to others will apply unless there is a local agreement between the CPS and the court that alters that arrangement.

III.28. Victim personal statements

III.28.1 This section draws attention to the Victim Personal Statement scheme, which started on 1 October 2001, to give victims a more formal opportunity to say how a crime has affected them. It may help to identify whether they have a particular need for information, support and protection. It will also enable the court to take the statement into account when determining sentence. In some circumstances, it may be appropriate for relatives of a victim to make a Victim Personal Statement, for example where the victim has died as a result of the relevant criminal conduct.

III.28.2 When a police officer takes a statement from a victim the victim will be told about the scheme and given the chance to make a Victim Personal Statement. The decision about whether or not to make a Victim Personal Statement is entirely for the victim. A Victim Personal Statement may be made or updated at any time prior to the disposal of the case. It will not normally be appropriate for a Victim Personal Statement to be made after the disposal of the case; there may be rare occasions between sentence and appeal when an update to the Victim Personal Statement may be necessary, for example, when the victim was injured and the final prognosis was not available at the date of sentence. If the court is presented with a Victim Personal Statement the following approach should be adopted:

(a) The Victim Personal Statement and any evidence in support should be considered and taken into account by the court prior to passing sentence.

(b) Evidence of the effects of an offence on the victim contained in the Victim Personal Statement or other statement must be in proper form, that is a witness statement made under section 9 of the Criminal Justice Act 1967 or an expert's report, and served upon the defendant's solicitor or the defendant, if he is not represented, prior to sentence. Except where inferences can properly be drawn from the nature of or circumstances surrounding the offence, a sentencer must not make assumptions unsupported by evidence about the effects of an offence on the victim.

(c) The court must pass what it judges to be the appropriate sentence having regard to the circumstances of the offence and of the offender, taking into account, so far as the court considers it appropriate, the impact on the victim. The opinions of the victim or the victim's close relatives as to what the sentence should be are therefore not relevant, unlike the consequence of the offence on them. Victims should be advised of this. If, despite the advice, opinions as to sentence are included in the statement, the court should pay no attention to them.

(d) The court should consider whether it is desirable in its sentencing remarks to refer to the evidence provided on behalf of the victim.

III.29. Support for witnesses giving evidence by live television link

III.29.1 This section of the Practice Direction is made pursuant to [rule 29.6 of the Criminal Procedure Rules 2005] and supersedes previous guidance given by the Senior Presiding Judges, Lord Justice Tasker Watkins in 1991 and Lord Justice Auld in 1998.

III.29.2 An increased degree of flexibility is now appropriate as to who can act as supporter of a witness giving evidence by live television link. Where a special measures direction is made enabling a vulnerable, intimidated or child witness to give evidence by means of a live television link, the trial judge will make a direction as to the identity of the witness supporter. Where practical, the direction will be made before the trial commences. In giving the direction, the trial judge will balance all relevant interests—see paragraph 1.11 of the guidance '*Achieving Best Evidence*'. The witness supporter should be completely independent of the witness and his or her family and have no previous knowledge of or personal involvement in the case. The supporter should also be suitably trained so as to understand the obligations of, and comply with, the National Standards relating to witness supporters. Providing these criteria are met, the witness supporter need not be an usher or court official. Thus, for example, the functions of the witness supporter may be performed by a representative of the Witness Service.

III.29.3 Where the witness supporter is someone other than the court usher, the usher should continue to be available both to assist the witness and the witness supporter, and to ensure that the judge's requirements are properly complied with in the CCTV room.

III.30. Treatment of vulnerable defendants

III.30.1 This direction applies to proceedings in the Crown Court and in magistrates' courts on the trial, sentencing or (in the Crown Court) appeal of (a) children and young persons under 18 or (b) adults who suffer from a mental disorder within the meaning of the Mental Health Act 1983 or who have any other significant impairment of intelligence and social function. In this direction such defendants are referred to collectively as "vulnerable defendants". The purpose of this direction is to extend to proceedings in relation to such persons in the adult courts procedures analogous to those in use in youth courts.

III.30.2 The steps which should be taken to comply with paragraphs III.30.3 to III.30.17 should be judged, in any given case, taking account of the age, maturity and development (intellectual, social and emotional) of the defendant concerned and all other circumstances of the case.

The overriding principle

III.30.3 A defendant may be young and immature or may have a mental disorder within the meaning of the Mental Health Act 1983 or some other significant impairment of intelligence and social function such as to inhibit his understanding of and participation in the proceedings. The purpose of criminal proceedings is to determine guilt, if that is in issue, and decide on the appropriate sentence if the defendant pleads guilty or is convicted. All possible steps should be taken to assist a vulnerable defendant to understand and participate in those proceedings. The ordinary trial process should, so far as necessary, be adapted to meet those ends. Regard should be had to the welfare of a young defendant as required by section 44 of the

Children and Young Persons Act 1933, and generally to parts 1 and 3 of the Criminal Procedure Rules (the overriding objective and the court's powers of case management).

Before the trial, sentencing or appeal

III.30.4 If a vulnerable defendant, especially one who is young, is to be tried jointly with one who is not, the court should consider at the plea and case management hearing, or at a case management hearing in a magistrates' court, whether the vulnerable defendant should be tried on his own and should so order unless of the opinion that a joint trial would be in accordance with part 1 of the Criminal Procedure Rules (the overriding objective) and in the interests of justice. If a vulnerable defendant is tried jointly with one who is not, the court should consider whether any of the modifications set out in this direction should apply in the circumstances of the joint trial and so far as practicable make orders to give effect to any such modifications.

III.30.5 At the plea and case management hearing, or at a case management hearing in a magistrates' court, the court should consider and so far as practicable give directions on the matters covered in paragraphs III.30.9 to III.30.17.

III.30.6 It may be appropriate to arrange that a vulnerable defendant should visit, out of court hours and before the trial, sentencing or appeal hearing, the courtroom in which that hearing is to take place so that he can familiarise himself with it.

III.30.7 If any case against a vulnerable defendant has attracted or may attract widespread public or media interest, the assistance of the police should be enlisted to try and ensure that the defendant is not, when attending the court, exposed to intimidation, vilification or abuse. Section 41 of the Criminal Justice Act 1925 prohibits the taking of photographs of defendants and witnesses (among others) in the court building or in its precincts, or when entering or leaving those precincts. A direction informing media representatives that the prohibition will be enforced may be appropriate.

III.30.8 The court should be ready at this stage, if it has not already done so, where relevant to make a reporting restriction under section 39 of the Children and Young Persons Act 1933 or, on an appeal to the Crown Court from a youth court, to remind media representatives of the application of section 49 of that Act. Any such order, once made, should be reduced to writing and copies should on request be made available to anyone affected or potentially affected by it.

The trial, sentencing or appeal hearing

III.30.9 Subject to the need for appropriate security arrangements the proceedings should, if practicable, be held in a courtroom in which all the participants are on the same or almost the same level.

III.30.10 A vulnerable defendant, especially if he is young, should normally, if he wishes, be free to sit with members of his family or others in a like relationship, and with some other suitable supporting adult such as a social worker, and in a place which permits easy, informal communication with his legal representatives. The court should ensure that a suitable supporting adult is available throughout the course of the proceedings.

III.30.11 At the beginning of the proceedings the court should ensure that what is to take place has been explained to a vulnerable defendant in terms he can understand, and at trial in the Crown Court it should ensure in particular that the role of the jury has been explained. It should remind those representing the vulnerable defendant and the supporting adult of their responsibility to explain each step as it takes place, and at trial to explain the possible consequences of a guilty verdict. Throughout the trial the court should continue to ensure, by any appropriate means, that the defendant understands what is happening and what has been said by those on the bench, the advocates and witnesses.

III.30.12 A trial should be conducted according to a timetable which takes full account of a vulnerable defendant's ability to concentrate. Frequent and regular breaks will often be appropriate. The court should ensure, so far as practicable, that the trial is conducted in simple, clear language that the defendant can understand and that cross-examination is conducted by questions that are short and clear.

III.30.13 A vulnerable defendant who wishes to give evidence by live link in accordance with section 33A of the Youth Justice and Criminal Evidence Act 1999 may apply for a direction to that effect. Before making such a direction the court must be satisfied that it is in the interests of justice to do so, and that the use of a live link would enable the defendant to participate more effectively as a witness in the proceedings. The direction will need to deal with the practical arrangements to be made, including the room from which the defendant will give evidence, the identity of the person or persons who will accompany him, and how it will be arranged for him to be seen and heard by the court.

III.30.14 In the Crown Court robes and wigs should not be worn unless the court for good reason orders that they should. It may be appropriate for the court to be robed for sentencing in a grave case even though it has sat without robes for trial. It is generally desirable that those responsible for the security of a vulnerable defendant who is in custody, especially if he is young, should not be in uniform, and that there should be no recognisable police presence in the courtroom save for good reason.

III.30.15 The court should be prepared to restrict attendance by members of the public in the court room to a small number, perhaps limited to those with an immediate and direct interest in the outcome. The court should rule on any challenged claim to attend.

III.30.16 Facilities for reporting the proceedings (subject to any restrictions under section 39 or 49 of the Children and Young Persons Act 1933) must be provided. But the court may restrict the number of reporters attending in the courtroom to such number as is judged practicable and desirable. In ruling on any challenged claim to attend in the court room for the purpose of reporting the court should be mindful of the public's general right to be informed about the administration of justice.

III.30.17 Where it has been decided to limit access to the courtroom, whether by reporters or generally, arrangements should be made for the proceedings to be relayed, audibly and if possible visually, to another room in the same court complex to which the media and the public have access if it appears that there will be a need for such additional facilities. Those making use of such a facility should be reminded that it is to be treated as an extension of the court room and that they are required to conduct themselves accordingly.

III.30.18 Where the court is called upon to exercise its discretion in relation to any procedural matter falling within the scope of this practice direction but not the subject of specific reference, such discretion should be exercised having regard to the principles in paragraph III.30.3.

III.31 Binding over orders and conditional discharges

III.31.1 This direction takes into account the judgments of the European Court of Human Rights in *Steel v United Kingdom* (1999) 28 EHRR 603, [1998] Crim LR 893 and in *Hashman and Harrup v United Kingdom* (2000) 30 EHRR 241, [2000] Crim LR 185. Its purpose is to give practical guidance, in the light of those two judgments, on the practice of imposing binding over orders. The direction applies to orders made under the court's common law powers, under the Justices of the Peace Act 1361, under section 1(7) of the Justices of the Peace Act 1968 and under section 115 of the Magistrates' Courts Act 1980. This direction also gives guidance concerning the court's power to bind over parents or guardians under section 150 of the Powers of Criminal Courts (Sentencing) Act 2000 and the Crown Court's power to bind over to come up for judgment. The court's power to impose a conditional discharge under section 12 of the Powers of Criminal Courts (Sentencing) Act 2000 is also covered by this direction.

Binding over to keep the peace

III.31.2 Before imposing a binding over order, the court must be satisfied that a breach of the peace involving violence or an imminent threat of violence has occurred or that there is a real risk of violence in the future. Such violence may be perpetrated by the individual who will be subject to the order or by a third party as a natural consequence of the individual's conduct.

III.31.3 In light of the judgment in *Hashman and Harrup*, courts should no longer bind an individual over 'to be of good behaviour'. Rather than binding an individual over to "keep the peace" in general terms, the court should identify the specific conduct or activity from which the individual must refrain.

Written order

III.31.4 When making an order binding an individual over to refrain from specified types of conduct or activities, the details of that conduct or those activities should be specified by the court in a written order served on all relevant parties. The court should state its reasons for the making of the order, its length and the amount of the recognisance. The length of the order should be proportionate to the harm sought to be avoided and should not generally exceed 12 months.

Evidence

III.31.5 Sections 51 to 57 of the Magistrates' Courts Act 1980 set out the jurisdiction of the magistrates' court to hear an application made on complaint and the procedure which is to be followed. This includes a requirement under section 53 to hear evidence and the parties before making any order. This practice should be applied to all cases in the magistrates' court and the Crown Court where the court is considering imposing a binding over order. The court should give the individual who would be subject to the order and the prosecutor the opportunity to make representations, both as to the making of the order and as to its terms. The court should also hear any admissible evidence the parties wish to call and which has not already been heard in the proceedings. Particularly careful consideration may be required where the individual who would be subject to the order is a witness in the proceedings.

III.31.6 Where there is an admission which is sufficient to found the making of a binding over order and/or the individual consents to the making of the order, the court should nevertheless hear sufficient representations and, if appropriate, evidence, to satisfy itself that an order is appropriate in all the circumstances and to be clear about the terms of the order.

III.31.7 Where there is an allegation of breach of a binding over order and this is contested, the court should hear representations and evidence, including oral evidence, from the parties before making a finding.

Burden of proof

III.31.8 The court should be satisfied beyond reasonable doubt of the matters complained of before a binding over order may be imposed. Where the procedure has been commenced on complaint, the burden of proof rests on the complainant. In all other circumstances, the burden of proof rests upon the prosecution.

III.31.9 Where there is an allegation of breach of a binding over order, the court should be satisfied beyond reasonable doubt that a breach has occurred before making any order for forfeiture of a recognisance. The burden of proof shall rest on the prosecution.

Recognisance

III.31.10 The court must be satisfied on the merits of the case that an order for binding over is appropriate and should announce that decision before considering the amount of the recognisance. The individual who is made subject to the binding over order should be told he has a right of appeal from the decision.

III.31.11 When fixing the amount of the recognisance, courts should have regard to the individual's financial resources and should hear representations from the individual or his legal representatives regarding finances.

Refusal to enter into a recognisance

III.31.12 If there is any possibility that an individual will refuse to enter a recognisance, the court should consider whether there are any appropriate alternatives to a binding over order (for example, continuing with a prosecution). Where there are no appropriate alternatives and the individual continues to refuse to enter into the recognisance, the magistrates' court may use its power under section 115(3) of the Magistrates Court Act 1980, and the Crown Court may use its common law power, to commit the individual to custody.

III.31.13 Before the court exercises a power to commit the individual to custody, the individual should be given the opportunity to see a duty solicitor or another legal representative and be represented in proceedings if the individual so wishes. Public funding should generally be granted to cover representation.

III.31.14 In the event that the individual does not take the opportunity to seek legal advice, the court shall give the individual a final opportunity to comply with the request and shall explain the consequences of a failure to do so.

Antecedents

III.31.15 Courts are reminded of the provisions of section 7(5) of the Rehabilitation of Offenders Act 1974 which excludes from a person's antecedents any order of the court 'with respect to any person otherwise than on a conviction'.

Binding over to come up for judgment

III.31.16 If the Crown Court is considering binding over an individual to come up for judgment, the court should specify any conditions with which the individual is to comply in the meantime and not specify that the individual is to be of good behaviour.

Binding over of parent or guardian

III.31.17 Where a court is considering binding over a parent or guardian under section 150 of the Powers of Criminal Courts (Sentencing) Act 2000 to enter into a recognisance to take proper care of and exercise proper control over a child or young person, the court should specify the actions which the parent or guardian is to take.

Security for good behaviour

III.31.18 Where a court is imposing a conditional discharge under section 12 of the Powers of Criminal Courts (Sentencing) Act 2000, it has the power, under section 12(6) to make an order that a person who consents to do so give security for the good behaviour of the offender. When making such an order, the court should specify the type of conduct from which the offender is to refrain.

Part IV Further Directions Applying in the Crown Court

IV.30. Modes of address and titles of judges

Mode of address

IV.30.1 The following judges, when sitting in court, should be addressed as 'My Lord' or 'My Lady', as the case may be, whatever their personal status:

(a) any Circuit Judge sitting as a judge of the High Court under section 9(1) of the Supreme Court Act 1981;

(b) any judge sitting at the Central Criminal Court;

(c) any Senior Circuit Judge who is the Honorary Recorder of the city in which he sits.

IV.30.2 Subject to paragraph 30.1, Circuit Judges, Recorders and Deputy Circuit Judges should be addressed as 'Your Honour' when sitting in court.

Description

IV.30.3 In cause lists, forms and orders members of the judiciary should be described as follows:

(d) Circuit Judges, as 'His [or Her] Honour Judge A' (when the judge is sitting as a judge of the High Court under section 9(1) of the Supreme Court Act 1981 the words 'sitting as a judge of the High Court' should be added);

(e) Recorders, as 'Mr [or Mrs] Recorder B'. This style is appropriate irrespective of any honour or title which the recorder might possess, but if in any case it is desired to include an honour or title the alternative description 'Sir CD, Recorder' or 'The Lord D, Recorder' may be used;

(f) Deputy Circuit Judges, as 'His [or Her] Honour EF, sitting as a Deputy Circuit Judge'.

IV.31. Transfer of cases from one circuit to another

IV.31.1 An application that a case be transferred from one Circuit to another should not be granted unless the judge is satisfied that:

(a) the approval of the Presiding Judges and Regional Director for each Region/Circuit has been obtained, or

(b) the case may be transferred under general arrangements approved by the Presiding Judges and Regional Directors.

IV.32. Transfer of proceedings between locations of the Crown Court

IV.32.1 Without prejudice to the provisions of section 76 of the Supreme Court Act 1981 (committal for trial: alteration of place of trial) directions may be given for the transfer from one location of the Crown Court to another of: (a) appeals; (b) proceedings on committal for sentence or to be dealt with.

IV.32.2 Such directions may be given in a particular case by an officer of the Crown Court, or generally, in relation to a class or classes of case, by the Presiding Judge or a judge acting on his behalf.

IV.32.3 If dissatisfied with such directions given by an officer of the Crown Court, any party to the proceedings may apply to a judge of the Crown Court who may hear the application in chambers.

IV.33. Allocation of business within the Crown Court

General

IV.33.1 Cases in Class 1 may only be tried by:

(1) a High Court Judge, or

(2) a Circuit Judge or Deputy High Court Judge or Deputy Circuit Judge provided (a) that, in all cases save attempted murder, such judge is authorised by the Lord Chief Justice to try murder cases, or in the case of attempted murder, to try murder or attempted murder, and (b) the Presiding Judge has released the case for trial by such a judge.

IV.33.2 Cases in Class 2 may be tried by:

(1) a High Court Judge

(2) a Circuit Judge or Deputy High Court Judge or Deputy Circuit Judge or a Recorder, provided that in all cases such judge is authorised to try class 2 cases by the Lord Chief Justice and the case has been assigned to the judge by or under the direction of either the Presiding Judge or Resident Judge in accordance with guidance given by the Presiding Judges.

IV.33.3 Cases in Class 3 may be tried by a High Court Judge, or in accordance with guidance given by the Presiding Judges, a Circuit Judge, a Deputy Circuit Judge or a Recorder. A case in Class 3 shall not be listed for trial by a High Court Judge except with the consent of a Presiding Judge.

IV.33.4 Appeals from decisions of magistrates shall be heard by:

(a) a Resident Judge, or

(b) a Circuit Judge, nominated by the Resident Judge, who regularly sits at the Crown Court centre, or

(c) an experienced Recorder or Deputy Circuit Judge specifically approved by or under the direction of the Presiding Judges for the purpose, or

(d) where no Circuit Judge or Recorder satisfying the requirements above is available and it is not practicable to obtain the approval of the Presiding Judges, by a Circuit Judge, Recorder or Deputy Circuit Judge selected by the Resident Judge to hear a specific case or cases listed on a specific day.

IV.33.5 Committals following breach (such as a matter in which a community order has been made, or a suspended sentence passed) should, where possible, be listed before the judge who originally dealt with the matter, or, if not, before a judge of the same or higher level.

Applications for removal of a driving disqualification

IV.33.6 Application should be made to the location of the Crown Court where the order of disqualification was made.

Absence of Resident Judge

IV.33.7 A Resident Judge must appoint a deputy to exercise his functions when he is absent from his centre.

Guidance issued by the Senior Presiding Judge and the Presiding Judges

IV.33.8 For the just, speedy and economical disposal of the business of the Circuits or a Circuit, the Senior Presiding Judge or the Presiding Judges, with the approval of the Senior Presiding Judge, may issue guidance to Resident Judges in relation to the allocation and management of the work at their court.

IV.33.9 With the approval of the Senior Presiding Judge, general directions may be given by the Presiding Judges of the South Eastern Circuit concerning the distribution and allocation of business of all classes of case at the Central Criminal Court.

IV.34. Settling the indictment

IV.34.1 Rule 14.1 of the Criminal Procedure Rules requires the prosecutor to serve a draft indictment not more than 28 days after service of the evidence in a case sent for trial, after the committal of the defendant for trial, or after one of the other events listed in that rule. Rule 14.2(5) provides that an indictment may contain any count charging substantially the same offence as one sent or committed for trial and any other count based on the prosecution evidence already served which the Crown Court has jurisdiction to try. Where the prosecutor intends to include in the draft indictment counts which differ materially from, or are additional to, those on which the defendant was sent or committed for trial then the defendant should be given as much notice as possible, usually by service of a draft indictment, or a provisional draft indictment, at the earliest possible opportunity.

IV.34.2 There is no rule of law or practice which prohibits two indictments being in existence at the same time for the same offence against the same person and on the same facts. But the court will not allow the prosecution to proceed on both indictments. They cannot be tried together and the court will require the prosecution to elect the one on which the trial will proceed. Where different defendants have been separately sent or committed for trial for offences which can lawfully be charged in the same indictment then it is permissible to join in one indictment counts based on the separate sendings or committals for trial even if an indictment based on one of them already has been signed. Where necessary the court should be invited to exercise its powers of amendment under section 5 of the Indictments Act 1915.

IV.34.3 Save in the special circumstances described in the following paragraphs of this Practice Direction, it is undesirable that a large number of counts should be contained in one indictment. Where defendants on trial have a variety of offences alleged against them then in the interests of effective case management it is the court's responsibility to exercise its powers in accordance with the overriding objective set out in part 1 of the Criminal Procedure Rules. The prosecution may be required to identify a selection of counts on which the trial should proceed, leaving a decision to be taken later whether to try any of the remainder. Where an indictment contains substantive counts and one or more related conspiracy counts the court will expect the prosecution to justify the joinder. Failing justification the prosecution should be required to choose whether to proceed on the substantive counts or on the conspiracy counts. In any event, if there is a conviction on any counts that are tried then those that have been postponed can remain on the file marked 'not to be proceeded with without the leave of the court'. In the event that a conviction is later quashed on appeal, the remaining counts can be tried. Where necessary the court has power to order that an indictment be divided and some counts removed to a separate indictment.

Multiple offending: trial by jury and then by judge alone

IV.34.4 Under sections 17 to 21 of the Domestic Violence, Crime and Victims Act 2004 the court may order that the trial of certain counts will be by jury in the usual way and, if the jury convicts, that other associated counts will be tried by judge alone. The use of this power is likely to be appropriate where justice cannot be done without charging a large number of separate offences and the allegations against the defendant appear to fall into distinct groups by reference to the identity of the victim, by reference to the dates of the offences, or by some other distinction in the nature of the offending conduct alleged.

IV.34.5 In such a case it is essential to make clear from the outset the association asserted by the prosecutor between those counts to be tried by a jury and those counts which it is proposed should be tried by judge alone, if the jury convict on the former. A special form of indictment is prescribed for this purpose.

IV.34.6 An order for such a trial may be made only at a preparatory hearing. It follows that where the prosecutor intends to invite the court to order such a trial it will normally be appropriate to proceed as follows. The draft indictment served under Criminal Procedure Rule 14.1(1) should be in the form appropriate to such a trial. It should be accompanied by an application under Criminal Procedure Rule 15.1 for a preparatory hearing. This will ensure that the defendant is aware at the earliest possible opportunity of what the prosecution propose and of the proposed association of counts in the indictment. It is undesirable for a draft indictment in the usual form to be served where the prosecutor expects to apply for a two stage trial and hence, of necessity, for permission to amend the indictment at a later stage in order that it may be in the special form.

IV.34.7 On receipt of a draft two part indictment a Crown Court officer should sign it at the end of Part Two. At the start of the preparatory hearing the defendant should be arraigned on all counts in Part One of the indictment. Arraignment on Part Two need not take place until after there has been either a guilty plea to, or finding of guilt on, an associated count in Part One of the indictment.

IV.34.8 If the prosecution application is successful, the prosecutor should prepare an abstract of the indictment, containing the counts from Part One only, for use in the jury trial. Preparation of such an abstract does not involve 'amendment' of the indictment. It is akin to where a defendant pleads guilty to certain counts in an indictment and is put in the charge of the jury on the remaining counts only.

IV.34.9 If the prosecution application for a two stage trial is unsuccessful, the prosecutor may apply to amend the indictment to remove from it any counts in Part Two which would make jury trial on the whole indictment impracticable and to revert to a standard form of indictment. It will be a matter for the court whether arraignment on outstanding counts takes place at the preparatory hearing, or at a future date.

Multiple offending: count charging more than one incident

IV.34.10 Rule 14.2(2) of the Criminal Procedure Rules allows a single count to allege more than one incident of the commission of an offence in certain circumstances. Each incident must be of the same offence. The circumstances in which such a count may be appropriate include, but are not limited to, the following:

(a) the victim on each occasion was the same, or there was no identifiable individual victim as, for example, in a case of the unlawful importation of controlled drugs or of money laundering;

(b) the alleged incidents involved a marked degree of repetition in the method employed or in their location, or both;

(c) the alleged incidents took place over a clearly defined period, typically (but not necessarily) no more than about a year;

(d) in any event, the defence is such as to apply to every alleged incident without differentiation. Where what is in issue differs between different incidents, a single 'multiple incidents' count will not be appropriate, though it may be appropriate to use two or more such counts according to the circumstances and to the issues raised by the defence.

IV.34.11 Even in circumstances such as those set out in paragraph IV.34.[10], there may be occasions on which a prosecutor chooses not to use such a count, in order to bring the case within section 75(3)(a) of the Proceeds of Crime Act 2002 (criminal lifestyle established by conviction of three or more offences in the same proceedings) for example, because section 75(2)(c) of that Act does not apply (criminal lifestyle established by an offence committed over a period of at least six months). Where the prosecutor proposes such a course it is unlikely that part 1 of the Criminal Procedure Rules (the overriding objective) will require an indictment to contain a single 'multiple incidents' count in place of a larger number of counts, subject to the general principles set out in paragraph IV.34.3.

IV.34.12 For some offences, particularly sexual offences, the penalty for the offence may have changed during the period over which the alleged incidents took place. In such a case, additional 'multiple incidents' counts should be used so that each count only alleges incidents to which the same maximum penalty applies.

IV.34.13 In some cases, such as money laundering or theft, there will be documented evidence of individual incidents but the sheer number of these will make it desirable to cover them in a single count. Where the indictment contains a count alleging multiple incidents of the commission of such offences, and during the course of the trial it becomes clear that the jury may bring in a verdict in relation to a lesser amount than that alleged by the prosecution, it will normally be desirable to direct the jury that they should return a partial verdict with reference to that lesser amount.

IV.34.14 In other cases, such as sexual or physical abuse, a complainant may be in a position only to give evidence of a series of similar incidents without being able to specify when or the precise circumstances in which they occurred. In these cases, a 'multiple incidents' count may be desirable. If on the other hand, the complainant is able to identify particular incidents of the offence by reference to a date or other specific event, but alleges that in addition there were other incidents which the complainant is unable to specify, then it may be desirable to include separate counts for the identified incidents and a 'multiple incidents' count or counts alleging that incidents of the same offence occurred 'many' times. Using a 'multiple incidents' count may be an appropriate alternative to using 'specimen' counts in some cases where repeated sexual or physical abuse is alleged. The choice of count will depend on the particular circumstances of the case and should be determined bearing in mind the implications for sentencing set out in *R v Canavan; R v Kidd; R v Shaw* [1998] 1 Cr App R 79.

IV.35. Voluntary bills of indictment

IV.35.1 Section 2(2)(b) of the Administration of Justice (Miscellaneous Provisions) Act 1933 allows the preferment of a bill of indictment by the direction or with the consent of a judge of the High Court. Bills so preferred are known as voluntary bills.

IV.35.2 Applications for such consent must not only comply with each paragraph of the Indictments (Procedure) Rules 1971, SI 1971/2084, but must also be accompanied by:
(a) a copy of any charges on which the defendant has been committed for trial;
(b) a copy of any charges on which his committal for trial was refused by the magistrates' court;
(c) a copy of any existing indictment which has been preferred in consequence of his committal;
(d) a summary of the evidence or other document which (i) identifies the counts in the proposed indictment on which he has been committed for trial (or which are substantially the same as charges on which he has been so committed), and (ii) in relation to each other count in the proposed indictment, identifies the pages in the accompanying statements and exhibits where the essential evidence said to support that count is to be found;

(e) marginal markings of the relevant passages on the pages of the statements and exhibits identified under (d)(ii).

These requirements should be complied with in relation to each defendant named in the indictment for which consent is sought, whether or not it is proposed to prefer any new count against him.

IV.35.3 The preferment of a voluntary bill is an exceptional procedure. Consent should only be granted where good reason to depart from the normal procedure is clearly shown and only where the interests of justice, rather than considerations of administrative convenience, require it.

IV.35.4 Neither the 1933 Act nor the 1971 Rules expressly require a prosecuting authority applying for consent to the preferment of a voluntary bill to give notice of the application to the prospective defendant or to serve on him a copy of documents delivered to the judge; nor is it expressly required that the prospective defendant have any opportunity to make any submissions to the judge, whether in writing or orally.

IV.35.5 The prosecuting authorities for England and Wales have issued revised guidance to prosecutors on the procedures to be adopted in seeking judicial consent to the preferment of voluntary bills. These procedures direct prosecutors:

(a) on the making of application for consent to preferment of a voluntary bill, forthwith to give notice to the prospective defendant that such application has been made;

(b) at about the same time, to serve on the prospective defendant a copy of all the documents delivered to the judge (save to the extent that these have already been served on him);

(c) to inform the prospective defendant that he may make submissions in writing to the judge, provided that he does so within nine working days of the giving of notice under (a) above. Prosecutors will be directed that these procedures should be followed unless there are good grounds for not doing so, in which case prosecutors will inform the judge that the procedures have not been followed and seek his leave to dispense with all or any of them. Judges should not give leave to dispense unless good grounds are shown.

IV.35.6 A judge to whom application for consent to the preferment of a voluntary bill is made will, of course, wish to consider carefully the documents submitted by the prosecutor and any written submissions timeously made by the prospective defendant, and may properly seek any necessary amplification. The judge may invite oral submissions from either party, or accede to a request for an opportunity to make such oral submissions, if the judge considers it necessary or desirable to receive such oral submissions in order to make a sound and fair decision on the application. Any such oral submissions should be made on notice to the other party, who should be allowed to attend.

IV.36. Abuse of process stay applications

IV.36.1 In all cases where a defendant in the Crown Court proposes to make an application to stay an indictment on the grounds of abuse of process, written notice of such application must be given to the prosecuting authority and to any co-defendant not later than 14 days before the date fixed or warned for trial ('the relevant date'). Such notice must:

(a) give the name of the case and the indictment number;

(b) state the fixed date or the warned date as appropriate;

(c) specify the nature of the application;

(d) set out in numbered sub-paragraphs the grounds upon which the application is to be made;

(e) be copied to the chief listing officer at the court centre where the case is due to be heard.

IV.36.2 Any co-defendant who wishes to make a like application must give a like notice not later than seven days before the relevant date, setting out any additional grounds relied upon.

IV.36.3 In relation to such applications, the following automatic directions shall apply:

(a) the advocate for the applicant(s) must lodge with the court and serve on all other parties a skeleton argument in support of the application at least five clear working days before the relevant date. If reference is to be made to any document not in the existing trial documents, a paginated and indexed bundle of such documents is to be provided with the skeleton argument;

(b) the advocate for the prosecution must lodge with the court and serve on all other parties a responsive skeleton argument at least two clear working days before the relevant date, together with a supplementary bundle if appropriate.

IV.36.4 All skeleton arguments must specify any propositions of law to be advanced (together with the authorities relied upon in support, with page references to passages relied upon) and, where appropriate, include a chronology of events and a list of dramatis personae. In all instances where reference is made to a document, the reference in the trial documents or supplementary bundle is to be given.

IV.36.5 The above time limits are minimum time limits. In appropriate cases the court will order longer lead times. To this end in all cases where defence advocates are, at the time of the plea and directions hearing, considering the possibility of an abuse of process application, this must be raised with the judge dealing with the matter, who will order a different timetable if appropriate, and may wish, in any event, to give additional directions about the conduct of the application.

IV.37. Citation of Hansard

IV.37.1 Where any party intends to refer to the reports of Parliamentary proceedings as reported in the Official Reports of either House of Parliament ('Hansard') in support of any such argument as is permitted by the decisions in *Pepper* v *Hart* [1993] AC 593 and *Pickstone* v *Freeman* [1989] AC 66 or otherwise must, unless the court otherwise directs, serve upon all other parties and the court copies of any such extract together with a brief summary of the argument intended to be based upon such extract. No other report of Parliamentary proceedings may be cited.

IV.37.2 Unless the court otherwise directs, service of the extract and summary of the argument shall be effected not less than 5 clear working days before the first day of the hearing, whether or not it has a fixed date. Advocates must keep themselves informed as to the state of the lists where no fixed date has been given. Service on the court shall be effected by sending three copies to the chief clerk of the relevant Crown Court centre. If any party fails to do so the court may make such order (relating to costs or otherwise) as is in all the circumstances appropriate.

IV.38. Applications for representation orders

IV.38.1 Applications for representation by a Queen's Counsel alone or by more than one advocate under Part IV of the Criminal Defence Service (General) (No 2) Regulations 2001 SI 2001/1437 made to the Crown Court shall be placed before the Resident Judge of that Crown Court (or, in his absence, a judge nominated for that purpose by a Presiding Judge of the circuit) who shall determine the application, save that, where the application relates to a case which is to be heard before a named High Court judge or a named Circuit Judge, he should refer the application to the named judge for determination.

IV.38.2 This does not apply where an application is made in the course of a trial or of a preliminary hearing, pre-trial review, or plea and directions hearing by the judge presiding at that trial or hearing.

IV.38.3 In the event of any doubt as to the proper application of this direction, reference shall be made by the judge concerned to a Presiding Judge of the circuit, who shall give such directions as he thinks fit.

IV.40. Video recorded evidence in chief

IV.40.1 The procedure for making application for leave to adduce a video recording of testimony from a witness under section 27 of the Youth Justice and Criminal Evidence Act 1999 is laid down in rule [29.7 of the Criminal Procedure Rules].

IV.40.2 Where a court, on application by a party to the proceedings or of its own motion, grants leave to admit a video recording in evidence under section 27(1) of the 1999 Act it may direct that any part of the recording be excluded (section 27(2) and (3)). When such direction is given, the party who made application to admit the video recording must edit the recording in accordance with the judge's directions and send a copy of the edited recording to the appropriate officer of the Crown Court and to every other party to the proceedings.

IV.40.3 Where a video recording is to be adduced during proceedings before the Crown Court, it should be produced and proved by the interviewer, or any other person who was present at the interview with the witness at which the recording was made. The applicant should ensure that such a person will be available for this purpose, unless the parties have agreed to accept a written statement in lieu of attendance by that person.

IV.40.4 Once a trial has begun if, by reason of faulty or inadequate preparation or for some other cause, the procedures set out above have not been properly complied with and an application is made to edit the video recording, thereby making necessary an adjournment for the work to be carried out, the court may make at its discretion an appropriate award of costs.

IV.41. Management of cases to be heard in the Crown Court

IV.41.1 This section of the practice direction supplements the rules in part 3 of the Criminal Procedure Rules as they apply to the management of cases to be heard in the Crown Court. Where time limits or other directions in the Consolidated Criminal Practice Direction appear inconsistent with this section, the directions in this section take precedence.

IV.41.2 The case details form set out in annex E should be completed by the Crown Court case progression officer in all cases to be tried on indictment.

Cases sent for trial

IV.41.3 A preliminary hearing ('PH') is not required in every case sent for trial under section 51 of the Crime and Disorder Act 1998: see rule 12.2 (which altered the Crown Court rule from which it derived). A PH should normally only be ordered by the magistrates' court or by the Crown Court where:

(i)   there are case management issues which call for such a hearing;

(ii) the case is likely to last for more than 4 weeks;

(iii) it would be desirable to set an early trial date;

(iv) the defendant is a child or young person;

(v)   there is likely to be a guilty plea and the defendant could be sentenced at the preliminary hearing; or

(vi) it seems to the court that it is a case suitable for a preparatory hearing in the Crown Court (see sections 7 and 9 of the Criminal Justice Act 1987 and sections 29–32 of the Criminal Procedure and Investigations Act 1996).

A PH, if there is one, should be held about 14 days after sending.

IV.41.4 The case progression form to be used in the magistrates' court and the PH form to be used in the Crown Court are set out in annex E with guidance notes. The forms provide a detailed timetable to enable the subsequent plea and case management hearing ('PCMH') to be effective.

IV.41.5 Where the magistrates' court does not order a PH it should order a PCMH to be held within about 14 weeks after sending for trial where a defendant is in custody and within about 17 weeks after sending for trial where a defendant is on bail. Those periods accommodate the periods fixed by the relevant rules for the service of the prosecution case papers and for making all potential preparatory applications. Where the parties realistically expect to have completed their preparation for the PCMH in less time than that then the magistrates' court should order it to be held earlier. But it will not normally be appropriate to order that the PCMH be held on a date before the expiry of at least 4 weeks from the date on which the prosecutor expects to serve the prosecution case papers, to allow the defence a proper opportunity to consider them. To order that a PCMH be held before the parties have had a reasonable opportunity to complete their preparation in accordance with the Criminal Procedure Rules risks compromising the effectiveness of this most important pre-trial hearing and risks wasting their time and that of the court.

Cases committed for trial

IV.41.6 For cases committed to the Crown Court for trial under section 6 of the Magistrates' Courts Act 1980 the case progression form to be used in the magistrates' court is set out in annex E with guidance notes. A PCMH should be ordered by the magistrates' court in every case, to be held within about 7 weeks after committal. That period accommodates the periods fixed by the relevant rules for making all potential preparatory applications. Where the parties realistically expect to have completed their preparation for the PCMH in less time than that then the magistrates' court should order it to be held earlier. However, to order that a PCMH be held before the parties have had a reasonable opportunity to complete their preparation in accordance with the Criminal Procedure Rules risks compromising the effectiveness of this most important pre-trial hearing and risks wasting their time and that of the court.

Cases transferred for trial

IV.41.7 In a case transferred to the Crown Court for trial under section 4(1) of the Criminal Justice Act 1987 or under section 53(1) of the Criminal Justice Act 1991 the directions contained in the case progression form used in cases for committal for trial apply as if the case had been committed on the date of the notice of transfer. A PCMH should be listed by the Crown Court to be held within about 7 weeks after transfer. That period accommodates the periods fixed by the relevant rules for making all potential preparatory applications. Where the parties realistically expect to have completed their preparation for the PCMH in less time than that then the magistrates' court should order it to be held earlier. However, to order that a PCMH be held before the parties have had a reasonable opportunity to complete their preparation in accordance with the Criminal Procedure Rules risks compromising the effectiveness of this most important pre-trial hearing and risks wasting their time and that of the court.

Plea and case management hearing

IV.41.8 Active case management at the PCMH is essential to reduce the number of ineffective and cracked trials and delays during the trial to resolve legal issues. The effectiveness of a PCMH hearing in a contested case depends in large measure upon preparation by all concerned and upon the presence of the trial advocate or an advocate who is able to make decisions and give the court the assistance which the trial advocate could be expected to give. Resident Judges in setting the listing policy should ensure that list officers fix cases as far as possible to enable the trial advocate to conduct the PCMH and the trial.

IV.41.9 In Class 1 and Class 2 cases, and in all cases involving a serious sexual offence against a child, the PCMH must be conducted by a High Court judge; by a circuit judge or by a recorder to whom the case has been assigned in accordance with paragraph IV.33 (allocation of business within the Crown Court); or by a judge authorised by the Presiding Judges to conduct such hearings. In the event of a guilty plea before such an authorised judge, the case will be adjourned for sentencing by a High Court judge or by a circuit judge or recorder to whom the case has been assigned.

Use of the PCMH form

IV.41.10 The PCMH form as set out in annex E must be used in accordance with the guidance notes.

Further pre-trial hearings after the PCMH

IV.41.11 Additional pre-trial hearings should be held only if needed for some compelling reason. Such hearings—often described informally as 'mentions'—are expensive and should actively be discouraged. Where necessary the power to give, vary or revoke a direction without a hearing should be used. Rule 3.9(3) of the Criminal Procedure Rules enables the Court to require the parties' case progression officers to inform the Crown Court case progression officer that the case is ready for trial, that it will proceed as a trial on the date fixed and will take no more or less time than that previously ordered.

IV.42. Juries

Jury service

IV.42.1 The effect of section 321 Criminal Justice Act 2003 was to remove certain categories of persons from those previously ineligible for jury service (the judiciary and others concerned with the administration of justice) and certain other categories ceased to be eligible for excusal as of right, (such as members of Parliament and medical professionals). Jury service is an important public duty which individual members of the public are chosen at random to undertake. The normal presumption is that everyone, unless mentally disordered or disqualified, will be required to serve when summoned to do so. This legislative change has, however, meant an increase in the number of jurors with professional and public service commitments. One of the results of this change is that trial judges must continue to be alert to the need to exercise their discretion to adjourn a trial, excuse or discharge a juror should the need arise. Whether or not an application has already been made to the jury summoning officer for deferral or excusal it is also open to the person summoned to apply to the court to be excused. Such applications must be considered with common sense and according to the interests of justice. An explanation should be required for an application being much later than necessary.

IV.42.2 Where a juror appears on a jury panel, it may be appropriate for a judge to excuse the juror from that particular case where the potential juror is personally concerned with the facts of the particular case or is closely connected with a prospective witness. Where the length of the trial is estimated to be significantly longer than the normal period of jury service, it is good practice for the trial judge to enquire whether the potential jurors on the jury panel foresee any difficulties with the length and if the judge is satisfied that the jurors concerns are justified he may say that they are not required for that particular jury. This does not mean that the judge must excuse the juror from sitting at that court altogether as it may well be possible for the juror to sit on a shorter trial at the same court.

IV.42.3 Where a juror unexpectedly finds him or herself in difficult professional or personal circumstances during the course of the trial, jurors should be encouraged to raise such problems with the trial judge. This might apply, for example, to a parent whose childcare arrangements unexpectedly fail or a worker who is engaged in the provision of services the need for which can be critical or Member of Parliament who has deferred their jury service to an apparently more convenient time, but is unexpectedly called back to work for a very important reason. Such difficulties would normally be raised through a jury note in the normal manner. In such circumstances, the judge must exercise his or her discretion according to the interests of justice and the requirements of each individual case. The judge must decide for himself whether the juror has presented a sufficient reason to interfere with the course of the trial. If the juror has presented a sufficient reason, in longer trials it may well be possible to adjourn for a short period in order to allow the juror to overcome the difficulty. In shorter cases it may be more appropriate to discharge the juror and to continue the trial with a reduced number of jurors. The power to do this is implicit in section 16(1) Juries Act 1974. In unusual cases (such as an unexpected emergency arising over night) a juror need not be discharged in open court. The good administration of justice depends on the cooperation of jurors who perform an essential public service. All such applications should be dealt with sensitively and sympathetically and the trial judge should always seek to meet the interests of justice without unduly inconveniencing any juror.

Jury oath

IV.42.4 The wording of the oath to be taken by jurors is: 'I swear by Almighty God that I will faithfully try the defendant and give a true verdict according to the evidence.' Any person who objects to being sworn shall be permitted to make his solemn affirmation instead. The wording of the affirmation is 'I do solemnly, sincerely and truly declare and affirm that I will faithfully try the defendant and give a true verdict according to the evidence.'

Guidance to jurors

IV.42.5 The following directions take effect immediately.

IV.42.6 Trial judges should ensure that the jury is alerted to the need to bring any concerns about fellow jurors to the attention of the judge at the time, and not to wait until the case is concluded. At the same time, it is undesirable to encourage inappropriate criticism of fellow jurors, or to threaten jurors with contempt of court.

IV.42.7 Judges should therefore take the opportunity, when warning the jury of the importance of not discussing the case with anyone outside the jury, to add a further warning. It is for the trial judge to tailor the further warning to the case, and to the phraseology used in the usual warning. The effect of the further warning should be that it is the duty of jurors to bring to the judge's attention, promptly, any behaviour among the jurors or by others affecting the jurors, that causes concern. The point should be made that, unless that is done while the case is continuing, it may be impossible to put matters right.

IV.42.8 The Judge should consider, particularly in a longer trial, whether a reminder on the lines of the further warning is appropriate prior to the retirement of the jury.

IV.42.9 In the event that such an incident does occur, trial judges should have regard to the remarks of Lord Hope at paras 127 and 128 in *R* v *Connors and Mirza* [2004] 2 WLR 201 and consider the desirability of preparing a statement that could be used in connection with any appeal arising from the incident to the Court of Appeal Criminal Division. Members of the Court of Appeal Criminal Division should also remind themselves of the power to request the judge to furnish them with any information or assistance under rule [68.23(1) of the Criminal Procedure Rules 2005] and section 87(4) of the Supreme Court Act 1981.

IV.43. Evidence of tape recorded interviews

IV.43.1 Where a suspect is to be interviewed by the police, the Code of Practice on Tape Recording of Interviews with Suspects effective from 10th April 1995 and issued under section 60 of the Police and Criminal Evidence Act 1984 applies. Where a record of the interview is to be prepared this should be in accordance with the national guidelines approved by the Secretary of State, as envisaged by Note E:5A of the Code.

IV.43.2 Where the prosecution intends to adduce evidence of the interview in evidence, and agreement between the parties has not been reached about the record, sufficient notice must be given to allow consideration of any amendment to the record or the preparation of any transcript of the interview or any editing of a tape for the purpose of playing it back in court. To that end, the following practice should be followed.

(a) Where the defence is unable to agree a record of interview or transcript (where one is already available) the prosecution should be notified no more than 21 days from the date of committal or date of transfer, or at the PDH if earlier, with a view to securing agreement to amend. The notice should specify the part to which objection is taken or the part omitted which the defence consider should be included. A copy of the notice should be supplied to the court within the period specified above.

(b) If agreement is not reached and it is proposed that the tape or part of it be played in court, notice should be given to the prosecution by the defence no more than 14 days after the expiry of the period in (a), or as ordered at the PDH, in order that counsel for the parties may agree those parts of the tape that should not be adduced and that arrangements may be made, by editing or in some other way, to exclude that material. A copy of the notice should be supplied to the court within the period specified above.

(c) Notice of any agreement reached under (a) or (b) should be supplied to the court by the prosecution as soon as is practicable.

(d) Alternatively, if, in any event, prosecuting counsel proposes to play the tape or part of it, the prosecution should, within 28 days of the date of committal or date of transfer or, if earlier, at the PDH, notify the defence and the court. The defence should notify the prosecution and the court within 14 days of receiving the notice if they object to the production of the tape on the basis that a part of it should be excluded. If the objections raised by the defence are accepted, the prosecution should prepare an edited tape or make other arrangements to exclude the material part and should notify the court of the arrangements made.

(e) Whenever editing or amendment of a record of interview or of a tape or of a transcript takes place, the following general principles should be followed:

  (i) Where a defendant has made a statement which includes an admission of one or more other offences, the portion relating to other offences should be omitted unless it is or becomes admissible in evidence;

  (ii) Where the statement of one defendant contains a portion which is partly in his favour and partly implicatory of a co-defendant in the trial, the defendant making the statement has the right to insist that everything relevant which is in his favour goes before the jury. In such a case the judge must be consulted about how best to protect the position of the co-defendant.

IV.43.3 If there is a failure to agree between counsel under paragraph IV.43.2(a) to (e), or there is a challenge to the integrity of the master tape, notice and particulars should be given to the court and to the prosecution by the defence as soon as is practicable. The court may then, at its discretion, order a pretrial review or give such other directions as may be appropriate.

IV.43.4 If a tape is to be adduced during proceedings before the Crown Court it should be produced and proved by the interviewing officer or any other officer who was present at the interview at which the recording was made. The prosecution should ensure that such an officer will be available for this purpose.

IV.43.5 Where such an officer is unable to act as the tape machine operator it is for the prosecution to make some other arrangement.

IV.43.6 In order to avoid the necessity for the court to listen to lengthy or irrelevant material before the relevant part of a tape recording is reached, counsel shall indicate to the tape machine operator those parts of a recording which it may be necessary to play. Such an indication should, so far as possible, be expressed in terms of the time track or other identifying process used by the interviewing police force and should be given in time for the operator to have located those parts by the appropriate point in the trial.

IV.43.7 Once a trial has begun, if, by reason of faulty preparation or for some other cause, the procedures above have not been properly complied with, and an application is made to amend the record of interview or transcript or to edit the tape, as the case may be, thereby making necessary an adjournment for the work to be carried out, the court may make at its discretion an appropriate award of costs.

IV.43.8 Where a case is listed for hearing on a date which falls within the time limits set out above, it is the responsibility of the parties to ensure that all the necessary steps are taken to comply with this Practice Direction within such shorter period as is available.

IV.43.9 In paragraph IV.43.2(a) and (d), 'date of transfer' is the date on which notice of transfer is given in accordance with the provisions of section 4(1)(c) of the Criminal Justice Act 1987.

IV.43.10 This direction should be read in conjunction with the Code of Practice on Tape Recording referred to in paragraph IV.43.1 and with Home Office Circular 26/1995.

IV.44. Defendant's right to give or not to give evidence

IV.44.1 At the conclusion of the evidence for the prosecution, section 35(2) of the Criminal Justice and Public Order Act 1994 requires the court to satisfy itself that the accused is aware that the stage has been reached at which evidence can be given for the defence and that he can, if he wishes, give evidence and that, if he chooses not to give evidence, or having been sworn, without good cause refuses to answer any question, it will be permissible for the jury to draw such inferences as appear proper from his failure to give evidence or his refusal, without good cause, to answer any question.

If the accused is legally represented

IV.44.2 Section 35(1) provides that section 35(2) does not apply if at the conclusion of the evidence for the prosecution the accused's legal representative informs the court that the accused will give evidence. This should be done in the presence of the jury. If the representative indicates that the accused will give evidence the case should proceed in the usual way.

IV.44.3 If the court is not so informed, or if the court is informed that the accused does not intend to give evidence, the judge should in the presence of the jury inquire of the representative in these terms: 'Have you advised your client that the stage has now been reached at which he may give evidence and, if he chooses not to do so or, having been sworn, without good cause refuses to answer any question, the jury may draw such inferences as appear proper from his failure to do so?'

IV.44.4 If the representative replies to the judge that the accused has been so advised, then the case shall proceed. If counsel replies that the accused has not been so advised, then the judge shall direct the representative to advise his client of the consequences set out in paragraph IV.44.3 and should adjourn briefly for this purpose before proceeding further.

If the accused is not legally represented

IV.44.5 If the accused is not represented, the judge shall at the conclusion of the evidence for the prosecution and in the presence of the jury say to the accused:

'You have heard the evidence against you. Now is the time for you to make your defence. You may give evidence on oath, and be cross-examined like any other witness. If you do not give evidence or, having been sworn, without good cause refuse to answer any question the jury may draw such inferences as appear proper. That means they may hold it against you. You may also call any witness or witnesses whom you have arranged to attend court. Afterwards you may also, if you wish, address the jury by arguing your case from the dock. But you cannot at that stage give evidence. Do you now intend to give evidence?'

IV.45. Pleas of guilty in the Crown Court

IV.45.1 Advocates must be free to perform their duty namely to give the accused the best advice possible and, if need be, in strong terms. It will often include advice that, in accordance with the relevant authorities and sentencing guidelines, a court will normally reduce a sentence as a result of a guilty plea and that the level of reduction will reflect the stage in the proceedings at which willingness to admit guilt was indicated. The advocate will, of course, emphasise that the defendant must not plead guilty unless he or she is guilty of the offence(s) charged.

IV.45.2 The defendant, having considered the advocate's advice, must have complete freedom of choice whether to plead guilty or not guilty.

IV.45.3 There must be freedom of access between advocate and judge. Any discussion must, however, be between the judge and the advocates on both sides. If an advocate is instructed by a solicitor who is in court, he or she, too, should be allowed to attend the discussion. This freedom of access is important because there may be matters calling for communication or discussion of such a nature that the advocate cannot, in the client's interest, mention them in open court, e.g. the advocate, by way of mitigation, may wish to tell the judge that reliable medical evidence shows that the defendant is suffering from a terminal illness and may not have long to live. It is imperative that, so far as possible, justice must be administered in open court. Advocates should, therefore, only ask to see the judge when it is felt to be really necessary. The judge must be careful only to treat such communications as private where, in the interests of justice, this is necessary. Where any such discussion takes place it should be recorded either by a tape recorder or a shorthand writer.

Pleas of guilty in the Crown Court: procedure

IV.45.4 This direction outlines the three routes by which a defendant may put forward a plea of guilty in the Crown Court, which are as follows:

a a plea of guilty to all or some of the charges on the basis of the prosecution case set out in the papers;

b a plea of guilty upon a basis of plea agreed by the prosecution and defence, or upon a basis of plea put forward by the defence but not contested by the prosecution; and c in cases involving serious or complex fraud conducted in accordance with paragraphs IV.45.16 to IV.45.28, below, a plea of guilty upon a basis of plea agreed by the prosecution and defence accompanied by joint submissions as to sentence.

(a) A plea of guilty to all or some of the charges on the basis of the prosecution case set out in the papers

IV.45.5 In many cases, defendants wishing to plead guilty will simply plead guilty to all charges on the basis of the facts as alleged and opened by the prosecution, with no dispute as to the factual basis and extent of offending alleged by the prosecution. Alternatively a defendant may plead guilty to some of the charges brought. When a defendant pleads guilty as set out above, the judge will consider whether that plea represents a proper plea on the basis of the facts set out by the papers. Where the judge is satisfied that the plea is properly grounded, sentencing may take place.

IV.45.6 Where the prosecution advocate is considering whether to accept a plea to a lesser charge, the advocate may invite the judge to approve the proposed course of action. In such circumstances, the advocate must abide by the decision of the judge.

IV.45.7 If the prosecution advocate does not invite the judge to approve the acceptance by the prosecution of a lesser charge, it is open to the judge to express his or her dissent with the course proposed and invite the advocate to reconsider the matter with those instructing him or her.

IV.45.8 In any proceedings, where the judge is of the opinion that the course proposed by the advocate may lead to serious injustice, the proceedings may be adjourned to allow the following procedure to be followed:

    a as a preliminary step, the prosecution advocate must discuss the judge's observations with the Chief Crown Prosecutor or the senior prosecutor of the relevant prosecuting authority as appropriate, in an attempt to resolve the issue;

    b where the issue remains unresolved, the Director of Public Prosecutions or the Director of the relevant prosecuting authority should be consulted;

    c in extreme circumstances the judge may decline to proceed with the case until the prosecuting authority has consulted with the Attorney General as may be appropriate.

IV.45.9 Prior to entering a plea of guilty, a defendant may seek an indication of sentence under the procedure set out in *R v Goodyear* [2005] 2 Cr App R 20; see paragraphs IV.45.29 to IV.45.33, below.

(b) A plea of guilty upon a basis of plea agreed by the prosecution and defence

IV.45.10 The prosecution may reach an agreement with the defendant as to the factual basis on which the defendant will plead guilty, often known as an 'agreed basis of plea'. It is always subject to the approval of the court, which will consider whether it is fair and in the interests of justice.

IV.45.11 *R v Underwood* [2004] EWCA Crim 2256; [2005] 1 Cr App R (S) 90 outlines the principles to be applied where the defendant admits that he or she is guilty, but disputes the basis of offending alleged by the prosecution:

    a. The prosecution may accept and agree the defendant's account of the disputed facts or reject it in its entirety. If the prosecution accepts the defendant's basis of plea, it must ensure that the basis of plea is factually accurate and enables the sentencing judge to impose a sentence appropriate to reflect the justice of the case;

    b. In resolving any disputed factual matters, the prosecution must consider its primary duty to the court and must not agree with or acquiesce in an agreement which contains material factual disputes;

    c. If the prosecution does accept the defendant's basis of plea, it must be reduced to writing, be signed by advocates for both sides, and made available to the judge prior to the prosecution's opening;

    d. An agreed basis of plea that has been reached between the parties must not contain any matters which are in dispute;

e. On occasion the prosecution may lack the evidence positively to dispute the defendant's account, for example, where the defendant asserts a matter outside the knowledge of the prosecution. Simply because the prosecution does not have evidence to contradict the defendant's assertions does not mean those assertions should be agreed. In such a case, the prosecution should test the defendant's evidence and submissions by requesting a *Newton* hearing (*R v Newton* (1982) 4 Cr App R (S) 388, (1982) 77 Cr App R 13), following the procedure set out in paragraph IV.45.13, below.

f. If it is not possible for the parties to resolve a factual dispute when attempting to reach a plea agreement under this part, it is the responsibility of the prosecution to consider whether the matter should proceed to trial, or to invite the court to hold a *Newton* hearing as necessary.

g. Subject to paragraph IV.45.12, where the prosecution has not invited the court to hold a *Newton* hearing, and where the factual dispute between the prosecution and the defence is likely to have a material impact on the sentence, if the defence does not invite the court to hold a *Newton* hearing the court is entitled to reach its own conclusion of the facts on the evidence before it.

IV.45.12 *R v Underwood* emphasises that whether or not pleas have been 'agreed' the judge is not bound by any such agreement and is entitled of his or her own motion to insist that any evidence relevant to the facts in dispute (or upon which the judge requires further evidence for whatever reason) should be called. Any view formed by the prosecution on a proposed basis of plea is deemed to be conditional on the judge's acceptance of the basis of plea.

IV.45.13 Where the defendant pleads guilty, but disputes the basis of offending alleged by the prosecution, the following procedure should be followed:

a. The defendant's basis of plea must be set out in writing, identifying what is in dispute;

b. The court may invite the parties to make representations about whether the dispute is material to sentence; and

c. If the court decides that it is a material dispute, the court will invite such further representations or evidence as it may require and decide the dispute in accordance with the principles set out in *R v Newton*.

IV.45.14 Where the disputed issue arises from facts which are within the exclusive knowledge of the defendant and the defendant is willing to give evidence in support of his case, the defence advocate should be prepared to call the defendant. If the defendant is not willing to testify, and subject to any explanation which may be given, the judge may draw such inferences as appear appropriate. Paragraphs 6 to 10 of *Underwood* provide additional guidance regarding the *Newton* hearing procedure.

IV.45.15 The Attorney General has issued guidance for prosecutors regarding their duties when accepting pleas and during the sentencing exercise titled *Attorney General's Guidelines on the Acceptance of Pleas and the Prosecutor's Role in the Sentencing Exercise*.

(c) Cases involving serious fraud—a plea of guilty upon a basis of plea agreed by the prosecution and defence accompanied by joint submissions as to sentence

IV.45.16 This section applies when the prosecution and the defendant(s) to a matter before the Crown Court involving allegations of serious or complex fraud have agreed a basis of plea and seek to make submissions to the court regarding sentence.

IV.45.17 Guidance for prosecutors regarding the operation of this procedure is set out in the *Attorney General's Guidelines on Plea Discussions in Cases of Serious or Complex Fraud*, published on 18 March 2009, referred to in this direction as the 'Attorney General's Plea Discussion Guidelines'.

IV.45.18 In this part—

a. 'a plea agreement' means a written basis of plea agreed between the prosecution and defendant(s) in accordance with the principles set out in *R v Underwood*, supported by admissible documentary evidence or admissions under section 10 of the Criminal Justice Act 1967;

    b. 'a sentencing submission' means sentencing submissions made jointly by the prosecution and defence as to the appropriate sentencing authorities and applicable sentencing range in the relevant sentencing guideline relating to the plea agreement;

    c. 'serious or complex fraud' includes, but is not limited to, allegations of fraud where two or more of the following are present:

      i. the amount obtained or intended to be obtained exceeded £500,000;

      ii. there is a significant international dimension;

      iii. the case requires specialised knowledge of financial, commercial, fiscal or regulatory matters such as the operation of markets, banking systems, trusts or tax regimes;

      iv. the case involves allegations of fraudulent activity against numerous victims;

      v. the case involves an allegation of substantial and significant fraud on a public body;

      vi. the case is likely to be of widespread public concern;

      vii. the alleged misconduct endangered the economic well-being of the United Kingdom, for example by undermining confidence in financial markets.

(i) Procedure

IV.45.19 The procedure regarding agreed bases of plea outlined in paragraphs IV.45.10 to IV.45.12, above, applies with equal rigour to the acceptance of pleas under this procedure. However, because under this procedure the parties will have been discussing the plea agreement and the charges from a much earlier stage, it is vital that the judge is fully informed of all relevant background to the discussions, charges and the eventual basis of plea.

IV.45.20 Where the defendant has not yet appeared before the Crown Court, the prosecutor must send full details of the plea agreement and sentencing submission(s) to the court, at least 7 days in advance of the defendant's first appearance. Where the defendant has already appeared before the Crown Court, the prosecutor must notify the court as soon as is reasonably practicable that a plea agreement and sentencing submissions under the Attorney General's Plea Discussion Guidelines are to be submitted. The court should set a date for the matter to be heard, and the prosecutor must send full details of the plea agreement and sentencing submission(s) to the court as soon as practicable, or in accordance with the directions of the court.

IV.45.21 The provision to the judge of full details of the plea agreement requires sufficient information to be provided to allow the judge to understand the facts of the case and the history of the plea discussions, to assess whether the plea agreement is fair and in the interests of justice, and to decide the appropriate sentence. This will include, but is not limited to: (i) the plea agreement; (ii) the sentencing submission(s); (iii) all of the material provided by the prosecution to the defendant in the course of the plea discussions; (iv) relevant material provided by the defendant, for example documents relating to personal mitigation; and (v) the minutes of any meetings between the parties and any correspondence generated in the plea discussions. The parties should be prepared to provide additional material at the request of the court.

IV.45.22 The court should at all times have regard to the length of time that has elapsed since the date of the occurrence of the events giving rise to the plea discussions, the time taken to interview the defendant, the date of charge and the prospective trial date (if the matter were to proceed to trial) so as to ensure that its consideration of the plea agreement and sentencing submissions does not cause any unnecessary further delay.

(ii) Status of plea agreement and joint sentencing submissions

IV.45.23 Where a plea agreement and joint sentencing submissions are submitted, it remains entirely a matter for the court to decide how to deal with the case. The judge retains the absolute discretion to refuse to accept the plea agreement and to sentence otherwise than in accordance with the sentencing submissions made under the Attorney General's Plea Discussion Guidelines.

IV.45.24 Sentencing submissions should draw the court's attention to any applicable range in any relevant guideline, and to any ancillary orders that may be applicable. Sentencing submissions should not include a specific sentence or agreed range other than the ranges set out in sentencing guidelines or authorities.

IV.45.25 Prior to pleading guilty in accordance with the plea agreement, the defendant(s) may apply to the court for an indication of the likely maximum sentence under the procedure set out in paragraphs IV.45.29 and following, below.

IV.45.26 In the event that the judge indicates a sentence or passes a sentence which is not within the submissions made on sentencing, the plea agreement remains binding.

IV.45.27 If the defendant does not plead guilty in accordance with the plea agreement or if a defendant who has pleaded guilty in accordance with a plea agreement successfully applies to withdraw his plea under rule 39.3 of the Criminal Procedure Rules, the signed plea agreement may be treated as confession evidence, and may be used against the defendant at a later stage in these or any other proceedings. Any credit for a timely guilty plea may be lost. The court may exercise its discretion under section 78 of the Police and Criminal Evidence Act 1984 to exclude any such evidence if it appears to the court that, having regard to all the circumstances, including the circumstances in which the evidence was obtained, the admission of the evidence would have such an adverse effect on the fairness of the proceedings that the court ought not to admit it.

IV.45.28 Where a defendant has failed to plead guilty in accordance with a plea agreement, for example in the circumstances set out in paragraph IV.45.27, above, the case is unlikely to be ready for trial immediately. The prosecution may have been commenced earlier than it otherwise would have been, in reliance upon the defendant's agreement to plead guilty. This is likely to be a relevant consideration for the court in deciding whether or not to grant an application to adjourn or stay the proceedings to allow the matter to be prepared for trial in accordance with the protocol on the Control and Management of Heavy Fraud and other Complex Criminal Cases, or as required.

Indications of sentence

IV.45.29 Prior to pleading guilty by any of the above routes, it is open to a defendant in the Crown Court to request from the judge an indication of the maximum sentence likely to be imposed if a guilty plea is tendered at that stage in the proceedings, in accordance with the guidance in *R v Goodyear*.

IV.45.30 Attention is drawn to the guidance set out in paragraphs 53 and following of *R v Goodyear*. During the sentence indication process and during the actual sentencing hearing, the prosecution advocate is expected to assist the court in sentencing by providing, where appropriate, references to the relevant statutory powers of the court, relevant sentencing guidelines and authorities, and such assistance as the court is likely to require.

IV.45.31 Whether to give such an indication is a matter for the discretion of the judge, to be exercised in accordance with the principles outlined by the Court of Appeal in *Goodyear*. Such indications should normally not be given if there is a dispute as to the basis of plea unless the judge concludes that he or she can properly deal with the case without the need for a *Newton* hearing. In cases where a dispute arises, the procedure in *R v Underwood* should be followed prior to the court considering a sentencing indication further, as set out in paragraphs IV.45.11 to IV.45.13, above. Following an indication of sentence, if a defendant does not plead guilty, the indication will not bind the court.

IV.45.32 Attention is drawn to paragraph 70(d) of *Goodyear* which emphasises that the prosecution 'should not say anything which may create the impression that the sentence indication has the support or approval of the Crown.' This prohibition against the Crown indicating its approval of a particular sentence applies in all circumstances when a defendant is being sentenced, including when joint sentencing submissions are made in accordance with the procedure set out in paragraphs IV.45.16 to IV.45.28 above.

IV.45.33 A *Goodyear* indication should be given in open court in the presence of the defendant but any reference to the hearing is not admissible in any subsequent trial; and reporting restrictions should normally be imposed (see paragraphs 76–77 of *Goodyear*).

IV.46. Majority verdicts

IV.46.1 It is important that all those trying indictable offences should so far as possible adopt a uniform practice when complying with section 17 of the Juries Act 1974, both in directing the jury in summing-up and also in receiving the verdict or giving further directions after retirement. So far as the summing-up is concerned, it is inadvisable for the judge, and indeed for advocates, to attempt an explanation of the section for fear that the jury will be confused. Before the jury retire, however, the judge should direct the jury in some such words as the following:

> 'As you may know, the law permits me, in certain circumstances, to accept a verdict which is not the verdict of you all. Those circumstances have not as yet arisen, so that when you retire I must ask you to reach a verdict upon which each one of you is agreed. Should, however, the time come when it is possible for me to accept a majority verdict, I will give you a further direction.'

IV.46.2 Thereafter the practice should be as follows: Should the jury return *before* two hours and ten minutes since the last member of the jury left the jury box to go to the jury room (or such longer time as the judge thinks reasonable) has elapsed (see section 17(4)), they should be asked: (a) 'Have you reached a verdict upon which you are all agreed? Please answer Yes or No'; (b) (i) If unanimous, 'What is your verdict?'; (ii) If not unanimous, the jury should be sent out again for further deliberation with a further direction to arrive if possible at an unanimous verdict.

IV.46.3 Should the jury return (whether for the first time or subsequently) or be sent for *after* the two hours and ten minutes (or the longer period) has elapsed, questions (a) and (b)(i) in paragraph IV.46.2 should be put to them and, if it appears that they are not unanimous, they should be asked to retire once more and told that they should continue to endeavour to reach an unanimous verdict but that, if they cannot, the judge will accept a majority verdict as in section 17(1).

IV.46.4 When the jury finally return they should be asked: (a) 'Have at least ten (or nine as the case may be) of you agreed on your verdict?'; (b) If 'Yes', 'What is your verdict? Please only answer Guilty or Not Guilty'; (c) (i) If 'Not Guilty', accept the verdict without more ado; (ii) If 'Guilty', 'Is that the verdict of you all or by a majority?'; (d) If 'Guilty' by a majority, 'How many of you agreed to the verdict and how many dissented?'

IV.46.5 At whatever stage the jury return, before question (a) is asked, the senior officer of the court present shall state in open court, for each period when the jury was out of court for the purpose of considering their verdict(s), the time at which the last member of the jury left the jury box to go to the jury room and the time of their return to the jury box and will additionally state in open court the total of such periods.

IV.46.6 The reason why section 17(3) is confined to a majority verdict of guilty and for the somewhat complicated procedure set out in paragraph IV.46.3 and paragraph IV.46.4 is to prevent it being known that a verdict of 'Not Guilty' is a majority verdict. If the final direction in paragraph IV.46.3 continues to require the jury to arrive, if possible, at an unanimous verdict and the verdict is received as in paragraph IV.46.4, it will not be known for certain that the acquittal is not unanimous.

IV.46.7 Where there are several counts (or alternative verdicts) left to the jury the above practice will, of course, need to be adapted to the circumstances. The procedure will have to be repeated in respect of each count (or alternative verdict), the verdict being accepted in those cases where the jury are unanimous and the further direction in paragraph IV.46.3 being given in cases in which they are not unanimous. Should the jury in the end be unable to agree on a verdict by the required majority (i.e. if the answer to the question in paragraph IV.46.4(a) be in the negative) the judge in his discretion will either ask them to deliberate further or discharge them.

IV.46.8 Section 17 will, of course, apply also to verdicts other than 'Guilty' or 'Not Guilty', e.g. to special verdicts under the Criminal Procedure (Insanity) Act 1964, verdicts under that Act as to fitness to be tried, and special verdicts on findings of fact. Accordingly in such cases the questions to jurors will have to be suitably adjusted.

IV.47. Imposition of discretionary life sentences

IV.47.1 Section 82A of the Powers of Criminal Courts (Sentencing) Act 2000 empowers a judge when passing a sentence of life imprisonment, where such a sentence is not fixed by law, to specify by order such part of the sentence ('the relevant part') as shall be served before the prisoner may require the Secretary of State to refer his case to the Parole Board.

IV.47.2 Thus the discretionary life sentence falls into two parts:

  (a) the relevant part, which consists of the period of detention imposed for punishment and deterrence, taking into account the seriousness of the offence, and

  (b) the remaining part of the sentence, during which the prisoner's detention will be governed by considerations of risk to the public.

IV.47.3 The judge is not obliged by statute to make use of the provisions of section 82A when passing a discretionary life sentence. However, the judge should do so, save in the very exceptional case where the judge considers that the offence is so serious that detention for life is justified by the seriousness of the offence alone, irrespective of the risk to the public. In such a case, the judge should state this in open court when passing sentence.

IV.47.4 In cases where the judge is to specify the relevant part of the sentence under section 82A, the judge should permit the advocate for the defendant to address the court as to the appropriate length of the relevant part. Where no relevant part is to be specified, the advocate for the defendant should be permitted to address the court as to the appropriateness of this course of action.

IV.47.5 In specifying the relevant part of the sentence, the judge should have regard to the specific terms of section 82A and should indicate the reasons for reaching his decision as to the length of the relevant part.

IV.47.6 Whether or not the court orders that section 82A should apply, the judge shall not, following the imposition of a discretionary life sentence, make a written report to the Secretary of State through the Lord Chief Justice as was the practice until 8 February 1993.

NOTE: Reference should also be made to the section on life sentences below.

IV.48. Life sentences for juveniles convicted of murder

IV.48.1 When a person is convicted of a murder committed when under the age of 18 the determination of the minimum term (previously tariff) applicable to his sentence has since 30 November 2000 been set by the trial judge, as it was and is for adults subject to discretionary life sentences: see section 82A of the Powers of Criminal Courts (Sentencing) Act 2000.

IV.49. Life sentences

IV.49.1 This direction replaces amendment number 6 to the Consolidated Criminal Practice Direction handed down on 18 May 2004 (previously inserted at paragraphs IV.49.1 to IV.49.25 of the Consolidated Criminal Practice Direction). Its purpose is to give practical guidance as to the procedure for passing a mandatory life sentence under section 269 of and schedule 21 to the Criminal Justice Act 2003 ('the Act'). This direction also gives guidance as to the transitional arrangements under section 276 of and schedule 22 to the Criminal Justice Act 2003 ('the Act'). It clarifies the correct approach to looking at the practice of the Secretary of State prior to December 2002 for the purposes of schedule 22 to the Act, in the light of the judgment in *R v Sullivan, Gibbs, Elener and Elener* [2004] EWCA Crim. 1762 ('*Sullivan*').

IV.49.2 Section 269 of the Act came into force on 18 December 2003. Under section 269 all courts passing a mandatory life sentence must either announce in open court the minimum term the prisoner must serve before the Parole Board can consider release on licence under the provisions of section 28 of the Crime (Sentences) Act 1997 (as amended by section 275 of the Act) or announce that the seriousness of the offence is so exceptionally high that the early release provisions should not apply at all (a 'whole life order').

IV.49.3 In setting the minimum term the court must set the term it considers appropriate taking into account the seriousness of the offence. In considering the seriousness of the offence the court must have regard to the general principles set out in schedule 21 to the Act and any other guidelines issued by the Sentencing Guidelines Council which are relevant to the case and not incompatible with the provisions of schedule 21. Although it is necessary to have regard to the guidance, it is always permissible not to apply the guidance if a judge considers there are reasons for not following it. It is always necessary to have regard to the need to do justice in the particular case. However, if a court departs from any of the starting points given in schedule 21 the court is under a duty to state its reasons for doing so.

IV.49.4 The guidance states that, where the offender is 21 or over, the first step is to choose one of three starting points: 'whole life', 30 years or 15 years. Where the 15 year starting point has been chosen, judges should have in mind that this starting point encompasses a very broad range of murders. At para.35 of *Sullivan* the court found that it should not be assumed that Parliament intended to raise all minimum terms that would previously have had a lower starting point to 15 years.

IV.49.5 Where the offender was 21 or over at the time of the offence, and the court takes the view that the murder is so grave that the offender ought to spend the rest of his life in prison, the appropriate starting point is a 'whole life order'. The effect of such an order is that the early release provisions in section 28 of the Crime (Sentences) Act 1997 will not apply. Such an order should only be specified where the court considers that the seriousness of the offence (or the combination of the offence and one or more other offences associated with it) is exceptionally high. Paragraph 4(2) of schedule 21 to the Act sets out examples of cases where it would normally be appropriate to take the 'whole life order' as the appropriate starting point.

IV.49.6 Where the offender is aged 18 to 20 and commits a murder that is so serious that it would require a whole life order if committed by an offender aged 21 or over, the appropriate starting point will be 30 years.

IV.49.7 Where a case is not so serious as to require a 'whole life order' but where the seriousness of the offence is particularly high and the offender was aged 18 or over when he committed the offence, the appropriate starting point is 30 years. Paragraph 5(2) of schedule 21 to the Act sets out examples of cases where a 30 year starting point would normally be appropriate (if they do not require a 'whole life order').

IV.49.8 Where the offender was aged 18 or over when he committed the offence and the case does not fall within paragraph 4(1) or 5(1) of schedule 21 the appropriate starting point is 15 years.

IV.49.9 18 to 20 year olds are only the subject of the 30 year and 15 year starting points.

IV.49.10 The appropriate starting point when setting a sentence of detention during Her Majesty's pleasure for offenders aged under 18 when they committed the offence is always 12 years.

IV.49.11 The second step after choosing a starting point is to take account of any aggravating or mitigating factors which would justify a departure from the starting point. Additional aggravating factors (other than those specified in paragraphs 4(1) and 5(1)) are listed at paragraph 10 of schedule 21. Examples of mitigating factors are listed at paragraph 11 of schedule 21. Taking into account the aggravating and mitigating features the court may add to or subtract from the starting point to arrive at the appropriate punitive period.

IV.49.12 The third step is that the court should consider the effect of section 151(1) of the Powers of Criminal Courts (Sentencing) Act 2000 (or, when it is in force, section 143(2) of the Act) in relation to previous convictions and section 151(2) of the Powers of Criminal Courts (Sentencing) Act 2000 (or, when it is in force, section 143(3) of the Act) where the offence was committed whilst the offender was on bail. The court should also consider the effect of section 152 of the Powers of Criminal Courts (Sentencing) Act 2000 (or, when it is in force, section 144 of the Act) where the offender has pleaded guilty. The court should then take into account what credit the offender would have received for a remand in custody under section 240 of the Act, but for the fact that the mandatory sentence is one of life imprisonment. Where the offender has been remanded in custody in connection with the offence or a related offence, the court should have in mind that no credit will otherwise be given for this time when the prisoner is considered for early release. The appropriate time to take it into account is when setting the minimum term. The court should normally subtract the time for which the offender was remanded in custody in connection with the offence or a related offence from the punitive period it would otherwise impose in order to reach the minimum term.

IV.49.13 Following these calculations the court should have arrived at the appropriate minimum term to be announced in open court. As paragraph 9 of schedule 21 makes clear, the judge retains ultimate discretion and the court may arrive at any minimum term from any starting point. The minimum term is subject to appeal by the offender under section 271 of the Act and subject to review on a reference by the Attorney-General under section 272 of the Act.

Transitional arrangements for new sentences where the offence was committed before 18 December 2003

IV.49.14 Where the court is passing a sentence of mandatory life imprisonment for an offence committed before 18 December 2003, the court should take a fourth step in determining the minimum term in accordance with section 276 of and schedule 22 to the Act.

IV.49.15 The purpose of those provisions is to ensure that the sentence does not breach the principle of non-retroactivity by ensuring that a lower minimum term would not have been imposed for the offence when it was committed. Before setting the minimum term the court must check whether the proposed term is greater than that term which the Secretary of State would probably have notified under the practice followed by the Secretary of State before December 2002.

IV.49.16 The decision in *Sullivan, Gibbs, Elener and Elener* [2004] EWCA Crim. 1762 gives detailed guidance as to the correct approach to this practice and judges passing mandatory life sentences where the murder was committed prior to 18 December 2003 are well advised to read that judgment before proceeding.

IV.49.17 The practical result of that judgment is that, in sentences where the murder was committed before 31 May 2002, the best guide to what would have been the practice of the Secretary of State is the letter sent to judges by Lord Bingham CJ on 10th February 1997, the relevant parts of which are set out at paras. IV.49.18 to IV.49.21 below.

IV.49.18 The practice of Lord Bingham, as set out in his letter of 10 February 1997, was to take 14 years as the period actually to be served for the 'average', 'normal' or 'unexceptional' murder. Examples of factors he outlined as capable, in appropriate cases, of mitigating the normal penalty were:

1. Youth.
2. Age (where relevant to physical capacity on release or the likelihood of the defendant dying in prison).
3. Subnormality or mental abnormality.
4. Provocation (in a non-technical sense), or an excessive response to a personal threat.
5. The absence of an intention to kill.
6. Spontaneity and lack of premeditation (beyond that necessary to constitute the offence: e.g. a sudden response to family pressure or to prolonged and eventually insupportable stress).
7. Mercy killing.
8. A plea of guilty, or hard evidence of remorse or contrition.

IV.49.19 Lord Bingham then listed the following factors as likely to call for a sentence more severe than the norm:

1. Evidence of a planned, professional, revenge or contract killing.
2. The killing of a child or a very old or otherwise vulnerable victim.
3. Evidence of sadism, gratuitous violence, or sexual maltreatment, humiliation or degradation before the killing.
4. Killing for gain (in the course of burglary, robbery, blackmail, insurance fraud, etc.).
5. Multiple killings.
6. The killing of a witness or potential witness to defeat the ends of justice.
7. The killing of those doing their public duty (policemen, prison officers, postmasters, firemen, judges, etc.).
8. Terrorist or politically motivated killings.

9. The use of firearms or other dangerous weapons, whether carried for defensive or offensive reasons.

10. A substantial record of serious violence.

11. Macabre attempts to dismember or conceal the body.

IV.49.20 Lord Bingham further stated that the fact that a defendant was under the influence of drink or drugs at the time of the killing is so common he would be inclined to treat it as neutral. But in the not unfamiliar case in which a married couple, or two derelicts, or two homosexuals, inflamed by drink, indulge in a violent quarrel in which one dies, often against a background of longstanding drunken violence, then he would tend to recommend a term somewhat below the norm.

IV.49.21 Lord Bingham went on to say that given the intent necessary for proof of murder, the consequences of taking life and the understandable reaction of relatives of the deceased, a substantial term will almost always be called for, save perhaps in a truly venial case of mercy killing. While a recommendation of a punitive term longer than, say, 30 years will be very rare indeed, there should not be any upper limit. Some crimes will certainly call for terms very well in excess of the norm.

IV.49.22 For the purposes of sentences where the murder was committed after 31 May 2002 and before 18 December 2003, the judge should apply the Practice Statement handed down on 31 May 2002 reproduced at paras. 49.23 to 49.33 below.

IV.49.23 This Statement replaces the previous single normal tariff of 14 years by substituting a higher and a normal starting point of respectively 16 (comparable to 32 years) and 12 years (comparable to 24 years). These starting points have then to be increased or reduced because of aggravating or mitigating factors such as those referred to below. It is emphasised that they are no more than starting points.

The normal starting point of 12 years

IV.49.24 Cases falling within this starting point will normally involve the killing of an adult victim, arising from a quarrel or loss of temper between two people known to each other. It will not have the characteristics referred to in paragraph 49.26. Exceptionally, the starting point may be reduced because of the sort of circumstances described in the next paragraph.

IV.49.25 The normal starting point can be reduced because the murder is one where the offender's culpability is significantly reduced, for example, because:

(a) the case came close to the borderline between murder and manslaughter; or

(b) the offender suffered from mental disorder, or from a mental disability which lowered the degree of his criminal responsibility for the killing, although not affording a defence of diminished responsibility, or

(c) the offender was provoked (in a non-technical sense), such as by prolonged and eventually unsupportable stress; or

(d) the case involved an over reaction in self-defence; or

(e) the offence was a mercy killing.

These factors could justify a reduction to 8/9 years (equivalent to 16/18 years).

The higher starting point of 15/16 years

IV.49.26 The higher starting point will apply to cases where the offender's culpability was exceptionally high or the victim was in a particularly vulnerable position. Such cases will be characterised by a feature which makes the crime especially serious, such as:

(a) the killing was 'professional' or a contract killing;

(b) the killing was politically motivated;

(c) the killing was done for gain (in the course of a burglary, robbery etc.);

(d) the killing was intended to defeat the ends of justice (as in the killing of a witness or potential witness);

(e) the victim was providing a public service;

(f) the victim was a child or was otherwise vulnerable;

(g) the killing was racially aggravated;

(h) the victim was deliberately targeted because of his or her religion or sexual orientation;

(i) there was evidence of sadism, gratuitous violence or sexual maltreatment, humiliation or degradation of the victim before the killing;

(j) extensive and/or multiple injuries were inflicted on the victim before death;

(k) the offender committed multiple murders.

Variation of the starting point

IV.49.27 Whichever starting point is selected in a particular case, it may be appropriate for the trial judge to vary the starting point upwards or downwards, to take account of aggravating or mitigating factors, which relate to either the offence or the offender, in the particular case.

IV.49.28 Aggravating factors relating to the offence can include:

(a) the fact that the killing was planned;

(b) the use of a firearm;

(c) arming with a weapon in advance;

(d) concealment of the body, destruction of the crime scene and/or dismemberment of the body;

(e) particularly in domestic violence cases, the fact that the murder was the culmination of cruel and violent behaviour by the offender over a period of time.

IV.49.29 Aggravating factors relating to the offender will include the offender's previous record and failures to respond to previous sentences, to the extent that this is relevant to culpability rather than to risk.

IV.49.30 Mitigating factors relating to the offence will include:

(a) an intention to cause grievous bodily harm, rather than to kill;

(b) spontaneity and lack of pre-meditation.

IV.49.31 Mitigating factors relating to the offender may include:

(a) the offender's age;

(b) clear evidence of remorse or contrition;

(c) a timely plea of guilty.

Very serious cases

IV.49.32 A substantial upward adjustment may be appropriate in the most serious cases, for example, those involving a substantial number of murders, or if there are several factors identified as attracting the higher starting point present. In suitable cases, the result might even be a minimum term of 30 years (equivalent to 60 years) which would offer little or no hope of the offender's eventual release. In cases of exceptional gravity, the judge, rather than setting a whole life minimum term, can state that there is no minimum period which could properly be set in that particular case.

IV.49.33 Among the categories of case referred to in paragraph IV.49.26 some offences may be especially grave. These include cases in which the victim was performing his duties as a prison officer at the time of the crime or the offence was a terrorist or sexual or sadistic murder or involved a young child. In such a case, a term of 20 years and upwards could be appropriate.

IV.49.34 In following this guidance; judges should bear in mind the conclusion of the Court in *Sullivan* that the general effect of both these statements is the same. While Lord Bingham does not identify as many starting points, it is open to the judge to come to exactly the same decision irrespective of which was followed. Both pieces of guidance give the judge a considerable degree of discretion.

Procedure for announcing the minimum term in open court

IV.49.35 Having gone through the three or four steps outlined above, the court is then under a duty under section 270 of the Act, to state in open court, in ordinary language, its reasons for deciding on the minimum term or for passing a whole life order.

IV.49.36 In order to comply with this duty the court should state clearly the minimum term it has determined. In doing so, it should state which of the starting points it has chosen and its reasons for doing so. Where the court has departed from that starting point due to mitigating or aggravating features it must state the reasons for that departure and any aggravating or mitigating features which have led to that departure. At that point the court should also declare how much, if any, time is being deducted for time spent in custody. The court must then explain that the minimum term is the minimum amount of time the prisoner will spend in prison, from the date of sentence, before the Parole Board can order early release. If it remains necessary for the protection of the public, the prisoner will continue to be detained after that date. The court should also state that where the prisoner has served the minimum term and the Parole Board has decided to direct release the prisoner will remain on licence for the rest of his life and may be recalled to prison at any time.

IV.49.37 Where the offender was 21 or over when he committed the offence and the court considers that the seriousness of the offence is so exceptionally high that a 'whole life order' is appropriate, the court should state clearly its reasons for reaching this conclusion. It should also explain that the early release provisions will not apply.

IV.50. Bail pending appeal

IV.50.1 The procedure for granting bail by a judge of the Crown Court pending an appeal to the Court of Appeal (Criminal Division) (see sections 1(2) and 11(1A) of the Criminal Appeal Act 1968, and section 81(1B) of the Supreme Court Act 1981) is described in the *Guide to Proceedings in the Court of Appeal Criminal Division*. This is available at Crown Courts and is to be found at (1983) 77 Cr App R 138 and [1983] Crim LR 145.

IV.50.2 The procedure is also set out in outline on Criminal Appeal Office Form C (Crown Court Judge's Certificate of fitness for appeal) and Form BC (Crown Court Judge's Order granting bail), copies of which are held by the Crown Court. The court clerk will ensure that these forms are always available when a judge hears an application under these provisions.

IV.50.3 The judge may well think it right (a) to hear the application for a certificate in chambers with a shorthand writer present; (b) to invite the defendant's advocate to submit before the hearing of the application a draft of the grounds of appeal which he will ask the judge to certify on Form C. The advocate for the Crown will be better able to assist the judge at the hearing if the draft ground is sent beforehand to him also.

IV.50.4 The first question for the judge is then whether there exists a particular and cogent ground of appeal. If there is no such ground there can be no certificate, and if there is no certificate there can be no bail. A judge should not grant a certificate with regard to sentence merely in the light of mitigation to which he has, in his opinion, given due weight, nor in regard to conviction on a ground where he considers the chance of a successful appeal is not substantial. The judge should bear in mind that, where a certificate is refused, application may be made to the Court of Appeal for leave to appeal and for bail.

IV.50.5 The length of the period which might elapse before the hearing of any appeal is not relevant to the grant of a certificate, but, if the judge does decide to grant a certificate, it may be one factor in the decision whether or not to grant bail. A judge who is minded to take this factor into account may find it advisable to have the court clerk contact the Criminal Appeal Office Listing Co-ordinator in order that he may have an accurate and up-to-date assessment of the likely waiting time. This can be very short. The Co-ordinator will require a general account of the weight and urgency of the case.

IV.50.6 Where the defendant's representative considers that bail should be applied for as a matter of urgency, the application should normally be made, in the first instance, to the trial judge, and the Court of Appeal may decline to treat such an application as urgent if there is no good reason why it has not been made to the trial judge.

PART V FURTHER DIRECTIONS APPLYING IN THE MAGISTRATES' COURTS

V.51. Mode of trial

V.51.1 The purpose of these guidelines is to help magistrates decide whether or not to commit defendants charged with 'either way' offences for trial in the Crown Court. Their object is to provide guidance not direction. They are not intended to impinge on a magistrate's duty to consider each case individually and on its own particular facts. These guidelines apply to all defendants aged 18 and above.

General mode of trial considerations

V.51.2 Section 19 of the Magistrates' Courts Act 1980 requires magistrates to have regard to the following matters in deciding whether an offence is more suitable for summary trial or trial on indictment:

(a) the nature of the case;

(b) whether the circumstances make the offence one of a serious character;

(c) whether the punishment which a magistrates' court would have power to inflict for it would be adequate;

(d) any other circumstances which appear to the court to make it more suitable for the offence to be tried in one way rather than the other;

(e) any representations made by the prosecution or the defence.

V.51.3 Certain general observations can be made:

(a) the court should never make its decision on the grounds of convenience or expedition;

(b) the court should assume for the purpose of deciding mode of trial that the prosecution version of the facts is correct;

(c) the fact that the offences are alleged to be specimens is a relevant consideration (although, it has to be borne in mind that difficulties can arise in sentencing in relation to specimen counts see *R* v *Clark* [1996] 2 Cr App R (S) 351 and *R* v *Canavan and others* [1998] 1 Cr App R (S) 243); the fact that the defendant will be asking for other offences to be taken into consideration, if convicted, is not;

(d) where cases involve complex questions of fact or difficult questions of law, including difficult issues of disclosure of sensitive material, the court should consider committal for trial;

(e) where two or more defendants are jointly charged with an offence each has an individual right to elect his mode of trial;

(f) in general, except where otherwise stated, either way offences should be tried summarily unless the court considers that the particular case has one or more of the features set out in paragraphs V.51.4 to V.51.18 and that its sentencing powers are insufficient;

(g) the court should also consider its power to commit an offender for sentence under sections 3 and 4 of the Powers of Criminal Courts (Sentencing) Act 2000, if information emerges during the course of the hearing which leads it to conclude that the offence is so serious, or the offender such a risk to the public, that its powers to sentence him are inadequate. This means that committal for sentence is no longer determined by reference to the character and antecedents of the offender.

Features relevant to individual offences

V.51.4 Where reference is made in these guidelines to property or damage of 'high value' it means a figure equal to at least twice the amount of the limit (currently £5,000) imposed by statute on a magistrates' court when making a compensation order.

Burglary: Dwelling-house

V.51.5 Cases should be tried summarily unless the court considers that one or more of the following features is present in the case *and* that its sentencing powers are insufficient. Magistrates should take account of their powers under sections 3 and 4 of the Powers of Criminal Courts (Sentencing) Act 2000 to commit for sentence, see paragraph V.51.3(l).

(a) Entry in the daytime when the occupier (or another) is present;

(b) Entry at night of a house which is normally occupied, whether or not the occupier (or another) is present;

(c) The offence is alleged to be one of a series of similar offences;

(d) When soiling, ransacking, damage or vandalism occurs;

(e) The offence has professional hallmarks;

(f) The unrecovered property is of high value: see paragraph V.51.4 for definition of high value;

(g) The offence is racially motivated.

Note: Attention is drawn to paragraph 28(c) of schedule 1 to the Magistrates' Courts Act 1980 by which offences of burglary in a dwelling cannot be tried summarily if any person in the dwelling was subjected to violence or the threat of violence.

Burglary: Non-dwelling

V.51.6 Cases should be tried summarily unless the court considers that one or more of the following features is present in the case *and* that its sentencing powers are insufficient. Magistrates should take account of their powers under sections 3 and 4 of the Powers of Criminal Courts (Sentencing) Act 2000 to commit for sentence, see paragraph V.51.3(g).

(a) Entry of a pharmacy or doctor's surgery;

(b) Fear is caused or violence is done to anyone lawfully on the premises (e.g. night-watchman, security guard);

(c) The offence has professional hallmarks;

(d) Vandalism on a substantial scale;

(e) The unrecovered property is of high value: see paragraph V.51.4 for definition of high value;

(f) The offence is racially motivated.

Theft and fraud

V.51.7 Cases should be tried summarily unless the court considers that one or more of the following features is present in the case *and* that its sentencing powers are insufficient. Magistrates should take account of their powers under sections 3 and 4 of the Powers of Criminal Courts (Sentencing) Act 2000 to commit for sentence, see paragraph V.51.3(g).

Breach of trust by a person in a position of substantial authority, or in whom a high degree of trust is placed;

Theft or fraud which has been committed or disguised in a sophisticated manner;

Theft or fraud committed by an organised gang;

The victim is particularly vulnerable to theft or fraud, e.g. the elderly or infirm;

The unrecovered property is of high value: see paragraph V.51.4 for definition of high value.

Handling

V.51.8 Cases should be tried summarily unless the court considers that one or more of the following features is present in the case *and* that its sentencing powers are insufficient. Magistrates should take account of their powers under sections 3 and 4 of the Powers of Criminal Courts (Sentencing) Act 2000 to commit for sentence, see paragraph V.51.3(g).

(a) Dishonest handling of stolen property by a receiver who has commissioned the theft;

(b) The offence has professional hallmarks;

(c) The property is of high value: see paragraph V.51.4 for definition of high value.

Social security frauds

V.51.9 [Superseded by the SGC, Magistrates' Court Sentencing Guidelines, see part 12 of Sentencing Guidelines in Supplement 1.]

Violence (sections 20 and 47 of the Offences against the Person Act 1861)

V.51.10 [Superseded by the SGC, Magistrates' Court Sentencing Guidelines, see part 12 of Sentencing Guidelines in Supplement 1.]

Public order act offences

V.51.11 [Superseded by the SGC, Magistrates' Court Sentencing Guidelines, see part 12 of Sentencing Guidelines in Supplement 1.]

Violence to and neglect of children

V.51.12 [Superseded by the SGC, Magistrates' Court Sentencing Guidelines, see part 12 of Sentencing Guidelines in Supplement 1.]

Indecent assault

V.51.13 [Superseded by the SGC, Magistrates' Court Sentencing Guidelines, see part 12 of Sentencing Guidelines in Supplement 1.]

Unlawful sexual intercourse

V.51.14 [Superseded by the SGC, Magistrates' Court Sentencing Guidelines, see part 12 of Sentencing Guidelines in Supplement 1.]

Drugs

V.51.15 [Superseded by the SGC, Magistrates' Court Sentencing Guidelines, see part 12 of Sentencing Guidelines in Supplement 1.]

Dangerous driving and aggravated vehicle taking

V.51.17 [Superseded by the SGC, Magistrates' Court Sentencing Guidelines, see part 12 of Sentencing Guidelines in Supplement 1.]

Criminal damage

V.51.18 [Superseded by the SGC, Magistrates' Court Sentencing Guidelines, see part 12 of Sentencing Guidelines in Supplement 1.]

Note: Offences set out in schedule 2 to the Magistrates' Courts Act 1980 (which includes offences of criminal damage which do not amount to arson) *must* be tried summarily if the value of the property damaged or destroyed is £5,000 or less.

V.52. Committal for sentence and appeals to Crown Court

V.52.1 Any case notes should be sent to the Crown Court when there is an appeal, thereby making them available to the judge if the judge requires them in order to decide before the hearing questions of listing or representation or the like. They will also be available to the court during the hearing if it becomes necessary or desirable for the court to see what happened in the lower court. On a committal for sentence or an appeal, any reasons given by the magistrates for their decision should be included with the notes.

V.53. Bail before committal for trial

V.53.1 [Rules 19.18 and 19.22 of the Criminal Procedure Rules 2005] apply to these applications.

V.53.2 Before the Crown Court can deal with an application it must be satisfied that the magistrates' court has issued a certificate under section 5(6A) of the Bail Act 1976 that it heard full argument on the application for bail before it refused the application. A copy of the certificate will be issued to the applicant and not sent directly to the Crown Court. It will therefore be necessary for the applicant's solicitors to attach a copy of the certificate to the bail application form. If the certificate is not enclosed with the application form it will be difficult to avoid some delay in listing.

Venue

V.53.3 Applications should be made to the court to which the defendant will be or would have been committed for trial. In the event of an application in a purely summary case, it should be made to the Crown Court centre which normally receives class [3] work. The hearing will be listed as a chambers matter unless a judge has directed otherwise.

V.54. Contempt in the face of the magistrates' court

General

V.54.1 Section 12 of the Contempt of Court Act 1981 gives magistrates' courts the power to detain until the court rises, someone, whether a defendant or another person present in court,

423

who wilfully insults anyone specified in section 12 or who interrupts proceedings. In any such case, the court may order any officer of the court, or any constable, to take the offender into custody and detain him until the rising of the court; and the court may, if it thinks fit, commit the offender to custody for a specified period not exceeding one month or impose a fine not exceeding level 4 on the standard scale or both. This power can be used to stop disruption of their proceedings. Detention is until the person can be conveniently dealt with without disruption of the proceedings. Prior to the court using the power the offender should be warned to desist or face the prospect of being detained.

V.54.2 Magistrates' courts also have the power to commit to custody any person attending or brought before a magistrates' court who refuses without just cause to be sworn or to give evidence under section 97(4) of the Magistrates' Courts Act 1980, until the expiration of such period not exceeding one month as may be specified in the warrant or until he sooner gives evidence or produces the document or thing, or impose on him a fine not exceeding £2,500, or both.

V.54.3 In the exercise of any of these powers, as soon as is practical, and in any event prior to an offender being proceeded against, an offender should be told of the conduct which it is alleged to constitute his offending in clear terms. When making an order under section 12 the justices should state their findings of fact as to the contempt.

V.54.4 Exceptional situations require exceptional treatment. While this direction deals with the generality of situations, there will be a minority of situations where the application of the direction will not be consistent with achieving justice in the special circumstances of the particular case. Where this is the situation, the compliance with the direction should be modified so far as is necessary so as to accord with the interests of justice.

V.54.5 The power to bind persons over to be of good behaviour in respect of their conduct in court should cease to be exercised.

Contempt consisting of wilfully insulting anyone specified in section 12 or interrupting proceedings

V.54.6 In the case of someone who wilfully insults anyone specified in section 12 or interrupts proceedings, if an offender expresses a willingness to apologise for his misconduct, he should be brought back before the court at the earliest convenient moment in order to make the apology and to give undertakings to the court to refrain from further misbehaviour.

V.54.7 In the majority of cases, an apology and a promise as to future conduct should be sufficient for justices to order an offender's release. However, there are likely to be certain cases where the nature and seriousness of the misconduct require the justices to consider using their powers under section 12(2) of the Contempt of Court 1981 Act either to fine or to order the offender's committal to custody.

Where an offender is detained for contempt of court

V.54.8 Anyone detained under either of these provisions in paragraphs V.54.1 or V.54.2 should be seen by the duty solicitor or another legal representative and be represented in proceedings if they so wish. Public funding should generally be granted to cover representation. The offender must be afforded adequate time and facilities in order to prepare his case. The matter should be resolved the same day if at all possible.

V.54.9 The offender should be brought back before the court before the justices conclude their daily business. The justices should ensure that he understands the nature of the proceedings, including his opportunity to apologise or give evidence and the alternative of them exercising their powers.

V.54.10 Having heard from the offender's solicitor, the justices should decide whether to take further action.

Sentencing of an offender who admits being in contempt

V.54.11 If an offence of contempt is admitted the justices should consider whether they are able to proceed on the day or whether to adjourn to allow further reflection. The matter should be dealt with on the same day if at all possible. If the justices are of the view to adjourn they should generally grant the offender bail unless one or more of the exceptions to the right to bail in the Bail Act 1976 are made out.

V.54.12 When they come to sentence the offender where the offence has been admitted, the justices should first ask the offender if he has any objection to them dealing with the matter. If there is any objection to the justices dealing with the matter a differently constituted panel should hear the proceedings. If the offender's conduct was directed to the justices, it will not be appropriate for the same bench to deal with the matter.

V.54.13 The justices should consider whether an order for the offender's discharge is appropriate, taking into account any time spent on remand, whether the offence was admitted and the seriousness of the contempt. Any period of committal should be for the shortest time commensurate with the interests of preserving good order in the administration of justice.

Trial of the issue where the contempt is not admitted

V.54.14 Where the contempt is not admitted the justices' powers are limited to making arrangements for a trial to take place. They should not at this stage make findings against the offender.

V.54.15 In the case of a contested contempt the trial should take place at the earliest opportunity and should be before a bench of justices other than those before whom the alleged contempt took place. If a trial of the issue can take place on the day such arrangements should be made taking into account the offender's rights under Article 6 of the European Convention for the Protection of Human Rights and Fundamental Freedoms (Rome, 4 November 1950; TS 71 (1953); Cmd 8969). If the trial cannot take place that day the justices should again bail the offender unless there are grounds under the Bail Act 1976 to remand him in custody.

V.54.16 The offender is entitled to call and examine witnesses where evidence is relevant. If the offender is found by the court to have committed contempt the court should again consider first whether an order for his discharge from custody is sufficient to bring proceedings to an end. The justices should also allow the offender a further opportunity to apologise for his contempt or to make representations. If the justices are of the view that they must exercise their powers to commit to custody under section 12(2) of the 1981 Act, they must take into account any time spent on remand and the nature and seriousness of the contempt. Any period of committal should be for the shortest period of time commensurate with the interests of preserving good order in the administration of justice.

V.55. Clerk retiring with justices

V.55.1 A justices' clerk is responsible for:
  (a) the legal advice tendered to the justices within the area;
  (b) the performance of any of the functions set out below by any member of his staff acting as legal adviser;
  (c) ensuring that competent advice is available to justices when the justices' clerk is not personally present in court; and
  (d) the effective delivery of case management and the reduction of unnecessary delay.

V.55.2 Where a person other than the justices' clerk (a 'legal adviser'), who is authorised to do so, performs any of the functions referred to in this direction he will have the same responsibilities as the justices' clerk. The legal adviser may consult the justices' clerk or other person authorised by the justices' clerk for that purpose before tendering advice to the bench. If the justices' clerk or that person gives any advice directly to the bench, he should give the parties or their advocates an opportunity of repeating any relevant submissions prior to the advice being given.

V.55.3 It shall be the responsibility of the legal adviser to provide the justices with any advice they require properly to perform their functions, whether or not the justices have requested that advice, on:
  (a) questions of law (including European Court of Human Rights jurisprudence and those matters set out in section 2(1) of the Human Rights Act 1998);
  (b) questions of mixed law and fact;
  (c) matters of practice and procedure;

(d) the range of penalties available;

(e) any relevant decisions of the superior courts or other guidelines;

(f) other issues relevant to the matter before the court; and

(g) the appropriate decision-making structure to be applied in any given case.

In addition to advising the justices it shall be the legal adviser's responsibility to assist the court, where appropriate, as to the formulation of reasons and the recording of those reasons.

V.55.4 A justices' clerk or legal adviser must not play any part in making findings of fact, but may assist the bench by reminding them of the evidence, using any notes of the proceedings for this purpose.

V.55.5 A justices' clerk or legal adviser may ask questions of witnesses and the parties in order to clarify the evidence and any issues in the case. A legal adviser has a duty to ensure that every case is conducted fairly.

V.55.6 When advising the justices the justices' clerk or legal adviser, whether or not previously in court, should:

(a) ensure that he is aware of the relevant facts; and

(b) provide the parties with the information necessary to enable the parties to make any representations they wish as to the advice before it is given.

V.55.7 At any time justices are entitled to receive advice to assist them in discharging their responsibilities. If they are in any doubt as to the evidence which has been given, they should seek the aid of their legal adviser, referring to his notes as appropriate. This should ordinarily be done in open court. Where the justices request their adviser to join them in the retiring room, this request should be made in the presence of the parties in court. Any legal advice given to the justices other than in open court should be clearly stated to be provisional and the adviser should subsequently repeat the substance of the advice in open court and give the parties an opportunity to make any representations they wish on that provisional advice. The legal adviser should then state in open court whether the provisional advice is confirmed or if it is varied the nature of the variation.

V.55.8 The performance of a legal adviser may be appraised by a person authorised by the magistrates' courts committee to do so. For that purpose the appraiser may be present in the justices' retiring room. The content of the appraisal is confidential, but the fact that an appraisal has taken place, and the presence of the appraiser in the retiring room, should be briefly explained in open court.

V.55.9 The legal adviser is under a duty to assist unrepresented parties to present their case, but must do so without appearing to become an advocate for the party concerned.

V.55.10 The role of legal advisers in fine default proceedings or any other proceedings for the enforcement of financial orders, obligations or penalties is to assist the court. They must not act in an adversarial or partisan manner. With the agreement of the justices a legal adviser may ask questions of the defaulter to elicit information which the justices will require to make an adjudication, for example to facilitate his explanation for the default. A legal adviser may also advise the justices in the normal way as to the options open to them in dealing with the case. It would be inappropriate for the legal adviser to set out to establish wilful refusal or neglect or any other type of culpable behaviour, to offer an opinion on the facts, or to urge a particular course of action upon the justices. The duty of impartiality is the paramount consideration for the legal adviser at all times, and this takes precedence over any role he may have as a collecting officer. The appointment of other staff to 'prosecute' the case for the collecting officer is not essential to ensure compliance with the law, including the Human Rights Act 1998. Whether to make such appointments is a matter for the justices' chief executive.

V.56. Case management in magistrates' courts

V.56.1 This section of the practice direction supplements the rules in Part 3 of the Criminal Procedure Rules as they apply to the management of cases in magistrates' courts. Where time limits or other directions in the Consolidated Criminal Practice Direction appear inconsistent with this section, the directions in this section take precedence. To avoid unnecessary and wasted hearings the parties should be allowed adequate time to prepare the case, having regard to the time limits for applications and notices set by the Criminal Procedure Rules and by other legislation. When those time limits have expired the parties will be expected to be fully prepared.

Cases to be tried summarily by the magistrates' court

V.56.2 The case progression form to be used is set out in annex E with guidance notes. The form, read with the notes, constitutes a case progression timetable for the effective preparation of a case.

Cases sent, committed or transferred to the Crown Court for trial

V.56.3 The case progression forms set out in annex E with guidance notes are to be used in connection with cases that are sent to the Crown Court for trial under section 51 of the Crime and Disorder Act 1998 and cases that are committed to the Crown Court for trial under section 6 of the Magistrates' Courts Act 1980. In a case transferred to the Crown Court for trial under section 4(1) of the Criminal Justice Act 1987 or under section 53(1) of the Criminal Justice Act 1991 the directions contained in the case progression form used for committal for trial apply as if the case had been committed on the date of the notice of transfer.

V.56.4 A preliminary hearing ('PH') is not required in every case sent for trial under section 51 of the Crime and Disorder Act 1998: see rule 12.2 (which altered the Crown Court rule from which it derived). A PH should be ordered only where such a hearing is considered necessary. The PH should be held about 14 days after sending.

V.56.5 Whether or not a magistrates' court orders a PH, a plea and case management hearing ('PCMH') should be ordered in every case sent or committed to the Crown Court for trial. The PCMH should be held within about 7 weeks after committal for trial, within about 14 weeks after sending for trial where a defendant is in custody and within about 17 weeks after sending for trial where a defendant is on bail.

Use of the forms: directions that apply by default

V.56.6 The case progression forms to be used in magistrates' courts contain directions some of which are determined by Criminal Procedure Rules or by other legislation and some of which are discretionary, as explained in the guidance notes. All those directions apply in every case unless the court otherwise orders.

The Lord Chief Justice of England and Wales 8 July 2002, as amended

ANNEX A

[This annex consists of a List of Practice Directions, Practice Notes and Practice Statements included in the consolidation. It is omitted.]

ANNEX B

[This annex consists of a List of Practice Directions, Practice Notes and Practice Statements not included in the consolidation, but no longer applicable in criminal proceedings. It is omitted.]

ANNEX C

Explanations for the imposition of custodial sentences: forms of words

The following forms may need to be adapted in the light of such provisions or practices as are in force affecting possible earlier release.

Forms of words are provided for use where the offender (a) will be a short term prisoner not subject to licence; (b) will be a short term prisoner subject to licence; (c) will be a long term prisoner; (d) will be subject to a discretionary sentence of life imprisonment.

Sentencers will bear in mind that where an offender is sentenced to terms which are consecutive, or wholly or partly concurrent, they are to be treated as a single term: section 51(2) of the Criminal Justice Act 1991.

(a) Total term less than 12 months

The sentence is () months.

Unless you are released earlier under supervision, you will serve half that sentence in prison/a young offender institution. After that time you will be released.

Your release will not bring this sentence to an end. If after your release and before the end of the period covered by the sentence you commit any further offence, you may be ordered to return to custody to serve the balance of the original sentence outstanding at the date of the further offence, as well as being punished for that new offence.

Any time you have spent on remand in custody in connection with the offence(s) for which you are now being sentenced will count as part of the sentence to be served, unless it has already been counted.

(b) Total term of 12 months and less than 4 years

The sentence is () (months/years).

Unless you are released earlier under supervision, you will serve half that sentence in a prison/a young offender institution. After that time you will be released.

Your release will not bring this sentence to an end. If after your release and before the end of the period covered by the sentence you commit any further offence you may be ordered to return to custody to serve the balance of the original sentence outstanding at the date of the further offence, as well as being punished for that new offence.

Any time you have spent on remand in custody in connection with the offence(s) for which you are now being sentenced will count as part of the sentence to be served, unless it has already been counted.

After your release you will also be subject to supervision on licence until the end of three-quarters of the total sentence. (If an order has been made under section 85 of the Powers of Criminal Courts (Sentencing) Act 2000: After your release you will also be subject to supervision on licence for the remainder of the licence period.) If you fail to comply with any of the requirements of your licence then again you may be brought before a court which will have power to suspend your licence and order your return to custody.

(c) Total term of 4 years or more

The sentence is () (years/months).

Your case will not be considered by the Parole Board until you have served at least half that period in custody. Unless the Parole Board recommends earlier release, you will not be released until you have served two-thirds of that sentence.

Your release will not bring the sentence to an end. If after your release and before the end of the period covered by the sentence you commit any further offence you may be ordered to return to custody to serve the balance of the original sentence outstanding at the date of the new offence, as well as being punished for that new offence.

Any time you have spent in custody on remand in connection with the offence(s) for which you are now being sentenced will count as part of the sentence to be served, unless it has already been counted.

After your release you will also be subject to supervision on licence until the end of three-quarters of the total sentence. (If an order has been made under section 85 of the Powers of Criminal Courts (Sentencing) Act 2000: After your release you will also be subject to supervision on licence for the remainder of the licence period. You will be liable to be recalled to prison if your licence is revoked, either on the recommendation of the Parole Board, or, if it is thought expedient in the public interest, by the Secretary of State).

(d) Discretionary life sentence

The sentence of the court is life imprisonment/custody for life/detention for life under section 91 of the Powers of Criminal Courts (Sentencing) Act 2000. For the purposes of section 82A of that Act the court specifies a period of (x) years. That means that your case will not be considered by the Parole Board until you have served at least (x) years in custody. After that time the Parole Board will be entitled to consider your release. When it is satisfied that you need no longer be confined in custody for the protection of the public it will be able to direct your release. Until it is so satisfied you will remain in custody.

If you are released, it will be on terms that you are subject to a licence for the rest of your life and liable to be recalled to prison at any time if your licence is revoked, either on the recommendation of the Parole Board, or, if it is thought expedient in the public interest, by the Secretary of State.

ANNEX D

[This annex consists of a list of forms for use in criminal proceedings and is omitted.]

ANNEX E

[This annex contains the forms to be used to facilitate case management and is omitted.]

Appendix 3 Control and Management of Heavy Fraud and other Complex Criminal Cases

A PROTOCOL ISSUED BY THE LORD CHIEF JUSTICE OF ENGLAND AND WALES – 22 MARCH 2005

Introduction

There is a broad consensus that the length of fraud and trials of other complex crimes must be controlled within proper bounds in order:

i.   To enable the jury to retain and assess the evidence which they have heard. If the trial is so long that the jury cannot do this, then the trial is not fair either to the prosecution or the defence.

ii. To make proper use of limited public resources: see *Jisl* [2004] EWCA Crim 696 at [113]–[121].

There is also a consensus that no trial should be permitted to exceed a given period, save in exceptional circumstances; some favour 3 months, others an outer limit of 6 months. Whatever view is taken, it is essential that the current length of trials is brought back to an acceptable and proper duration.

This Protocol supplements the Criminal Procedure Rules and summarises good practice which experience has shown may assist in bringing about some reduction in the length of trials of fraud and other crimes that result in complex trials. Flexibility of application of this Protocol according to the needs of each case is essential; it is designed to inform but not to prescribe.

This Protocol is primarily directed towards cases which are likely to last eight weeks or longer. It should also be followed, however, in all cases estimated to last more than four weeks. This Protocol applies to trials by jury, but many of the principles will be applicable if trials without a jury are permitted under s. 43 of the Criminal Justice Act 2003.

The best handling technique for a long case is continuous management by an experienced Judge nominated for the purpose.

It is intended that this Protocol be kept up to date; any further practices or techniques found to be successful in the management of complex cases should be notified to the office of the Lord Chief Justice.

1. The Investigation

(i) The role of the prosecuting authority and the judge

a.   Unlike other European countries, a judge in England and Wales does not directly control the investigative process; that is the responsibility of the Investigating Authority, and in turn the Prosecuting Authority and the prosecution advocate. Experience has shown that a prosecution lawyer (who must be of sufficient experience and who will be a member of the team at trial) and the prosecution advocate, if different, should be involved in the investigation as soon as it appears that a heavy fraud trial or other complex criminal trial is likely to ensue. The costs that this early preparation will incur will be saved many times over in the long run.

b.   The judge can and should exert a substantial and beneficial influence by making it clear that, generally speaking, trials should be kept within manageable limits. In most cases 3 months should be the target outer limit, but there will be cases where a duration of 6 months, or in exceptional circumstances, even longer may be inevitable.

(ii) Interviews

a. At present many interviews are too long and too unstructured. This has a knock-on effect on the length of trials. Interviews should provide an opportunity for suspects to respond to the allegations against them. They should not be an occasion to discuss every document in the case. It should become clear from judicial rulings that interviews of this kind are a waste of resources.

b. The suspect must be given sufficient information before or at the interview to enable them to meet the questions fairly and answer them honestly; the information is not provided to give the suspect the opportunity to manufacture a false story which fits undisputable facts.

c. It is often helpful if the principal documents are provided either in advance of the interview or shown as the interview progresses; asking detailed questions about events a considerable period in the past without reference to the documents is often not very helpful.

(iii) The prosecution and defence teams

a. *The Prosecution Team*
    While instructed, it is for the lead advocate for the prosecution to take all necessary decisions in the presentation and general conduct of the prosecution case in court. The prosecution lead advocate will be treated by the court as having that responsibility.

    However, in relation to policy decisions, the lead advocate for the prosecution must not give an indication or undertaking which binds the prosecution without first discussing the issue with the Director of the Prosecuting authority or other senior officer.

    "Policy" decisions should be understood as referring to non-evidential decisions on: the acceptance of pleas of guilty to lesser counts or groups of counts or available alternatives: offering no evidence on particular counts; consideration of a re-trial; whether to lodge an appeal; certification of a point of law; and the withdrawal of the prosecution as a whole (for further information see the 'Farquharson Guidelines' on the role and responsibilities of the prosecution advocate).

b. *The Defence Team*
    In each case, the lead advocate for the defence will be treated by the court as having responsibility to the court for the presentation and general conduct of the defence case.

c. In each case, a case progression officer must be assigned by the court, prosecution and defence from the time of the first hearing when directions are given (as referred to in paragraph 3 (iii)) until the conclusion of the trial.

d. In each case where there are multiple defendants, the LSC will need to consider carefully the extent and level of representation necessary.

(iv) Initial consideration of the length of a case

If the prosecutor in charge of the case from the Prosecuting Authority or the lead advocate for the prosecution consider that the case as formulated is likely to last more than 8 weeks, the case should be referred in accordance with arrangements made by the Prosecuting Authority to a more senior prosecutor. The senior prosecutor will consider whether it is desirable for the case to be prosecuted in that way or whether some steps might be taken to reduce its likely length, whilst at the same time ensuring that the public interest is served.

Any case likely to last 6 months or more must be referred to the Director of the Prosecuting Authority so that similar considerations can take place.

(v) Notification of cases likely to last more than 8 weeks

Special arrangements will be put in place for the early notification by the CPS and other Prosecuting Authorities, to the LSC and to a single designated officer of the Court in each Region (Circuit) of any case which the CPS or other Prosecuting Authority consider likely to last over 8 weeks.

(vi) Venue

The court will allocate such cases and other complex cases likely to last 4 weeks or more to a specific venue suitable for the trial in question, taking into account the convenience to witnesses, the parties, the availability of time at that location, and all other relevant considerations.

2. Designation of the Trial Judge

(i) The assignment of a judge

a. In any complex case which is expected to last more than four weeks, the trial judge will be assigned under the direction of the Presiding Judges at the earliest possible moment.

b. Thereafter the assigned judge should manage that case "from cradle to grave"; it is essential that the same judge manages the case from the time of his assignment and that arrangements are made for him to be able to do so. It is recognised that in certain court centres with a large turnover of heavy cases (e.g. Southwark) this objective is more difficult to achieve. But in those court centres there are teams of specialist judges, who are more readily able to handle cases which the assigned judge cannot continue with because of unexpected events; even at such courts, there must be no exception to the principle that one judge must handle all the pre-trial hearings until the case is assigned to another judge.

3. Case Management

(i) Objectives

a. The number, length and organisation of case management hearings will, of course, depend critically on the circumstances and complexity of the individual case. However, thorough, well-prepared and extended case management hearings will save court time and costs overall.

b. Effective case management of heavy fraud and other complex criminal cases requires the judge to have a much more detailed grasp of the case than may be necessary for many other Plea and Case Management Hearings (PCMHs). Though it is for the judge in each case to decide how much pre-reading time he needs so that the judge is on top of the case, it is not always a sensible use of judicial time to allocate a series of reading days, during which the judge sits alone in his room, working through numerous boxes of ring binders.

See paragraph 3 (iv) (e) below.

(ii) Fixing the trial date

Although it is important that the trial date should be fixed as early as possible, this may not always be the right course. There are two principal alternatives:

a. The trial date should be fixed at the first opportunity – i.e. at the first (and usually short) directions hearing referred to in subparagraph (iii). From then on everyone must work to that date. All orders and pre-trial steps should be timetabled to fit in with that date. All advocates and the judge should take note of this date, in the expectation that the trial will proceed on the date determined.

b. The trial date should not be fixed until the issues have been explored at a full case management hearing (referred to in subparagraph (iv), after the advocates on both sides have done some serious work on the case. Only then can the length of the trial be estimated.

Which is apposite must depend on the circumstances of each case, but the earlier it is possible to fix a trial date, by reference to a proper estimate and a timetable set by reference to the trial date, the better.

It is generally to be expected that once a trial is fixed on the basis of the estimate provided, that it will be **increased** if, and only if, the party seeking to extend the time justifies why the original estimate is no longer appropriate.

(iii) The first hearing for the giving of initial directions

At the first opportunity the assigned judge should hold a short hearing to give initial directions. The directions on this occasion might well include:

a. That there should be a full case management hearing on, or commencing on, a specified future date by which time the parties will be properly prepared for a meaningful hearing and the defence will have full instructions.

b. That the prosecution should provide an outline written statement of the prosecution case at least one week in advance of that case management hearing, outlining in simple terms:
   i. The key facts on which it relies.
   ii. The key evidence by which the prosecution seeks to prove the facts.

The statement must be sufficient to permit the judge to understand the case and for the defence to appreciate the basic elements of its case against each defendant. The prosecution may be invited to highlight the key points of the case orally at the case management hearing by way of a short mini-opening. The outline statement should not be considered binding, but it will serve the essential purpose in telling the judge, and everyone else, what the case is really about and identifying the key issues.

c. That a core reading list and core bundle for the case management hearing should be delivered at least one week in advance.

d. Preliminary directions about disclosure: see paragraph 4.

(iv) The first Case Management Hearing

a. At the first case management hearing:
   i. The prosecution advocate should be given the opportunity to highlight any points from the prosecution outline statement of case (which will have been delivered at least a week in advance).
   ii. Each defence advocate should be asked to outline the defence.
   If the defence advocate is not in a position to say what is in issue and what is not in issue, then the case management hearing can be adjourned for a short and limited time and to a fixed date to enable the advocate to take instructions; such an adjournment should only be necessary in exceptional circumstances, as the defence advocate should be properly instructed by the time of the first case management hearing and in any event is under an obligation to take sufficient instructions to fulfil the obligations contained in S 33–39 of Criminal Justice Act 2003.

b. There should then be a real dialogue between the judge and all advocates for the purpose of identifying:
   i. The focus of the prosecution case.
   ii. The common ground.
   iii. The real issues in the case. (Rule 3.2 of the Criminal Procedure Rules.)

c. The judge will try to generate a spirit of co-operation between the court and the advocates on all sides. The expeditious conduct of the trial and a focussing on the real issues must be in the interests of **all** parties. It cannot be in the interests of any defendant for his good points to become lost in a welter of uncontroversial or irrelevant evidence.

d. In many fraud cases the primary facts are not seriously disputed. The real issue is what each defendant knew and whether that defendant was dishonest. Once the judge has identified what is in dispute and what is not in dispute, the judge can then discuss with the advocate how the trial should be structured, what can be dealt with by admissions or agreed facts, what uncontroversial matters should be proved by concise oral evidence, what timetabling can be required under Rule 3.10 Criminal Procedure Rules, and other directions.

e. In particularly heavy fraud or complex cases the judge may possibly consider it necessary to allocate a whole week for a case management hearing. If that week is used wisely, many further weeks of trial time can be saved. In the gaps which will inevitably arise during that week (for example while the advocates are exploring matters raised by the judge) the judge can do a substantial amount of informed reading. The case has come "alive" at this stage. Indeed, in a really heavy fraud case, if the judge fixes one or more case management hearings on this scale, there will be need for fewer formal reading days. Moreover a huge amount can be achieved in the pre-trial stage, if all trial advocates are gathered in the same place, focussing on the case **at the same time**, for several days consecutively.

f. Requiring the defence to serve proper case statements may enable the court to identify:
   i. what is common ground and
   ii. the real issues.
   It is therefore important that proper defence case statements be provided as required by the Criminal Procedure Rules; Judges will use the powers contained in ss 28–34 of the Criminal Proceedings and Evidence Act 1996 (and the corresponding provisions of the CJA 1987, ss. 33 and following of the Criminal Justice Act 2003) and the Criminal Procedure Rules to ensure that realistic defence case statements are provided.

g. Likewise this objective may be achieved by requiring the prosecution to serve draft admissions by a specified date and by requiring the defence to respond within a specified number of weeks.

(v) Further Case Management Hearings

a. The date of the next case management hearing should be fixed at the conclusion of the hearing so that there is no delay in having to fix the date through listing offices, clerks and others.
b. If one is looking at a trial which threatens to run for months, pre-trial case management on an intensive scale is essential.

(vi) Consideration of the length of the trial

a. Case management on the above lines, the procedure set out in paragraph 1 (iv), may still be insufficient to reduce the trial to a manageable length; generally a trial of 3 months should be the target, but there will be cases where a duration of 6 months or, in exceptional circumstances, even longer may be inevitable.
b. If the trial is not estimated to be within a manageable length, it will be necessary for the judge to consider what steps should be taken to reduce the length of the trial, whilst still ensuring that the prosecution has the opportunity of placing the full criminality before the court.
c. To assist the judge in this task,
   i. The lead advocate for the prosecution should be asked to explain why the prosecution have rejected a shorter way of proceeding; they may also be asked to divide the case into sections of evidence and explain the scope of each section and the need for each section.
   ii. The lead advocates for the prosecution and for the defence should be prepared to put forward in writing, if requested, ways in which a case estimated to last more than three months can be shortened, including possible severance of counts or defendants, exclusions of sections of the case or of evidence or areas of the case where admissions can be made.
d. One course the judge may consider is pruning the indictment by omitting certain charges and/or by omitting certain defendants. The judge must not usurp the function of the prosecution in this regard, and he must bear in mind that he will, at the outset, know less about the case than the advocates. The aim is achieve fairness to all parties.
e. Nevertheless, the judge does have two methods of pruning available for use in appropriate circumstances:
   i. Persuading the prosecution that it is not worthwhile pursuing certain charges and/or certain defendants.
   ii. Severing the indictment. Severance for reasons of case management alone is perfectly proper, although judges should have regard to any representations made by the prosecution that severance would weaken their case. Indeed the judge's hand will be strengthened in this regard by rule 1.1 (2) (g) of the Criminal Procedure Rules. However, before using what may be seen as a blunt instrument, the judge should insist on seeing full defence statements of all affected defendants. Severance may be unfair to the prosecution if, for example, there is a cut-throat defence in prospect. For example, the defence of the principal defendant may be that the defendant relied on the advice of his accountant or solicitor that what was happening was acceptable. The defence of the professional may be that he gave no such advice. Against that background, it might be unfair to the prosecution to order separate trials of the two defendants.

(vii) The exercise of the powers

a. The Criminal Procedure Rules require the court to take a more active part in case management. These are salutary provisions which should bring to an end interminable criminal trials of the kind which the Court of Appeal criticised in *Jisl* [2004] EWCA 696 at [113]–[121].
b. Nevertheless these salutary provisions do not have to be used on every occasion. Where the advocates have done their job properly, by narrowing the issues, pruning the evidence and so forth, it may be quite inappropriate for the judge to "weigh in" and start cutting out more evidence or more charges of his own volition. It behoves the judge to make a careful assessment of the degree of judicial intervention which is warranted in each case.

c. The note of caution in the previous paragraph is supported by certain experience which has been gained of the Civil Procedure Rules (on which the Criminal Procedure Rules are based). The CPR contain valuable and efficacious provisions for case management by the judge on his own initiative which have led to huge savings of court time and costs. Surveys by the Law Society have shown that the CPR have been generally welcomed by court users and the profession, but there have been reported to have been isolated instances in which the parties to civil litigation have faithfully complied with both the letter and the spirit of the CPR, and have then been aggrieved by what was perceived to be unnecessary intermeddling by the court.

(viii) Expert Evidence

a. Early identification of the subject matter of expert evidence to be adduced by the prosecution and the defence should be made as early as possible, preferably at the directions hearing.
b. Following the exchange of expert evidence, any areas of disagreement should be identified and a direction should generally be made requiring the experts to meet and prepare, after discussion, a joint statement identifying points of agreement and contention and areas where the prosecution is put to proof on matters of which a positive case to the contrary is not advanced by the defence. After the statement has been prepared it should be served on the court, the prosecution and the defence. In some cases, it might be appropriate to provide that to the jury.

(ix) Surveillance Evidence

a. Where a prosecution is based upon many months' observation or surveillance evidence and it appears that it is capable of effective presentation based on a shorter period, the advocate should be required to justify the evidence of such observations before it is permitted to be adduced, either substantially or in its entirety.
b. Schedules should be provided to cover as much of the evidence as possible and admissions sought.

4. Disclosure

In fraud cases the volume of documentation obtained by the prosecution is liable to be immense. The problems of disclosure are intractable and have the potential to disrupt the entire trial process.

i. The prosecution lawyer (and the prosecution advocate if different) brought in at the outset, as set out in paragraph 1 (i)(a), each have a continuing responsibility to discharge the prosecution's duty of disclosure, either personally or by delegation, in accordance with the Attorney General's Guidelines on Disclosure.
ii. The prosecution should only disclose those documents which are relevant (i.e. likely to assist the defence or undermine the prosecution – see s. 3 (1) of CPIA 1996 and the provisions of the CJA 2003).
iii. It is almost always undesirable to give the "warehouse key" to the defence for two reasons:
    a. This amounts to an abrogation of the responsibility of the prosecution;
    b. The defence solicitors may spend a disproportionate amount of time and incur disproportionate costs trawling through a morass of documents.
    The Judge should therefore try and ensure that disclosure is limited to what is likely to assist the defence or undermine the prosecution.
iv. At the outset the judge should set a timetable for dealing with disclosure issues. In particular, the judge should fix a date by which all defence applications for specific disclosure must be made. In this regard, it is relevant that the defendants are likely to be intelligent people, who know their own business affairs and who (for the most part) will know what documents or categories of documents they are looking for.
v. At the outset (and before the cut-off date for specific disclosure applications) the judge should ask the defence to indicate what documents they are interested in and from what source. A general list is not an acceptable response to this request. The judge should insist upon a list which is specific, manageable and realistic. The judge may also require justification of any request.
vi. In non-fraud cases, the same considerations apply, but some may be different:
    a. It is not possible to approach many non-fraud cases on the basis that the defendant knows what is there or what they are looking for. But on the other hand this should not be turned

into an excuse for a "fishing expedition"; the judge should insist on knowing the issue to which a request for disclosure applies.

    b. If the bona fides of the investigation is called into question, a judge will be concerned to see that there has been independent and effective appraisal of the documents contained in the disclosure schedule and that its contents are adequate. In appropriate cases where this issue has arisen and there are grounds which show there is a real issue, consideration should be given to receiving evidence on oath from the senior investigating officer at an early case management hearing.

5. Abuse of Process

i. Applications to stay or dismiss for abuse of process have become a normal feature of heavy and complex cases. Such applications may be based upon delay and the health of defendants.

ii. Applications in relation to absent special circumstances tend to be unsuccessful and not to be pursued on appeal. For this reason there is comparatively little Court of Appeal guidance: but see: *Harris and Howells* [2003] EWCA Crim 486. It should be noted that abuse of process is not there to discipline the prosecution or the police.

iii. The arguments on both sides must be reduced to writing. Oral evidence is seldom relevant.

iv. The judge should direct full written submissions (rather than "skeleton arguments") on any abuse application in accordance with a timetable set by him; these should identify any element of prejudice the defendant is alleged to have suffered.

v. The Judge should normally aim to conclude the hearing within an absolute maximum limit of one day, if necessary in accordance with a timetable. The parties should therefore prepare their papers on this basis and not expect the judge to allow the oral hearing to be anything more than an occasion to highlight concisely their arguments and answer any questions the court may have of them; applications will not be allowed to drag on.

6. The Trial

(i) The particular hazard of heavy fraud trials

A heavy fraud or other complex trial has the potential to lose direction and focus. This is a disaster for three reasons:

a. The jury will lose track of the evidence, thereby prejudicing both prosecution and defence.

b. The burden on the defendants, the judge and indeed all involved will become intolerable.

c. Scarce public resources are wasted. Other prosecutions are delayed or – worse – may never happen. Fraud which is detected but not prosecuted (for resource reasons) undermines confidence.

(ii) Judicial mastery of the case

a. It is necessary for the judge to exercise firm control over the conduct of the trial at all stages.

b. In order to do this the judge must read the witness statements and the documents, so that the judge can discuss case management issues with the advocates on – almost – an equal footing.

c. To this end, the judge should not set aside weeks or even days for pre-reading (see paragraph 3 (i)(b) above). Hopefully the judge will have gained a good grasp of the evidence during the case management hearings. Nevertheless, realistic reading time must be provided for the judge in advance of trial.

d. The role of the judge in a heavy fraud or other complex criminal trial is different from his/her role in a "conventional" criminal trial. So far as possible, the judge should be freed from other duties and burdens, so that he/she can give the high degree of commitment which a heavy fraud trial requires. This will pay dividends in terms of saving weeks or months of court time.

(iii) The order of the evidence

a. By the outset of the trial at the latest (and in most cases very much earlier) the judge must be provided with a schedule, showing the sequence of prosecution (and in an appropriate case defence) witnesses and the dates upon which they are expected to be called. This can only be prepared by discussion between prosecution and defence which the judge should expect, and say he/she expects, to take place: See: Criminal Procedure Rule 3.10. The schedule should, in so far as it relates to Prosecution witnesses, be developed in consultation with the witnesses, via the Witness Care Units, and with consideration given to their personal needs. Copies of the schedule should be provided for the Witness Service.

b. The schedule should be kept under review by the trial judge and by the parties. If a case is running behind or ahead of schedule, each witness affected must be advised by the party who is calling that witness at the earliest opportunity.

c. If an excessive amount of time is allowed for any witness, the judge can ask why. The judge may probe with the advocates whether the time envisaged for the evidence-in-chief or cross-examination (as the case may be) of a particular witness is really necessary.

(iv) Case management sessions

a. The order of the evidence may have legitimately to be departed from. It will, however, be a useful for tool for monitoring the progress of the case. There should be periodic case management sessions, during which the judge engages the advocates upon a stock-taking exercise: asking, amongst other questions, "where are we going?" and "what is the relevance of the next three witnesses?". This will be a valuable means of keeping the case on track. Rule 3.10 of the Criminal Procedure Rules will again assist the judge.

b. The judge may wish to consider issuing the occasional use of "case management notes" to the advocates, in order to set out the judge's tentative views on where the trial may be going off track, which areas of future evidence are relevant and which may have become irrelevant (e.g. because of concessions, admissions in cross-examination and so forth). Such notes from the judge plus written responses from the advocates can, cautiously used, provide a valuable focus for debate during the periodic case management reviews held during the course of the trial.

(v) Controlling prolix cross-examination

a. Setting **rigid** time limits in advance for cross-examination is rarely appropriate – as experience has shown in civil cases; but a timetable is essential so that the judge can exercise control and so that there is a clear target to aim at for the completion of the evidence of each witness. Moreover the judge can and should indicate when cross-examination is irrelevant, unnecessary or time wasting. The judge may limit the time for further cross-examination of a particular witness.

(vi) Electronic presentation of evidence

a. Electronic presentation of evidence (EPE) has the potential to save huge amounts of time in fraud and other complex criminal trials and should be used more widely.

b. HMCS is providing facilities for the easier use of EPE with a standard audio visual facility. Effectively managed, the savings in court time achieved by EPE more than justify the cost.

c. There should still be a core bundle of those documents to which frequent reference will be made during the trial. The jury may wish to mark that bundle or to refer back to particular pages as the evidence progresses. EPE can be used for presenting all documents not contained in the core bundle.

d. Greater use of other modern forms of graphical presentations should be made wherever possible.

(vii) Use of interviews

The Judge should consider extensive editing of self serving interviews, even when the defence want the jury to hear them in their entirety; such interviews are not evidence of the truth of their contents but merely of the defendant's reaction to the allegation.

(viii) Jury Management

a. The jury should be informed as early as possible in the case as to what the issues are in a manner directed by the Judge.

b. The jury must be regularly updated as to the trial timetable and the progress of the trial, subject to warnings as to the predictability of the trial process.

c. Legal argument should be heard at times that causes the least inconvenience to jurors.

d. It is useful to consider with the advocates whether written directions should be given to the jury and, if so, in what form.

(ix) Maxwell hours

a. Maxwell hours should only be permitted after careful consideration and consultation with the Presiding Judge.

b. Considerations in favour include:

   i. Legal argument can be accommodated without disturbing the jury;

   ii. There is a better chance of a representative jury;

   iii. Time is made available to the judge, advocates and experts to do useful work in the afternoons.

c. Considerations against include:

   i. The lengthening of trials and the consequent waste of court time;

   ii. The desirability of making full use of the jury once they have arrived at court;

   iii. Shorter trials tend to diminish the need for special provisions e.g. there are fewer difficulties in empanelling more representative juries;

   iv. They are unavailable if any defendant is in custody.

d. It may often be the case that a maximum of one day of Maxwell hours a week is sufficient; if so, it should be timetabled in advance to enable all submissions by advocates, supported by skeleton arguments served in advance, to be dealt with in the period after 1:30 pm on that day.

(x) Livenote

If Livenote is used, it is important that all users continue to take a note of the evidence, otherwise considerable time is wasted in detailed reading of the entire daily transcript.

7. Other Issues

(i) Defence representation and defence costs

a. Applications for change in representation in complex trials need special consideration; the ruling of HH Judge Wakerley QC (as he then was) in *Asghar Ali* has been circulated by the JSB.

b. Problems have arisen when the Legal Services Commission have declined to allow advocates or solicitors to do certain work; on occasions the matter has been raised with the judge managing or trying the case.

c. The Legal Services Commission has provided guidance to judges on how they can obtain information from the LSC as to the reasons for their decisions; further information in relation to this can be obtained from *Nigel Field, Head of the Complex Crime Unit, Legal Services Commission, 29–37 Red Lion Street, London, WC1R 4PP.*

(ii) Assistance to the Judge

Experience has shown that in some very heavy cases, the judge's burden can be substantially offset with the provision of a Judicial Assistant or other support and assistance.

Index